Lamani Woman

THE TRIBES AND CASTES OF BOMBAY

THE
TRIBES AND CASTES OF BOMBAY

BY

R. E. ENTHOVEN

Companion of the Order of the Indian Empire, Commander of the Order of Leopold II, Indian Civil Service, Superintendent of Ethnography, Bombay Presidency

Issued under the orders oj the Government of Bombay

VOLUME II

ISBN: 978-93-5128-445-1(HB)

ISBN: 978-93-5128-443-7(Set)

First Published in 1922
Indian Reprint in 2017

Published by

Kalpaz Publications
C-30, Satyawati Nagar,
Delhi – 110052
E-mail: kalpaz@hotmail.com
Website: kalpazpublications.com
Ph.: +91-9212142040

TRIBES AND CASTES OF BOMBAY.

GHANCHIS or oilmen, from *ghání* an oil-press, numbering 35,828 (1901), including 21,220 males and 14,608 females, are found all over Gujarát, chiefly in large towns and villages. Though they have Rajput tribal surnames, such as Gohil, Jhála, Padhiár, Parmár, Solanki, etc., they claim descent from the Vániás of Modhera in North Gujarát, but no evidence is forthcoming in favour of this claim. They appear to be an occupational caste recruited from Vániás and Kanbis, members of which castes are still admitted by the Ghánchis. Name and origin.

Ghánchis are fair, their women being strong and occasionally handsome. Except that the clothes of those who deal in oil are dirty and spotted with oil, in their dress Ghánchis closely resemble Vániás and Kanbis.

Ghánchis have nine endogamous divisions of a territorial type. They are :— Divisions.

1. Ahmedábádi.	4. Kambháti.	7. Pátni.
2. Bharuchi.	5. Modh.	8. Sidhpuria.
3. Champáneri.	6. Pancholi.	9. Surti.

They all call themselves Modh Ghánchis, and were probably originally one group. But, as usual in Gujarát, the Modh Ghánchis of Sidhpur who settle in Surat become 'Sidhpuria' Modh Ghánchis and intermarriage ceases in consequence. Of the above divisions, Modhs and Sidhpuriás rank highest, the other divisions eating food cooked by them, while the former do not eat food cooked by the other six. None of the nine divisions intermarry.

Marriages are prohibited between near relations and within seven degrees of relationship. Marriage with a wife's sister is allowed after the death of the wife. Marriage is generally infant. Polygamy is permissible after making provision for the maintenance of the first wife. Polyandry is unknown. Widows are allowed to remarry. A widow may marry a younger brother of her deceased husband, but never the elder. Divorce, though rare, is allowed with the sanction of the caste *panch*. Divorced wives are allowed to marry again by the widow remarriage form.

Except that in South Gujarát the bridegroom goes to the bride's house hid in a flower veil and that the bride and bridegroom worship Marriage ceremonies.

Hanumán immediately after they are married. Ghánchi marriage ceremonies do not differ from those performed by Kanbis. The widow remarriage ceremony is very simple. The widow and her new intended husband are seated facing each other on two low wooden stools, and the ends of their garments are tied into a knot by a priest who is an Audich Bráhman. Next, Ganpati is worshipped and a remarried widow throws grains of rice over them and brings their heads into close contact, thus completing the ceremony.

Religion. Ghánchis follow the Hindu Law of inheritance, sometimes excluding daughters. They belong to many sects, Kabirpanthi, Rámánandi, Rámsnehi, Shaiva, Swáminaráyan, Vallabhácharya, and worshippers of Bahucharáji. Their family goddess is at Modhera, where many go on pilgrimage. They observe the regular Hindu fasts and feasts, believe in exorcism, witchcraft and omens, and visit all popular places of Hindu pilgrimage. Their priests are Bráhmans.

They burn their dead except children under eighteen months old, who are buried. Their birth and death ceremonies are similar to those of Kanbis.

Ghánchis mostly keep to their hereditary occupation of pressing and selling sesame, cocoanut, castor and linseed oil. Some earn a living by lending money, by selling grain, fruit, vegetables and sweetmeats, by selling milk and clarified butter, by tillage, by labour, and in Cutch by making bamboo baskets.

Food. Except Modhs and Sidhpuriás, they eat the flesh of goats, sheep, fowls and fish, and drink liquor. Socially they rank almost equal to Sutárs and calico-printers, though Golá-Ghánchi is a common synonym in Surat for low caste groups in contradistinction to the Bráhman Vánia classes.

GHANTECHOR.—A sub-division of Koravas.

GHANTICHOR.—A synonym for Bhámta.

GHARDHERA.—A synonym for Bábria.

GHATI.—A sub-division of Nhávis, Chámbhárs and Kumbhárs; a local name applied in Bombay to all labourers from the Deccan as distinguished from Konkani, and in Gujarát to all domestic servants from the Deccan.

GHATKAMBLE.—A sub-division of Mahárs.

GHATOLE.—A synonym for Nemádi Báris; a sub-division of Khándesh Kunbis.

GHERMEHDI.—*See* under Minor Musalmán castes.

GHISADIS or tinkers, also called Bailne Kumbárs or outside ironsmiths in Belgaum, numbering (1901) 3,255, including 1,640 males and 1,615 females, are found scattered in small numbers throughout the Deccan, Konkan and the Karnátak. The name Ghisádi seems to come from the Maráthi *ghisne, i.e.*, to rub. According to their own story they are called after a certain Ghisádi who overcame and killed a famous gymnast. They have no memory of any earlier home, but their home tongue, which is a corrupt Gujaráti suggests that they were formerly settled in Gujarát. They now wander from place to place during the fair weather, living in temporary sheds called *páls* formed by fixing two forked poles in the ground, laying a third pole in the forks of the two uprights, and stretching a cloth or large blanket over the horizontal pole so as to form a tent with sloping sides and open ends. Name and origin.

There are no endogamous divisions of the caste, nor do there appear to be any exogamous sub-divisions above families having the same surname. The commonest surnames are Chaván, Charváse, Kátkar, Padvalkár, Powár, Sálunke, Selár, Shinde, Suryavanshi and Khetri. Divisions

Marriages are prohibited within four degrees of relationship on the boy's side and three degrees on the girl's side. A member of the caste can marry his father's sister's or mother's brother's daughter. He cannot marry his mother's sister's daughter. A man may marry two sisters, and two brothers may marry two sisters. Marriage is infant as well as adult. Baby-girls are sometimes married by tying the marriage garland to the cradle. Women occasionally remain unmarried till they are thirty. If a girl is guilty of sexual indiscretions with a casteman, the latter is compelled to marry her, and the parents of both the parties are either fined or made to give a feast to the caste people. If the offence is committed with a man of a lower caste, the offender is turned out of the caste. Polygamy is allowed and practised, but polyandry is unknown.

The offer of marriage is made by the boy's father, who has to pay to the girl's father a sum known as *dej*, varying from Rs. 25 to Rs. 100. The betrothal takes place either a day or even a year or two before the marriage, when the boy's father presents the girl with a robe and a bodice-cloth and feasts the caste people. On the day before the marriage the *devak* or marriage guardian is installed at the houses of both the parties. It consists of *pánchpálvi, i.e.*, leaves of five kinds of trees, *viz.*, mango, *umbar* (Ficus glomerata), *jambhul* (Syzigium jambolanum), *shami* (Prosopis spicigera), and *rui* Marriage ceremonies.

(Calotropis gigantea). The *devak* is placed on a dish with a *dhán** or shovel and taken to the temple of Máruti with music by a band of friends accompanied by two married couples, one from the bride's and the other from the bridegroom's house, whose skirts are tied together. There the *devak* and Máruti are worshipped, a betelnut and a pice are placed before the image of the god, and the *devak* is brought back and placed before the household gods until the ceremony is ended. The family gods are worshipped, a goat is slain in their name and the caste people are feasted. In Belgaum and Bijápur the custom of installing the *devak* appears to have died out; in its place a *goundhal* dance is performed to propitiate the gods. The marriage ceremonies are (1) rubbing the bride and the bridegroom with oil, (2) *halad* or applying turmeric paste to the boy and the girl, (3) *simántpujan* or reception of the bridegroom by the bride's father at the village gate, (4) *varadhawa* or going of the bridegroom in procession to the girl's house for the marriage, (5) *kanyádán* or making a gift of the bride to the bridegroom, (6) *rukhawat* or sending sweetmeats to the bridegroom by the bride's father, (7) the marriage sacrifice, and (8) *varát* or taking the bride to the bridegroom's house in procession after the marriage is over. The essential and binding portion consists in the bride and the bridegroom walking round the sacrificial fire.

The re-marriage of widows is permitted. A widow cannot marry her mother's sister's, father's sister's or maternal uncle's son, or a member of her late husband's section. A widow's marriage can be celebrated on the dark nights of any month except *Chaitra*, *Ashvin* and *Bhádrapad*. The ceremony consists in worshipping Ganpati and Varuna, applying red powder to the widow's forehead, the filling of her lap by a Bráhman priest, and the mutual utterance of each other's name by the couple. A bachelor is not allowed to marry a widow. Divorce is not allowed. The caste follow the Hindu law of inheritance.

Religion. Ghisádis are Hindus and chiefly belong to the Várkari and Kabir sect. Their family deities are Bahiri, Báláji of Giri in the Madras Presidency, Bhawáni, Khandoba, Satvái, Yamái, Kálamma, Ambábái and Yellamma, and they also worship the village gods and gods of the boundary. The *tulas* or sweet basil plant, the banyan tree and *umbar* (Ficus glomerata), weapons, sacred books and account books are worshipped. Offerings of goats and fowls are made to Khandoba on Sundays and to Janái or Jokhái on Tuesdays, Fridays or Sundays.

* Before the passing of the Arms Act a sword was used in the place of a *dhán*.

When cholera or small-pox breaks out Mariái and Shitaládevi are propitiated by offerings of goats and cooked food. Ghisádis make pilgrimages to Alandi, Dehu, Jejuri, Pandharpur and Tuljápur. They observe all the Hindu holidays. They are great believers in soothsaying and witchcraft. Their priests are the ordinary local Bráhmans.

The married dead are burnt, the unmarried being buried with head to the north. The ordinary funeral rites are observed; but in the case of violent death, if the corpse is not found, an image of wheat flour is made in the name of the dead and the funeral rites are performed over it. The ceremony of *shráddha* is in use. **Death.**

The principal occupation of the Ghisádis is working in iron. They are wandering tinkers, and make horse-shoes, iron spoons, sickles, reaping hooks and other field tools including cart axles and wheels. In the Belgaum district they are at times of assistance to robbers, supplying them with spear-heads, and other weapons.

They eat goats, sheep, deer, hare, poultry and fish, and drink liquor. **Food.**

GHODA.—A synonym for Gauda.

GHOGARI.—A sub-division of Bráhmans and Dasa Deswál Vániás.

GHOGATTUNYA.—A sub-division of Dhangars.

GHOGHVA.—A sub-division of Modh Vániás.

GHOSI.—A sub-division of Ahirs.

GIDBIDKI JOSHI.—A synonym for Joshi.

GIJGE.—A sub-division of Holayás.

GIRASIA.—A title applied to Rajput landlords.

GIRNARA.—A sub-division of Bráhmans.

GOALBAN.—A sub-division of Ahirs.

GODE BHOI.—A sub-division of Bhois.

GODHWAL.—A sub-division of Bráhmans.

GODMALVI.—A sub-division of Bráhmans.

GODVAN.—A sub-division of Mahárs.

GOJRA.—A sub-division of Meghváls.

GOL.—A synonym for Golla.

GOLA.—A synonym for Khavás.

Name and origin.

GOLAS, also known as Ránás or Rice pounders, numbering 16,167 (1901), including 8,442 males and 8,725 females, are found all over Gujarát and Káthiáwár. According to their story, they were originally Rajputs of Chitor in Mewar who called themselves slaves or *golas* to protect themselves from the persecution of Parashurám. In token of a Rajput strain the word Rána is always added to the name Gola, and in some places the caste is known by the name Rána only. The fact seems to be that they were domestic slaves of Rajput families and are of mixed descent in consequence.

According to another story, when pursued by Parashurám, they hid themselves in a temple of Mahádev. As they were long without food, Párvati, Shiva's consort, took pity on them and brought them earthen pots or *goras* filled with curds. In their hungry scramble, the pots fell to the ground and were broken to pieces. After eating as much of the curds as they could pick up, they went to Shiva to ask his advice. To make some provision for the refugees, Shiva changed his discus into a mill, his arrows into pestles, his ash-balls into mortars, his rosary beads into a sieve, and his shield into a winnowing fan. He then ordered them to make their living by pounding rice. According to this story, Gola is a corruption of *gora* an earthen pot. Clearly the tradition is a mere play on words.

Divisions.

The Golás are variously described as belonging to the Káshyap or Vijasani *gotra*. They are named after the places in which they reside, *e.g.*, Dabhoia (those residing in Dabhoi), Vadodaria (those living in Baroda), Pádaria, Khambáti, Bharuchi, Surti, Jambusaria, etc.

The tribal surnames are as follows :—

Agásia	Jádhav	Sitpuria
Andhária	Kátakia	Solanki
Chávda	Manhora	Takoria
Chodhávála	Nagaretha	Tunvar
Chohán	Pánchshadia	Vághela
Daladia	Pat	Vághmar
Divadia	Parmár	Varsadia
Gobil	Pasia	Vehirjia
Hirvania	Sámalia	

Marriages are prohibited between persons bearing the same surname, and within five to seven degrees of relationship. A Gola cannot marry a girl from a family to which a girl is given from his own. Marriage with a father's sister's, mother's sister's or mother's brother's daughter is not allowed. Two brothers are allowed to marry two sisters, the younger sister being married to the younger brother. Girls are married from five to seven, boys up to twelve. Polygamy is allowed if the first wife has no issue, her children are short lived, or she has some physical defect. Divorce is not allowed. Marriage with a second wife can be effected after paying a penalty of Rs. 1,000 to the castemen and after providing for the maintenance of the first wife. If a wife becomes deformed at a very early age, the penalty is only Rs. 100. Polyandry is unknown.

Marriage negotiations are commenced by the girl's father through the family priest. Betrothals take place sometimes immediately, and sometimes years, before marriage. A betrothal is seldom broken. The dowry settled on the girl varies from Rs. 25 to Rs. 100 according to the means of the boy's parents. It is paid in the form of ornaments and articles of dress. The bridegroom's parents are not allowed to receive a dowry. If they are discovered receiving it secretly, they are forced by the castemen to pay it back to the parents of the bride, and in addition to pay a fine of Rs. 51 to the caste. Except that they are less detailed, the marriage ceremonies of Golás do not differ from those performed by Kanbis. Marriage ceremonies.

Widow remarriage is allowed. The levirate is permitted, but is not compulsory. The permission of the caste *panch* is required for the marriage of a widow, which is obtained after the payment of a fine of Rs. 25. In some places, the fine ranges from Rs. 4-4-0 to Rs. 8-4-0. A widow remarriage can be celebrated on a Sunday, Tuesday or Thursday after night-fall. It cannot take place on a new-moon day or the day previous. The ceremony takes place at the widow's father's house in the verandah or courtyard. The bride and bridegroom are seated on low wooden stools, and an image of Ganpati made of wheat flour is worshipped, a Bráhman priest officiating. A flower garland is put on the wrist of the bride and on the neck of the bridegroom. A bunch of flowers is fixed in the bridegroom's turban, and a marriage garland made of red thread is worn by both. Next, a wheat flour lamp with seven wicks fed with *ghi* is lighted and the couple are made to bow to the lamp. The priest then puts the lamp in an earthen pot and covers it with a sieve. Until this is done, nobody is allowed to be present at the ceremony, as it is a belief that if an unwidowed woman were to see the lamp she would become a widow. Next, five, seven or nine unwidowed women, one by one, daub the brows of the bride and bridegroom with red powder and throw grains of rice over their heads, which concludes the ceremony. On the day following, the bridegroom returns to his house with his bride after nightfall. Should a bachelor desire to marry a widow, he is first married to a *shami* bush. Divorce is not allowed. The caste follow the Hindu law of inheritance.

Religion. The Golás were originally Shaivas, their chief god being Mahádev. They are now Bijpanthis, Kabirpanthis, Rámánandis, Shaivas, Svámináráyans, Satráms, and Udásis. In Kaira, like Mátia Kanbis, they belong to the Porána sect. Except the Porána Golás, who worship their saints' tombs and a heap of flowers, they respect all Hindu gods, but keep no idols in their houses. The minor deity specially worshipped is the goddess Khodiár *máta*. They believe in witchcraft, exorcism, the regular Hindu omens and the influence of the evil eye. They are careful to observe the regular Hindu fasts and feasts. During the whole of the *adhika* or intercalary month, bands of as many as fifty men and boys go to the river to bathe every morning, singing hymns and songs. They have their religious heads who occasionally visit them, and are paid about a rupee by each family. The animals they worship are the cow on *Sankránt* day and the donkey on New Year's day. A redpowder mark is made on the donkey's forehead, a flower wreath is thrown round its neck, and a cocoanut is offered to it and the kernel distributed to caste-people. They visit the ordinary places of Hindu pilgrimage. Their priests are chiefly Audich, Ráyakval, Meváda and Shrimáli Bráhmans. They do not wear the sacred thread, but at the time of performing death ceremonies, some hang a cotton thread across their shoulders.

Death ceremonies. The dead are burnt. Children under eighteen months old are buried. The death ceremonies are of the standard type. The castemen are feasted for one to four days. The *shráddha* and *mahálaya* are performed for the propitiation of the deceased. If a person meets a violent death and the corpse is not found, an idol is made in his name and burnt with the same details as in the case of ordinary death.

The Gola is held in little respect; a slovenly Vánia is called a Gola in contempt. The Golás and Ghánchis are the first on the lower side of the boundary line between high and low caste Hindus. Though Golás rank among the first of lower class Hindus, a certain contempt attaches to them, partly owing to their unskilled profession, their love of drink and their poverty, and partly owing to their fondness for riding donkeys. In Central Gujarát, a Gola ordinarily rides on a donkey; and in South Gujarát, on the *Holi* festival he is specially hired and grotesquely dressed and paraded on a donkey's back, with the beating of drums.

Though some profess to be vegetarians, even scrupling to eat snake gourds, pumpkins and carrots, the Golás eat, besides coarse food-grains, fish, fowl and the flesh of the goat, deer, hare and antelope. They drink liquor to excess. Food.

GOLAK.—A sub-division of Bráhmans.

GOLALARE.—A synonym for Alkari.

GOLLA.—A sub-division of Gavlis.

GOLLAS or Gols, also known as Gopáls in the Belgaum district, are a tribe of wandering cowherds and medicine-sellers. At the Census of 1901 they numbered approximately 7,214 including 3,629 males and 3,585 females. The largest number was recorded in Dhárwár, and they were also found in small numbers in Belgaum, Bijápur, Kanara, the Southern Marátha Country and Ratnágiri. The Golla cowherds and the Golla medicine-sellers, though originally one and the same tribe, are now two distinct communities, the former being found only in Kanara. They are described below separately. The original home of the tribe appears to be Telangan, and most of them speak Telugu at home. It is said that about a hundred years ago during a great famine in Telangan, many of the tribe migrated northwards in search of food, some of them taking to the profession of administering medicines, and thus forming a separate caste. At the Census of 1901 the Gollás numbered 855,221 in Madras, 281,714 in Hyderabad, and 143,249 in Mysore. All Gollás claim Krishna as a casteman, which suggests their connection with the Gollás and Gaulis of the north; and it is possible that, in their wanderings, some of the northern Gollás may have settled in the south. There is now, however, nothing in common between the northern Gollás and Gaulis and the southern Gollás except their occupation and the similarity between their names. Name and origin.

The Gollás who are medicine-sellers appear to be recruited from many castes such as Maráthás, Vaidus, etc. In Dhárwár and Belgaum they have come under the influence of Lingáyatism. They have six endogamous divisions, which neither eat together nor intermarry. They are as follows:— Endogamous divisions.

1. Advi or Telugu Gollás.
2. Hanam Gollás or Bhingis.
3. Krishna Gollás or Yádavs.
4. Kenguri Gollás.
5. Páknák Gollás.
6. Shástra Gollás.

Of these the Advi Gollás are most numerous. The Páknák Gollás have a tradition that they were brought into the Badámi sub-division of Bijápur from the Advani or Adoni country as shepherds when that sub-division was thinly populated. The Kenguri Gollás rear white sheep and are found mostly in the Nizam's territory.

Exo-gamous divisions. The Gollás of the Dhárwár district have five exogamous divisions as follows :—

1. Ambir Vandlu.
2. Bindu Vandlu.
3. Chesru Vandlu.
4. Galla Vandlu.
5. Gobbar Vandlu.

The exogamous divisions of the Bijápur Gollás are identical with surnames. They are More, Pavár, Shinde and Yádav. These surnames and the fact that their ceremonies and customs also are like those of Maráthás suggest that there is a strong infusion of Márátha blood among the Gollás of Bijápur. Marriage is infant as well as adult. Polygamy, widow marriage and divorce are allowed and practised but polyandry is unknown. The Golla women of Dhárwár are said very rarely to commit adultery, and even for adultery a man may not divorce his wife. If a woman is taken in adultery, a hole about two feet deep is dug in the ground, and the adulteress is made to stand in the hole. Thorns are spread round the edge of the hole, and the woman is made to sit on the thorns with her feet in the hole, as if on a chair. A grindstone is set on her head, and she is made to drink three small teaspoonfuls of cowdung mixed with water. The people of the caste lecture her ; she is considered to be purified, and her husband continues to live with her.

Marriage ceremonics. The marriage and other ceremonies of the Bijápur Gollás are the same as those of Maráthás. The only difference is that the bride's father gets Rs. 26 as the price of his daughter and in return gives four feasts. The marriage ceremonies of the Dhárwár Gollás are as follows :—

When a marriage is settled, a shed with twelve posts is built in front of the bride's hut and twelve earthen pots filled with water are kept at the posts, worshipped, and allowed to remain there five days. On the first day friends and relations are feasted on animal food in honour of their gods. On the second day the bride and bridegroom are rubbed with turmeric and bathed ; on the third day a feast of sweet cakes and animal food is given ; and on the fourth day the maternal uncles of both the bride and bridegroom tie yellow wristlets or *kankans* to the couple's right wrists, their brows are marked with turmeric powder, and marriage coronets of oleander or *bangot* leaves are fastened round their heads. The bridegroom ties the lucky thread round the bride's neck, betelnuts and leaves are served to the guests, and five married unwidowed women sing songs and call with a loud voice *Jai bhagiams*, that is, may the bride and bridegroom prosper. On the fifth day caste people are feasted on flesh and liquor, and five married unwidowed women take the bride and bridegroom into the bridal chamber, from which time they live together as husband and wife. When he sends the bride to her husband's house, her father presents his son-in-law with a dog. Should the bride afterwards wish to visit her parents she is not allowed to go alone or even with a member of the bridegroom's family. The husband himself must go with her, stay for three days, and return with her. When a girl arrives at puberty a branch of the *lakki* tree is fixed in the floor of one of the rooms in the house, and the girl is made to sit under the branch for three days, and on the fourth day she is bathed and is pure. No future monthly sickness is held to make a woman impure.

The Dhárwár Gollás worship Hanumán, Hulgeva, and Yellamma. **Religion.** On some Tuesday or Friday, at any time during the year, they wash the images of Hanumán and Yellamma and burn incense before them. To Hanumán they offer flowers, sandal paste, plantains and cocoanuts, and to the goddess Yellamma they offer a goat which is partaken of by themselves. They have no spiritual teacher. They believe in sorcery, witchcraft and soothsaying. They do not respect Bráhmans or call them to their ceremonies. The Belgaum Gollás worship the ordinary Bráhman gods and have the greatest respect for Máruti, whose image, along with those of Venkoba, Narsoba, and Yellamma they keep in their houses. They respect Bráhmans and call them to their marriages. Both the Dhárwár and Belgaum Gollás employ Jangams to conduct the death ceremonies. The family gods of the Bijápur Gollás are Venkoba, Tulja-Bhawáni, Margái, Yellamma of Saundatti in Parasgad, and Mira Saheb of Miraj. They offer goats to Tulja-Bhawáni and feast on the flesh. On Tuesdays and Fridays in the month of *Shrávan* they take only one meal in the evening. They keep the leading Hindu holidays. They worship village and local deities, but profess not to believe in witchcraft or soothsaying. They have no priests, but they call Bráhmans to conduct their marriages. The Hanam Gollás are married by a *guru* or religious teacher of their own caste. Their chief house god is Somnáth. The religious teacher of the Krishna Gollás is also a man of their own caste and is called Ushtum. Both he and a Bráhman attend their marriages. Their great god is Krishna.

The Gollás of Dhárwár and Belgaum bury their dead; in other places the dead are either burnt or buried. In Dhárwár, on the third day after death, a Lingáyat priest is called, his feet are washed, three copper coins are placed on his right foot and two on his left, incense is burnt before them, and a few drops of the water in which the feet have been washed are sipped by the members of the family. The priest gives them white ashes, which they rub over their body and are purified. The Gollás of the Belgaum district mourn for five weeks, when they call a Jangam, who makes them pure by ringing a bell and blowing a conch-shell.

)ccupa-ion. The Gollás are hereditary medicine-sellers and beggars. Besides drug-selling, they draw out guineaworms with a pin, and bleed with the help of a copper cup. After the end of October, when the rainy season is over, they spend about three months in the woodlands and wastes looking for roots, herbs, fruits, and bulbs. They carry these herbs and other cures and oxydes of metals and minerals in two bags formed by tying together the four ends of a square ochre-coloured cloth, and fastened one at each end of a stick which they carry on their shoulder. They hawk their drugs, calling as they go, 'A doctor to cure wind; doctor to draw out guineaworm'. They cure liver and spleen diseases by branding with a red-hot iron. Before prescribing a medicine they go through the form of feeling the pulse. In addition to housework their women plait mats of wild date *ichalu* (K.) *shindi* (M.) leaves Phœnix sylvestris, and help the men when they are at work in the fields.

ood. They eat the flesh of goats, sheep, the hare, domestic fowls and wild game, and drink liquor. They eat from Bráhmans, Lingáyats, Rajputs, Maráthás and Sonárs, but not from Dhangars, Vaddas, Kolhátis, Koravas and Jingars.

KANARESE GOLLAS, who are cowherds, are, according to Buchanan[1] partly of Telugu and partly of Karnátak descent. They are divided into Gollás proper, Hál-Gollás, Háv-Gollás, Kad-Gollás Kemper-Gollás and Ur-Gollás, who neither eat together nor intermarry. Marriages are prohibited between persons of the same stock. Girls are married between nine and twelve, and even after attaining puberty; boys between fifteen and twenty. Polygamy and widow marriage are allowed and practised. Their chief gods are Krishna, Shiva under the terrible form of Kálbhairav, and Párvati. They worship the ordinary Hindu gods and goddesses, offering blood sacrifices to mothers or female powers, and employing Shrivaishnav Bráhmans whom they greatly respect. They believe that after death good men become gods, and bad men devils. They know nothing of the transmigration of the soul. Though none of them wear the *linga*, their spiritual guide is a Lingáyat and lives at Mápkali about fourteen

(1) Mysore, I. 347; II. 8.

Gondhalis.

miles North of Wodda-Ballápur in Mysore. They bury their dead. Their funeral and other ceremonies do not differ from those of the Lingáyats. They were formerly noted for their honesty in carrying Government treasure. They are now chiefly husbandmen and milk and butter sellers. They eat fish, fowls, sheep and deer and drink liquor. They rank next to the cultivating classes.

GOMBIADISO.—A sub-division of Kilikets.

GOMITRA.—A sub-division of Bráhmans.

GOMTIWAL.—A sub-division of Bráhmans.

GONDS, numbering 542 (1901), including 270 males and 272 females, are chiefly found in Surat and Násik. They are immigrants from the Central Provinces, where they are found in large numbers.(1)

GONDHALIS, numbering 11,682 (1901), including 5,863 males and 5,819 females, are found all over the Presidency except Gujarát. The largest number are found in the Kolába, Sátára, and Khándesh districts and in the Kolhápur State. They take their name from the word *gondhal* meaning a confused dance. They are a class of religious minstrels recruited from many castes, and, like the Vághes and Murlis, are generally children offered to gods in fulfilment of vows. They state that the founders of their caste were the sage Jamadagni and his spouse Renuka, and that they came into the Deccan two or three hundred years ago from Máhur and Tuljápur in the Nizám's Territory, which are their original places of residence. They call themselves the sons or devotees of the goddess Bhaváni, and wear round their neck a garland of yellow shells called the Bhaváni cowris. Being the devotees of the goddess Bhaváni they enjoy the same semi-sacred position among the lower class Hindus of the Deccan as the Bráhmans enjoy among the higher classes. Name and origin.

In the beginning of the seventeenth century when the worship of the goddess Amba Bhaváni of Tuljápur had spread far and wide in the Deccan and when every Marátha house re-echoed her praises, the Gondhalis were held in great esteem and their songs were much in favour. It was a time of religious and political activity. The people had suffered much from the oppression of the Musalmáns and were eagerly looking for something divine to free them from the yoke of their foreign oppressors. As the Hindu gods are supposed to be not so easily won by prayers and offerings as the goddesses and especially as the latter are supposed to enjoy greater power for good or for evil in this age of Káli, the goddesses were appealed to for help, and Amba Bhaváni of Tuljápur was the foremost among them to respond readily to the prayers of her devotees.

(1) Census of India, 1911, Vol. X, Part I, page 218.

She appeared to many in dreams, helped others in their difficulties, and showed hidden treasures to a favoured few. But in the case of the Gondhalis the goddess did more than that. She appeared in the body of some one or other of the Gondhalis in their *gondhal* dances and enabled them to foretell past and future events and to perform many other miracles. It was at this time that some of the great Marátha poets, like Wáman Pandit, Shridhar, and Rámdás, flourished. The writings of these men, especially of Wáman and Rámdás, though full of pious and philosophical sentiments and free from vulgar and ungrammatical expressions, were read by very few and understood by a still smaller number. Such was not the case with the songs of the Gondhalis. The *powádas* of the Gondhalis, being composed in a rude, simple, home language of of the Maráthás, were understood by the masses and admired. Consequently, the sentiments the songs of the Gondhalis embodied did not fail to make a permanent impression on the mind of the audience. If, on the one hand, the religious and political writings and teachings of the poet Rámdás, the spiritual guide of Shiváji, enlightened and enlivened the minds of the few who could read and write, and impressed them with ideas of freedom and patriotism, on the other hand, the simple songs of the Gondhalis tickled the fancy, gratified the pride, and roused the patriotism of the unlettered mountaineers of the Western Gháts, and made a deeper impression on their minds. In those days certain plays, called *tamáshás* and *lalitas*, were a favourite form of amusement with the masses, and in these plays the Gondhalis played no unimportant part. The songs which the Gondhalis sang in these plays, and which related the exploits of the heroes of the Rámáyana and Mahábhárata, or the fights of Amba Bhaváni, Malhári, or other gods, with the *rákshasas*, or demons, were attentively listened to by thousands, admired by hundreds, and learnt by not a few. The Gondhalis used also to sing the praises of the living, and he whose praises were sung by them, and in whose name the *danka*, or sacred drum was beaten, was considered to be highly honoured.

Endogamous divisions.

The Gondhalis are divided into eight endogamous divisions, *viz.*, (1) Bráhman, (2) Dhangar, (3) Marátha, (4) Kumbhár, (5) Kadamrai, (6) Renukrai or Picháti, (7) Máli, (8) Akaramáse, who neither eat together nor intermarry. All these divisions except the last perform the dance as described below. The Bráhman Gondhalis perform the dance with a *bhaden* or the lower half of an earthen pot filled with combustible materials set on fire, corresponding to the *divati* of the other Gondhalis. The Kadamrai and Renukrai Gondhalis maintain that they are the only hereditary Gondhalis, the other branches being mere musicians belonging to other castes. Kadamrais are socially the superiors of the Renukrais.

The exogamous sub-divisions of the caste are identical with surnames. The surnames and names of males and females of the Marátha Gondhalis are the same as among the Marátha Kunbis. The surnames of the Kumbhár Gondhalis are Badge, Dhembe, Gangávan, Garud, Jugle, Jádhav, Panchángi, Thite, Vaid and Varáde. Those of the Renukrai and Kadamrai Gondhalis are Bekre, Bhandáre, Dhamál Dungu, Gáikwád, Ghátekar, Gurádkar, Jádhav, Jagtáp, Kále, Kolhátkar, Maráthe, Máherkar, Palaskar, Renke, Shinde, Supalkar, Tarte, Thite, Tipke, and Uble. In Dhárwár, they have the surnames Garod, Gurne, Panchángi, and Wugde. Persons bearing the same surname cannot intermarry. Sameness of *devak* is also a bar to intermarriage. The *devaks* of Gondhalis are the same as those of the Maráthás; but the *pánchpálvi* or leaves of five trees, the mango, the *shami* (Prosopis spicigera), the *palas* (Butea frondosa), the *umbar* (Ficus glomerata), and the *rui* (Calotropis gigantea) are the most common. Exogamous divisions.

Marriages are also prohibited between persons between whom a former connection cannot be traced. Girls are married before they attain puberty, boys up to 20 or 25 years. If a man is well-to-do and his children die in infancy, he marries his infant son, while in the cradle, with a girl of similar age. Polygamy and widow remarriage are allowed and practised, but polyandry is unknown. Divorce is allowed. A divorced woman is not allowed to marry again during the life-time of her husband. The caste follow the Hindu law of inheritance.

Gondhalis belong to the Hindu religion. They worship all Hindu gods and goddesses, but the chief objects of their worship are Bhaváni of Tuljápur, Ambábái of Kolhápur, Yellamma of Belgaum, Renuka of Máhurgad in the Nizám's Territory, Jokhái of Kolhápur, Janái at Karhád, Tukái at Kondanpur, Khandoba, and *Asras* or the river or water nymphs. They make pilgrimages to the shrines of these deities. They are their votaries and beg and perform the *gondhal* dance in their name. They observe all the Hindu fasts and feasts and also the Musalmán Moharrum. The nine nights in *Navarátra* which end in *Dasara* day is their biggest festival. On Tuesdays and Fridays they eat only once, these days being sacred to their goddesses. Because their family goddess at Mahurgad sleeps on a cot, they do not allow their women in child-bed to lie on a cot but on the ground. They have no spiritual teacher. Their priests are the local Bráhmans. Religion

They resemble the Marátha Kunbis in their ceremonies and customs. But in their marriage ceremony, in addition to the *devak*, they also tie to the chief post of the marriage booth a drum or *sambal*, Marriage and investiture.

a *chavak* or one-stringed fiddle, a garland of cowrie shells, and their begging bag. The ceremony of investing their boys with a garland of sacred shells is peculiar to the caste. This ceremony is performed when the boy is about ten or twelve years of age. On a lucky day relations and caste-men are invited to dine. When they have come, the head-man of the Gondhalis or some other elderly member of the caste spreads rice on a low wooden stool, puts a pot filled with water on it, tells the boy's father to put a rupee and a quarter or other silver coins in the pot, and closes its mouth with mango leaves and a cocoanut. He then tells the boy to worship the pot (which is supposed to represent Amba Bhaváni) with flowers, sandal-paste, and incense. The Gondhali then ties a garland of yellow shells round the boy's neck, and repeats in his ear the name of the goddess Bhaváni and some other mystic words. The guests are then feasted and the ceremony comes to an end.

The Gondhal dance.

Gondhalis make their living chiefly by performing the *gondhal* dance. They also beg in the name of the goddess Bhaváni, and sing songs religious, historical, and amorous. Amongst the Maráthás, Shimpis, Sonárs, Deshasth Bráhmans, and some other castes of the Deccan it is customary to perform a *gondhal* dance on the occasion of a thread-girding and marriage ceremony. The dance may be briefly described as follows.

A few days before the ceremony the Gondhalis are invited to dine and are sumptuously fed. In the evening friends and relations are invited to witness the dance. In the centre of the hall, on a low wooden stool, the head of the Gondhalis spreads a bodice-cloth and on it some handfuls of rice. On the rice is placed a pot filled with water, and on the mouth of the pot are placed some mango leaves. On the pot is placed a tray filled with rice, and in it a *ták* or image of the goddess Bhaváni. The owner of the house then worships the image with sandal-paste, redlead, turmeric and flowers, burns incense before it, offers it fruit and money, and then bows down before it. The head of the Gondhalis now stands in front of the goddess, and on his right hand stands one of his comrades holding a lighted torch in his hand. Other companions of the head Gondhali stand behind him, one of them playing on a double drum called *sambal*, another on a stringed instrument called *tuntune*, and the third striking two metal cups one against the other. The head Gondhali now worships the *divti* or lighted torch with sandal-paste, turmeric, and flowers, and bows to it, and says, "O goddess Bhaváni, of Tuljápur, come to witness the *gondhal* dance." In this way he repeats the names of several gods and goddesses, and invites them to witness the performance. He then sings a song relating to the deeds of Bhaváni, Malhári, Ráma, or some other hero, walking to and fro, and his comrades play on their instruments. After a few minutes he stops and explains to the audience the meaning of his song. He again repeats another song, walks to and fro again, and stops to explain the meaning. In this way he continues his story till daybreak. After the narrative is over, the head Gondhali, if desired by the audience, sings songs describing the exploits of Shiváji, or some other Marátha hero, and if he be a clever man, he amuses the audience by singing some new ballads composed by himself or some other Gondhali. Occasionally one of the Gondhalis becomes possessed and pretends to foretell future events. At about daybreak a lighted lamp or camphor is waved round the goddess, the *divti* or sacred torch is extinguished in milk or clarified butter, and the ceremony comes to an end.

The dead are either burnt or buried.

Food. In food they resemble the Marátha Kunbis. In the social scale they stand lower than the Maráthás, who will not eat food cooked by them.

GONDVAN.—A synonym for Godvan Mahár.

GONGADIKARS (also known as Gonigas), numbering 69 (1901), including 62 males and 7 females, are found only in the Kanara district. They are immigrants from Mysore and are cultivators by occupation.(1)

GONIGA.—A synonym for Gongadikar.

GOPAL.—A synonym for Golla; a sub-division of Mahárs.

Name and origin. **GOPALS** are a wandering tribe of cattle owners, tumblers and beggars who appear to have originated in children offered to the gods, re-inforced by refugees, from several castes. They have apparently been recruited from Marátha Kunbis, Dhangars, Kásárs, Sonárs, Sális, Vanjáris, and even Mahárs. The caste numbers (1901) 3,504 including 1,814 males and 1,690 females. Of these the greater number (2,385) are found in Khándesh whence they wander in the fair season with their cattle over the neighbouring district of Násik and the Berárs. It is admitted that they still accept recruits from the Kunbis. The name Gopál is derived from *go* a cow and *pál* protector. Their touch is impure, and they are socially degraded, some of them eating flesh.

(1) Census of India, 1911, Vol. XXI, Part I, p. 167.

Endogamous divisions.

The endogamous divisions of the caste are :—

Bhil.	Marátha.
Gujaráti.	Vir.

The bulk of them appear to be Marátha Gopáls. The Virs are named after Virbhadra whom they worship.

Exogamous divisions.

The exogamous divisions are of special interest as they indicate the sources of recruitment. The chief *kuls* are :—

1 Bhingal.	8 Gire.	15 Kákapáth.	22 Pavár.
2 Chaván.	9 Gurav.	16 Kánade.	23 Sáli.
3 Dadiv.	10 Hanbar.	17 Kásár.	24 Sonár.
4 Dhangar.	11 Hatkar.	18 Koli.	25 Vanjári.
5 Dhogade.	12 Jádhav.	19 Lonáre.	
6 Gáikwád.	13 Jangam.	20 Magar.	
7 Gajákos.	14 Kadam.	21 Nikam.	

Marriages are prohibited between members of the same *kul*. Sameness of *devak* is no bar to intermarriage, the whole tribe having the same *devak*, *viz*., the *pánchpálvi*. A member of the tribe cannot marry his father's sister's or mother's sister's daughter. He may marry his mother's brother's daughter. A man may marry two sisters and two brothers may marry two sisters. Polygamy is allowed and practised, but polyandry is unknown.

Boys are generally married up to the age of twenty-five, girls before they come of age. If a girl remains unmarried till after puberty, her parents have to pay a fine of Rs. 15 to the tribesmen. If a girl commits sexual indiscretions before marriage, she is allowed to remain in the tribe on her father's paying a fine or giving a dinner to the tribesmen.

Marriage ceremonies.

The offer of marriage comes from the boy's father, who has to pay a bride-price of from Rs. 10 to Rs. 150 to the girl's father. The day for the marriage is fixed by a Bráhman who conducts the service. The marriage ceremonies of Gopáls resemble those of the Kunbis.

The remarriage of widows is permitted. A widow cannot marry her father's sisters' or mother's sister's son or a member of her late husband's section. The widow's intended husband has to pay a fine of Rs. 10 to the tribesmen. A widow remarriage is celebrated during the dark fortnight of any month. The ceremony consists in pouring water on the feet of the couple and tying into a knot the ends of their garments. The faces of the remarried pair are not seen for three days after the marriage. A feast is given to the tribesmen on the fourth day after the marriage. Should a bachelor desire to marry a widow, he is first married to a *rui* bush (Calotropis gigantea). The marriage tie is not a very binding link.

Divorce is allowed with the sanction of the headmen of the tribe if the husband and wife do not agree, the husband is impotent, or the wife's conduct is bad. The man who wants a divorce has to pay a fine of Rs. 3-8 to the tribe. If a woman wants to marry another man, she can obtain a divorce from her husband by repaying the marriage expenses incurred by him. A woman divorced on account of adultery can remain in the tribe by paying a fine of Rs. 3-8 to the tribesmen, and can remarry by the widow remarriage form. If she repeats the offence, she is excommunicated. The Hindu law of inheritance is followed.

Religion. Gopáls belong to the Hindu religion. The special object of their worship is Khandoba of Madhi in Gamthadi, where a fair is held on the full-moon day of *Mágh*, when the first flag is set up by this tribe. Their family deities are the Devi of Tuljápur in the Nizam's territory. Khandoba of Jejuri in Poona, Mariái and Mhasoba. Every family among them offers a she-buffalo to Khandoba, calls her *Jáni*, rears her with care, and does not load her or sell her milk and butter, but presents her to Bráhmans. They worship all local gods and observe all the Hindu holidays. The Musalmán saints are venerated. When an epidemic breaks out, goats and fowls are offered to Mariái. They believe in soothsaying, witchcraft and evil spirits. Their marriages are conducted by Deshasth Bráhmans, the other ceremonies by the caste elders.

Death. The dead are buried in a sitting position with face to the east. The tribesmen are feasted on any day between the third and thirteenth and once at the end of the sixth month, and again at the end of the year. For the propitiation of the deceased ancestors the *Mahálaya* is performed either in the *Mahálaya paksha* or All Souls Fortnight in *Bhádrapad* or during the *Diwáli* holidays.

The Gopáls are reported to have once earned a living by weaving mats. They are now cowherds, and some of them cultivate small holdings. But the bulk of the tribe earn their living by acrobatic feats with bamboos and by begging. Many are day labourers.

Food. They eat flesh except beef and pork, and drink liquor. They have no objection to eat the leavings of the higher castes.

GOPALGANI.—A sub-division of Kolhátis.

GOPAL KALI.—A synonym for Rangári Shimpi.

GORE.—A sub-division of Bene Israels.

GORE MARATHA.—A sub-division of Kumbhárs.

GORKHODIA.—*See* under Minor Musalmán Castes.

GORWAL.—A synonym for Godhwál.

GOTRANG.—A sub-division of Holayás.

GOVALVAL.—A sub-division of Vániás.

GOVARDHAN.—A synonym for Golak.

GOYALVAL.—A synonym for Govalvál.

Name and origin. **GUDIGARS** or sandalwood carvers, also called Gaudchitrakas, numbering 359 (1901), including 154 males and 205 famales, are found in small numbers in Sirsi, Siddápur, Honávar, Ankola and Kumta *tálukás* of the Kanara district. Twenty-three were returned in the Dhárwár district at the time of the 1901 census. They style themselves Chitárs or Chitrakas, the name given by Manu to artisans, and claim to be Kshatriyas. They came to Kanara from Goa after the establishment of Portuguese rule, and have substituted Kanarese for Konkani except on the coast, where Konkani is still spoken by them. They claim to belong to the Káshyap, Kaundanya, Vasishtha, Vatsa, Gautam and Bháradwája *gotras*; but their claim is not admitted by the Bráhmans, who consider them Shudras.

Marriage ceremonies. Marriages are prohibited between members of the same *gotra*. A member of the caste may marry his father's sister's or mother's brother's daughter. He cannot marry his mother's sister's daughter. A man may marry two sisters and two brothers may marry two sisters. Polygamy is allowed and practised, but polyandry is unknown. Girls are married between nine and twelve, boys between sixteen and twenty.

Boys are girt with the sacred thread before marriage, which consists of the following ceremonies :—

Vágnischaya or the settlement of the marriage. This takes place in the presence of castemen, when sugar and betelnuts are distributed.

Simantpujan.—In this the bridegroom is received on the border of the bride's village by her father and presented with articles of dress.

Phule Khovane or decking the hair with flowers, is performed a few days before the *Simantpujan*. In this the boy's mother goes with some unwidowed women to the girl's house, presents her with an ornament, decks her hair with flowers, and fills her lap to the accompaniment of music. The marriage service is conducted after the fashion of Bráhmans.

The essential portions are *Phule Khovane* and the *Kanyádán*. The remarriage of widows is not permitted. A husband can divorce a wife on the ground of her misconduct. A woman who misconducts herself is excommunicated.

Religion. The caste follow the Hindu law of inherintance and belong to the Hindu religion. Their family gods are Nágesh, Raulnáth, Lakshmi-Náráyan, Mhálsa, Shántádurga, Káveri and Kámákshi, whose shrines are in Goa. They worship all local and village gods and observe all the Hindu holidays. They make pilgrimages to Tirupati, Dharmasthal, Gokarn and Rámeshwar. Their spiritual guides are the Smárt head of the Shringeri monastery in Mysore and the head of the Rámchandrapur *matha*. They reverence Musalmán saints. When an epidemic breaks out goats and fowls are offered to the Mareyamma goddess of Sirsi. Their priests are Havik Bráhmans.

Death. The dead are burnt. Their death ceremonies resemble those of the local Vánis.

The hereditary occupation of the caste is carving, inlaying and painting. They paint boards for various purposes and do all sorts of turning work. They carve sandalwood, ivory and ebony with great skill. They also work on the lathe in wood, making beautiful lacquered articles. It is usual for them to work only to order, and the finest specimens of their skill can only be procured in this way. A few own land under the Rayatvári system.

Food. They eat the flesh of goats, fowls and fish and drink liquor. They rank next to Vánis and eat at the hands of the Havik Bráhmans only.

GUGLI.—A sub-division of Bráhams.

GUJAR.—A sub-division of Ahirs, Láds, Dhedas, Chárans, Darjis, Kumbhárs, Telis, Kunbis, Sonis, Sutárs; also a synonym for Gurjar. A term applied to all Gujarátis in the Deccan and Konkan.

GUJARATI.—A sub-division of Kolhátis, Gopáls, Sagars, Gavandis, Bhadbhunjás, Rabáris, Vanjáris, Ods, Bhávsárs, Mális, Khatris, Lohárs.

GUJAR-GUPI.—A sub-division of Khojáhs.

GULIK.—A sub-division of Holayás.

Name and origin.

GURAVS, numbering 108,887 (1901), including 54,818 males and 54,069 females, are found all over the Presidency except in Gujarát. They are a class of temple ministrants, and consist of the following endogamous divisions or sub-castes :—

(1) Shaiva Gurav, or Nagari, Nilkanth, Svayambhu Gurav.

(2) Kadu Gurav, or Junari, Kotsáne, Gasrat Gurav.

(3) Hugar, Jeer, or Malgar, who are mostly Lingáyats.[1]

(4) Jain Gurav.

(5) Konkani Gurav or Bhávik.

None of these divisions intermarry with the others. The common bond is their occupation as temple servants. The Hugars or Jeers are of particular interest, inasmuch as they contain three religious groups, the Lingáyats or *linga* wearers, the Hindus who wear the sacred thread, and a mixed group wearing both the sacred thread and the *linga* (see LINGAYAT).

These various divisions are generally styled indifferently Gurav. The Kadu Guravs rank below the Shaiva group. From their names Nagari and Junari it seems possible that the division occurred when the Ahmednagar and Bijápur (Junnar) kingdoms formed separate political entities, and that the division is an instance of the influence of political boundaries on caste fission. The example of Gujarát tends to show that different political control fosters differences in social practices, which are commonly the origin of new castes.

The Jain Guravs are found only in the Málvan *táluka* of the Ratnágiri district. It is not clear why they are called Jain. In the accounts received regarding them there is no trace of any respect paid by them to Jain Tirthankars. There is a Shaiva temple at Váingani, a village in the Málvan *táluka*, which is called the Jain Rámeshwar temple, probably after the Jain builder, and it may be that the present Jain Guravs are the descendants of Jains who had taken to the worship of Shiva under the influence of Lingáyatism.

The Koli and Marátha ministrants at the temples of Shiva and other deities often describe themselves as Guravs, but they have not formed themselves into separate castes, and are members of the general Koli or Marátha community. They cease to call themselves Guravs when they cease to minister at temples.

So far as the Deccan is concerned, the Shaiva Guravs are considered superior to the other Gurav castes. They are invested with the sacred thread, and abstain from flesh and liquor, and their observances and ceremonies approach those followed by the Deshasth Bráhmans. The following particulars apply to them.

SHAIVA GURAVS are also called Pujári and Devalak, but they are generally known by the name Gurav only. The word *Pujári*, meaning worshipper, is often used by devotees for ministrants at the temples of Shiva and of other deities. The word *Devalak* is used in the Sanskrit account of the caste.

The origin of the caste is thus related in the 43rd chapter of the Shiva Purán :—

The Bráhman sage Dadhichi, devoted to the worship of Shiva, had to proceed on a journey to attend a council of Bráhmans. Before his departure he initiated his son Sudarshana into the secrets of the worship of Shiva, and entrusted his duties to him during his absence. After some days *Maháshivarátra* or Shiva's night arrived. On this day all people fasted and attended Shiva's temple, but Sudarshana, who, in the evil association of his wife Dushkala (ill-behaved), had allowed himself to go astray, instead of fasting and passing his time in the worship of Shiva, returned to his house after the morning worship and slept with his wife. Next day he went to Shiva's temple without bathing. All this enraged Shiva, who cursed him so that his wife died of the effect of the curse.

When the sage Dadhichi learnt his son's misfortune, he returned home, prayed to Shiva, and through the intercession of Párvati secured a boon which conferred upon Sudarshana and his descendants the privilege of workshipping Shiva before all and the right to all offerings made at his temples.

It is therefore enjoined that a Gurav must be feasted with Bráhmans at the completion of the worship of Shiva, and that a Gurav should worship Párvati first. Sudarshana and his descendants lost their Bráhmanhood. Sudarshana's four sons were appointed by Shiva himself as chief ministrants to the four quarters of the earth. All Shaiva Guravs claim descent from these four sons of Sudarshana.

Shaiva Guravs have both the Bráhmanical system of *gotras* and the surname groups of the lower castes. The restrictions upon intermarriage are regulated mainly by surnames, as many families do not know their *gotras*, a fact which tends to show that the Bráhmanical system must have been adopted by the caste at a later stage with a view to raise themselves into the social scale. The surnames and *gotras* known so far are as follows :—

Surname.	*Gotra.*
Bendre	.. Shándilya.
Upádhye	.. Do.
Kále	.. Do. Vasishtha, Vatsa.
Agláve	.. Nityandan.
Thorát	.. Gargya.
Jámdár	.. Have no *gotras.*
Kshiraságar	.. Have no *gotras.*
Sálunke	.. Have no *gotras.*
Bhagwán	.. Have no *gotras.*
Gáikwád	.. Have no *gotras.*

Marriages are prohibited between members having the same surname or *gotra.* A member of the caste may marry his mother's brother's daughter, but not his father's sister's or mother's sister's daughter. A man may marry two sisters, and two brothers may marry two sisters. Girls are married between five and thirteen, as a rule before they come of age ; boys between twelve and twenty-five. Polygamy is allowed and practised if the first wife is barren, ill-behaved, or subject to some incurable disease. There is no limit to the plurality of wives. (A Gurav of Hadapsar, a village near Poona, has more than five wives). Polyandry is unknown.

Boys are girt with the sacred thread between seven and eleven. The ceremony is performed with the same details as amongst the Bráhmans, but *puránokta mantras* are used instead of the *vedokta* which are used by the latter.

Marriage ceremonies. The offer of marriage comes from either side, more generally from the girl's father. Both dowry and bride-price are allowed, the amounts varying according to the means of the parties, but never exceeding Rs. 100. The day for the marriage is fixed by an astrologer. The service is conducted by a priest who is a caste-man, or, in his absence, by a Bráhman. When the wedding day is fixed, invitations are sent round beginning with the house gods, for whom written cards are placed in the household shrine. The marriage consists of the following ceremonies :—

Akshad.—On a lucky day the relatives of the bride and bridegroom go together in procession to the temples of Ganpati and Devi to invite the god and goddess and offer them cocoa-nuts, betel-leaves, betel-nuts, copper coins, and a pinch of rice grains coloured red with *kunku* (red powder). The priest accompanying the procession invokes the god and the goddess to be present at the wedding and ward off all evil. Next, a married pair from each party go round inviting friends and relations.

Simant-pujan.—In the evening previous to the marriage day the ceremony of *simant-pujan*, or worship at the boundary, takes place. In this ceremony the parents of the girl with their relatives go to the bridegroom's house with the following articles : uncooked rice, wheat, cocoanuts, betel-nuts, betel-leaves, red powder, turmeric powder, turmeric roots, garlands, flowers, milk, sugar, sweetmeats, and articles of dress such as a turban, a coat, a pair of waist-cloths and bodice-cloths. There they first worship Ganpati (represented by a betel-nut), Varuna (represented by a water-pot), a lamp, and the earth ; and then wash the feet of the bridegroom and offer him a dress. Next, the bride's mother washes the feet of the bridegroom's mother and fills her and her female relations' laps with wheat and pieces of dry cocoa-nut kernel. The guests assembled are presented with betel-leaves and betel-nuts, and Bráhmans with money gifts.

Vágnischaya or the ceremony of oral promise, takes place at night. In this ceremony the bridegroom's parents with their relations go to the bride's house with a dress and ornaments for the bride. First, the fathers of the bride and bridegroom present each other with a cocoa-nut and embrace each other. Next, they seat themselves on a carpet facing each other, and the bride is brought and made to sit in front of her father facing the bridegroom's father, who presents her with the ornaments and dress brought for her. After presenting betel-leaves and betel-nuts to the guests and distributing money to the Bráhmans the party returns to the bridegroom's house.

Turmeric ceremony.—In the morning of the wedding day the girl is rubbed with turmeric paste at her house by some unwidowed women of both sides, the remaining portion of which is taken to the boy's house, where he is rubbed with it similarly.

Dev-pratishta or God-installing.—Before the ceremony begins, the bride with her parents is bathed in hot water by some unwidowed women. After changing clothes and bowing to the house gods and the elders, the bride's parents with the bride begin the ceremony, which consists of the worship of planets (represented by betel-nuts), Ganpati, Varuna, and *avighna kalasha.* The *avighna kalasha* is an earthen jar, daubed with white and red colours. It contains turmeric roots, betel-nuts, a copper coin, and sweetmeats, and its mouth is covered with an earthen lid tied to it with a piece of cotton thread passed round several times. It is prayed to ward off all evil. This ceremony takes place at the bridegroom's house also.

Gauri-pujan.—This is performed only by the bride. The bride, with some of her female friends, worships in the house the goddess Párvati or Gauri, and sits there till the wedding time, repeating the word "Gauri".

Rukhawat.—When the time for the wedding draws near, a party from the bride's house takes several dishes of sweetmeats to the bridegroom's house and serves them to the bridegroom and his relations. Then the bridegroom is worshipped, garlanded, and is presented with articles of dress by the bride's father (a turban, a coat, a waist-cloth, and a shoulder-cloth). The priest then asks the bridegroom to bow to the house gods and the elders. The bridegroom, garlanded, dressed in new clothes, with a finger-mark of lamp-black on his either cheek, and his forehead daubed with redpowder, is taken in procession on a horse to the bride's house, the females walking just behind him and the males behind the females.

When the procession reaches the bride's house, cooked rice mixed with curds is waved in the bridegroom's face. In the meanwhile the bride's mother washes the feet of the bridegroom's mother, who returns to her place, as she has not to hear the marriage verses. Next, the bridegroom is taken off the horse and is led to the marriage booth, where the priests set two low wooden stools and make the bride and bridegroom stand on them facing each other. They hold a silk cloth between them that they may not see each other, and ask the bridegroom to bring before his mind's eye the image of his family god. They repeat marriage verses, and they and the assembled guests and relatives throw reddened rice grains over the pair. When the verses end, the screen is removed with a noise of clapping and drums and pipes. Guests, relations, and friends resume their seats, and are presented with betel-leaves, betel-nuts, flowers, sweet scents, etc. Money is also distributed amongst Bráhmans.

Madhuparka.—The bride's parents wash the bridegroom's feet, worship him, and give him a mixture of honey, milk, curds, sugar *ghi*, etc., to drink, and present him with a cow, bull, or cash, etc. Next, the bride and bridegroom garland each other. The priest passes cotton thread round the pair twelve times, which is then taken off and divided into two parts. The pair are made to fasten these on each other's wrists.

Kanyádán.—In this the parents of the bride hand her over to the bridegroom's care and request him to treat her well during her life-time.

Marriage sacrifice, or Lájáhoma.—The pair are led to the altar where fire is kindled. The priest asks them to worship the fire and throw parched rice and *ghi* into it. Next, he asks them to take mutual oaths that they will be each other's partners during their life-time for weal or woe. These oaths are taken in the presence of the fire, the earth, the priest, and gods.

Saptapadi.—Seven small heaps of rice are made on the altar and a betel-nut is placed on each of them. The priest recites *mantras* and the bridegroom lifts the bride's right foot and places it on the heaps in succession. When the seventh heap is crossed the marriage is complete.

Sun-mukh.—The bridegroom's mother puts on the bride all the ornaments made for her and looks at her face.

Sáde, or Robe ceremony.—The bride is presented with a robe and bodice, and her lap is filled with wheat, a cocoa-nut, and some fruits, by the priest and some unwidowed women.

Bride-giving.—The parents of the bride sit in front of the newly married pair. After worshipping the bridegroom they say to him, "we here give you this good-natured daughter, well-nourished and healthy, and request you to treat her kindly". The pair are then made to sit on the laps of the nearest relations while the priest repeats the above words.

Varát.—The procession, both of the bride and bridegroom. The bridegroom then takes the bride to his house in a palanquin or carriage with music, and accompanied by males and females on both sides.

Lakshmi pujan.—The goddess of wealth is worshipped by the pair at the bridegroom's house.

Naming.—The maiden name of the bride is changed and she is given a new name by which she is known afterwards in her husband's family. Betel packets and sugar are distributed to the party assembled and money to Bráhmans.

Exchange of feasts ends the ceremony.

Widow remarriage is allowed in the case of childless widows, but till recently it was not looked on with favour. A widow must marry either a widower or a married man. She cannot marry a member of the *gotra* of her father or of her deceased husband. A widow remarriage can take place on any auspicious day of the year during any month except *Ashádha*, *Bhádrapad*, and *Pausha*. It is always performed at night when the moon has set or not risen. A priest (member of the caste, or in his absence a Bráhman) and one or two widows are present on the occasion. The widow and her new husband are seated together on low wooden stools in a separate room (all relations sitting out of the room). They put on ornaments and new clothes, the priest makes them worship Ganapati, Varuna, a lamp, and the earth, and applies turmeric and red powder to the widow's forehead, fills her lap with wheat, a cocoa-nut, and some fruits, and asks the pair to garland each other. The skirts of their garments are tied together and they are told to bow to the house gods and the elders, which completes the union. A feast and presentation of betel packets end the ceremony.

Divorce is allowed in the case of infidelity on the part of the wife, with the sanction of the caste *panch*. It is effected by passing a deed in writing on a stamped paper to the effect that the husband no longer wants the wife and that there is no objection to her marrying whomsoever she likes. The document is signed by the husband and attested by the *panch*. But divorces are rare. A divorced woman can marry again after the widow re-marriage system.

Religion. The caste follow the Hindu law of inheritance and belong to the Hindu religion. They are followers of the Shaiva sect and worship chiefly Shiva and his incarnations. They have the privilege of worshipping these gods (morning and evening) before any other castes (including Bráhmans). Hence worship performed before a Gurav has done his is considered to be in bad form. Minor gods, such as Khandoba, Bhairav, Ambábái and Satvái; the cow, the bull, the cobra, the horse; and the banyan, *pipal* (Ficus religiosa), *umbar* (Ficus glomerata), and the sweet basil plant are also worshipped. Musical instruments (such as the double drum and stringed instruments), weapons (such as sword, mace, trident), and sacred books also form the objects of their worship. Khandoba and Bahiroba are worshipped generally daily (by village Guravs), but especially on Sundays. Ambábái or Párvati is worshipped daily. When an epidemic like cholera or small-pox breaks out they propitiate Ambábái by worshipping her and by pouring water over her idol continuously. The goddess Satvái is twice worshipped—on the fifth day after a child-birth, and on the twelfth if the child is a girl, and on the thirteenth if it is a boy. As amongst other Hiudus, the sweet basil, banyan, and the *pipal* trees are the special objects of worship of the female sex. They observe all the Hindu holidays and go on pilgrimage to Benares, Rameshwar, Gaya, Pandharpur, and other important and holy places of the Hindus, giving preference to those of Shiva. Their spiritual guide is Shankarácharya. Their priests are men of their own caste. In their absence Bráhmans are employed, who are received on terms of equality by other Bráhmans.

Death ceremonies.

The dead are burnt. Infants who have not cut their teeth are buried. When a person is on the point of death, money is distributed among Bráhmans according to the means of the family. After death the body is placed on a white blanket with its feet to the south. The corpse is then taken out of the house, placed in a sitting position on a low wooden stool, the crown of the head is rubbed with *ghi*, the body is bathed in hot water, and it is dressed in a loin cloth if a male, and in a robe and a bodice if a female. It is then laid on a bamboo bier with the head either to the south or to the east and a string is passed over it. If the deceased has no issue, the face is covered with a piece of cloth. A small piece of gold, two or three small pearls, and some basil leaves are put into the mouth, and flowers, red powder, and betel leaves are spread over the body. The son or male heir of the deceased walks in front carrying fire in an earthen pot, which is placed on a triangular bamboo frame suspended by means of strings attached to each of the corners of the frame. The bier is carried by four men (or more if necessary) who walk behind. At a small distance from the burning ground the bier is placed on the ground and the bearers change sides. The son or male heir picks up a stone (called the life-stone or *ashma*) and places a few grains of rice and a copper coin on the spot. When the party reaches the burning ground they put down the bier, untie the corpse, and place it on a pyre of wood or cow-dung cakes. The son or male heir dips the ends of his garments into water and wrings it into the mouth of the deceased. The priest then repeats *mantras* and the pyre is kindled. When the skull is broken the son or male heir bathes in the river, and taking on his shoulder an earthen jar filled with water, walks thrice round the funeral pyre. At the end of each round one of the party breaks a hole in the pot by the life-stone. When the rounds are complete the son drops the earthen pot and beats his mouth with his hand. The party then bathe and return to the house of the deceased to see the lamp lighted on the spot where the dead person breathed his last.

A male is burnt naked; a female in a robe and bodice.

On the second or third day after death the ashes are thrown into water.

If a woman dies within ten days after delivery, nails are driven into the thresholds of the house and *rála* (Italian millet) seeds are strewn behind the corpse from the house to the burning ground. Her remains are generally thrown into water the same day.

On the tenth day the son or the male heir goes to the river with a priest, makes a small triangular mound of earth, and spreads *darbha* grass over it after it is sprinkled with cow-dung and cow-urine. On this heap of earth he places five small earthen pots filled with water and throws in each of them a few barley and sesamum seeds. He closes the mouths of these pots with small but thick wheat cakes and places over each a ball of cooked rice. A small red flag is erected near each pot. On the heap in the middle he places the life-stone, which is worshipped with water, white clay, sesamum and barley grains, flowers, frankincense, etc., and is prayed to accept the offering. If crows eat the balls, especially the one to the right hand side, it is believed that the deceased has left behind no wish unfulfilled. Next, each mourner pours over the life-stone a handful of water with a few grains of sesamum and barley, and the son or the heir throws the life-stone into the river.

On the eleventh day the son and the priest go to the river. The son bathes in the river, makes sixteen balls of wheat flour and one of cooked rice, places them in a line from left to right on a piece of *darbha* grass, and worships them with sandal-wood paste, sesamum and barley seeds, flowers, and basil leaves, etc. Next, a sacrificial fire is kindled, in which a mixture of cooked rice, *ghi*, and a few seeds of sesamum and barely is thrown thirty-two times. The chief mourner then returns home and presents to Bráhmans water-pots, a pair of shoes, an umbrella, a lamp, a bedding, a pair of waist cloths, rice, wheat, pulses, and a cow.

In some families eleven balls of earth and eleven balls of cooked rice are made. Earthen balls are first placed in a line from left to right on pieces of *darbha* grass and then rice balls in the same way. They are worshipped with an offering of cooked food.

On the twelfth day the *sapindi shráddha* is performed in a *dharmashála* or on the river-side. The chief mourner cleanses the place with cow-dung and cow-urine. He places three pieces of plantain leaf on pieces of *darbha* in a line facing north, one for his grandfather, one for his great-grandfather and the third for his grandfather's grandfather; two pieces facing east, one for Kámdev and one for Kuldev; and one for the deceased facing north-east. The images of all (excepting the deceased) are represented by pieces of *darbha*. They are worshipped with water, sandal-wood paste, rice grains, sesamum and barley seeds, flowers, basil leaves, frankincense, etc., and are offered cooked food, such as rice, sugar, vegetables, *ghi*, lemon, and ginger, and are asked whether they are satisfied. What remains of the cooked rice is made into four balls—three small and one large—which are placed on *darbha* grass and worshipped. The large ball is divided into three equal parts by a blade of *darbha* grass. The three small balls (representing grandfather, great-grandfather, and grandfather's grandfather) are mixed up with the three parts of the large ball one by one. They are then placed in a vertical line and worshipped, the chief mourner saying, " I have united my dead father with the *pitras* or ancestors. " The party then return home and uncooked articles of food are given to Bráhmans.

On the thirteenth day a ceremony is performed at the house of the deceased in which forty-five balls of rice are placed on *darbha* grass and worshipped, and the corpse-bearers and other caste-men are feasted.

On the fourteenth day a betel-nut representing Ganpati is worshipped, and prayers are made that no sort of trouble may befall the family. Next, an earthen jar filled with water is placed on a piece of *darbha* grass, sesamum and barley seeds, and a copper coin are put into it, and its mouth is covered with mango leaves and pieces of *darbha* grass. This is called *shánti kalash.* It is worshipped and the water contained in it is sprinkled over the members of the deceased's family. Money and uncooked articles of food are given to Bráhmans and caste-men are feasted. This brings the death ceremonies to an end.

In the case of violent death, if the corpse is not found, the funeral rites are performed by *pálásh vidhi*. In the case of childless ancestors an adopted son or the heir of the deceased performs the ceremonies.

For the propitiation of deceased ancestors a member of the caste is fed every month during the first year. The *shráddha* is performed annually on the anniversary of the deceased, and the *paksha* on that day of the latter half of *Bhádrapad* which corresponds to the day of death.

Occupation.

The hereditary occupation of the caste is temple service. They dine on the offerings made to gods. They also make and sell leaf plates and cups, and in villages furnish flowers and leaf plates to the villagers, for which they receive grain allowances or *balutás*. They are good musicians and play on the double drum, stringed instruments, and harmonium. Some of them are *pátils* and *kulkarnis*. Some are in private service. Very few are petty Government servants. Some hold *inám* lands in the name of the gods they worship. A few hold service *ináms* (*mokása, pátilki,* and *kulkarniki*). Some take lands on lease which they cultivate themselves.

They eschew flesh, fish, and liquor. They take food only from Bráhmans who smoke with them.

JUNARI or KADU GURAVS differ from the Shaiva Guravs in eating flesh and drinking liquor and in performing their ceremonies after the fashion of the Kunbis. Their *devak* or marriage guardian consists of the leaves of the *vad* or banyan tree, which they tie to a post of the marriage booth and worship. They dine with the Kunbis.

KONKANI GURAVS are also known as Bhávik Guravs. They resemble the Konkani Maráthás in their customs and ceremonies, but they do not perform the *hom* or marriage sacrifice, the binding portion of the marriage ceremony consisting in putting garlands by the pair round each other's neck. Their *devak* consists of a twig of *kalamb* (Anthocephalus cadumba) which they will not cut either for building purposes or for fuel. Their priests are the local Bráhmans. They either burn or bury the dead. Besides ministering at temples, they also slaughter animals offered to the gods and play on the clarion or *sanai* at marriages. They eat the flesh of goats, sheep, fowls, deer, hares, pigs, and fish. They are much respected by the lower castes as they are believed to have influence over the gods whose worshippers they are.

LINGAYAT GURAVS have three endogamous divisions: those who wear the *linga,* those who wear the sacred thread, and those who wear both the sacred thread and the *linga.* They are the ministrants of Máruti or Hanumán, the monkey god and village guardian, who wears both the sacred thread and the *linga,* and is worshipped both by Bráhmanic Hindus and Lingáyáts. Their chief family stocks are Ishvar and Káshyap. Members of the same stock may not intermarry. Their priests, who are members of the caste, marry the daughters of ordinary Guravs after initiation, but will not give them their daughters in marriage. Girls are married from four to twelve before attaining puberty; boys from six to twenty. Polygamy is allowed and practised, but polyandry is unknown. The offer of marriage comes from either side. The boy's father has to pay a *teru* or bride-price to the girl's father, which the latter should not accept if he is well off. The day for the marriage is fixed by the family priest who conducts the service. The *Báshtagi* or the betrothal ceremony first takes place, in which the boy's father with relations and friends goes to the girl's house and presents her with ornaments and articles of dress. The marriage booth is then erected, and the boy and the girl are rubbed with turmeric paste and oil by five unwidowed women. On the following day the *devakárya* is performed and five to twenty-five unwidowed women are feasted. Next, the *airani* is installed, *i.e.*, four earthen jars are placed at the four corners of a square, a fifth is set in the middle, and a cotton thread passed round the necks of the jars is cut and fastened to the wrists of the boy and the girl. The boy and the girl are rubbed with oil and seated near the jars with some of their relations and bathed with the water in the jars. Marriage verses are then repeated and sacred grains of rice are thrown over the heads of the pair. This is the binding portion of the ceremony. The remarriage of widows is permitted. Divorce is allowed. A divorced woman is permitted to remarry if the cause of divorce be not adultery, in which case she is excommunicated. The caste follow the Hindu law of inheritance.

Guravs are non-Panchamsáli Lingáyats entitled to *ashtavarna* rites (*see* LINGAYAT). The chief deities of their worship are Shiva, Máruti, Sarasvati, Rámeshvar, and family ghosts who are deified to prevent them from bringing sickness into the house. Their priests are men of their own caste. Their religious teacher is also a man of their caste. Those who wear the *linga* bury and the rest burn their dead.

Besides ministering at temples some are astrologers and fortune-tellers and others are husbandmen. Some are musicians who beat the *sambal* or tabor at Bráhman, Sonár, and Lingáyat weddings, accompanied by Korvis who blow the *sanai* or clarion. They also make the brow-horn or *báshing* of flowers which the bridegroom wears. They sometimes, but seldom, as it is against their religion, play the drum or fiddle for their spiritual followers, the dancing girls, or Kalávants. They also sell *bel* (Ægle marmelos) leaves and flowers and flower garlands, which has led them to be called Hugars, *hu* in Kanarese meaning a flower. They do not use flesh or liquor.

JAIN GURAVS resemble local Bráhmans in matters of religion and custom, though they have a system of divisions by *devaks*. Their *devaks* consist of the *kalamb* (Anthocephalus cadumba) and the *audumbar* (Ficus glomerata), both of which are most common in the southern part of the Ratnágiri district. They abstain from flesh and liquor and do not take food and water from any Hindu caste, even from Bráhmans. They are mainly servants in village temples which, though dedicated to Bráhmanic gods, have still by their sides broken remains of Jain images. This, and the fact that most of the temple land grants date from a time when Jainism was the State religion, support the theory that the Jain Guravs are probably Jain temple servants who have come under the influence partly of Lingáyatism and partly of Bráhmanism. A curious survival of their Jainism occurs at *Dasara, Shimga,* and other leading festivals, when the village deity is taken out of the temple and carried in procession. On these occasions, in front of the village god's palanquim, three, five, or seven of the villagers, among whom the Gurav is always the leader, carry each a long, gaily-painted wooden pole resting against their right shoulder. At the top of the pole is fastened a silver mask or hand, and round it is draped a rich silk robe. Of these poles, the chief one, carried by the Gurav, is called the Jain's pillar, *Jainácha khámb* (Bom. Gazetteer, Vol. X. p. 119).

GURJAR.—A sub-division of Bráhmans and Vániás.

GURU.—A sub-division of Bráhmans.

GURUSTHAL.—A sub-division of Jangams.

HABBU.—A sub-division of Bráhmans.

HABSHI.—A synonym for Sidi.

HADIA.—A sub-division of Dhedas.

HAIG.—A sub-division of Kabbaligars.

HAIGA.—A synonym for Havik.

HAJAM.—*See* Náhvi or Hájám; a sub-division of Vanjáris.

HAJURI.—A synonym for Khavás.

HAKIM.—*See* under Minor Musalmán Castes.

HALABE.—A sub-division of Devángs.

HALAI.—A sub-division of Memans.

HALALKHOR.—A synonym for Bhangi.

HALDE.—A sub-division of Mális.

HALE.—A sub-division of Hanbars.

Name and origin.

HALEPAIK, * a caste of Toddy-drawers numbering (1901) 51,930, including 26,805 males and 25,125 females, residing, with the exception of a few emigrants, entirely in the district of Kanara. They would seem to be connected with the Billavas or Divars of South Kanara, and perhaps with the Tiyans of Malabar, who are also toddy-drawers by profession. Little is known for certain regarding the original home of this caste; but from the fact that the *swámi* or high priest

* The materials for this article were supplied by Mr. J. A. Saldanha.

of one division lives at Anegundi (Vijayanagar) and that the caste tradition connects them with the kingdom of Vijayanagar it would seem probable that they were at one time very largely employed in the service of the Vijayanagar kings, and formed an important element in the fighting forces of the Hindu kingdom of the south. At the present day they are mostly found on the coast, in the *tálukás* of Ankola, Kumta, and Honávar, and are only met with in any numbers above the Gháts in the *tálukás* of Sirsi and Siddápur. Apart from the mystery concerning their origin, the Halepaiks are interesting on account of their totemistic organization, which is described below.

Endogamous divisions.

The caste consists of two endogamous divisions :—

1. Tengina Divar or Tengina Makkalu.
2. Bainu Divar or Kán Divar.

The Tengina Makkalu, or "Children of the Cocoanut tree," live on the coast. They also style themselves Námdhar and Trinámdhar Paiks. The Bainu Halepaiks take their name from *bainu*, the sago-palm, and reside above Gháts. The bar against intermarriage seems to be in origin geographical, and is similar to the barrier that exists between the Konkani and Deshasth Maráthás, who are also separated by the wall of the Western Gháts, once a formidable obstacle to social intercourse. The natural consequence of the bulk of the caste residing in the more civilized regions of the coast has been to engender a certain contempt for their less cultivated fellow caste-men living in the above-ghát jungles. This feeling manifests itself in the practice which is rapidly gaining in popularity among the former, of styling themselves Námdharis and Trinámdharis, and a feeling of superiority over the latter that has worked powerfully towards producing the present completely endogamous sections. The Námdharis and Trinámdharis bear the marks of the Rámánuja sect, the Trinámdharis being the social superiors of the Námdharis. Many Halepaiks returned themselves as Námdharis at the census of 1901. It is usual to derive the name Halepaik from *hale* old, and *paik* a soldier. Taken in connection with the name Komárpaik, another Kanarese caste, the derivation is not improbable; and it gains in probability from the fact that both the Halepaiks and Komárpaiks, at the advent of British rule, were notorious as a troublesome tribe of banditti who appeared to be warriors by profession. They would seem to have been at one time a favourable recruiting ground for the kings of Vijayanagar and the *poligars* or petty chiefs of Kanara. Some further light is thrown on the origin of the caste by the synonym of "Divar" which would appear to be another form of "Tivar" an Islander. The Tiyans of Malabar are Tiyars, and their name also takes the form of Iravar, Illavar, and Billavar. A tradition in Malabar relates how certain Dravidian tribes in Malabar migrated to Ceylon, whence they returned to Travancore to spread northwards along the coast. Hence the term Islanders. Anthropometrical examination of the Halepaiks and Tiyans would probably throw much light on the supposed identity of these castes.

The Halepaiks speak Kanarese. Those on the coast are fluent in Konkani also. The names in common use are—Maria, Timma, Ira, Hanama, Venka, Gidda, Shiva, Krishna. Females bear the same names with the termination *i*. The males suffix "Naik," *i.e.* "Chief", to their names, corresponding to the Marátha "Rao" and "Desai."

Exogamous divisions.

The Halepaiks have a totemistic social organization. Each exogamous section known as a '*bali*' (*lit.* a creeper) is named after some animal or tree which is held sacred by the members of the same. This animal, tree or flower, etc., seems to have been once considered the common ancestor of the members of the *bali* and to the present day it is both worshipped by them, and held sacred in the sense that they will not injure it. Thus the members of the Nágbali, named apparently after the Nágchampa flower, will not wear this flower in their hair, as this would involve injury to the plant. The Kadavebali will not kill the elk (Kanarese *Kadave*) from which they take their name. The *balis* are very numerous. The names and origins of some of the most important are given below. The existence of these totem divisions seems to establish the Dravidian origin of the caste.

Tengina Divars :—

Name.		Derivation.
1. Shetti bali	..	Shetli or Shetti = a fish.
2. Honne bali	..	Honne = a tree (*Pterocarpus marsupium*).
3. Chendi bali	..	Chendi = a tree (*Cerbera odállum*).
4. Tolana bali	..	Tola = a wolf.
5. Devana bali	..	Devana = a tree (*Artemesia phalleris*).
6. Hole bali	..	Hole = a tree (*Terminalia arjuna*).
7. Bhairana bali	..	Bhairana = a bird.
8. Kendi bali	..	Kandi = a tree (*Prosopis spicigera*).
9. Handi bali	..	Handi = a pig.
10. Nág bali	..	Nágchampa = a tree (*Mesua ferrea*).
11. Vali bali	..	Vali = a creeper.

	Name.		Derivation.
12.	Shige bali	..	Shige = soap-nut (*Acacia concinna*).
13.	Ajjane bali	..	Ajja = a tree (*Antiaris toxicaria*).
14.	Kanne bali	..	Kanna = a tree.
15.	Shivana bali	..	Shivani = a tree (*Gmelina arborea*).
16.	Ganga bali	..	Ganga = the river Gangávali.
17.	Salyan bali	..	Saler = a porcupine.
18.	Manál bali	.	Manál = a tree (*Pithocolobium dulce*).
19.	Shire bali	..	Shire = a tree (*Gynan dropsis pentaphylla*).
20.	Arashina bali	..	Arasina = turmeric (*Curcuma longa*).
	Bainu Divars—		
1.	Mahár bali	..	Mahár = a low caste, or Mhád—the palm tree.
2.	Bangár bali	..	Bangár = gold.
3.	Kadave bali	..	Kadave = the elk.
4.	Sarpana bali	..	Sarpa = a snake.

and several of the *balis* already given, *i.e.*, Nos. 1 to 6 inclusive.

The Holebali and Mahárbali are held to be socially inferior and the girls of these sections alone may be married to members of the other *balis*. A special feature of these *balis* is that they are traced through females, not through males. This practice suggests the former prevalance of polyandry, and serves to confirm the opinion that the original home of the caste was in Southern India. *Balis* of the same kind are found among many castes in North Kanara, notably the four Vakkal castes, *i.e.*, Hálvakki, Gám, Kot and Kare and the following others :—

Ager	Haslár	Mukri.
Ambig	Kumbhár	Suppalig
Harakantra	Moger	Uppár.

Many of these also reckon descent through females.

Comparing the Halepaiks with the Tiyans of Madras, it will be noted that, in addition to the common appellation of 'Divar,' the castes resemble each other in being divided into *balis*, in tracing descent through females, and in their occupation of toddy-drawers. In appearance they are not dissimilar. The Tiyans practise polyandry to the present day in South Malabar. They are supposed to have imported the cocoa-palm into India between the 1st and 5th century A.D.

The coast and above-ghát Halepaiks do not intermarry nor do they dine together. It has been seen that the former are further divided into the Námdhari and Trinámdhari, who will intermarry, with the reservation that, when a member of the Trinámdhari division wishes to marry a girl of the Námdhari group, both the bride and bridegroom have necessarily to receive *mudrádhárana* (*i.e.*, branding with the metal stamps of Shankha and Chakra, which are the marks of the followers of Vishnu) for their purification. *Mudrádhárana* is not necessary when a Trinámdhari marries a Trinámdhari girl or when a Námdhari marries a Trinámdhari girl, though there is no objection to any person undergoing it at any time for bodily purification. The Námdharis are not allowed to bear on their foreheads the three vertical marks of the Trinámdharis, and it appears that the Trinámdharis occupy a comparatively superior position in the caste. But the Námdharis of Konalli maintain that there is no distinction between the two divisions in any respect, and that the two divisions intermarry freely without any distinction whatever and are on a footing of equality.

The members of the same *bali* cannot intermarry, nor are marriages allowed between paternal cousins even though they belong to different *balis*. But a man may marry his maternal uncle's daughter; also a deceased wife's sister.

Origin of the Caste. The origin of the caste is still a subject of speculation. According to the account given by the leaders of the caste, which has been obtained from the religious head of the caste, *viz.*, Lokacháriya of Sagar in Mysore, the origin of the Halepaiks is as under:—

"During the reign of Vijaya Rámabhupála of Vijayanagar, Bhámini, the wife of one of the king's servants Ranganaika, by the blessing of the goddess Laxmi, bore a son, who was born at Kumarakshetra in the kingdom of Vijayanagar on Friday, the 7th of the bright half of *Kartika* in the year Sadharana, 1143, of the Shaka era. The boy was named Naráyan. One day the boy was playing in the street, when Gopala Krishna Raja, the son of Vijaya Ráma Bhupála, happened to pass by in a chariot. Attracted by the royal bearing of the child, he placed him in his chariot and took him with him to his palace. At 16 years the boy, who had been educated as a prince of the royal family, managed important affairs of State, distinguished himself as a commander of the Vijaynagar army and conquered many new territories. The king, admiring his valour, made him the ruler of a State, gave him a large retinue, and invested him with all the marks of royalty. In course of time, however, Nárayan met his father Ranganaika, who had grown old since the loss of his son, and came to know that he was the lost son of the man Ranganaika and Bhámini. When the king Gopála Krishna discovered Náráyan's humble origin, he placed him in charge of the mint, and gave him the village of Halepaikas, a *jaghir*, to be enjoyed by him and his descendants. In course of time some of his descendants started on a pilgrimage. They went to Rámeshwar, Káshi, Tirupati, Shriranga, and thence to Udapi and Gokarn, and visited the then ruling sovereigns of this part of the country, namely, Venkatappa Naik of Ikkeri and Sankanna Naik of Keladi. They were appointed to honourable posts under the Anegundi and Chandávar sovereigns and thus came to reside in Chandávar, in Kumta *táluka*."

It is unfortunate that this story of the origin of the caste seems to have no foundation in the history of Vijayanagar; nor have the places Kumarkshetra and Halepaik been identified. The story refers to Shaka 1143, *i.e.*, A. D. 1221; but the kingdom of Vijaynagar was not founded till about the year A. D. 1336.

The habits of the caste are settled. The Halepaiks in Kanara district are well organised communities and are distributed over twelve *shimes*, or territorial divisions, namely :—

Among Coast Halepaiks :—

1. Chandávar.
2. Mirjan.
3. Gersappa.
4. Ankola.

Of these four divisions, the Chandávar *shime* occupies the first place and Konalli near Chandávar is the recognized head-quarters of the caste, being known as the *Tai-sthala* or mother-place. There is no peculiarity in regard to the shape or material of their dwellings.

Among Highland Halepaiks :—

1. Yellápur.
2. Sonda.
3. Karur.
4. Sirsi.
5. Helur.
6. Banavasi.
7. Islur.
8. Bilgi.

Of these 8 *shimes*, the Bilgi *shime* occupies the highest place, the head-quarters of which is at Bellhali, where is a *math* presided over by a *guru* who is a Trinámdhari. Each *shime* consists of a number of village settlements presided over by a hereditary headman, called *Buddhivant*, who presides at meetings of the castemen settling disputes, or referring them to the *yajamán*. A *yajamán* is the head of several *shimes* and is entitled to collect dues from those within his jurisdiction. The Halepaiks do not admit outsiders into the caste.

Marriage ceremonies. The girls among coast Halepaiks, are married before they attain puberty, *i.e.*, when they are 5 to 12 years of age ; there is no restriction, of age with regard to males. Sexual license before marriage is not recognized nor tolerated. Among highland Halepaiks girls are married even at the age of 16. Polygamy is permitted, but polyandry is not. A man may marry any number of wives. A married woman cannot marry again during the lifetime of her husband, after she has been divorced.

When a match is approved of by the parents of the bride and bridegroom, they cast the horoscopes of the boy and girl to be married, and consult the local deity. This is done in the same way as receiving *prasád*, *i.e.*, the fall of a flower from the body of the deity is taken as an indication of its approval. If the horoscopes agree and the deity approve of the settlement, the father of the would-be bridegroom, accompanied by friends and relations, takes flowers in a plate to the house of the bride. These flowers are put on the body of the bride, and the parents of the bride fill the plates with betel-nut and betel-leaves, and offer them to the parents of the bridegroom. On the next day, or on any subsequent day fixed, the bridegroom takes in his hand a cocoanut, betelnut, betel-leaves, and a small knife, enveloped in a piece of red cloth, which are to be placed before the *tulsi* or sacred basil plant. He is taken to the bride's house in procession, where he and his would-be bride are made to stand before the *tulsi*, and the wedding ceremony takes place. The principal ceremonies are :—

(1) The joining of the hands of the bride and bridegroom and pouring a pot of milk over them by their parents. This is known as the *dháre* ceremony.

(2) The tying of ends of their garments by the maternal uncle of the bride.

(3) The throwing of rice by the priest and elders.

(4) The garlanding of the bride and bridegroom by each other.

After garlanding, the marriage cannot be dissolved, though the marriage settlement may be broken at any time before it. The marriage feasting continues for two days more, and on the fourth day the *báshing*, or ornamental head—dress of the bridegroom, is tied to the principal post inside the house and the ceremony is over. The bridegroom has to pay the bride's parents the *tera* as bride-price, which varies from Rs. 20 to Rs. 100. In order to save this payment, double marriages are sometimes arranged. Thus, when a girl is taken from a family, another girl who is a near relation of the bridegroom is also married to a member of the bride's family. If this mutual exchange is not feasible, the bridegroom is sometimes adopted by the parents of the bride as a domestic son-in-law (*mane-alaya*). In this case the bridegroom has not to pay the bride-price, but there is a mutual agreement that the son-in-law should stay and work at the bride's house, receiving some of the profits of her parents.

Remarriage of widows is permitted but is looked upon with disfavour by the community. A widow cannot marry her husband's younger or elder brothers. She may marry any other person who is not of her *bali*.

A man who is to marry a widow must be a married man, whether the first wife or wives may or may not be alive when he marries the widow. The man who intends to marry a widow must obtain the permission of his community by a payment of Rs. 12 to the leaders of the caste. The marriage must take place at midnight. The persons to be married should sit on a mat of cocoa-palm leaves behind the *tulsi-katta*. Four or five widows then give the widow bangles, a *mugati* or nose-ring, and a *shire* or loin cloth, which are all brought by the husband for the occasion. The widow puts these on and the marriage is complete. The married pair must go to their house before daybreak. The married widow must herself mark her forehead with a red paint, which is the usual mark of a married woman. The married couple are regarded as socially degraded and the husband is not allowed to take part in caste meetings, nor may the pair take a leading part at any auspicious ceremony. A man married to a widow may not perform the marriage of his children. There is no intercourse in respect of food or marriage between the pair and the relations of the former husband of the widow. This is the opinion of the Mirján *shime*. There are several instances of widow marriages at Mirján, Kodkani, Hiregutti, Bargi, Sanekatta, and Hanehalli. But the Halepaiks of the Chandávar *shime* say that widow marriage is not permitted among them, and that those who have married widows are regarded as outcaste. In the Bilgi *shime* the widows who are detected having gone astray are taken to the *math* at Bellhalli near Siddápur, and are disposed of for a price to any man in need of a wife, provided he is already a married man. This is regarded as a marriage. The practice appears to be confined to the Bilgi *shime*.

Divorce depends upon the pleasure of the husband, and there is no particular form by which it is effected. A divorced wife may remain in the caste so long as she follows the caste rules. She is not permitted to remarry during the lifetime of her husband.

The members of the caste in North Kanara follow the Hindu law of inheritance, but in South Kanara the Halepaiks follow the Aliya Santan law of descent through females.

Religion. They belong to the Hindu religion and are followers of Rámánuja. Venkataráma of Tirupati with his servant Hanumán are their deities of special worship. There appear to be no particular reasons for this preference beyond the fact that they are the followers of Rámánuja, and that almost all the Shudra castes in North Kanara worship the same deities. Their worship and Rámánuja's Vaishnavism appear to have been imported into Kanara, rather than brought this side by the Halepaiks or other low castes. Tátáchári, residing at Tirupati, is the Guru of the Námdharis and Lokachari, who resides at Tirukolam in the Sagar district of the Mysore territory, is the Guru of the Trinámdharis. But both the sub-divisions also respect the Gurus of each other. A Námdhari can become a Trinámdhari by having *mudrádhárana* and sprinkling of holy water from the Ayyas of Hospet. The Guru of the highland Halepaiks resides at Anegundi. He occasionally (once in four or five years) visits the district, and sells the powder or material for imprinting the name or mark on their foreheads. In Kanara general control over the highland Halepaiks is exercised by a Trinámdhari Halepaik of the Bellhalli Math near Siddapur, whom they term Guru or Swámi, but he is subordinate to the Swámis of Anegundi.

They pay respect also to other Hindu gods and worship the local minor deities, such as Gráma-Devati, Masti, Jataga, etc., like other Shudras, but have no special minor gods and patron saints. They keep the Hindu festivals of *Diváli*, *Dasara*, and *Chauti*.

They employ Trinámdhari Vaishnava Bráhmans from Sagar district for their religious purposes. These Bráhmans are not respected as Bráhmans in Kanara. They are called *Tirtha* givers or Ayyas. Of the local Bráhmans, none but Saklápuri and Karnátak Bráhmans act as priests to them. Havik and other Bráhmans are not allowed to officiate as priests to the caste, on pain of being put out of caste.

Death ceremonies. They commonly burn their dead, except in the case of those who die of small-pox, who are buried, as is also customary among all other Hindu castes of this part of the country. In both cases the dead body is laid on its back. The ashes are collected on the ground on the third day and thrown into a river.

Of the two sub-divisions of the coast Halepaiks, *viz.*, Trinámdhari and Námdhari, the first (Trinámdhari) perform *shráddha* for propitiation of their ancestors on the date of death, and *mahálaya* in the latter half of *Bhádrapada* for the propitiation of ancestors in general. The Námdharis perform the *mahálaya* only. There are no special forms of these ceremonies for childless ancestors and men who have died a violent death. This at least is the practice followed by the Halepaiks of the Mirján *shime.* Those of Konalli in Chandávar *shime,* who are more disposed to imitate Bráhmanical ritual, say that *shráddhas* and *mahálayas* are performed by both the sects according to the form in which these ceremonies are performed by Bráhmans. The highland Halepaiks perform only *mahálayas.*

They believe their original occupation to have always been agriculture. Their hereditary profession was mainly that of toddy-drawers until recently. The restrictions of the Forest and Abkári Departments have driven the Halepaiks on the Gháts to other occupations. The coast Halepaiks too do not find toddy-drawing as lucrative an occupation as before. Their present occupations are agriculture, toddy-tapping, quarrying and stone-cutting, carpentry, smithy, trade, cart-driving, and Government service as village servants. Occupation.

Some of them are tenure-holders of Government lands, occupancy and non-occupancy ryots without any special privileges in respect of rent. Several of them are landless day-labourers. None of them are nomadic cultivators.

As artizans they work in wood and metal and any other material except leather. They are not hunters by profession, but they hunt a hog, a stag, a hare, etc., for their own food. The Halepaiks of Konalli however do not hunt any animal.

There is no special implement or mode of working of the caste, nor is there any particular occupation which raises any of them above the others.

They do not habitually prostitute either their married or unmarried women.

They eat the following:—Flesh of fowl, pigeon, and sheep, pork from wild hog, fish (of the varieties known as Bangdi, Tori, Shetti, Tora, Madjali, etc.), white rats, rabbits, tortoises, stag and deer. There is no special article of food the abstaining from which may raise them above other castes. But they are prohibited from eating Food.

monkeys, cow's flesh, crocodiles, snakes, lizards, jackals, house rats, and insects. The coast Halepaiks also do not drink wine or liquor. But this restriction does not obtain among the highlanders.

They eat *pakki* and *kachchi* from the hands of all Bráhman castes and from Nádors, Vánis, Hálvakki Vakkals and Maráthás, and not from the hands of any other castes.

The only Hindu castes which eat *pakki* or *kachchi* or drink and smoke with them are Agers, Mukris and Chamárs. At their marriage and other ceremonies the Suppalig and Bhandári musicians may not play music, on pain of being put out of caste. The Halepaiks employ only the Halleer and Ager musical bands for this purpose. They rank higher than the Agers, Mukris and Chamárs, and are at the top of the Asprishya Shudras. All castes of Bráhmans, and Nádors who are Sat-Shudras, regard them as such.

The pretensions of the highland Halepaiks, on the other hand, do not reach so high as those of the coast sub-caste. They do not appear as sophisticated by contact with civilization as their brethern on the coast. They admit that they eat *kachchi* at the house of Halvakki and Kot Vakkals, while none of the Vakkal castes would eat *kachchi* from the hands of the Halepaiks. In the estimation of all, except the coast Halepaiks themselves, all classes of Halepaiks are regarded as impure, standing below the Vakkals, who correspond to the Kunbis of the Deccan.

HALGE.—A sub-division of Berads; a synonym for Bile.

Name and origin. **HALLEERS**, numbering 2,079 (1901), including 1,078 males and 1,001 females, are found entirely in the Kanara district. According to local tradition, when the Sonda chiefs were reigning at Panjim in Goa, the Halleers were their musicians and lived in the village of Kuppali. Originally they are believed to have emigrated from Tirupati in North Arcot. They came to Kanara about eight or ten generations ago, and settled at Majáli and Bád near Kárwár, gradually spreading southwards as far as Honávar. The Halleers in Kárwár style themselves Vájantris, the general term for musicians, and refuse to have any connection with their brethren in Gokarn, Hiregutti, and Hegde. These so-called Vájantris declare that the rest of the Halleers rank with the impure castes, and are not allowed to play at temples and at the thread or marriage ceremonies of Bráhmans, being employed only by the lower castes. According to the Bombay Gazetteer, all Halleers are held to be impure, and it is probable that the Kárwár Halleers are now endeavouring to raise themselves to a level with other musicians not considered impure, by imitating their manners and customs, and disclaiming connection with their brethren in the south. The latter apparently have not yet adopted the usages of the higher castes.

There are neither endogamous nor exogamous sub-divisions of the caste.

Intermarriages can take place between those families only with whom a former connection can be traced. A member of the caste may marry his father's sister's or mother's brother's daughter. He cannot marry his mother's sister's daughter. A man may marry his deceased wife's sister. Two brothers may marry two sisters. Polygamy is allowed and practised, the number of wives a man can have at a time being limited to four. Polyandry is unknown. Boys are generally married between fifteen and twenty-five; girls between eight and thirteen, as a rule before coming of age. If a girl remains unmarried till after she attains puberty, her parents have to pay a fine to the caste *panch.* Misconduct on the part of an unmarried girl is generally connived at; but if the man involved be a Christian or a Musalmán, she is turned out of the caste.

Marriage ceremonies.

The offer of marriage comes from the boy's father, who has to pay a sum of Rs. 5 to the girl's mother. The day for the marriage is fixed by the village astrologer. The ceremony is conducted either by a Karnátak Bráhman or by an elderly member of the caste. About eight or ten days before the marriage takes place the betrothal ceremony, which is known as *phule khovane,* is performed, in which the girl is dressed in a new robe and her hair decked with flowers. On the marriage day the boy and the girl are rubbed with turmeric paste and oil, a marriage coronet is put on the boy's head, and he is taken in procession to the girl's house. When he is seated, rice grains, a cocoanut, and five plantains are offered to each of the village gods and to the family gods of the parties. The boy's father then presents the girl with some articles of dress and ornaments, which she puts on and seats herself next to the bridegroom. The pair then put garlands round one another's necks. The essential portion of the ceremony consists in the decking of the girl's hair with flowers.

The remarriage of widows is permitted. The widow has to return to the relations of her deceased husband the clothes and ornaments received from him. The widow bathes and puts on a new robe presented to her by her new husband. She is then seated by his side, redpowder is applied to her forehead, and a lucky necklace is tied round her neck, this completing the ceremony. A bachelor is not allowed to marry a widow.

A husband can divorce a wife on the ground of her misconduct. A divorced woman can marry again after the fashion of the widow remarriage ceremony.

Religion. The caste follow the Hindu law of inheritance and belong to the Hindu religion. They chiefly worship village gods, such as Vetál, Dád, Beer, and Mhasti, the special object of their devotion being Mámái or Mahámái, whose fane is at Chitakule near Sadáshivgad to the north of Kárwár. Their family gods are Mahádev of Bád in Kárwár, Venkatesh of Ankola, and Sailkárdev of Májáli, nine miles north of Kárwár. They worship their musical instruments on the *Dasara* day. Goats and fowls are offered to the village gods, of which the heads are received by the worshippers at the temples, and the bodies by those who make the offerings. They make pilgrimages to Tirupati and Pandharpur, and observe all the Hindu holidays. They have great faith in soothsaying, witchcraft, and evil spirits. Sickness of all kinds is believed to be the work of spirits. Ghádi and Komárpaik magicians are consulted to devise a cure. Their spiritual guide is the head of the Shringeri monastery in Mysore. Their ceremonies are usually conducted by members of the caste. Occasionally Karnátak Bráhmans are employed to conduct marriages, and they are considered degraded on this account. They are readmitted into their caste only after performing a penance.

Death. The dead are either burnt or buried. On the tenth day after death a sweet basil plant is planted on the spot where the corpse was burnt or buried; and a tender cocoanut, a lamp, and a flag of cotton-rag are placed by its side. On the eleventh day a feast is given to relations. The *shráddha* is not performed.

Occupation. Halleers are hereditary musicians. They are employed by many classes of Hindus at marriage and other ceremonies. The Halleers near Gokarn appear to be employed chiefly by the lower castes. They have an hereditary right to perform at the village temples. Their instruments are the drum or *dhol*, double drum or *sammel*, the timbrel or *kánsál*, the clarionet or *sanai*, the brass horn or *shriti*, the cornet or *kahalo*, and the horn or *shing*. A few of them are carpenters. They catch fish for their own use. They do not catch crocodiles or tortoises.

Food They eat the flesh of goats, sheep, hares, fowls, and fish, and drink liquor. They eat the leavings of Bráhmans. They consider themselves superior to those who eat certain kinds of flesh from which they abstain.

HALMANE.—A sub-division of Holayás.

HALVAI.—A functional group of confectioners.

HALVAKKI VAKKALS, numbering between 20,000 and 30,000, also known as Gávdás, are found only in the Kanara district. In 1881 the number was returned as 26,395; but at the subsequent census enumerations no reliable figures were obtained owing to the caste being confused with other cultivating castes, such as the Kunbis, the word Kunbi being the Maráthi equivalent of the Kanarese *Vakkal*. Vakkal or Vakkalig in Kanarese signifies cultivator, and the term Vakkal is not therefore a caste name, but a profession. In the Bombay Presidency and Mysore the Vakkals are the Kanarese cultivating castes. The Mysore Gazetteer (Vol. I, p. 229) includes Reddis, Nonabas, and even Halepaiks under the name of Vakkalig. **Name and origin.**

In Kanara the caste is chiefly found in the *tálukas* of Kárwár, Ankola, Kumta, and Honávar, where they have numerous centres. The name of the caste is commonly said to be derived from the Kanarese *hálu* (milk-white) and *akki* (rice), probably because the Hálvakki Vakkals are the chief growers of the better kind of rice (*hálakki* in Kanarese meaning table rice). The caste is also found in Mysore. They seem to be among the earliest settlers on the coast. They have now lost all tradition of connection with Mysore, but a trace perhaps remains in their worship of Venkataráma of Tirupati in North Arcot.

The caste seems once to have been the great landlord caste of Kanara, and subsequently to have given place to Haviks, Gaud Sárasvats, and Lingáyats. It is still a common tradition that their women intermarried with the early Havik settlers, and evidence is forthcoming to render this tradition not improbable.

The names in common use among men are Bira, Nága, Goli, Timma, Kuppa, Goinda; and among women, Tulsi, Karijádevi, Shivi, Gangi, Nági, Timmi, and Putti. The men add *gavda*, literally a headman, to their names, some interposing the honorific *appa* or *anna*, as Birappagavda or Venkannagavda. Female names are generally formed by substituting "*i*" for "*a*," "*u*," or "*o*" at the end of the names of the males.

There are no endogamous divisions of the caste, which is divided into *balis* or exogamous sections, of which the following are the most important:— **Divisions.**

1. Baler bali .. Balai = plantain tree.
2. Balina bali .. Bali = a sea fish (*Trichnirus lapturus*).

3.	Bargal bali	..	Barga = hog deer.
4.	Bhairan bali	..	Bhairana = a bird.
5.	Devi bali	..	Devi = goddess.
6.	Dyávana bali	..	Dyava = the tortoise.
7.	Gurvina bali	..	Gurani = prickly plant (*Ichnocarpus*).
8.	Hole bali	..	Hole = a tree (*Terminalia arjuna*).
9.	Kadsan bali	..	Kadachi = a shrub.
10.	Kadvin bali	..	Kadave = the elk.
11.	Kodkal bali	..	Kodkal = a monkey.
12.	Kunte bali	..	Kunti = a tree (*Murraya exotica*).
13.	Kedagi bali	..	Kedagi = fragnant screw-pine (*Pandanus odoratissimus*).
14.	Machholi bali	..	Machchu or Machchi = an axe used for cutting trees.
15.	Majkal bali	..	(Unknown).
16.	Manál bali	..	Manál = a tree (*Pithocolobium dulce*).
17.	Manjal bali	..	Manjála = saffron.
18.	Muskinbali	..	Muskin = a river fish.
19.	Nág bali	..	Nág champa (*Mesua ferrea*).
20.	Shirin bali	..	Shirkal= a tree (*Gynandropsis pentaphylla*).

The enquiries conducted into the significance of these *balis* seem to show that they are true totemistic divisions though tending to lose their original character as the sections of the caste advance in the social scale. Thus the *kedagi* is the screw-pine commonly found in the streamlets and rivers of Kanara. The members of the Kedagi bali will neither cut the tree nor pluck its flowers. Those of the Bargal bali will not kill or eat the *barga* or mouse-deer. The followers of the Shirin bali, named after the *shirkal* tree will not sit in the shade of the tree, and refrain from injuring it in any way. Descent in reference to *balis* is traced through males, the caste in this point differing from the majority, who either trace their *bali* through females or through both sexes, the latter presumably being the intermediate stage betweem the older fashion and the modern system.

Persons of the same *bali* cannot intermarry. A boy cannot marry a paternal uncle's daughter but he may marry his father's sister's daughter. He cannot marry his maternal aunt's daughter, but he may marry his mother's brother's daughter. There are no other prohibitions on intermarriage. A man may marry his deceased wife's sister.

Hálvakki Vakkals live in isolated villages peopled by families of their caste, with a strong and elaborate social organization to preserve purity of morals, simplicity of manners, and strict adherence to the customs handed down from their forefathers. Their settlements lie between the western slopes of the Sahyádris and the sea. They stretch from the Kálinadi near Kárwár on the north to the Shirávati near Honávar on the south. This tract is divided into five social groups or circles known as *shimes* : Hebbánkeri or Honávar, Chandávar or Kumta, Gokarn or Katgál, Ankola, and Nádgeri or Kárwár. Each of these village groups has a *shime-gauda* or group-headman, and each village or hamlet in the group has its village-headman or *urgauda.* The five group-heads or *shime-gaudas* are under a chief or *arás gauda* who has a minister or *pradhán-gauda.* The civil head or *arás-gauda* has as colleague a religious head or *guru-gauda,* who holds the rank of a *swámi* and helps the civil head to enforce discipline. The religious head is a layman of the caste who marries in the caste and eats with the members. His office is hereditary and his duty is to fix the expiation of any offence proved against a member of the caste. He does not join in the ordinary meetings of the caste, but when an offence is proved before the civil head, the civil head fixes the fine and refers the matter to the religious head, who names the expiation suitable to the offence. The religious head is treated with much respect by the people, even by the civil head. The headquarters of the civil head are at Hegde, four miles east of Kumta, those of the minister at Válgalli three miles, and those of the religious head at Talgod five miles from Kumta. The offices of all the headmen, including the civil head, the minister, and the religious head, even that of the *kolkár* or beadle, are hereditary. The functions of the village heads are to call meetings to enquire into ordinary breaches of social rules ; to dispose of minor offences against time-honoured customs by fines up to Rs. 5 ; and to report to the group-head or *shime-gauda* serious matters in which a heavier punishment is deemed necessary. The group-head or *shime-gauda* hears complaints against the decisions of the heads of the villages in his group and has power to put out of caste or to levy an unlimited fine. The village head is treated with much respect by the villagers, who offer him betel leaves and nut and give him the highest place at any village meeting. The village groups in turn show a like respect to the group-head and the group-head to the civil head. Each village-head has a beadle or *kolkár*, who carries messages from the village-heads to the people and to the group-heads. At certain intervals the civil head and the religious head, with the help of the minister or *pradhán*, call a general caste council to settle social disputes, punish the refractory, or re-admit the penitent. A penitent is allowed back to caste on paying a fine varying from Rs. 16 to Rs. 100. The general caste meetings and councils are held at uncertain intervals, generally once in three or ten years, at any convenient place fixed by the civil and the religious heads. The council lasts seven to twenty days and sometimes a month, during which the members are fed and other expenses met by contributions of food or of cash. The ordinary charges vary from Rs. 100 to 300, besides the materials and labour supplied by the people in making the council hall. The right of being members of caste committees, *jati-budvantike*, and of receiving certain complimentary offerings, called *mánmaryáde*, are jealously guarded by some of the richer families. The peculiar and apparently very ancient organization of this caste shows no sign of decay.

Girls are married from the age of eight to sixteen, there being no rule that they should be married before the age of puberty. Boys are married between twelve and eighteen. Sexual license before marriage with a member of the caste is tolerated, though nominally condemned. Polygamy is permitted, but polyandry is unknown.

Marriage ceremonies.

The offer of betrothal generally comes from the boy's family. When a match is proposed the eldest male member of the boy's family asks a Havig priest whether the marriage will be prosperous, and with some of the people of the family, goes to the girl's house, where he is treated to rice, curry, and *paisa*, that is, rice, molasses, and cocoanut milk cooked together. After the meal the elder walks up to the mother or any other near kinswoman of the girl, drops into her hand a couple of betel leaves and nuts with a two or four anna silver coin, and asks the girl's name. The woman tells the girl's name, and all the people present chew betel leaves and nuts, when the boy's party return home. Before the marriage, at both the bride's and bridegroom's, a shed of bamboo and cocoa-palm leaves is raised for the guests. The shed is plain and has no marriage altar as in the guest-sheds made by high class Hindus. To the post of the shed, which is first fixed in the ground, they tie mango sprays, and call the post *muhurtmed* or auspicious post. No other ceremony is observed in connection with this post. They do not bring new pots from the potter, nor do they in any way require the potter's help in their marriage service. A day or two before the wedding the boy's father again goes to a Havig priest, asks him to name a lucky hour for holding the wedding, and pays him four annas for his services, together with two pounds of rice, a cocoanut, and betelnuts, and leaves. On the evening before the wedding day all caste people are invited. Next day they come, each with a cocoanut or a pound of rice, which they present to the boy's mother, and sit on mats spread in the marriage hall. Early on the wedding morning his mother rubs the bridegroom with turmeric paste and bathes him with water out of the ordinary bathing pot. They then lead him to the wedding hall and seating him by an arch of *atti* (Ficus glomerata) branches, sing Kanarese songs, and bathe him with water from two new earthen pots called *kumbhas*, using five smaller pots called *gadiges*. At the same time the bride is bathed by five women at her house. When the bathing is over, the bridegroom is dressed in a waist-cloth, a long white coat falling to his ankle, and a head-scarf. The bridegroom and bride and their parents fast during the whole day. A metal pot called *talige*, filled with water, and with mango leaves and a cocoanut in its mouth, is set on a metal tray with a small quantity of rice. The bridegroom, wearing the marriage coronet, walks to the sweet basil plant, and bowing before it and the image of the patron god which is under it, sets a cocoanut before them. A dinner is served to all except the bridegroom and his parents, and a dinner is also given in the bride's house. The bridegroom then enters the house and bows to the ground before the cocoanut god and offers a cocoanut to it, and holding a few betelnuts, and leaves and a cocoanut in his hands, leaves his house for the bride's, generally between nine and eleven at night. He is accompanied by his house people and guests and by a Bhoi fisherman who leads the procession carrying a lighted torch. Close behind the bridegroom walks his best-man, who is his brother-in-law, cousin, or other near relative. The best-man is called *chanchi-kusa* or box-carrier because he bears on his head a rattan box called *chanchi* containing betelnuts and leaves, tobacco, three robes, a wooden comb, and a small metal vial with eye-salve and another with vermilion paste. The box also contains flowers, the lucky necklace, and some gold and silver ornaments worth Rs. 10 to Rs. 20. The bridegroom's sister walks by his side with a tray containing the water-pot or *talige*. When the procession has started the women sing Kanarese songs, two of them leading the chorus with shouts of *suve*, from *shubh* happy or prosperous. When the bridegroom draws near the bride's house, her father comes out with a small metal pot called *chambu* full of water, washes the bridegroom's feet, and leads him to the sweet basil plant, near which is an arch of *atti* (Ficus glomerata). In front of the basil plant the washerman spreads a clean white cloth for the bridegroom to walk on, and receives eight annas, one or two pounds of rice, and a cocoanut. When in front of the basil plant the bridegroom bows to it, while the women of the bride's house wave lighted lamps before his face. He then enters the house and presents the bride with one of the three roben worth about Rs. 4 which were brought in the cane-box, and in this she dresses herself as soon as the bridegroom has gone back to the marriage hall. On his return to the marriage hall, the bridegroom is seated on one of two low wooden stools, which are placed close to the sides of the arch, and soon after the bride is brought by her parents and seated on the empty seat beside the bridegroom. Married women then rub one of the bride's and bridegroom's arms with turmeric paste and wash it off with water taken from the water-pots or *kumbhas*. Then the bridegroom presents the girl's mother with a robe worth Rs. 2, one of the three robes brought in the best-man's box. The couple then rise, pass through the arch, walk three times round it, and move to a wooden seat or *mancha*, in front of which they stand face to face separated by a curtain held by two young men, relations of the bride. The parents of the bride then join the right hands of the bride and bridegroom, and pour milk on them from a small metal pot. This is known as the *dhâre* ceremony and is the binding portion of the marriage service. When the milk pot is emptied, the curtain is drawn to one side and the pair sit together on the bench, while the guests throw rice on their brows, wishing them good luck, and the women wave lighted lamps before their faces, sprinkling grains of rice on their brows and singing Kanarese songs. When this is over the bridegroom gives the bride a second robe, worth Rs. 2, the last of the three brought in the best-man's box, and the maternal uncle of the bride makes them rise from the seat, and tying the ends of their garments, leads them into the house, where they bow to the cocoanut-god, break a cocoanut before it, and sit on a mat spread in the ante-chamber, and are given refreshments in separate dishes. The bridegroom, for fear of being considered a glutton, eats nothing and, when pressed, feigns want of appetite; but he eats to his heart's content when all the guests have gone. On ordinary days the wife eats in her husband's dish without washing it, after he has eaten; but during the marriage ceremonies she eats from a separate dish in company with other women. Next evening the married couple with their guests return to the bridegroom's house, bow before the basil plant and Venkatarâma, and break the cocoanut which was offered to them, and then bow to the ancestral cocoanut and break the cocoanut that was offered to it. The marriage coronet is then taken from the bridegroom's head and next day is fastened to the chief post of the house. The ceremony ends with a dinner. At none of their marriage ceremonies or processions is there any instrumental music; the only music is the women's songs. A marriage costs the girl's father about Rs. 60 and the boy's father about Rs. 100. The boy's father has to pay to the girl's father *tera*, or bride-price, varying from Rs. 20 to Rs. 64. In order to save this payment, double marriages are sometimes arranged; but if this is not feasible, the bridegroom is sometimes adopted by the parents of the bride as a domestic son-in-law (*mane-alaya*), in which case the bridegroom has not to pay the bride-price, but there is a mutual agreement that the son-in-law should stay and work at the bride's house, receiving some of the profits of her parents.

The marriage of widows is allowed and practised. The widow's new husband should, if possible, be a widower, and in any case he must be a married man. No special ceremonies attend a widow's marriage, except that her new husband gives her a fresh robe and that she leaves her parents' house by the back door. Widow marriage is regarded with disfavour.

A husband is allowed to divorce a wife. A divorced wife cannot remarry during the life-time of her husband.

Like most other Kanara castes, the Hálvakki Vakkals have come under the influence of the Vaishnavism of Rámánuja. Their family god is an unhusked cocoanut, which is kept in a shed near the sweet basil plant and worshipped daily, and their patron deity is Venkatráma of Tirupati and his attendant Hanumán. One of their favourite places of worship is a temple of Hanumán at Chandávar in Kumta. The ministrant is a Havig Bráhman, but the Hálvakkis have the right to receive the *prasád* or flowers used in adorning the god.

They also worship the village gods and goddesses by sacrificing goats and fowls before their idols, and the unhusked cocoanut, which represents the head of their family. Whenever they can afford the Rs. 5 to Rs. 10 which the journey costs, they go on foot to Tirupati. On their return, during the rest of their life, they keep Saturday as a fast and abstain from animal food till they propitiate the god and feast the community. On the first fair day after the feast the pilgrims, with a band of their caste fellows, hunt in the woods, and feed on any deer or hog they may kill. Every year, a few days after *Yágadi* or New Year's Day, that is, near the end of April, they celebrate the day of Venkatarámа, calling it *Haridina* or *Harisheve*, that is, Hari's Day or Hari's Propitiation. Eight days before the *Haridina*, metal vessels are cleaned and earthen cooking vessels are broken and new ones brought from the potter. The houses and yards and the sweet basil altar are smeared with cowdung. On Hari's Day the basil plant is ornamented with sugarcane and festoons of flowers and mango twigs, and the image of Venkatarámа is worshipped by one of the caste people, who, by several pilgrimages to Tirupati, has earned the title of *Dás* or servant of the god. The worship begins about one in the afternoon and lasts for three hours. The priest or *dás* repeats Kanarese hymns in honour of Hari, and offers fruits, flowers and betel leaves and nuts, burning frankincense and waving a lighted lamp. The guests, at the end of every hymn, shout Govind! The men, women, and children who have been asked to the feast have to fast from sunrise till four in the afternoon, when a dinner is given of rice, vegetables, fried rice, pulse, cakes called *vadás*, and *paisa.* The basil worship is repeated on the next day and a small dinner is given to relations and friends, the cost of the whole varying from Rs. 20 to Rs. 100 according to the means of the family. This entertainment marks the beginning of the agricultural year. The four months before it (December—March) are a time of comparative leisure, during which the Hálvakki Vakkals attend car festivals and other yearly fairs. They also, at a cost of Rs. 10 to Rs. 40, hold a social feast called *hagna*, from *hagran* fight, which lasts six days, during which, every morning and evening, the house gods are worshipped and neighbours and kinsmen are feasted. In the evening the women sing songs while the men play on globe-shaped earthen drums or *ghumtás* with one end open and the other covered with a lizard skin. This drum forms an excellent accompaniment to the women's voice. To the singing and playing they sometimes add a masquerade dance, differing little from the round *Shimga* or *Holi* dance. In this, men alone take part dressed like Europeans, Bráhmans, soldiers, constables, and messengers.

In the houses of those whose ancestors have visited Tirupati is kept an image of Venkatarámа, a miniature human figure about six inches high carved in red sandalwood and covered with gold leaf. The image is set in the *vrindávan* or basil altar. Part of their earnings is set aside as an offering to Venkatarámа. It is laid beneath the sweet basil plant at the time of worship and is then removed and dropped into a hollow bamboo through a small slit at the upper end of one of its joints. The head of the family every now and again adds a coin to the store. When the bamboo is full the contents are taken out and sent to Tirupati to be presented to the god. This practice of setting apart savings for the god is called *chakra kattuvadu,* that is, the tying of four-anna pieces. The savings are considered sacred, and even in times of necessity are carefully kept for the god.

Their other holidays are full and new moons, the eclipses, the *Sankránt* in January, *Holi* in March-April, *Yugádi* in April, *Diváli* in October-November, *Aliyan Amváse* or son-in-law's new moon in October-November, and the hook-swinging or *bhánd* festival.

They believe in soothsaying, witchcraft, and the power of spirits, exorcising them when there is sickness by the help of Ghádi and Komárpaik soothsayers. They observe birth, naming, marriage and death ceremonies. They also believe in ceremonial impurity, holding a family to be impure for three days after a birth or after a death, and women for four days once a month.

They respect and consult Bráhmans, but do not employ them to perform any ceremonies.

Death ceremonies.

The bodies of deceased persons are usually burnt except those dying of small-pox or cholera, women dying in child-birth, and children under seven years of age, which are buried. When sickness takes a fatal turn the nearest relation of the dying man feeds him with gruel from a shell spoon, resting his head on his lap. When signs of death appear, the *Dás* or some elderly member of the family calls out the name of Hari and Govinda. When the man is dead the body is brought out, washed, covered with a new shroud, and laid on a bier. As they draw near the burning-ground, the bearers set down the bier, pick a small stone and lay it by the side of the corpse. They address it as the spirit of the dead and promise it a resting place and food till the spirit has been formally called back to join its ancestors in the family cocoanut. The bier is then lifted and taken to the burning-ground, where the body is burnt without further ceremony. Before the party return home, the chief mourner offers cooked rice and a young cocoanut to the life-stone and repeats the offerings on the second and third days. On the third day the chief mourner goes to the burial-ground, and gathering the ashes in a conical mound, offers the dead a fresh cocoanut and rice cooked without salt. On their return, the faces and the heads, except the top-knot, of the male mourners, are shaved, the house is cleaned by a fresh coating of cowdung, and the washerman sprinkles water over the people and over the house. After the house has been cleaned and the people purified by the washerman, the chief mourner goes to the family cocoanut, worships it, and asks the spirit of the latest deceased to join its ancestors in the cocoanut. In the evening dinner is given to a few of the castemen. On the twelfth day a feast is given to the whole community, when a person of the age and sex of the deceased is fed and presented with betelnuts and leaves, tobacco, and a new robe of small value. Every year a feast is held in honour of the deceased ancestors when caste people are feasted and offerings are made to the ancestors.

Occupation. The Hálvakki Vakkals are now chiefly husbandmen, but they hire themselves as labourers when their services are not required at home. Their daily wages are four annas for a man and two annas for a woman. The women and children never work, except in the fields, being paid in grain worth 1½ to 2 annas. They have the monopoly of making roofs of bamboos and coir rope and also of building the tops of the great temple-cars or *raths*. Some of them are good physicians, using roots and barks to cure fever, carbuncles, inflammation of the lungs, and liver diseases. They are paid only their boarding, with in some cases the present of a blanket worth Re. 1 to Rs. 3. Besides house work the women help the men in the fields and also plait mats of grass or sedge called *lava*, worth 3 annas to Re. 1 according to size and quality. They are successful cultivators, but their custom of spending as much as Rs. 40 to Rs. 100 on their marriages often forces them to borrow money at twelve to twenty-four per cent. In many cases the principal remains unpaid for generations, the interest being regularly paid and the bonds on which the money is lent being renewed by the borrower or his heirs. A Hálvakki Vakkal seldom begs, the old and infirm being supported by their neighbours in return for such light work as they can do.

Food. Their staple food is rice and *rági*. They are very fond of molasses and *paisa*. They eat tame animals like fowls and goats sacrificed to the village deities, as also fish and wild animals killed in hunting, such as hogs, rabbits, and deer, provided they are not sacred to the *bali* to which the eater belongs. They do not eat bison, crocodiles, snakes, lizards, jackals, and insects. They never touch liquor, and carry their dislike of it so far that they never stand under a cocoanut tree while it is being tapped.

HALVEKARI.—A sub-division of Láds.

HANAM.—A sub-division of Gollas.

Name and origin. **HANBARS,** also known as Krishna Gollas, numbering 23,917 (1901), including 11,951 males and 11,966 females, are found chiefly in Belgaum, Bijápur and the Southern Marátha Country. The name Hanbar means a possessor of cattle with upright horns. According to their caste rules they ought to live in forests, keep herds of cattle, and sell milk and clarified butter, eat only once a day, wearing a wet cloth, and never look at a lamp or engage in tillage. Now-a-days they do not adhere to these rules; many of them till land, and a few serve as messengers and labourers or field workers.

Hanbars consist of the following endogamous divisions:— Divisions.

(1) Hosa or New Hanbars.

(2) Hale or Old Hanbars.

(3) Bile Shriyas.

(4) Bannad Shriyas.

In Belgaum the *Hosa* or New Hanbars and *Hale* or Old Hanbars eat together and intermarry, but in Kanara neither interdining nor intermarriage is allowed. Bile Shriyas and Bannad Shriyas do not eat together or intermarry. All Bijápur Hanbars are Bile Shriyas; the Bannad Shriyas are found only in the hilly country. The Hanbars of Kanara are said to have come from Kalyán in the Nizám's Dominions; but all communication with their Kalyán caste-fellows has ceased. The surnames among the Hanbars of Bijápur district are, Boluya, Hosurya, Kiriya and Kuriya.

The *bedagus* or exogamous divisions are as follows:—

1. Annil.	5. Gudael.	9. Nandana.
2. Bannada.	6. Gundya.	10. Sindaga.
3. Chandana.	7. Houma Kasturi.	11. Tambilta.
4. Chuncha.	8. Hounana.	12. Tragari.

Sameness of *bedagu* but not merely sameness of surname is a bar to intermarriage. In Belgaum district among the Hanbars the sameness of *devak* is a bar to intermarriage. In Kanara they have no *devaks*. Families who have the same gods are considered to belong to one stock and therefore to be too closely related to allow of intermarriage. A man may marry his father's sister's or mother's brother's daughter. He cannot marry his mother's sister's daughter. A man may marry two sisters, and two brothers may marry two sisters. They do not admit outsiders into their caste.

Boys are married at any age. Girls must be married before the age of puberty. Girls guilty of sexual indiscretions before marriage are turned out of the caste. Polygamy is permitted but polyandry is unknown.

Marriage ceremonies. The offer of marriage comes from the boy's father. The auspicious day for marriage is fixed by a Deshasth Bráhman, who also conducts the marriage service. The boy's father pays money to the girl's father. The betrothal known as *báshtagi* is performed in the presence of the castemen. Then comes *devakárya,* which consists in holding a dinner for the propitiation of the marriage guardian deity. The bride and bridegroom are then rubbed with turmeric paste, and the ceremony is known as *Arishina* (*i.e.* turmeric). When the marriage is celebrated, grains of rice are tied to the ends of the bride's and bridegroom's garments and are also thrown over the heads of the couple by the assembly. The bride and bridegroom are then taken on a horse or a bullock to the temple. This is known as *Eterisuvadu.* The marriage ceremony ends with the performance of the *Nagvali* ceremony, a feast of rice and millet.

Widow remarriage is allowed. A widow may marry her father's sister's or mother's brother's son. A widow remarriage can be celebrated on an auspicious day in any month except *Paush.* Divorce is allowed. A woman convicted of adultery is turned out of her caste.

Religion. They follow the Hindu law of inheritance. They say that they do not believe in witchcraft or sorcery, but have faith in soothsaying. When a soothsayer is consulted, a packet of betelnut and leaves and a copper coin or two are laid before him, when he opens his book and, after reflection, gives an answer therefrom.

Hanbars are Hindus by religion and worship Shiva, Máruti, Yellamma, etc. Their family god is Alamprabhu, whose shrine is at Alatgi in Kolhápur State. They worship minor deities, such as Khandoba. Animals and trees sacred to the Hindu religion are revered by them. Sacrifices of goats and fowls are made to their gods and are partaken of by the offerers. They worship the images of their dead ancestors amd make offerings of cooked food. They fast on Fridays and keep the usual Hindu holidays. When an epidemic breaks out they prepare wooden images of Durgavva and Murgavva and worship them. Their family priests are Deshasth Bráhmans, who officiate at their marriages, and are consulted regarding lucky days and names for their children.

Death. They bury or burn their dead. The bones and ashes of the dead when burnt are thrown into a river or a pond. Caste-men are feasted on the eleventh day after death. Every year in the month of *Bhádrapad* Bráhmans are worshipped, water in which their feet have been washed is drunk, and presents are made to them. No ceremonies are performed for the propitiation of childless ancestors and persons who have died a violent death.

Occupation.

The Hanbars are frequently husbandmen. They grow both watered and dry crops. They are skilful husbandmen, being helped by their women and children. Some of them are field labourers. Their busy season is from June to December and their slack season from January to May.

Food.

They eat the flesh of goats, sheep, fowls and fish. They drink liquor.

The following customs are peculiar to the Hanbars of Bijápur district:—

Bijápur Hanbars.

In settling marriages, the boy's father visits the girl's house and presents her with fifty betelnuts and fifty leaves and four pounds of sugar. Caste-people are asked to attend, and sugar is put into the girl's mouth in the presence of all. The boy's father pays the girl's mother one to five rupees, betel and sugar are served, and the caste-people withdraw. The boy's father is treated to a dinner of rice, pulse and stuffed cakes. For the betrothal or *báshtagi,* the boy's father again calls at the girl's house with a present of four pounds of dry dates, four pounds of betelnut, fifty leaves, twelve pounds of sugar, two pounds of cocoa-kernel, a piece of bodice-cloth and five turmeric roots. The girl is seated on a blanket, her lap is filled with rice and five kinds of fruit, and her mother is paid ten rupees in the presence of the caste-people met at the house. The guests are feasted on sugar rolly-polies, rice and clarified butter, and a day is fixed for the marriage by the village *joshi* or astrologer. On the happy day the bride's party lead the bride to the bridegroom's and they remain there till the marriage is over. In the evening the couple are rubbed with turmeric paste and on the next day the gods are propitiated. On the third day the couple are bathed, dressed in white, and taken to bow in Máruti's temple. On their return to the bridegroom's they stand face to face in the yard before the house, separated by a turmeric cross or *nandi* marked cloth held between them by the maternal uncle of the bride. A thread wristlet to which a piece of turmeric is tied is bound round the right wrist of each of the couple and they are blessed and rice is thrown over them. Then comes the *dhuru* or earth-offering, in which rice and cakes are set in a dish, which the couple are made to worship, and they are feasted on the rice and cakes in company with five married women. The other guests and caste-people are feasted and in the evening the couple are made to visit the temple of Máruti, where they place a lighted lamp before the god, bow to him and return home. Then they bow before their family gods, and in the presence of caste-people the parents of the girl formally make her over to the bridegroom's mother. The party of the bride are feasted on *nagvali*, a dish of rice and millet boiled together and mixed with clarified butter and molasses, cakes, rice and pulse.

The patron deities of Hanbars of Bijápur are Máruti, Mangalavva and Yellamma. They bathe once a week and visit the temple of Máruti and bow before the image. On other days they perform no worship before their morning meal and none of them have images of their gods in their houses. They visit the shrines of Mangalavva at Mangalgad in Bágevádi and of Yellamma at Parasgad in Belgaum. Once a year they sacrifice a goat to the god or goddess, who guards their fields and to Mangalavva or mother luck at the end of the festival held in her honour. They keep no Hindu holidays except the Cobra's Fifth or *Nágpanchmi* in *Shrávan* or July-August, and the *Mágh* full moon or *Mághi Pournima* in February. They never fast. They have a teacher of their own caste, whose office is hereditary. They pay no respects to Bráhmans and do not ask them to their ceremonies. Their priests belong to their own caste. They perform both marriage and death ceremonies.

When a person dies, a peg is driven into the wall and the body is bound to the peg in a sitting posture. If the deceased is a man he is dressed in a waistcloth and headscarf, and, if she is a woman, in a robe and bodice. The body is laid in a blanket or coarse cotton cloth and carried to the burying ground and buried. A stone is laid on the grave. Some burn their dead. On the third day they visit the place, worship the stone that was laid on the grave, and leave an earthen pot or *moga*, Indian millet flour boiled in water, and a second earthen pot full of water. They wait for a time to see whether a crow touches them, and return home. On the fourth, fifth, or sixth day the house is cowdunged; the chief mourner with the four corpse-bearers have their heads shaved and this purifies them. They then dine at the house of the dead. Within a month after the death a waistcloth or robe is left in the place where the death occurred, and the caste-people are feasted. They perform no memorial or *shráddha* ceremonies.

HANDE GURUBA.—A sub-division of Handevants.

HANDE KURUBA.—A synonym for Lingáyat Kuruba.

HANDERAUT.—A sub-division of Handevants.

HANDEVANT.—A sub-division of Lingáyats.

HANDEVAZIR.—A sub-division of Handevants; a synonym for Lingáyat Kuruba.

HANDEYAWA.—A sub-division of Handevants.

HANSA.—A synonym for Mánbháv.

HANSOTI.—A sub-division of Gandhariás and Khárvás.

HARALI.—A sub-division of Chámbhárs.

HARAN PARDHI.—A sub-division of Párdhis.

HARIDASAS are a small tribe of cattle breeders, found chiefly in East Khándesh.

HARKA.—A sub-division of Kolhátis.

HARAKANTRAS, * a class of fishermen, numbering 6,092 (1901), including 2,904 males and 3,188 females, are found entirely in the Kanara district on the sea-coast towns and villages from Kárwár to Honávar. According to some, the name Harkantra is derived from *Harikarta* a maker of cocoa fibre ropes. This derivation does not seem to be correct as none of the Harkantras make ropes. According to others, the caste is named after Harikantra, their supposed common ancestor. This statement also seems to lack foundation in fact. The most probable derivation of the term Harkantra appears to be *harkat* meaning obstruction. In this connection a story is told that formerly the Ambigs, Harakantras and Bhois were one and the same caste. On one occasion three brothers of the caste went fishing and caught a large number of fish. At the time of distributing the fish a quarrel arose between the brothers, and in the struggle that ensued, the fishing net was torn in pieces. One of the brothers took away a piece of the net and began to catch fish with this piece. For so doing he was outcasted, and his offspring were called Harkantras. The second brother took another piece of the torn net and used it after mending. His descendants were called Ambigs. The third brother carried away in a basket the fish caught by the three and sold it. He was the founder of the Bhois. Outsiders often mistake the Harakantras, Bhois and Ambigs for each other, as they all follow the same occupation and their features show a strong resemblance. It is possible that in their origin they were more closely connected than at present. But the castes can be distinguished from one another by the way in which they throw the fishing net and carry fish to the market for sale. The Harakantras throw the hand-net from the

Name and origin.

* The materials for this article were supplied by Mr. V. L. Ugrankar.

level of the elbow, jerking it sideways from the left to the right. The Ambigs throw it just in front from the level of the head. The Bhois toss it round the waist. The Harakantra women carry fish to the market on their shoulders in bamboo or wicker baskets, the Ambigs on the head in the same kind of baskets, while the Bhois carry it in bags of cadjan leaves.

Harakantras speak Kanarese like the other lower castes of Kanara. Some know Konkani and Hindustáni. The names in common use among men are Pursu, Ráma, Goida, Jáju, Mailya, Gutti, Pokka, Dongya, Bhika, Bhiva, Lingu, Tippa, Hanma, Chikka; and among women, Pursi, Jiri, Devi, Bhimi, Jethu, Tippi, Sukri, Nagi, Putti, Demi, Chikkai, Iru, Káli and Honma.

Harakantras are a well-organized community. A group of four or more villages has a headman called *budvant*, a secretary called *chaulgo*, and a messenger known as *kolkár*. These with the adult male members of the community form a committee who have power to decide caste disputes and the punishment for breaches of caste rules. The principal committees of the caste are at Kárwár and Mirján. An appeal against the decision of the committee lies to a special committee convened for the purpose, consisting of the Kárwár and Mirján *budvants* as presidents and the representatives of the caste from all other villages as members. A second appeal lies with the agent of the Shankaráchárya of the Shringeri monastery who resides at Gokarn. Petty offences are punished with fines varying from annas two to rupees ten, grievous offences such as adultery and eating with members of lower castes, with excommunication. The offices of the *budvant*, *chaulgo* and *kolkár* are hereditary. In case the rightful incumbent is too young or otherwise incompetent, the next-of-kin officiates or another efficient and elderly member of the community is elected as a substitute.

Exogamous divisions.

Harakantras have numerous exogamous divisions of a totemistic nature known as *balis*, in common with most other castes in Kánara of a similar social standing. Instances of these *balis* are—

1. Chandi bali.
2. Devan bali.
3. Galtan bali.
4. Hole bali.
5. Iránaikan bali.
6. Málgijetti bali.
7. Kágáljetti bali.
8. Kanne bali.
9. Káyanmane bali.
10. Kimane bali.
11. Kusale bali.
12. Sherogáran bali.
13. Sukri bali.
14. Timman bali.
15. Tolana bali.

No member of the section will injure in any way the tree, animal or other object giving its name to the *bali* to which he belongs.

A member of the caste may marry his daughter to his sister's son. Sisters' children cannot intermarry. A man may marry his deceased wife's sister. He cannot marry his brother's wife's sister during the wife's lifetime. Polygamy is allowed and practised, the number of wives a man may have at a time being usually restricted to two. Polyandry is unknown. Girls are generally married from ten to twelve, always before attaining puberty; boys from fifteen to twenty-five.

Marriage ceremonies.

The negotiations for marriage begin with the boy's father, who has to pay a *teru* or bride-price of from Rs. 8 to Rs. 32 to the girl's father. The betrothal takes place about ten days before marriage, when a feast is given to the boy's party by the girl's father. A match cannot be broken off after the betrothal ceremony has been performed.

About three days before the marriage the boy's party go to the girl's house, and present her with flowers and a gold or silver ornament. The girl is decked in these, and the boy's party is treated to a dinner by her father. This is known as the *Oppali* ceremony.

On the next day, a lucky day for the marriage is fixed by a Havik priest, and invitations for the marriage are sent round. On the same day marriage booths are erected at the houses of both the boy and the girl. The *muhurta medha* or auspicious post of the marriage booth at the boy's house is made of the *jámba* (Xylia dolabriformis) and at the girl's house of the *kindal* (Terminalia paniculata) tree. Outside the marriage booth, at both the houses, is raised a small arch or canopy of Indian fig leaves, which are brought by a boy dressed in holy clothes, after offering a cocoanut to the tree. The *bali* or marriage guardian, which consists of rice grains, a cocoanut, betel leaves and nuts placed on a piece of new cloth in a winnowing fan, is then worshipped, and a feast called *chhaprade uta* (booth-dinner) is given to the caste people.

Early next day the bridegroom, dressed in marriage attire with a marriage coronet fixed on his head and a cocoanut and a couple of betel leaves in his hands, starts in procession for the girl's house. When they near the girl's house the procession stops, and some of the party go to the girl's house and present her with betel leaves and nuts and flowers and a robe. This part of the ceremony is called *kai-yele.* The girl puts on the robe and the wedding chaplet. In the meantime the main body of the procession arrives, and is received at the entrance of the marriage booth by the girl's father. The bridegroom is received by the girl's mother, who waves round his face a plate containing lighted lamps and turmeric water. The bridegroom puts annas four into the plate. He is then led to the marriage altar, the bride is brought and made to stand facing him, a cloth is held between them and they are made to throw flower garlands round each other's necks. Next, the bride's parents join the right hands of the bride and bridegroom and pour over them milk or water (*dhâre* ceremony), which is the binding portion of the marriage ceremony. Five unwidowed women wave lighted lamps round the faces of the pair and throw grains of rice over their heads. The bride's father makes presents of clothes, etc., to the bridegroom, leads the pair into the house, seats them near the *bali*, and gives them some molasses to eat. A feast to the caste people ends the day's proceedings.

Next morning the bride and bridegroom are rubbed with turmeric paste, and seated under the canopy of Indian fig leaves, where are placed two big earthen jars filled with water and five smaller jars empty. The bride's mother holds a tray containing a cocoanut, rice grains, betel leaves, etc., over their heads, and her father pours water into the tray five times from the earthen jars. At each time both of them throw grains of rice over the couple's heads. This ceremony is performed by all the guests in order of their social rank. Next, the pair are taken into the house and made to play a game with a ring, after which they are led into the marriage booth. In the afternoon a feast is given to the caste people by the girl's father. This fourth day ceremony is called *Muyyi*, and the feast *Muyyi uta.*

On the fifth day, at high tide as a rule, the bridegroom returns to his house with his bride. On their arrival, the *Muyyi* ceremony is again performed, and the bride and bridegroom are led into the house over grains of rice strewn on their path, the former holding a lighted lamp into her right hand. Near the *devak* the bridegroom's father takes the couple into his lap and gives them molasses to eat, the bride's maiden name is changed, and she is give a new name. This ceremony is known as *Gharabharan.* When it is over, a dinner is given to the caste people by the boy's father. The same afternoon the marriage coronet is taken off the bridegroom's head and the chaplet off the bride's head, and the parties on both sides are free to enjoy their favourite palm-juice drink, from which they have been abstaining from the commencement of the marriage.

On the next day the newly married pair go in procession to the temple of their family deity to bow to the god, and thence to the caste headman and other leading members of the caste. Next the bridegroom goes to his father-in-law's house with his bride to stay there for five days, which is called *pánch partávan*. This ends the marriage ceremonies.

The remarriage of widows is permitted with the sanction of the caste committee. A widow cannot marry a member of her deceased husband's *bali*. She may marry her mother's brother's son, but not her mother's sister's son. Before the marriage takes place, she has to return to the relations of her deceased husband the ornaments, etc., received from him. A widow remarriage is celebrated at a late hour at night on any day during the year. No priest attends. Only a few widows and male relations of the parties are present. The widow bathes, breaks the bangles on her wrists, and puts on a robe and new bangles presented by her intended husband. The pair are then seated side by side and *ukda* rice (rice prepared after boiling the paddy) is waved over their faces by the widows present, which completes the ceremony. Neither a remarried widow nor her husband are allowed to take part in any religious or social ceremony. A bachelor is not allowed to marry a widow. Adultery on the part of women is punished with excommunication. The caste follow the Hindu law of inheritance with this peculiarity that even self-acquired property is subject to partition at the time of a division.

Harakantrás belong to the Hindu religion. They worship all Hindu gods and goddesses and all plants and animals held sacred by the Hindus. The special deities of their veneration are Kodibira (*Kodi* cruel and *bira* a hero), Balebira (*bale* net and *bira* a hero) and Belebanta (*bele* seashore and *banta* a soldier), whom they consider their guardian deities, and who are propitiated whenever an epidemic breaks out, or there is a storm in the sea, or there is a scarcity of fish. Of the minor gods they worship by preference Somanath, Mariamma, Hulidevata (the god who has power to prevent tigers from doing harm to the people), Vanadevate (the forest-goddess), Birs, Jatgas and Vetál (the chief of ghosts). They hold the whale (Kan. *tiva* M. *devamása*) in great awe as they consider it a dangerous fish, and whenever they chance to come across it in the seas, propitiate it by vows to feed maidens with presents of bodice cloths, bangles, etc., immediately on reaching land. The Musalmán saints are venerated. They observe almost all the Hindu holidays and make pilgrimages to Tirupati, Gokarn, Dharmasthal and Pandharpur. They have great faith in omens, sorcery, soothsaying, and lucky and unlucky days. To meet a fisherman or fisherwoman carrying fish the first thing on starting on business or on a journey is considered a lucky omen. In other Religion.

respects on this point they resemble the other Hindus. They believe in evil spirits and have so much faith in their power to do good or evil that all calamities are attributed to their working, and consequently they are propitiated in various ways. Their priests are the Havik or Karnátak Bráhmans.

Death ceremonies.

The dead are generally buried in a lying position with head to the north. Those who can afford the expenses burn their dead. Persons who have made pilgrimages to Tirupati and other sacred places must be buried in a sitting position. The standard funeral rites in use among the lower castes are observed. Even in the case of burial, fire is carried with the corpse to the burning ground and is enkindled on the grave after the corpse has been buried. The bones and ashes are collected on any odd day between the third and eleventh day after death, and thrown into a stream or the sea. On this occasion an offering of cooked rice, cakes, fish curry and a cocoanut is made to the deceased near the grave, and the chief mourner gets his head and moustaches shaved. The mourning ends on the eleventh day, when all the male members of the family who are fatherless have their heads and moustaches shaved. The house is purified by sprinkling all over it soda and ashes brought from a washerman, and all members of the deceased's family sip *panchagavia* (five products of the cow) brought by the family priest. On the twelfth day a casteman having no father is invited to dinner and is presented with articles of dress, five pice, a metal plate and a metal drinking pot.

For the propitiation of the deceased ancestors cows are fed on the new-moon day of every month, and every year on the new-moon day of *Bhádrapad* crows are fed and castemen are feasted. Persons meeting a violent death are considered to become violent spirits, and in order to prevent disturbance from them, they are consulted through mediums and their desires fulfilled.

Occupation.

The hereditary occupation of the caste is catching and selling fish, and bearing palanquins and litters. They do all kind of work connected with fishing. They own small boats and use about fifteen kinds of nets, which are known also to the other fishing castes of Kanara. They do not catch crocodiles or tortoises. A new boat is launched into the sea on a lucky day, decorated with garlands and flowers. The guardian deities and spirits are worshipped on the occasion, and molasses and cocoa-kernel are distributed. Those who can afford it give a dinner to the caste people. They decorate their boats with garlands and flowers also on the *Dasara* and Cocoanut holidays.

Some of the Harakantras are sea-farers. But they are not skilled sailors. A sailor is given annas 3 a day with food. Some are unskilled carpenters and earn 3 to 6 annas a day in villages below the Ghats and 5 to 8 annas a day in villages above the Ghats. A few are office peons and messengers. When the sea is stormy or they cannot put to sea, they work as day labourers, or spin hemp yarn or weave nets.

Harakantras eat the flesh of goats, sheep, stags, deer, hares, boars, wild and domestic fowl, fish and all sort of wild game. They drink liquor, but have a special liking for palm-juice, which is drunk by men, women and children almost every day. Food.

They eat food cooked by all higher castes except Sonárs, whom they hate so much that they will not carry their palanquins or even stay under their roof after sunset. They eat *kacchi* also with lower castes except the Halepaiks, Bhandáris, Komárpaiks, Marátha Kunbis, all the fishing castes of Kanara except their own, and the degraded classes. Only the depressed classes eat food cooked by the Harakantras.

HARSOLA.—A sub-division of Vániás; a synonym for Harsolia.

HARSOLIA.—A sub-division of Bráhmans.

HARSORA.—A synonym for Harsola.

HARVAVIA.—A sub-division of Dublás.

HASLARS or Hulsavars, numbering 2,277 (1901), including 1,269 males and 1,008 females, are found in isolated settlements in the Sirsi and Honávar *tálukás* of the Kanara district. They rank amongst the impure classes, and live on the outskirts of towns and villages like Mahárs and Chámbhárs. They seem to have come from Shimoga in north-west Mysore, where the caste is found in large numbers, speaking the same language and following the same customs as Kanara Haslárs. Name and origin.

There are two endogamous divisions of the caste, (1) Haslár and (2) Bant Haslár, who neither eat together nor intermarry. Their exogamous divisions known as *balis* are as follows:— Divisions.

1. Ane bali .. *Ane* = elephant.
2. Betta bali .. *Betta* = the cane.
3. Kanne bali .. *Kanne* = a virgin.
4. Shendi bali .. *Shendi* = the toddy tree.
5. Shetti bali .. *Shetti* = a fish.
6. Shirin bali .. *Shire or Shirkal* = a tree (*Gynandropsis pentaphylla*).

These *balis* are totemistic. Members belonging to the same *bali* cannot intermarry.

A Haslár may marry his father's sister's or mother's brother's daughter. He cannot marry his mother's sister's daughter. Marriage with a deceased wife's sister is allowed, and brothers are allowed to marry sisters. Polygamy and widow remarriage are allowed, and practised, but polyandry is unknown.

Marriage ceremonies. The offer of marriage comes from the boy's father, who has to pay a sum of Rs. 10 to the girl's father. The marriage and other ceremonies of Haslárs do not differ from those of Mukris. They follow the Hindu law of inheritance, and though they profess Hinduism, they do not worship any of the regular Hindu gods. The chief objects of their worship are the Jatgás and Mhastis, and Hathgudi and other minor gods. They do not make pilgrimages. They observe only the *Dasara*, *Yágudi*, and *Holi* holidays. They are much afraid of the spirits of the dead, whom they believe to have the power of harming them. They offer them cocks, sheep and fruit, and have much faith in sooth-saying and witchcraft. They trace all disease to the working of unfriendly spirits, against whom they employ *Ghádis* or exorcists. The dead are either burnt or buried. All their ceremonies are conducted by *budvants* or headmen of the caste.

Haslárs make their living by working as labourers in fields and gardens. They are paid both in cash and in grain. Some of them take land on lease from superior holders.

Food. They eat the flesh of goats, sheep, fowls, wild pigs and venison, and drink liquor. They rank with Mukris above Mahárs and below Halepaiks.

HATGHADE.—A sub-division of Kumbhárs.

Name and origin. **HATIS**, * numbering 2,231 (1901), including 1,118 males and 1,113 females, are found mostly in the Soráth division of Káthiáwár. They are residents of the historic district of Malia Hatma under Junágad State. Accoring to the Hátis they are descendants from the Sisodia Rajputs of Chitor, Háthising being the common ancestor. Those who reside out of Malia Hatma are nicknamed Jáda (thick or large) and those who live in Hatma Malia permanently are nicknamed Pátala (thin or small), though the Pátalás are the more numerous of the two. Some Hátis are known as Jogia Khumáos, and are supposed to have descended from Jogaji (brother of Háthising) who ruled at

*The materials for this article were supplied by Mr. K. G. Pandit, B.A., LL.B.

Ránpur Bhesán. The Jogias and Hátis being descended from a common ancestor cannot intermarry.

The Hátis have two exogamous divisions, Sakháyat and Avartia, Divisions. closely corresponding with the divisions bearing the same name among the Káthis. The names in common use are, Bhojo, Desur, Devo, Háthising, Joga, Khimo, Matra, Pithait, etc. Some of the surnames can be traced to some brave ancestor, *e.g.*, Lákháni (from Lákho), Bhojag (from Bhojo), Fakiráni (from Fakiro), Bhuráni (from Bhuro); while one to a village, *viz.*, Keshoja (from the village Keshod). These five are the principal *kuls* (family stocks) of the Sakháyat Hátis. The Sakháyat Hátis intermarry with the Avartia Hátis and also with the Avartia Káthis, but not with the Sakháyat Káthis. At times they intermarry with the Ahirs also. Subject to these rules, a Háti may marry his father's sister's or his mother's brother's daughter, but not his mother's sister's daughter. Two sisters can be married simultaneously, or a younger sister may be married on the death of the elder sister. Two brothers may marry two sisters.

Girls are generally married at the age of ten and may remain unmarried till after they come of age. Boys are married at about twenty. A girl committing sexual indiscretions can remain in the tribe by paying a fine to the tribesmen. Polygamy is allowed though not common. Incompatibility of temper, failure of issue, and misconduct of the wife justify the husband in taking to a second wife. Polyandry is unknown.

The offer of marriage comes from the boy's father. A Rájgor Marriage ceremonics. Bráhman acts as a mediator between the parties and is paid as remuneration sums varying from As. 8 to Rs. 5. These negotiations are called *Sagái*. The boy's father has to pay the girl's father a sum of money known as *des*. In exchange for the *des*, clothes and ornaments are sometimes presented to the girl; this ceremony is called *Sayurtun*. The day for the marriage is fixed by a Bráhman, a note stating the day being written and carried to the boy's father by the family priest. This is known as *lagna mokalvun* (the sending of the marriage note). The girl's father takes the note, seats the priest on a wooden cot, makes a *chándlo* (a mark with red powder) on his forehead, and presents him with a cocoanut and a silver coin. This is called *layna vadhávavun* (welcoming the marriage). Two days before the marriage, booths are put up at the houses of both the bride and bridegroom. On the day previous to the marriage day a fruit *bhindol* is tied to the wrist of both the bride and the bridegroom, saffron or turmeric powder mixed with water is applied to their cheeks and foreheads; Ganpati is also worshipped. On the night of the marriage day the bridegroom goes in procession through the village and is welcomed by the villagers with presents of dry dates. This is known as *Kulekun*. The procession moves on to the residence of the bride, where they are received by the bride's party. The bridegroom is taken into the marriage booth and welcomed by the bride's mother (*Pomkhavu*). The bride and bridegroom are garlanded with one garland for the two. Next, the family priest comes with the bride's father and reads the marriage bans, which are then placed between the hands of the couple. Marriage hymns are chanted and the bride handed over (*Kanyádán*). The bride and bridegroom are then made to walk four times round the marriage altar, which is the binding portion of the marriage service. A dinner is held and the ceremony concludes.

The remarriage of widows is permitted. A widow is permitted, if she so choose, to cohabit with her late husband's younger brother. If she wishes to remarry outside her husband's family, she must first get a deed of separation (with or without paying a fine, as the caste allow). She may marry her mother's brother's or father's sister's son, but not her mother's sister's son. A widow remarriage is celebrated on any auspicious day. Three or four respectable relatives from either side, as also three or four near relatives of the intended husband, are called as witnesses. Cash and ornaments as agreed upon are presented to the widow by her intended husband through her father. The widow is then dressed and decked with ornaments. The mother of the intended husband, or, in her absence, some other woman of the caste, applies red powder to the foreheads of the pair, a present of five coins is made to the widow's mother, molasses or sugar is distributed among all present, and the ceremony is over. No additional ceremonies are performed in the case of a bachelor marrying a widow.

Divorce is allowed. Suspicion as to the wife's chastity or actual misconduct on her part or discord between the husband and wife are sufficient reason for obtaining a divorce. Either party has the right of seeking a divorce. But to justify a divorce on the part of the wife, the husband must either have turned a recluse, contracted a loathsome disease, or shown signs of impotence. A divorced wife can marry again by the widow remarriage form. Calling the wife sister or mother simultaneously with the tearing off of a piece of her head-dress is a sufficient ceremony for a divorce. Forbidding a wife to enter her husband's house is also thought sufficient proof of a divorce.

Sons cannot claim partition during the father's life-time, but can claim maintenance. Daughters cannot claim the mother's *Stridhan* unless it has been given away by the latter during her life-time. With such limitations, the community is governed by Hindu law.

The tribe is Hindu in religion. They belong to the Swáminániyan and Rámdási sect. Shankar and Vishnu are worshipped. Their family deities are Nága and Chámunda. The cow is worshipped in the month of *Bhádrapad* on the *Ganesh Chaturthi* day. Offerings are made to deities in times of epidemic diseases. Their priests are Bráhmans. **Religion.**

The dead are burnt. Infants and children under two years and a half are buried as well as persons suffering from leprosy, the belief being that leprosy is a disease which burns the body and that another burning is not necessary. Both at burning and burial the corpse is laid with head to the north. The bones and ashes of the deceased are kept in an earthern pot and thrown into the Dáma-kund (pool) in the Girnár hills near Junágadh. **Death ceremonies.**

To pacify a deceased ancestor, an annual *shráddha* is held. If a man dies leaving no issue, as a formality, a male calf is married to a female calf, and this mock marriage is called *lila paranávi*. If a person meets a violent death, a stone idol made in his name or stones resembling his feet are kept near the house gods on the ninth day of the dark half of *Bhádrapad*.

The Hátis believe themselves to have once been a warrior class and history supports this belief. Very often the Malia Hátis have fought with Junágad and kept that State at bay, and their belief is that had Pithait Háti not been treacherously seized, they would have this day remained masters of 124 villages. Even now they occupy many villages, *viz.*, Malia, Khorasa, Lathodra, Kosod, Pánkhán, Eklera, Shimoroti, Shilodhar, Vadála, Dhanej; but very few of them are landed proprietors. Many are small Vatandars, some cultivate the soil as day labourers, and others serve as *Pasaitas* (village policemen).

They eat the flesh of goats, sheep, scaly and scaleless fish, and drink liquor. They would eat with Ahirs, Rabáris, Bharváds, Kumbhárs and Mahias. The Káthis, Rájputs, Babrias and Chárans would eat with them. **Food.**

HATKAR.—*See* Devàng, Hatkar, Jád, Koshti or Sáli. A sub-division of Dhangars.

HATODE.—A sub-division of Kumbhárs.

HATTIKANKAN.— A sub-division of Kurubas.

HAVIG.—A synonym for Havik.

HAVIK.—A sub-division of Bráhmans.

HEBBE GAUDA.—A synonym for Mukri.

HEDSHI.—A sub-division of Mahárs.

HELA.—A sub-division of Bhangis.

Name and origin.

HELAVS, literally cripples, numbering (1901) 1,088 including 557 men and 531 women, are a class of religious beggars found in Belgaum, Bijápur, Dhárwár and the Kanara districts. In some respects they resemble the Pánguls, a Hindu begging caste, but differ from them in being Lingáyats. The caste is said to have come from the territory about Kalyán in the Nizám's dominion. The tradition regarding its origin is, that in the twelfth century when Jainism was predominant and Lingáyatism was declining, the god Shiva ordered his *pramáths*, or attendants, to visit the earth and revive Lingáyatism. The Helavs claim to be descended from one of these *pramáths* or attendants named Vakkalabhringi (*i.e.*, one-legged Bhringi) who, on coming down to the earth, wore ochre-coloured clothes, sat on a bullock, and went from house to house singing the praises of the god Shiva. In imitation of him, the Helavs, when going begging, hide one of their legs in a blanket even at the present day.

Divisions.

There are no endogamous divisions of the caste. There are ten exogamous sub-divisions known as Yarasanava, Bommalinganava, Andhakanava, Somadevanava, Kunchayanava, Tankanava, Bandiyava, Immadiyava, Bhimashettiyava, Yakapattinava. The Bombay Gazetteer mentions the sub-divisions Parsabátenava, Sádrinava, Pankranava and Vanmanava.

A member of the caste is prohibited from marrying his brother's paternal uncle's, or maternal aunt's daughter; but he may marry his elder sister's, paternal aunt's, or maternal uncle's daughter. He is not allowed to marry two sisters. Marriage is generally infant. Polygamy is permitted, but a man marries a second wife only when he has no issue by the first wife or in case of her misconduct.

Marriage ceremonies.

The boy's father generally commences negotiations for a marriage, the day for which is fixed by a Jangam or a Joshi. The ceremony is conducted by an elderly member of the caste, who is called for the time being Kattemaneyava or headman and is paid Rs. 5 by the boy's father. The boy's father has to pay Rs. 30 to the girl's father as brideprice. The boy and the girl are rubbed with turmeric on a Monday or Thursday and the marriage takes place on the next day. The essential portion consists in throwing sacred grains of coloured rice on the bride and bridegroom, who are made to sit opposite each other on low stools with a curtain bearing a turmeric cross between them until the critical moment. The lucky thread or *mangalsutra* is then fastened on the bride's neck by a married woman. In the evening Máruti is worshipped, and the priest of Máruti places half a cocoanut, filled with ashes, in the bride's lap.

The remarriage of widows is permitted. The widow cannot marry her husband's elder or younger brother or a man of the sub-division to which her husband belonged. The marriage takes place at night. Castemen are present, but they do not witness the ceremony. Unwidowed women are not allowed to be present on the occasion. The ceremony consists in taking the widow and her new husband into a room, seating them side by side, and the tying round the widow's neck of a marriage badge by another widow. On the next day a dinner is given to the caste people.

Divorce is not known although a husband may abandon his wife owing to her infidelity or on account of her quarrelsome disposition. The caste follows the Hindu law of inheritance.

Religion.

In religion they appear to be Lingáyats of the third class, without *ashtavarna* rites [see LINGAYATS]. They wear the *linga* or phallic emblem characteristic of all Lingáyat castes. They worship by preference Basava as they believe that the founder of their caste came down to the earth with him to propagate the Lingáyat religion. An alternative belief is that Basava, the founder of Lingáyatism, took a *pángul* or lame beggar under his protection and from this convert the Lingáyat Helavs are descended. The Bombay Gazetteer states that their family deities are Revaneshwar and Yellamma, and that they make images and worship their dead ancestors to prevent them from bringing sickness into the family. On *Shrávan* or July-August Mondays they take only one meal in the evening, and keep *Shivrátra* in January-February as a total fast. They believe in soothsaying and witchcraft. They do not beg on Hindu holidays. They have neither priests, nor a *guru* or religious teacher. Their religious ceremonies are either conducted by experienced men of the caste or by Jangams. The dead are buried, the married in a sitting posture with the legs crossed and face to the east or north, the unmarried in a lying position with the head to the west or south. For the propitiation of ancestors, a ceremony is performed on the full moon day of *Jyeshtha* or the 10th day of the bright half of *Ashvin* when new clothes and cooked food are offered to their silver images. No special rites are performed for the propitiation of childless ancestors or men who have died a violent death. The ceremony of *Shráddha* is not performed.

They are hereditary beggars. When they go begging they sit on a bullock and wrap the body from the neck down in a quilt or white sheet to prevent people seeing their feet, which are tied to their thighs. They alone have the privilege of passing through the village gate without alighting from their bullock. They say that originally they were genealogists and lived upon the charity of their patron families, whose houses they visited and sung praises of their ancestors. They are now mostly husbandmen and day-labourers.

They habitually prostitute their unmarried women. When a girl is grown up she is made to undergo all the forms of a marriage without a bridegroom and is dedicated to Máruti, in whose name she carries on prostitution. She does not lose caste on this account.

Food. According to one account they abstain from eating flesh and drinking liquor. According to the Bombay Gazetteer they eat goats, hares, fowls and fish, and they drink liquor.

HELMAR.—A sub-division of Kolis.

HESI.—A sub-division of Berads.

HIJDA.—A synonym for Pávaya.

HINDUSTANI.—A sub-division of Dhors.

HIRE KURVINS.—A sub-division of Devángs.

HIR PANJNIGAR. —A sub-division of Pánjnigárs.

HOLAR.—A sub-division of Mahárs; A synonym for Holaya.

HOLAYAS, known also as Holárs or Valers in the Deccan and as Jambus elsewhere, number 106,465 (1901), including 51,705 males and 54,760 females, and are found all over the Karnátak and above the Sahyádris in Kanara, in parts of the Southern Marátha Country, and in Poona, Sátára and Sholápur. Of this number, 884 were shown as Lingáyats at the Census of 1901. According to some, the term Holaya is derived from the Kanarese *hola* a field, the word Holaya meaning a field-labourer. According to others, it comes from *hole* meaning dirty. The latter derivation is rendered probable by the fact that Holayás are an impure tribe, whose touch is defiling.

The tribe is represented in large numbers in Mysore and Madras. In South Kanara, they are also called Raneru or kings. Sir W. Elliot[1] is inclined to make the Holaya a Whaliar, which in early Kanarese

---

(1) 1869, J. Eth. Soc. Lond. I. 103.

is written Poliyár ; and the Támil Polaiyar is the same word. According to tradition, Parashurám's Bráhmans were driven out by low class chiefs, one a Moger or fisher, the other a Holaya. In later times, though the two stories perhaps belong to the same event, the Kadamba or Mayurvarma Bráhmans about A. D. 700 were driven out by a Holayar chief named Nanda and were brought back by Nanda's son.(1) According to another tradition(2) the Kadambas of Banavasi destroyed Hubásiga, the king of the mountain Chándáls, and annexed his dominions.

The Holayas of Dhárwár assert that the first Holaya was named Jambu. At that time, men were miserable and unsafe, living on an earth that swayed on the face of the waters. Jambu made its foundation sure by burning his son alive. In reward for this sacrifice the earth was called Jambudvipa or Jambu's land.

According to Sir W. Elliot the Holayas are the remains of the early race to whom the Deccan impure classes and the Konds and Gonds belong. In proof of the fact that in Mysore the Holayas are sons of soil, that is, are the earliest remaining race, Captain Mackenzie notices(3) that the village watchman, who is a Holaya by caste, settles boundary disputes and receives a burial-fee. In the Deccan and Konkan, this function is still performed by the impure Mahár, who also is known as son of the soil (*Bhumiputra*).

The Holayas are one of the aboriginal tribes of Southern India. In Mysore, where they number about five and a half-lakhs, they have still totemistic social divisions. This, and the facts that they feed on carrion, that they have no Bráhman priests, and that they are held impure, are indications of their primitive origin.

Holayas are dark, middle-sized, muscular with fairly regular features. In their dress and ornaments they resemble the Mahárs. Those of their women who are Basavis or prostitutes, unlike married women, wear rings on their great toes.

The home tongue of the Holayas in the south of the Presidency is Kanarese, and of those living in the Deccan, Maráthi. The names in common use among men are Basappa, Hanma, Mallappa, Ninga, Rámappa, Rudra, Vithu and Yella ; and among women, Basavva, Gangavva, Hanmavva, Tuljavva and Udchavva.

Holayas are bound together by a strong caste feeling. In the Karnátak, their social disputes are settled by their headman, the

(1) Buchanan's Mysore, III. 163. (2) Rice's Mysore, I. 194.
(3) 1873, Ind. Ant. II. 65.

Chalvádi, and some leading men of the caste, and any one who disobeys their decision is driven out. In Kanara, they have a hereditary headman called Gataga, who performs their ceremonies and settles their disputes. Offences against the community, such as eating with lower castes, are punished by fines. When a married woman commits adultery, both the guilty parties are put out of caste, and are not re-admitted until their heads have been shaved and their tongues branded.

Endogamous division.

The Holárs of the Karnátak have two divisions, Proper and Potrajas, who neither eat together nor intermarry. The endogamous divisions found amongst the Deccan Holárs are as follows :—

Ayavle	Gotrang	Hálmane
Birlinge	Gulik	Mánvat
Dhanvat	Jávir	Namdáse
Gárode	Kámle	Pársha
Gijge	Karde	Vágár.

These divisions eat together but do not intermarry.

Exogamous divisions.

The exogamous divisions of the Deccan Holayas are known as *bhávkis* in Sholápur and as *kuls* in other places. They are as follows :—

Ail	Háthikát	Mhetre
Badanvar	Hedge	Námdás
Devak	Honmáre	Navir
Dhoble	Jáve	Páras
Edve	Kámble	Párse
Elve	Kengár	Povár
Gováre	Khandekar	Lonvane
Gorve	Longar	Tormal
Gulve	Máne	Torne.

Marriages are prohibited between members belonging to the same *kul*. Sameness of *devak* is also a bar to intermarriage. Every *kul* has a separate *devak*. These *devaks* include an axe (*kurhád*), the whirler of a spinning wheel (*chát*), leaves of five trees (*pánchpálvi*) and the sun-flower.

A Holaya can marry his mother's brother's daughter. He cannot marry his father's sister's or mother's sister's daughter. Marriage with a wife's sister is allowed. Two brothers are allowed to marry two sisters. Polygamy is allowed and practised, but polyandry is unknown. A husband can divorce his wife with the sanction of the caste *panch* if she is unchaste. The ceremony prescribed for divorce is the performance of funeral rites in the name of the divorced wife, who can then marry again by the widow remarriage form. Girls are generally married between five and fifteen, boys between twelve and twenty. Sexual intercourse before marriage is generally allowed, but if a girl becomes pregnant, the offence has to be condoned by the payment of a fine and giving a dinner. If the man involved belong to another caste, the girl is said to be excommunicated; though this appears doubtful.

Birth ceremonies.

When a child is born, its navel-cord is cut and buried in the front yard of the house. A stone is laid over it, and the mother and child are bathed upon the stone. On the fifth day, Indian millet is cooked into thick gruel, a small stone is kept in the lying-in room, and *five* lumps of Indian millet gruel are set round the stone on a piece of cloth which has been dipped in turmeric powder and water. The five lumps of porridge and a little coarse sugar are served in five dishes, and *five* married unwidowed women are asked to eat the food. On the ninth day, *five* sorts of grain, Indian millet, *togari* (Cajanus indicus), *besru* (Phaseolus mungo), wheat and *madki* (Phaseolus aconotifolius) are boiled together and seasoned in a little oil, and *five* unwidowed women are called and fed with Indian millet gruel and coarse sugar. The women lay the child in a cradle and sing. On the twenty-ninth day the child is taken to the temple of their goddess Adchava, and is laid before the idol. The *pujári* or ministrant cuts a betel leaf in the shape of a pair of scissors, and with them goes through the form of cutting the child's hair, whether it is a boy or a girl. They ask the ministrant to find from the goddess what name should be given to the child. The ministrant consults the goddess, and remains for a while in silent study. He then suddenly utters a name, and that name is given to the child. Flowers, turmeric and red powder are laid before the goddess, and all go home. Next day, or on some future day, the hair of the child's head is cut.

Amongst the Deccan Holárs, on the fifth day, two figures are traced in charcoal on the door of the lying-in room, and an elderly woman worships them as the goddess Satvái. The figures of the goddess are offered wheat, bread and rice, and the mother brings her child and bows before them, and the ceremony is over. On the twelfth day, the mother worships *five* pebbles out of doors and offers them bread and rice. A child is named when it is a month old, the name being given by a Bráhman priest. Their children's hair is clipped any day between four months and four to eight years after birth. *Five* pebbles are worshipped at some distance from the house or in the bush, a goat is offered, and they return and feast.

Marriage ceremonies.

The offer of marriage comes from the boy's father, who has to pay a bride-price of from Rs. 20 to Rs. 100 to the girl's father. The day for the marriage is fixed in some places by a Bráhman astrologer; in others by a Jangam. The ceremony is conducted either by an elderly castemen or by a Lingáyat Chalvádi. In the *Báshtagi* or betrothal the boy's father places a cocoanut and annas 1¼ before the girl's house gods, seats the girl on a blanket, marks her brow with vermilion, presents her with a robe and a bodicecloth, and gives a bodicecloth to her mother. Sugar is handed to the guests. The girl's father treats the boy's father to a feast of boiled rice, wheat flour balls and molasses water. On the wedding day the bride's party go to the bridegroom's. If the bride is of age, she walks; if not, she is taken on a bullock. As they draw near the boundary of the bridegroom's village, his party go and meet them with two plates, one with lighted lamps and the other with burning incense. Both plates are waved round the bride and her party. The bride's party also wave lamps and incense round the bridegroom's party and they come together to the bridegroom's. Next day the boy and girl are rubbed with turmeric paste and bathed in a *surgi* or square with a drinking pot at each corner, a cotton thread being passed several times round the necks of all the vessels. A married woman waves a lamp before the boy and girl, the boy is dressed in new clothes, and the girl in a white robe and yellow bodice. The girl stands on a low stool or on a stone slab, and opposite her the boy stands in a basket containing rice, bits of a leather strap, and a whip. The boy fastens the *Mangal Sutra* or lucky string on the girl's neck, and an elderly Holaya recites a verse or two out of the marriage service and drops rice on the pair. Other guests join him in throwing rice, and the ceremony ends with a caste feast. In some places, the bride and bridegroom are seated on a blanket, and the lucky thread is fastened by the officiating priest. Next day, the boy's father presents the girl with a robe and bodicecloth, and her mother with two robes. The heads of the boy and girl are decked with marriage coronets and they are seated on a bullock, the girl sitting in front of the boy. The procession is headed by some men beating *halkis* or bell-less tambourines. The procession halts at the temple of the village Máruti, where the pair give a cocoanut to the ministrant, who breaks it before the god and returns half of it to the pair, with ashes from the god's censer. After bowing before the god the party return in procession to the boy's. Next day the girl is taken to her village. After some days the *Gharbharni* or housefilling takes place, in which the girl is taken to the boy's house and is given a robe and bodice. When a girl comes of age, she is made to sit by herself for three days, and is fed on boiled rice mixed with cocoa-kernel scraping and coarse sugar. On the fourth day she is taken to a *bábhul* tree and made to touch it with her right hand. She then comes home, bathes and is purified.

The marriage ceremonies of the Deccan Holayas resemble those of the Mahárs, the essential portion being the pouring of water over the joined hands of the bride and bridegroom (*dháre*).

The remarriage of widows is permitted. A widow cannot marry her mother's brother's or mother's sister's son, or a member of her deceased husband's *kul*. She may marry her father's sister's son. A widow remarriage is celebrated on a dark night or on a new-moon day. Kinsfolk on both the sides attend the ceremony. The widow and her intended husband are seated on low wooden stools or on a bullock's packsaddle, the widow's lap is filled, and her brow is marked with red powder. A feast is then held, which completes the ceremony. It is considered unlucky to see the faces of the remarried pair for three days after the marriage. A bachelor is allowed to marry a widow after he has been married to a *shami* tree (Prosopis spicigera).

Holayas follow the Hindu law of inheritance and profess Hinduism. Most of them neither worship Bráhman gods nor call Bráhmans to conduct their ceremonies. The family deities of the Karnátak Holayas are Dyámavva, Durgavva, Adchavva, Yellavva, Margavva, Hirodya, and Shaktivva. The chief object of worship of the Kanara Holayas is Venkataráma. The ministrants of Durgavva, Margavva and Shaktivva are Holayas. Holayas keep the holidays of *Holihunmi*, *Ugádi*, *Nágpanchami*, *Dasara* and *Diváli*. They make pilgrimages to Parasgad in Belgaum, Tuljápur, Shingnapur, Pandharpur, Jejuri, and to the shrine of Jotiba in Ratnágiri. Goats and he-buffaloes are offered to Murgavva and Ambábái and Khandoba. Parts of the offerings are given to the servants of the deities, and parts are partaken of by the offerers themselves. Musalmán saints are venerated. Sometimes both men and women vow to rub themselves with *huttegi* or sandal paste in the name of Yellamma. The devotee strips her clothes off, rubs her body with oil, bathes, smears the whole body with sandal paste, and covers it with *nimb* leaves from head to foot. The devotee then goes to a temple of Yellamma, bows before the goddess, offers her dressed food, and returns home. On the way to and from the temple the devotee shouts aloud *Udho, Udho,* that is Victory, Victory. The spiritual teacher of the Karnátak Holayas is a man of their own caste who lives in Bellary, and the teacher of those in Kanara lives in Tirupati. They are great believers in sorcery, witchcraft and soothsaying. Religion.

When a Holaya has all daughters and no son, he makes one of his daughters a Basavi and keeps her in his house to look after him. To make a Holaya girl a Basavi, on a lucky day the girl is taken to a temple of the goddess Adchavva with flowers, cocoanuts, and betel-nuts and leaves. The *pujári* or ministrant of the goddess worships the idol, ties a lucky thread of gold and glass beads round the girl's neck, rubs her brow with white cowdung ashes, and tells her that she has been made a Basavi, and from that day is free to act as courtezan.

From that day she maintains her parents and attends on the idol on great days, driving off the flies from the idol with a fan. After the death of her parents she inherits their property as a son would, and her daughters are freely taken in marriage.

Death ceremonies.

The dead are buried. The married dead are carried to the burial ground seated in a cloth or blanket, the unmarried in a lying position. A Lingáyat Chalvádi washes the face of the corpse, rubs it with white ashes, puts a small piece of gold into its mouth, and fills the pit with salt. The body of a Basavi or female devotee is buried with the same rites as the body of a married woman. The unmarried dead are buried without washing the face, applying white ashes, or putting a piece of gold in the mouth. On the fifth day the deceased's house is cowdunged and the deceased's clothes are washed, incensed with frankincense, and presented with a sweet dish. Holayas observe mourning for ten days, during which they consider themselves impure. They do not perform the *shráddha*.

Occupation.

The main occupation of the Kanarese Holayas is removing dead animals, making sandals, and ordinary field work, especially at harvest time. They skin dead cattle and sell the hides and horns. They sweep the village *chávdi* and remove dead cattle, for which the husbandmen pay them in grain at harvest time. Some are village watchmen and some are in charge of village ponds. Under former Governments they had to carry the baggage of Government officials from village to village without pay.

The Holayas of the Deccan maintain themselves chiefly as musicians and songsters. They are engaged at the marriages of Kunbis and other castes of similar standing. They also work in leather like their Kanarese brethren.

Food.

The staple food of Holayas is Indian millet bread, pulse, chillies and vegetables. In Kanara, rice forms the principal article of their food. They eat carrion, cows, sheep, pig, jackals, fowls and game, and drink liquor. Some Holayas do not eat from Dhors, Mángs and

Samgárs or even from Nhávis and Parits. In the social scale they occupy the same place as the Mahárs of the Maráthi-speaking districts and the Dhedas of Gujarát. Like the Mahárs, their touch, even contact with their shadow, is considered to defile.

POTRAJAS or Buffalo kings differ in some respects from the Holayas proper. The story of the origin of their name is that their ancestor became the husband of Dyámavva, an incarnation of the great goddess Lakshmi. They lived together for several years and had children. At Dyámavva's request the Holaya brought his mother to their house. As they were eating some of Dyámavva's sweetmeats the mother said to the son, "How like this is to a roasted búffalo tongue." Dyámavva, finding how she had been deceived and degraded, burnt her house, slew her children, and, pursuing her husband who had taken the form of a buffalo, killed him. The descendants of the husband are called Potrájás, that is Buffalo kings. They are a small body and are found in only a few villages of the Dhárwár district. On Dyámavva's fairs, which last for eight days, several male buffaloes representing the Holaya who married Dyámavva and a number of sheep representing his children are slaughtered before the deity. The officiating Potrája tears open the throat of a lamb with his teeth, and drinks its blood. On the last day of the fair, in a state of stark nakedness, he carries cooked rice on his head all round the village, throwing away a little, and slaughtering a sheep at each of its corners. On his return he receives a large share of the slaughtered buffaloes and sheep. In other respects Potrájás do not differ from Holayas.

HOLGE.—A sub-division of Mángs.

HOLIA.—A sub-division of Kolhátis.

HOLIACHIBALKI.—A synonym for Athnikar.

HOLKAR.—A sub-division of Dhangars.

HONA.—A sub-division of Rabáris.

HOSA.—A sub-division of Hanbars.

HUGAR.—A sub-division of Lingáyats.

HULSAVA.—A synonym for Mahár.

HULSAVAR.—A synonym for Haslar.

HUMAD.—A synonym for Ummad.

HUMBAD.—A synonym for Ummad.

HUSSAINI BRAHMAN.—*See* under minor Musalmán Castes; a synonym for Sahadev Joshi.

HUVALE.—A synonym for Holár Mahár.

IDHVAL.—A synonym for Indhvál.

ILGARS or palm-tappers, also called Kaláls and Shindigárs, are found chiefly in Dhárwár, Bijápur and Belgaum. Their main calling is that of tapping palms. They have four divisions, (1) Kaudanya, (2) Kárunya, (3) Kátunya and (4) Váschalya. The first two eat together and intermarry, but do not eat or marry with the third or fourth. They have several family stocks which are exogamous. Their family deities are Basava, Tuljá-Bhaváni, Hanumán Yellamma and Ratnaray. They show great respect for the *linga*. Their spiritual teacher is a Lingáyat priest named Ajayya. They employ both Bráhman and Lingáyat priests. They bury their dead in Lingáyat fashion. Their other ceremonies resemble those of Kabbaligars. They eat fish and the flesh of goats, sheep, deer, hare and domestic fowls. Except in Bijápur, they do not drink liquor; and they nowhere drink palm juice, which they explain by saying that the wild date palm is their sister.

INDHVAL.—A sub-division of Bráhmans.

INDORIA.—A sub-division of Kolis.

ISRIA.—A sub-division of Dublás.

ISTARI.—A sub-division of Khatris.

JAAFARI.—A sub-division of Bohorás.

JAD.—*See* Deváng, Hatkar, Jád, Koshti or Sáli.

JAILVAL.—A synonym for Jelvál.

Distribution.

JAINS numbering 536,116 (1901), including 297,672 males and 256,444 females, are chiefly found in the Gujarát districts and States, Cutch and Káthiáwár and in the southern part of the Deccan, the Karnátak and the States of the Southern Marátha Country. They are divided into two territorial groups, (1) the Jains of Gujarát and (2) the Jains of the Deccan, who neither eat together nor intermarry and differ considerably in ceremonies and customs, though the main principles of their religion are the same.

Divisions.

The Jain religion is not opposed to the observance of caste, with the result that Jain divisions are found in many castes of the Presidency. No intermarriage between the Hindu and Jain division of a caste is recognized.

The following are the chief castes divisions in which Jains are recorded:—

A. (*Gujarát.*)

(1)	Agarwál Váni	(3)	Bhátia
(2)	Bhavsár or Chippa	(4)	Bhojak

(5) Chaturtha
(6) Chhatri or Khatri
(7) Desháwál Váni
(8) Gandhi
(9) Gurjar Váni
(10) Halvái or Kandoi
(11) Hardás.
(12) Humbad or Umbad Váni
(13) Jat or Jati
(14) Kásar, Kansár, Bogár or Baligar
(15) Khadáyata Váni
(16) Kumbhár
(17) Kunbi
(18) Lád Váni
(19) Lohána
(20) Márwádi or Osvál Váni
(21) Mewáda Váni
(22) Modha Váni
(23) Narsingpuri Váni
(24) Nima or Nema Váni
(25) Pánchál
(26) Porwád or Porwál Váni
(27) Sevak
(28) Shetwál
(29) Shrimáli Váni
(30) Soni or Sonár
(31) Sorthia Váni

B. (*Deccan*).

(1) Charutha or Chaturtha
(2) Kásár, Bogár or Baligar
(3) Pancham
(4) Shetwál
(5) Upádhya

The Gujarát castes will be found for the most part described under VANI. Of the Deccan divisions the Upádhyás are the priests, who will take daughters in marriage but will not give their daughters to the other divisions. Charuthas or "fourths" are Shudras or husbandmen. It is said that these are the original "Charodas" of the Goanese Native Christians, who have three caste divisions. Panchams or "fifths" are traders and are said* to be Jains who allow widow re-marriage. The name and the practice would seem to suggest some connection with Lingáyat Panchamsális (*see* LINGAYAT). Owing to this practice the other Deccan Jain castes stand aloof from them, and will not intermarry. Where a caste has a Hindu and a Jain subdivision it is usual to describe the former as '*Meshri*' and the latter as '*Shrávak*'.

Name and origin.

Jains take their name from the fact that they are followers of the 24 Jins or conquerors, commencing with Rishabh or Adinabh and ending with Mahávir or Vardhmán. (*See* page 133 *infra*).

Párasnáth or Párshavanáth, literally the *náth* or lord, who comes next to the last Jin Vardhmán is said to have been the son of king Ashvasen by his wife Váma or Báma Devi of the race of Ikshváku.

* Bombay Gazetteer, Volume XXII, p. 117.

He is said to have been born at Benares, to have married Prabhávati, the daughter of king Prasen Jit, to have adopted an ascetic life at the age of thirty, and to have practised austerities for eighty days, when he gained perfect wisdom. Once while engaged in devotion his enemy Kamath caused a great rain to fall on him. But the serpent Dharanidhar or the Nág king Dharan shaded Párasnáth's head with his hood spread like an umbrella or *chhatra,* whence the place was called Ahichhatra or the snake umbrella.(1) Párasnáth is said to have worn only one garment. He had a number of followers of both sexes, and died performing a fast at the age of 100 on the top of Samet Shikhar in Hazáribágh in West Bengal. His death occurred 250 years before that of the last or twenty-fourth Jin Mahávir. Mahávir or Vardhmán, who was also of the Ikshváku race, is said to have been the son of Siddhárth prince of Pavan by Trisala and to have been born at Chitrakut or Kundgrám perhaps the modern Chitarkot a great place of pilgrimage seventy-one miles west of Alláhábád. He is said to have married Yashoda, the daughter of prince Samarvir, and to have by her a daughter named Priyadarshana, who became the wife of Jamáli, a nephew of Mahávir's and one of his pupils who founded a separate sect. Mahávir's father and mother died when he was twenty-eight, and two years later he devoted himself to austerities which he continued for twelve and a half years, nearly eleven of which were spent in fasts. As a Digambar or sky clad ascetic he went robeless and had no vessel but his hand. At last the bonds of action were snapped like an old rope and he gained *keval* or absolute unity of spirit and became an Arhat, that is, worthy or Jin, that is, conqueror. He went to Pápapuri or Apápuri in Bihár and taught his doctrine. Of several eminent Bráhmans who became converts and founded schools or *ganas,* the chief was Indrabhuti or Gautama, who preached his doctrines at the cities of Kaushambi and Rájgrih and died at the age of sevent-two at Apápuri in South Bihár between B.C. 663 and 526.(2)

Like the Buddhists, the Jains reject the Vedas, which they pronounce apochryphal and corrupt and to which they oppose their own scriptures or Angas. As among Buddhists confession is practised among Jains. Great importance is attached to pilgrimage, and four months or the *cháturmás,* that is, four months from the eleventh of *Ashádh* or July-August to the eleventh of *Kártik* or October-November, in the year are given to fasting, the reading of sacred books, and

(1) General Cunningham has identified the ancient Ahichhatra with the present Rámanagar in Rohilkhand in Upper India. Cunningham's Ancient Geography, I. 359.

(2) Rice's Mysore and Coorg, 1, 374, 375.

meditation. They attach no religious importance to caste. Jains like Buddhists are of two classes, *yatis* or ascetics and *shrávaks* or hearers. Jains like Buddhists admit no creator. According to them the world is eternal, and they deny that any being can have been always perfect; the Jin became perfect but he was not perfect at first. Both Buddhists and Jains worship, though under different names, twenty-four lords each with his sign and his attendant goddess or *shásan devi* :—

Jain Saints.[1]

Name.	Sign.	*Shásandevi* or Attendant Goddess.	Name.	Sign.	*Shásandevi.* or Attendant Goddess.
Rishabh or A'dinath.	Bull.	Chakreshvari.	Vimalnáth.	Boar.	Vidita.
			Anantnáth.	Falcon.	Ankusha.
Ajitnáth.	Elephant	Ajitbala.	Dharmanáth.	Thunder-bolt.	Kandarpa.
Shámbhav.	Horse.	Duritári.	Shantináth.	Antelope.	Nirváni.
Abhinandan.	Monkey.	Kálika.	Kunthunáth.	Goat.	Bala.
Sumati.	Curlew.	Mahákali.	Arnáth.	*Nandyáv a r t* or pleasing.	Dhárini.
Padmaprabh.	Lotus.	Shyáma.	Mallináth.	Water jar.	Dharanpriya
Supárshv.	Lucky Cross or *Svastik.*	Shánta.	Muni Suvrat.	Tortoise.	Naradatta.
Chandra-prabh.	Moon.	Bhrikuti.	Niminánth.	Blue Water Lily.	Ghándári.
Pushpadant.	Crocodile.	Sutaraka.	Neminánth.	Conch Shell.	Ambika.
Shital.	Cruciform symbol or *Shrivats.*	Ashoka.	Párshvnáth.	Cobra.	Padmávati.
Shreyánsh	Rhinoceros.	Manavi.	Vardhmán or Mahavir.	Lion.	Siddhayika.
Vásupujya.	Buffalo.	Chanda.			

On the whole Jainism is less opposed to Bráhmanism than Buddhism is, and admits some of the Bráhman deities, though it holds them inferior to their *chovishi* or twenty-four saints. Jainism, of which there are traces in South India as early as the second century before Christ and to which the great stone figure of Gomateshvar at Shrávan Belgola in Mysore is believed to belong, was a ruling religion in the Deccan at least as early as the fourth or fifth century.[2]

In Gujarát Jains speak Gujaráti. Deccan Jains speak Kanarese at home and Maráthi abroad, which they call Aré Mátu or the language of the Arés, a name by which the Maráthás are known in the extreme south of the Presidency. In their Kanarese the last syllable is always Language.

(1) Rice's Mysore and Coorg, I, 374.

(2) Bombay Gazetteer, Volume XXIV, pages 133-34.

very indistinct. They name their children after the *arhats* or worthies of the present, past and future ages, after the parents of the *arhats*, after the pious and great men and after Bráhmanic gods and local deities. Like Bráhmanic Hindus, Deccan Jain parents sometimes give their children mean names to avert early death as Kallappa from *Kallu* (K) stone, Kádappa from *kád* (K) forest, Dhondu from *dhondu* (M) stone.

Ceremonies.

Of the sixteen sacraments or *sanskárs*, which are nearly the same as the sixteen Bráhman sacraments, Jains perform thread-girding marriage, puberty, and death. Except that the texts are not Vedic the rites do not differ from those performed by Bráhmans. Their birth ceremonies are the same as those of Bráhmans like whom on the fifth day they worship the goddess Satvái.

Thread girding.

Boys are girt with the sacred thread between eight and sixteen. A boy must not be girt until he is eight. If, for any reason, it suits the parents to hold the thread-girding before the boy is eight, they add to his age the nine months he passed in the womb. A Jain astrologer names a lucky day for the thread-girding, a booth is raised before the house and an earth altar or *bahule* a foot and a half square is built in the booth, and plantain trees are set at its corners. Pots are brought from the potter's and piled in each corner of the altar, and a yellow cotton thread is passed round their necks. Over the altar is a canopy and in front is a small entrance hung with evergreens. Invitation cards are sent to distant friends and kinsfolk. A day or two before the thread-girding the invitation procession consisting of men and women of the boy's house with music and friends starts from the boy's. They first go to the Jain temple, and the father or some other relation with the family priest lays a cocoanut before the god, bows before him, and asks him to the ceremony. They visit the houses of their friends and relations and ask them to attend the ceremony. The Jains have no *devak* or family guardian worship. The boy and his parents go through the preliminary ceremonies as at a Bráhman thread-girding. The boy's head is shaved and he is bathed and rubbed with turmeric. The astrologer marks the lucky moment by means of his water-clock or *ghatka*, and as it draws near, music plays and guns are fired. The priest repeats the lucky verses and throws red rice over the boy. The boy is seated on his father's or, if the father is dead, on some other kinsman's knee on a low stool. The knot of his hair is tied and he is girt with a sacred thread or *jánve* and a string of *kush* grass is tied round his waist. The priest kindles the sacred fire, betel is served to the guests, and money gifts are distributed among priests and beggars. The boy has to go and beg at five

Jain houses. He stands at the door of each house and asks the mistress of the house to give him alms saying, "Oh lady be pleased to give alms."[1] The alms usually consists of a waistcloth, rice, or cash. Great merit is gained by giving alms to a newly girded boy, and many women visit the boy's house for three or four days to present him with silver or clothes. After begging at five houses the boy returns home, and a feast to friends and kinsfolk ends the first day. The *sodmunj* or grass-cord loosening is performed usually after a week and sometimes between a week from the thread-girding and the marriage day. The loosening is generally performed near a *pipal* (Ficus religiosa) tree. The boy is bathed, the rite of holiday calling or *punyáhavachan* is gone through as on the first day, music plays, and flowers, sandal paste, burnt frankincense, and sweetmeat are offered to the *pipal* tree. The boy bows before the tree and the priest unties the cord, from round his waist. The boy is dressed in a full suit of clothes, declares that he means to go to Benares and spend the rest of his life in study and worship, and sets out on his journey. Before he has gone many yards, his maternal uncle meets him, promises him his daughter's hand in marriage, and asks him to return home and live among them as a householder or *grihasth*. The boy is escorted home with music and a band of friends and a small feast to friends and kinsfolk ends the ceremony.

Marriage. Boys are married between fifteen and twenty-five and girls before they come of age. As a rule the boy's father proposes the match to the girl's father, and when they agree, an astrologer is consulted, who compares the birth papers of the boy and the girl and approves the match if he thinks the result will be lucky and if the family stocks and branches or *shákhás* of the boy and the girl are different. Then on a lucky day the boy's father visits the girl's house with a few friends, including five kinswomen, and are received by the girl's father and mother. The girl is seated on a low stool in front of the house gods, and the boy's father presents her with a robe and bodice and a pair of silver chains or *sánkhlis* and anklets or *válás*. Her brow is marked with vermilion and decked with a network of flowers. The women of the boy's house dress the girl in the clothes and ornaments brought by the boy's father and the boy's father puts a little sugar in her mouth. Packets of sugar and betel are handed among the guests and the asking or *mágni* ends in a feast to the guests. As a rule marriage takes place two or three years after betrothal. Every year the boy's parents have to send a present of a string of cocoa-kernel and some

(1) The Sanskrit runs: *Bhavati bhikshám dehi.*

fried rice on the Cobra's Fifth or *Nágpanchmi* in July-August and this they have to continue to do till the girl comes of age. When the boy is fifteen or sixteen and the girl is ten or eleven the parents think it is time they were married, and send for and consult an astrologer. He compares their horoscopes, consults his almanac, and names a lucky day for the marriage. The ceremony as a rule lasts five days. On the first day two married girls in the bride's house bathe early in the morning, wear a ceremonial dress, and with music and a band of friends go to a pond or a river with copper pots on their heads, lay sandal-paste, flowers, rice, vermilion, burnt frankincense, and sweetmeats on the bank in the name of the water goddess, fill the pots with water, and mark them with vermilion, set a cocoanut and betel leaves in the mouth of each, cover them with bodice-cloths, and deck them with gold necklaces. They then set the waterpots on their heads, return home, and lay them on the earthen altars. Flowers, vermilion, burnt frankincesnse and sweetmeat are offered to the pots and five dishes filled with earth are set before them sprinkled with water from the waterpots, and mixed seed grain is sown in the earth. Friends and kinsfolk are asked to dine at the house and the sproutoffering or *ankurárpan* is over. The bridegroom is bathed at his house and lights a sacred fire or *hom*, puts on a rich dress, and goes on horseback with music and friends carrying clothes, ornaments, sugar, and betel packets to the bride's house. The bride's party meet him on the way and the bridegroom is taken to the bride's house and seated outside of the house on a seat of *audumbar* or *umbar* (Ficus glomerata.) The bride's parents come out with a vessel full of water, the father washes his future son-in-law's feet and the mother pours water over them. The bridegroom is then taken to a raised seat in the house, seated on it, and presented with clothes, a gold ring, and a necklace. The bridegroom's parents present the ornaments and clothes they have brought for the bride, packets of betel and sugar are handed among friends and kinspeople, and the first day ends with a feast to the bridegroom's party. The bridegroom returns home with his party, is rubbed with turmeric and clarified butter, and bathed by five married women seated in a square with an earthen pot at each corner and a yellow thread passed five times round their necks. The bride is bathed in a similar square at her house. On the third day the bride and bridegroom bathe, dress in newly washed clothes, and starting from their homes meet at the Jain temple. The priest attends them, and the pair bow before the idol. The priest makes them repeat the five-salutation hymn which every Jain ought to know and warns them to keep the Jain vow or *Jain vrat* of not-killing or *ahinsa* and of leading a pure moral life. The pair are treated to sweetmeats, each by their own people, and the family gods and the cork marriage coronet or *báshing* are worshipped at both houses. Men and women from both houses go with music and ask their friends and kinspeople. In the afternoon, when all meet, the women take their seats in the booth and the men inside of the house, and all eat at the same time. On the fourth day the actual marriage ceremony begins. Friends and relations are asked to both houses. The bridegroom is rubbed with fragrant oil, and with about fifteen of his relations again kindles the sacred fire, dresses in r ch clothes, and goes to the bride's house on horseback with music and friends. On the way he is met by the bride's party and taken to a raised *umbar* (Ficus glomerata) seat. While he is seated on the *umb r* seat a couple from the bride's house, generally the bride's parents, come and wash his feet. The bridegroom thrice sips water, puts on the new sacred thread offered him by the bride's priest, and swallows curds mixed with sugar which the couple have poured over his hands. The father-in-law leads the bridegroom by the hand to a ready-made seat in the house. Before the seat a curtain is held, and two heaps of rice, one on each side of the curtain, marked with the lucky cross or *svástik* and crowned with the sacred *kush* grass. A short time before the lucky moment the bride is let out by her friends and made to stand on the rice heap behind the curtain, the bridegroom standing on the rice heap on the other side. The guests stand around and the priests recite the nine-planet lucky verses or *navgrah mangaláshtaks*. The astrologer marks the lucky moment by clapping his hands, the musicians redouble their noise, the priests draw aside the curtain, and the pair look at each other and are husband and wife. The bridegroom marks the bride's brow with vermilion and she throws a flower garland round his neck. They fold their hands together and the bride's father pours water over their hands. They then throw rice over each other's head, and the priests and guests throw rice at the pair. The priests tie the marriage wristlets on the hands of the pair. The bridegroom then sits on a low stool facing east, and the bride on another stool to his left. The priest kindles the sacred or *hom* fire and the bridegroom feeds the fire with offerings of parched rice held in a dish before him by the bride. Then the priest lays seven small heaps of rice each with a small stone at the top in one row. The bridegroom, holding the bride by the hand, touches the rice and the stone on each heap with his right toe, moves five times round the heaps, the priest shows the pair the Polar star or *dhruv*, and the payment of a money gift to the priest completes the day's ceremonies. The hems of the pair's garments are knotted together and they walk into the house and bow before the waterpots which are arranged on the first day, and are fed with a dish of milk and clarified butter. Next day the bride's parents give a feast to the bridegroom's party and to their own kinspeople. In the morning the pair are seated in the booth and young girls on both sides join them. The pair first play betel-nuts for a time and the bridegroom takes some wet turmeric powder and rubs it five times on the bride's face, who gathers it and rubs it on the bridegroom's face. The bridegroom is given a betel packet to chew, chews half of it and hands the rest to the bride. Thus he chews the five betel packets, and the bride in her turn chews another five, each time handing half of the betel packets to the bridegroom to chew. Next morning the sacred fire is again kindled and the serpent is worshipped. The pair then dine at the bride's and play with betelnuts. The pair are seated on horseback, the bride before the bridegroom, and taken to the Jain temple, where they walk round the god, bow before him, and ask his blessing. They then walk to the bridegroom's with music and friends.

Before they reach it every part of the house is lighted and a long white sheet is spread on the ground from the booth door to the god-room. When the pair attempt to cross the threshold the bridegroom's sister blocks the door and does not allow them to enter. The bridegroom asks her why she blocks the door. She says, Will you give your daughter in marriage to my son? He answers, Ask my wife. The sister asks the wife and she says, I will give one of my three pearls in marriage to your son. Then she leaves the door, the pair walk into the house, bow before the house gods, and a feast of uncooked provisions to those that do not eat from them and of cooked food to friends of their own caste and to kinspeople ends the ceremony.

Though forbidden by their sacred book, all Jains except Upádhyás or priests allow widow marriage. They say the practice came into use about 200 years ago. If a woman does not get on well with her husband, she may live separate from him but cannot marry during her husband's lifetime. When a girl comes of age she sits apart for three days. On the fourth she is bathed and her lap is filled with rice and a cocoanut and the rest of the age-coming does not differ from a Bráhman age-coming.(1)

Religion.

The religion of the Jains may be treated under five heads: the temple worship of the twenty-four saints and their attendant goddesses; holy places and holy days; the worship of house gods; the worship

(1) Bombay Gazetteer, Volume XXIV, pages 140—144.

of field guardians; and the irregular worship of evil disease-causing spirits. The chief Jain doctrine is that to take life is sin. Like Buddhists they believe that certain conduct has raised men above the gods. Twenty-four saints have gained perfection. To each of these a sign and an attendant goddess have been allotted, and these form the regular objects of Jain temple worship. The Jains belong to two main sects, the *shvetámbars* or white-robed and *digambars* or sky-clad, that is, the naked saint worshippers. The bulk of the Deccan Jains are Digambars. Temple worship is the chief part of the Jain's religious duties. Their temples are called *bastis* or dwellings, but can easily be known from ordinary dwellings by their high plinths.

The temple consists of an outer hall and a shrine. The walls of the outer hall are filled with niches of the different Bráhmanic deities and attendant goddesses. In the shrine is an image, generally of the twenty-third saint Párasnáth, which is generally naked. The images in most cases are of black polished stone two feet to three feet high, either standing with the hands stretched down the sides or in the seated cross-legged position. Temple worship is of four kinds, daily worship, eight-day or *ashtánhiki* worship, wish-filling or *kalp* worship, and the five blessing or *panch kalyáni* worship. In the daily temple worship the image of the saint is bathed by the temple ministrant in milk and on special days in the five nectars or *panchámrits* water, tree sap or *vriksh ras*, that is sugar, plantains, clarified butter, milk and curds. The priest repeats sacred verses, sandal paste is laid on the image, and it is decked with flowers.

Jains perform the *ashtánhiki* or eight-day worship three times in a year from the bright eighth to the full-moon of *Shrávan* or July August, in *Kártik* or October-November, and in *Phálgun* or February-March. Only the rich perform the wish filling or *kalp* worship as the worshipper has to give the priest whatever he asks. Except the goat-killing the five-blessing or *pánch kalyáni* worship is the same as the Bráhmanical sacrifice. According to the Jain doctrine bathing in holy places does not cleanse from sin. Jains make pilgrimages to Jain holy places, Uru Jayantgiri or Girnár in South Káthiáwár sacred to Nemishvar or Neminá th, Pavápur near Rájagriha or Rájgir about fifty miles south of Pátna sacred to Vardhmán Svámi, Sammedh-giri properly Samet Shikhar or Párasnáth hill in Hazáribágh in West Bengal sacred to Párasnáth where are feet symbols or *pádukás* of the twenty-four Jain *arhats* or worthies, and in the south, the stone figure of Gomateshvar in Shrávan Belgola in Mysore, and Mudbidri in South Kanara. They make pilgrimages to Benares, which they say is the birthplace of Párasnáth who was the son of Vishveshvar, the chief Bráhman deity of the place. The leading religious seats of the Jains are Delhi, Dinkánchi in Madras, Vingundi in South Kanara, and Kolhápur. Any poor Jain may visit these places and is fed for any number of days, but on pain of loss of caste he must beg from no one who is not a Jain.

Jain ascetics keep ten fasts in every lunar month, the fourths, the eighths, the elevenths, the fourteenths, and the full-moon and no-moon. They keep all Bráhmanic holidays, and in addition the week beginning from the lunar eighth of *Ashádh* or June-July, of *Kártik* or October-November, and of *Phálgun* or February-March, and they hold a special feast on *Shrut Panchmi* or Learning's Fifth on the bright fifth of *Jyeshth* or May-June. Of the twenty-four minor goddesses who attend on the twenty-four saints the chief are Kálika and Jválámálini and Padmávati, who probably are the same as the two popular Bráhman goddesses Bhaváni and Lakshmi.

Besides the twenty-four attendant goddesses, Jains believe in all Bráhmanic deities, placing them below their saints or *tirthankars*. They pay special respect to the Bráhman goddess Sarasvati who is represented by a sacred book resting on a brazen chair called *shrut skandh* or learning's prop and in whose honour in all Jain temples a festival is held on the bright fifth of *Jyeshth* or May-June. To these guardian goddesses and saints two beings are added, Bhujval or Goval of Shrávan Belgola in Mysore, distinguished by the creepers twining round his arms, and Nandishrami, a small temple like a brass frame. Besides these they worship a brass wheel of law or *dharm-chakra* which is said to represent five classes of great deities or *Parameshthis*, a verbal salutation to the whole of whom forms the Jain's daily prayer. The Jains think their book and temple gods the *arhats* or worthies, the *siddhs* or perfect beings, the *ácháryás* or godfathers, the *upádhyás* or priests, and the *sádhus* or saints are too austere and ascetic to take an interest in every-day life or to be worshipped as house guardians. For this reason their house deities are either Bráhmanic or Lingáyat gods.

As among Bráhmanic Hindus the house deities are kept in a separate room, generally next to the cooking room in a *devára* or shrine of carved wood. The images are generally of metal three to four inches high. Among the images is not unusually the mask or bust of some deceased female member of the family who has afflicted the family with sickness and to please her had her image placed and worshipped among the house gods. Besides the usual Bráhmanic or Lingáyat house deities several families have a house image of Párasnáth, but the worship of Párasnáth as a house image is not usual. As among Bráhmanic Hindus, the daily worship of the house gods is simple chiefly consisting in a hurried decking with flowers. On holidays the images are bathed in milk, and flowers, sandal-paste, rice, burnt frankincense, and camphor and cooked food are laid before them. Women are not allowed to touch the house gods. During the absence of the men of the house the temple priest is asked to conduct the daily worship. Another class of Jain deities are the *kshetrapáls* or field guardians, the chief of whom are Bhairav and Brahma. In theory Jains do not believe in spirits. The learned are particularly careful to disavow a belief in spirits and even ordinary Jains dislike to admit the existence of such a belief. Still, enquiry shows that a belief in spirits is little less general than among the corresponding Bráhmanic classes. They believe in spirit-possession and call their family spirits *pitrad* or fathers. Though they profess not to believe that infants are attacked by spirits, they perform the ceremonies observed by Bráhmanic Hindus in honour of Mothers Fifth and Sixth, which seem to form a part of the early rites on which the customs of all Hindu sects are based. Besides the spirit attacks to which children are specially liable on the fifth and sixth days after birth, Jain children are liable to child seizures or *bál grahas,* probably a form of convulsions, which Jain women say is the work of spirits. Educated and religious Jains who object to the early or direct form of spirit action believe in the more refined *drisht* or evil eye as a cause of sickness. According to the popular Jain belief all eyes have not the blasting power of the evil eye. Care must be taken in cutting the child's navel, for if any of the blood enters its eyes their glance is sure to have a blasting or evil power. Unlike most Bráhmanic Hindus, Jains do not believe that a woman in her monthly sickness is specially liable to spirit attacks. In their opinion a woman runs most risk of being possessed when she has just bathed and her colour is heightened by turmeric, when her hair is loose, and when she is gaily dressed, and happens to go to a lonely well or river bank at noon or sunset. Boys also are apt to be possessed when they are well dressed or fine-looking or when they are unusually sharp and clever. Jains profess not to hold the ordinary Bráhmanic belief that the first wife comes back and plagues the second wife. Still they hold in great terror Jakhins, that is, the ghosts of women who die with unfulfilled wishes. Among Jains as among other Hindus, Jakhins plague the living by attacking children with lingering diseases. When a child is wasting away, Jain parents make the Jakhin a vow that if the child recovers the Jakhin's image shall be placed with their family gods. If the child begins to recover as soon as the vow is made the house people buy a silver or gold mask or *ták* of Jakhin, lay sandal-paste and flowers on, and sweetmeats before, it, and set it in the god room with the other house gods. Five married women, who are asked to dine at the house are presented each with turmeric, vermilion, betel, and wet gram, and a special offering or *váyan* consisting of five wheat cakes stuffed with sugar clarified butter and molasses is made in the name of the dead woman who is believed to have turned Jakhin and possessed the child. The women and men guests dine with the family and take the special offering or *váyan* home. The image is daily worshipped with the house gods with great reverence as it generally represents the mother or some near relation of the worshipper. This Jakhin worship is common among Jains. Jains have no professional exorcists or charmers chiefly becuase their place is filled by the Jain priests. When sickness is believed to be caused by spirit-possession the priest is consulted. He worships the goddess Padmávati or Lakshmi and gives the sick holy water or *tirth* in which the goddess' feet have been washed. If the holy water fails to cure, the priest consults his book of omens or *shakunvanti*, adds together certain figures in the book and divides the total by a certain figure in the tables of the book, and by referring to the book finds what dead relation of the sick person the quotient stands for. If it is a woman she has become a Jakhin and should be worshipped along with the family gods. The priest then mutters a verse over a pinch of frankincense ashes or *angara* burnt before the gods and hands it to the sick man to be rubbed on his brow. If the ash-rubbing and the Jakhin worship fail to cure the sick man the priest prepares a paper or *bhoj* or birch leaf called a *yantra* or device marked with mystic figures or letters and ties it in a silk cloth or puts it in a small casket or *táit*, mutters verses over it, burns frankincense, and ties it round the possessed person's arm or neck. If the amulet is of no avail the priest advises an *anushthán* or god-pleasing. The head of the house asks the priest to read a sacred book before the temple image of one of the saints or to repeat a text or *mantra* or a sacred hymn or *stotra* some thousand times in honour of one of the saints. The priest is paid for his trouble, and when the sick man is cured the god-pleasing ends with a feast to priests and friends. If even the god-pleasing fails, the sick man, if he is an orthodox and particular Jain, resigns himself to his fate or seeks the aid of a physician. Unlike the men, Jain women are not satisfied without consulting exorcists and trying their cures. Exorcists are shunned by men Jains because part of the exorcists' cure is almost always the offering of a goat or of a cock. A

Jain man will seldom agree to such a breach of the chief law of his faith, but Jain women secretly go to the exorcists and do as they are advised. When all remedies are of no avail Jains sometimes take the sickman to a holy place called Tavnidhi fifteen miles south-west of Chikodi, and he or some relation on his behalf worships the spirit-scaring Brahmanidhi until the patient is cured. The Jains profess to have no sacred pools, animals, or trees that have a spirit-scaring power. When an epidemic rages a special worship of Jindev is performed.(1)

To every Jain temple one or more priests or Upádhyás are attached. They belong to the Chaturth or the Pancham division and are supported by the Jain community, taking the food offerings, cloth and money presents which are made to the gods and goddesses. Besides temple priests, every village which has a considerable number of Jains has an hereditary village priest called *grámopádhya* who conducts their ceremonies and is paid either in cash or in grain. The village priests, who are married and in whose families the office of priests is hereditary, are under a high priest called *dharmádhikári* or religious head, a celibate or ascetic by whom they are appointed and who has power to turn out any priest who breaks religious rules or caste customs. The village priest keeps a register of all marriages and thread-girdings in the village, and the high priest, whose authority extends over all Jains under his jurisdiction, makes a yearly circuit gathering contributions or sends an agent to collect subscriptions, from the persons named in the village priests' lists. The office of high priest is elective. The high priest chooses his sucessor from among his favourite disciples.(2)

When a Jain is on the point of death a priest is called in to repeat verses to cleanse the sick person's ears, to quiet his soul, and if possible to drive away his disease. When recovery is hopeless a ceremony called *sallekhan vidhi* or tearing rite is performed to sever the sick person from wordly pleasures and to make him fit for the life he is about to enter. Sometimes the sick man is made to pass through the ceremony called *sannyás grahan* or ascetic vow-taking with the same rites as among Bráhmans. When these rites are over and death is near the dying man is made to lie on a line of three to four wooden stools and the names of gods and sacred hymns are loudly repeated. After death the body is taken outside of the house, bathed in warm water, dressed in a waist and a shoulder cloth, and seated cross-legged on a low stool leaning against the wall. A bier is made, the deceased is laid on it, and the whole body including the face is covered with a Death.

(1) Bombay Gazetteer, Volume XXIV, pages 137—140.

(2) Bombay Gazetteer, Volume XXIV, page 136.

white sheet. Jewels are put into the dead mouth and fastened over the eyes. Four kinsmen lift the bier and, followed by a party of friends, walk after the chief mourner, who carries a firepot slung from his hand. To perform Jain funeral rites, from the first to the thirteenth day, six men are required, the chief mourner who carries fire, four corpse-bearers, and a body-dresser. Music is played at some funerals, but on the way no coins or grain are thrown to spirits and no words uttered. The party moves silently to the burning ground and the chief mourner is not allowed to look behind. About half-way the bier is laid on the ground and the cloth is removed from the dead face, apparently to make sure that there are no signs of life. They go on to the burning ground and set down the bier. One of the party cleans the spot where the pyre is to be prepared and they build the pyre. When it is ready the bearers lay the body on the pile and the chief mourner lights it. When the body is half consumed the chief mourner bathes, carries an earthen pot filled with water on his shoulder, and walks three times round the pile. Another man walks with him and at each turn makes a hole in the pot with a stone called *ashma* or the life-stone. When three rounds and three holes are made, the chief mourner throws the pot over his back and beats his mouth with the open palm of his right hand. The *ashma* or life-stone is kept ten days and each day a rice ball is offered to it. As a rule the funeral party stops at the burning ground till the skull bursts. If they choose, some of the party may go home, but as a rule the six mourners must remain there till the body is consumed, when each offers a flour-ball and a handful of water to the life-stone and returns home. A lamp is set on the spot where the dead breathed his last, and kept there burning for at least twenty-four hours. On the second day the six chief mourners go to the burning ground and in the house put out the fire with offerings of milk sugar and water. On the third day they gather the deceased's bones and bury them somewhere among the neighbouring hills. Except offering a rice ball to the life-stone from the first to the tenth day, nothing special is performed from the fourth to the ninth day. The family are held impure for ten days. On the tenth the house is cowdunged and all members of the family bathe and each offer a handful of water called *tilodak* or sesame water to the dead. The house is purified by sprinkling holy water and the sacred or *hom* fire is lit by the priest. On the twelfth the clothes of the deceased are given to the poor, and rice balls in the name of the deceased and his ancestors are made and sandal-paste, flowers, vermilion, frankincense, and sweetmeat are offered them. The temple gods are worshipped and a feast to the corpse-bearers and dresser ends the twelfth day ceremony. On the thirteenth the *shráddha* or mind-rite is performed and a few friends and relations are asked to dine. A fortnightly and monthly ceremony is performed every month for one year and a feast is held every year for twelve years. According to rule the widow's head should be shaved on the tenth, but the practice is becoming rare; still, her lucky thread and toe ornaments are taken away and she is not allowed to wear a black bodice or robe. When a *sanyási* or ascetic dies his body is carried in a canopied chair instead of an ordinary bier. The body is laid on the pyre and bathed in the five nectars or *panchámrits* milk, curds, clarified butter, plaintain, and sugar. Camphor is lighted on the head and the pile is lit. At a *sanyási's* funeral only five men are required. A fire-carrier is not wanted as fire can be taken from any neighbouring house to light the pile. The family of the dead are impure for only three days, and no balls are offered to the dead. When an infant dies before teething it is buried, and boys who die before their thread-girding are not honoured with the rice-ball offering. No special rites are performed in the case of a married woman, a widow, or a woman who dies in child-bed. No evil attaches to a death which happens during an eclipse of the sun or the moon. In the case of a person who dies at an unlucky moment, Jains perform the same rites as Bráhmanic Hindus.(1)

Occupation.

In spite of political changes many Jains are hereditary village and district officers. Strict Jains object to tillage because of the loss of life which it cannot help causing. Still they do not carry their objection to the length of refusing to dine with Jain husbandmen. Among Deccan Jains the husbandmen are the largest and most important class, with a head priest of their own who lives at Nandni about eighteen miles east of Kolhapur. Except some of the larger landholders, who keep farm servants, the Jain landholders, with the help of their women, do all parts of field work with their own hands. They are the hardest working husbandmen, making use of every advantage of soil and situation. In large towns like Kolhápur and Miraj Jains are merchants, traders, and shopkeepers dealing chiefly in jewellery, cotton, cloth, and grain. Most Kásárs deal in bangles or work as coppersmiths, and others weave and press oil. Some Jains live by begging, but any one who asks alms from a man who is not a Jain is put out of caste.(2)

Food.

Jains are strict vegetarians and do not use animal food on loss of caste. Every Jain filters the water he uses in drinking or cooking for

(1) Bombay Gazetter, Volume XXIV, pages 144—146.

(2) Bombay Gazetter, Volume XXIV, pages 135—136.

fear of killing insect life. He also takes his food before sunset in case of destroying any animal life by eating in the dark. No Jain tastes honey or drinks liquor, and monks and religious Jains abstain from fresh vegetables.

JAIN GURAV.—A sub-division of Guravs.

JALGAR.—A synonym for Zárekari.

JAMBU.—A sub-division of Bráhmans ; a synonym for Holaya.

JAMBUVANT.—A synonym for Jambu.

JAMPHODA.—A synonym for Bhangi.

JANAV DEVANG.—A synonym for Kulácháradavaru.

JANDE.—A sub-division of Kurubás.

JANGDE.—A sub-division of Kattais.

JANTI OD.—A synonym for Gáda Od.

JARIA.—A sub-division of Lodhás.

JAS.—A sub-division of Berads.

JAS AGRI.—A synonym for Sudh Agri.

JATS(1) numbering 2,230 (1901), including 1,542 males and 728 females, are immigrants from the Punjab. They are found in the City of Bombay and scattered in small numbers all over the Deccan and Gujarát.

JATI.—A class of Jain mendicant devotees.

JAT LOG.—A sub-division of Kanjáris.

JAT OD.—A synonym for Gáda Od.

JATWE.—A sub-division of Kattais.

JAVAL.—A sub-division of Bráhmans.

JAVERI.—A synonym for Johári.

JAVIR.—A sub-division of Holayás.

JAYAKRISHNIYA.—A synonym for Mánbháv.

JEER.—A synonym for Hugar.

JELVAL.—A sub-division of Vániás.

JETHIMAL.—A sub-division of Modh Bráhmans.

JHADE.—A sub-division of Mahárs.

JHAROLA.—A sub-division of Bráhmans and Vániás.

JHARORA.—A synonym for Jhárola.

---

(1) Tribes and Castes of the North-Western Provinces and Oudh, Volume III; pp. 25—40.

JHILKA.—A sub-division of Lohárs.

JHOLIWALA.—A sub-division of Vaidus.

JINGAR.—A sub-division of Mochis and Mángs.

JINGARS, known also as Dalsingars, Digwáns and Káranjkars, numbering 3,077 (1901), including 1,541 males and 1,536 females, are found in small numbers scattered over the Deccan, Konkan and the Southern Marátha Country, as well as in Khándesh and Kanara. The word Jingar is derived from the Persian *jin* a saddle, and the traditional occupation of the caste is saddle-making. It is to be noted that the manufacture of native saddlery, which formerly contained no leather but was made with cloth, felt, cotton rope, metal work, embellished with embroidery and ornamental metal bosses, involves a knowledge of handicrafts generally confined to separate castes, and thus the Jingars are also known as Jádas (weavers), Lohárs (blacksmiths), Otáris (metal-casters), Sonárs (goldsmiths), Tárkars (wire-makers), Chitáris (painters), etc.; but within the three divisions mentioned below, they all dine and intermarry freely, showing that they are distinct from the castes bearing these occupational names. The term Káranjkar means fountain-makers, and it seems that in the days when it was the fashion to lay out gardens, probably during the period of Musalmán rule in the Deccan, the caste was employed to construct the fountains of which traces remain at such centres as Bijápur and Ahmednagar. The caste prefers to style itself Arya Somavanshi Kshatriya, or Aryan Kshatriyas of the Moon division. In appearance they would seem to belong to a higher social position than is usually allotted to them, and it is a fair inference that they attained great importance in the days when the annual equipment of large military forces led to an extensive demand for saddlery. With the decay of this occupation they have been forced to take to making wooden toys, decorating houses and pursuing other allied occupations, and have sunk considerably in the social scale owing to their gradual impoverishment. The local barbers now refuse to shave them on the ground that they are impure, and they are therefore obliged to employ Pardeshi barbers. Some years ago an action for libel was brought against the barbers by the Poona Jingars, but the charge was thrown out. Name and origin.

The reason for considering the Jingars impure is possibly their working in leather, which they have now-a-days to use in making saddles—the occupation of leather-working and the castes who follow it being considered impure all over the Presidency. Against this theory, however, it must be noted that, their impurity was maintained by the Bráhmans in the days of the Peshwás, and the charge may have been an attempt of the Bráhmans to dispose of the Jingar claim to Kshatriya rank.

In support of their claim to Kshatriya origin the castemen relate the following story, which, they state, is given in the *Brahmánd purán*.

The gods and sages were once engaged in performing a sacrifice in Brihadáranya, when Jánumandal, a giant, the grandson of Vritrásur, endowed with Brahmadev's blessing and made invincible, appeared with the object of obstructing the sacrifice. The gods and sages fled to Shiva. In Shiva's rage a drop of sweat fell from his brow into his mouth. It assumed human form and was called Mauktik or Muktádev. Muktádev fought with Jánumandal and defeated him. The gods and sages, pleased with his prowess, enthroned him as their king and went to the forests. Muktádev married Prabhávati, the daughter of the sage Durvás, by whom he had eight sons, who married the daughters of eight other Rishis. He left the charge of his kingdom to his sons and with his wife withdrew to the forest to do penance. In the height of their power the sons one day slighted the sage Lomaharshan, who cursed them, saying that they would lose their royal power and their right to perform Vedic ceremonies, and would wander in misery. Muktádev, on coming to know of the curse, implored Shiva to have mercy on his sons. Shiva could not recall the sage's curse, but to lessen its severity added that Muktádev's sons might perform the Vedic rights stealthily, that they would be known from that day forward as Aryaskhatris, and would follow eight callings *chitragárs* or painters, *swarnagárs* or goldsmiths, *shilpakárs* or artists, *patakárs* or weavers, *reshim karmi* and *patvekárs* or silk-workers, *lohárs* or ironsmiths, and *mritikákars* and *dhátu-mritikákars* or potters and metal and earth-workers.

Divisions. There are three divisions of the caste, Jingars and Chitárs who eat together and intermarry, and a third division known as Kadus, *i.e.*, those who have violated the caste rules, with whom no member ofthe above divisions interdines. They have ten *gotras*, Bháradwája, Vasishtha, Gautam, Angira, Kanva, Gárgya, Jámadagnya, Kaundanya, Káshyap, Atri, Jámbalya and Sánkhyáyan; and five *pravars*, Garga, Shándilya, Kapil, Gokarn and Kanva. But it seems that they have adopted this Bráhmanical system at a recent date with the object of confirming their assumed Kshatriya origin, as in regulating marriages attention is mainly paid to surnames, which are exogamous. The fact that their chief *devak* or marriage guardian is the *pánchpálvi* and that every section has a separate *devak* also points to their being of the same origin as most of the lower castes in the

Decccan. Their commonest surnames are, Ghodake, Chaván, Jádhav, More, Korade, Yande, Bhagat, Surve, Dukare, Bháleráo, Jondhale, Ambale, Avate, Shinde, Nágare, Kadam, Pimpale, etc.

A member of the caste cannot marry his father's sister's or mother's sister's daughter. He may marry his mother's brother's daughter. Marriage with a wife's sister is allowed even during her life-time. Two brothers are allowed to marry two sisters. Girls are generally married before the age of twelve, boys before they are thirty: sometimes girls remain unmarried even till they attain puberty. Sexual license before marriage is not tolerated. A girl guilty of misconduct is relegated to the Kadu division of the caste. Polygamy is allowed and practised, but polyandry is unknown.

Marriage ceremonies.

The offer of marriage comes from the boy's father, who has to pay a sum of money to the girl's parents if they are poor. If the girl's parents are well-to-do, they pay a dowry of from Rs. 10 to Rs. 100 to the boy. The day for the marriage is fixed by a Bráhman who conducts the service. The principal ceremonies are *kunku lávane*, that is the betrothal, *Halad* or rubbing the bride and bridegroom with turmeric paste, *Punyáhavachan* or the Holy-day-blessing, the installation of the *devak* which consists of the *pánchpálvi*, a hammer, a stuffed cake, etc., *Simántpujan* or the reception of the bridegroom by the bride's father, *Lagna* the marriage proper, and *Varát* or the returning of the bridegroom in procession to his house with his bride. The essential portion consists in throwing sacred grains of rice over the bride and bridegroom.

The remarriage of widows is permitted amongst the Jingars of the Deccan, but it is strictly forbidden amongst the Karnátak and Kanara Jingars. A widow is not allowed to marry her father's sister's, mother's sister's, or mother's brother's son, or a relation of her deceased husband. The ceremony takes place at night on the new-moon day during any month except *Ashádh*. The heads of the caste *Pancháyat* are present on the occasion. Unwidowed women are not allowed to attend the ceremony. A Bráhman priest makes the pair worship Varuna, which is represented by a water-pot, and brings the pot in close contact with the heads of the pair, which completes the union. They are then locked in a room for the night and the rest of the party retires. Early in the following morning the pair go to a temple of Máruti as it is considered unlucky to see their faces before they have done so. Should a bachelor desire to marry a widow he is first married to a *shami* bush (Prosopis spicigera).

A husband can divorce a wife on the ground of her misconduct or incompatibility of temper. In the former case the woman is turned out of the caste, and generally becomes a prostitute. In the latter, she is allowed to remarry after the widow remarriage ceremony.

Religion. The caste follow the Hindu law of inheritance and belong to the Hindu religion. Most of them are followers of the Várkari sect. They worship all Bráhmanic and local gods, observe all the Hindu fasts and feasts, and make pilgrimages to all the sacred places of the Hindus, but particularly to Shiva Kánchi or the modern Conjeveram in Madras, where there is a shrine of Muktádev, the supposed founder of the caste. All the plants and animals held sacred by the Hindus are worshipped. The family deities of the Deccan Jingars are Khandoba, Bahiroba, Narsoba and the goddess Bhaváni of Tuljápur and Kolhápur; of those residing in Kanara, Venkataráma nd Mailárling; and of the Karnátak Jingars, Malaya. Goats and fowls are offered to the goddess Mhálsa on the full-moon days of all months except *Shrávan*. These offerings are received by the officiating priests. When an epidemic breaks out, a cart filled with cooked rice sprinkled over with red powder and a he-buffalo are moved in procession through all the streets of the village, and the cart is left beyond the village boundary, the buffalo being set at liberty. This ceremony is known as *Bali kádhane* or the procession of the offering. The spiritual guide of the Deccan Jingars is the Shankaráchárya of Shringeri, of the Karnátak Jingars, Shankar Bhárati. It is said that the Jingars keep the sixteen Bráhmanic *Sanskárs* or sacraments, but enquiries show that this is not the case, the caste members being not even aware of the names of most of the *Sanskárs*. There appear to be only two such *Sanskárs* observed by the Jingars as are not observed by the lower castes. They are the *Chaul*, that is the hairclipping ceremony, and *Upanayan* or the thread-girding. The latter ceremony is not performed after the Bráhmanical ritual, but the boy is invested with the sacred thread when the other members of the caste renew theirs in the month of *Shrávan*. The priests of the Deccan Jingars are the Yajurvedi Deshasth Bráhmans, those of the Karnátak and Kanara Jingars are either Deshasth, Konkanasth or Havik Bráhmans.

Death. The dead are burnt. Children who have not cut their teeth are buried. The ordinary funeral rites are observed. The bones and ashes are consigned to water. For the propitiation of the deceased ancestors the *Shráddha* and *Mahálaya* are performed every year.

The hereditary occupation of the caste is said to be saddle-making, Occupation.
occupation but most of them have given up this occupation. They now follow a variety of callings such as casting metal, carving stones, painting, making toys and figures of clay and cloth, carving wood, and repairing boxes, padlocks and watches. They also make *vinas* or lyres, *sárangis* or fiddles and other musical instruments. The Jingars of Gokák in the *táluka* of that name, and of Deshmur in the Sampgaon *táluka* of the Belgaum district are famous for their wooden toys and for life-like imitations of fruit and figures of men and animals. Their skill as craftsmen was rewarded by the Peshwás by gifts of lands and houses. A few of them hold land under the Rayatwári system.

They eat the flesh of goats, sheep, fowls, hares, deer and fish, and Food.
drink liquor. They eat at the hands of Bráhmans only and drink and smoke with the Maráthás. No caste, however low, eats food prepared by them, a proof of the degradation attached to them, the cause of which is doubtless to be found in their working in leather.

JIRAIT.—A sub-division of Mángs.

JIRE.—A sub-division of Mális.

JOGAR.—A sub-division of Jogis.

JOGI.—A sub-division of Vanjáris.

JOGIS numbering 10,974 (1901), including 5,760 males and 5,214 Name and origin.
females, are found scattered in small numbers all over the Presidency. The term Jogi is derived from the Sanskrit *yoga*, union, and means a follower of the Yoga of Pátanjal school of philosophy. It is popularly applied to all who lead a life of asceticism. The Jogis form a religious brotherhood founded by the saint Gorakhnáth. They are nicknamed Kánpháte or slit-eared, because they make big holes to the lobes of their ears, in which they wear large thick ivory, clay, bone or fish scale ear-rings. They are also called Náths after their founder Gorakhnáth.

They have two divisions of a territorial type, (1) Gujarát Jogis Divisions.
and (2) Marátha Jogis, who include the Karnátak and Kanara Jogis. The former are pure ascetics. The latter have two divisions, regular and secular. The regular Jogis live by begging, the secular Jogis in addition to begging also work as husbandmen and labourers. Some breed buffaloes and dogs, and some make and sell smooth black stone vessels. They have twelve endogamous divisions: (1) Are, (2) Balgár, (3) Berak, (4) Bhorpi, (5) Dombári, (6) Davarji, (7) Jogár, (8) Ker, (9) Kindri, (10) Kurub, (11) Mendar, and (12) Murád. They have twelve clans, each of which belongs to one of the twelve orders said

to have been founded by twelve disciples of Gorakhnáth. Marriages are prohibited between members of the same clan or order.

The restrictions upon intermarriage are the same as those among Maráthás. Widow marriage is allowed. They eat goats, sheep, hares, deer, wild pigs and fowls, and drink liquor. Except that they initiate their boys in their order at the age of twelve, and that they bury their dead, their ceremonies do not differ much from those of the surrounding cultivating castes.

JOGIA KHUMAO.—A synonym for Háti.

JOGTI.—A sub-division of Mahárs; a synonym for Jogtin.

JOGTINS, numbering 23 (1901), including 9 males and 14 females, are found chiefly in Poona and Sátára. They are a religious order recruited from all castes of Hindus. The order is kept up by children dedicated to the goddess Yellamma. The boys thus dedicated are known as Jogtis. They marry girls of the castes to which they belong, and observe their respective caste rules. Jogtins are not allowed to marry. They make their living by begging in the name of the goddess.

JOHARIS or Javeris, numbering 846 (1901), including 448 men and 398 women, are chiefly found in Khándesh, Sholápur, Ahmednagar, Násik and Poona. Their occupation is dealing in jewelry, the name johári being derived from *javáhir* (jewelry).

Name and origin.

The caste is believed to have come from Northern India during the time of the Peshwás for purposes of trade, but it no longer inter-marries with the parent stock. It is said that the caste is formed of children of a Shudra father by a Vaishya mother. The fact of each of the sub-divisions having a separate *devak* or god of the exogamous section suggests an original totemistic organization. As a rule outsiders are not admitted into the caste, but sometimes young boys of other castes are admitted without performing any ceremony, when they become *dahámáses* of the *ardháduba* section.

Endogamous divisions.

There are three endogamous divisions of the caste Báramáse, Akaramáse, and Dahámáse, the first being superior to the other two, and the second being superior to the third. The names Akaramáse and Dahámase probably mean eleven and ten *másás*,(1) that is one and two *másás* short of the full *tola*, as these two divisions are

(1) A *mása* is a measure of weight among goldsmiths amounting to nearly 6½ grains and being one-twelfth of a *tola*, the goldsmiths' common measure.

formed of the illegitimate children of the members of the caste and the outsiders admitted into the caste.

There are 22½ exogamous sub-divisions of the caste, known as Gaud, Gujar, Lava, Ráthod, Bhatti, Bhais, Agdode, Sonyáráthod, Badgujar, Bám, Dasavantas, Shishode, Digoa, Kápasha, Nathiyán, Thák, Sonyáphadya, Kativále, Suni, Sarvativále, Pathiván, Gadria, and Ardháduba, the last being the half sub-division. The full sub-divisions are found only among the Báramáses, the half sub-division being formed from the other two divisions. Marriages cannot take place in the same sub-division. Sameness of *devak* is a bar to inter-marriage. **Exogamous divisions.**

Marriages are prohibited between descendants on the paternal uncle and maternal aunt's side. A member of the caste may marry his father's sister's or maternal uncle's daughter. He is allowed to marry two sisters, and brothers may marry sisters.

Boys are generally married from the age of ten to twenty, and girls even after they attain puberty. Sexual license before marrigae is not tolerated. If a girl commits sexual indiscretions she is turned out of the caste unless the man involved is a casteman, when she is allowed to remain in the caste as his mistress, and her children by him are admitted to the *ardháduba* exogamous section. Polygamy is allowed and practised. In theory a man can marry any number of wives, but in actual life no instance is found of a man having more than three. Polyandry is unknown.

The offer of marriage is made by the boy's father. The settlement of the marriage day and the ceremony itself are entrusted to the caste priest. The most important of the marriage ceremonies are *Vágnischaya, Simántpujan, Lagna, Bhovari-phirane, and Kanyádán.* The first three appear to be copied from the Deshasth Bráhmans. The *Bhovari-phirane, i.e.,* walking round the sacred fire, corresponds to the Bráhmanic *Saptapadi* and is the binding portion of the ceremony. *Kanyádán, i.e.,* giving away of the bride, consists in tying together both the hands of the bride and bridegroom separately with a cotton thread and placing thereon copper coins and pouring water on them by all present. It is believed that by performing this ceremony the whole caste get the *punya* (merit) of making a gift of a daughter. In Násik their marriages are always celebrated at night after nine o'clock, the bridegroom wearing a yellow or red robe reaching to the feet. The *devaks* or marriage guardians of the caste consist of he *pánchpálvi., i.e.,* leaves of five kinds of trees, which are tied to a post **Marriage ceremonies.**

of the marriage booth, every exogamous section having a separate *devak*.

Remarriage of widows is allowed, but it is not much in vogue. A widow is not allowed to marry her mother's sister's son or a relation of her deceased husband. A widow's marriage is always celebrated on a dark night, but especially on the last day of the month. No woman is allowed to be present on the occasion. Only a priest and a male member of the caste are present. The widow and her new husband are seated on a bullock's packsaddle and made to worship Ganpati. The priest then fills the widow's lap and makes the couple drink milk from the same cup, this being the essential portion of the ceremony. It is considered unlucky for unwidowed women to see the widow's face three days before or after the marriage takes place. A bachelor is not allowed to marry a widow. Divorce is allowed. A divorced woman can remarry according to the *pát* (widow remarriage) ceremony. The caste follow the Hindu law of inheritance.

Religion. They are Hindus and belong to the Nának sect. They worship all the Hindu deities and the *tulas* or sweet basil plant. The Joháris of Poona seem to specially reverence Rám, the seventh incarnation of Vishnu, and the hero of the Rámáyan. They observe all the Hindu holidays, their chief holidays being *Rámnavami*, *Gokuláshtami*, and *Navarátra*. They make pilgrimages to Oudh, Gokarn, Gokul Vrindávan, Tuljápur, Pandharpur and other places. Pearls and precious stones are worshipped on the *Dasara* and the *Rákhi Paurnima* day. Images of dead ancestors are installed among the house gods, and worshipped daily along with them. The offerings consist of articles of daily food. If cocoanuts are offered they are taken by the officiating priests. Vows are sometimes made to Musalmán Pirs, and if they are successful, the things promised are offered to them. When cholera breaks out, the goddess supposed to preside over the disease is propitiated by offerings of water. The religious teachers of the caste are *Udásis*, a sect of Gosávis from the Punjab, who are Nánakpanthis in belief and have a monastery, *akháda* or *math*, at Trimbak. Joháris profess not to believe in witchcraft or in evil spirits. The priests of the caste are, as a rule, Kanojia Bráhmans, but in their absence Deshasth Bráhmans are employed.

Death. They either burn or bury the dead, burning being more common. At burial the corpse is laid with the head turned to the south. The ordinary funeral rites are performed, and a feast is given to the caste people on the twelfth day. Those who have not the means to give this feast are not allowed to perform the obsequies till they are in a position to give the feast. They perform the *shráddha*.

The occupation of the caste is dealing in pearls, corals, diamonds and other precious stones, and in glass beads. They buy old gold and silver lace, and embroidered clothes, burn them and extract the gold and silver. Their women keep small haberdashery shops, selling wooden and tin boxes, combs, marbles, looking glasses, tops, whistles, dolls, and small brass cups and dishes. The Poona Joháris appear to be hereditary beggars, dealing in old lace and ribands, and professing a knowledge of physic. Occu pation.

The Bombay Gazetteer states that the Joháris of Poona and Sholápur are vegetarians and take no liquor, but a more correct view seems to be that they eat goats, domestic fowls and fish and that they drink liquor. Food

JOSHIS, also known as Budbudki, Gibidki or Chudbudki Joshis, Davaris, or Pingles, numbering 34,716 (1901), including 17,472 males and 17,244 females, are found scattered all over the Presidency, but especially in the Deccan, Konkan and the Karnátak. They are a caste of wandering beggars and fortune-tellers recruited from numerous sources. The term Joshi means an astrologer. It is a corruption of the word *Jyotishi*, which means an astronomer or astrologer. The terms *Budbudki*, *Gidbidki*, and *Chudbudki* are onomatopœic names for a small hour-glass shaped drum, three or four inches in diameter, which the Joshis play as an accompaniment to the songs which they sing as they walk begging from door to door. Another name for the drum is *daur*, which has given rise to the caste synonym of Davari. The name Pingle has its origin in their practice followed by these astrologers of consulting the *pingala* or spotted owlet, *Carine brahma*, before starting on their begging rounds in the early morning. The Joshis appear to be recruited from Maráthás, Dhangars, Mális and other castes of Marátha origin. Name and origin.

They have two endogamous divisions, *i.e.*, Proper and *Akarmáshe* or bastard, who eat together but do not intermarry. Their exogamous sub-divisions known as *kuls* are, Bhise, Bhosale, Chaván, Gáikwád, Garud, Gháti, Jádhav, Kadam, Máne, Náikal, Povár, Shingan, and Shinde—all common *kul* names among Maráthás and kindred castes. Divisions.

The restrictions on intermarriage are the same as amongst Marátha Kunbis. Polygamy, widow marriage and divorce are allowed and practised, but polyandry in unknown. Boys are married between ten and twenty-five, girls before they come of age.

The marriage is preceded by betrothal, when the girl is presented with a robe and bodice. Her brow is marked with red powder and feasts are given. On the marriage day, the guardian or *devak*, consisting Marriage ceremonies.

of the leaves of five trees or *pánchpálvis*, is tied to a post of the booth with a hatchet, two wheaten cakes, and a lighted earthen lamp. A sheep is offered to the guardian, and the caste is feasted. The boy and girl are rubbed with turmeric at their homes. The boy then proceeds on horse-back to the girl's house, where both the boy and girl are made to stand in bamboo baskets half full of rice, with a curtain held between them. Marriage verses are then repeated, and rice grains thrown over the couple by all assembled, and the ceremony is complete.

The marriage ceremony of the Bijápur Joshis differs somewhat from the above. Two water pots are placed in the marriage booth, one for the bride and the other for the bridegroom, with five copper coins and five betelnuts in each, and a string is wound round their necks. When a Bráhman is present at the wedding he ties a piece of turmeric root to each string, and binds one on the bride's wrist and one on the bridegroom's. He also ties the *mangalsutra* or lucky thread round the girl's neck. In Belgaum, the caste meet, and the Bháts throw rice on the boy's and girl's heads, the ceremony ending with a dinner.

Religion. Joshis belong to the Hindu religion. Their family gods are Kedáreshvar, Shidoba, Bhaváni, Yellamma, Khandoba, Bahiroba and Mariái. Another god specially worshipped is the Vithoba of Pandharpur, whose shrine they occasionally visit. They do not make pilgrimage to any other place. They observe the leading Hindu holidays. During *Shrávan* they take food from no one and eat only one meal a day. On the *Dasara* day they offer goats and sheep to Bhaváni, the flesh of which is eaten by themselves. Goats are also offered to Musalmán saints. Some of the Bijápur Joshis grow the beard in honour of a Musalmán saint called Yemána Sáheb. They believe in divination and soothsaying. They are said not to practise witchcraft and to have no faith in the evil eye. They believe Tuesday and Friday are lucky days and the rest unlucky. Their spiritual guide lives at Chitgupa in the Nizám's country, and is named Shidoba. In Belgaum, their priests are Bháts. In Bijápur, Bráhmans are sometimes employed to conduct marriages. In Dhárwár, marriages are conducted by Bráhmans and the other ceremonies by priests of their own caste who are called *Ganácháris*. In Kanara, the Chitpávan or Karháda Bráhmans officiate at their ceremonies.

Death. The dead are buried, except lepers, who are burnt. At burial the corpse is placed in a sitting position. The body is slung from a pole and carried to the burial ground on the shoulders of two men. On the third day wheat bread, rice and milk are laid on the spot where the dead was buried. In some places, a goat is killed and flesh and bread are taken to the grave. Mourning is observed ten days and caste-fellows are feasted on the twelfth. A *shráddha* is performed on the death day of the deceased.

Occupation. The main occupation of Joshis is to wander from house to house and village to village telling fortunes and begging. A Joshi got up for a begging tour is a quaint figure. He is dressed in a large dirty white turban with a red cloth turned over it, a long white coat reaching below his knees, and a tattered silk-bordered shoulder-cloth. In one hand is a staff and in the other the eponymous drum. A knotted cord is fastened to the drum, and when the drum is shaken the knot strikes against the membrane of the drum and makes a tinkling sound. Some Joshis carry in one hand a book or almanac, by referring to which they pretend to foretell fortunes. Some have a bag by their side containing *chintámani*, a collection of pictures on small pieces of cardboard. These pictures are used as guides in fortune telling. It is a common practice of the Joshis to rise at three in the morning, and go to some ruined buildings or large trees outside of the village, where they consult the spotted owlet or *pingala*, whose notes they profess to understand. About four or five o'clock they come back into the village, and, standing at the door of each house and sounding their drum, awaken the people and tell their fortunes. Their forecast sometimes includes one or two not unlikely misfortunes, and this fact induces the inmates, growing uneasy, to come out and ask the Joshi how the misfortune can be avoided. He tells them what to do, receives a fee as a reward, and wanders on from house to house till nine in the morning. The occupation is declining in popularity as few believe in the prophecies. In the Bijápur district some of the caste hold *grám Joshi* or village astrologer's rent-free lands.

Food. Joshis eat fish and flesh, and drink liquor. It is said that they eat the leavings from Bráhmans, leaf plates. They rank themselves with Maráthás, but Maráthás will not eat with them because they take alms from Mahárs and Mángs and receive cooked food from persons with whom Maráthás do not eat.

JUNA.—A sub-division of Shrigaud Bráhmans.

JUNAGADHI.—A sub-division of Lodhás.

JUNARE.—A sub-division of Devángs.

JUNARI.—A sub-division of Guravs and Nhávis.

JUNNARE.—A sub-division of Mahárs.

JYAPHOLONDI.—A sub-division of Alkaris.

Name and origin.

KABBALIGARS numbering 75,753 (1901), including 38,796 males and 36,957 females, are found all over the Karnátak, chiefly along the banks of the Bhima and Krishna, and in Kanara on the banks of the Gangávali river. Of this number 2,845 returned themselves as Lingáyats at the census of 1901. They are also known by the following names :—

1. Ambi, Ambig or Ambekar.
2. Bárkar or Bárekari.
3. Bhillakabberu.
4. Kabber or Kabher.
5. Gangimakkalu.
6. Jád.
7. Sungar or Sunnakallu Bestha.

At the 1901 census 15 of them returned themselves as Durga Murgis, on account of their practice of carrying an image of Durga Murgavva when begging, as do also the Berads.

The name Ambi or Ambig is derived from the Sanskrit *ambu* water, and is chiefly in use in Kanara. The term Gangimakkalu means river-children, and is equivalent to the English term fisherman, being applied to many castes who fish in rivers, but the caste members endeavour to connect it with the sacred Ganges in order to raise themselves in the public estimation. The terms Sungar and Jád are occasionally applied to Kabbaligars who have taken to the occupation of these two castes, *viz.*, lime-burning and weaving. The origin of the other names has not been traced.

The Kabbaligars are largely represented in Mysore by the Besthas, for whom the synonyms Kabber, Kabbaligar, Ambig, Gangimakkalu and Sungar are also in use. The first two names are in use in Shimoga, and the term Ambig in the south-western portions of the state bordering on British territory. Another synonym for Sungar or lime-burning Kabbaligars is Sunnakallu Bestha.

It is alleged that the original home of the Kabbaligars was in the Bellary District of Madras. Telugu is the home speech of one of their divisions. This and the fact that the *hálagamb* and *dháre* ceremonies are performed amongst them at the time of marriage support the theory of a southern origin. The survival of a totemistic organization amongst the division of the caste living in Kanara seems to point to the same conclusion. All traces of totemism have disappeared from among the Karnátak Kabbaligars, who have adopted a system of *bedagus* or family stocks. The caste in places is adopting Bráhmanical *gotras*; and they have hit upon a somewhat singularly sounding Garuda Gandharva *gotra* instead of the usual Káshyap. The caste is loosely organised. Many girls remain unmarried and follow prostitution as a calling, and this, in the case of most of their divorced women, is the chief means of livelihood. Members of higher castes such as the better classes of Lingáyats, Jains, Maráthás, Raddis, etc., may be admitted into the caste. The new comer is shaved, the tip of his tongue is branded with burning cotton, and he is then called upon to give a dinner to the caste people.

The Kabbaligars are a powerful and fine-looking class of men, rather dark, with regular features. They and the Kurubas are the sturdiest class in the Karnátak. In the Karnátak, their dress is a head-scarf and a pair of knee-breeches; and a shoulder-cloth thrown over the shoulders. The women wear the ordinary robe and bodice without passing the lower end of the robe between the legs. Both men and women wear a few ornaments of brass and silver. The dress of the Kanara Kabbaligar men is much the same as that of their Karnátak brethren. The women wear the robe, drawing the upper end over the left shoulder and then throwing it back over the right shoulder. They wear no bodice; but adorn their hair with the white flowers of the betel-palm, the leaves of the *páchche* plant, and *aboli* flowers. Both men and women rub their brows with cowdung ashes.

The Kabbaligars speak Kanarase. The division who beg from door to door speak Telugu amongst themselves and Kanarese with others. The names in common use among men of the Karnátak Kabbaligars are, Básappa, Bhikáppa, Bhimappa, Kallappa, Mallappa, Ningappa, Ráyappa, Siddáppa and Sadrappa; and among women, Bhimavva, Gangavva, Lakshmavva, Mallavva, Nágavva, Sangavva, Sedavva, Sindhavva and Somavva. The names of male Kabbaligars in Kanara are, Badka, Basva, Dema, Durgu, Govind, Iva, Jetti, Kitna, Manju, Mhásti, Rama, Timma and Venka; and of women, Basoi, Bhimi, Devi, Gangi, Gauri, Gutti, Jetti, Mhásti, Putti, Sukri, Sutti and Tulsi. The Karnátak Kabbaligars have an hereditary headman known as Kattimani who settles social disputes at meetings of the caste men. He has the power to excommunicate and readmit members of the caste. The headmen of the Kanara Kabbaligars are known as Budvants.

The endogamous divisions of the Karnátak Kabbaligars are as follows :— Endogamous divisions.

1. Ambig.
2. Bailgammar.
3. Bailugar.
4. Bhoi.
5. Bovar.
6. Durga Murgi.
7. Haig.
8. Kabber.
9. Lingáyat.
10. Lohagár.
11. Mosalegár.

Each of the above divisions except the Lingáyat is again split up into three *kuls, viz.*, Hanjukul, Jokumárkul, and Navilkul, which are endogamous. All divisions eat from the Lingáyats, but they neither eat nor intermarry with one another. The Kabbers marry girls from the Ambigs but do not give their daughters in marriage to them, as the latter prostitute their women and are hence considered to be lower in status.

The Kanara Kabbaligars have four endogamous divisions as follows :—

1. Gauda or Handmaid.	3. Koli or Boatman.
2. Mashal or Torchman.	4. Pátrachandri or Singer.

Those women of the last division who are favoured with good looks do not marry, but earn their living by singing and prostitution.

Exogamous divisions. The Karnátak Kabbaligars have 101 exogamous sub-divisions known as *bedagus*, the chief of which are as follows :—

1. Aggadava.	12. Chatak.	23. Mávlig.
2. Alagasandhi.	13. Haggadava.	24. Nadgaddeyava.
3. Ambisáni.	14. Halasig.	25. Nátgar.
4. Anigundiyava.	15. Halmaneyava.	26. Patigár.
5. Antyagár.	16. Harigar.	27. Sarvandig.
6. Arelladava.	17. Jálgár.	28. Sunagár.
7. Bellannava.	18. Kallusagat.	29. Talvár.
8. Benneyava.	19. Kundangár.	30. Tapadava.
9. Bhandárdava.	20. Lakshmisagat.	31. Teppagár.
10. Bhilluger.	21. Mallashetti.	32. Tolanbandi.
11. Byátigar.	22. Másál.	33. Vagir.
		34. Yaluk.

The Kanara Kabbaligars are split up into exogamous sub-divisions known as *balis*, of which the following have been recorded :—

1. *Anebali* (*ane* elephant). 2. *Gangábali* (*Ganga* the river *Gangávali*).

It is commonly alleged that the members of the *Anebali* will not allow their women to wear ornaments of ivory, and that they worship the elephant. The *Gangábali* are accustomed to make offerings to the river *Gangávali*. Members of the *Anebali* must marry outside that sub-division, and similarly, in the case of members of the *Gangábali*, marriage must be with members of some other *bali*. These *balis* are therefore truly exogamous.

A Kabbaligar may marry his sister's, father's sister's or mother's brother's daughter. According to some, marriage with a mother's sister's daughter is also allowed. Two sisters can be married simultaneously, and brothers are allowed to marry sisters. Polygamy is allowed and practised, but polyandry is unknown. Girls are married either before or after they come of age. In Kanara, it is a rule that girls must be married before they attain puberty. If a maiden indulges in sexual intercourse with a fellow casteman, she is either married to him or is fined and made to give a dinner to the caste people. If she is guilty of misconduct with a member of a higher caste, the penalty is a fine and a dinner to the caste people. But if her misconduct results in pregnancy, in addition to the above punishment, she loses the privilege of marrying according to the first marriage form, though she is free to marry after the widow marriage ritual. Many of the girls who become pregnant remain unmarried and follow prostitution. This does not involve loss of caste, but marriage connections with the children of such women are not allowed in the case of the offspring of married couples. Girls committing adultery with members of lower castes are said to be excommunicated. Polygamy is allowed and practised but polyandry is unknown.

Marriage ceremonies.

The offer of marriage comes from the boy's father, who has to pay a *teru* or bride-price of from Rs. 12 to Rs. 100 to the girl's father. The day for the marriage is fixed by a Bráhman priest, who conducts the service. The principal ceremonies are as follows :—

1. *Sákheri.*—The boy's parents with friends and relations go with sugar, cocoanuts and betel leaves to the girl's home and lay the articles before the house gods. They ask some people to attend, put a little sugar in the girl's mouth, and hand betel to the guests. A feast of rice and curry and vermicelli is served, and the boy's party and guests withdraw.

2. *Báshtagi, Hasaruville,* or *Ville.*—A few days after, the bridegroom's party go to the bride's with a robe, four pieces of bodice cloth, five halves of dry cocoa-kernel, five pieces of turmeric, five pieces of molasses, two hundred betel leaves, and gold and silver ornaments ; and dress the bride in the robe, make her sit before the god, and lay in her lap rice, cocoa-kernels, ornaments and betel leaves. The girl's mother is presented with a robe and a bodice cloth. The boy's party are then feasted with sweet rice gruel, and next day with bread and sweetmeats, and they return home.

3. *Arashina or turmeric rubbing.*—On an appointed day the bride's party take the bride to the bridegroom's, and both the bride and bridegroom are rubbed with turmeric paste.

4. *Devakárya.*—Next day the *Devakárya* or god-pleasing ceremony is performed. A log of wood of the *umbar* (Ficus glomerata) is thrown into a pond or well, and then brought home in procession after sunset by unwidowed women, one of whom brings a jar filled with the water of the pond or well. The jar is supposed to represent the deceased ancestors. It is covered with a piece of new cloth, placed near the household gods, and worshipped with offerings of sweet dishes. The log of the *umbar* wood is cut into two parts. One is called the *hálagamb* or milkpost and the other *handargamb* or marriage-booth post. The posts are planted and worshipped and the marriage booth is then erected. The *devak* or marriage guardian is then installed. Two men, one from the boy's house and the other from the girl's, cut two twigs of an *Ingli* tree and keep them in a temple. Next, a party goes in procession to the temple, women wave lamps before the twigs, and the twigs are brought home and tied to the *handargamb*. To the end of the twigs is tied a bundle containing five betelnuts, five betel leaves, five pice, a turmeric root, and one half of a dry cocoa-kernel. The twigs are then worshipped and a dinner is given to the caste people.

5. *Airanikelu.*—In the evening, the party go to a potter's with ten pounds of millet, ten quarter-anna pieces, and food enough for a holiday meal. They bring from the potter's four small pots or *mogás*, two middle sized pots or *gádgás*, a large pot or *ghágar*, and two pot-covers, and lay them before the house gods. A *suragi* or square is formed with the *mogás* in the marriage booth and the *ghágar* is placed in the middle of the square. The *mogás* are filled with coloured water, a pice is dropped into each, and the mouths of the *mogás* are covered with mango-leaves. Five cotton threads are passed round the *mogás* and the boy and some of his near relations are seated near the *ghágar* in the middle of the square, and bathed with the water contained in the *mogás* to the accompaniment of music. The girl is bathed similarly at her house.

6. *Lagna or the marriage proper.*—On the third day the bride and bridegroom and their mothers sit together, bathe and dress in new clothes. Next, a marriage coronet is put on the boy's head and he is given milk to drink. The boy is then taken on a bullock's back to a temple, breaks a cocoanut before the image of the god in the temple, and offers him the marriage coronet intended for the girl. Next he

takes back the coronet and the party return home. The boy and the girl are then made to stand face to face, a cloth is held between them, marriage verses are repeated, and grains of rice coloured red are thrown over the bridal pair by the guests. The pair also throw rice grains on each other's heads. A lucky necklace is then placed on the girl's neck, *kankans* or marriage wristlets are tied round the wrists of both, and the ends of their garments are tied into a knot (*brahmagantu*). The girl's maternal uncle joins the hands of the couple and pours water over them (*Dhâre*), which is the binding portion of the service.

7. *Meravanige.*—On the night of the fourth day, marriage coronets are put on the heads of the boy and girl, and they are taken in procession on a bullock's back to a temple. After returning home, they are bathed and made to play with water dyed with turmeric paste, and a feast is held. Next, the marriage coronets are taken off the heads of the pair, and they are taken to the girl's father's house, where the boy is presented with brass and copper vessels. The boy then returns home with his bride, which ends the marriage.

Among the Kabbaligars of Kanara, animal food is not used either at the boy's or the girl's house from the commencement to the end of the marriage ceremonies.

The remarriage of widows is permitted. A widow can marry her father's sister's son or mother's brother's son, but not her mother's sister's son. She cannot marry a member belonging to her late husband's or father's *bedagu*. A widow remarriage can be celebrated on any dark night except a new-moon day, in any month except *Ashâdh* and *Paush*. A few leading castemen and widows only attend the ceremony. The widow is made to wear an old robe, she is taken into a dark room, and a lucky necklace is placed on her neck by another widow, which completes the ceremony. In some places the ceremony consists in the widow's putting on the dress presented by her intended husband and in tying into a knot the ends of the pair's garments; while in others, the locking up of the widow and her intended husband in a room for the night is the only ceremony. On the following morning the face of the widow is not seen until she has bathed. A dinner is then given to the caste people. A bachelor desirous of marrying a widow is first married to a *rui* bush (Calotropis gigantea). Divorce is allowed if there is disagreement between husband and wife, or the wife is found to be unchaste. Divorced women can marry again by the widow remarriage form, or take to a life of prostitution. The caste follow the Hindu law of inheritance.

Like most castes of the Karnátak, the Kabbaligars have not Religion. escaped the influence of Lingáyatism. Just as a Kuruba or shepherd, if he rises to the position of a village headman, generally puts on the *linga* and calls himself a Hande Vazir, so the Kabbaligar *pátil* as at Akalvadi in Bijápur, and the Kabbaligar *kolkár* or *pátil's* servant as at Bágevádi and Mungoli in Bijápur, are occasionally Lingáyats. Such cases are rare, because few Kabbaligars have risen to high position. The family gods of the Karnátak Kabbaligars are Bharmappa, Opliparmánand, Mailárling, Basavanna and Virbhadra; and their family goddesses are Dyámavva, Durgavva, Gangavva, Hulgavva and Bhaváni. These and the god Máruti are the chief objects of their worship. Goats and fowls are offered to the goddesses on Tuesdays and the *Dasara* day and whenever they are worshipped. The Karnátak Kabbaligars make pilgrimages to Hampi, Gokarn and to the shrine of Yellamma. They keep all Hindu holidays, especially *Gudipádva* or New Year's day, *Vatapaurnima*, *Nágpanchami*, *Dasara* and *Diváli*. They never fast, and have no spiritual teacher. When cholera or small-pox breaks out, they do not work on Tuesdays and Fridays, and the village goddess is propitiated with offerings of water, food and articles of dress. The lap of the goddess' idol is filled, it is carried in a chariot in procession, a fair is held, and he-buffaloes and fowls are sacrificed. The Kabbaligars believe in soothsaying, spirits and ghosts, but some profess to have no faith in witchcraft. The well-to-do amongst them instal images of their deceased ancestors amongst their household gods, and worship them with offerings of goats on festive occasions and on holidays. Musalmán saints are venerated. Their marriages are conducted by Bráhmans and the death ceremonies by Jangams or the caste elders.

The objects of special worship of the Kanara Kabbaligars are the god Basava, whose image, in the form of a bull carved on a metal plate four or five inches square, is kept in their houses for daily worship, and the goddess Gangávali, to whose shrine they make pilgrimages at the festival of the *Gangáshtami* day. They also make pilgrimages to Tirupati, Gokarn and Dharmasthal. The religious teacher of some is the head of the Shringeri monastery; of others the head of the Lingáyat monastery at Chitaldurg in Mysore. They keep all Lingáyat festivals, the leading Hindu holidays, and the festivals of *Haridina* and *Panvár*. Their family deities are Guttiamma of Banavási in Sirsi, Mailárdeva of Dhárwár, Yellamma of Parasgad in Belgaum, and Basava and Maridevi of Sirsi. Their priests are either Karnátak or Havik Bráhmans.

Death. The Karnátak Kabbaligars bury their dead, except persons dying of leprosy, who are burnt under the belief that if buried they prevent the rain falling. In Kanara, the married dead are burnt, the unmarried being buried. At burial the unmarried are laid with head to the north, the married are seated. The funeral rites of the Kanara Kabbaligars resemble those of the Bánjigs. In the Karnátak also their death ceremonies mostly resemble those of the Lingáyats, the marked difference being that, after the funeral party return home, they bathe in cold water holding *durva* grass and *patri* or *bel* leaves in their hands, which they wash in a metal pot full of water placed on the cow-dunged spot where the deceased breathed his last. On the third day the mourners take *rági* gruel or *ámbli* and millet bread to the grave, lay them on the grave, and burn incense close by. They retire to some distance to allow the crows to feed on the offerings. If the crows do not eat the cakes, it is held a bad omen, and the food is given to a cow. On the fifth day the corpse bearers are feasted. They slaughter a sheep and feed the castemen on the ninth. In some places, on the ninth or eleventh day, water in which a Jangam's feet have been washed is sprinkled all over the house of the deceased. Next, a jar filled with water is placed near the gods and, if the deceased was a male, it is covered with a man's waistcloth, and if a female, with a woman's robe. The jar is then worshipped with an offering of cooked food containing goat's or fowl's flesh. Some of the food is laid on the spot where the corpse was buried, and the caste is feasted. During the fifth or some other odd month after death, a mask or *mukhavata* if the deceased was a man, or a top-like vessel if the deceased was a woman, is brought from a local goldsmith and is laid among the house gods. To these a waistcloth or a robe is offered and a goat is killed before them. If the deceased was a great drinker, spirituous liquor is also offered; and if he leaves a son, the latter presents clothes to a person of the age and sex of the deceased on the *márnavami*, that is, the day before the *Dasara*, and during the *Diváli* holidays. Once in every two, three, four or five years, the castemen are feasted for the propitiation of the deceased ancestors, when the masks of the deceased, or in their absence the household gods, are worshipped with offerings of articles of dress.

Among the Kanara Kabbaligars, on the twelfth day after death, a feast is given to the corpse-bearers and caste people, and crows are fed. At night an exorcist is called to release the spirit of the deceased from the control of the ill-disposed spirit Ráhu, and to give it over to that of the favourably disposed spirit Guttu. On the thirtieth day after death, a man of the age and sex of the deceased is feasted, and crows are fed, when the spirit of the deceased is supposed to have joined the spirits of the other ancestors. This is repeated every thirtieth day during the first twelve months, and after that once a year during the latter half of the month of *Bhádrapad*.

Occupation. The hereditary occupation of the caste is fishing, ferrying and palanquin-bearing. In Kanara they are also employed as sailors. They have no objection to catching crocodiles and tortoises. Some hold *inám* land for performing village service, while others hold lands under the *Rayatvári* and *Bhágdári* systems. Some take land on lease from superior holders, and some are day labourers. Some have taken to making lime and weaving cloth. In Kanara, some are petty shopkeepers dealing in rice and curry stuff, and some keep bullock carts for hire.

Food. They eat the flesh of goats, sheep, fowls, hares, deer, fish, etc., and drink liquor. They hold themselves superior to those who eat beef, pork, rats and jackals.

KABBER.—A sub-division of Kabbaligars.

KABHER.—A synonym for Kabbaligar.

KABIR.—A sub-division of Kolis.

KABULE.—A sub-division of Mahárs.

KABULI and BADAKSHANI.—A sub-division of Khojahs.

KACHA.—A sub-division of Mális.

KACHARIS or glass-bangle makers, numbering 395 (1901), including 232 males and 163 females, are found in Ahmednagar, Poona, Sátára, Násik, and the Akalkot State. In the year 1891 they were returned as numbering 918. There are two endogamous divisions of the caste, Maráthás and Lingáyats, who do not eat together or intermarry. The Marátha Káchāris resemble the Marátha Kunbis in religion and customs. The Lingayat Káchāris are non-Panchamsáli Lingáyats entitled to the *Ashtavarna* rites. They eschew flesh and liquor and do not differ from the other Lingáyats in religion and customs.

The Káchāris make black and green glass bangles. They buy broken pieces of bangles from Márwár Vánis and other hawkers, melt them, and cast them afresh. Their working tools are earthen pots, a *mus* or pestle, and iron bar or *salai*.

KACHHAVASI.—A sub-division of Alkaris.

KACHHELA.—A sub-division of Chárans.

KACHHIS, numbering 385 (1901), including 178 males and 207 females, are found chiefly in Poona. A few are recorded in Rewa Kántha, Násik, Belgaum and Sátára. They relate that their forefathers were employed in Aurangzeb's army and came with him to the Deccan. They were not regularly paid, and at his death in 1707 at Ahmednagar they left the army and settled at Aurangabad as fruitsellers, whence they gradually spread into the adjoining Deccan districts. The caste is largely represented in the United Provinces, where it has numerous sub-divisions. Name and origin.

There are two main divisions of the caste, Márwári and Pardeshi, who neither eat together nor intermarry. Each of these groups is again divided into the following endogamous divisions :— Endogamons divisions.

1. Bundele-Gwálhere or those residing about Bundelkhand and Gwalior.

2. Narbhari or those residing on the banks of the Narmada.

3. Kárbhoi or Dhimár, who are fishermen and palanquin-bearers.

4. Maláo, who rear fruit gardens.

None of these divisions eat together or intermarry.

Their exogamous sub-divisions or *kuls* are as follow :— Exogamous divisions.

Name of divisions.	Its *kuls*.
Bundele-Gwálhere	..Lakadvále, Rojanvále, Bhaisvále, Ghátvále, Agarvále, Elchya.
Narbhari	..Kulathe, Arafe, Amore, Sonore, Kamare, Vade, Khandore, Mithore.
Kárbhoi or Dhimár	..Pachalondhe, Kachore, Tilathe, Panduro, Kuchate, Limbáre.

The Maláos state that they have no sub-divisions.

Marriages are prohibited between members of the same *kul* and within three degrees of relationship. A member of the caste cannot marry his father's sister's, mother's sister's or mother's brother's daughter. He may marry two sisters and two brothers may marry two sisters. Polygamy is allowed if the first wife is barren or not liked by her husband. Instances are known of men having six or seven wives at a time. Polyandry is unknown. Girls are married up to the age of twelve, which limit is transgressed in the case of poor people, who keep their girls unmarried even till they come of age. Boys are married up to the age of twenty. If a girl commits sexual indiscretions with a casteman, both are made to give a dinner to the caste people. If the offence is committed with a man of an impure caste, the girl is put out of caste.

Marriage ceremonies. The offer of marriage comes from the boy's father. The day for the marriage is fixed by the caste priest who conducts the service. The principal ceremonies of marriage are as follow :—

1. *Sagái* or the betrothal.

2. *Mathána.*—In which the earth on the road is worshipped by women, some of which is brought and placed on a low wooden stool near the house gods.

3. *Rajjega.*—The ceremony of singing songs in honour of the goddess.

4. *Mátápuja.*—In which a goddess is installed and worshipped by the bridegroom, after which he is rubbed with turmeric paste.

5. *Mándav.*—The ceremony of giving a feast to the caste people in the marriage booth.

6. *Varát.*—In which the bridegroom is taken in procession to the girl's house. He is seated in an adjoining house till the following ceremonies are performed on the girl :—

1. *Chadháva.*—Dressing the girl in the dress presented to her by the boy's parents.

2. *Bhátpashtai.*—The ceremony of feeding the girl with rice and milk by her relations.

3. *Binnáki.*—In which the girl is carried in a palanquin four or five yards from the house, where songs are sung by women. The girl is then brought back and bathed and a *kankan* is tied to her wrist.

Next, a *chauk*, that is an octagon six feet in length and four in breadth, is formed on the ground with turmeric powder, red powder, and quartz powder, a low wooden stool is placed over it and the bridegroom is brought and seated on the stool. The girl is brought and seated by his side, and the marriage is performed in the ordinary way, the essential portion being the *saptapadi*.

The *devak* or marriage guardian of the Káchhis consists of an axe or *kurhád* and the *Pánchapálvi* or leaves of the five trees—Ficus religiosa *pipal*, F. glomerata *umbar*, F. indica *vad*, F. infectoria *nándruk*, and the mango, which they tie to a post of the marriage hall at both the boy's and the girl's houses.

The remarriage of widows is permitted. A widow cannot marry her father's sister's, mother's sister's or mother's brother's son, or a a member of her late husband's section. A widow remarriage is celebrated on a dark night at the widow's house. A barber pair, a Bráhman, relations, and the caste headmen are present on the occasion. The widow is taken to a stream by the barber's wife and bathed. Next, she puts on a new robe and bangles, and a pot filled with water is placed on her head by the barber's wife. She then returns home and enters the house in the presence of the company assembled, which completes the ceremony. A bachelor is not allowed to marry a widow. Divorce is allowed if the husband and wife do not agree, or the wife's conduct is bad. A divorced woman may marry again by the widow remarriage form. The caste follow the Hindu law of inheritance.

Káchhis belong to the Hindu religion. They worship the usual Hindu gods and goddesses and observe all the Hindu holidays. The chief object of their devotion is the goddess Bálàji. They make pilgrimages to Tuljápur in the Nizám's dominions, Chatarshingi in Poona, Saptashring in Násik and Mahurgad in the Berárs. Their priests are Upper India Bráhmans. Religion.

The dead are either burnt or buried. The ashes of the burnt are consigned to water on the third day after death. The bones are thrown into a river on the full-moon day of *Kártik*. The caste is feasted on the third day after death and on the day following the anniversary of the deceased. For the propitiation of the deceased ancestors, uncooked articles of food are given to the caste priest and castemen are feasted on the *Akshatritiya* day. The *shráddha* is not performed. Death.

The hereditary occupation of the caste is selling fruit. They take fruit gardens on lease from their owners. The Dhimárs or Karbhois have given up this occupation and taken to fishing and palanquin-bearing. The Maláos grow water-melons and sweet-melons. The other two divisions have not abandoned the hereditary occupation. Occupation.

They eat the flesh of goats, sheep, fowls, and fish and drink liquor. Food.

KACHHIAS, numbering 17,320 (1901), including 8,957 males and 8,363 females, are found in all the Gujarát districts and Native States, but chiefly reside in Ahmedabad, Broach, Kaira, Surat and Rewa Kántha. In addition to 17,320 Hindus, 101 have returned themselves as Muhammadans at the census of 1901. The Káchhiás are also known as Pastágia, meaning fruit sellers, and Kunkara. The Káchhiás are said to be Kanbi and Koli cultivators who took to the growing of garden produce. Name and origin.

Divisions. They contain nine divisions, three of which are found in north Gujarát and six in the south. The three Gujarát divisions are the Ajwáliás or bright fortnighters, the Andháriás or dark fortnighters, and the Khambhátiás or Cambay men. Of these, Andháriás are the lowest, the other two sub-divisions neither eating nor marrying with them. The Ajwáliás and Khambátiás eat together but do not intermarry. The six south Gujarát divisions are Ahmedábádi, Khamár, Khatri, Koli, Máli and Sangaria. Of these, the Ahmedábádis, who are also called Kanbis and are said to have moved to Ahmedábád from Chámpáner, rank highest. Except that the other five divisions eat food cooked by Kanbi Káchhiás, the six sub-divisions do not eat together and do not intermarry.

Marriages are prohibited within four or five degrees of relationship on the mother's side, and entirely on the father's side. Marriage with a mother's sister's daughter, maternal uncle's daughter and father's sister's daughter is not allowed. Marriage with a wife's sister is allowed during the wife's life-time or after her death. Two brothers may marry two sisters. The Káchhiás have formed certain territorial groups and must form marriage connections within those groups. Sometimes the taking of a girl from outside these groups is allowed. But instances of giving a girl outside these groups are punished by fines. Girls are married before they are eight and boys up to ten. Polygamy is permitted but polyandry is unknown.

Marriage ceremonies. The offer of marriage generally comes from the bride's father. The auspicious day is fixed by the village Joshi, and the service of marriage is conducted either by an Audich Bráhman or a village priest commonly called a *gor*. The custom of paying a dowry is not in vogue. When the bride's father is very poor, he is paid money to defray the marriage expenses. The bridegroom's father gives to the girl ornaments and clothes worth Rs. 30 or upwards. This is termed a *pallo*, and becomes the bride's property. The ceremony of betrothal is performed at any time before marriage. Their marriage ceremony does not differ from that of the Leva Kanbis. Three or four days before the marriage day, Ganpati is installed and worshipped. Sometimes Ganpati is worshipped on the marriage day, but never before the marriage booth is erected. The bridegroom goes in procession to the girl's house and is received by his mother-in-law. Then marriage verses are repeated and the bride is brought by her maternal uncle and seated before the bridegroom. The hands of the pair being joined, sacred verses are repeated. This is the essential portion of the ceremony. Next the ceremony of *swastiáhaváchan* is performed, for which the leaves of five kinds of trees are required. These trees are generally the *nágarvel*, *pipal*, mango, *aso*, *umbar*, *sitaphal*, etc. Sacrifices are performed, and the bride and bridegroom take five turns round the fire. This is called *mangalphero*. Next the bride and bridegroom feed each other with *kansár* brought by the bride's mother. Then red powder is applied to the foreheads of the couple. Lastly, the bridegroom takes the bride to his house and Ganpati is worshipped.

Widow remarriage is allowed. A widow cannot marry her father's sister's son, maternal uncle's son or mother's sister's son. She may marry the younger brother of her deceased husband if she chooses. A widow remarriage is brought about either by the widow's parents or by other near relatives. A widow remarriage is celebrated on Sunday, Tuesday or Thursday. The new husband of the widow goes to the widow's house with his kinsmen. Only males take part in this ceremony. The father of the widow receives them. The widow then puts on the ornaments presented by her new husband. They are then seated on two low wooden stools, and the priest leads them to the worship of Ganpati. The ceremony of *swastiáhaváchan* is gone through. Four unwidowed women daub the foreheads of the widow and her new husband with red powder, throw rice grains over their heads, and bless the new couple. This is the principal part of the ceremony. A bachelor wishing to marry a widow is first married to a *Shami* tree.

Divorce is allowed, and a husband or a wife can divorce each other by mutual consent, notified by their signing the caste book. A fine of Rs. 31 is paid to the caste. When the wife obtains a divorce, the marriage dowry is refunded to the husband. A divorce is effected in the presence of the headman of the caste, and it is usually termed a *Chhuta Chhedákarva* or *Phárkat ápvi*. The act of divorce consists in tearing a piece of cloth from the garments of the husband and wife or in the wife's taking off her bangles. A woman divorced for no misconduct is allowed to marry a second time, and her marriage is conducted in the form of widow remarriage. A woman divorced for adultery with a man of a lower or higher caste is turned out of her caste.

They follow the Hindu law of inheritance. They believe in exorcism, sorcery and omens.

Religion.

Except the Andháriás of north Gujarát and the Khatris of south Gujarát, the Káchhiás belong to different religious sects. The Khambhátiás and the Ajwáliás in north Gujarát are Bijpanthis, and a few of them in the Panch Maháls are Shaivas, Vallabhácháryas and Swámnáráyans. The south Gujarát Káchhiás are Shaivas, Kabirpanthis or followers of goddesses. They have household gods and visit their temples daily or on high days. They go on pilgrimages to Benares, Dwarka, Jagannath, Dakor and Mathura. They keep the ordinary fasts and feasts. Some among them become holy men or *bhagats* and live in their temples. One of these holy men named Santrám has a temple at Nadiád and is the founder of a new sect. The patron saint of some of the Káchhiás is Gangábhạrati and his *gádi* is said to be at Kocharpaladi, a village in Ahmedábád district. They worship the cow and, in small-pox epidemics, the donkey, who is the bearer of the small-pox goddess. They worship the cobra on the fifth of *Shrávan sud* in August, painting its image on the housewall and worshipping it. They also worship and hold sacred trees such as the sweet basil, *pipal* and *samdi*. They worship Muhammadan saints and make offerings of *Malida*. The Andhária and Khatri Káchhiás are, like Mátia Kanbis, followers of Imám Sháh, and observe half Hindu half Musalmán rites. Besides ordinary Hindu holidays, they fast during the Ramzán, and hold those Fridays sacred which fall on a new moon day. They do not respect the ordinary Hindu gods, and do not visit their temples, but go to Pirána instead of to Hindu places of pilgrimage. They employ Bráhmans for religious and ceremonial purposes.

Death.

For the performance of funeral rites a class of Bráhmans known as Káyta are employed. The other Bráhmans have no intercourse with Káytas, and consider them to be degraded. Káchhiás burn their dead. Children 18 months old are buried with their heads northwards. The ashes and bones of the dead are thrown into a river or are sent to a holy place if their means permit.

Occupation.

The hereditary occupation of the caste is growing garden crops and selling vegetables. They are helped by both their wives and children in raising and selling vegetables. Their busy season is during the four cold weather months. Some Káchhiás have taken to new pursuits. In north Gujarát they have opened grocers' shops, and some, especially the Khambhátiás, have taken to handloom cottoncloth weaving. In south Gujarát some are bricklayers, carpenters and sawyers, some sell pounded turmeric, and some, especially the Máli Káchhiás, drive bullock-carts for hire or are in private service. Some are agricultural labourers.

Food.

They do not consume flesh or liquor.

They eat *pakki* at the hands of Kolis, Dhárálás, Thákardás and such other castes. All Bráhmans excepting priests and Tapodhans, Meshri Vániás, Shrávaks except Shrimáli Shrávaks, Sutárs, Sonis eat *pakki* prepared by men of this caste. They will not take either *pakki* or *kacchi* at the hands of Mochis, Vághris, Bhils, etc.

KACHHI MEGHVAL.—A sub-division of Meghváls.

KADAMRAI.—A sub-division of Gondhalis.

KADHARVAL.—A synonym for Katrivál.

KAD HAVIK.— A synonym for Bándi.

KADIA.—*See* under Gavandi.

KAD KONKAN.—A synonym for Bándi.

KADU.—A term applied to a sub-division of a caste consisting of offspring born of irregular unions.

KADVA.—A sub-division of Kanbis.

KAFSHGAR.—*See* under Minor Musalmán castes.

KAGZI.—*See* under Minor Musalmán castes.

KAHANAMIA.—A sub-division of Dhedas.

Name and origin.

KAHARS, or Bundeli Bhois, numbering 1,182 (1901), including 646 males and 536 females, are found mostly in the Deccan and in small numbers in Ahmedábád, Broach, Surat, and Sind. They say that they came into the Deccan from Bundelkhand in Upper India during the time of Aurangzeb. This is extremely probable. At the present day the Kahárs in the United Provinces of Agra and Oudh number over 200,000. It may be assumed that the original immigrants were *pálki*-bearers in the train of the Mughal Emperor. They have since severed all connection with the parent stock and adopted the customs and ceremonies of the local castes of similar social standing.

Divisions.

There are no endogamous divisions of the caste, neither have they any exogamous sub-divisions above families bearing the same surname. The commonest surnames are Bhandáre, Gangole, Kachare, Lachure, Ladke, Lakreyda, Libre, Luchnáre, Mehere, Padre and Sámbre. Persons bearing the same surname cannot intermarry.

A member of the caste cannot marry his father's sister's, mother's sister's, or mother's brother's daughter. He may marry two sisters, and brothers may marry sisters. The habit of the caste is settled. Outsiders are not admitted into this caste. Boys are married between ten and twenty-five, girls before they come of age. Polygamy is allowed and practised, but polyandry is unknown.

Marriage ceremonies. The marriage ceremonies of Kahárs resemble those of the Maráthás. The chief of these are: The installation of the *devak*, which consists of the leaves of the *shami* (Prosopis spicigera). These are tied to a post of the same bush planted in the marriage booth, and to this is tied a turmeric root in a piece of yellow cloth. An earthen jar and lid are brought in procession from a potter's, placed near the *devak*, and worshipped. *Halad*, or rubbing the bride and bridegroom with turmeric paste and oil. *Kanyádán*, or handing over of the bride to the bridegroom; and *Saptapadi*, or walking seven times round the sacrificial fire, which they call *Lotapáta*.

The remarriage of widows is permitted. The ceremony consists in the putting on of a new robe and bodice by the widow, after which red powder is applied to her forehead. Should a bachelor desire to marry a widow, he is first married to an earring worn by him. A husband can divorce a wife on the ground of her misconduct. A divorced woman can marry again after the fashion of the widow remarriage ceremony.

Religion. The caste follow the Hindu law of inheritance and belong to the Hindu religion. They worship all Bráhmanic and village gods, and their fishing nets, and observe all the Hindu holidays. Their priests are Upper India Bráhmans.

Death. The married dead are burnt, the unmarried being buried. Their death ceremonies are the same as those of Bhois or Kunbis. Unlike Kunbis, they do not remember the dead in *Bhádrapad*, but perform the *shráddha* of those who die between February and October on *Diváli* in October, and of those who die between October and February on *Shivarátri* in February. The married dead are alone entitled to these honours, and on these days any member of the caste can join the dinner party unasked.

The hereditary occupation of the caste is palanquin-bearing and catching and selling fish. Some of them grow vegetables and tobacco.

Food. They eat fish and the flesh of goats, sheep and game animals but not of game birds. They drink liquor. They rank above Bhois and eat at the hands of Kunbis.

KAIJI.—A sub-division of Kaikádis.

Name and origin. **KAIKADIS,** numbering 7,595 (1901), including 3,629 males and 3,966 females, are found chiefly in the Deccan, and in small numbers in the Karnátak and the Southern Marátha Country. They are a wandering tribe and were once notorious robbers; but they have now adopted comparatively settled habits, though some of them still commit thefts and indulge in house-breaking. They state that their original

Kaikadi woman.

home was Telangana, which seems probable from their language, a mixture of Kanarese and Telugu. Some speak incorrect Maráthi, greatly interspersed with Telugu words. The tribe is loosely organized, and appears to have been recruited at times from other criminal tribes such as the Bhámtás, Lamáns, etc.

Endogamous divisions

There are nine endogamous divisions of the caste: (1) Borivále, (2) Dhuntale or Chor, (3) Kámáthi, Kusubatanvále or Lálbájárvále (4) Káiji, (5) Lamán, (6) Mákadvále, Kunchevále or Khulkhulevále, (7) Ur Kaikadi, from the Kanarese *uru* a village, (8) Váibase, and (9) half-caste Kaikádis known as Bhámtás or Tuhliás. The Boriváles and Váibases are of settled habits and look on the other divisions as their social inferiors. The Kámáthis are basket-makers, and their women make a livelihood as prostitutes; the Mákadváles wander from place to place exhibiting performing monkeys; the Káijis are flute-players and performers of magic; the Lamáns make bullock's pack-saddles; Ur Kaikádis are musicians and basket-makers, and Bhámtás, who are the offspring of intermarriages between Bhámtás and Kámáthis, are pick-pockets. The Kaikádis have a certain affinity with Ods and Kolhátis by reason of their keeping donkeys. They call them ass-brothers and invite them to conferences on caste questions.

Exogamous divisions.

There are five clans in the tribe: Jádhav, Máne, Gáikwád, Madhavant, and Povár. Of these the Jádhavs have two septs, Madhu and Sapátsar; and the Mánes two, Mának and Malájur. In some parts these clan names have become surnames and the clans are called Sátapádi, Melpádi, Kávádi, Mendharegutti and Sangádi. Marriages are prohibited between members of the same clan.

A member of the caste may marry his father's sister's or mother's brother's daughter; he cannot marry his mother's sister's daughter. A man may marry two sisters, and two brothers may marry two sisters. Members from higher castes are said to be admitted into the tribe on their paying a certain amount of money to the tribesmen, which is spent on a feast. After two or three generations the new comers are considered to be the social equals of the other members of the tribe. Marriage is infant as well as adult. Sexual immorality is generally connived at—one of the clans following prostitution as a calling. Polygamy is allowed and practised, but polyandry is unknown.

Marriage ceremonies.

The offer of marriage comes from the boy's father, who has to pay a bride-price of from Rs. 25 to Rs. 100 to the girl's father. The day for the marriage is fixed by a Bráhman who sometimes conducts the service, but in some districts the Kaikádis do not call in Bráhmans for the marriage ceremony. The *devaks* of the Kaikádis consist of the *pánch pálvi, i.e.*, the leaves of five trees, or the leaves of the *pipri* (Ficus tseila), mango, or of the *umbar* (Ficus glomerata). The *devak* is tied, along with an axe and a piece of bread, to a post of the marriage booth. In most places their marriage ceremonies resemble those of the local Kunbis, the essential portions being the *homa* or the marriage sacrifice, the tying of the *kankans* or marriage wristlets round the wrists of the bride and bridegroom, and the fastening of the lucky necklace round the girl's neck. In some places the throwing of the sacred grains of rice over the pair is the only operative ceremony.

In Khándesh and Belgaum the marriage is subject to a condition which requires the son-in-law to live with his wife's family and help to support them until he has three children. If separated from his wife by mutual consent, the husband is bound to make an allowance to his wife's parents.

Amongst the Dhuntale Kaikádis the marriage is conducted by the caste *panch*. A bough of the *pipal* tree (Ficus religiosa) is put in an earthen jar. The jar is taken to a pond, filled with water, brought home and placed on the ground. The bride and bridegroom are seated before the jar, rice grains are thrown over their heads by the caste *panch*, and the bride's brother knots the hems of the pair's garments, thus completing the ceremony.

The remarriage of widows is permitted. A widow can marry her father's sister's or mother's brother's son; she cannot marry her mother's sister's son or a member of her late husband's section. The widow who wishes to remarry has to pay to the relations of her deceased husband the expenses incurred by him in marrying her. A widow remarriage is celebrated on a dark night, except a new-moon day. A Bráhman priest and widowed women and male members on both sides are present on the occasion. The widow and her new husband are seated on a bullock's pack-saddle, Ganpati is worshipped, and the Bráhman priest applies red powder to the widow's forehead and fills her lap. Next, the pair are made to drink milk from the same cup, and this completes the union. In some places the widow remarriage ceremony consists merely in tying into a knot the hems of the couple's garments. Should a bachelor desire to marry a widow, he is first married to a *shami* bush. Divorce is allowed if there is disagreement between husband and wife, or if the wife's conduct is bad. A divorced woman can marry again by the widow remarriage form.

Religion. The caste follow the Hindu law of inheritance and belong to the Hindu religion. They worship the usual Bráhmanic gods and goddesses, and observe the leading Hindu holidays. They also worship all local and boundary gods, and Bahiroba, Bhaváni, Mariái, Phirangái, Tukái, and Yamái, whose images they keep in their houses with the masks or *táks* of their ancestors. Their family gods are Máruti, Bahiroba of Sonári near Sholápur, Khandoba of Jejuri, and Bhaváni of Tuljápur. They make pilgrimages to Alandi, Jejuri, Sonári, Tuljápur, and Pandharpur. Their religious teachers or *gurus* are Gosávis, whose advice they take on all important matters. They believe in sorcery, witchcraft, soothsaying, omens, and lucky and unlucky days, and consult oracles. When an epidemic breaks out, goats and fowls are offered to the deity supposed to preside over the disease, and in the case of cholera a he-buffalo is also offered jointly by the whole tribe. The Musalmán saints are reverenced, particularly by the Khándesh Kaikádis, who, in common with many Khándesh Hindus, have a deep reverence for Dávulmalik, the famous saint of Mulher in Sátára. His devotees keep a stick, *juli*, in their houses wrapped in a green cloth or bag in some recess in honour of the saint, and it is no unusual thing to keep the saint's *juli* and the image of Khanderáo side by side. The priests of the tribe are the Deshasth Bráhamns in the Deccan; but the use of Bráhmans is not yet universal in the tribe.

Death.

The dead are either burnt or buried. Mourning is observed for three, five, nine, ten, or twelve days. The four corpse-bearers are held impure for five days, and are not only avoided by others, but do not even touch each other. On their return from the funeral the corpse-bearers are asked to dine at the house of the deceased. Next day they go to the burning ground, throw the ashes into water, place on the spot two earthen jars filled with water, and return home. On the fifth day a *nimb* (Azadirachta indica) branch is dipped in cow's urine, the head of the chief mourner is touched with it, and he is shaved by the barber, as are the heads of the four corpse-bearers, and their shoulders are rubbed with sweet oil. A goat is killed on the third, fifth, or thirteenth day, and caste-men are feasted. An image or *ták* of the deceased is made and installed amongst the household gods. It is worshipped on the *Dasara* and *Diváli* holidays. They do not observe death-days or perform the *shráddha*.

Occupation.

Kaikádis are notorious as thieves and are always under the eye of the police. They are hereditary basket-makers. They make baskets of many sizes of bamboos, the branches, leaf, fibres, and stalks of the *tarvad* tree (Cassia auriculata), of *bábhul* (Acacia arabica) twigs, and cotton and *tur* stalks. Husbandmen smear these baskets with cowdung and store grain in them. They also make reed sizing-brushes used by weavers, snares for catching birds and deer, bird's cages, and children' toys. Some beg by exhibiting snakes. They carry sand, earth, bricks, tiles, and stones on their donkeys, remove sweepings and filth, and of late have taken to tillage. Some are labourers.

Food. They eat fish and the flesh of goats, sheep, deer, hares, fowls, and pigs, and drink liquor. They rank below Kunbis and above the impure classes.

KAJULE.—A sub-division of Gaud Sárasvat Bráhmans.

KAKAPURI.—A sub-division of Kolis.

KAKAR.—*See* under Minor Musalmán Castes; a sub-division of Mángs.

KAKARMUNDI.—A sub-division of Berads.

KAKODIA.—A sub-division of Vághris.

KALACHUDAVALA.—A sub-division of Kadva Kanbis.

KALAIGAR.—*See* under Minor Musalmán Castes.

KALAIS or, **KALANS** numbering 2,619 (1901), including 1,298 males and 1,321 females, are found in small numbers throughout the Presidency. They are distillers and liquor-sellers and belong to the great Kalwár Tribe of Northern India.(1)

KALAN.—*See* under Kalál or Kálan. A sub-division of Bhandáris.

KALANDAR.—*See* under Minor Musalmán Castes.

Name and origin. **KALAVANTS** also called Naikins, numbering 2,012 (1901), including 693 males and 1,319 females, are found chiefly in the Kanara and Ratnágiri districts. The male offspring of the Kalávants are called Gáns. They derive their name from the Sanskrit *kala* art, and are singers and dancers by profession. They claim descent from the *Apsaras* (heavenly dancing girls) and *Gandharvas* (heavenly singers) of the Hindu mythology, and give as proofs of their claim their hereditary services in connection with the Hindu temples. Their original home appears to be Vijayanagar, where a very large number of such women were kept to wait on the king. They went to Sonda and the Kanara coast after the capture of Vijayanagar by the Musalmáns. Paes, in his account of Vijayanagar, refers to the women who belong to the temples, all girls born of whom belong to the temple. "These women are of loose character, and live in the best streets that are in the city. They are

(1) Tribes and Castes of the North-Western Provinces and Oudh, Vol. III, pp. 106-113.

very much esteemed and are classed among those honoured ones who are mistresses of the captains. These women are allowed even to enter the presence of the wives of the king, and they stay with them and eat betel with them, a thing which no other person may do, no matter what his rank."*

There are six endogamous divisions of the Kalávants, which neither eat together nor intermarry. They are— **Endogamous divisions.**

1. Konkani.	4. Lingáyat.
2. Maráthá.	5. Telang.
3. Karnátak.	6. Musalmán.

The Telangs being foreigners do not come within the scope of this survey.

The Konkani Kalávants have exogamous divisions represented by surnames which are local in origin. They are Bándodkár, Borikár, Jotkár, Kakodkár, Návekár, Parvatávaile, Phátarpekár, and Shirodekár. Members bearing the same surname neither eat together nor intermarry. **Exogamous divisions.**

Formerly, at the age of eight or nine years, girls underwent a form of marriage called *shes*, in which a girl dressed as a man and holding a dagger or *katár*—the emblem of Kártikeya, their family deity—in her hand acted as a bridegroom. On this occasion girls were invested also with ankle bells and upper garments, which every Kalávant has to wear in a concert or dance. The ceremony was performed with great pomp at considerable expense; but the High Court having ruled marriages under this form to be criminal offences, it is now performed with less show and after a girl has attained her majority. **Marriage ceremonies.**

As all Kalávants lead a life of prostitution, the Gáns have to marry girls of outcaste people, whom they buy at a cost of Rs. 100 to Rs. 300. But as many are unable to pay such a heavy bride-price, the majority of them remain single.

Inheritance was formerly through females only. But it has been now decided by the High Court that property should be divided equally between males and females. Kalávants having no issue adopt girls of outcaste people, whom they purchase, and on whom the *shes* ceremony is performed. Girls who have attained puberty are ineligible for adoption.

Kalávants worship all Bráhman and village gods. Their family goddesses are Mhálsa, Kántra, Shántádurga and Shánteri Kámákshi **Religion.**

* "A Forgotten Empire." Sewell, pages 241-42.

whose shrines are in Goa. Their patron deity is Kártikeya, the god of war. They have great faith in soothsaying, witchcraft and evil spirits. Their priests are the Chitpávan, Karháda or Havik Bráhmans. They make pilgrimages to Gokarn, Rámeshwar, Benares, Dharmasthal, and Pandharpur. They offer blood sacrifices to the *Ammas* or *Shaktis.* They observe all the Hindu holidays and worship their musical instruments on the *Dasara* day. The dead are burnt. Their death ceremonies do not differ from those of the Konkani Maráthás.

The hereditary occupation of Kalávants is singing and dancing. The well-to-do employ them to sing and dance at thread and marriage ceremonies and on other grand occasions. They are also engaged to dance in Hindu temples, and in return enjoy the produce of certain temple lands. The Gáns accompany the Kalávants on an oblong two-faced drum called *mridanga;* the timbrel or *tál,* the fiddle or *sárangi,* and the double-drum or *tabla.* A troop of Kalávants is known as *táfa* and includes one to four Kalávants and three to four Gáns. Besides singing and dancing, Kalávants also act as courtesans. Many have left their home and gone to Bombay, Kolhápur and Mangalore to make their fortunes. Women of other prostitute classes, such as Devlis, Bándis, Adbatkis, and Padiárs, are not hired to dance unless they are invested with the scarf and bells by a member of the Kalávant community. Even after investiture, Kalávants look down on other dancers and refuse to perform with them. It is the special privilege of Kalávants to dance in temples, and they oppose the attempts of Bhávins to usurp this privilege.

Food. They eat fish and the flesh of goats, sheep and fowls and drink liquor.

MARATHA KALAVANTS resemble the Konkani Kalávants in all details.

KARNATAK KALAVANTS are known as Pátradavarus or shawl weavers. They claim to represent the heavenly dancing girls Rambha and Urvasi. As among the Konkani Kalávants, girls are invested with ankle bells and scarves at the age of seven years, and are made to undergo a form of marriage called *halpudi* when they are twelve. The ceremony is celebrated like the *shes* of the Konkani Kalávants, with this difference, that the bridegroom is represented, not by a *katár* or dagger, but by a *madli* or double drum. Their family god is Mailár, whose chief shrine is at Gudguddápur in Ránebennur *táluka,* Dhárwár, and their family goddesses are Guttemma and Hulgemma. Their spiritual teacher is Ayyappa, who is a Kshatriya by caste. A peculiar custom of the caste is that, if any one strikes a Pátrad with a shoe, though she may have done nothing wrong, the girl loses caste and has to pay a fine and undergo penance before she is allowed to re-enter the caste.

LINGAYAT KALAVANTS do not differ in any important particular from the Lingáyat courtesans or Sáibs (*see* Lingáyat).

No class of Hindus eats food cooked by Kalávants. Food.

KALE.—A sub-division of Bene Isráels

KALE KUNBI.—A sub-division of Kunbis.

KALINGA.—A sub-division of Bráhmans.

KAL KAIKADI.—A synonym for Adivi Korava.

KALSABAD.—A sub-division of Lohárs.

KALU.—A sub-division of Ods.

KALWADAR.—A synonym for Bhámta.

KAMAR.—A Kanarese term for Lohár.

KAMATHIS or Telugus, numbering 4,790 (1901), including 2,511 males and 2,279 females, are found chiefly in the city of Bombay, the Deccan, Karnátak and Thána. The term includes a few scattered immigrant members of Munurvárs, Golevárs, Gullodás, Mungalollás and Sálodás, who speak Telugu and came to the Presidency some hundred years ago from Hyderabad and Madras. They rank generally with Maráthás, but follow Telugu customs. They follow a variety of callings, but their commonest occupation is some form of more or less skilled labour.

KAMATHI.—A sub-division of Kaikádis.

KAMATI.—A synonym for Bhámta.

KAMBAYA.—A sub-division of Dhors.

KAMBLE.—A sub-division of Mahárs.

KAMLE.—A sub-division of Lohárs and Holayás.

KAMLIS numbering 1,156 (1901) including 596 males and 560 females, are found in the Thána district. They state that they came from Káthiáwár more than 500 years ago, and that they were formerly known as Kamb Rajputs. They are husbandmen and palm-juice drawers. They allow widow marriage. Their chief gods are Máruti, Ganpati, and Mahádev. Their priests are Gujaráti Bráhmans. They burn their dead. They eat the flesh of goats, sheep, hares, deer and fowls and drink liquor.

KAMLIA.—*See* under Minor Musalmán castes.

KAMTI.—A synonym for Kanadi Máli.

Name and origin.

KANBIS [1] number 924,921 (1901), including 474,371 males and 450,550 females.

The term Kanbi merely indicates the occupation of a cultivator; but the majority of Gujarát Kanbis are probably Gujars in origin, and in this differ markedly from the Kunbi of the Deccan and Konkan, who is, for the most part, of common stock with the Marátha.

All Ahmádábád Kanbis are addressed as Pátidárs, a title of distinction. In Kaira (Charotar) only Levás are called Pátidárs, others being termed simply Kanbis. Other titles commonly used are Desái, Amin and Patel.

Endogamous divisions.

Kanbis have seven endogamous divisions. They are :—

(1) Anjna.	(4) Kadva.	(7) Momna.
(2) Dángi.	(5) Leva.	(8) Pattani.
(3) Gujar.	(6) Matia.	(9) Uda.

Of the above divisions, Levás and Kadvás eat together, but do not intermarry. Udás do not interdine or intermarry with any other division. Pattanis eat with Levás and Kadvás, but do not marry with them. Levás and Kadvás do not associate with Matiás, Anjnás, Momnás, and Dángis, and, except that Anjnás and Dángis eat together, none of these divisions interdine or intermarry.

In religion, ceremonies and customs, the Levás, Kadvás, Anjnás Dángis, Udás and Pattanis differ only in a few details. The Matiás and Momnás, who are half Hindus half Musalmáns, differ considerably from the other divisions and from one another. The points common to Levás, Kadvás, Anjnás, Dángis, Udás and Pattanis are described below, the peculiarities of each being described separately under each. The Matiás and Momnás are described in full separately.

Town Kanbis closely resemble Vániás in appearance, dress and ornaments. Village Kanbis are darker and stronger.

Language.

Kanbis speak Gujaráti. The names in common use among men are Amra Bakor, Bhago, Bhimo, Chhota, Dalsukh, Dhori, Gordhan, Govind, Hira, Jetha, Kalo, Kesho, Kheta, Khushál, Ládha, Lakho, Lallu, Magan, Megha, Nárán, Narsing, Punja, Ranchhod, Ruda, Rupa, Shiva, Soma, Vala, Vasta, Vishrám. The tendency of late is to use full names ending in 'ji,' 'Bhai,' 'Dás,' 'Lál,' 'Chand,' etc., for the short names given above, *e.g.*, Bhimji for Bhimo, Ranchhodji for Ranchhod, and so on.

The names in common use among women are Amba, Aval, Bena Chanchal, Dáhi, Devi, Diváli, Heta, Jiwa, Kanku, Káshi, Kunvar,

(1) The terms Kanbi and Kunbi are synonyms meaning cultivator; but the former is usually applied to cultivating castes in Gujarát while Kunbi denotes the similar occupational caste in the Deccan and Konkan.

Ládu, Lakhama, Lál, Mani, Megha, Párvati, Rádha, Rámu, Rudi, Rupadi, Seji, Sona, Teja. As among men the tendency of late is to add 'ji,' etc., to the old names, so among women commonly 'bái' is added to the names, *e.g.*, Kunvarbái, Dáhibái, etc. In Káthiáwár 'ba' is added instead of 'bái.'

Opprobricus names such as Punjo, Ladho, Natho or Nathu are often given to boys whose elder brothers have died in infancy.

Marriages are prohibited between members belonging to the same exogamous section. A man cannot marry a woman of the section to which his mother, his paternal grandmother or maternal grandmother belongs. He cannot marry his father's sister's, mother's sister's or mother's brother's daughter. In other cases, two families having common ancestor relationship on the maternal side in either case are allowed to intermarry if the common ancestor is removed to the fourth or fifth degree. A Kanbi may marry his deceased wife's sister, and brothers may marry sisters. Marriage is mostly infant. Kanbis allow widow marriage. Polygamy is allowed and practised, but among Pátidárs it is very rare. If a husband divorces his wife, no money is paid, but if the wife claims a divorce she has to pay her husband money enough to meet the cost of his second marriage. Divorces are asked and granted if the husband and wife do not agree. The children are either kept by the father or taken by the mother. As a rule, grown children stay with the father. Divorced women are allowed to remarry by the widow remarriage form.

Pregnancy.

During the seventh month of a woman's first pregnancy, on a day fixed by the astrologer, the lap-filling or *kholobharni* takes place. A woman who has all her children alive lays in the pregnant woman's lap 5¼ or 10½ lbs. of clean rice, plantains, betelnuts, a cocoanut and red-powder. The pregnant woman empties the rice from her lap into a winnowing-fan, and from the winnowing-fan the rice is again passed to the pregnant woman's lap. After this has been repeated seven times, the rice is put into a new earthen jar. Seven balls made of the dung of a goat and a mouse, seven bundles of cotton-thread, seven figs of the banyan tree, seven betelnuts, seven almonds, seven dry dates and seven copper coins, and a rupee and a quarter worth of silver coins, are put along with the rice in the jar. A red cotton thread is wound round the jar's mouth, and in the mouth a cocoanut is placed. The pregnant woman, with the help of a family-priest, worships the cocoanut and the jar. After the worship is over, besides small cash presents, the priest receives the seven copper coins from the jar. The jar and its other contents are put aside and are carefully preserved.

The pregnant woman receives presents in clothes from her father, and on the wrist of her right arm a silver armlet called a *rákhdi* or guard with a golden bead is tied by her husband's sister. The woman continues to wear the silver armlet till her delivery, after which it is returned to the husband's sister with an additional cash present if the child is a boy. The ceremony ends with a dinner to friends and relations. During the interval after this ceremony and the time when the woman goes to her father's house for confinement, she is invited to dinner by her relations and friends and receives a present of Re. 1 to Rs. 5 or a robe. This is known as *váyanu*. In the course of the seventh or ninth month the woman goes to her father's house to be confined.(1)

Birth ceremonies.

Kanbi women go to their father's house to be confined. When a woman's time is come, a barber's wife or any other skilled woman is called and attends the child and its mother every morning generally for ten days. Besides a set of woman's clothes, she is given about Re. 1 if the child is a boy and about annas eight if the child is a girl. On the birth of a child the family astrologer is asked to note the time by some of the Pátidárs and, in the case of the birth of a son, a barber or a messenger of any caste is sent to give the news to the child's father. The messenger takes with him the footmarks of the child impressed on a piece of paper with redpowder. The relations and friends of the child's father gather on hearing the news. The barber is feasted and paid from Rs. 2 to Rs. 5. The child's father distributes molasses and sugar to his relations and friends. As soon as it is born, the child is bathed in warm water, and about ten inches of the navel cord is left uncut and tied to a red cotton thread, which is wound round the child's neck. For three days the child is fed on a liquid mixture of clarified butter, molasses and castor-oil called *golthuthi* or *chátu*, and on the fourth day it is suckled. Cowdung ashes are rubbed on the navel daily for three or four days, at the end of which the cord dries and is separated from the navel. On the sixth day the *chhati* ceremony is performed. In the evening, on a footstool near the mother's bed, are laid a piece of paper, an inkstand, a reed-pen, red rice, flowers, a rupee, a few copper pice, a lamp fed with clarified butter, some molasses, some cocoa-kernel, and a piece of the waistcloth of a man whose children are all alive. These things are taken away in the morning. The silver and copper coins are melted along with other similar coins and made into an anklet or wristlet for the child, and the piece of the waistcloth is made into a *jabhla* or small coat. On the

(1) Bombay Gazetteer, Vol. IX, Part I, page 161.

morning of the tenth day the woman bathes, but continues impure for twenty-five days more in the case of a son and for thirty days in the case of a daughter. On the morning of the thirty-fifth or fortieth day she bathes, worships the sun, the well and the door-post and is pure. Four or five months after the birth the woman is sent to her husband's house. The woman's father, besides making presents of cash, ornaments and clothes to the child and its mother, gives the child a cradle, a small mattress, and pillows. Except that the name is fixed by the family astrologer, no naming ceremony is performed. The child is named on the sixth or twelfth day or on a lucky day in the first, second or third month, when a Bráhman priest attends and worships Ganpati. Four boys in the case of a boy, or four girls in the case of a girl, rock the child in a piece of cloth, and the father's sister names the child. The father's sister receives a robe or *sádi*, a piece of silk for a bodice, and the Bráhman priest from Re. 1 to Rs. 2 in cash.(1)

Instead of the Bráhmanic thread, some of the Kanbis wear a rosary of beads made of the stem of the basil plant or some other material. Some of the Pátidárs in Kaira and Broach have of late taken to wearing the sacred thread and claiming to be twice-born. Among those who wear the rosary, some time when they are between seven and eleven years old, both boys and girls are taken to the religious head or *guru*, who binds the rosary round the neck of the novice. Besides a day's food the *guru* receives about Rs. 2 as the initiati n fee. The offer of marriage comes from either side. If the boy's father accepts the offer the girl's father's family-priest goes to the boy's house, where, in the presence of the assembled guests, the boy worships a Ganpati painted in red on a low wooden stool. The boy's brow is marked with redpowder, and he is given a turban, a cocoanut and a rupee. Cash presents are made to the priest and the barber, and a dinner is given to the family. Betrothals may be broken at any time before marriage. If the betrothal is broken by the boy's father, the girl's father gets back the amount he has paid, but if the girl's father breaks off the engagement none of the betrothal money is returned. As a rule, the amount to be paid to the bridegroom is settled at the time of betrothal. The amount varies according as the parties are of family *kulia* or of no-family *akulia*. A bridegroom of high family gets a dowry of from Rs. 1,000 to Rs. 2,000 while a no-family bridegroom has to pay from Rs. 500 to Rs. 1,000 to the bride. Landlords or *Pátidárs* marry their daughters

(1) Bombay Gazetteer, Vol. IX, Part I, pp. 157-158.

before they are eleven, and the ordinary peasant Kanbis between eleven and sixteen.

Marriage ceremonies.

The marriage-day is fixed by the Bráhman astrologer. Five or six days before the marriage, the father of the bride sends a roll of paper or *langanpatri* with the family-priest. The names of the bride and bridegroom and the time for the marriage in hours and minutes are written on the roll. The priest takes the roll to the bridegroom's house and presents the roll along with a rupee to the bridegroom's mother. The priest is feasted and is given a cash present. Three or four days before the marriage the parents of the bride and bridegroom, each in their own house, worship a Ganpati painted on the house wall. Two days before the marriage-day, the parents, each at their own house, perform the *grahashánti* or planet-pleasing ceremony. The bride and bridegroom, each at their homes, are then rubbed every morning and evening with a mixture of turmeric-powder, parched *adad* (Phaseolus mungo) flour, and camphor, and are given sweetmeats by friends and relations. The rubbing of the mixture is repeated daily till the marriage-day, and women-relations sing songs in the mornings and evenings for a week or till the marriage is over. On the marriage-day the brother of the bridegroom's mother gives him presents in cash and in clothes, and the brother of the bride's mother gives the bride presents in ornaments and clothes. Marriage preparations then begin. At the house of the bride a square or *chori* of four posts of *shami* (Prosopis spicigera) wood is raised with either five or seven coloured earthen pots piled conewise at each post. At the house of the bridegroom the relations and friends of the bridegroom gather and take their meals. The bridegroom bathes and puts on ornaments and rich clothes. A *kanku* mark is made on his forehead and right cheek, lampblack is applied to his eyes, a lampblack mark is made on his left cheek, and rice, seven betelnuts, two or three betel-leaves, a rupee and a cocoanut are put in the hollow of his two joined hands. Four women whose first husbands are alive by turns touch the bridegroom's nose with four millet stalks dipped in wet *kanku* which are thrown to each of the four quarters of heaven. The bridegroom's sister waves over his head a copper pot containing seven betelnuts, a rupee and a few crystals of salt. The pot is wrapped in a handkerchief and is held in the sister's right hand, who, after waving it round her brother's head, passes it over her right shoulder. The bridegroom then sits on a horse or in a carriage. The procession sets out from the bridegroom's house with music, the men ahead, the bridegroom in the middle, and, except among *Pátidárs*, the women behind singing songs.[(1)] The bridegroom's mother, with a hood of palm-leaves, keeps in her hand a lamp fed with clarified butter. The procession stops at the outskirts of the bride's village. The bridegroom and his elderly relations sit on a carpet, while the young relations drive in bullock carts to the bride's house, the swifter the bullocks the larger share of grain and spices they get. The bride's relations, both men and women, with a barber and with music, go out to receive the bridegroom and his party. The men of the two parties greet each other with the words *Rám-Rám* and an embrace. The barber gives molasses and water to the bridegroom and his party to drink, and is paid a rupee by the bridegroom's father. The bridegroom and his party are conducted with music to a house which is set apart for them, and the bride's relations return to the bride's house. About an hour later three or four female relations of the bride, among them her sister or her brother's wife, go with music to the bridegroom's lodging. They take *siro* or wheat-flour mixed with clarified butter and sugar and give five pinches of it to the bridegroom to eat. The bridegroom eats the *siro* and gives about Rs. 3 to the bride's sister or brother's wife. About eight or ten in the evening of the marriage day the bridegroom and his relations go with music to the bride's house. At the entrance the bridegroom is received by the bride's mother, who shows him a miniature plough, arrow, pestle, and churnstaff. He is led to the marriage-booth, where he sits on a wooden stool and, with the help of the family-priests of the bride and bridegroom, worships Ganpati. After the worship the bride, dressed in ornaments and clothes presented to her by her mother's brother, is brought in and set by her mother's brother on a stool opposite the bridegroom. The parents of the bride then worship Ganpati and the great toe of the bridegroom's right foot. Wreaths of red thread are thrown round the necks of the bride and the bridegroom. Their hands are joined, and over their hands a piece of cloth is thrown. The hems of their clothes are tied together and their feet are washed with water. In the central square or *chori* a fire is lighted, and clarified butter, barley and sesame are offered to it. With their hands one upon another the couple walk together four times round the fire. The bride and bridegroom then feed each other with coarse wheat-flour mixed with clarified butter and molasses served by the bride's mother. After he has finished eating, the bridegroom catches his mother-in-law's robe and does not loosen his hold till he has received a handsome present. The

(1) Among *Pátidárs* no women, even the mother of the bridegroom, attend a boy's wedding.

bridegroom in his turn pays about Rs. 3 to the bride's younger brother or sister. The bride and the bridegroom worship Ganpati, and the ceremony is over. The bridegroom and his relations then go to their lodging. On the second day the opium-serving ceremony takes place. The bride's male relations go with music to the bridegroom's house, where *kasumba* or opium-water is served. *Kesar* or saffron water is served to those who object to opium-water. The bride's relations then return to their house, and the bridegroom and his relations go to the bride's house to receive presents, the value of which depends on the wealth and social position of the giver. The bride's father then makes presents in cash or in clothes to Bráhmans, his family barber, his Máli or gardener, and his Kumbhár or potter. The family priest of the bride then dips his hand in wet *kanku* and applies it to the coats of the bridegroom's male relations. The bride and bridegroom then worship the marriage booth and go in carriages with music to the bridegroom's house with his relations. Before they start, the bride's mother worships the spokes of the carriage-wheel and gives a cocoanut to be crushed by the wheels. For two days the bridegroom's relations are feasted by the bride's father, and on the third day they go to their village with the bride and the bridegroom. After entering the house the bride and bridegroom worship Ganpati and, as among Vániás, play a game of chance.(1)

Nátra or the remarriage of widows is permitted by all Kanbis, but among the well-to-do it is rarely resorted to. A widow cannot marry her deceased husband's brother or a member of his section except among Lewás, Kadvás and Pattanis in Cambay, where marriage with a younger brother of the deceased husband is allowed. The parents of the widow usually receive a sum of from Rs. 25 to Rs. 75 from the intended husband, but a man can marry a widow without making any payment. Sometimes the widow is also presented with some ornaments. *Nátra* is celebrated on Sunday or Tuesday, less often on Thursday. It always takes place at night. The widow is conducted by *five* relations of her new husband from her parent's house. There is little ceremony. The couple are seated facing each other, and in front of them is placed an earthen pot containing a lighted lamp fed with *ghi*. The pair are asked to look down into the pot, and as they do so their heads touch, which completes the ceremony. In some places, Ganpati is worshipped, after which the widow puts on new bangles presented by her intended husband. Sometimes the widow wears a new robe, and, taking on her head a brass pot filled with water,

(1) Bombay Gazetteer, Vol. IX, Part I, pp. 158-160.

enters the house of her intended husband. In some localities a Bráhman priest is called, who ties red thread round the right wrists of the bride and bridegroom.

Religion. As a class, Kanbis are very religious. Unlike Vániás and other high classes, the Kanbis belong to many sects, Bijmárgis, Dádupanthis, Kabirpanthis, Mádhavgarnis, Pranámis, Rámánandis, Shaivs, Svámináráyans, and Vallabbácháryas. A few are Jains. They worship all Hindu gods and goddesses, and respect Musalmán saints. Though very few keep images in their houses, they often visit the temple of their sects. They are careful to respect Bráhmans and their spiritual leaders and to give grain in charity to the poor of the village and to travellers. To their religious heads or *gurus* they show much reverence, paying them about Re. 1 on occasions of a marriage or of a death, and besides food about Rs. 2¼ on the *kanthi* or rosary ceremony. To their *guru* they also pay a small fee whenever he goes to their town or village. They have much faith in sorcery, witchcraft, and the influence of the evil eye. In sickness or in difficulty they consult a sorcerer, generally a Koli or Vághri, a Bráhman, or a religious beggar, Hindu or Musalmán. They believe in omens and signs. On the lucky *Akhátrij* or third day of *Váishákh sud* (April) they begin to take manure to their fields. On the fourth of the first fortnight of *Bhádarvo* (September) they worship Ganpati in order that his carrier the rat may not destroy their crops. Before sinking a well and before each season's first ploughing the ground is worshipped by making *kanku* or vermilion marks and sprinkling rice over the marks. Before watering the ground for the first time, the water in the well is worshipped to increase its nourishing power. Rice and *kanku* are thrown into the water, a lamp fed with clarified butter is laid near the well's mouth, and a cocoa-kernel is offered to the water-god. To guard against too great rainfall the village headman and other husbandmen go with music to the village reservoir and offer flowers, *kanku* and a cocoanut. Of four-footed animals, they hold the cow sacred, and of birds the *nilkanth* or jay and the *chás* or kingfisher on *Dasara* Day (September-October). For three days from the 13th to the 15th of *Bhádarva sud* (September-October), Kanbi women fast and worship a cow and feed her with barley, and on the fourth day they drink cow's milk mixed with a few grains of barley found in the dung. They observe the ordinary Hindu fasts and feasts and occasionally make pilgrimages locally to Ambáji, Bahucharáji, Dákor, Dwárka, and Unái; and among more distant holy places to Alláhábád, Banáres, Badrikedár, Gokul, Jagannáth, Mathura, and Shrináthji, Rámeshwar, Násik and Pandharpur.(1)

(1) Bombay Gazetteer, Volume IX, Part I, pp. 156-157.

Death ceremonies.

When a Kanbi is on the point of death the family-priest, who is generally an Audich Bráhman, and other Bráhmans of the village are called, and a lamp fed with clarified butter is placed near his bed. The dying person worships Vishnu, and gives, besides presents in cash and clothes, a cow or the value of a cow in cash to the priest. To each of the other Bráhmans, besides presents of cash, the dying man makes gifts of wheat, husked rice, pulse, salt, and rusty nails and shovels. If well off, he sets apart sums of money to be spent after his death on works of public charity, sinking wells, making halting places on the roadside, and supplying water to thirsty travellers. Friends and relations come to visit the dying man, and, as the end draws near, they utter the name of Rám near his ear. One of the female relations sweeps the floor of the entrance room and cow-dungs a portion of it of the length and breadth of a man. The cowdunged space is strewn with sesame and barley seeds, *tulsi* leaves, and *darbha* grass. The head of the dying man is shaved, he is bathed with hot water and his brow is marked with *gopichandan* or milkmaid's earth, and the body is laid on its back with the head towards the north on the freshly cowdunged floor. Ganges water and some gold, silver and coral, a pearl, a piece of crystal, and a basil leaf are placed in the mouth. A ball of unbaked millet flour and a rupee are given to a Bráhman. When life is gone, the nearest relations raise the life-cry or *prán-pok* a call to bring back the spirit. Among the Pátidárs of Ahmedabad the name of the deceased is written on a tile with a piece of charcoal and it is sent to the relations of the deceased by a Bhangi to inform them of the occurrence. Caste-people(1) go to the house of death, the men to bear the body to the burning ground, the women to mourn. Two or three of the mourners bring from the market two bamboo poles, several short lengths of bamboo, coir string, and a piece of red silk if the deceased is a married woman, or of white cotton cloth if the deceased is either a man or a widow. The poles and pieces of bamboo and the coir string are made into a ladder-shaped bier and from each corner a cocoanut is hung. The corpse is laid on the bier and tied to it by the coir strings. The body is covered with the white or red cloth, and over the cloth red powder and flowers are strewn. The bier is raised on the shoulders of four of the nearest relations and is borne forth feet first, preceded by one of the nearest relations carrying an earthen or copper vessel with fire and cakes of cowdung. The relations and caste-fellows follow calling the words *Rám bolo bhái, Rám* (Call Rám, brothers, call Rám). The female mourners follow the body for some distance weeping. Then they stop, beat their breasts, return to

(1) The Kanbi funeral procession is large as by caste rules the attendance of one man from each house is enforced on pain of fine.

the house and bathe either in well-water or in a river. Midway between the house and burning-ground the male mourners halt and set down the bier. The nearest relations cease to weep and the bier is borne head foremost to the burning-ground. When the burning-ground is reached, the bearers lay the corpse almost uncovered with the head to the north on a pile of a man's length of wood and cowdung cakes. A little butter is dropped into the dead mouth and the chief-mourner, generally the eldest son of the deceased, puts some fire near the face, and the other mourners set the pyre ablaze. Two or three of the older men stay near the body while it is being burnt, keeping the pile in order; others sit afar, talking and making merry if the deceased was old, and with a certain sadness and regret if the deceased was young. When the body is almost consumed, a little clarified butter is poured on the flames. The mourners bathe and return weeping to the house of the deceased and then to their homes. Letters telling friends and relations in distant villages are sent either by post or by carrier. On the second or third day the chief-mourner and two or three of the nearest relations go to the burning-ground. The ashes and bones are gathered and are thrown into a river or a pond, and an earthen jar filled with water is set where the body was burned. The mourners bathe, and with wet clothes return home, weeping. They take with them a few of the bones and keep them in the house till some member of the family goes on a pilgrimage and throws them into the sacred Narbada or Ganges. After the mourners return from the burning-ground an earthen pot is filled with water and milk and placed on the roof of the house. The nearest relations remain impure for ten days, during which they touch no one, do not approach the house gods, do not visit the temples, do not change their clothes, and do not shave. On the tenth day men shave the head and moustaches; girls and married women wash their hair with clay or with soapnut, the floors are cowdunged, and all earthen drinking pots which have been touched during the ten days are replaced by new ones. The mind-rite or *shráddha* ceremony is performed by the chief-mourner from the tenth to the thirteenth day, on the eleventh with the help of a Káyatia Bráhman, and on the other three days with the help of the family-priest. During the four days of the *shráddha* ceremony the chief-mourner, instead of a turban, wears a linen cloth wound round his head. On the thirteenth day his father-in-law presents him with a new turban and the linen cloth is removed. On the thirteenth day the family-priest is given, besides a few ornaments and a complete set of clothes, a sleeping cot, some pillows, and some brass or copper vessels. Friends and relations are feasted from the tenth to the thirteenth day, and the caste-people on the twelfth and on the thirteenth. If the deceased was a wealthy man, presents in grain, in clothes, and in cash are given to Bráhmans, to religious beggars, and to the poor. Female mourners go to the house of the deceased to weep and mourn, morning and evening, for a month if the deceased was of mature age, and for six months if the deceased was young. During the first year, as among other Hindus, monthly, half-yearly and yearly mind-rites or *shráddha* are performed, and a yearly *shráddha* in all subsequent years and an additional *shráddha* during the latter half of *Bhádrarvo* (September-October). Landlords or Pátidárs and headmen of villages call all the villagers to dinner on marriage and death feasts. This custom has ruined many families.[(1)]

Food. Except Anjnás, Kanbis neither eat flesh, nor drink liquor.

Though many town Kanbis are skilled weavers of silk and cotton, dealers in cloth and grain, and some have risen to high positions in Government service or made money in trade or as money-lenders, the bulk of the Kanbis are husbandmen. Many are village headmen or *mukhis*, that is, police headmen, and enjoy allowances in cash and land. The officiators are chosen from the *Matádárs*, that is, those who have the right to sign village papers. They are very jealous of their rights, which give them a certain position and influence, and which go to show that they are the original *vatandárs* of the village. Gujarát Kanbis do not enlist as soldiers. Kanbis, especially those of the Kadva and Leva divisions, are capital husbandmen. They are learned in the properties of every soil and minutely acquainted with the wants of every crop.

ANJNA KANBIS are found chiefly in North Gujarát. In appearance they are more like Kolis than other Kanbis, and, like Rajputs, some of their names end in *sing*, such as Dánsing, Harising, Rájsing, Umsing. They have twenty-three clans, who eat together and intermarry. Some of the Anjnás of Cutch are Jains.

DANGI KANBIS are found in Mahi Kántha. Originally Anjnás, with whom they dine but do not intermarry, they are said to have lost their position by adopting the dress and language of Bhils. Many of them live in Mewár and have marriage and other relations with the Mahi Kántha Dángis.

GUJAR KANBIS are found in East and West Khándesh. They consist of eight sub-divisions, (1) Anála, (2) Dále, (3) Dore, (4) Gari, (5) Kadva, (6) Khápra, (7) Londhári or Bád and (8) Reva

(1) Bombay Gazetteer, Vol. IX, Part I, pp. 161-163.

or Leva. There are a few families of Dáles on the banks of the Tápti in Sháháda and Taloda and in Ráver towards Barhánpur. The Deshmukhs of Jámner are said to be Gari Gujars, but they claim equality with and call themselves Reva Gujars. Revás or Levás appear to be an offshoot of the Gujarát Levás. They consider themselves a very superior caste, eschew flesh and liquor and eat only at the hands of Bráhmans. Kadvás, Análás and Dáles are found only in small numbers. Kadvás appear to be a branch of the Gujarát Kanbis of the same name, and, like the parent stock, celebrate their marriages once in twelve years. The Londháris are said to have acquired the name Londhári from their being exclusively employed in ginning cotton. The Kháprás are a mixed or inferior class.

KADVA KANBIS are chiefly found in Ahmedábád and in the Kadi *táluka* of the Baroda State. They are closely connected with the Levás. According to one story, the Kadvás are descendants or followers of Kush, the second son of Rám and Sita ; according to another, they are sprung from clay figures fashioned by Uma or Párvati, the wife of Shiva. Shiva at Uma's request inspired the figures with life and founded for them the village of Unja about forty miles north of Ahmedábád, where a temple was raised in Uma's honour. This village and temple all Kadva Kanbis consider the chief seat of their tribe, and to it they resort from long distances to pay their vows. Some state that they came to Gujarát from Kábul through the Punjab, which is supported by the names of some of their *shákhás* or sections. Except in Surat they have no sub-divisions. In Surat there are three sub-divisions, one calling themselves Lálchudáwálás from their women wearing red bracelets, the other Káláchudáválás from their women wearing black bracelets, and the third Ahmedábádis from Ahmedábád. These three divisions eat together, but for the last thirty-five years have ceased to intermarry. As among Leva Kanbis they have Kulia and Akulia sections in south Gujarát, the relations between which are the same as those between similar branches of the Levás. A Kadva Kanbi can divorce his wife at will, but in north Gujarát the wife cannot divorce the husband without his consent or after she has borne a child. Kadvá's marriages are celebrated once in every nine, ten or eleven years. Efforts are of late being made to reduce this period to five years by some and to one year by others, and a few marriages have also been celebrated accordingly. But the community as a whole has not yet accepted the reform. There are fifty-two original *shákhás* or exogamous sections, mostly called after the names of villages in the Punjab. At present

Kadvás marry outside their villages and call themselves after their village, *e.g.*, Narodia from Naroda. Thus, new *shákhás* are continually in process of formation. The original fifty-two *shákhás* with a few of such new *shákhás* are given below :—

The old original fifty-two Shákhás.

1	Amrita	.. From	Amritsar.
2	Bakha ..	.. ,,	a place near Gopálganj.
3	Bhemat ..	.. ,,	Bhám near Hoshiápur.
4	Bhua ..	.. ,,	Bhoa near Láhore.
5	Bhut ..	.. ,,	Bhutána near Lodhiána.
6	Chawelia ..	.. ,,	Chawidsa near Amritsar.
7	Chechat ..	.. ,,	Chechat near Kotah.
8	Cheniár .	.. ,,	Chenári near Bahawad.
9	Chhapala ..	.. ,,	Chhapal near Mhow.
10	Chopada ..	.. ,,	Chopada, Khándesh.
11	Dáni	.. ,,	Dána Awal near Jalandar.
12	Dhánkania ..	.. ,,	Dhánakatti near Faridpur.
13	Dhántodwa .	.. ,,	Dhampur near Gonda Belámpur.
14	Dhekál ..	.. ,,	Dhekál near Faridpur.
15	Dholu ..	.. ,,	Dhol near Mujafarpur.
16	Diwani ..	.. ,,	Diwanganj near Bhopál.
17	Dokotara ..	.. ,,	Dakot kul.
18	Gámi ..	.. ,,	Gambár near Montgomery.
19	Gogada ..	.. ,,	Goga near Bháwalpur.
20	Goti ..	.. ,,	Got, Sharif Málwa.
21	Harania ..	.. ,,	Har near Mednipur.
22	Hoti ..	.. ,,	Hoti near Pesháwar.
23	Juwátar ..	.. ,,	Juwa near Itáwah.
24	Kadawátar ..	.. ,,	Kaláli near the Godávari river.
25	Kalára ..	.. ,,	Kála near Jhelum river.
26	Kálpuncha ..	.. ,,	Kálsaya near Ludhiána and Ambálla.
27	Karanáwat ..	.. ,,	Karandáh near Gashipur.
28	Katwar ..	.. ,,	Káth near Matoda.
29	Kodal ..	.. ,,	Konda near Gwálior.
30	Kuwára ..	.. ,,	Kumargeri near the Godávari.
31	Lahuwot ..	.. ,,	Láhore.
32	Lákod ..	.. ,,	Lákoda near Láhore.
33	Láli ..	.. ,,	Lár near Gorpur.
34	Majitia ..	.. ,,	Majit Mandi near Amritsar.
35	Mándalot ..	.. ,,	a village in Mewád.
36	Mandawia ..	.. ,,	Mandi, Punjáb.

37 Manwar .. .. From Manor near Bareli.
38 Mogala .. .. „ Mogalpur near Láhore.
39 Mokát .. .. „ Moka near Beláji.
40 Munját .. .. „ Munja near Gujaranwála.
41 Páhán .. .. „ a place near Gonda, Balrámpur State.
42 Pokár .. .. „ Pokáran near Miraj.
43 Phok .. .. „ Phuk near Lárkhána.
44 Rusát .. .. „ a village near Delhi.
45 Sákaria .. .. „ Sákari in Khándesh.
46 Shethia .. .. „ Shethgadh near Bareli.
47 Shirwi .. .. „ Shirwa near Miraj.
48 Sorotár .. .. „ Sontár near Punial.
49 Tilat .. .. „ Tilatu near Shahábád.
50 Wagada .. .. „ Wagada near Detroj, taluka Viramgám.
51 Wághoda .. .. „ a place in East Khándesh.
52 Wijayat

New Shákhás.(1)

1 Aduwaya† .. .. 23 Hematpara.†
2 Apara .. .. 24 Itál.
3 Baládiwádás† .. .. 25 Jhampadia.
4 Báloki .. .. 26 Kachhar.
5 Bálwot .. .. 27 Kága.
6 Bária* .. .. 28 Kajáwit.
7 Bhila .. .. 29 Kalatia.
8 Buhát .. .. 30 Kálwelia.
9 Chámbdáwádás† .. .. 31 Kangali.
10 Chávda* .. .. 32 Kank.
11 Chhotia .. .. 33 Kanotra.
12 Chulgar† .. .. 34 Kapáli.
13 Daridria .. .. 35 Karur (near Multán).
14 Darjia .. .. 36 Kasatia (Káshtia)†.
15 Dábhi* .. .. 37 Káshmir.
16 Dhola .. .. 38 Katármal.
17 Ghargada .. .. 39 Kawar.
18 Gohela* .. .. 40 Khoda.
19 Gol* .. .. 41 Khud.
20 Gomát .. .. 42 Kondha.
21 Gowál .. .. 43 Kutriwádás†.
22 Hádi. .. .. 44 Lákadia.

(1) Of these *shákhás* those marked * are taken from Rajput clans and those marked† are found only among the Ahmedábád City Pátidárs.

New Shákhás—contd.[1]

45 Lodáwádia†.	.. ..	56 Rátol*.
46 Lodhia.	.. ..	57 Sábawa.
47 Makwána*.	.. ..	58 Sawándhara.
48 Mándu.	.. ..	59 Shenur.
49 Menia.	.. ..	60 Sutaria.
50 Metalia.	.. ..	61 Trágadi.
51 Moghara.	.. ..	62 Ujalia.
52 Padia.	.. ..	63 Wághela.*
53 Parewa.	.. ..	64 Wanod.
54 Patiad.	.. ..	65 Wenjáwat.
55 Pemát.	.. ..	66 Widalia.

There are various social grades among them, the Ahmedábád City Kadvás being the aristocracy of the caste. Until a few years ago, children about a month old and even unborn children were married, on the hypothesis that the sexes would prove correct. The mothers actually walked round the altar in the marriage booth to sanctify the agreement. This custom has now become extinct. As Kadva marriages are celebrated periodically, suitable husbands for girls are frequently not available. The difficulty is overcome as follows :—The girl is married to a bunch of flowers on the general marriage day and then the flowers are thrown into a well or river. The girl thus becomes a widow, and may contract a second informal marriage (*nátra*) on any suitable opportunity. An alternative is to induce some married man to go through the ceremony of marriage on payment of a small sum of money on condition that he divorces the girl immediately. The divorced girl may then contract a second marriage.

The auspicious season for holding marriages is fixed in the following way. A few Bráhman priests and astrologers with the two headmen of Unja go together to worship Uma in her temple. After worship lots are drawn, and according as the lot falls, the year on which the lot falls or the following year is declared the proper time. When the year is known, the astrologers name a special day. The day always comes in *Vaishákh*. For the sake of those prevented from sickness or other cause, a second day is chosen about a fortnight later than the first. As soon as these days are fixed, Bráhmans start to spread the news on every side. Wherever they go they are received with honour and rejoicing. At Ahmedábád they are met outside the city in the Asarva suburb. The whole Kadva community comes to

(1) Of these *shákhás* those marked * are taken from Rajput clans and those marked † are found only among the Ahmedábád City Pátidárs.

Dáda Hari's well, and after worshipping Ganpati and Umáji, the headman of Asarva reads out the names of the lucky days.

LEVA KANBIS are the largest division of Gujarát Kanbis. They are found all over Gujarát, but chiefly in the *tálukas* of Anand, Nadiád and Borsad in the Kaira district. They are found also in Cutch, where they have two territorial divisions, Halái and Vághadia, who eat together but do not intermarry. The Gujarát Levás consist of two groups, Pátidárs or shareholders and Kanbis or husbandmen. The Pátidárs do not give their daughters in marriage to the Kanbis, but take their daughters on payment of a handsome dowry. Further, the Pátidárs of thirteen villages in the Charotar (part of Kaira district) are called Kuliás or men of family, and do not give their daughters in marriage to the Pátidárs outside these villages, who are called Akuliás or men of no family. In Kulia families servants draw water and perform menial household duties. Their women do not appear abroad, and, as stated above, widow marriage is forbidden. As among Vániás, Levás have *gols* or groups of villages formed for the purpose of taking brides. Marriages are generally performed between members of the same *gol*, but the areas of *gols* are not permanently fixed.

Before the introduction of British rule, Kulia Pátidárs acted as farmers of revenue and as middlemen between Government and the husbandmen, and in most cases were found to have exacted the most ingenious and crushing taxes. Though under the survey settlement, they have lost this uncontrolled power of exaction, they have still much influence and are admitted to have a higher social position than the common husbandmen.

"For many years after the introduction of British rule, in spite of their skill and their steady work, their extravagance at marriages kept the Kanbis in a state of depression. The competition to marry their daughters into the higher families was keen, and great sums were paid to secure the honour. In A. D. 1848, to put a stop to this evil, Mr. Fawcett, the Magistrate of Ahmedábád, induced the chief men of the Kanbi caste to pass an agreement reducing marriage expenses and promising not to seek husbands for their daughters among the Kaira families. These agreements were enforced till, in A. D. 1852, the Judge of Ahmedábád decided that they were not legally binding. The restriction was accordingly discontinued, and, for nearly twenty years, no further attempt was made to interfere with the Kanbi marriage customs. In A. D. 1871 information collected in connection with a measure for the suppression of infanticide (Act VIII of 1870), showed among the Kanbis a startling excess in the number of males over females. Inquiries were made, and the result seemed so suspicious that in April 1871 the provisions of the Infanticide Act were applied both to the Leva and Kadva Kanbis. The result of more complete information has been to show that the fears of Government were excessive. The Kadva Kanbis were declared wholly exempt from the provisions of the Act, and in the case of the Leva Kanbis, the restrictions were reduced to a simple registration of births and deaths."(1)

MATIA KANBIS, from *mat* opinion, are found only in the Jalálpur and Bárdoli *tálukás* of Surat. They are half Hindus, half Musalmáns by religion. That they were originally Leva Kanbis of Ahmedábád is proved by the traces of relationship still subsisting between Leva and Matia Kanbis, and by the surnames of Kothia and Bavalia from the villages of Koth and Bavla in Dholka. About 300 years ago a company of Leva Kanbis on their way to Benares are said to have passed a night at the village of Garmatha, about ten miles south-west of Ahmedábád. Imám Sháh, a Musalmán recluse, was at that time living in Garmatha. According to one story, Imám Sháh spoke to the pilgrims, and learning that they were going to Benares told them that if they would carefully listen to his doctrines they would visit Benares without the trouble of going there. Some of the pilgrims paid no attention to what Imám Sháh said, and went to Benares. Others who trusted in Imám Sháh saw Benares, bathed in the Ganges, and feasted the Bráhmans, all without leaving Garmatha. Astonished at this miracle they adopted Imám Sháh as their spiritual head. According to another account they were saved from becoming Musalmáns by becoming the followers of Imám Sháh.

Till lately there were no divisions among Matiás, but, during A. D. 1880, from 150 to 175 families formed themselves into a separate caste, calling themselves Vaishnav Matiás as distinguished from the original or Pirána Matiás. This division is due to the preaching of an ascetic Nirmaldás of Surat, who told the Matiás of their Leva Kanbi origin. Some of his hearers looking with hatred on their half-Hindu half-Musalmán customs, started on a pilgrimage to Benares and were put out of caste. The seceding or Vaishnav Matiás have joined the Rámánandi and Dádupanthi sects. They worship the images of Narsingji, Thákorji, and sometimes the *linga* of Mahádev. They observe the ordinary Hindu fasts and go on pilgrimage to

(1) Bombay Gazetteer, Vol. IX, Part I, p. 167.

Alláhábád, Benares, Jagannáth and Mathura. The Vaishnav Matiás and Piràna Matiás do not eat together. Since the split no old betrothals have been broken and no new betrothals have been made. The Vaishnav Matiás have abandoned all Musalmán customs and in all respects live like Leva Kanbis. But Leva Kanbis do not dine with them, and they do not intermarry.

Pirána Matiás closely resemble Leva Kanbis in appearance, speech and dress. Marriages are forbidden within seven degrees of relationship either on the father's or on the mother's side. Girls are sometimes married when they are six months old, but generally between five and eight, and boys between eight and twenty. Widows are allowed to marry, the widow of a man marrying his younger brother. Divorce is lawful. A bachelor cannot marry a divorced woman or a widow unless he first marries a *shami* (Prosopis spicigera) tree. A widow who marries again wears an ivory bracelet plated with gold. The marriage ceremonies of Matiás do not differ from those of Leva Kanbis. They are conducted by their family priests, who are Audich or Modh Bráhmans.

As a rule a Matia woman gives birth to her first child at her father's house. On the birth of a first child, if it is a boy, its foot-prints are marked with wet *kanku* on paper, and the paper is carried by a barber to the father, who gives him a present of about Rs. 2. On the sixth day the goddess Chhathi is worshipped. On the twelfth day the woman worships the threshold, the doorpost and the nearest well in the street by rubbing on them sandal-dust and *kanku*. Near the well she ties two cowdung cakes together by a cotton thread. The children of the street are given boiled wheat and *juvár* mixed with molasses. For forty days the woman is held impure and cannot touch anything in the house. She never leaves the house if she can help it, and if she is forced to go out she carries with her a sickle or a knife to ward off evil spirits. On some day between the thirty-fifth and the fortieth the woman bathes, and the floor of the lying-in-room is scraped. The woman is then purified by the sin-removing *láhe-utárni* ceremony. After this the child is named by a Bráhman astrologer. When the child is two or three months old the woman goes to her husband's house. No ceremonies are performed when a child is first fed with cooked food.(1)

They follow the Atharva or fourth *Ved* and call themselves *Satpanthis*, followers of truth. They worship the tombs of the Musalmán saints whose mausoleums are at Pirána, Ahmedábád, Navsári,

(1) Bombay Gazetteer, Vol. IX, Part I, p. 170.

and Burhánpur. Their sacred book is the collection of religious precepts called *Shiksha Patri* made by Imám Sháh, the saint of Pirána. Some of them learn the book by heart and gain the name of *káka* or devotee. The *kákás* are laymen, and like the rest of the Matiás maintain themselves by tilling the soil. One special family of *kákás* officiates at some of their ceremonies and are the agents through whose hands all presents pass to the saintly descendants of Imám Sháh at Ahmedábád, Navsári and Burhánpur. The Matiás include three religious divisions, *Pánchiás* or followers of Surabhái's mausoleum, the third of the five Pirána shrines, so called from the five devotees who at first managed the institution, *Sátiás*, from the seven original managing devotees, who are the followers of Baba Muhammad's mausoleum, the fourth of the Pirána shrines ; and *Athiás*, from the eight devotees who managed the institution, who are the followers of Bákar Ali's mausoleum, the fifth Pirána shrine. Except in being called after different saints, these divisions do not differ in belief or in practice. Sin-removing or *láhe-utárni* is their chief ceremony. A woman after child-birth or monthly sickness, a cow or a buffalo after calving, a person who has accidentally defiled himself by the sight of a woman in child-bed, and all those who have broken caste rules by using forbidden articles of food, are made to pass through the sin-removing ceremony. At the house where the purifying ceremony is to be performed various dishes of sweetmeats are prepared. The village *káka* is called and comes accompanied by an assistant called *khal káka*. The *káka* brings with him four copper coins, an earthenware cup, and frankincense. He also brings with him in a small portable tin or brass box, peashaped balls made of white chalk or rice-flour mixed with milk or sandal-dust brought from the tomb of one of the saints. On entering the house the *káka* goes into the kitchen, lights a lamp fed with clarified butter, and mutters a text. While his chief is saying a prayer the *khal káka* calls for a brass plate and in the plate piles from five to eight heaps of cooked rice according as the host is a Pánchia, a Sátia, or a Athia Matia. After the *kalmo* or prayer is over the *káka* sits bowing on a waistcloth spread on the ground. He then burns frankincense and murmurs a second prayer. After the second prayer he spills a circle of wheat grains in a brass plate, and, inside the circle, sets four coins and on the coins a cup. Into the cup he pours a mixture called *nur* or light made of sugared-water, milk and white chalk or rice from the saint's tomb. When this is ready the *khal káka* brings the brass plate with the heaps of rice, and over each heap the *káka* sprinkles the mixture from the earthenware cup repeating a text at each sprinkling. The text for each sprinkling is different, but each ends in *Lá-iláha-illaláh, Muhammad ar-Rasul-*

alláh or *Imám Sháh-Nur-Ali Muhammad Sháh.* The brass plate with the heaps of cooked rice is then put aside and the person to be purified is called in. The man or woman to be purified stands near the *káka* and bows to him, and after being sprinkled with the mixture from the earthenware cup, sits down. He or she then presents a silver or copper coin to the *káka,* who washes it with water, and gives the water along with the mixture from the cup to the man or the woman to drink. The heaps of rice in the brass plate are mixed by the *khal káka* with the rest of the cooked articles and distributed among the guests. The puriying fee is 8 annas for a woman after childbirth and for a buffalo after she has calved, 4 annas for a cow after she has calved, and ¼ anna for those who have broken caste rules. These fees are sent by the *káka* to the saint's tomb at Ahmedábád, Navsári, or Burhánpur. Besides these presents every Matia cultivator sends once a year to the saints through the *káka* three and a half *mans* (140 pounds) of husked rice and one rupee for each of his ploughs.

Matiás hold the second day of every Hindu lunar month sacred, and when the second falls on a Friday they fast for the whole day and do not eat until they have seen the moon. They keep the Ramzan fast, some of them eating no solid food during the whole month. Their other Musalmán holidays are the *Uras* or Saint's Day and the two preceding Sandal Days. On these days they do no work, and spend their time in feasting or in visiting the shrines of their saints in Navasári. Besides these Musalmán holidays they observe as days of feasting *Holi* February-March, *Akhátrij* April-May, *Diváso* June-July, *Balev* July-August, and *Diváli* October-November. Their chief places of pilgrimage are Navsári, Pirána, Burhánpur, and Vemál, seven miles from Miágám in Broach, which they visit on great days or whenever they have leisure. The *káka* accompanies the pilgrims to these places. At Pirána, Navsári and Vemál the pilgrims visit only the saint's tombs. But at Burhánpur the pilgrims worship the great toe of their living saint. The spiritual guide sets his foot on a heap of not less than a hundred rupees contributed by one or two pilgrims. After it has been set on the heap of rupees the leader's foot is washed, rubbed with a fragrant substance, and the right great toe is kissed by each pilgrim in turn. The *káka* who accompanies the pilgrims receives from the spiritual head presents in clothes and ornaments both for himself and his wife.(1)

The Matiás bury the dead. A dying person is bathed and laid on the ground, the *káka* standing near and reading texts. When life is

(1) Bombay Gazetteer, Vol. IX, Part I, pp. 168-170.

gone, the body of the deceased, if a man, is dressed in cotton trousers, a shirt and a cap, and if a woman, in a silk robe, a bodice and a petticoat. It is laid in a Musalmán bier and carried to the burial-ground, which is generally on the bank of a stream. The bearers do not take off any of their clothes or their shoes. On reaching the burial-ground the bearers, without removing any of the clothes, lay the body in a pit and fill the pit with earth. After the body is buried the mourners purify themselves by each holding a piece of frankincense in his hand and muttering two half-Hindu half-Musalmán prayers. The first prayer runs: In the name of Alláh the pitiful, the merciful, of Satgor or Satgur Pátra, of Brahma and Indra, of Imám Shah, of the spotless spiritual Vishnu and of Ali Muhammad Sháh. The second prayer is in these words: The incense burns, evil goes and faith wins (now is the time to) mercy implore.

The funeral party go to the house of mourning, and there the deceased's family feast them with sweet wheat-balls. The mourners eat a mixture of split pulse and rice cooked in a neighbour's house. Like Hindus, Matia women weep and beat their breasts for ten days, and for ten days the sin-removing *láhc-utarni* ceremony is daily performed. Friends and relations from the villages round, summoned by a Bhangia, come to mourn, and are feasted with wheat-flour mixed with clarified butter and sugar. Unlike Hindus, the nearest relations do not consider themselves impure for ten days. No death ceremonies are performed and no rice balls are offered to the spirits of the deceased. Caste people are feasted on the tenth and eleventh days after a death or on any day between the thirteenth and the twentieth, if the eleventh or twelfth falls on a Sunday or a Tuesday. On the first feast-day after a death each family of Matiás sends the chief mourner half a *man* (twenty-pounds) of husked rice, and, besides the rice, friends and relations give eight annas. These presents, along with the clothes, bed and bedstead of the deceased, are sent to the shrine of the saints at Burhánpur, Navsári, Ahmedábád, or Vemál. Besides these presents the chief mourner sends on his own account a money present, and if rich he sets apart a mango tree for the exclusive use of the saint. The aggregate amount of death-presents which go to their saints varies from Rs. 15 to Rs. 100. The Bráhman priest receives some presents on the eleventh day, not in his character of priest, but in return for the help he gives in feasting the caste-people.

Like Leva and Kadva Kanbis, Matiás are strict vegetarians, eating neither fish nor flesh and drinking no spirits. Caste rules forbid the use of assafœtida, garlic, onions and narcotics, and those who break the rule have to be purified before they are let back into caste.

MOMNA KANBIS are found almost entirely in Cutch, nearly two-thirds of the Kanbis in Cutch being Momnás. "Descendants of Hindus of various castes, they are, according to one account, said to have been converted to the Musalmán faith by Imám Sháh, and a portion of them to have fled, after the great Momna revolt and defeat (1691) in Gujarát, to Cutch and settled at Shikra in Vágad. According to another account they were Leva Kanbis converted and called Momnás or *Momins,* believers, by Pir-sadar-ud-din who is said to have become their independent pontiff, *imám.* Slightly made and dark, the Momnás shave the head except the top knot, and the face except the upper lip. The men wear coats, trousers, and three-corned overhanging turbans. Dark in colour, their women wear petticoats, jackets, and head clothes. Their home tongue is Gujaráti without any noticeable peculiarities. Untidy, but sober, quiet and hardworking, Momnás work chiefly as husbandmen and labourers. Very few are rich or well off, and many are in debt, but as a class they have enough for their daily wants. Shiáhs in faith, they are Musalmáns in little more than name, their habits, feelings, and general mode of thought being Hindu. The ordinary form of salutation among themselves is the Shrávak phrase, *johár, johár,* and with others the ordinary Hindu form, *Rám, Rám*; although not knowing why, they keep the *Janmáshtami* and *Diváli* holidays, dressing in their best and feasting. Though according to their own accounts they believe in Shet Sayad of Pátan, the cultivators devote one-twentieth part of their income, and the labourers a rupee a year each, to Imámsháh's shrine at Pirana. Marrying among themselves, they form a separate body with, at Mánkuva near Bhuj, a headman, *patel,* who settles all disputes. He has also the power of fining and excommunicating any one who breaks caste rules. His sanction is also necessary for widow marriage, any widow marrying without his consent being excommunicated. Murder and adultery are punished by excommunication, the offender being allowed to rejoin on paying a fine. They do not associate with Musalmáns, eat no flesh, do not circumcise, say no five daily prayers, and do not keep the Ramzán fast."(1)

The tendency nowadays with Momnás is not to be called Musalmáns even in name. They style themselves Leva Pátidárs or Leva Kanbis, and except for a few tenets of their religion, which are Muhammadan, are in all respects Hindus. They claim descent from Leva Kanbis, and state that their ancestors were converted at Pátan by a Sayad who met

(1) Bombay Gazetteer, Vol. V, pages 90-91.

them there, and by taking them to the Ganges and bringing them back in a trice, induced them to become Musalmáns. Many of late have reverted to Hinduism by adopting the tenets of the Swáminaráyan sect; and though they form an endogamous division, they dine with the other Momnás and have departed little from the customs and practices of the Momnás proper, except from such as are opposed to their new faith. They admit Momnás proper into their division, the condition being to accept the Swáminaráyan creed.

The rules regulating the restrictions on intermarriage are the same as those among Leva Kanbis. Polygamy is permissible, but polyandry is unknown.

The marriage ceremonies of Momna Kanbis differ in some particulars from those observed by Levás. They do not erect the *chori* or marriage altar or kindle the sacrificial fire. The essential ceremony amongst them is the *Duva,* in which the bride and bridegroom are seated in front of a low wooden stool on which three lights are kept burning. It is alleged that these three lights represent the Hindu Trinity, Brahma, Vishnu and Mahesh. The hands of the pair are then joined by the *Mukhi* or headman of the caste, who is in charge of the caste *Khána* (place of worship), and he recites the *Duva.* Other ceremonies such as drawing up the marriage deed, *mándva* or erection of the marriage booth, and the like, are similar to those performed by Leva Kanbis.

The marriage of widows is permitted. A widow cannot marry a brother of her deceased husband or a member of his section. The parents of the widow's intended husband have to give about four maunds of *kichri* (mixture of rice grains and spilt pulse) and three maunds of *ghi* to her parents, which is intended for feasting the marriage party. The same ceremony is gone through as in the case of a first marriage, the essential portion being the *Duva.*

Divorce is permitted at the instance of a husband only. A wife cannot obtain a divorce at her own will. Divorced women are allowed to remarry.

Momnás profess a religion which is neither strictly Hindu nor Musalmán, though they are very particular about being called Hindus, and object to being called Momnás, as in Gujarát those who go by the name Momna are pure Musalmáns following Musalmán customs and ceremonies. They call their religion *Sat panth* or the True Path, while it is popularly known as *Khána* or *Pirana panth.* Their place of worship is called *Khána*, though they prefer it to be called *Dharmashála*. There is a *pát* or low wooden stool in the *Khána*, on which on certain occasions a *ghat* (water jar) is placed. The Momnás call this *pát* the *pát* of Brahma. From the *ghat* the devotees often sip water made holy by the earth of Pirána. Their ceremonies are conducted by the *Mukhis* or headmen of the caste, the tendency of late being not to employ Bráhmans as far as possible.

Momnás bury their dead. A funeral feast is given to the castemen on the third or any other convenient day after death. Every year in the month of *Bhádrapad* on the day corresponding to the day of death, a preparation of *ghi*, flour and sugar is taken to the place of worship and distributed to children and other persons who may be present.

Like other Kanbis, Momnás are strict vegetarians. They do not eat with Musalmáns. Rajputs, Darjis, Lohárs, Valands, etc., will eat food cooked by Momnás.

UDA KANBIS are a division once part of the Levás. They are followers of a Bhagat named Uda. They are peculiarly exclusive in their habits and would not drink from a brass or copper pot touched even by a Bráhman. They are generally Kabir Panthis.[1]

KANCHGARS, numbering about 198 (1901), including 100 males and 98 females, are found chiefly in Kanara. Their surnames, which they take from places in Goa, and the fact that the shrine of their family god Kásárpál is also in Goa, seem to show that they originally belonged to that locality. They make vessels of copper and brass and cast articles in brass, copper and bell metal. Girls are married before they come of age. Widow marriage is forbidden. Boys are girt with the sacred thread between ten and twelve. Their priests are Havik Bráhmans. In ceremonies and customs they follow Gudigars.

KANDHI.—A sub-division of Telis.

KAN DIVAR.—A synonym for Bainu Divar.

KANDOI.—A synonym for Halvái.

KANDOLIA.—A sub-division of Bráhmans.

KANE.—A synonym for Pál Kolháti.

KANGAR.—A sub-division of Dhangars.

KANHERJIN.—A sub-division of Vanjáris.

---

(1) Baroda Census Report, 1901, Part I, p. 468.

KANJARIS, numbering 6[1] (1901), including 3 males and 3 females, are found chiefly in Poona, Sátára and Belgaum. Their origin is obscure, but some accounts assign them Gujaráti as their home language, and it is probable that they have been recruited in many directions. They are a wandering tribe of beggars, and in Sátára are notorious thieves. They also make and sell brushes or *kunchás* used by weavers in cleaning wool. They have two divisions (1) Kuncha Bándhanáre and (2) Jat Log, who neither eat together nor intermarry. Marriages are prohibited between members having the same surname. Marriage is infant as well as adult. The remarriage of widows is permitted. Divorce is not allowed. The chief objects of worship of Kanjáris are Mariái and Musalmán Pirs. They declare that they are neither Hindus nor Musalmáns. They have neither religious teachers nor priests. The married dead are burnt and the unmarried buried. For the propitiation of deceased ancestors they perform *pitar*, that is, they feed castemen on the anniversary of the death. Kanjáris eat fish and the flesh of goats and fowls and drink liquor. They eat food cooked by Maráthás, Kolis, Dhangars, Thákurs and Musalmáns, but not by Márwáris, Telis, Mahárs and Mángs. None except Mahárs and Mángs will eat food cooked by them.

MUSALMAN KANJARIS, numbering 10 (1901), including 7 males and 3 females, are found in Ahmednagar, Sholápur, Dhárwár, Bijápur and Belgaum. Many must have returned themselves simply as Musalmán. They appear to be a quite distinct community from their Hindu namesakes, making their living by rearing and selling poultry. They are supposed by some to be converts from the Od or Párdhi tribes and by others representatives of the Hindu Kanjár tribe which is now extinct. Except that they say that they are Sunnis of the Hanafi school and ask the Kázi to register their marriages, they are almost Hindu in religion, worshipping and offering vows to Hindu gods and keeping Hindu festivals. They marry only among themselves and form an organised society with a headman of their own, who, with the concurrence of the majority, can fine any one who breaks their caste rules. They hold a low position among Musalmáns.

KANKALIA.—A sub-division of Bháts.

KANKAVA.—A sub-division of Dhors.

KANKORIA.—A sub-division of Vághris.

KANNAD.—A synonym for Kánade.

(1) The census figures are clearly incorrect, many having apparently returned their original caste names.

Kanjari woman.

KANOJIA.—A sub-division of Bháts

KANPHATE.—A synonym for Jogi.

KANSAR.—A synonym for Kásár.

KANSARAS or Coppersmiths, from *kánsu* bell-metal, numbering about 15,554 (1901), including 8,230 males and 7,324 females, are found in most large towns in Gujarát, Káthiáwár and Cutch. They state that their original home was Pávágad, twenty-nine miles east of Baroda. According to their story, there lived five brothers at Pávágad who were great devotees of Kálka Máta and worshipped her by beating bell-metal cymbals. The goddess was so pleased with their devotion that she told them to make a living by beating metal. From beating brass they advanced to making brass, copper and bell-metal vessels. Name and origin.

In appearance, dress and language Kansárás resemble Vániás and Kanbis.

Kánsárás have four endogamous divisions of a territorial type: Divisions.

Chámpáneris,	Sihorás,
Márus,	Visnagrás,

who neither eat together nor intermarry. Their surnames are:

Bagáya.	Bhatti.	Kársakariya.	Solanki.
Bármeya.	Gohel.	Parmár.	

Marriages are not allowed between near relations. Except among Visnagrás, widows are not allowed to marry, the widow sometimes marrying her husband's younger brother. Divorce is only allowed in south Gujarát.

Kansárás are Hindus of the Rámánandi, Shaiva and Vallabháchárya sects. Their family goddess is Kálka Máta, who is held in high reverence by followers of all the sects. They worship all Hindu gods and goddesses, keep the ordinary fasts and feasts, and visit the usual places of local pilgrimage, chiefly the shrines of Ambáji, Bahucharáji and Kálka. Their great holiday is the bright ninth of *Aso* (October), on which they perform a sacrifice and, at midnight, dance and leap, holding a wreath of *karena* or oleander flowers in one hand and a lighted torch in the other. One of the revellers, inspired by the goddess, professes to cut off his tongue with a sword. They have not much faith in witchcraft, exorcism and omens. Their priests are Audich, Meváda, Shrigaud and Shrimáli Bráhmans. Religion.

Except that some Cutch Kansárás, on the sixth day after the birth of a child, paint part of the wall of the lying-in room red, light Ceremonies.

a lamp fed with clarified butter near the red mark, dress the child in a necklace of false pearls and make it bow to the painted wall, the birth ceremonies of Kansárás do not differ from those of Kanbis. Except that in parts of Central Gujarát on the marriage day the bride-groom, when he goes to the bride's house, holds a dagger, Kansára marriage ceremonies do not differ from those of Kanbis. A pregnancy ceremony is performed during the seventh month after a woman's first conception. In Cutch some Kansárás do not bind a bracelet or *rákhdi* to the pregnant woman's arm ; in Central Gujarát, while passing from her father's to her husband's house, the woman, holding a cocoanut in her hands, walks with her brother along the road underneath a canopy formed by a piece of cloth held at the four corners by four female relations. The brother holds up the cocoanut in his sister's hands. With these differences, the pregnancy ceremonies are the same as those performed by Kanbis. Except that in Central Gujarát a knife is laid near the corpse when it is tied to the bier, that the four male relations bathe before taking the corpse out of the house, that if the deceased dies without a son his sister's son walks in front and holds in his hand a pot containing live charcoal, and when the party reach the burning ground, lights the pile, and that sweet balls are thrown to dogs, the Kansára funeral is like a Kanbi funeral.

Occupation. The hereditary occupation of Kansárás is making vessels of copper and brass. Those who work in particular metals are called by the name of the metal : copper-workers Támbághada, brass-workers Pitalghada, and gold-workers Sonára Kansárás. The last have already formed themselves into a distinct endogamous group in certain places by ceasing to marry with the parent caste, and the others may perhaps, in course of time, crystallize into similar endogamous occupational groups. In some places, notably in Sihor in Káthiáwár and in Kadi and Visnagar in North Gujarát, where there are remarkably good workmen in brass and copper, the Kansárás, in addition to the ordinary household vessels, turn out delicately carved ornaments such as penholders, inkstands, betel boxes, idols, lamps and bells. Besides working in brass and copper, some Kansárás move about the town tinning plates and mending vessels.

Food. Kansárás are vegetarians except a few in Cutch who eat fish and goats' flesh, and drink liquor.

KANSARA SONI.—A sub-division of Sonis.

KAPDIS, numbering 909 (1901), including 478 males and 431 females, are found chiefly in Cutch and Pálanpur. They are a religious order leading a life of celibacy, and keep up their order by recruiting. Most disciples are Lohánás, but disciples may be taken from any Hindu caste except from the degraded classes. They are devotees of the temple of Ashapura Máta at Mádh about fifty miles north-east of Bhuj. They live by begging and on the income of the land attached to the temple.

KAPIL.—A sub-division of Bráhmans.
KAPOL.—A synonym for Kapil ; a sub-division of Vániás.
KAPOLA.—A synonym for Kapol.
KAPUR.—A sub-division of Khatris.
KAR.—A sub-division of Bhois.
KARAD.—A sub-division of Vániás.
KARADE.—A sub-division of Kolis.
KARAGIR.—A synonym for Nhávi.
KARALIA.—*See* under Minor Musalmán castes.
KARANJKAR.—A synonym for Jingar.
KARATIA.—A synonym for Darbhia.
KARBELIA.—A sub-division of Bráhmans.
KARBHOI.—A sub-division of Kachhis.
KARDE.—A sub-division of Holayás.
KARE.—A sub-division of Ganigs.

KARE VAKKALS, or black Vakkals, are found in the forest tracts and remote villages of Ankola *táluka* and a few in the forest tracts of Sirsi, Kárwár, Kumta, Honávar, Siddapur, and Yellápur *tálukas* of the Kanara district. They are styled *kare* or black, because they are darker than the other Vakkal castes. Name and origin.

They speak Kanarese like the Hálvakki Vakkals ; a few speak Konkani. The common names among men are, Kariya, Giriya, Shiva, Tipa, Venka, and Timma ; and among women Rámi, Gangi, Gubbi, Gopi, Dodakka, Sannakka, and Subbi. The men add *gauda* or headman to their names.

The caste is divided into several *balis* or exogamous sub-divisions of which the following is as complete a list as it has been found possible to secure :— Exogamous divisions

(1) Arashina bali	..	Arsina = turmeric. (*Curcuma longa.*)
(2) Chendi bali	..	Chendi = a tree. (*Cerbera odollam*).
(3) Honne bali	..	Honne = a tree. (*Pterocarpus marsupium*).

(4) Shetti bali	..	Shetti = a fish.
(5) Migan bali	..	Miga = a chital. (*Axis maculata*).
(6) Shire bali	..	Shire = a tree. (*Gynandropsis pentaphylla*).
(7) Vadkan bali	..	(Unknown).

The trees and animals giving their names to these divisions are treated with respect, and are never cut or injured in any way by the members of the division called after them. The *bali* is traced through males. It will be seen that with two exceptions these *balis* are also found among the Gám Vakkals.

The habits of the caste are settled. They have a social organization somewhat on the lines of the Hálvakki Vakkals though less elaborate, as the community is more dispersed and does not possess so much cohesion. They are distributed over twelve *shimes* or territorial divisions.

Each village has a headman called *grámgauda* or *budvant*, and each *shime* is under the control of a *shimegauda*. The village heads have only the power of fining up to a certain limit; but the *shime* headmen may impose unlimited fines, and outcaste or re-admit offenders as well as hear appeals against the decisions of the village headmen.

Ceremonies.

The ceremonies of Kare Vakkals do not differ materially from those of the Hálvakki Vakkals. Widow re-marriage and polygamy are allowed and practised; polyandry is unknown. Their chief objects of worship are Venkataráma of Tirupati, Jatga, Hulidev or the tiger-god, Karidev of Shiveguli in Ankola and the village mothers *ammas* or *shaktis*, to whom they offer blood sacrifices. They have a strong belief in ghosts, sooth-saying and witchcraft. They either burn or bury the dead.

They are husbandmen and field labourers and generally tenants, only a few holding land. Their form of tillage is the *kumri* or wood-ash tillage, and some of them still burn patches of forest land to rear crops of *rági* and vegetables.

Food.

The ordinary food of the Kare Vakkals is rice and *rági*, but they eat fish, fowls, sheep, goats, and wild animals such as pig and deer. They drink liquor, though the practice is nominally condemned.

KARHADA.—A sub-division of Bráhmans.

KARKHELIA.—A sub-division of Bráhmans.

KARNATAK.—A territorial name.

KAS.—A synonym for Halde Máli.

KASAB.—A synonym for Kasái.

KASAIS or Khátiks, numbering 8,860 (1901), including 4,500 males and 4,360 females, are found scattered in small numbers in every part of the Presidency, performing the work of butchers. In Ahmednagar district they belong to the Dhangar caste and eat but do not marry with Kunbis and Mális. In the Kanara district they claim to be descendants of the sun and to belong to the Káshyap and Kaundanya family stocks, and persons of the same stock do not intermarry. They appear to have been recruited from Dhangars, Maráthás and Kunbis who took to killing sheep and goats when the Musalmán incursion into the Deccan created a demand for such food. They perform birth, marriage and death ceremonies similar to those of the Kunbis. Polygamy is allowed and practised, but widow remarriage is forbidden among the Kasáis of the Kanara district. Name and origin.

They worship all Bráhmanic gods and keep all Hindu fasts and feasts. Their family gods are Devi of Tuljápur in the Nizám's country, and Khandoba of Jejuri in Poona. They keep the images of their gods in the house, and offer them sandal paste, flowers, and food on Mondays, and on full-moon and new-moon days. Their priests are local Bráhmans, who conduct their marriages. They have no religious teacher of their own and cannot tell to what sect they belong. The family goddess of the Kasáis of the Kanara district is Yellamma, whose shrine is at Kulburga in the Nizám's country, and their family priests are Havik Bráhmans, to whom they pay great respect. They go on pilgrimage to Dharamsthal in South Kanara and to Chandragutti in Mysore. Religion.

Formerly the business of Kasáis was confined to selling sheep and goats, the slaughtering work being done by Musalmáns. Now they act as butchers as well as meat-sellers, while a few are husbandmen and labourers. Their women, besides minding the house, grind corn and help their husbands in selling mutton, and the children take the animals to pasture outside of the town. Occupation.

They eat fish and the flesh of goats and sheep and drink liquor. Food

KASAR.—*See* Támbat or Kásar.

KASARE.—A sub-division of Mahárs.

KASBATI.—*See* under Minor Musalmán castes.

KASBINS, numbering 144 (1901) including 62 males and 82 females, are found in Thána, Belgaum, Bijápur, Kanara and Ratnágiri. They are low class courtezans without any training or accomplishment. They are generally recruited from women who have been divorced or deserted by their husbands and all married and unmarried women and widows who have left their relations and friends of their own accord and have chosen to live as prostitutes. Being recruited from many castes, it is doubtful whether the Census figures are at all accurate, for many Kasbins would return themselves as of the caste to which they formerly belonged. They generally belong to the lower classes. They do not eat together unless they happen to belong to the same caste. They do not go through any form of marriage or other ceremony like the dancing girls. They are not allowed to wear ankle bells or to sing, dance or sit in a public assembly.

KASHIKAPDI.—A synonym for Tirmáli.

KASHTI.—A synonym for Solesi.

KAST.—A sub-division of Bráhmans.

KASTH.—A synonym for Kást.

KATABU.—A synonym for Kiliket.

KATANI UPPAR.—A sub-division of Uppárs.

KATARIS, also known as Kharádis, are a small caste of wood carvers, found principally in Káthiáwár and parts of Gujarát. There are a few Kátáris found here and there in the Deccan, but they appear to be Marátha Kunbis following the occupation of wood carving.

MUSALMAN KATARIS, generally known by the name Kharadi, numbering 302 (1901), including 151 males and 151 females, are found chiefly in Gujarát and the Deccan. They form a large body at Ahmedábád and are said to be converts from the Hindu caste of the same name. In Surat and other places in Gujarát they seem to be a mixed class. They marry only among themselves and are Sunnis of the Hanafi school in religion. Their customs do not differ from those of ordinary Musalmáns.

KA-THAKUR.—A sub-division of Thákurs.

KATHAR.—A sub-division of Vánis.

Name and origin.

KATHIS,(1) numbering 21,601 (1901), including 11,182 males and 10,419 females, are almost entirely found in the *tálukás* of Jetpur, Chital, Jasdan and the surrounding villages in Káthiáwár. They date their origin from the times of the Mahábhárat or the Great War. The Pándavs, after having been beaten at the gaming board by the Kauravs. were pledged to remain in concealment for twelve years

(1) The materials for this article were supplied by Mr. K. G. Pandit, B.A., LLB.

on pain of forfeiting their estate should they be discovered during this period. After wandering for seven years they came to Gujarát and took refuge in the town of Virát, now called Dholka. Duryodhan, the head of the Kauravs, got scent of this and marched upon Virát with a large army. But he could not get into the walls of the town, much less discover the Pándavs. Karan, his minister, suggested the course of driving off the cattle of the ruler, which would bring out the true Rajputs as protectors of cattle. It was, however, considered disgraceful for a Rajput to stoop to cattle-lifting: so Karan struck his staff on the ground and produced a newly created man who was called *káth, i.e.*, stick, and who, in return for his carrying off the cattle, was to be granted immunity to commit theft, especially of cattle, in all future time. The Káthis claim to be the descendants of this *káth* and give this legend as a proof of their right to commit robbery. It is not difficult to understand this legend when it is borne in mind that the Káthis were a race of marauders whose profession was that of plunder and robbery as late as 1808, when the British Government put a stop to it in the interests of peace and prosperity. Another tradition current among the Káthis as to their origin is to the effect that they are a tribe of the solar race, and the offspring of the sun directly through Karan, the famous warrior of the Mahábhárat. They came to Thán from Pawar (between Sind and Cutch) and thence drove away the Bábriás, who, in their turn, captured Bábriávád. There is still a temple dedicated to the sun on the Mandwa hill at Thán, but strangely enough it is no longer visited by the Káthis as a sacred place.

History.

The true original Káthis are called Avartiás, while the descendants of Dhan Vála of Dhank, a Rajput who married the daughter of Umro Patgar a Káthi, are called Sakháyats and fall under three branches—(1) Vála, (2) Khumán and (3) Káchar—who are said to have been the three sons of Dhan Vála by the Káthi wife. Dhan Vála was of course put out of caste by the Vála Rajputs of Dhank and banished the territory. This took place about the year 1400 A.D. according to the Káthi tradition. Dhan led his Káthis back to Cutch from whence they had come. From Cutch, however, they were afterwards driven forth on account of quarrels with the ruling chief who was said to have dishonoured one of their women and whom they murdered, and were consequently banished by his successor. There was a pitched battle at Thán, in which the Káthis won. Finding the country quite good and agreeable grazing ground for their cattle, they settled there and built a temple in honour of the sun, who is an object of worship among the Káthis to this day and whose symbol is used on all their deeds. Vála the first son of Dhan occupied Jetpur. Khumán the second son took Chotilla, and Káchar settled at Mithiáli. Just about this time a wealthy merchant of Amreli, annoyed by the exactions and oppression of the officers of the Junágadh Nawáb, sought refuge at Chital. He offered the Káthis half of whatever portion of his property they could recover for him. The Káthis made a raid on Amreli and recovered the merchant's property, and then resolved to put him to death and keep it for themselves. They were dissuaded from this by one of their women, and not only gave the merchant back all his goods, but refused to take the share which he had promised them. They had their reward, for not only did the merchant settle at Chital, but others, attracted by the report of such generosity, established themselves there also. The neighbouring proprietors put themselves under the protection of the Káthis, and in A.D. 1760 the Nawáb of Junágadh ceded to them the important districts of Mendarda, Bhilka and Jetpur. The Káthis, finding that honesty was the best policy, gave up plunder and soon gained a name for good government.

It would appear that the description of Vála, Khumán and Káchar as the three sons of Dhan is inaccurate for two reasons, *viz.*, (1) the improbability that the number of Vála Káthis from one common ancestor, who was co-eval with 500 Vála Rajputs then alive, should have so far exceeded the latter that the proportion of Vála Káthis is now ten to one ; and (2) the names Khumán and Káchar have not persisted as names among Káthis, though it is a very common custom among Hindus to name a grandchild after the grandfather.(1)

It is possible that the Káthis entered Káthiáwár from Málwa and also from Multán in the Punjáb ; the Vála Káthis from Málwa and the Khumán and Kháchar Káthis from the Punjáb, and that their original residence in the twelfth century **B. C.** was in Asia Minor (Kurdistan). The features of the Káthis, their stature and their habits lead to a strong inference that they are of Scythian origin. In the Assyrian inscriptions there is a tribe described as Khatti. This corresponds to the Hittites of the Old Testament, and, according to Campbell, may refer to the Káthis. In the Assyrian wars appears the very significant name of Comain, who could bring into the field an army of 20,000 followers. The Khattis seem to have been

---

(1) Campbell's theory is probably correct, *viz.*, that some Káthis succeeded in getting themselves recognised as Rajputs and the rest did not—*vide* Bom. Gaz. Vol. IX, pt. I, p. 260.

fond of horses and of serving as mercenaries in internecine wars. The Khattis during subsequent wars towards the latter part of the twelfth century **B. C.** seem to have been defeated and driven eastwards, for we find them opposing Alexander the Great at Sangala. Arrian in describing them speaks of them as roving tribes. During the reign of Shálivâhan after 1169 A.D. Káthis appear as dwelling near the Aravali mountains. They must have lived in and about Málwa till about the fourteenth century, when it is likely they came to Cutch and from thence to Saurâshtra. From their own traditions it is easy to gather that the Bábriás and Ahirs preceded them. Among them the Válás came first and were followed by the Khumáns, the Kháchars coming last. The districts of Málwa near Rewa Kantha are still called Káti. The word Thân, also observable in Multán, leads to the conjecture of their having come through the Punjáb. The Bábriás serve as a connecting link between the Káthis and Ahirs, freely intermarrying with either.(1)

Divisions. In addition to the two divisions of the Káthis mentioned above, *viz.*, Avartia and Sakháyat, there is a third division recognized as Káthis. This consists of the Khawads of Jhálâwád, especially those round Anandpur, Paliád and Sejakpur. They intermarry with the Sakháyats and are fully entitled to Káthi status.

The Vála division of the Sakháyats has twenty sub-divisions. They are as follows :—

Bhojag.	Gige.	Karpada.	Vajmal.
Bhogra.	Govalia.	Kasturia.	Vala.
Chak.	Hudad.	Lalu.	Vikma.
Derva.	Jogia.	Rajdadia.	Waikha.
Far.	Kajra.	Vaja.	Wardad.

The Kháchars(2) have the following sub-divisions :—

Chomadia.	Hipa.	Kháchar.
Dadu.	Jebalia.	Khavás.
	Lomasaria.	

The sub-divisions found among Khumáns are :—

Chanda.	Jhammar.	Man.
Chandsur.	Khumán.	Motia.
Jogia.	Lumsar.	Manijani.
	Waland.	

(1) Abul Fazl, writing in A.D. 1590, says of the district of Sorath : there are many Káthis in this country whose caste is that of Ahir. *Ain-i-Akbari.*

(2) Kháchar may be a form of Khazar or Gujar and suggests a connection with the Gujar invasion of India in the sixth century A.D.

The Avartia Káthis have ninety-three sub-divisions, the chief of which are the following:—

Barad.
Basia.
Bhambla.
Boricha.
Chávda.
Dangar.
Dhadhal.
Jallu.
Jebalia.
Jhánjaria.
Jhilaria.
Katial.
Khakharia.
Kharak.
Lalu.
Maitra.
Makvána.
Málavia.
Manjharia.
Mosha.
Nata.
Padva.
Pálav.
Patgar.
Sindhav.
Turia.
Virda.
Wáchhada.
Wank.
Winchia.

Some of the above names obtain among the Bábriás and Ahirs, clearly showing the close relationship between the three tribes.

Some of the names of the sub-divisions are traceable to some brave ancestor, others to the place inhabited, *e.g.*, Lalu from Lalo and Jogia from Jogáji, and Jhilaria and Khakharia from the villages of those names. It will further be seen that some of the names in the different sub-divisions agree.

Marriage. The Sakháyats intermarry with the Avartiás or Babriás or Ahirs but never among themselves, even if the sub-divisions be different. A Káthi can marry his father's sister's or mother's brother's daughter but not his mother's sister's daughter. Two brothers can marry two sisters. The same man can marry two sisters simultaneously or one after the other. Polygamy is allowed. A Káthi, unless he is rich, has rarely more than one wife and her influence is considerable. Divorce is allowed with the sanction of the caste *panch*. A divorced woman can remarry. There is no fixed age limit to marriage though girls are rarely married before they attain puberty. This is probably the result of the tribe having been one of nomadic and predatory instincts with a record of past service as mercenaries. They often robbed the other tribes of their grown-up girls and lived with these as man and wife. A relic of this custom is still to be noticed in their marriage ceremonies for, when the bridegroom's party are about to enter the bride's village, the bride's party come out of the village and oppose the bridegroom's party with stones and brickbats, after which they are allowed admission.

The offer of marriage comes from the boy's side. The marriage ceremonies are of the standard type obtaining among tribes of similar standing in Káthiáwár. The officiating priests are Modh Bráhmans the family priests being Rájgors, the bards Chárans, and the personal attendants Gadhvis. Chárans and Gadhvis bear the same relation to a Káthi which Bháts and Khavásas bear to a Rajput.

The remarriage of widows is permitted. So long as the deceased husband's younger brother is alive his widow must remain with the latter as his wife even if she have children by the former, unless she takes a vow not to remarry for the rest of her life, in which case she is entitled to food and raiment. But if the deceased husband be a younger brother, the widow can marry outside the family. The ceremony consists in the distribution of molasses to the relatives of the pair who may be present and the presentation to the widow of clothes by the intended husband.

The tribe is governed by Hindu law. The partition between the brothers is always equal and consequently the big Káthi States have in the past been split up into petty estates. The Jetpur *táluka* alone has fourteen shareholders. Recently the British Government has recognized the principle of primogeniture, the cadets or *bhayats* being paid only *jiwani*. As regards *stridhan*, on a woman's death the whole of her moveable property goes to the nearest relative along with the children.

Káthis belong to the Hindu religion. Most of them are followers **Religion.** of the Shaiva sect, some are Vaishnavs and a few followers of the Swáminaráyan and Rámánuja sects. They worship by preference the sun. Each subdivision has a separate family deity such as Wáchhado, Chámunda, etc. In some families images of the original ancestors (*suro puro*) are installed and worshipped. Káthis observe all the Hindu fasts and feasts. Their priests are the Modh Bráhmans. Their *gurus* or religious teachers are the Atits.

The dead are burnt except infants who have not cut their teeth **Death.** and lepers who are buried. The corpse is laid with head to the north. The bones and ashes of the burnt are thrown into the village river or stream or the sea if near. Those who can afford it have them thrown into the Ganges. The *shráddha* is performed every year on the anniversary of the death.

Káthis believe their original occupation to be that of soldiers. Most of them are now tálukdárs or petty land-holders. Some are in service and some are day-labourers.

Káthis eat meat, fowl and fish. On no account is a deer killed or **Food.** eaten. The lapwing is held in high esteem, so much so that in *shráddhas* instead of throwing rice balls to be eaten by crows, the Káthis throw them to lapwings, who are supposed to be acceptable to the deceased. They drink liquor and opium extract. They eat food cooked by Khánts, Sagars, Ahirs, Bábriás, Bharváds, Hátis, Mahiás, Rajputs, Valandas, Khavásas and Atits who can eat with one another and with the Káthis.

KATHIARA.—*See* under Minor Musalmán Castes.

KATHIGOR.—A sub-division of Audich Bráhmans.

KATHIVALE.—A synonym for Mahár.

KATHKARI.—A synonym for Kátkari.

KATHODI.—A synonym for Kátkari.

KATHODIA.—A synonym for Kátkari.

Name and origin.

KATKARIS,(1) also known as Káthkaris, Káthodis and Káthodiás, numbering 75,710 (1901), including 37,317 males and 38,393 females, are found chiefly in that part of the Western Ghats, with the outlying spurs, that is found in the Thána and Kolába districts, in the States to the east and north-east of Surat, and along the base of the Sahyádris between the Poona and Násik roads. Of the above number 15 were shown as Musalmáns at the 1901 census, probably as a result of an error in handling the census returns. The term Kátkari seems to be derived from the Maráthi *kát* or *káth,* catechu, the thickened juice of the *khair* (Acacia catechu) tree, and *karne* to make, the whole meaning "makers of catechu", the original occupation of the tribe still pursued by some of their number. The term Káthodi is similarly derived from *káth* (catechu) and *vadi* (a cake), which would give the meaning "(sellers of) cakes of catechu". Káthodia is the Gujaráti form of Káthodi and is in use only in Gujarát.

The Kátkaris, who are probably of Bhil origin, are believed to have come from the north, and to have been originally settled in the Gujarát Athávisi, the present district of Surat. They have a division named Athávar to this day. According to their story, they are descended from the monkeys which the god Ráma took with him in his expedition against the demon-king Rávan of Ceylon. They say that when Ráma became victorious, he blessed the monkeys and made them human beings. From their appearance, customs and religion it would appear that they are an aboriginal tribe little influenced by Bráhmanism. Their peculiar dialect contains certain words common among the Bhils and their customs, to some extent, indicate a Bhil origin.

(1) Much of the information contained in this article was contributed by the Revd. A. Wilkie Brown.

Kátkari women were formerly said to carry off men of other castes. The youth's friends regarded him as an outcaste and he then joined the Kátkaris, living with one of their women.(1) The Kátharis are reported by Dr. Wilson to have similarly compelled strangers to join their community.(2) No relic of the custom has been traced, but in some parts of the Thána district members from higher castes such as Várlis, Kolis, Thákurs and Kunbis are still admitted into the tribe on their paying a sum of Rs. 5, which is spent in treating the tribesmen to liquor.

Formerly the Kátkaris chose their settlements in the forest to suit their convenience, selecting a spot that promised good hunting or tillage, and leaving it as convenience dictated. Even to the present day, an epidemic of sickness will induce the people of a *váda* to vacate it and settle elsewhere in the neighbourhood, following a practice common among the Bhils. Their dwellings are low thatched huts, built of *kárvi* and mud. The huts are square or rectangular.

Kátkaris, according to the *Bombay Gazetteer*, are much darker and slimmer than the other forest tribes. The Sons and some of the Dhors shave the face and head, and wear a very marked top-knot. But the northern cow-eating Kátkaris generally have long matted hair and wild beards. The women of both divisions are tall and slim, singularly dirty and unkempt. They are strong, healthy and hardy, and pass through child-birth with little trouble or pain. They are said, sometimes when at work in the fields during the rains, to retire behind a rice bank, and give birth to a child, and, after washing it in cold water, to put it under a teak-leaf rain-shade and go back to their work. The Kátkari children can always be known by their gaunt pinched look.

The chief peculiarity of the dress of Kátkari women is the number of bead necklaces they wear, and the glass and metal bangles which cover almost the whole of the forearm. They wear a robe tightly wound round the waist and drawn up between the thighs. One end is thrown loosely over the shoulder, and for the rest, body and limbs are bare. Bodices are worn only on great occasions. They also wear long hanging ear-rings in both the top and bottom of the ear. The unmarried women may wear coloured necklaces, but no toe-rings. The married women wear black necklaces along with the coloured ones, and toe-rings.

(1) Trans. Bom. Geog. Soc., Vol. I, 329.

(2) Dr. Wilson's Aboriginal Tribes, p. 20.

The men generally wear a very coarse waist cloth and a waist belt of leather, or plaited grass or coloured cord, to which is attached their tobacco pouch and a wooden support to carry their *koita* or sickle. Sometimes they wear bangles on the wrist or upper arm.

The girls of the Kátkaris are tattooed about the age of six. The operation is generally performed by professional tattooers from the Deccan. On the forehead is tattooed a representation of *tulsi* or sweet basil plant, on the forearm, Krishna's mark in the form of a milkmaid, on the temples a trident, and on the cheeks and chin a *til* mole.

In intercourse with other castes the Kátkaris speak Maráthi rather clipped and mutilated. Among themselves they use a patois which, on examination, proves to be a slightly disguised Maráthi with many Gujaráti and Hindustáni words. A tendency is noticeable to get rid of the personal, not the tense, inflections in verbs. Thus *kothe gelás* becomes *kusigel.* There are some peculiar words in use, such as *suna* a dog, *hiru* a snake, *narak* a bear, *akti* fire, and *vádis* a wife. The names in common use among men are Dhaku, Chimya, Pandu and Pavalya ; and among women, Bhagvathi, Chimi and Tulsi. There is no special superstition about the naming of children. Indeed there is often a pleasing directness in this matter, as when a peculiarly dark baby is called Kálya, or one with a protruding navel is called Bendya. In such cases another name is given for use on occasions of ceremony. They have a headman called Naik whom they consult on all occasions and obey.

Endogamous divisions.

There are five endogamous divisions of Kátkaris :—

1. Athávar.
2. Dhed or Dhor.
3. Sidhi.
4. Son or Marátha.
5. Varap.

The Son or Marátha Kátkaris do not eat cow's flesh, and are allowed to draw water at the village well and to enter Kunbis' houses and temples. The Dhors eat cow's flesh, and, like the Mahárs, are held to be impure. Athávars are looked down on as inferior by the Son Kátkaris. Sidhis are doubtless African immigrants in origin. Varaps or reverts may have been either Christian or Musalmán. Dhors or Dheds are beef-eaters and therefore the lowest of the tribe, socially. Son and Dhor divisions are found also among the Kolis. Dhor is commonly supposed to mean cattle-eating, and Son either golden, red (Sanskirt *shon*), or foreign (Dravidian *son* or *sonag*).(1) The Son

(1) Caldwell, 2, 569.

Kátkaris declare that at one time there was no such division as the Dhor Kátkaris, but that many generations ago, under stress of famine, some of the tribe took to feeding on the carcasses of cattle, and since that time the two sections have been distinct. There is some probability in this explanation, as in many places, notably in the Kolába district, the customs of both sections are identical. But it is equally possible that the Son division arose from abandoning the primitive habit of feeding on beef, with a view to rise in the social scale.

The exogamous divisions of the tribe are represented by surnames. They are as follows :— Exogamous divisions.

Ahir.	Gángoda.	Misál.	Selár.
Bágle.	Gharyáre.	Mora.	Suvar.
Baraph.	Gotarna.	Mukane.	Vághmáre.
Bhoi.	Hilam.	Murkhute.	Valne.
Chaván.	Jáma.	Pátkar.	Valvi.
Dhárkar.	Kámdi.	Pavár.	Várdi.
Diva.	Khutale.	Saura.	Vatáse.
Gáikvád.	Máje.	Savad.	Wágh.

It is commonly alleged that many of the above names such as More, Vághmáre, ect., are totemistic in origin, though reverence for the totem is no longer observable. Thus, the headman of the Kátkari *váda* of Wawarla, near Karjat in the Kolába district, Dhákumarya Vághmáre, of name, had a son who fell ill. He went to a Thákur who was supposed to have some skill as a doctor, and asked for medicine. The Thákur prescribed a draught of water and earth on which a tiger had micturated. Traces of a tiger's presence were found and the required earth carefully collected. The medicine was prepared and given to the boy, who rapidly came out in eruptions like large blisters. The father hastened to the Thákur, who was for a moment nonplussed. Then an idea occured to him and he asked Dháku what his surname was. "Vághmáre," was the reply. "That explains it," said the Thákur. "Since your name is Vághmáre, we should not have used the tiger in your son's case."

Dhors have no restriction on intermarriage among different families. But amongst Sons marriage is prohibited between members bearing the same surname. First cousins are not allowed to marry, though second cousins may. Marriage with a wife's younger sister is allowed. Two brothers are allowed to marry two sisters. Girls are generally married between twelve and fifteen and boys between twelve and twenty-five. Sexual license before marriage is not recognised. Should a girl become pregnant before marriage, the fault would be condoned by marriage, but the ceremony would be performed with widow remarriage rites. Polygamy is permitted when the first wife is barren. Sometimes when a man becomes well-to-do and owns a number of cattle, he takes a second wife as an additional helper. In this case it is looked upon rather as a mark of a man of substance. Polyandry is unknown.

Birth ceremonies.

Before the birth of a child a midwife is called in, and after the birth she stays for five days washing the child and the mother twice a day. Among the Dhors, if the child is a girl, the midwife stays for four days only. They employ no Bráhman to draw up a horoscope or to name the child. Among Sons the name is given on the fifth day after birth by some elderly relation, when caste fellows and friends are treated to liquor and a dance. Among Dhors, no limit is set to the number of days within which a child should be named, and the name is chosen not by some elderly relation, but by a medium into whose body a spirit, *dev*, has entered. They wait till some one is possessed, and then go and ask him to name their child. They have not generally to wait long, as spirit possession is common among Kátkaris. In Gujarát, on the sixth day after a birth, the goddess Chathi is worshipped, and some rice figures of the goddess are set on the ground with a lamp near them. The father or mother names the child and the guests are fed on thick cakes and liquor.

Marriage ceremonies.

In Kolába, the marriage ceremonies of both the Son and Dhor Kátkaris are identical. In Thána, they greatly differ. The offer of marriage is made by the boy's father, who has to pay a *dej* or bride-price of Rs. 5 to the girl's father. A day before the marriage a booth is erected at the houses of both the boy and the girl, one of the posts of which must be of the *umbar* (Ficus glomerata) tree. To this post are tied leaves of the *jámbhul* (Eugenia jambolana) and mango trees. In Thána, among Sons, the boy and girl are rubbed with turmeric at their houses on the day before the marriage. On the marriage day the boy goes to the girl's house wearing a white turban and waistcloth, and covered by a red and white sheet. His father presents the girl with a red bodice and green robe, and she retires and dresses in her new clothes. On returning, she takes one of two garlands prepared by her parents and places it round the bridegroom's neck, and he in turn throws the other round her neck. They are then made to stand facing each other, and a cloth is held between them. The marriage is performed by a Kátkari, who from his virtuous life has been chosen by the tribe to be the marriage priest or Gotarni. On one side of the cloth sits the Gotarni and on the other side sit four elders. To each of the elders the boy's father gives a copper coin, rice, betelnut and leaves, and they sit with these gifts in their hands. The Gotarni, seated on a blanket spread on the ground, sprinkles rice in lines and cross lines, and, in the middle of the rice, places the copper coin. He then, followed by the four elders, stirs the rice with his closed fist in which he holds the betelnut and copper coin. At last he opens his hand, leaving the betelnut and coins lying among the rice on the blanket. The other four elders do the same. The cloth is then pulled aside, and the Gotarni, advancing, ties the hem of the bridegroom's sheet to the hem of the bride's robe, and together they walk five times round the marriage hall. Meanwhile a low wooden stool is set near the rice on the blanket, and is sprinkled with lines of rice by the Gotarni. When the bride and bridegroom are seated on the stool, their friends seize their heads and knock them together over the rice. They then feed one another with cooked rice, and the girl gets a new name, by which she is called by her husband and her people. The character of the feast depends on the means of the parents. They are not bound to feast the whole tribe, and, for the most part, each guest brings his own bread and eats it with the rest, the host providing fermented palm juice. After drinking, the guests as a mark of joy go outside and strike their sticks into the family dust heap. This ends the marriage, and after some music, a dinner is given to the guests. The bridegroom passes that night with the bride, but, on the first or second day after, both go to the bridegroom's house accompanied by the Gotarni, and by their relations and friends. When they reach the bridegroom's house, the hems of their garments are tied and they are seated on a low wooden stool. In front of this stool twenty-two small heaps of rice are set in a row, and the bride touches the heaps, one after another, as fast as she can, with her thumb and left big toe, uttering her husband's name every time she touches them until she is out of breath. Next day they take off their garlands and wash away the turmeric, but for four days more they keep the house. On the fifth, balls of rice flour and molasses are made and laid in a plate, and the bride, bearing this plate on her head and followed by her husband, goes to her parents' house and presents the balls to them. With this the marriage ceremonies end.

Dhor Kátkaris celebrate their marriages in any of the fair weather months except *Paush*. Among them the bridegroom is rubbed with turmeric the day before the marriage. On the marriage day, the bridegroom comes from his parent's house, and sits a little way from the marriage booth at the bride's house. The bride, with some elderly female relation, comes out, and, following the elderly woman, walks five times round the bridegroom. Then passing a piece of cloth round his neck and holding the two ends in her hands, she gently draws him towards her, saying 'Up, bridegroom, and come into the marriage hall.' In the marriage hall the guests are met, and, when the bride and bridegroom come in, a cloth is stretched between them, each holding two of the corners. The bridegroom says to the bride, *urel ani purel,* 'There is enough and to spare', and throws his end to the bride. She replies *náhin urel ani nahin purel,* 'There is not enough and to spare', and throws it back to him. This they repeat five times and then dress each other in new clothes, brought by the bridegroom, a speckled red sheet for himself and a robe and a red bodice for the bride. After this they are seated on a blanket on which five elders have been sitting, one at each corner and one in the middle, each holding in his hand a copper coin, betelnut and leaves, and a few grains of rice given by the bridegroom's father. Before the bride and bridegroom sit down the five elders empty the contents of their hands in the middle of the blanket, and on this heap of betelnuts and rice the bride and bridegroom are seated. Then the bride and bridegroom cover one another's heads with garlands, and with the distribution of liquor, the ceremony comes to an end. The bridegroom and the guests spend the night at the bride's house, and next morning the bridegroom leaves for his parents's house. After weeping on her parents' neck, the bride, when the hem of her robe has been tied to the hem of the bridegroom's sheet, starts for her new home, drawing the bridegroom after her. On the third day both come back to the bride's house, and the bride washes the bridegroom, anointing his head with cocoanut oil and combing his hair. They stay three or four days with her parents, and then leave for their home.

The marriage ceremonies of the Kolába Kátkaris are as follows:—

The elders of the bridegroom's village take the boy to another Kátkari hamlet. They call on the *Náik* and ask him if there is any marriageable girl there. The *Náik* asks who the boy is. He is produced and the party is invited to spend the night there. In the evening the villagers are summoned and are informed of the object of the visit. The *Náik* invites any one who has a girl to give in marriage to speak. The father of a possible bride asks who that boy is. Again he is produced, and if he finds favour and there is no objection otherwise, the parent or guardian of the girl says so and agrees to give her in marriage. The girl is brought and shown to the strangers. If she finds favour, the boy's father distributes *pánsupári*, which he has brought with him for the purpose. This ceremony being over, the bride's party ask for the usual betrothal money—generally one rupee, though in the case of the bridegroom's father being comparatively well-off, a larger sum might be given. The father of the bride is also asked to give his contribution to the betrothal money, which amounts to four annas as a rule for every rupee contributed by the bridegroom's father. The bride's father then asks if the wedding is to take place at once or the following year. If it is to be deferred, they proceed to the ceremony of tying on the marriage necklace, for which a further contribution of two rupees is levied on the bridegroom's father. The visitors remain as guests for the following day, and the ceremony of fastening the necklace takes place in the evening. The necklace is put into the boy's hands who fastens it on the girl's neck in the presence of the *panch*. The day after the bridegroom's party return home.

If the wedding is to take place without delay, after the ceremony just described is over, the boy's father fixes the wedding day in consultation with the *panch*. The Kátkaris do not consult Bráhmans in these questions. Any one present who has a reputation for special knowledge of days and seasons may be consulted. The months for weddings are *Márgashirsha*, *Mágha*, *Vaishakh* and *Shimga*. Two days before the wedding day, the boy's father sends a messenger to the girl's parents to remind them and to tell them to put on the *halad* or turmeric powder. Afterwards he takes five mango leaves and places them in a row. On each leaf he places a little turmeric powder, red powder, red lead and lampblack. These leaves he places in some spot outside the village, thereby propitiating the *vansh* or typical five ancestors of the tribe, whom it is the custom of most primitive tribes to worship.

Then five girls are selected to apply the turmeric powder to the bridegroom, which they proceed to do, reserving half the quantity, which is sent with half a maund of rice, some salt and spices to the bride, who must with her own hands take the gift from the messengers. Next day the bridegroom's party sets out for the wedding, accompanied by musicians. On leaving the village a cocoanut is broken, and on reaching the bride's village, the bridegroom alights at the house of the headman or *Náik*. The bride's maternal aunt comes there with a present and he gives her a small sum of money, from two to four annas. She accompanies him to the marriage pandal in front of the bride's dwelling, whither he is carried on some one's shoulder. The bride's brother is seated on the top of the pandal and, as the bridegroom is about to enter, he sprinkles him with water. The bridegroom gives him a small present of money, generally two pice, and enters. The bride is then brought out into the pandal and the couple are made to sit together.

Preparations are then made for bathing. The bride is told to place her hand on the bridegroom's head. She then takes off her outer garments, and the two are made to stand opposite each other. The bridegroom places his left hand on the bride's head, and as they stand in this position, five girls pour water over them. When the bathing is over, a cloth is held between them, and a new robe is put in the bridegroom's hand. He throws it to the bride and says, "Take it". She throws it back to him and says it is not enough. Again he throws it to her, saying, "It is very big : there is enough and to spare".

The bride then goes into the house, puts on the robe and comes out to sit beside the bridegroom. Then five married women sit down in front of them. In their hands they hold a betelnut, a pice, and some rice, with which they make a circle on the ground. On this a brass tray is placed and rubbed backwards and forwards until the rice, pice and betelnuts are mixed up, and the shape of the figure is gone. The bride and bridegroom are then told to grasp their great toes. The five men lift them up in this position and deposit them on the rice. The bridemaids place the brass tray behind the bride. The men then throw rice on the heads of the couple and what is left is thrown into the tray. Of the money, three pice are given to the bride and two pice to the bridegroom. When this is done the marriage ceremony is complete.

Following on this, however, the bridegroom has to fasten a necklace of black beads on the bride's neck. Two balls of rice are then made up, and one is given to each. The bridegroom puts his in his mouth, takes it out again immediately, and gives it to the bride to eat. She gives her ball of rice to him, which he eats. The pair then put some more turmeric powder on each other's faces, and have then to repeat each other's names, always a source of amusement owing to the reluctance of the bride to pronounce her husband's name in public.

Next day the married couple go to the bridegroom's village, escorted by a party of musicians. The headman comes out to meet them, ties a little money, a betelnut and some rice in a corner of the husband's cloth, and again tying this to a corner of the bride's robe, accompanies them round the village, where they visit each house in turn.

The day after, the bridegroom bathes the bride, and washes off the turmeric powder. Before entering the house again, the bridegroom's sister puts a bar across the door, and they have to remain without. He asks his sister why she is keeping him there. She replies " You must give your daughter to my son ". The bridegroom says to the bride, " She asks for our daughter. Shall we give her ? " The bride says, " Yes ". The bridegroom tells his sister that they agree to give their daughter to her son, and then, withdrawing the bar, she lets them in.

Afterwards they take off the bride and bridegroom's *báshings* or marriage coronets and fasten them on the bridegroom's head back and front. The headman goes out of the village and the bride and bridegroom following him, ask, " Whither are you going ". He replies, " To Benares ". They beg him not to go and return home. They all come back. The *báshings* are taken from the bridegroom and placed in the bride's hands. He then lifts her up and carries her to the house. For five days the couple remain at home. On the sixth day they prepare balls of rice flour which they cook. Of these the bride breaks one, which they share. The remainder are sent to the bride's parents, who distribute them one to each household. This terminates the marriage ceremonies.

The remarriage of widows is permitted. A widow cannot marry her mother's sister's or mother's brother's son or a member of her late husband's section. A widow remarriage can be celebrated on any day. The widow's intended husband presents her with a robe and bodice and glass bangles, and her father with Rs. 2 or 3, if he can afford it. Next, he ties a *mithla* (a neck ornament) round the widow's neck, and the widow puts a turban over his head, which completes the ceremony. In some places, the ceremony consists simply in holding a meeting of the tribesmen at night and in treating them to liquor; while in others, joining the hands of the couple is sufficient to validate the marriage.

Should a bachelor desire to marry a widow, he has first to marry a *rui* bush (Calotropis gigantea). This ceremony consists in the bachelor putting a marriage coronet on his head and going round the bush five times. As he walks, he passes a cotton thread round the tree. In some places, bachelors are allowed to marry widows without any ceremony.

Divorce is allowed with the permission of the headman of the tribe, if the husband and wife do not agree, if the husband marries another woman or abandons his wife in favour of another, or if the wife is unchaste. Divorce is known by the name of *dáva* or *samjut* and is effected in the following manner :—The first husband with some arbitrators goes and sits at the door of the second husband. A consultation is held between them and the arbitrators of the second husband and the *dáva* is settled by a payment of Rs. 5 by the second husband to the first. If the second husband is unable to pay the amount in cash, he gives a buffalo, a bullock or some other thing in exchange. The remaining sum is spent on drink. The second husband has to drink a portion of the liquor drunk by the first. The latter then takes off the string of glass beads round the neck of the divorced wife, and the former ties a new one in its place. Next, the first husband breaks a straw in two parts, which completes the divorce. In some places, the divorce is effected by breaking an earthen pot and performing funeral rites in the name of the divorced wife,. while in others, no ceremony of any sort is observed. Wives who have been divorced may marry again by the widow re-marriage form. Adultery is usually compounded by the payment of a fine of from five to ten rupees. The parents of the woman also may be called upon to pay a fine if she is still an inmate of their house. If the person with whom the offence is committed belong to a lower caste, the woman is excommunicated.

Religion.

The religion of the Kátkaris, so far as they have any, is animism. They have no sacred books, neither have they any spiritual guides. They do not appear to say any prayers themselves, or to employ others to say prayers for them. Their chief object of worship is the tiger-god, who is supposed to look with peculiar favour upon them and very seldom harms them, and they are disinclined to shoot him. His image is generally set up in the forest or on the boundary of the village. But in parts, as in Karjat, where forests and tigers are scarce, there are many Kátkari hamlets without a tiger-god. What worship there is among the Kátkaris is paid to the Kunbi village god, *gámdev*, and to such minor gods as Máolya, Mhasha, Vetál, Jarimari and Hirva. Red lead, cocoanuts and fowls are offered to these gods and to evil spirits, which are greatly dreaded. In Gujarát, Bhildev is worshipped. In a Dhor Kátkari's house there may sometimes be seen devil gods whom they call *Cheda*. This is the soul of a dead relation which has become a spirit, *bhut*, capable of entering the bodies of men. It is this close connection with, and power over, spirits that makes the Kátkari so dreaded by the Kunbi. The latter credits him with the power of the evil eye, and with being able by means of his spirits to compass the death of his enemies. Among the Dhors the only holidays are *Shimga* and *Diváli*, to which the Sons add the fifteenth of *Bhádrapad* when they perform ceremonies in honour of the deceased.

Death ceremonies.

Among Kátkaris, when a person dies of cholera, he is buried until the outbreak of cholera is over, when the body is dug up and burnt. In the same way, in some parts of Kolába, if a death takes place in wet weather, the corpse is buried for a time between two hurdles and is afterwards dug up and burnt. The men who have to carry out the exhumation are plied with drink and have their nostrils stuffed with onions to enable them to carry out the task. In other cases the dead are burnt at once. If the death happens at night, the funeral is put off till the next day. But the corpse has to be watched all night, and to cheer the watchers special music is played. On the upper surface of a common brass plate a lump of wax is stuck, and, in the wax, a thin stick about nine inches long. When the finger and thumb are passed down this stick, it vibrates with a weird drone or hum. To this accompaniment the mourners chant all night long, crouching round a fire outside the house. When the time comes to prepare the body, it is washed with warm water mixed with turmeric. The waistcord and loincloth are thrown away and new clothes put on. If they can afford it, a piece of new cloth is wound round the head and another cloth is laid under and drawn over the body. The cloth is sprinkled over with red and sweet-scented powder and a pillow of rice is laid under the head. About half way to the burning ground, the pall-bearers stop and lower the bier, while the chief mourner hides a copper coin under a stone. At the burning ground the corpse is laid on the pile. A hole is torn in the face cloth, some rice and a piece of silver or copper are laid in the mouth, and the pile is lighted at both ends. While it burns the chief mourner walks round it five times with an earthen water jar in his hand. Then, knocking a hole in the jar, he sprinkles the pyre and dashes the jar to pieces on the ground. When the burning is over the Dhors leave the bones and embers as they are; but the Sons gather them into a heap, quench the embers, and lay a stone over them. On the twelfth day after the death the Sons of Karjat cook a hen with split pulse and some rice. The hen and pulse are divided into two equal parts, and one-half left in the house and the other half, with the whole of the rice, taken by the chief mourner to the stone under which the copper coin was left. He lays part of the rice and half of the hen and pulse on the stone, and the rest of the food he sets on the stone that covers the dead man's ashes. Over this stone he builds a little hut to shade the deceased's resting place. On his return home, he divides the share of victuals that was left in the house among some fasting children, and entertains his neighbours, friends and relations with rice and liquor.

In Gujarát, on the third day, the mourners visit the burning ground and gather the ashes, throw a little into the village, and, on the top of the ash-heap, place some cooked rice. Then, in front of them, in the deceased's name, the chief mourner feeds young children on cooked rice.

Occupation

Kátkari children are great plunderers of birds' nests and very sharp in finding them. The men seldom commit deeds of violence, but are notorious for constant petty thefts. Many of them, both men and women, have found permanent employment in Bhiwandi as rice cleaners, and numbers, both in Bhiwandi and Karjat, have two or three months' steady work a year as field labourers. Some of them still make *káth* or catechu, the thickened juice of the *khair* (Acacia catechu). A few partly support themselves by tillage. They never take land on a regular lease or grow rice. They till uplands, *varkas*, either waste or taken from the Government holders, or on agreement to share the produce. They burn brushwood, *ráb*, on the plot of ground and use the hoe, but never the plough. When their supply of grain is finished, they gather and sell firewood and wild honey, and, with their bows and arrows, kill small deer, hares and monkeys. When these fail, they dig in old threshing floors for rats, eating the rats and taking their stores of grain, or they steal from fields and threshing floors. In the rains, they build dams across the streams, under which ingenious basket-traps are inserted. A small opening in the dam just over the mouth of the basket creates an eddy in which the fish are caught and carried into the basket. Their women work hard, both as labourers and in bringing into market the head-loads of wood their husbands have gathered in the forests.

Food.

The every day food of Kátkaris is *náchni*, *vari*, field rats, squirrels, porcupines, lizards, snakes, monkeys, civet cats, deer, wild pigs, doves and partridges. They drink liquor. They (except the Dhors) do not eat the flesh of the cow and the brownfaced monkey, who, they say, has a human soul. About thirty-five or forty years ago an immense encampment of Kátkaris in Nándgaon in the Násik district was attacked by an epidemic. This they believed to be a punishment for killing and eating the sacred Hanumán monkeys on Mahádev's hill. They accordingly fled the country and only returned there in small numbers after ten or fifteen years.

Kátkaris take food from all castes except Mángs, Mahárs, Chámbhárs and Musalmáns. But they never eat leavings, even those of a Bráhman. The only caste who eat from the hands of Kátkaris are the Mahárs.

KATRIVAL.—A sub-division of Vániás.

KATTAIS, Pardeshi Mochis, or Pardeshi Chámbhárs, numbering 134 (1901), including 78 males and 56 females, were recorded at the 1901 Census only in Ahmednagar and Násik. The Census figures are misleading as many of them described themselves as Chámbhárs at the 1901 Census. Kattais are found in large numbers also in Poona, Sátára, Bombay, etc. The Kattais are of Upper India origin and it is probable that they formed part of the following of a Mughal camp. Tradition relates that they followed Alamgir when he came into the Deccan. **Name and origin.**

The Kattais are divided into Ahirwáre, Játwe, Doravre, Jángde, Kurule, Dohor, Malai, Nákshe, Dhuse, etc., endogamous divisions which eat together. The first three divisions, *viz.*, Ahirwáre, Játwe and Doravre divisions, are found in the Násik district. Kattais are considered lower than Chámbhárs and higher than Mahárs. Their exogamous divisions are :— **Divisions.**

Ahirwáre.		Játwe.		
Imple.	Lunse.	Bedwal.	Naroti.	Sainwál.
Károle.	Páncle.	Dholpuri.	Narwar.	
Kharke.	Puchhe.	Kapune.	Páraye.	
Láchore.	Shahápure.	Mháwar.	Pipras.	

Boys are married between fifteen and twenty-five, and girls before they come of age. Polygamy and widow remarriage are allowed and practised, but polyandry is unknown. The offer of marriage comes from either side. The day for the marriage is fixed by an astrologer. The marriage is celebrated after midnight and before daybreak. The marriage ceremony is simple enough. The bridegroom's father's sister's husband ties the ends of the bride's and bridegroom's garments into a knot and asks them to walk round a pillar of *saralli* wood. Some twenty-one porcelain pots are arranged in four rows round the pillar. The bridegroom walks seven times and the bride five times. Their *devak* ceremony consists in digging up some earth and worshipping it near the house gods. This is termed *meher*. **Marriage.**

Kattais are Hindus of the Náth sect. The special object of their worship is Venkatráma of Tirupati in North Arkot. Their family **Religion.**

deities are Bálâji of Tirupati, Devi of Tuljápur, Mahádev of Trimbakeshvar in Násik and Vithoba of Pandharpur in Sholápur. They observe all the leading Hindu holidays. Their priests are Upper India Bráhmans.

Death. The dead are burnt. The ordinary funeral rites are observed. A feast is given to the friends and relations of the deceased on the 13th day after death.

Occupation. The hereditary occupation of the caste is making shoes and harness. They have not abandoned this occupation, which is well paid. The women of the Doravre division sift gold and silver dust from rubbish or ashes gathered at village goldsmiths' shops.

Food. Kattais eat the usual kind of flesh. The Ahirwáre Chámbhárs eat the flesh of dead cattle including cows. They drink liquor. They eat at the hands of Marátha Chámbhárs.

KAVALETTU.—A sub-division of Berads.

KAVI.—A synonym for Bhát.

KAYAKADA.—A sub-division of Jangams.

Name and origin. **KAYASTHS,** numbering 2,246 (1901), including 1,247 males and 999 females, are found in small numbers in all parts of Gujarát. They belong to the great writer caste of the same name in Northern India, and appear to have been brought into Gujarát by the Muhammadan conquerors at the close of the sixteenth century when (A.D. 1573—1583) Gujarát became part of the Mughal empire. "Under the arrangements introduced by the emperor Akbar Surat was placed in a special position. The city and neighbouring districts were administered by *mustadis* or clerks of the crown, who held directly from the court of Delhi, and were not subordinate to the viceroy of Gujarát. Though the governor of the city does not seem ever to have been a Káyasth, the work of collecting the revenues of the *aththávisi* or twenty-eight divisions subordinate to Surat was entrusted to Káyasths. Till A. D. 1868 in the English villages, and up to the recent times (A. D.1895) in the Baroda *aththávisi* villages, the sub-divisional accountants or *majmundárs* were mostly Káyasths."(1) In the Cutch State, to this day, most of the state officials are Káyasths.

Káyasths claim descent from Chandragupta, registrar to the mythological Dharmarája, the judge of the dead. They state that they are called Káyasths, because Chitragupta was born of the body (*káya*)

(1) Bom. Gaz., Vol. IX, Part I, p. 60

of Brahma. The term Káyasth often occurs in Sanskrit literature and in inscriptions, in the sense of a writer. These references do not throw any light on the origin of the caste. There are also a number of traditions connecting them with one or other of the ancient Kshatriya dynasties, one of which states that they are descendants of Chandrasena, who is also claimed as a common ancestor by the Káyasth Prabhus of the Deccan. The similarity in their names and occupation is believed by some to be an indication of their original identity. But this is not supported either by tradition or customs followed by the castes, which have nothing in common.

Regarding the origin of Káyasths Sir Herbert Risley writes as follows :—

"Putting tradition aside, and looking, on the one hand, to the physical type of the Káyasths, and on the other to their remarkable intellectual attainments, it would seem that their claim to Aryan descent cannot be wholly rejected, though all attempts to lay down their genealogy precisely must necessarily be futile. It appears to be at least a plausible conjecture that they were a functional group, developed within the Aryan community, in response to the demand for an official and literary class, which must in course of time have arisen. This class would naturally have been recruited more largely from the peaceful Vaishyas and Shudras than from the warlike Kshatriyas, while the Bráhmans would probably have held aloof from it altogether."(1)

The Káyasths of Northern India have twelve endogamous divisions, of which only three are found in Gujarát. They are— Endogamous divisions.

(1) Bhatnagra.

(2) Máthur.

(3) Válmik.

None of these divisions either eat together or intermarry. The Bhatnagrás are found in Ahmedábád, Baroda and in small numbers in Surat. According to the *Padma Purán*, they were given this name because one of the twelve sons of Chitragupta was sent with a sage named Bhat to found Srinagar, of which he was afterwards administrator. The Bhatnagrás have two divisions—Visás and Dasás—of which the former ranks higher. The Visás formerly refused to eat food cooked by the Dasás. They take Dasá girls in marriage, but do not give their girls to Dasás. The Máthurs, as their name shews, come from Mathura,

(1) Tribes and Castes of Bengal, Part I, p. 439.

their original home. They are found in Ahmedábád, Surat, Baroda, Cutch and Káthiáwár.

Exo-gamous divisions.

The exogamous divisions of the caste are known as *nukhs*, and seem to suggest a Sind origin, as most of them, like the *nukhs* found in Sind, end in *áni*. The principal *nukhs* are—

1. Dámáni.
2. Govindjiáni.
3. Gujaráti or Mánek-Bhanderi.
4. Hariáni.
5. Jágáni or Sámáni.
6. Kasturia.
7. Khimjiáni.
8. Khira.
9. Kothári.
10. Márwádi.
11. Meghrájáni.
12. Pashaviáni.
13. Pátáni.
14. Ranchodáni.
15. Sindi or Bhimáni.
16. Singajiáni.
17. Sorathia.
18. Thávàni.
19. Topasia.

Most of the above *nukhs* are named after ancestors, many being of comparatively recent origin. It is said that, about 300 years ago, Káyasths had a quarrel with their bards, who kept their genealogies. From that time the bards ceased to serve them, and all knowledge about their *gotras*, *nukhs*, etc., was lost to the caste.

The Káyasths of Hállár, Gujarát and Cutch do not marry with one another. Marriages are prohibited between members of the same *nukh*. Marriage with a father's sister's, mother's sister's and mother's brother's daughter is not allowed. Marriage with two sisters is allowed, and brothers are allowed to marry sisters. Polygamy is permissible, but polyandry is unknown. Widows are not allowed to re-marry. Divorce is forbidden.

Girls are generally married between ten and thirteen, boys between fourteen and sixteen. The boy's parents have to give to the girl ornaments worth about Rs. 700. The marriage ceremonies among the different sub-divisions of Káyasths vary considerably, and differ in many details from the standard marriage ceremonies obtaining in Gujarát. They are as follows :—

Marriage cere-monies.

Among the Válmik Káyasths there is no fixed time for betrothal. It takes place sometimes days and sometimes years before marriage. The chief part of the ceremony is the comparison of the boy's and girl's horoscopes. The contract is only verbal, but it is seldom broken. On various occasions, between betrothal and marriage, the boy and girl go to the house of their fathers-in-law to dine and receive presents. Marriage takes place on a day fixed by the astrologer. Five or six days before the marriage comes the booth-consecrating or *mándva murt* ceremony. The father of the girl sits in a courtyard and worships Ganpati. Four relations who have only once been married and who are not widowers are asked to help the father in digging a small pit and laying therein a small twig of the *shami* (Prosopis spicigera) tree, together with honey, milk, curds and rice. The four helpers receive balls of boiled milk and sugar *pendás*. The same ceremony takes place at the bridegroom's house. Two or three days before the marriage the bride and the bridegroom accompanied by children go to the house of their fathers-in-law and worship Ganpati. They are given plantains, sweetmeats and a few coppers. On the day of the marriage, at the bride's, and a day or two before at the bridegroom's house, the *grahashánti* or planet-propitiating ceremony takes place, and the bride and bridegroom are rubbed with turmeric. On the marriage day, at noon, at both the bride's and and the bridegroom's house, caste people, especially women and children, are asked to dinner. Just before sunset, the usual time for performing the wedding ceremony, the bridegroom goes to the bride's house in procession. At the entrance to the marriage booth the husband of one of the wife's sisters stands near a footstool on which the bridegroom stands, and the girl's mother throws wheat and flour balls in four directions and shows her son-in-law a miniature plough, a grinding pestle, a churning staff, and an arrow, and pulls his nose. The bridegroom is then led by the mother-in-law into the marriage booth and seated on a wooden stool underneath a bamboo canopy. The bride is brought by the maternal uncle and seated on a wooden stool opposite the bridegroom, and a piece of cloth is held up by two men so that the bride and the bridegroom may not see each other. The Vallabhácháryа Mahárája is invited to be present till the hand-joining ceremony is over. He is given cash by the parents of the bride and bridegroom. The Mahárája gives clothes to the bride and bridegroom. After the recital of a few *mantras* or prayers by the priest and other Bráhmans in the presence of the Mahárája, the hands of the bride and bridegroom are joined and the cloth is removed. Then the bridegroom's parents and other relations leave the marriage hall as if in anger. The parents of the bride go to call them back, and, after making presents of cash and clothes, bring them again into the marriage hall. The bride and bridegroom then walk four times round the fire, the bridegroom if he is young reciting one or two marriage songs taught him by a *mehetáji* or teacher. When the four rounds are completed the bride and bridegroom feed each other with a handful of *kansár* (wheat-flour mixed with clarified butter and molasses). The bride and bridegroom then start in a palanquin to the bridegroom's house. At the bridegroom's house the mother of the bridegroom receives the pair at the entrance. The bride and bridegroom worship the goddess and play cards. On the marriage day the bridegroom's father gives a caste dinner. On the second or third day after marriage the bridegroom and bride go in procession to the bride's house, where they are bathed and dressed in rich clothes and ornaments. On this day two white doves—a male and a female—are brought to the bride's house, each in a Bráhman's hand. The birds are tied together by a red thread which is put round their necks. The bride and bridegroom oil them, smooth their feathers, make them look in a mirror, and mark their brows with redpowder and grains of rice. When the worship is over the doves are taken away by the owner, who is generally a Musalmán and who, besides cooked food, is given half a rupee. After the dove-worship the bride and bridegroom oil and comb each other's hair, and beat each other with a twisted handkerchief. After this the bridegroom takes his bride to his house. Five or six days after the marriage the family goddess is worshipped and removed, the bride and bridegroom again oil and comb each other's hair and a caste dinner is given.(1)

Among the Máthur Káyasths, a day before the marriage, the bride is attired in rich male dress and her face is hidden by a closely-woven flower-wreath (*shero*). In the evening she is mounted on a mare and led in procession to the bridegroom's house. She is received at the marriage booth (*mámdva*) by the oldest male relative of the bridegroom, who takes her on his lap. The bridegroom's priest then comes with a dish of cocoa-kernels and almonds. The oldest male relative rubs her brow with redpowder, a costly robe is given her, a flower garland thrown round her neck, and cocoa-kernel and almonds are put in the pockets of her coat. She goes home with all these things, in the same way as she came. During the time she is in the booth the bridegroom is not allowed to come near her or see her face.

On the marriage day, at the house both of the bride and of the bridegroom, the planets are worshipped, and the bride and bridegroom are bathed. After bathing, the bridegroom's head is covered with a red scarf, one end of which is plaited with his hair, and a silver pendant (*gophni*) is fastened to it. He wears a red cotton waistcloth, and a piece of red cloth is tied round his breast. Gold necklaces are put on his neck—some passing underneath the right arm, some underneath the left arm—and his legs are adorned with anklets. All this makes him look like a woman. Over the headscarf he wears a hood

(1) Bombay Gazetteer, Volume IX, Part I, pages 62-63.

of thick-stemmed palm-leaves (*Caryota urens*) and his face is hidden by a closely woven flower-wreath. Thus dressed, with his father and a band of his relations and friends, he sets out for the bride's. When the party reaches the bride's, some of her relations, by way of joke, set a winnowing fan on the head of the bridegroom's father. Before he is ushered into the booth the bridegroom is shown a model spinning wheel and plough. After entering the booth the bridegroom stands on a wooden stool and changes his red waistcloth for a white one. If he is not grown up he is set on his maternal uncle's shoulders and the bride is brought in on the shoulders of her maternal uncle. Thirteen *karena* or oleander twigs are laid one after another in the bride's right hand. The bride and bridegroom are carried round the booth on their uncle's shoulders, the object of the girl's uncle being to give her the chance of striking the boy with one of the twigs, and the object of the boy's uncle being to give the boy the chance of snatching the twig out of the girl's hand. The bridegroom's friends help him in trying to snatch the twigs from the bride's hands, and the mimic fight is the cause of much merriment. Then follows the hand-joining, the ceremony being the same as among Bráhmans, except that it takes place near the family goddess and not in bamboo canopy or *máhera* in the booth.

The marriage ceremonies of Bhatnagra Káyasths are similar to those performed by the Máthurs.

Káyasths, like their brethren in Northern India, were originally Shákt́ás or *Devi*-worshippers. On their migration into Gujarát they could not escape the influence of Vaishnavism, which had its hold on Gujarát, and most of them adopted the tenets of the Vallabhácharya and Rámánuja sects. A few in Cutch are followers of the Rádhávallabi or Parnámi sect. Some of the Máthurs are Sháivas. Each family has a family goddess or *kuldevi*, some form of Káli, Durga or Amba. They worship such minor gods as Hanumán, Kshetrapál or the Snake-god, Yaksha and Pábu. Their priests generally belong to the Audichya, Modh, Shrimáli, Parásar and Sáchora divisions of Bráhmans. The Bhatnagrás and Máthurs invest their boys with the sacred thread with full Bráhmanic rites. **Religion.**

Káyasths burn their dead except children under two years old, who are buried. The funeral rites are of the standard type except that a small silver coin is placed in the mouth of the deceased before cremation. The ceremony of *shráddha* is performed annually on the anniversary of the death and on the day corresponding to the day of death in the dark half of *Bhádrapad*. A ceremony called *dhro* is **Death.**

performed also in the bright half of *Bhádrapad,* for the well-being of the deceased. In the case of childless ancestors and persons who have died a violent death, in addition to the usual rites, ceremonies called *Náráyan Bali* and *Báwani Kriya* are performed at some holy place, such as Bet Dwárka, Sidhápur, Pátan or Gaya, on or about the full-moon day either of *Chaitra* or *Kártik.*

Occupation. The hereditary occupation of Káyasths is clerical work. Many of them are in State employ, some of them holding offices of high trust and position. Under the Musalmáns, and for some time after the introduction of British rule, a knowledge of Persian was required in a Government clerk, and in this language most of the Káyasths were proficient. Of late years they have lost the monopoly they once enjoyed as Government clerks.

Food. Káyasths are strict vegetarians and do not indulge in drink. They eat food cooked by Kshatris, Lohánas, Bhansális, Kansárás, Depalas and Pátni Sonis. Members of these castes and Gujarát Sárasvat Bráhmans will eat food cooked by them.

KAYASTH PRABHU.—A synonym for Chándraseniya Káyasth Prabhu : *see* under Prabhu.

KAYAT.—A sub-division of Khatris.

KAYATIA.—A synonym for Darbhia.

KAYIT.—A sub-division for Láds.

KELASI.—A synonym for Nhávi.

KEMP.—A sub-division of Gánigs.

KENGURI.—A sub-division of Gollas.

KER.—A sub-division of Jogis.

KHADAPE.—A sub-division of Gaud Sáraswat Bráhmans.

KHADAYATA.—A sub-division of Bráhmans and Vániás.

Name and origin. **KHALPAS,** numbering 9,570 (1901), including 4,848 males and 4,722 females, are found chiefly in Broach, Surat and Rewa Kántha. The word Khálpa is derived from *Khal* or *Chhal,* the outer skin, Khálpás being tanners and workers in leather. The Khálpás are also known as Chamadias, Chhadias, Chamárs or Dabgárs. They admit to the caste members of other castes except Bhangias, Mángs and the very lowest, and appear to have originally sprung from a Rajput ancestor and a low caste woman.

They are divided into the following endogamous divisions :— Divisions.

1. Khambatia or Cambay.
2. Kothariya.
3. Nadia.
4. Patani.
5. Saria.
6. Tipra.

The Khambatia and Patani or Molávar divisions are hypergamous, the Khambatias marrying a Patani girl, but not giving a girl to a boy of the Patani sub-division. The *kuls* are, in some instances, named after places, *e.g.*, Dholkya, Sorathi, etc., but a number of common Rajput family names are found among them, *e.g.*, Bhadkia, Chaván, Chávda, Kataria, Kansaria, Makwána, Parmár, etc.

Marriages cannot be performed between members of the same *kul*. Where *kuls* do not exist, marriages cannot be formed within seven degrees of relationship. Marriage with a maternal uncle's daughter, father's sister's daughter and mother's sister's daughter is not allowed. Marriage with a wife's younger sister is allowed during the wife's lifetime or after her death. Two brothers may marry two sisters.

Girls are married before they attain the age of puberty. Only the poorest remain unmarried till puberty. Boys are married from five years of age. Sexual license in the case of unmarried girls is forbidden, but is not infrequent. On detection, a girl committing sexual indiscretions with a man of her caste, is generally married to the man involved. If he is unwilling to accept her, he is fined and a dinner is given to the castemen. She is then married to another member of the caste. If a girl is guilty of sexual indiscretions with a man of a higher or lower caste she is fined. Polygamy is permitted but polyandry is unknown.

Marriage ceremonies.

The offer of marriage either comes from the bride's or bridegroom's father. A marriage is settled with the help of a casteman styled *Vastalio* or *Kárbhári*. The bride's father receives from the bridegroom's father a gift of money known as the *dej* or *pallo*. The auspicious day for the ceremony is fixed by a Gáruda Bráhman who is either a Khálpa or a Dheda, and who conducts the service. The following are the principal ceremonies.

When a marriage is settled the first ceremony is the *Ghan Murt* or rice pounding ceremony. Three, five or seven days before the marriage date the bride and bridegroom are rubbed with turmeric paste. A day before the marriage, at the bridegroom's house, and on the marriage day at the bride's house, Ganpati is worshipped, and the planets are propitiated. Two earthen pots filled with water are taken, two cocoanuts are placed in the mouths of these pots and they are worshipped. This is the installation of the marriage guardian deity. On the marriage day, the bridegroom with friends and relations proceeds to the bride's village. At the outskirts of the bride's village, the party are met by the bride's parents. At night the bridegroom is taken in procession to the bride's house. There the bride's mother meets the bridegroom, and presenting him with a miniature plough, a grinding pestle, and a churning stick, leads him to the marriage hall. He is seated on a cot facing the east. The bride's maternal uncle or her sister's husband places a necklace of glass-beads round her neck, puts bracelets on her arms and carries her into the hall, where she is seated to the left of the bridegroom. The ends of the bride and bridegroom's robes are knotted together, their hands are joined, and the Gáruda Bráhman recites verses. When this is over, a *chori* sacrificial fire is kindled, and the bride and bridegroom throw *ghi* into it. They then take four turns round the fire. This completes the marriage ceremony.

Widow remarriage is allowed. A widow cannot marry her father's sister's, mother's sister's, or maternal uncle's son. She may marry the younger brother of her deceased husband if she likes. A widow remarriage is brought about either by the parents of the widow or by the widow herself. It is celebrated on Tuesday, Thursday or Sunday. On the occasion of a widow remarriage the widow is decorated with the ornaments given by her new hubsand, and seated opposite the bridegroom on a low wooden stool. The skirts of the couple's garments are tied together, the priest then leads them to the worship of the deity, after which the couple throw grains of rice over each other. This completes the ceremony. Sometimes the ceremony consists in holding a cocoanut between the heads of the bridal pair and bringing them in contact. A bachelor wishing to marry a widow is first married to a *shami* tree.

Divorce is allowed. Both husband and wife can apply for a divorce. The party applying has to pay to the other a sum settled by the caste *panch*. The permission of the headman of the caste and of the relatives and friends is necessary for a divorce. Divorce is known as *Chhuta Chheda Karva, Chhedo phadi apvo* or *Talak apvi*. A woman divorced for adultery with a man of her caste, or with a man of a higher caste is allowed to marry a second time, her marriage being performed as a widow remarriage. But when she has committed adultery with a man of lower caste, she may be turned out of her caste. She is frequently allowed to re-enter the caste by undergoing purification. The process involves the drinking of a mixture of cowdung and cow's urine. Her nails are also cut, and she is required to jump over a burning fire seven times.

Religion. Khálpás follow the Hindu law of inheritance and belong to the Hindu religion. Some are followers of Rámánand, Kabir and Rohidás faith. They worship Shiva, Vishnu, Rám, Máta and other gods of high caste Hindus. The cow, the basil plant, the *pipal* tree, the cobra and the mongoose are worshipped by them. They go on pilgrimage to Unai, Dakorji and Shuklatirtha. Their leading holidays are *Diváli* (October-November), *Dasra* (September-October), *Nágpanchmi* (July), *Shila Saptami* and *Balev* (August-September). They take vows to Muhammadan saints and make offerings of cocoanuts, sweetmeats, etc., when their objects are achieved. They worship their dead ancestors and prepare images of them, which are installed in the compounds of their houses. These are worshipped on the 14th of the latter half of the month of *Ashvin*. When cholera and small pox are raging Khálpás worship the goddess Máta or Káka Balia. Offerings of food are given to them. Some offer annual sacrifices, but it is not usual to kill the animals offered. A limb is cut, and they are then released. Khálpás employ Gáruda or Kalátia Bráhmans for religious and ceremonial purposes.

Death. They bury or burn their dead. Small children are buried. The deceased is laid in a grave on his back, the head being turned towards the north. In some places persons dying of cholera, small-pox, snake bite and leprosy are buried to prevent the spread of the disease. When the body is consumed the ashes and bones are thrown into water. The castemen are feasted on the 11th or 12th day. For the propitiation of ancestors in general they perform *Shráddha* ceremonies in the latter half of the month of *Bhádrapad*.

Occupation. Their hereditary occupation is the tanning and colouring of leather, the making of leather buckets, bags and ropes, and the repairing of old shoes. The leather is chiefly made from the skins of buffaloes, bullocks and cows. Khálpás generally receive their supplies of hides from Dhedás and Musalmán butchers. They seldom work with goat or sheep skins.

Food. They eat the flesh of goats, sheep, beef, fowls, fish and ducks. They drink liquor. They eat *pakki* at the hands of Mahárs, Mángs and Bhangiás. No higher caste will receive anything at their hands.

KHAMAR.—A sub-division of Kachhias.

KHAMBHATI.—A sub-division of Khárvás, Kachhias, Khálpás, Kumbhárs, Lohárs, Mochis, Shrigaud Bráhmans, Ghánchis.

KHAMBHATIA.—A synonym for Khambháti.

KHANDE KHARVA.—A sub-division of Konkani Khárvas.

KHANDESHI.—A territorial name. A sub-division of Bhois, Nhávis, Kunbis, Sonárs.

KHANDEVAL.—A sub-division of Vánias.

Name and origin. **KHANTS** (1) numbering 13,423 (1901), including 6,733 males and 6,690 females, are found chiefly in the Gir villages under the Junágad State in Káthiáwár. The chief of the tribe claims descent from a Bhatti Rajput.(2) The leading families are known by the title of Mer, which is said to mean elder or chief, and to be derived from the old Gujaráti word *mer* meaning the largest bead in a necklace. But it seems probable that these families have a strain of late Koli, that is Mhed, Mand or Mer blood in them. One of their early leaders Dhándh Khánt was the son of Sonang Mer, and is said to have conquered Dhandhuka, and to have founded Dhándhalpur in Panchál. Another leader, Pátal Khánt, is related to have conquered Petlád. But their most famous leader was Jesa or Jesing, by whose help the Emperor Muhammad Toghlak took Junágad (A. D. 1330) from Ra Kengár. In return for their help the emperor is said to have bestowed on the Khánts the hill of Girnár and the twenty-four villages of Bilkha Chavisi. A century later, when Mahmud Begada conquered Junágad (A. D. 1472), he found the Khánts dwelling in the Girnár. The tribe believe that their eponymous ancestor was Márkand, the son of Káshyap.

Divisions. They have so many sub-divisions corresponding with the Rajput clans that it seems probable they were once either Rajputs or personal attendants on Rajput chiefs. The chief sub-divisions are as follows :—

Bária.	Dhawal.	Mher.	Vála.
Chávda.	Jádhav.	Parmár.	Válukia.
Dadhavla.	Lalukia.	Rathod.	
Damera.	Makwana.	Surviya.	

Marriages are prohibited between members of the same sub-division. A Khánt may marry his father's sister's or mother's brother's daughter, but not his mother's sister's daughter. A man may marry two sisters simultaneously or one after the death of the

(1) From materials supplied by Mr. K. G. Pandit, B.A., LL.B.

(2) The following verse is quoted regarding the marriage of the Khánt maiden by Páloji Bhati: *Jag kahe Jesalmer, atali bal utat parno Bhil Padmani; Khatri Pátal, Khánt*; that is, the world-famous Jesalmer of exceeding great strength married the Bhil Padmani, Khátri Pátal (married) the Khánt.—Col. J. W. WATSON.

other. Two brothers may marry two sisters. The rest of the sub-divisions would generally hesitate to marry among the Gohel Khánts, who form a division by themselves. Girls are generally married between fifteen and twenty, boys a little later. Cases of misconduct before marriage are rare. Should they occur, the parties, if of the same tribe, are compelled to marry. If one of the parties be of a different caste or tribe, a fine of from Rs. 200 to Rs. 500 is levied on the tribe and a series of dinners is given for seven consecutive days. Polygamy is allowed and practised, but polyandry is unknown.

The proposals for betrothal are made by the boy's father through a mutual friend, who is given some money for the purchase of *keda kharach* and *kusumbo* (opium solution). The *des* or bride-price is Rs. 100 or upwards according to the means of the boy's father. The marriage ceremonies resemble those of the Vánjhás in every detail. Marriage.

The re-marriage of widows is permitted, the first claimant to the widow's hand being the deceased husband's younger brother. If the widow is not inclined to live with him, she may marry anybody she chooses outside the prohibited limits. There is nothing peculiar about the ceremony. The widow's intended husband presents her with a few clothes and ornaments, and molasses are distributed among those present. Divorce is allowed. A divorced woman can re-marry on paying a fine to the former husband, which is paid by the second husband. The tribe is governed by Hindu law with the same modifications as in the case of the Vánjhás.

Khánts belong to the Hindu religion. They worship Shankar and all other Hindu gods and goddesses. Their favourite deity is the goddess Shakti or Durga. They observe all the Hindu holidays, and those who can afford the expense go on pilgrimages. The *khijadia* tree is greatly venerated. Its branches are not cut nor are the leaves plucked on any account. It is worshipped on the *Dasara* day. Islám Pir is held in great reverence, cocoanuts being offered, lamps lit or bedsheets offered to poor people or a sweet preparation called *malindo* given to the Pir in his honour. When an epidemic breaks out, Durga, Shankar or Máruti is propitiated. The caste priests are *gors*. Religion.

Infants dying under a year old, persons dying of small-pox and *bhagats* (recluses) are buried. Lepers are cast into the water. Persons dying of snake-bite or accidents are burnt on the village land. The rest are burned at the village burning ground. The corpse is placed in a lying position with head to the north. The burnt ashes are thrown into the river, and the bones are put in an earthen jar and, Death.

if possible, thrown into the Dáma pool in the Girnár hills. Little trinkets of gold or silver and clothes belonging to the deceased are given away as presents to the Bráhman performing the funeral ceremonies. On the eleventh day after death an image of the deceased is made and worshipped. In memory of the unmarried dead a young male and a female calf are married. In the case of childless ancestors and accidental deaths, caste dinners are held or money is given in charity.

The Khánts believe that they were originally a class of marauders. Subsequently they took to agriculture as a more respectable calling. Some of them are now landholders and others day-labourers earning a few annas a day.

Food.

They eat the flesh of goats, sheep, scaly and scaleless fish, and drink liquor. They eat and drink with Káthis, Ahirs, Mers, Kadias, Kumbhárs, Bharváds, Rabáris, Ságars, Talabda Kolis and Káthi Bhils. Kanbis, Vániás and Bráhmans accept only uncooked food from them.

KHAPRA.—A sub-division of Gujar Kanbis.

KHAR.—A sub-division of Kolis.

KHARADIS or Sanghádiás are found principally in Káthiáwár. They claim descent from Káshyap Rishi, and state that their regular line of descent is from Birbal (the witty minister of Akbar) who introduced into the caste the custom of widow remarriage. They appear like Vánjhás, Sutárs, and Saránias to have been originally Khatris or dyers. They have such Brahmanical *gotras* as Bháradwája, Kaundinya, etc., but they do not affect intermarriage. They have six exogamous sections each with a separate family-deity. Marriage with a father's sister's, mother's sister's or mother's brother's daughter is prohibited. Divorce is not allowed. Most of the Kharádis are Hindus. Some are Jains. They are turners and do ornamental wood-work. They eat food cooked by Khatris and Vániás.

Name and origin.

KHARAKS,* numbering 5,897 (1901), including 2,995 males and 2,902 females, are found principally in Káthiáwár and also in Ahmedábád. They chiefly reside on the eastern coast of Káthiáwár in Bhávnagar territory. Their Bárot lives at Pethalpur, two miles from the sacred place of Gopinath on the Bhávnagar coast. Formerly Gariadhar was their head-quarters.

The caste believe themselves to have once been Rajputs. They relate that, when Parashurám began the extirpation of the

* From materials supplied by Mr. K. G. Pandit, B.A., LL.B.

Kshatriyas, some of them took refuge in the temple of Mátáji, who promised to save them provided they renounced Kshatriya ways and became Vaishyas. They agreed to this. Their claim to Kshatriya origin is very doubtful. Their names, profession and very docile ways clearly point to their having been originally Vaishyas carrying on trade in grain which they carried from place to place on the backs of donkeys. The name Khárak is probably a contracted form of Kharwahanka (donkey-drivers). Subsequently they took to cultivation and are now an agricultural class in Káthiáwár. Their bards say that they started from Bhinmala in Northern India and thence descended to Ujjain, that subsequently they took up their abode in Dholka and Gariadhar (under Palitana) at which place there was a great famine. They took to carrying grain on the backs of donkeys, and were tauntingly called Kháraks, which brought about a quarrel between them and the other Vánias so that they left those parts and, separating from the rest of the community, took to cultivation. In customs and mode of life they closely resemble Kanbis.

Divisions.

There are no endogamous divisions of the caste. They have exogamous sections (some of the sub-sections having a common ancestor being grouped under a section) the chief of which are as follows :—

1. Solanki Valia and Thánh Valia.
2. Khimáni and Tádha.
3. Koládia, Sánghani, Boláni, Kába and Khodiphád.
4. Bhojáni.
5. Kansára and Suráni.
6. Kágda.
7. Bhoot.
8. Daiya.
9. Sentha.
10. Kápadia.
11. Kámalia.
12. Rathod.
13. Sebhádia.
14. Bhálálha.
15. Koocha.
16. Jália.
17. Makodia.
18. Umchadia (Umchada village).
19. Navelhia.
20. Gohel.

Sub-sections cannot intermarry among themselves, nor sections. Marriage with mother's brother's daughter or with father's sister's daughter or with mother's sister's daughter is prohibited. During the life-time of the first wife her sister cannot be taken as a second wife. Two brothers may marry two sisters. Betrothals are generally made when the children are infants. Marriage takes place between the age of ten and twelve. Polyandry is unknown, but polygamy is allowed. The grounds on which the marriage of a second wife is allowed are trivial. Generally barrenness or contraction of an incurable disease on the part of the first wife is sufficient. No one in the caste is known to have more than two wives.

Marriage ceremonies.

Betrothal is known as *sagái* or *veswál.* The girl's father makes an offer through a *gor* (village priest) who is generally a Táláwadi Audich Bráhman. He carries a cocoanut with him to the boy's father and gets Rs. 5 in case the offer is accepted. From the time of betrothal up to the time of marriage an annual present *Hárdo* consisting of two cocoanuts, five seers of sugar, five seers of dry dates, and a piece of cotton fabric has to be sent to the house of the girl's father. On the marriage day a dinner is given by the bride's father to the people of the caste, and in lieu of this the bridegroom's father gives the cost of eight maunds of *ghi* calculated at three-fourths of the bazar price. This forms part of the *Des* or marriage endowment with the presents of the annual *hrádo.* The day for the marriage is fixed by the *gor,* who writes a note stating the day and carries it to the boy's father (*lagan lakhavun* and *lagan mokalvun*). The boy's father accepts the note (*lagna vadhávavun*) and signifies such acceptance by making with red powder a mark (*chándlo*) on the *gor's* forehead, presenting him with a cocoanut and a silver coin. Two days before the marriage, booths are put up at the houses of both the bride and the bridegroom. On the day previous to the marriage a fruit *mindhol* is tied to the right wrist of the bridal pair, and saffron or turmeric powder mixed with water is applied to their cheeks and foreheads. Kshetrapál (protector of the field) is worshipped and is the presiding deity of the marriage booth. On the night of the marriage day the bridegroom approaches the bride's village, where he is received by the bride's party (*sámaiyun*) and brought in procession into the village (*fulekun*). The bridegroom is taken into the marriage booth and welcomed by the bride's mother (*ponkhvun*). The bride is brought and seated near the bridegroom. The couple then walk four times (*Fera ferva*) round the altar, and this is the binding portion of the marriage service. The newly married pair bow to the girl's family deity, a feast is held at the expense of the bridegroom's father, and the bridegroom returns to his house with his bride, thus completing the marriage.

Widow remarriage is allowed, but a widow is strictly prohibited from marrying her late husband's brother. The officiating priest is the *gor,* who seats the couple on wooden seats, makes a *chándlo* on their foreheads, and receives Rs. 20 as reward. The bridegroom presents a suit of new clothes to the bride. On the day following, early in the morning the widow goes to a river (to fetch water) or to the village well with her face veiled, and on filling water unveils her face, thus casting off the evil which is supposed to attach to her remarriage. On returning, the pair see each other's faces in a vessel containing liquified *ghi*. A dinner is then given to the caste people in the village, the cost of which is divided. This brings the ceremony to a close. Divorce is permitted but not encouraged. Only the husband can seek it, the usual ground being the wife's misconduct or incompatibility of temper. The divorce is effected by the husband calling his wife by the name of sister or mother. The caste is governed by Hindu law with certain modifications. The sons are entitled to a separate residence and maintenance, but not to partition if the father is disinclined towards the latter. The daughters cannot claim any part of the *stridhan* of their deceased mother, which goes to the sons, or their heirs according to law.

When they were Vániás, the Khâraks were Jains. When they took to cultivation, they became staunch Vaishnavas. Their chief god is Thákorji and their family deity is Khodiar. Whenever an epidemic breaks out, they make an offering every week (called *mánta*) of *lápsi*, a kind of wheat pudding, molasses, etc. On Hindu holidays, all of which they observe, they give alms to Bráhmans. Their priests are the Tálâwadi Audich Bráhmans who are not any way inferior in status to the other Bráhmans.

Death. The dead are burnt, except children under eighteen months old, who are buried in a lying position with head to the north. The ashes are thrown into the sea, if near, or buried in a pit near a watercourse so as to be carried away by the rain water. The unburnt bones are carried to Nakatinga (Nishkalanka) which is about sixteen miles from Bhávnagar. In honour of the dead a *shráddha* is held once a year on the ninth day of the dark half of *Bhádrapad*. If the deceased has no child a male calf is married to a female calf by a mock ceremony called *Nil parnávavi*.

Occupation. The Khâraks believe themselves to have once been a trading class. They are now cultivators. Many are landed proprietors though owning very small tracts seldom exceeding a hundred acres.

Food. They neither eat flesh nor drink liquor. They eat with Sutárs and Kanbis.

KHARCHA.—A sub-division of Dublás.

KHARCHI.—A synonym for Lenkávale.

KHARI.—A sub-division of Bhois.

KHAROLA.—A sub-division of Shrigaud Bráhmans.

KHAROTE.— A sub-division of Vániás.

KHAROVAVA.— A sub-division of Alkaris.

KHARPATIL.— A synonym for Agri and Khárva.

KHARSE.— A sub-division of Mahárs.

Name and origin.

KHARVAS or Khárvis, numbering 36,036 (1901), including 18,946 males and 17,090 females, are found in the ports of Cutch, Káthiáwar, Cambay, Gujarát, Thána, the Konkan, Kanara, Janjira, and in the city of Bombay, 112 being recorded at the port of Aden. The term Khárva is a Persian word signifying a sailor and is consequently applied somewhat indiscriminately to those leading a seafaring life. Another derivation of the term is from *khár* (salt land), Khárvás being found cultivating salt lands on the coast to this day. They are also known as Khár Pátils. The following account deals with all Khárvás that do not come under any other well-known caste name for those following the occupation of sailors, such as Máchhis, Ambis or Kolis.

Endogamous divisions.

The endogamous divisions of the caste are—

1. Rájput.	4. Hánsoti.	7. Konkani.
2. Koli.	5. Surati.	8. Musalmán.
3. Khambháti.	6. Barochi.	

In Gujarát, Khárvás claim Rajput descent. The tradition regarding their origin in Surat and Cambay is to the effect that, having taken to salt-manufacture and sea-faring, they sunk and came to be called Khárvás, but this seems to be a play on the word *khára* (salt). Their Cutch tradition is that they fled from Jhálávad during the persecution of the Emperor Ala-ud-din Khilji in A. D. 1294, and were sheltered by a Máchhi, whose example led them to take to sea-faring. Another account attributes a still earlier origin to the caste, which is said to date from the times of Mahmud of Ghazni (1024 A.D.). The Porbandar Khárvás and also those in Mangrol, Navánagar, Vanákbárun near Diu, and Verával consider that some of them came from Dwárka and some from the Bhávnagar Coast, and disclaim all connection with Cambay Khárvás. Of the three classes of Khárvás in Káthiáwar, *i. e.*, Rajput, Koli and Musalmán, the Rájputs probably date from the time (A. D. 746) of the Anhilváda dynasty, which assigned them a special quarter in Gogha (1). They eat with Rajputs and follow Rajput customs. The Koli Khárvás are the descendants of pirates who used to infest the Southern Káthiáwar Coast and have a strong infusion of Koli blood.

(1) *Rás Mála*, p. 245.

They have such local names as Talájia in Bhávnagar, and Shiále from Shiálset near Diu. They are found chiefly in Bhávnagar, Jáfarábád near Diu, Mahuva and Talája, and do not differ from Kolis in their ways. Musalmán Khárvás in Cutch are known as Bhadálás.

Exogamous divisions. The Rajput Khárvás in Cutch have seven clans—Chávda, Gohil, Tethava, Jhála, Parmár, Ráthod and Solanki, and those in Káthiáwar—Gohil, Jhála, Ráthod and Solanki. The South Gujarát Khárvás are of four divisions of a territorial type—Barochi, Hánsoti, Khambháti and Surati. The Khambhátis rank highest, and, while marrying with the daughters of the other divisions, they do not give their own girls in marriage to them. The other three divisions inter-dine but do not inter-marry. The Khambhátis have twelve divisions, the chief of which are Katiála, Máchhi, Mujáfaria, Ságaria, Vádia, and Vejporia, who inter-marry freely. Marriage does not take place between persons who are related to each other in any way. A man may marry his wife's sister, either during the wife's lifetime or after her death. Two brothers may marry two sisters. Except some Khambháti families, all Khárvás allow polygamy, but the permission of the first wife is usually necessary. Polyandry is unknown. There is no strict rule regarding the marriageable age of boys and girls, although marriage after the age of puberty is not favoured.

Marriage ceremonies. The offer of marriage comes either from the girl's father or the boy's parents. The boy's father has to give to the girl ornaments worth about Rs. 30 which are known as *pallun*. The day for the marriage is fixed by the family priest. The first ceremony in a marriage is the drawing up the marriage deed or *lagna lakhávavu* followed by *mándva muhurt* or booth consecrating. Next, the bride and bridegroom are rubbed with turmeric paste. This is followed by the *grahashánti* or planet propitiation. The boy then goes in procession to the bride's house for the marriage. *Mindhal* (wristlets) are tied on the bride and bridegroom. The essential portion is the *mangalphero* or walking round the sacrificial fire.

The re-marriage of widows is permitted. A widow cannot marry her father's sister's, mother's sister's, or mother's brother's son. Marriage with a deceased husband's brother is preferred. A widow re-marriage is celebrated on a Sunday, Tuesday or Thursday with the assistance of the family priest. The widow and her intended husband are seated on two low wooden stools. They worship Ganpati and throw rice grain over each other, which completes the ceremony. Divorce is allowed. A divorced woman is allowed to re-marry. A woman taken in adultery can remain in the caste by paying a fine to the caste people. The Hindu law of inheritance is followed with this restriction, that a son cannot claim a part of the ancestral property during the lifetime of his father.

Religion. Khárvás profess Hinduism. Some of them are followers of Swáminaráyan and some of Kuberji, regularly attending the temples of their faith and worshipping at home the image of the founder. The goddesses Ambáji, Bahuchara, Bhádrakáli are also worshipped and pilgrimages are made to Dákor, Dwárka and Benáres. In Cutch they are Vaishnavs and worship the goddesses Ashápura, Harsad, Luna, Monamaya, Rhoji and Chámunda, and in Porbandar the Dedvádi, Mámai, Padmani, Porávál and Veravari *mátás* or mothers. In Mándvi they worship the god Murlimanoharji, set him in a fourwheeled car or *rath* on the 10th of *Shrávan Vad* (July-August) and draw it to a pond in which they bathe the image. They also worship the cow, the planets and the elements. Such as ply their own craft worship the sea and their newly-moored craft on *Nárelpurnima* or cocoanut day, the fullmoon of *Shrávan*. All Khárvás are strong believers in omens, spirits, witchcraft, the evil eye and exorcism. They observe all the Hindu holidays and offer goats to the *mátás*, which are partaken of by themselves. Their priests are Bráhmans.

Death. The dead are burnt. Children under eighteen months old are buried head northwards. The bones and ashes of the burnt are consigned to water. Propitiative ceremonies are performed on the eleventh, twelfth and thirteenth day after death with the assistance of the family priest. A sacred thread of two strands is worn when performing *shráddhas* in memory of deceased ancestors.

Occupation. As a class Khárvás are bold and enterprising, and generally honest and true to their word. The Surat Khárvás are hardy sailors and are known as the best builders of bridges in all parts of India. The Cambay Khárvás were deep-sea sailors and saltmakers ; but since the decline of Cambay as a port, and the closing of the salt-works on the introduction of the Imperial salt duty in A. D. 1878, they have taken to labour, house-building, and especially tile-turning. Very few of them are sailors. They remain away for employment during the fairweather months ; and have in many Gujarát towns, and to some extent also in Bombay, monopolised the work of skilled tile-turners. In Ahmedábád and other inland towns, besides tile-turning, Khárvás weave oakum thread, make brooms and mats, trade in, rather than catch fish, and sometimes cultivate. Their women also in Surat and Broach work in coir, make ropes, do field work, and serve as labourers.

In the coast towns and villages of Surat and Broach, Khárvás ply boats and serve in country craft and steamers. But the hardiest sailors are of Ránder and Gogha in Gujarát, and of the Káthiáwár and Cutch ports from Bhávnagar to Mándvi. They are skilful and daring seamen. They man the country craft that visit Zanzibár, Aden, and the whole coast of India, east as far as Singápore, and are also largely employed and well known as lascars in steam-boats running between Bombay and Europe.

Except such as have adopted the Swáminaráyan and Kuberji faith, all Khárvás eat fish and the flesh of goats and fowls, and drink liquor. Food.

KONKANI KHARVAS have two divisions, Proper and Khánde or sword-wearing Khárvás. The latter are probably those Khárvás who in piratical times used to go armed with swords. In Bombay City they are divided into *bháji* or vegetable grower, *nalia* or tile turners and *mith* or salt workers. The Kanara branch are said to have come into the district from Goa, where they were of importance before the rise of Portuguese power. Groups of families having the same family deities are exogamous. The chief family deities are as follows :—

1. Báneshvar.	5. Mhálsa.
2. Dámodhar.	6. Ravalnáth.
3. Kudtari.	7. Shánteri Kámákshi
4. Mahámáyi.	8. Kàtyayani Devi.

The shrines of the first seven deities are in Goa territory, showing the former connection of the caste with Goa. The shrine of Katyayani Devi is in Avarsa, a village in the Ankola *táluka* of the Kanara district, to which the deity is reputed to have been brought from elsewhere.

The home tongue of the Konkani Khárvás is Konkani, though some talk Kanarese. The names in common use among men are Ananta, Bhim, Ballu, Boti, Bhikaro, Devappa, Fullayya, Irayya, Jáya, Komár, Murári, Omu, Paik, Pursayya, Ráma, Rupo, Shivayya and Tondo ; and among women, Devái, Gauri, Gangái, Huvái, Kurshi, Lakshmi, Manju, Mhálái, Párvati, Rumái, Sántái and Shesái. The men add to their names the words Bhimi, Mesta and Tándel.

The caste has a chief headman known as the Subraya Ráut who resides in Belikeri, four miles north of Ankola. Each village has a committee of *chaugulas* formed of the leading members of the community under the presidency of a headman called *budvant* or wise man. The *budvant* settles all social disputes according to the opinion of the majority of the *chaugulás*, and refers difficult and contested questions to the *ráut*. The *ráut* submits to the head of the Shringeri monastery any complicated question which he finds difficult to settle. The decisions of the heads of the caste are enforced by *kolkárs* or messengers. Adultery by women is punished with expulsion from the caste. In cases of assault with sandals, the assailed as well as the assailant are fined and sent to Gokarn to be purified. On their return they have each to give to the community a pot of toddy, which is drunk with boiled fish.

Girls are married before they attain maturity. Polygamy is allowed and practised. Widow re-marriage is permitted but seldom practised. Widowers only can marry widows. Polyandry is unknown.

Marriage ceremonies. The offer of marriage comes from the boy's father, who has to pay a bride-price of Rs. 16 to the girl's father. The day for the marriage is fixed in consultation with a Bráhman. The ceremony is conducted by the caste Bráhman. The marriage lasts five days. Booths of cadjan leaves are erected at the houses of both the boy and the girl. On the marriage day the bridegroom, wearing a *báshing* (marriage coronet), goes in procession to the bride's house.

The party is received at the entrance to the marriage booth by the girl's father with the same ceremony as among Gám Vakkals. The party enter the booth over a clean white sheet spread by the village washerman. The *budvant* then passes a cotton thread round the necks of the bride and bridegroom, joins their hands, and pours water over them (the *dháre* ceremony). The other ceremonies are the same as among the Gám Vakkals, with the exception that on the fifth day the bride is formally made over to the bridegroom's mother. Then the bridal party goes in procession to the bridegroom's house. The bridegroom's father sits on a heap of rice grains, seats the bride on his left thigh and the bridegroom on the right. The girl is then given a new name, by which she is known afterwards in her husband's family. This terminates the marriage.

Religion. The Konkan Khárvás are particularly devoted to Ammás, Játkás and Mhastis, though they worship all Hindu gods. They also pay great reverence to Hanumant of Chandávar, whose image is once a year carried in a palanquin through the coast villages, when the people pay tithes and make offerings which are received by the Havik priest who is in charge of the palanquin. They greatly revere the Roman Catholic Saints, and offer flowers, oil, candles and gold and silver ornaments in fulfilment of vows to the Virgin Mary and St. Francis

Xavier. Feasts are held on Good Friday. They make pilgrimages to Tirupati, Gokarn, Dharmasthal, Rámeshvar and Pandharpur. Their religious teacher is the head of the Smárt monastry at Shringeri in Mysore. Their priests are Havik and Karnátak Bráhmans.

Death ceremonies. The dead are either burnt or buried. On the twelfth day after death a *ghádi* or exorcist is called to release the soul of the deceased from the control of the killing spirit Ráhu, and to place it under the control of a guardian spirit. The ceremonial impurity ends on this day, and the corpse-bearers and relatives of the deceased are feasted. After a short time the *ghádi* frees the soul from the control of the guardian spirit and allows it to join the group of the family spirits. Crows are fed on the twelfth day, on the last day of the month and year, and on the anniversary of the deceased, in order to pacify the deceased. The *mahálaya* is also performed, when members of the caste are feasted.

Occupation. The chief occupation of the Konkan Khárvás is sailing coasting craft. Like many sailor castes they also lay and turn tiles in the monsoon. Some are salt-water fishermen, their fishing boats and nets being the same as those of the Ambigs. Some work as carpenters, especially as boat-builders. They also work as house servants and labourers and occasionally as husbandmen. Like other fishing classes they carry palanquins. The women husk rice and make coir rope.

Food. They eat fish and flesh except beef and pork, and drink liquor.

KHARVI.—A synonym for Khárva and Gábit.

KHATAVAN.—A sub-division of Devángs.

KHATIK.—*See* under Minor Musalmán Castes. A synonym for Kasái.

Name and origin. **KHATRIS** or Weavers, numbering 38,574 (1901), including 19,987 males and 18,587 females, are found all over the Presidency. They call themselves Kshatris or Kshatriyas and claim a Kshatriya origin, those in Gujarát claiming to be Brahma Kshatris. As a rule they are tall and fair and they wear the sacred thread. Like the Brahma Kshatris, their favourite objects of worship are Devis or goddesses, and even in the south of the Presidency their home tongue is interspersed with many Hindustáni words. These facts would seem to suggest that they originally belonged to the great Kshatri race of the Punjáb, but the custom of widow marriage which obtains amongst them, and their ceremonies which closely resemble those of Kunbis in the Deccan, of Smárt Deshasth Bráhmans in the Karnátak and of Vániás in Gujarát, would suggest some admixture at least of local castes and tribes. In Dhárwár, the tradition regarding their origin is, that they are the descendants of seven sages Bháradwája, Jamadgni, Káshyap, Kátyáyan, Válmik, Vashishtha and Vishwámitra. The Poona, Násik and Ahmednagar Khatris relate that, in order to avoid being slain by Parashurám, they were told by the goddess Hingláj to assume the name of Khatris and to take to weaving. The Násik Khatris further state that their original ancestor was Kártavirya. There is a tradition in Ahmednagar to the effect that they formerly lived in Sahasrárjuna in Mundugad, the old capital of Málwa. The Sholápur Khatris state that they came there about a hundred years ago from Cheul in Kolába. The Khándesh Kshatris claim Sahasrárjun to be their common ancestor. The Gujarat Khatris say that they came into Gujarát from Sind in the sixteenth and seventeenth centuries, tempted by the strong European demand for their cloth.

Khatris are hereditary silk and cotton weavers. They weave women's robes, waist-cloths, shoulder-cloths and bodice-cloths. Besides weaving they string on wire or thread gems and pearls, make fringes, threads for necklaces, tassels, netted work, and hand and waist ornaments. Their industry has been much crippled since the introduction of machine-made piece-goods.

Divisions. The social organization of the caste is very intricate. It cannot be said with certainty how many endogamous divisions they have. Broadly speaking, they may be said to consist of the following groups :—

1. Brahma Khatri.
2. Gujaráti.
3. Istari.
4. Kapur Khatri.
5. Karnátak.
6. Káyat.
7. Marátha.
8. Sahasrárjuna.
9. Surti.
10. Somavanshi.
11. Suryavanshi.

The above divisions neither eat together nor intermarry. The Maráthás, Gujarátis, Surtis, and Karnátaks are of the territorial type. The Somavanshis claim descent from *soma* the moon, the Suryavanshis from *surya* the sun, and the Sahasrárjunas from a mythological hero of that name. Brahma Khatris are an offshoot of the Khatris, claiming a superior status or they represent the Brahma Kshatris proper (*see* BRAHMAKSHATRI). The origin of the other divisions is unknown.

The above divisions are described below under Marátha, Gujaráti and Karnátak Khatris.

MARATHA KHATRIS have the following surnames :—

Báji.	Chingi.	Magaji	Sálunke.
Bákháve.	Kankrej.	Mule.	Tak.
Barad.	Katyáre.	Pakhále.	Tavarej.
Bhánde.	Kháde.	Pancháng.	Teli.
Bichhave.	Khámbe.	Ráthor.	Váyada.

They have also *kuls* and *gotras* as follows :—

Kuls.

Bhángde.	Konka.
Chaván.	Kukare.

Gotras.

Bháradwája.	Páráshar.
Gautam.	Shándilya
Jamadagni	Válmiki.
Káshyap	Vashishtha.
Nárad.	

In some places marriages are prohibited between members belonging to the same *kul*, in others sameness of *gotra* is a bar to intermarriage, while again in some places both *gotras* and *kuls* must be different for the contracting parties. Many members do not know to which *gotra* they belong, in which cases either *kuls* or surnames are considered in settling marriages. Marriage with a father's sister's, mother's sister's, or mother's brother's daughter is not allowed. A man may marry two sisters and brothers may marry sisters. Girls are generally married between five and twelve, boys between seven and twenty-five. Polygamy is permissible, but polyandry is unknown. The marriage ceremonies of Marátha Khatris are similar to those of Marátha Kunbis except that in Ahmednagar they have *devaks* consisting of earthen pots brought from the potters and marked white and red. A married couple sets them at the corners of a square and lays before them sandal paste, flowers and vermilion, with food or sweetmeats. The goddess Devi is propitiated with an offering of a goat, and the bridegroom visits the bride's, where the priest or Khatribhat blesses the couple with lucky rice and kindles the sacred fire. The couple throw mango, *jámbul* (Eugenia jambolana), *rui* (Calotropis gigantea), *umbar* (Ficus glomerata), and *shami* (Prosopis spicigera) leaves on the fire and their brows are marked with vermilion, to which rice is stuck. The ceremony ends with a feast. Next day the bridegroom's party take three to five goats to the bride's house, where these are killed and the party is treated to a sumptuous feast.

The remarriage of widows is permitted. Divorce is allowed. A woman divorced for bad conduct is turned out of the caste.

Marátha Khatris follow the Hindu law of inheritance and belong to the Hindu religion. Except that in Khándesh they employ Audich Bráhmans and in Ahmednagar members of their own caste known as Khatribhats to officiate at their ceremonies, that in some places their death ceremonies are conducted by the caste elders, and that they invest their boys with the sacred thread, they do not differ in their religious beliefs and practices from Marátha Kunbis.

The dead are burnt except boys who have not been girt with the sacred thread. The latter are buried. The death ceremonies of Khatris do not differ from those performed by the local Bráhmans.

Food. They eat fish and the flesh of goats, sheep and fowls, and drink liquor.

GUJARATI KHATRIS are Vaishnavas by religion, but most of them prefer the worship of Devi, especially of Hingláj Máta. Except that they allow widow marriage, their customs differ little from those of Vániás. They live, as a rule, on vegetable food, but many in south Gujarát eat flesh and drink liquor to excess.

KARNATAK KHATRIS have no sub-divisions or family stocks. They allow polygamy and forbid widow marriage. Their family gods are Ganpati and Mahádev and their family goddesses Tuljá-Bhaváni and Yellamma. They keep the leading Hindu fasts and feasts and make pilgrimages to Ambábai at Tuljápur in Sátára. Their spiritual teacher is Shankaráchárya. Their marriage and death ceremonies differ little from those of Smárt Deshasth Bráhmans. Before a marriage a *gondhal* dance is preformed. Boys are girt with the sacred thread at the age of eight years. The dead are burnt. Boys who die before they are girt with the sacred thread and girls who die before they are married are buried. Karnátak Khatris eat flesh and are excessively fond of intoxicating drinks.

KHATRIGOR.—A sub-division of Audich Bráhmans.

Name and origin. **KHAVAS** or Golas (1) are personal attendants, numbering 25,217 (1901), including 12,424 males and 12,793 females, found in most parts of Gujarát, Káthiáwár and Cutch in the households of Rajput Chiefs

(1) Compiled from materials supplied by Mr. K. G. Pandit and the *Bombay Gazetteer*, Vol. IX, Part I.

and Rajput landlords or Girásiás. They are also called Hajuris or "of the Presence" in Rewa Kántha, Vajirs or ministers in Pálanpur and elsewhere Lundás or household slaves. The term Khavás is also applied to all the personal servants of a Rajput Chief or of a Girásia, whether they are Rajputs, Kolis, Dhánkás or Musalmáns. These Khavás have nothing in common except their occupation. They follow the religion and customs of their respective castes.

The Khavás proper are recruited from members of all castes, except the impure classes. They appear to fall into two classes: Khavás and Golás, of whom the former are superior in rank, though originally there appears to have been no distinction between them, and Khavás freely married Golis or female Golás. The necessity for men of position having round them a trusty set of servants led to the gradual elevation of the Khavás over the Golás, a superiority which the descendants retain. A Gola may rise to the rank of a Khavás, while a Khavás may sink to the condition of a Gola. Both are so far bondsmen that it is customary to sell or pass them from house to house.

Corresponding to the male Khavás and Golás are female Khavásans and Golis. The domestic position and work of these two classes is the same, but the Khavásan is the more respectable as she does no work except waiting on her mistress. The Khavásans, who are known among the higher Rajput families as Vadhárans or Chokris, that is maid-servants or female attendants, are the daughters of Khavás. They have an independence which is denied to the Golis. They or their parents have the right to decide where they will take service, and whether or not they will accompany their young mistresses into other families. The Golis are girls either of the province or of outside districts. Those of the province are the daughters of destitute parents who have been thrown for maintenance on the charity of the Girásiás, and perform service in return for their food and clothes. In the Rájputána famine of A.D. 1869 many girls were received into the houses of Káthiáwár Girásiás. Till A.D. 1878, Bháts and Chárans made a regular trade of bringing girls from Márwár into Cutch. The girls were either kidnapped or lured from their homes by promises. Sometimes they were sold in payment of debts by their parents and guardians direct to the Bháts and Chárans, who brought them to Cutch for sale; and sometimes their parents and guardians sold them to their creditors who re-sold them to Bháts and Chárans. After they were brought to Cutch, the Bháts and Chárans used to take the girls from village to village, and sell them to some land-holder.

The price was mutually settled, and a deed of sale was drawn up. These girls were in much demand among all classes of Rajputs, especially among Jádejás, as their custom is to give one or more male and female servants as part of the dowry of a daughter. In A.D. 1865 by notification, the people of Káthiáwár were warned against importing African slaves, and in A. D. 1869 against kidnapping and selling girls. Though in Rajput households the Golis, like the Khavásans, are fed, clothed and well treated, unlike Khavásans their wishes are seldom consulted when sent with their young mistress as a portion of the dowry. An implied proprietary right still exists over them, and in former times claims for their restitution used occasionally to be made to political officers. The Golis are of easy virtue, and are seldom married. If they are married, it is with a member of their own caste, and the marriage tie is by no means strong. Should the Chief dismiss a Gola, he is not allowed to take his wife with him. She and her family remain at the Chief's, and are handed over to another Gola. The practice may be said to be almost promiscuous cohabitation, controlled either by the authority of the Chief or by a sense of propriety. An intrigue with a Goli is considered disgraceful to a member of another class. When a Goli is found with child by a man of another caste, her mistress forces her to declare the name of the father, who, if a wealthy person, is compelled to pay a fine. No fault is imputed to the woman. The children swell the ranks of Golás and Golis, who, in process of time, rise to the position of Khavás and Khavásans. It not unfrequently happens that a Goli or Khavásan with good looks attracts the attention of a Chief, and instances are not wanting of such Golis and Khavásans being raised to the rank of a Chief's wife.

As the States in Káthiáwár began to be dismembered, employment could not be found for all the Khavás with Rajput Chiefs, which led to the liberation of many, who have formed a distinct community and marry only among themselves. Some of these are fairly educated, leading a decent married life, serving as clerks, artisans, etc. Some are land-holders, notable among them being the Tálukdár of Amrau under the Jám of Návánagar, and the Erdás of Porbunder.

Khavás claim descent from the Royal families of Jaipur, Márwár, Udaipur and Cutch, and state that even at present their kinsmen are petty land-holders in Málwa and are called Thákardás or chieflings. They are a mixed class, with, no doubt, a strong strain of Rajput blood in their veins.

Khavás look and dress like Rajputs, some of their men and women being remarkably handsome. They have several sub-divisions, the chief of which are as follows :— Exogamous divisions.

Name of sub-division.	Family deity.
Bárad	Mohmayi.
Bhatti	Kálika.
Chaván	Chámunda.
Chávda	Durga.
Makvána	Bechráji.
Parmár	Sikotar.
Solanki	Váchhdo.
Zála	Mohmayi.

The above sub-divisions are exogamous so far that, whenever regular marriages take place, the bride and bridegroom must belong to different sub-divisions. Marriage with a maternal uncle's daughter is allowed, but not with a mother's sister's or father's sister's daughter. Marriage with two sisters is allowed, and brothers are allowed to marry sisters. There is not, and cannot be, a limit of age for the marriage of girls ; but among that section of the Khavás who have formed a separate community, girls are generally married between twelve and fourteen. There is no limit of age in the case of the marriage of boys. Polygamy is permitted, but polyandry is unknown. Widows are allowed to remarry. Marriage with a deceased husband's brother is not permitted. The widow's intended husband has to pay her Rs. 50 known as *des*. A bachelor may not marry a widow. Divorce is allowed with the consent of both parties. If the wife wants to enforce a divorce without the consent of the husband, she has to pay a fine of 700 *koris* (Rs. 175). A similar act on the part of the husband would entail on him a fine of 200 *koris* (Rs. 50). The caste *panch* have to be satisfied of the propriety of the divorce, and a fine of Rs. 5 called *dád* has to be paid to the caste, a dinner being also given.

Khavás are governed by the Hindu law of inheritance somewhat modified, *e.g.*, a son cannot claim partition but only maintenance during the life-time of his father. So also daughters have no right to the *stridhan* of their deceased mother unless the latter has parted with it and disposed of it during her life-time. In their religion and ceremonies they follow Rajputs. They worship the *pipal*, *tulsi* and *kadamba* trees, and will not injure them on any account. Their priests are Audich or Kanojia Bráhmans. Religion.

Khavás are personal attendants on Rajput Chiefs and Girásiás, and cultivators and day labourers. In former times the Golás used sometimes to accompany the corpse of their Chief to the funeral pile and burn themselves with it. When their widowed mistress breaks her bracelets, the maids break theirs, but afterwards get fresh ones. They receive food, lodging and clothes, and if their position in the family entitles them to it, ornaments also, but no money. As their duties are light and as all their wants are supplied by their masters, who defray the expenses connected with their births, marriages and deaths, they are well off.

Food. They eat the flesh of the goat, sheep, boar, antelope, spotted deer, hare, fowls, partridges and quails and drink liquor.

In Káthiáwár, twelve castes can meet and eat at a common table including Khavás, *viz.*, Rajputs, Kumbhárs, Bharváds, Valands, Bhois, Pakhális, Chárans, Ahirs, Mers, Gulasavas and Atits.

KHEDAWAL.—A sub-division of Bráhmans.

KHEDWA.—A synonym for Khedawál.

KHEDWAYA-MOMNA.—A sub-division of Khojáhs.

KHELKARI.—A synonym for Kolháti.

KHETARPHADI.—A sub-division of Dhors.

Name and origin. **KHETRIS**, Chhetris or Mustigars, a caste of husbandmen, numbering 15,390 (1901), including 7,962 males and 7,428 females, are found chiefly in Belgaum and Bijápur, a few being recorded in the Southern Marátha Country and in Kanara. The word Khetri is said by some to be a corruption of the Sanskrit Kshatriya, and their ancestors are said to have come from Central India. But a more probable derivation seems to be the Sanskrit *kshetra* or field, which is indicative of their occupation. The origin of the term Mustigar is unknown.

Divisions. There appear to be two endogamous divisions of the caste, of a territorial type, the Karnátak Khetris and the Kanara Khetris, who neither eat together nor intermarry. The Karnátak Khetris have no surnames or family-stock names, but persons known to belong to the same family do not intermarry.

The names in common use among men are Rámayya, Rangáppa and Timappa: and among women, Bálávva, Dyámavva, Girevva, Hanmavva, Malavva and Ráyavva. The men generally add *Mustiger* or *Chhetri* to their names. Their home tongue is Kanarese. They are bound together by a strong caste feeling and settle social disputes at meetings of adult castemen under the hereditary headman or *Kattimani*, whose opinion carries great weight in all caste matters. Any one who fails to accept the headman's decision is put out of caste. Breaches of rules are punished by a fine which generally takes the form of a caste feast. Polygamy and widow marriage are allowed and practised, but polyandry is unknown.

Marriage ceremonies.

Boys are married between fifteen and twenty-five, and girls between eight and twenty. At the engagement or marriage-fixing ceremony a party comes from the boy's to the girl's. The girl is dressed in a robe presented to her by the boy and her lap is filled with rice and a cocoanut, plantains, and betelnuts and leaves. Betel leaves and nuts are handed among the guests and the men from the bridegroom's house withdraw. On the *báshtagi* or betrothal the girl wears another robe given by the bridegroom with ornaments and a bodice, and, before the house gods, her lap is filled with rice and five kinds of fruit. A day or two before the marriage the god-pleasing or *devakárya* is performed in front of both houses and attended by friends and relations, and her parents take the girl to the bridegroom's village. The girl's party is lodged at a house close to the boy's and on the same day he is treated to a dinner at the bride's. At the bride's house five married women rub the couple with turmeric paste. In the morning, with the help of the men, five married women build a booth. At noon, caste people are feasted, and before sunset the bride's kinswomen bring pots from the potter's. A square called *surgi* with an earthern pot at each corner is made ready, a thread is passed round the necks of the pots, the couple and their mothers are seated in the square, and they are bathed in warm water. The thread that was passed round the pot necks is twisted into four separate cords and tied round the wrists of the couple and their mothers. Lights are waved round them to guard them from the evil eye and other evil influences, and they bow before the bride's family gods, come out, and fall prostrate in the booth. On the third or marriage day, the bridegroom's kinswomen ask the bride to accompany the bridegroom to his house. The bride agrees and starts followed by a married man carrying an earthern pot called *surgi bhum*, or the square earth-offering, holding vermicelli, rice, and raw sugar, and by a married woman with an earthen vessel filled with water on her head. At the bridegroom's the man is presented with a turban and the woman with a bodice, and the couple are received by the boy's household. Sweetmeats and water are laid before the family gods, the hands and feet of the couple are washed with the water, and they are fed with the sweetmeats along with ten married women, five from each house. The marriage party visits the shrine of the local Máruti, and the bridegroom and bride are dressed in rich clothes and decked with ornaments. At a lucky hour they are made to stand in the booth face to face on low stools covered with millet and five copper coins, and separated by a curtain of which the centre is marked with a red Jain cross or *svástik*, which they call *mandi* and consider the goddess of good fortune. Threads are tied round the wrist of the bride and bridegroom, and, at the lucky moment, the priest throws red rice over them and fastens the lucky necklace round the bride's neck. Betelnuts and leaves are handed to the guests and money to the Bráhmans. The hems of the couple's garments are knotted together and they bow to the family gods and elders. Next comes the *Bhuma Jevan* or earth-offering feast, when the couple with five married women on each side feast on cakes, rice, and clarified butter brought in equal quantities from the two houses. Friends and relations are feasted at the bridegroom's, and the couple are rubbed with turmeric and made to splash each other with turmeric water. The ceremony ends with presents of clothes made by the relations of the couple. They are then seated on a bullock, taken to Máruti, before whom they break a cocoanut, and return home. Lastly they both play at hide-and-seek. The girl is formally handed by her parents to the care of the bridegroom's mother. The bride's relations return home and the wedding ceremonies are over.

Religion. Khetris belong to the Hindu religion. Their family deities are Kálamma, Máruti, Venkatarama of Tirupati and Yellamma, and they also worship other Bráhmanic and local gods. They keep the usual Bráhmanic and local Hindu fasts and feasts, make pilgrimages to the shrines of their family gods, and visit local fairs held in honour of Hindu and Musalmán saints. They keep two special holidays, the full-moon of *Ashvin* and *Bahuláshtami* or the dark eighth of *Márgashirsha.* They believe in soothsaying and evil spirits. They ask Deshasth Bráhmans to officiate at their ceremonies, and after a birth or death ask Oshtama Bráhmans to purify them with *tulsi* (sweet basil) water. Their marriages are conducted by three men, a Deshasth Bráhman, the *Kattimani* or caste headman, and an Oshtama.

Death ceremonies. The dead are burnt. After death the body is bathed, set close to a wall, and tied in a sitting position to a peg fixed in the wall. It is wrapped in a blanket, laid on a bier, and taken by four men to the burning ground, where the pile is prepared, and the body burnt. When the pile is nearly consumed, the chief mourner walks three times round it with an earthern pot on his shoulder, pierces three holes in the pot, throws the pot over his shoulder, and beats his mouth with the back of his right hand. Gifts are given to Bráhmans, and the Mahár, who is called the son of the soil, is given something as the price of the land which was used for the pyre. On the third day the ashes of the deceased are gathered and thrown into water. On the fifth, the chief mourner worships three stones in the name of the deceased, and offers them boiled rice without looking to see whether or not it is touched by a crow. On the eleventh day the friends and relations are treated to a rich feast of boiled mutton and wheat cakes. A month after the death goats are killed and caste people are feasted. The anniversary or death-day mind-feast or *shráddha* at the end of the year is optional.

The chief and hereditary calling of Khetris is husbandry. Some also work as labourers and cart-drivers. They are successful husbandmen but poor gardeners. They eke out their field profits by the sale of dairy produce, but as a class they are poor and debt-burdoned. Occupation.

They use all kinds of animal food except beef and pork, and drink liquor. Food.

KANARA KHETRIS have two *gotras*, Bháradwája and Káshyap, which are exogamous. They have no surnames. The names in common use among men are Putappa, Mudiyana, Irranna, and Huchanna; and among women, Shitamma, Irrama, Pukamma and Lingamma. They speak Kanarese. Polygamy is allowed, widow marriage is forbidden, and polyandry is unknown. Girls are married before they come of age, and boys between sixteen and twenty-five. When a match is proposed, the village *joshi* or astrologer, who is asked to see whether the match will prove lucky, comes to the houses of the bridegroom and bride, and, after comparing their horoscopes, fixes a time for the marriage. The ceremony lasts four days. In the morning of the day before the wedding five women from the bridegroom's house and five from the bride's visit the bride and the bridegroom in their houses and rub them with turmeric paste. On the first day the bridegroom, dressed in a waistcloth, a long white coat, and a head-scarf and wearing the marriage coronet, goes in procession with a knife, betel leaves and a cocoanut in his hands to the bride's house. When he reaches the bride's house, her father comes forward, washes his feet, and leads him into the booth, where he sits on a bench, and is presented with clothes. A cloth curtain is then held in front of him by two men, the bride is led in, and the bride and bridegroom stand facing each other separated by the curtain. The priest repeats texts and, at the proper time, the curtain is withdrawn, and the bridegroom and bride throw strings of flowers round each other's necks.

and the parents of the bride pour water on their joined hands (the *dháre* ceremony). Then the evil-averting strings called *Kankandora* are tied round their hands and the bridegroom puts round the neck of the bride the lucky necklace, the sign of married life. Five large betelnuts are tied to the ends of the bridegroom's and bride's robes who sit side by side and have the ends of their robes tied together. Gifts of money are made to Bráhmans and caste people are feasted. Women sprinkle red rice on the brows of the pair and wave lighted lamps round them. The second and the third days pass in the bride's house in entertainments. On the fourth evening the bride and bridegroom, seated either in a palanquin or on horse or bullockback, are taken to the village temple to bow to the god. On the fifth day the pair go in procession to the bridegroom's, where a feast is given. This concludes the marriage ceremony.

Religion. The Kanara Khetris are Hindus of the Vaishnava sect. They worship all Vaishnava gods, especially Venkataráma, who is their family god. They make pilgrimages to his shrine at Tirupati. Of the sixteen Bráhmanic sacraments they observe seven, *Garbhádhán* or puberty, *Shemanti* or pregnancy, *Námakarana* or naming, *Chaula* or shaving, *Upanayana* or thread-girding, *Viváha* or marriage, and *Shráddha* or funeral rites. They believe in soothsaying and consult professional mediums who generally belong to the Halepaik caste. Their spiritual teacher is Tátiáchári, a Shrivaishnava Bráhman, who lives at Terkavlur in South Arcot. He is a married man and comes on visitation tours generally once in three years, when his adherents pay him 4 annas to Rs. 4 according to their means. The Tátiáchári enquires into breaches of social discipline, punishes offenders, and re-admits the excommunicated. Fines levied for misdemeanours belong to the teacher, whom all hold in such high respect that they prostrate themselves at his feet and worship him when he visits them. Their priests are Karnátak Bráhmans.

Death. The dead are burnt. On reaching the burning ground the body is placed on the funeral pile which has been made ready by a Mahár or other low-caste man. The shroud is taken off and given with $1\frac{3}{8}$ annas and two pounds of rice to the Mahár. Logs of wood are piled over the body and the chief mourner sets fire to the pile. When the body is consumed the chief mourner offers the deceased cooked rice, and all except the mourners go to bathe in some pond or spring. When they have bathed, they accompany the chief mourner to his house and retire to their homes. On the twelfth day after death all the mourners shave their faces and swallow the five products of the cow. Crows are then fed and caste people feasted, and a *shráddha* is held on every anniversary day.

The main occupation of the caste is husbandry. Some have their own lands, while others take land on lease, either on condition of sharing the produce equally or of paying the land-owner a fixed quantity of grain or money. Some are petty shopkeepers. They deal in rice, fruit, spices and oil, which they buy wholesale from the producers. Occupation.

They neither eat flesh nor drink liquor. They rank with Maráthás. Food

KHETRI KOMARPANTH.—A synonym for Komárpaik.

KHICHADYA.—A sub-division of Modh Bráhmans.

KHIKRI.—A sub-divisoin of Dhangars.

KHILARI.—A sub-division of Dhangars.

KHILLARI.—A synonym for Gavli.

KHISA KATRA.—A synonym for Bhámta.

KHODIA.—A sub-division of Pália Dublás.

KHOJAHS, numbering 50,837 (males 25,555, females 25,282) at the 1901 Census and 52,367 (males 26,387 and females 25,980) at the 1911 Census are scattered all over Gujarát, in Cutch, Káthiáwár, in the Portuguese territories of Diu and Daman, in Bombay City, Thána, Khándesh and Sind; and beyond the Presidency in Calcutta, the Punjab, Kashmir, Kábul, Dárdistán, Nagar Hunza, (1) Bahrein, Bandar Abbas, Mina, Linga, Kism, Karbala, and Sháh Najaf, and, in Arabia proper, in Maskat, Aden and Sheher Mukalla. There is a flourishing colony of Khojáhs in Zanzibar. The term Khojáh has the sectarian sense of "honourable convert(2)". Khojáh is the form used in India for the Persian Khwájah, "a rich or respectable man; a gentleman; an opulent merchant(3)". Name and origin.

Khojáhs are Ismáiliás of the Nazárian sub-division, who separated in A. D. 1094 from the Mustaálian Ismáilians on a question regarding the succession to the throne of the Fátimite Khiláphat in Egypt(4). The cause of Nazár, the elder son of Al-Mustansirbillah History.

(1) Bombay Gazetteer, Vol. IX, Part II, p. 36.

(2) The great Khojáh case of 1866, pp. 10—12.

(3) Hughes-Dictionary of Islam (1885), p. 277. It is said to be of Turkish origin and to mean also bard, teacher, and also, like *Máulá* both serf and master. (Burton's Sind 412. Bombay Gazetteer, Vol. IX, Part II, p. 36.) But the modern Persian and sectarian senses are as given in the text.

(4) Founded in A.D. 910 (A.H. 299) by Obeidullah, who first assumed the title of al-Máhdi.

(A.D. 1036-1095), one of the claimants to the Egyptian succession, was espoused and energetically promoted, especially in Persia, where it subsequently rose to be supreme, by Hasan Sabah, an Ismailian missionary, who was born at Rai, about fifteen miles south of Teheran and now in ruins, in the beginning of the eleventh century. Hasan founded the order of the Fidáwis or Fidáis or devotees known in Europe probably from their leader's name as the Assassins[1]. Hasan concentrated his power at Alamut or the Falcon's Nest, an impregnable hill fort on the borders of the Persian district of Dailem, about 200 miles north of Kazwin, which, with a small section of the surrounding country, he had acquired in the latter part of the eleventh century partly by stratagem, partly by purchase, from the commandant of the Seljuk emperor Malak-sháh (A.D. 1072—1092). After gaining Alamut, Hasan resolved to cease acting as *dai* or missionary and political emissary of the Fátimites, and, though he did not yet arrogate to himself the title of *Unrevealed Imám*, he made himself known by the convenient style of *Shaikh-ul-Jabal* Lord, or, according to the Crusaders, Old Man of the Mountain, a title which two of his immediate successors continued to use. Before his death at an advanced age in A.D. 1124, Hasan had the satisfaction of leaving his order flourishing and bidding fair to undermine by his Fidáwi's poignard[2], as well as by the levelling force of his doctrines, the neighbouring monarchies of Islám. His successors becoming the terror of kings and the authors of revolutions, ruled from the confines of Khurásán to the mountains of Syria and from the Caspian Sea to the Mediterranean[3]. Hasan (A.D. 1163, H. 559), the son of Muhammad, the son of Buzurg-Umeid, the fourth ruler on the pontifical throne of Alamut, threw aside the mystery with which the son of Sabáh had deemed it politic to surround his doctrines. He declared himself the Unrevealed Imám and preached that no action of a believer in him could be a sin[4]. He is called

(1) On the other hand Sir Joseph Arnould observes: It is likely enough that the etymology insisted upon by Silvestre de Sacy should be correct and the origin be the word by which the Ismáiliás of Alámut and Massiat were designated in the eastern languages. This name is *Hash-shi-shin*, a word derived from the use of Hashish *bháng* or hemp-water with which Hasan and his successors subdued the souls while they inflamed the energies of the Fidáwis whom they employed as their instruments. (The great Khoják case of A.D. 1866). Against this derivation it is to be noted that not one of the Arab or Persian historians of the time designates the Ismáilias by the title of *Hash-shi-shins*. All call them Mulahidah or heretics. (Elliot, II.-353-337; Farishtah-Persian Text, II, 645-646).

(2) The primary meaning of fidáwi from the Arabic *fidá* to ransom is scapegoat. The Ismáilia Fidáwis were the volunteers of the order courting death for its glory. Sir Joseph Arnould styles them the self-offering or devoted. The Great Khoján Case of 1866, page 9.

(3) Von Hanmer's Assassins by Lee, 77-88, 91-92.

(4) Von Hanmer's Assassins, by Lee, 109.

the " Ruler of the world who loosened the bonds of the Law ". No Khojáh mentions his name without the words *A'la Zikri-his-Salam.* Peace be to his name.(1) It is through this Hasan that his Highness the Agha Khan traces his decent from Ali.(2) The Indian Khojáhs further believe that Hasan was the first of their Imáms to send a missionary to India. The name of this missionary was Nur Satágur.(3) In the beginning of the reign of Sultánah Rasiah (A.D. 1237-1240) Minháj-us-Siráj the author of the Tabakát-i-Násiri(4) speaks as an eye-witness of the *Mulahidah* heretics of Hindustán being reduced by a person with some " pretentions to learning called Nur the Turk " (probably Nur Satagár, the missionary of Hasan Zikri-his-salám), " flocking to him in large numbers from all parts of Hindustán such as Sind, Gujarát, the environs of Delhi, and the banks of the Ganges and Jamna." Minháj-us-Siráj goes on to say that when Nur preached the rabble gathered around him. He used to call the learned Sunnis *Nasibis*, or enemies of Ali and usurpers of his patrimony, and their followers *Marjis* or hopefuls. On Friday the 6th of Rajab H. 634 (March 1237) his followers to the number of a thousand men, inflamed by his fulminations against the orthodox, and armed with swords, shields, arrows and other weapons, attacked the Jáma Mosque of Delhi and slew many of the congregation assembled there till they were routed with great loss by the officers of the Empress Rasiah. According to the Khojáh accounts Nur-uddin, or as they call him Nur Satágur, came from Deilam to Pátan in Gujarát, when that country was goverened by a Hindu prince, apparently the Solanki Bhima II (A.D. 1179-1242). He made a number of converts by ordering the idols of a Hindu temple to speak and bear testimony to the truth of his mission. He is said to have returned to Persia shortly after converting the Hindu ruler of Pátan secretly to his faith.(5) On his second visit to Gujarát he married the daughter of Rája Surchand, chief or governor of Navsári near Surat. His success as a proselytiser and his wealth exciting the envy of his followers, he was killed by Chách, one of his two leading

---

(1) Mir Khond on the authority of Yusuf Sháh Kátib (or the Scribe) relates that over the door of the library of Alámut, Hasan had caused the following couplet to be engraved :—

Bar-dasht tauaui-shar-abataid-i-I' sadi.
Makhdum-i-rusgar-aala-Zikri-his-salam.

With the help of God he hath undone the collar of the Law,
The ruler of the world, He of blessed memory.
Von Hanmer's Assassins—Wood, 108-100.

(2) The great Khojáh case of 1866, page 9, paragraph 1.
(3) The Khojáh Vratant, 155.
(4) Elliott, II.—335-336
(5) The Khojáh hymn called Ramat in the Khojáh Vratant, 155.

disciples while he was absorbed in *samádhi* or contemplation. The name Nur Satágur "Teacher of pure light" which he took in addition to his own name Nur-ud-din or Nurshâh and the practice of the Hindu abstraction or *samádhi* show the process by which the first Ismailla preachers succeeded in converting Hindus. (1) The Ismália preachers gained their chief success among the Afghán tribe of Lohánás. According to the tribe-legends preserved by the Khojáhs the Lohánás are descended from Lava, a son of Ráma, who founded the tribe of the Ráthors to which the Lohánás belong. According to another story, of which there seem to be several versions, Rája Jaichand of Kanauj took to wife an Afghán woman who was made captive after the defeat of Shaháb-ud-din Ghori (A.D. 1178) and who in revenge caused Jaichand's death. Jaichand's son, to quiet his father's angry spirit, was advised to feed many Brahma-Kshatris. The Kshatris refused and fled to Lahuragadh. The title Khwájáh meaning Lord which they received on their conversion to Islám from their *Pir* Sadr-ud-din seems a translation of the title Thakkar or Thákur by which Lohánás are addressed. In support of this it is to be noticed that in Hálár or North-east Káthiáwár Khojáhs are still addressed by the Lohána title of Thakkar and wear their waist cloths in Lohána fashion. Further the language of the Khojáhs and of some of their Sindi religious hymns contains a liberal mixtúre of Punjábi words which are also present in the language of the Káthiáwár Lohánás.

A later element of strength in the Khojáh community is of Káshmir origin. Farishtah(2) mentions the *Cháks*, originally a race of sun-worshippers, who called themselves *Raushanias* The People of Light. During the reign of Fateh-sháh of Káshmir (A.D. 1458-59; H. 864) these *Cháks* were converted to the Ismáili's faith by a missionary from Irák. This was Shams-ud-din, the second Ismáilia missionary to India, who, according to the Khojáh hymns, was able to work miracles.(3) Shams-ud-din settled at Uch in Baháwal-

(1) Another Ismáilia missionary Sadr-ud-din adopted the Hindu names of Sahdeva and Harchand. Apart from its popularity with Hindus the adoption of a Hindu name was in agreement with the Sufi (tasaw-wuf) rule as laid by Saádi (A.D. 1258):—

Saddiya gar wasl khahi Sulh kun ba kahs o am ;
Ba Musalmans Allah Allah, ba Hunudan Ram Ram.

Saàdi if thou wishest union, live at peace with low and high ;
With the Muslim call on Allah, with the Hindu Rám Rám cry.

(2) Persian Text, II, 647.

(3) Farishtah notices that he met with elders of the Nur Baksh order in Badakhshán. He found they differed in no way from the orthodox either in appearance or in ostensibly following the rules of the *Sunnah* or tradition. He says a son of Nur Baksh showed him Nur Baksh's book, in which he found much to admire. Farishtah Persian Text, II, 643.

pur about eight miles south of Multán, where his shrine still exists.[1] The followers of Shams-ud-din number about 75,000 in the Punjab and Káshmir. Many of his Bhoi (porter), Sonár (goldsmith) and Kására (coppersmith) converts, though still believing in him, have gone back to Hinduism, and many who never ceased to be Hindus continue to believe in him. According to the Khoját accounts Shams-ud-din is the disciple of Nur Satágur whom Shams served under the name of Chote. Farishtah gives A.D. 1496 as the date of Shams Chote's arrival in Káshmir.[2]

About A.D. 1430 Sadr-ud-din known as the third Pir was appointed head of the Khojáhs of Káshmir, Sind and the Punjab and was the first Pir to found a *Khánah* or Khoját religious lodge. He conceived the idea of taking all the Khojáhs of India to visit the Unrevealed Imám in Persia. The huge army of pilgrims travelled till they reached Gujarát in the Punjab. At Gujarát to test the faith of his headmen, the *Pir* betook himself to the house of a prostitute seemingly forgetful of the sacred errand on which he had persuaded his followers to start. Two of the headmen lost faith in Sadr-ud-din. But Trikam, the Sind Mukhi, though vilely repulsed, satisfied the demands of the prostitute and took his *Pir* with him to the camp of pilgrims. At the next encampment the faith of the followers was still more rudely tested. The Sind headman alone passed the ordeal unscathed. In the end the *Pir* went alone to Alamit. He saw the Imám incarnate, returned to Uch, died and was buried at a village called Jetpur near Uch.

As about A.D. 1200 Nur-Satágur had converted Gujarát, so one of his successors Rámde, originally a Tuwar Rajput sowed the seed of the Ismáilia faith in Cutch and Káthiáwár. About A.D. 1430, from the Ismáilia lodge (*khánah*) he had established at Kotda in Sind, Pir Sadr-ud-din started the first tythe-gathering wallet (*jholi*) on its rounds from the Himalayas to the Vindhya range. It was Pir Sadr-ud-din who, to impart everlasting vigour to the tree of the Ismáilia faith, engrafted into it the name of Ali, and also the name of Agha Islám Sháh an ancestor of his Highness the Agha Khán, as Ali's

---

(1) One of the most famous of Shams Chote's miracles was the calling to life of the dead son of a powerful noble of Uch. The Pir said: In the name of Allah thou that art dead arise. The corpse did not stir. Then Shams-ud-din said: In the name of Shams thou that are dead arise, and the boy drew up and stretched out his hands and feet, yawned, sneezed, and was one of the living. Farishtah (Persian Text, II. 643) seems to think that much of the success of Shams-ud-din in converting the Chak sun worshippers was due to the happy accident that the missionary's name was "Sun of the Faith" *Shams-ud-din.*

(2) Major Biddulph's Tribes of the Hindu Kush 124.

incarnation, together with the nine Avatárs of his Vishnu-worshipping followers. Up to Pir Sadr-ud-din's time Adam and the Prophet of Islám were unknown in the Hindu Pantheon. Adam is now introduced as Vishnu and the prophet of Islám as Mahesh. Again, as Islám Sháh was the incarnation of Ali, so Nur-Satágur was the incarnation of Brahma and Sadr-ud-din was the incarnation of Bálaráma. The last of the Imáms, the coming Mahdi, was explained to be the *Nishkalanki* or stainless Avatár, whose appearance was looked for by the Saktipanthis as the millennium.*

After Sadr-ud-din came Kabir-ud-din who was succeeded by Imám-ud-din known in Gujarát as Imám Sháh. Imám Sháh was not well received by the Sind Khojáhs and had to withdraw to Persia where, after visiting the Imám at Kekht, he returned to India in A.D. 1452. Disgusted with his Sind followers he turned his footsteps towards Gujarát and was favourably received by Mahmud Begada (A.D. 1459-1511). Imám-ud-din founded a new sect in Gujarát with opinions differing in some minor points from the doctrines of the Ismáilia faith. The Khojáhs possess to this day a hymn composed by Imám Sháh called the *janázah* or Bier in which he describes his journey to the heavens through the power of the Imám, and his meeting with Pralhádha, Harischandra, Yudhisthira, Sadr-ud-din and others. Imám Sháh died in A.D. 1512. His disciples, who belong to the class of Momnás, are to be found in Ahmedábád, Kaira, Cambay, Baroda, Bhávnagar, Surat, Khándesh and Cutch. Owing to the deviation of his teaching from the doctrines laid down by the older Khojáh *Pirs* and owing to his denouncing the Khojáh practice of levying *dassondh* or tythes, Imám Sháh was excommunicated by Abdas-salám, the son of Islám-sháh, the unrevealed Khojáh Imám of the time. In Gujarát after the death of Pir Imám-ud-din (A.D. 1512) active proselytizing ceased. About A.D. 1594 Kapura Lohána and some other Khojáhs carried the tythe wallet of the Indian Ismáilias to Kekht in Persia, the residence of Agha Abd-us-Salám the unrevealed Imám. To supply the want of a missionary Agha Abd-us-Salám wrote in Persian for the guidance of his Indian followers a book called the *Pandyád-i-Jawánmardi*, that is, the Maxims of Fortitude. This book transliterated and translated into Sindi and Gujaráti forms part of the scriptures of the Khojáhs and is regarded with a veneration which gives the book the twenty-sixth place in the list of the Khojáh *Pirs* or saints. The mystic strain in their faith the

* For further details of the Hinduized presentation of the Ismáiliah faith see below.

Khojáhs trace to certain allegorical traditions of the Prophet and Ali. (1)

About the middle of the sixteenth century the backsliding of the Punjáb Khojáhs to Sunniism showed the need of a vice-pontiff in India. The Imám summoned one Dáud or Dádu, a descendant of a powerful family of Sind Khojáhs, and invested him with the mantle of a Pir. The day of Dádu's investiture is still celebrated by the Khojáhs as the Shah's Id. About 1549 (Samvat A.D. 1606) Pir Dádu, owing to the hostility of the Sumrás, left Sind and settled in Jámnagar. Here they were honourably received by the Jám and at his request forty more families of Khojáhs were invited. A plot of land near the town was assigned to them and round it they raised a wall, one of whose gates is still known as Dádu's Gate. After converting some Káthiáwár Lohánás, Dádu went to Bhuj, the capital of Cutch in the reign of Ráo Bhármal I (A.D. 1585-1631). Here a rain-compelling miracle procured the Pir many converts. Pir Dádu died in A. D. 1594 and was succeeded by his son Sadik, after whom the title of Pirship became extinct, the deputy of the Imám being henceforth styled *Vakil*. Owing to family dissensions Sádik's grandson moved from Bhuj to Hálár in Káthiáwár. In A.D. 1844 the Khojáh Imám Agha Sháh Hasan Ali discontinuing the appointment of local Khojáhs as his *Vakils* sent out his nephew to Cutch as his deputy. A year later (A.D. 1845), Agha Sháh Hasan Ali better known as his Highness the Agha-Khán himself came to India and was the first Ismáilia unrevealed Imám to settle in this country. He was eighteenth in descent from Ruknuddin Khur Sháh during whose tenure of the Ismáilia pontificate in A.D. 1255, Haláku Khán the Tartar massacred the Ismáilia population of Persia, and dismantled their forts.

Khojáhs are split up into seven divisions(2). They are as follows :— Divisions.

(1) Atlai-Khurásáni.

(2) Badakhsháni and Kábuli.

---

(1) Ali being asked how he came to know Allah replied: I came to know my Maker from the weakness of my own purpose. In justification of their belief in incarnations the Khojáhs put forward the argument about Godhead in Man furnished by a tradition which they attribute to the Prophet: I am the 'Mim' less Muhammad. This is *Ahad*, the One and Unique Allah. (That is, without its three *ms* or *mins* Muhammad becomes *Ahad*). A scoffer asked Ali; What is Allah? The Prince of the Faithful replied: Hast thou been at sea in a sinking ship? Though the winds sang thy dirge and the waves threatened to engulf thee like the veritable black valley of Jehanna, even then did no small benign voice whisper to thee 'Thou shalt be saved'. That voice, oh thou of little belief, was Allah. The Khojáhs are fond of the Prophet's saying: Think not on the being, think on the bounty of God. Khojáh Vratant 1-10.

(2) The Khojáh Vartánt, p. 255.

(3) Gujar-Gupti.
(4) Khedwáya Momna.
(5) Mochi-Momna.
(6) Multáni.
(7) Soni-Lohár.

Birth. Khojáhs have many observances and customs differing from those of regular Musalmáns. The *chhatti* or sixth day ceremony after birth differs from that performed by regular Gujárat Musalmáns. Near the bed of the mother is placed a *bájot* or wooden stool, on which after the child and mother have been bathed and dressed, on the evening of the sixth day are placed a reedpen, an inkstand, a blank book, a knife and a garland of flowers. The pen, ink and paper are intended for the Goddess of Fortune who is believed to write the destiny of the newborn child. A *chaumukh* four-sided butter-fed dough lamp is also placed on the stool and lighted and close to the lamp is set a box of Chinese crackers. As each of the female relatives of the family comes in she strews a little rice near the stool, lays on the ground her present of gold or silver wristlets and anklets for the child and, bending over the mother and her newborn babe, takes their *baláyen* or ills upon herself by passing her hands over them and cracking her finger joints against her temples. The little one is then laid on the ground on the strewn rice and the mother rises and worships the child by bowing towards it and to the *chaumukh* or four-faced lamp on the stool. Crackers are then let off and the child is laid in its mother's lap.

Marriage. The Khojáh marriage keeps a relic of the marriage by purchase which they believe once obtained among them. Three or four days before the marriage the fathers or male guardians of the marrying pair meet one evening at the Jamá-át Khánáh or assembly lodge with their friends and relatives and the Mukhi or other Jamá-át officer. The officer registers the names of the bride and bridegroom in a register kept under the order of his Highness the Agha Khán. The father of the bridegroom gives Rs. 5¼ to the father of the bride. The sum is received by the girl's father and handed to the Jamá-át officer as the marriage contribution to the fund. The bridegroom's friends place before the Jamá-át officer a copper or brass tray containing from five to ten *seers* of sugar. The Jamá-át officer, after repeating the hallowed names of the Five or *Panj-tan*, that is, Muhammad, Ali, Fátimáh, Hasan and Husein declares "I do hereby begin the wedding of Mehr Ali, son of Karam Ali, with Rábiáh, the fourth daughter of Padamsi Punja, to wed as did wed Fátimáh, the bright-faced lady, daughter of our Lord and Prophet

Muhammad (on whom be peace) with the Lord and the leader, the receiver of the testament of the Chosen and Pure, the Lord Ali, the son of Abu Talib." The sugar tray is then placed before the bride's father who, in token of ratifying the compact, tastes a pinch of the sugar which is then distributed among those present. This is the verbal compact.

On the morning of the next day, the written agreement is prepared. A thick parchment-like sheet of blank paper is taken together with trays full of dried fruit and sugar to the bride's house by the bridegroom's father and his friends accompanied by the Jamá-át officers. The Jamá-át scribe begins the writing with the names of the five holy persons and the names of the four archangels in the four corners. Then are entered the names of the contracting parties with those of their fathers and grandfathers, the amount of the marriage portion, the names of the chief Jamá-át officers of the day, and the dates on which the chief marriage ceremonies are to be preformed. Saffron water is sprinkled over the sheet of paper, which, together with the sugar and dried fruit, is laid before the bridegroom's father. The bridegroom's father lays the sheet on the ground and on it places an iron nail and four betelnuts and throws some rice over it. Then folding it he wraps it and the betelnuts in an unused silk or cotton handkerchief and takes it away. Except that in Bombay the *Nikah* ceremony is performed by his Highness the Agha Khán himself and outside Bombay by his officers, the ceremonies that follow possess no note-worthy peculiarity.

The religion of the Khojáhs is Shiáh Ismáiláism. To the simple Sunni *Kalimah* or profession of faith "there is no God but Alláh and Muhammad is His Prophet" the Shiáh adds "and Ali, the companion of Muhammad, is the Vicar of God". The elevation of Ali to an almost equal place with the Prophet is the distinctive tenet of the Shiáhs.(1) The whole religious life of the Shiáh is steeped in a current of thoughts, beliefs, traditions and observances having their source in Ali, the Lady Fátimáh, and their two sons Hasan and Husain, four venerated names which with that of the apostle of God compose the Pentad or Panj-Tan of the holy family of Islám. To revere Ali as the Vicar, still more as the incarnation of Alláh, to go on pilgrimage to Sháh Najaf, the supposed place of Ali's martyrdom, 120 miles southwest of Baghdád, and at Karbála to bow the forehead on moulds **Religion.**

(1) Etymologically Shiáh means separatist, which is probably the correct derivation. The term was originally applied to those pure-blooded members of Ali's family who fell early victims to the hostility of the Sunni Umayad Khalifáhs of Damascus (A.D. 661—745). Sir Joseph Arnould in the great Khojáh case of 1866,

of Karbála clay and to drink the holy clay dissolved in water are practices as meritorious in the eyes of the Shiáh as they are forbidden in the estimation of the Sunni. The Sunni prays with folded arms five times, the Shiáh with his arms straight by his side three times a day. The Shiáh venerates Ali and Fátimáh and execrates the memory of the first three Khalifáhs. The Sunni reverences the first three Khalifáhs equally with Ali and the Lady Fátimáh. The Shiáh laws of marriage, divorce and inheritance, though drawn from the same source, are completely opposed to the Sunni laws. The Khojáhs, like the Memans, follow the Hindu law of inheritance.(1) The Sunni considers it his duty, if he can afford it, to make a pilgrimage to Mecca and Madina. With the Shiáh it is an act of merit if he has visited the shrines of Ali and Husain.(2)

The Shiáhs are divided into two classes, the *Isna-asharis* or Twelvers who believe in the twelve Imáms, the descendants of Ali. To this branch of the Shiáh faith belong the regular classes of the Persian and Indian Shiáhs. The other branch is that of the Seveners or *Sábins* who are called Ismáilians because they reckon seven Imáms and make Ismáil, the son of Muhammad, the son of Jaáfar Sadik, the last of the revealed Imáms. The difference between the Twelvers and the Seveners starts from the seventh Imám. The power of the Seveners originated with the dynasty of the Fátimis in Egypt (A.D. 910—1171) founded by Obeidullah (A.D. 910) who through Muhammad Habib, the son of Jaáfar Musaddik, who claimed descent from Ismáil, the seventh and according to the Ismáilias the last of the revelaed Imáms. Muhammad, the son of Ismáil, and his son Jaáfar Musaddik and his son Muhammad Habib are called by the Ismáilias their *Maktum* or Concealed Imams in contradistinction to Obeidullah, the asserter of the rights of the family of Ismáil to the Khiláphat, a Revealed Imám. On the establishment of the Fátimite dynasty in Africa

(1) During the absence of his Highness the Agha in Calcutta in A.D. 1846-47 and 1848 litigation was carried on and concluded which again divided the Khojáhs of Bombay into two hostile parties. It was the well-known case as to the rights of female inheritance among the Khojáhs, called Sarjun Mir Ali's case, in which Sir Erskine Perry in A.D. 1847 pronounced a learned judgment, founded on the evidence of caste-usage and custom, against the rights of Khojáh females to inherit according to the rules of Muhammadan law. The great Khojáh case of 1866.

(2) Sir Joseph Arnould, on whose judgment in the great Khojáh case of A.D. 1866 much of the above contrast is based, thus sums the differences: In a word agreeing in reverencing Muhammad as the Prophet and the Kuraan as the word of Alláh the Sunnis and Shiáhs agree in little else except in hating each other with the bitterest hatred. (The great Khojáh case.) The Shiáh calls the Sunni a *Nasibi* and a *Kháriji*, a usurper and an outgoer. The Sunni retorts by calling the Shiáh a *Ráfzi* or rejecter. Sir Richard Burton (Alf Lailah-wa-Lailah, IV, 44, note I) says: The Shiáhs have no ground to feel offended at the word *Rafzi* being applied to them as the name was taken from their own saying *Imma rafadhna hum* verily we have rejected or renounced them, that is the first three Khalifahs.

(A.D. 910) the Ismáilia doctrines were first publicly taught at Mahdia, a city founded by Obeidullah afterwards surnammed Al Mahdi and after the conquest of Egypt, by the fourth Fátimite Ali-Muizz (A.D. 953—975) at Cairo. Towards the close of the eleventh century (A.D. 1072—1092) the power of the Ismáilias was established at Alamut in Persia by Hasan Sabáh. The doctrines of the Ismáilias of Persia remained without change till the year A.D. 1163 when the fourth successor of Hasan Sabáh, Alazikri-his-salám, abrogated the rule of secrecy and promulgated his doctrines and transferred the Imámate from the Fátimite to himself.(1) From Alázikri-his-salám the Khojáhs derive the succession and descent of their present Imám his Highness the Agha Khan. For the presentation of the Ismáilia faith in inviting form to the Shakti-worshipping Lohánás, see above. In addition to the equations there given the five Pándavas were equated with the first five famous Ismáilia pontiffs. Among the Mátapanthis each of the four Yugas or epochs has its preacher or *bhakta*. To the first epoch is assigned as *bhakta* Pralháda, to the second Harischandra, and to the third Yudhishthira. Instead of the fourth Balabhadra or Balaráma Pir Sadr-ud-din, the third Khojáh missionary, added his own name. The four sacrifices(2) of the four *jugas* were confirmed as were also confirmed the *Ghat Páth—Mantra* or prayer and ritual of the Shaktipanthis. Instead of Shaktipanthi Sadr-ud-din adopted the name of *Satpanth* or True Doctrine for his new faith. The Khojás repeat the hymns of Sadr-ud-din with great devotion and never name him but with extreme reverence. The forms of Khojáh prayer and ritual are laid down in the Book of Pandyádi Jawán Mardi by Agha Abdus Salám Sháh, one of the Khoja Imáms. The book is translated into old Hindu Sindi. Before the time of Pir Dádu (about A.D. 1550) the form of worship prescribed to the Khojás was daily attendance at the *khanáh* or prayer lodge and the repetition on a rosary of 99 or 101 beads the names *Pir-Sháh*(3) or *Sháh Pir*. Pir Dádu ordered his followers to pray three times a day like the Shiáhs, repeating the above words in their prayer and also repeating the names of all the Imáms down to the present Imám. The Khojáh prays sitting, mentally addressing his prayers to the Imám for the time. He also makes prostrations at stated intervals. The new moon, Muharram and Ramazán prayers are repeated in the Jamáat-Khánah with the Pir as Leader. While the prayer reciters are assembling a man stands at the chief entrance. He demands the

(1) Von Hanmer's Assassins, by Lee—20-109.

(2) The Balidána, the first Yuga sacrifice being the elephant, the second the horse, the third the cow, the fourth the goat. Khojáh Vratant, 195.

(3) Sháh, literally King, allegorically means *God*, and *Pir*, the Prophet. Khojáh Vratant, 239-40.

Khojáh shibboleth or watchward of every person seeking admission. The newcomer says : *Hai Zindah,* Oh, thou living one, and the Janitor answers *Kayámpáya* I have found him alike and true.(1) The Khojah's three daily prayers are : Morning prayer *Subo-ji-nimáz* between 4 and 5 a.m. ; evening prayer *Maghrib* or *Sánanji nimáz* at dusk ; and night prayer *Isáji nimáz* between 8 and 9 p.m., generally at home. Next to prayer the most important act of devotion is the counting of the names of the Pirs on a rosary of 101 beads made of Karbála clay. Third in importance is the Khojáh sacrament the *Ghat páth* or Heart-prayer. Except on holidays, Saturdays and Mondays, when in Bombay the Imám presides, the sacrament is held after the morning prayers at the chief Jamá-át-Khánah by the Jamá-át officers. Karbála clay is dissolved in a large bowl of water, and as each of the congregation rises to leave the lodge he goes to the person presiding, lays before him from 2 annas to 2 rupees and kisses his hand. He receives a small cup of the sacramental water which he drinks and retires.

Besides the *Dassondh* or tithe and the *Petondh* a smaller contribution, the Khojáh has to pay his Imám about sixteen minor contributions varying from $\frac{1}{4}$-5 annas to Rs. 1,000.(2) These he pays as the *zakát* or purification ordered by the Kuran. Besides these when pressed for money the Imám sends round the *Jholi* or wallet demanding an extraordinary levy of the tenth or fifth part of the whole of a Khojáh's possessions. This is called the *Bakkas*, a corruption of *bakshish* or voluntary gift. Though it once caused the defection of a large number from the community the Khojáhs have more than once cheerfully paid the *Bakkas.* It is known to have been paid in A.D. (1839-40).(3)

The *Dassondh* is levied on each newmoon day of every month, each Khojáh dropping into a cloth bag kept in the Jamá-át-Khánah for the purpose as much as he is inclined to pay, generally the tenth part of his monthly earnings. The *Kánga* is the contribution due for the initiation of a Khojáh child. It is paid by the parents at any

(1) It is said that Pir Kabir-u-din, the fourth Ismáilia missionary (A.D. 1448) in one of the visits to the Imám at Deilam, was addressed by the Imám as *Hai-zindah.* Oh living one. In reply the Pir said *káyámpáya* I have found him alive (meaning himself). These words repeated in a Khojáh's devotions possess a merit equal to the gift of a horse in charity. Khojáh Vratant, 212.

(2) The Khojáh Vratant at page 244 gives the names of some of the chief dues as: 1. *Sarshur*, 2. *Leko*, 3. *Choko*, 4. *Chopdo*, 5. *Samar-chhanto*, 6. *Marnu-parnu*, 7. *Chandranu-pirana.* 8. *Bhai-bhuki*, 9 *Darya Bakas*, 10. *Chhati mundu.* 11. *Gulfu*, 12. *Phoda-phodi*, 13. *Mata-salamati*, 14. *Mohur*, 15. *Sadamaji*, 16. *Kango.* The *Dassondh* and *Petondh*, though large dues, are not regularly paid. Many Khojáhs do not pay them at all.

(3) Sir Joseph Arnould's Judgment in the great Khojáh case of 1866, page 11,

time after the child has reached the age of four to twelve. This is the Khoján substitute for the *Bismilláh* ceremony of the regular Musalmáns.

Besides the *Ramazán* and the *Bakr Ids*, two holidays which they enjoy jointly with other Musalmáns, the Khojáhs observe nine other yearly holidays. They are as follows (1) :—

Katl.—Assassination of the Imam Ali ..	21st Ramazan.
Lailat-ul-Kadr.—Night of preordainment of Destinies	23rd Ramazan.
Id-i-Ghadir	18th Zir Hajjah.
Ashurah	9th and 10th Muharram.
Chihillum	21st of Safar.
Katl-i (Assassination of) Imam Hasan	29th ,,
I'd-i-Maulad (Husein's Birthday) ..	17th of the 1st Rabi.
The Nauruz or vernal Equinox	kept according to the Pársi calculation.
Birthday of his Highness Agha Khan	2nd November.

A remarkable feature at a Khoján's death is the *samarchhánta* or Holy Drop. The Jamá-át officer or the Mukhi asks the dying Khoján if he wishes the *samarchhánta*. If the dying person agrees, he or she bequeaths Rs. 5 to Rs. 500 or any larger amount to the Khoján Jamá-át. A Sindi-knowing Khoján is then called in to read the Book of the Ten Incarnations, *Das-Avatár*. A Jamá-át officer dilutes a cake of Karbála clay in water, and, to save the departing soul from the temptation of the Archfiend, who is believed to be present, offering a cup of false nectar, moistens the lips, and sprinkles the rest of the water on the face, the neck and the chest of the dying Khoján. The touch of the Holy Drop is believed to relieve the death agony as completely as among the Sunnis does the recital at a death-bed of the Chapter of the Kurán known as the Surah-i-Yásin. If the deceased is old and gray-haired the hair after death is dyed with *henna*. A garland of cakes of Karbála clay is tied round the neck of the corpse. If the body is to be buried locally two small circular patches of silk cloth cut from the covering of Husain's tomb, called *chashmáhs* or spectacles, are laid over the eyes. If the body is to be buried in the sacred soil of Karbála, the viscera are removed before the body is bathed, the hollow is filled with camphor and the incision carefully sewn. (2) After it is bathed and shrouded, the body is laid in a bier and Death.

(1) Bombay Gazetteer, Vol. IX, Part II, p. 49.

(2) This is doubtful. Some say the Shiáh in common with orthodox sections believe that it is sacrilege amounting to a mutilation to even handle the body roughly after death. They say that the viscera are not removed, but that a stout cotton ribbon about two inches in breadth is wound tightly and closely round the body of the corpse beginning from the toes and ending at the throat. After the body is deposited in the coffin the remaining space in the coffin is filled with finely pounded *henna* powder. The powdered *henna* absorbs all the moisture which the body exudes and prevents smell.

taken to a mosque and the prayers for the dead are repeated over it. It is then placed in an air-tight tin-lined coffin which is afterwards enveloped in tarred canvas. As long as the coffin lies at a mosque awaiting shipment the services of a Shiáh Mulláh are engaged at Rs. 5 to Rs. 50 to keep on reading the Kurán over the body. The coffins of dead Khojáhs are carried by steamer and transhipped at the mouth of the Euphrates into smaller river-craft and by them are landed at Baghdád ten or twelve days after leaving Bombay.* At Baghdád professional coffin-carriers take charge of them and carry the coffins by mule or camel to Karbála. The steamer freights vary from Rs. 200 to Rs. 400 : the Baghdád camelmen charge no less than Rs. 20 to Rs. 40 for each coffin ; and the final internment charges at Karbála are heavy ranging from Rs. 100 for the deposit of the coffin in the vaults (*Sardab*) below Husain's shrine to Rs. 2,000 to Rs. 5,000 for a grave on the Karbála side.

Occupation. The Khojáh enyoys a good business reputation. A keen jealous spirit of competition is the chief trait in the Khojáh character. Though called "*Tundás*" that is, beliefless epicures,† the Khojáhs have a great regard for their religion, the tenets ofwhich they observe faithfully. They are neat, clean, sober, thrifty, ambitious and in trade enterprising and cool and resourceful.‡ They are great travellers by land and sea, visiting and settling in distant countries for purposes of trade. They have business connections with the Punjab, Sind, Calcutta, Ceylon, Burma, Singápore, China and Japan ; with ports of the Persian Gulf, Arabia and East Africa, and with England, America and Australia. Khojáh boys go as apprentices in foregin Khojáh firms on salaries of Rs. 200 to Rs. 2,000 a year with board and lodging.

On their first settlement in the towns of Gujarát the Khojáhs were parched grain-sellers, fuel-sellers, old embroiderymen (*zaripuránás*) and bricklayers. They now enjoy assured and powerful positions in the ivory, horn, cotton, hide, mother of pearl, grain, spice, fishmaw, shark-fin, cotton seed, furniture, opium and silk trades. They have also gained high places in the learned professions as doctors, engineers and lawyers.

KHOKHAR.—*See* under Minor Musalmán Castes.

KHOMBHADIA.—A sub-division of Karád Vániás.

---

* All these details relate to conditions prevailing before the War.

† Bombay Gazetteer, Vol. IX, Part II, p. 44; *Tunda* is presumably the Maráthi word meaning—"sleek, complacent from the Skt. *tunda* a belly."

‡ Like most successful trading races they have acquired a reputationf or crooked dealing. The proverb.—"A Meman will be faithless though he read seventy Qurans" is quoted by Risley. The People of India—1st Edition, 1908, App. I, p. XXVI. According to Risley Meman in this proverb means Khojáh.

KHOSARE.—A synonym for Kochare Mahár.

KHOT.—A synonym for Javal.

KHOTI.—A sub-division of Machhis.

KHOTIL.—A sub-division of Bhils.

KHOTRA.—A synonym for Náde.

KHUDANE.—A sub-division of Vanjáris.

KHULKHULEVALE.—A synonym for Mákadvále.

KHUTE.—A synonym for Khutekar.

KHUTEKAR.—A sub-division of Vaidus, Dhangars.

KILIKETS or Katabus, also known as Chhatris, numbering about 900, and not recorded separately at the Census of 1901, are a caste of wandering beggars recruited from many castes, notably from Bágdis, Budbudkis, and Gondhalis. They claim descent from a Kshatriya, who is said to have followed the Pándavs in their wanderings after the loss of their kingdom, and hence style themselves Chhatris. But an examination of their manners and customs tends to show that they are recruited from several castes in the Karnátak with no claim to Kshatriya rank. Like many other wandering castes, they have no Bráhman priests; they change their abode frequently, feed on pork, and their women, like the Korava women, are expert tattooers. They rank low in the social scale. Name and origin.

There are two divisions of the tribe, Minahidiyo and Gombiadiso, but they are not forbidden to eat together or intermarry. The Minahidiyos (Kan. *mine* fish, *hidiyo* catcher) make their living by catching and selling fish, and the Gombiadisos (Kan. *gombi* doll, *adiso* exhibitor) by exhibiting leather dolls. The tribe is divided into thirteen clans, which are exogamous. The first ten of these clans hold tribal offices. The names of the clans are as follows:— Divisions.

1. Ganáchári.
2. Shiváchári.
3. Neknár or Kattimani.
4. Pánchángi or Bhandári.
5. Shindya or Halmani.
6. Sálva or Hogaluvike.
7. Sásnik.
8. Mohria.
9. Shingán or Harkári.
10. Dhruv or Mattimani.
11. Vákuda.
12. Dorkar.
13. Dhumalkar.

This tribal organization is said to have been the work of Hanmantráv Narsing of Haveli in Poona. He became headman of the tribe and called himself Sar-Ganáchári. The office of Ganáchári is hereditary in his family. He was joined by Shiváchári who brought with him Neknár Pátil, to whom was given the office of Kattimani. The Pátil was joined by a Gondhali of Máhergad to whom was given the title of Pánchángi or Bhandári. The Gondhali brought over to their side Shindya, who was made Halmani. He was joined by Sálva, who afterwards became Hogaluvike. Lastly the Sásniks and Mohrias joined them. Shingán and Dhruvs have joined them within the last thirty or forty years, and have been made Harkáris and Mattimanis. The Vákudás, Dorkars and Dhumalkars have joined within the last thirty years. A representative from each of these clans must attend at every Kiliket marriage, and each has certain functions assigned him in the ceremony. The Dhruv or Mattimani brings all the wheat, rice and other stores that may be required; the Shingán or Harkári bids the guests to the wedding; the Ganáchári must give the order for the marriage and throw the rice on the happy pair; the Shiváchári draws the cross called *nandi* on the curtain and holds it between the bride and bridegroom. The Shindya or Halmáni spreads a blanket for the couple; the Sásnik strews rice on it; the Neknár or Kattimani ties the hems of the married couple's clothes into a knot; and the Pánchángi does five things: makes a serpent of earth on *Nágpanchami* in the month of *Shrávan*, distributes provisions equally among his castemen, takes Rs. 9 from the bridegroom, spends Re. 1 in betel-leaves and nuts, and distributes the remaining sum equally among his caste people, and lastly prepares fire for smoking tobacco at caste meetings. If anyone of these office-bearers refuse to attend, the Kilikets are put to grave inconvenience. Many years ago the Mohrias, whose business it was to weave peacock feathers at the marriage, refused to perform their office. They were put out of caste and marriages have since been performed without the help of peacock feathers. These various office-bearers are remunerated as follows:—

		Leaves.	Betelnuts.	Pice.
Ganáchári	..	5	5	5
Shiváchári	..	4	4	4
Neknár or Bagli Pátil	..	4	4	4
Pánchángi	..	4	4	4
Shindya	..	2	2	2
Sálva	..	2	2	2
Sásnik	..	2	2	2

The Mohria, having quarrelled with the whole body of the Kilikets does not attend the marriages, which take place without him. But if the bride or bridegroom belongs to the Mohria clan, the Mohria claims his two betel-leaves, two betelnuts and two pice.

The Ganáchári, who belongs to the chief clan, performs the Diksha or purifying ceremony. If a male is outcasted for intercourse with a female of a lower caste he cannot be readmitted into the caste. If a female becomes pregnant by a man of a lower caste she is not allowed to remain in the caste. But if she commits adultery with a man of her own caste, she is purified by the Ganáchári, who gets five pice for the purpose.

The Kilikets are bound together by a strong caste feeling. At the same time, they have no central authority or referee to settle disputes. The Neknárs are called Pátils or Kattimanis, but the Ganácháris seem to be the leading clan. Their name comes first in the list, it is they who perform the Diksha or purifying ceremony on persons readmitted into caste, they play a leading part at marriages, and are then presented with a turban and coat. Every member of the community is obliged to share his earnings equally with the caste people. A hunter must divide his game, and when a fisherman catches the *ándhali* or big blind fish he must share it with the caste. At the same time, he is allowed to keep any money he may make by the sale of the fish.

The home tongue of the Kilikets is a dialect of Maráthi mixed with many Kanarese words, *bislo* for *baslo* I sat; *bardun dila* for *lihun dila* gave in writing; *apni* for *hukum* order; *henang* for a girl; and *gandag* for a boy. *Engyáni* and *gandgyáni* are their peculiar terms for bride's and bridegroom's parties. The names in common use among men are Bápu, Bhima, Dakulya, Dundya, Fakirana, Gidya, Gudadya, Haibati, Hanmanta, Lakshman, Ráma, Shettanna, Támanna and Yellappa; and among women, Basakka, Bhimavva, Gangavva, Hulgakka, Jekavva, Kallamma, Lakkavva, Mugakka, Narsavva, Shavantravva, Tayavva and Yellavva. They live outside villages in little reed cabins like Vaddas or Kolhátis. These flimsy little huts are water-tight and the Kilikets live in them all through the rains. The huts are so small that there is scarcely room to stand upright, and, in obedience to custom, they are moved from place to place at the end of every third month. Sometimes this rule is not kept, and instead of moving the hut the fire-place is moved from one corner of the hut to another. Polygamy and widow marriage are allowed and practised, but polyandry is unknown. Girls are married at any time; there is no rule that they should be married before they come of age.

The offer of marriage comes from the boy's parents, who have to bear the whole cost of the marriage. At the engagement, the boy's **Marriage ceremonies.**

father puts glass bangles on the girl's wrists, and places Rs. 2 in her hands to meet the expense of a feast given to persons present at the ceremony. Shortly after the boy's father goes to the girl's house for the betrothal or *báshtagi* when he pays Rs. 5 to the girl's father who feasts him. On the day before the day fixed for the beginning of the marriage ceremonies, the boy's father goes to the girl's village and feasts his caste people on wheat cake and mutton. Next day a marriage booth is raised and wheat, a goat, rice, robes, a bodice cloth, dry cocoa-kernel, and betelnuts are carried to the girl's house by the boy's father. The bride and bridegroom are rubbed with turmeric paste and bathed in warm water, and the day ends with a caste feast given jointly by the two fathers. On the third day the Pánchángi or Bhandári receives Rs. 9 from the boy's father and spends Re. 1 in distributing betel-leaves to the guests. The bride and bridegroom are dressed, and the bridegroom is made to stand outside the marriage booth while the bride stands in the booth. The Shiváchári holds the curtain with a central turmeric cross between the bride and bridegroom and rice is handed to the guests. The Sálva proclaims aloud the name of the god and the ancestry of the bride and bridegroom, the curtain is removed, the bride gives a packet of betel to the bridegroom, and the Neknár ties the hems of the couple's clothes into a knot. The Shindya spreads a blanket for the couple, and the Sásnik strews rice on it. When the couple have sat on the blanket, the Ganáchári ties a tinsel chaplet to the bridegroom's brow, adorns the bride's head with a network of flowers, encircles their right wrists with *kankans* or wristlets in which pieces of turmeric are tied, and throws grains of rice on their heads. After the Ganáchári, the other caste office-bearers, each in the order of his rank, throws grains of rice and lastly the guests shower rice. The bride's father feasts his caste people on *polis* or sugar rolly-polies and boiled rice. On the fifth day the bride and bridegroom go on foot in procession to worship a god and the girl's father gives a caste feast. On the sixth day the bride and bridegroom are made to sit on a blanket and to mention each other's name; and the bride is handed by her mother to her mother-in-law. The seventh is day is marked by no ceremony. On the eighth the booth is taken down, the friends and relations of each party are treated to a dinner of *polis* or sugar rolly-polies, and the house-entering ceremony is performed. On the ninth day the guests return to their homes, and the marriage is over.

Religion.

The two leading deities of Kilikets are Mahádeva and Durgavva. Mahádeva is said to be found only in the house of the head of the

Ganácháris, but many have Durgavva in their sheds and worship her themselves. They also worship Bhaire, Hulgemma, Máyava and Yellamma. Those who have no image of Durgavva, on her great day, a Tuesday about *Mágh* full-moon, make an image of meal and worship it. They do not keep the sweet basil plant or worship it. They worship their leather pictures and offer them *polis* or sugar rolly-polies on *Ganesh-chaturthi*, the bright fourth of *Bhádrapad.* They keep all leading Hindu fasts and feasts, and a few sometimes make pilgrimages to Parasgad in Belgaum and to Pandharpur in Sholápur. They profess to have no faith in soothsaying, and to have no relations with exorcists. When a Kiliket is possessed by a ghost he or she is made to sleep near the show-box for three or four days and this scares the ghost away. Their priests are members of their Ganáchári clan and the head Ganáchári is their spiritual teacher.

Death ceremonies.

The dead are buried in a grave like a Lingáyat grave. When a Kiliket dies, the body is washed with warm water and dressed, and if it is a married woman the hair is decked with a network of flowers. If the deceased was married the body is kept in a sitting position by a string fastened to a peg driven in the wall; if unmarried, the body is laid on its back. So long as the body remains in the house, it is covered with garlands and bouquets of flowers, and with red and scented powders. It is carried to the burial ground in a worn out blanket, and is buried sitting, if married and lying if single. When the burial is over, the funeral party bathe and return to the house of mourning, throw blades of *durva* grass in a pot filled with water which is placed on the spot where the dead person breathed his last, smoke tobacco, and go home. The mourners do not dine at home. Their friends and relations ask them to eat a meal of bread and *chàtni* or relish. On the third day the mourners go to the burial ground and lay two offerings, one on the stone which was placed on the top of the grave and the other twenty-four feet from the grave. These offerings are of millet grit mixed with molasses and oil and laid on two leaves. They stand far off for fear they may frighten the crows. If the crows eat the offering it is well, the deceased has left no wish unfulfilled. If the crows refuse to eat, the mourners pray to the dead. If even then the crows do not eat they give the offerings to a cow. The mourners bathe, return home and ask the four persons who carried the body to a meal. On the eleventh day the house is washed with cowdung, the clothes are washed and a feast is given. Before a month is passed a goat is killed in honour of the house gods, a brass image of the deceased is made and placed among them and the caste is feasted. As is the case with several other castes, the bodies of pregnant women are burnt, to prevent the Gárudis digging them up and using their bones as charms.

Occupation. The chief occupation of the Kilikets is to show at night, before a light, transparent pictures painted in brilliant colours on skin, representing Lakshmana, Rámchandra, Sitábai, Hanumant, Rávan, the Pándavs and Kauravs, and many other heroes and gods, the character of the show closely resembling that of the Chitrakathis or picture-showmen of the North Konkan and Deccan. At harvest time they go from village to village collecting grain which the husbandmen give them in charity. Their women are expert tattooers and are paid in grain and old clothes. They tattoo women of all castes. South of the Krishna where hills and undergrowth abound, the men are paid in grain by the villagers to destroy wild pigs which do great damage to the crops. Some of the Kilikets fish with nets. The Ganácháris hold rent-free or *inám* lands in Bágalkot, Bádámi and Hungund in the Bijápur district though they do not till them with their own hands. Some work as field labourers.

Food. They eat fish and the flesh of sheep, goats, hares, deer, fowls and pigs, and drink liquor. They rank below Kabbaligars and above Vaddás and Koravas, from whom they do not eat.

KINDRI.—A sub-division of Jogis.

KIRADS, numbering 152 (1901), including 72 males and 80 females, are found in small numbers only in Poona. They are petty traders. They are immigrants from the United Provinces.(1)

KIRAT.—A synonym for Bhil Berads.

KIRLOSKAR.—A sub-division of Gaud Sárasvat Bráhmans.

KIRPAL.—A sub-division of Bhandáris.

KIRVANT.—A sub-division of Bráhmans.

KITTE.—A sub-division of Bhandáris.

KOCHARE.—A sub-division of Mahárs.

KODAG MALLAVA.—A sub-division of Mallavas.

KOKALVAR.—A sub-division of Mángs.

KOLGHAS, numbering 5,849 (1911), are a very primitive tribe who, though lowly, refuse intercourse with Bhangis. They are

(1) Tribes and castes of the North-West Provinces and Oudh, Vol. III, pp. 282—284.

chiefly found in the States to the south-east of Surat. They do not respect Bráhmans, neither have they priests of their own tribe. They worship only a few of the minor Hindu deities, and their ceremonies are of the primitive type. Polygamy and widow marriage are allowed and practised. The offer of marriage comes from the boy's father, who has to pay Rs. 3 to the girl's father. Some days before the marriage, the boy's father goes to the girl's house and presents her with a robe and a pair of solid brass armlets. The day for holding the marriage is fixed on this occasion. On the marriage day the bridegroom with his parents and friends, and some Kokna musicians playing the *mudhul* drum, goes to the girl's house. The boy and girl are seated face to face on a blanket and while the women of both parties sing songs, the bride and bridegroom's skirts are tied and each of them utters the other's name. Then the whole party, men and women, dance together in pairs, the bride and bridegroom joining. After the dancing is over, dinner is served and when dinner is finished the bride and bridegroom, their skirts still tied, are carried on his friends' shoulders to his father's house. On reaching the bridegroom's house the skirts are untied. The bride stays with her husband for two or three days, and, after spending two or three days more with her father, returns to her husband.

Kolghás chiefly worship Hanumán, Bhil Dov and Kákábalia the small-pox goddess. They have no priests. The dead are burnt, the funeral pyre being lighted at both ends. While returning home from the burning ground the funeral party have a drink of toddy. On the third day the ashes are gathered, and sprinkled over with toddy. Those who can afford it give funeral feasts.

Kolghás are hereditary servants, labourers, and wood-cutters. Their condition is very poor, some of them having to eat roots, and at times to fast two or three days together.

KOLHATIS or tumblers, numbering (1901) 4,611 including 1,922 males and 2,689 females, are found in the Deccan, Karnátak, Kanara, Kolába, and Thána. In addition to 4,611 Hindus, 68 returned themselves as Muhammadans in 1901. The Kolhátis are generally known as Dombáris in the Karnátak and as Khelkaris in the Ahmednagar district. The Dombáris appear to be socially inferior to the rest of the Kolhátis. The caste is much mixed, being recruited from numerous sources, and largely dependent on the prostitution of its women. Name and origin.

Endogamous divisions.

They consist of the following endogamous divisions :—

1. Marátha.
2. Gujaráti.
3. Dukre or Potre.
4. Pál or Káne.
5. Harka.
6. Vale or Valiar, that is Holia, also called Mahár Dombárs.
7. Gopalgani.
8. Are.
9. Musalmán.

The Gujaráti, Marátha, Dukre or Potre, and Pál or Káne subdivisions are found in the Poona district. The Pál or Káne divisions appear to be Maráthás from the similarity of their surnames. The Gujaráti Kolhátis claim Rajput descent and bear Rajput names. The meaning of the term 'Dukre' or 'Potre' is not clear; but 'Dukre' appears to be derived from *dukar* a pig, and may refer to those who keep pigs. The Dukre division eat beef and pork and are held socially inferior to Pál or Káne Kolhátis. In Ahmednagar district the Marátha Kolhátis are again sub-divided into *Khare* (proper) and *Akaramáshe* or bastard. Marátha Kolhátis are reported in the Bombay Gazetteer to invest their boys with the sacred thread. The village *joshi* is asked to their house, and the boy's brow is marked with vermilion and rice, collyrium is put in his eyes, and he is rubbed with turmeric paste. He is then bathed and presented with the thread by the priest. In Belgaum, the endogamous divisions are Vale or Valiar, that is, Holia, also called Mahár Dombárs, Gopalgani, and Musalmán. In the Bijápur district, Gujaráti, Dakshani, *i. e.*, Marátha Kolhátis, and Are, are the three endogamous divisions. None of these divisions either eat together or intermarry. In the Sátára district they speak a mixture of Gujaráti, Maráthi, and Hindustáni; in Sholápur a mixture of Gujaráti and Maráthi; in Ahmednagar Poona, and Násik a mixture of Maráthi, Gujaráti, Kanarese, and Hindustáni. The Vale Dombárs and Gopalgani Dombárs speak Kanarese and Marátha respectively. According to the tradition related by the Marátha Kolhátis, the founder of their class was a man named Nát or dancer and nicknamed Kola, born of a Teli father by a Kshatriya mother. Kolhátis are also commonly said to be the children of Shudras by Kshatriya wives. The commonest surnames among the Marátha Kolhátis, which are all exogamous, are Nilkanth, Dalkar, Lákhe, Davalkar, Aundhare, Jádhav, Kachre, Musle, Powar, etc. Marriage with a father's sister's and mother's sister's daughter is prohibited within three generations on the girl's side and four on the boy's side. When the boy and girl are brought up by one foster mother, marriages are prohibited even though the boy and girl belong to two different families. Marriage with a wife's sister is allowed. Two brothers may marry two sisters. Like other wandering tribes they live in huts of matting in the outskirts of villages and towns. The sides and back of the hut are closed by three mats, the front is open and the top is covered by a fourth mat. Every family has two huts, one for cooking and the other for sleeping and sitting. They keep donkeys, which they use in travelling from place to place. Some Marátha Kolhátis have purchased houses and settled down, although they are forbidden to do so by their caste rules. Kolhátis admit outsiders, such as Maráthás, Sonárs, Shimpis, Lohárs, Sutárs, etc., into their caste. The convert is given the flesh of a pig to eat as a condition of being admitted.

They marry their boys before they are twenty-five and their girls even after they attain puberty. Sexual intercourse before marriage is not allowed. Among them marriage in the case of girls is optional. When the girl attains the age of puberty she is called on to choose between marriage and prostitution. If, with her parent's consent, she decides to lead a married life, she is well cared for and carefully watched. If she chooses to be a tumbler and a prostitute, she is taken before the caste council, a feast is given, and with the consent of the council she is thereupon declared a prostitute. In the Sátára district, the children of unmarried girls are considered outcastes, while in the Poona district they are not considered to be so degraded, but they may not marry with legitimate Kolháti children. If a girl commits sexual indiscretions with a man of her caste or with a man of a higher or lower caste before marriage, she is allowed to remain in her caste either by paying a fine or by giving a dinner to her caste-men. If the man involved be of her caste, she is married to him. In some cases, however, she is made a prostitute. Among the Gujaráti Kolhátis marriage is compulsory in such a case irrespective of the caste of the man involved. Polygamy is permitted but polyandry is unknown.

Marriage ceremonies.

The offer of marriage generally comes from the boy's father, who pays to the girl's father from fifty to two hundred rupees as the price of thebride. Occasionally, to avoid such payments, a double marriage is arranged between two families. The marriage ceremony is conducted by either the Bráhmans or more usually by the caste-men and consists of the following ceremonies:—(1) *Sagai* or *Mágni*.—When a marriage is settled the bridegroom's father goes to the bride's house with the head-man of the caste. The bride is offered a sugar packet, a waist cloth, a bodice, and some ornaments. *Pán-supari* is distributed, and the bridegroom's father treats his guests to a feast or to liquor in a liquor shop. Afterwards the parents of the bride and bridegroom announce to their guests the fact of their having entered into a marriage contract. Marriages are not dissolved after this ceremony has been performed. (2) *Halad* (or turmeric paste rubbing). —Turmeric paste is applied to the bride and bridegroom, and they are bathed by kinswomen, who sing songs. The bride and bridegroom's brows are marked with red powder and marriage coronets are tied to their brows. The boy is given a dagger to hold, and keeps it in his hand till the completion of the marriage ceremony. (3) *Devakárya* —Boughs of mango, *umbar* (Ficus glomerata), *rui* (Calotropis gigantia), *shami* (Prosopis spicigera), *jambul* (Eugenia jambolana) are brought by a man and his wife, relations of the bride or bridegroom, in a plate containing a burning lamp. The skirts of the bridal pair are tied into a knot and a cloth is held over them by four men. They are then led with music to the marriage booth, when the parents of the bride or bridegroom worship them, as also ropes and an axe. Then a dinner of goat's flesh is offered to the castemen. The following are the two different modes of *devak* worship observed among the Kolhátis in Sholápur and Poona districts: (i) Two earthen pots are whitewashed and worshipped, and a bunch of mango leaves is tied to a pot in the marriage hall. This pot is known as the guardian *devakárya* or *devak*. (ii) On the first day, generally a Sunday, they hold the *devak* or marriage guardian ceremony, when both at the boy's and girl's a metal water-pot is placed in a metal plate and filled with water. Five betelnuts and turmeric powder are dropped into it, and the mouth of the pot is closed with a cocoanut. Frankincense is burnt before the pot, the cocoanut is broken, and all present partake of it. (4) *Gadagner.*—The bridge and bridegroom are fed by their relatives. (5) *Telsádi.*—The lap of the bride is filled with dates, cocoa-kernels, betelnuts, and turmeric roots. (6) *Marriage.*—The bride and bridegroom are seated over two leaf plates placed on a *bahula* of turmeric powder, the bride facing the west and the bridegroom the east. A curtain is held between them and the Bráhman priest recites marriage verses (*sávdhán*) at the end of each verse. When the recitation is over, they clap hands, and the bride and bridegroom exchange seats. A cotton thread is twice passed round them five times. The bride's parents then worship the bridegroom and he is presented with a brass plate, a copper pot, a pair of of shoes, and a *dhoti*. Marriage bracelets are then tied to the wrist of the bride and bridegroom with turmeric roots. The bride is decorated with ornaments, and the marriage string of glass beads is tied round her neck. The bride and bridegroom are then seated over a square of rice grains drawn on a blanket, and the bride's lap is filled with turmeric roots, cocoa kernels, dates, almonds, etc., and the ends of their garments are tied into a knot. They are then led to make a bow to the house gods, and the bride and bridegroom call each other by their names. Their relatives then put sugar into their mouths. This is known as *osangli-bharne*. They are then taken to the boy's house. A large feast ends the ceremony. The following simple form of marriage ceremony is adopted by some. On the marriage day the bride and bridegroom are bathed and are given a new waist-cloth to wear, turmeric paste being applied to them. The bridegroom is then taken to the bride's house, where the kinsfolk on both the sides meet. The bride and bridegroom are seated under a cloth and the bride's mother ties the ends of the bride and bridegroom garments into a knot. They then go to make a bow to the house gods. The knots are then untied and the marriage ceremony ends.

Widow marriage is allowed. A widow cannot marry her mother's sister's son, father's sister's son, or any member of her deceased husband's family. She can marry her maternal uncle's son. A widow remarriage is celebrated during dark nights. Sunday is held to be a lucky day for the ceremony. The widow hands over her ornaments to relatives of her deceased husband, a custom known as *garsul-zada*. The widow is given a new waist-cloth to wear and her brow is marked with red powder. The couple then seat themselves on a square of grain, and the widow's lap is filled with dates, cocoa kernels, etc., The couple conceal themselves in woods for one night and return to their homes the next day. A feast is then given to the castemen. A widow may marry a third time, but in that case she has to hold a cock by her side when the marrige ceremony is performed. A bachelor is allowed to marry a widow if he has first been married to a *rui* tree.

Divorce is not allowed. In Poona district if a woman commits adultery with a man of her caste or with a man of a higher or lower caste, her hair and the moustache and hair of her husband are shaved and their tongues are branded with hot gold at a caste meeting. When a husband and wife do not agree, the husband relinquishes all his rights over his wife in exchange for a sum of money: this is termed *sandkhat-karne*.

Kolhátis follow the Hindu law of inheritance. They have great faith in soothsaying, sorcery, and the evil eye.

Kolhátis belong to the Hindu religion. They worship Mahádev and Máruti, who was a wrestler like themselves. They observe Religion.

almost all Hindu holidays. They make pilgrimages to Jejuri, Alandi, Shingnapur, Pandharpur, Kolhápur, Dákor, etc., but the motives which induce them to visit the sacred places are more selfish than religious, as they find opportunities of exhibiting their athletic feats on these occasions. They worship the minor deities Khandoba, Mariái, Bahiroba, Janái, Jokhái, Mhasoba, etc. ; but their favourite, and, as they say, their only living gods are the bread-winners or hunger scarers, the drum, the rope, and the balancing pole. They hold the cow sacred and worship the sweet-basil and the *ápta*. To their goddesses they make a sacrifice of goats on *Dasara* day, or also on Tuesday or Friday in any month, and to Khandoba on any Sunday. The sacrifice is eaten by the offerers. They worship the images of their dead ancestors and make sacrifices of goats, etc., for their propitiation. They revere Muhammadan saints. When an epidemic breaks out, they propitiate Mariái and sacrifice a goat outside the village boundary.

Death ceremonies. They bury their dead. The body is laid on its back in the grave with the head turned northwards. It is washed with hot water and is laid on a bamboo bier covered with a new shroud. Red powder and flowers are sprinkled over it. If the deceased be a woman whose husband is still alive, the body is washed by a married woman and wrapped in a new waist-cloth, bangles being put on the arms. Red powder, turmeric powder, and flowers are offered to the dead. The chief mourner walks ahead of the bier holding in his hand a burning cowdung cake. A halt is made midway to the burial ground, and grains of rice and a pice are thrown over the place where the bier is put down. The bearers change sides without looking back. When the interment is complete the chief mourner applies his hand to his mouth and calls aloud. All then retire to their houses. The grave is levelled on the third day. The chief mourner goes to the burial ground taking with him in a winnowing-fan, milk, cow 's urine, cooked rice and three cakes. One cake and a little of the cooked rice are thrown on the place where the bier was put down on the way to the grave. The grave is then levelled, cow's urine and milk are sprinkled over it, and a cake and some rice are placed at each end of the grave. This is known as *máti-savadne.* On the eleventh day all go to the burial ground and prepare a small triangular platform of earth, a cone of which must point to the south. Three small porcelain pots of earth filled with water are placed at each cone, and in their mouths are placed three cakes and three balls of rice. Red flags are also pitched close by. A crow is required to touch the ball pointing to the west. When the crow touches the ball at

Koli fishermen of Thana.

once, it is thought that the dead has left behind no desire. Sometimes artificial crows of *darbha* grass are prepared. On the thirteenth day the caste-men are feasted. For the propitiation of ancestors in general they observe the *shráddha* ceremony in the month of *Bhádrapad* and on the 3rd of the bright half of the month of *Vaishákh*.

Occupation. Both men and women of the Kolhátis are tumblers and beggars. Many of the women are prostitutes. Kolhátis kidnap high-caste girls to bring them up as prostitutes, and they are for this reason kept under the eye of the police. The Gopalgani women are experts in persuading men to visit them, and to pay them well. For this purpose the best looking girls are set apart for prostitutes and called *sonchedis* or golden daughters. Kolhátis also make and sell small buffalo-horn pulleys, mattresses, combs, and dolls. Kolháti women are expert tattooers. Any one working for hire is put out of caste, but is readmitted on paying a fine varying from a handful of betel leaves to ten rupees. Some of the Kolhátis in Poona district were given *inám* lands by the Peshwás for their skill in athletic games. Their appliances are a drum, a flute, a leather strap, and five poles fifteen to twenty feet long. Boys and girls are trained to tumble at the age of five and are good tumblers at the age of eleven.

Food. They eat fish, and the flesh of goats, sheep, fowls, ducks, and wild boars, and also drink liquor.

Name and origin. **KOLI** a term of vague meaning covering a number of tribes of inferior status which have little in common beyond a position inferior to the Kunbi or cultivating caste. Probably the term Koli has been used for centuries to describe the greater part of the original inhabitants of the Presidency so long as they adhered to a tribal organization. Dr. J. Wilson (Aboriginal Tribes) translates Koli as clansman, and this closely represents its significance. A Koli settling down to agricultural pursuits in the Deccan frequently becomes a Kunbi and thus helps to recruit the Maráthás. In Gujarát Kolis gain an improved status by intermarriage with Rajputs. The term Koli is almost certainly the origin of the word coolie, applied promiscuously in India by Europeans to manual labourers. The derivation of the word itself has not been satisfactorily traced. In the Census of 1901 Kolis numbered, 1,714,107 (males 882, 606, females 831, 501) and in 1911, 2,006,121 (males 1,040, 310, females 965,811). Gujarát Kolis differ very widely from those of the Deccan and Konkan, who have much in common. A fragment of the late Rev. Jonn Wilson's printed in 1876, gives a description of the aboriginal tribes of the Presidency based on personal observation and a study of their language and customs. He regards the Bhillas as the most independent and isolated of the aboriginal tribes but lays stress on the change of physique produced by good food, climate and occupation. He quotes with approval the opinion of another competent observer who says that the (Bhillas) natives of the plains " are scarcely to be distinguished from the other classes of society, though exposure, fatigue and poverty have left their accustomed marks in the diminutive figure and deep lined countenance of the hardy denizen of the hill". Kolis or Kulis he describes as not so independent as the Bhillas, " being intermingled in most districts with the Hindu cultivators ". He regards them as the aborigines of the plains as the Bhillas are of the hills, and states his conviction that " they do not differ in race from the Kulambis or Kunbis". Their physical appearance is hardly distinguishable from the Kunbis, their touch does not defile, and the Kulambis in Gujarát sometimes take their wives from them more or less secretly *. Koli chiefs of pure blood are difficult to distinguish from the Rajputs who have actually admitted their Koli blood. Habitat and occupation, he believes, have the greatest effect on their physical appearance. No complete list of the Kolis is attempted but he mentions the Talabda as the most numerous and respectable, the Son Koli as the original inhabitant of Bombay Island, the Ráj Koli of Jawhár and the North Konkan, the Mahádev and Malhár of the Deccan, and the Khárvas and Agaris of Surat and Thána. Lastly the Dhudias†, Chaudharis‡, Wárlis, Kátkaris, Dubalás and Thákurs§ are described as further offshoots from the great Koli tribe with more or less marked characteristics and customs engendered by their isolation in special surroundings. The latter are the descendants of the Thákurs of Gujarát, who fled to the hills in the time of Mahmud Begada's persecutions and induced others to join them. They are described as indistinguishable from the Wárlis now.

* This practice is common at the present day. The Kanbi or Patidar caste of North Gujarát are very short of women. Brokers therefore obtain Koli girls and palm them off on bachelor or widower Kanbis as of their own caste. The practice is so common that there is no real deception. The Kanbi marries the girl, and all goes well unless some one from spite makes the girl's origin public. Then the husband has to clear himself by prosecuting the brokers for cheating and convictions are often obtained. Competent observers say that of the wives of Patidars in Ahmedabad City quite a large proportion are really Kolis. The Intercaste Marriage Bill so much discussed in 1918-19 would, if passed into law, regularize the practice; and it is noteworthy that the introducer of the bill is himself a Patidar.

† Modern spelling Dhodias.

‡ Modern spelling "Chodhras".

§ These are not included under Koli in recent censuses.

The Kolis of the Deccan and Konkan have the following divisions :— Endogamous divisions.

Agri	Marátha
Ahir	Marvi
Band	Mendale
Bhil	Meta or Dhangar
Bhiláve or Bhiràle	Musale or Bhandu
Chanchi	Nehre
Dhor or Tokre	Ráhtádkar
Helmar	Shingtoki
Kabber	Son
Karáde	Solesi also called Káshti or Lállangoti.
Khár	Suryavanshi
Konkan	Tankri
Kulparna	Táyade
Mahádev, Dongar or Ráj	Thánkar or Christian
Malhár, also called Kunum, Chumli, Pán or Pánbhari	Wali.

Of the above, the main groups are the Malhár Kolis, the Mahádev Kolis, the Son Kolis and the Dhor Kolis. The latter are the lowest in the social scale and eat beef and the flesh of animals found dead in the jungle. The Chief of the Jawhár State is a Mahádev Koli, and either this fact or the mixture of Rajput blood which they claim probably accounts for the synonym Ráj, and for their high social position. For the rest, Malhár and the Mahádev Kolis closely resemble Maráthás and in some districts are almost indistinguishable from them. These groups are described below separately.

GUJARAT KOLIS present numerous difficulties in classification, mainly owing to the varying nomenclature employed in different areas and the extreme vagueness of our Koli informants. The highest families in the social sense prohibit widow remarriage in imitation of the Rajputs, and the same is true of the Khánt and Bária Kolis of the north and of the Pateliás or Patelia Kolis of the Panch Mahāls and the Rewa Kántha. These high caste Kolis have given brides to Rajputs, and, failing Rajput husbands, to Molesaláms or converted Rajputs. They never give their daughters to the lower Kolis such as Pagis, Kotwáls and Pátanwádiás. There are several general terms in use among Kolis such as Dhárála and Talábda, and while in some districts these terms have a definite significance, in others they have none, and General description.

even where there is a definite significance this will vary from district to district. In Kaira, where Kolis are most numerous, all except the Kolis proper or Pátanwádiás are known as Dhárálás, a term which includes the Khánt, Bária and Talábda Kolis, the latter being further subdivided into Vághelás, Pagis, Kotwáls and Báriás. Thus a Bária Koli is totally distinct from a Talábda Bária and a Rajput clan name like Vághela or Parmár may or may not give some indication of a Koli's marriage group. Over the border in the Ahmedabad district, the term Dhárála is never used, and the Koli aristocracy is represented by the Koli Patelia or Talábda, while the Thákarda or Pagi, holding a distinctly inferior position and proclaiming his baser blood in every line of his features, intermarries with the numerous lower class Dhárálás of Kaira. To add to the confusion, in the Gujarát districts of Broach and Surat, Talábda denotes precisely the better class Koli; while Thákarda is a title assumed by the higher families among the Chunvália Kolis of Viramgám, who are also said to be the common Kolis of Cutch and to be found in Pálanpur and the Mahi Kántha*. Little light is thrown upon the problem by the examination of social customs and ceremonies. Amongst all Gujarát Kolis who allow widow remarriage (*vide* supra) *diyarvatu* or marriage with the late husband's younger brother is allowed and in some cases expected. It is at least probable that the custom is commoner than has been reported, and a competent observer has stated that amongst some of the Gujarát Kolis the younger brethren claim marital rights over the elder brother's wife, but no confirmation of this interesting trace of polyandry has been obtained. For the rest all Kolis follow somewhat laxly the prevailing Hindu customs of their locality. In the circumstances it is only possible to give a list of the Koli endogamous groups reported from the various districts and to indicate, where possible, such relationship as may be presumed to exist.

Exogamous divisions.

Exogamous groups have been reported from Pálanpur and the Mahi Kántha, the Panch Maháls and Cutch, but it is very doubtful whether marriages are regulated in practice by a consideration of these clan or family names, and careful inquiry has disclosed that the important group with mostly all Kolis of the present day is the village. In no case is marriage within the village permitted, and in some cases a regular cycle of villages has been found to exist, brides being given from village A to village B, from village B to village C, and

*The confusion is rendered worse by the deliberate attempts made at each census by individuals to get themselves enumerated as members of a higher group than the one to which they really belong (V Bom. Census Report, 1911, Pt. II, pp. 195-196 and an interesting note by the late Mr. W. O. Alcock there quoted).

so on. The main endogamous groups as reported from the various districts are given below :— Endogamous divisions.

Pálanpur Agency— (1) Thákarda.
(2) Koli.

Mahi Kántha— (1) Talábda.
(2) Chunwáliya.
(3) Pátanwádia.
(4) Charotaria (*i.e.*, from the Kaira Charotar, presumably Talábdás).

Ahmedabad— (1) Talábda or Patelia.
(2) Thákarda or Pagi.
(3) Chunwália.

Of these (2) and (3) will feed together; (2) intermarry in Kaira over the border with the lower class Dhárála, presumably Talábda Pagis; (3) vary in social status *inter se.* Many are Tálukdárs and assume the title of Thákarda which is not to be confounded with the name Thákarda Pagi. They probably correspond with the Thákardás of Pálanpur and the Chunwáliás of Cutch. (1) are a distinct and prosperous group like the Talábdás and Mansororariás of South Gujarát.

Kaira— (1) Khánt, a Káthiáwár tribe of undoubtedly high social position said to be subdivided into (*a*) Dábhi, (*b*) Makwána.
(2) Bária; also of high repute socially.
(3) Talábda; subdivided into (*a*) Vághela, (*b*) Pagi, (*c*) Kotwál, (*d*) Bária.
(4) Pátanwádia or Koli.

Of these—(3) call themselves Dhárálás and (1), (2) and (3) are all said to be Dhárálas but the names Khánt Bária are more commonly given. (4) are a large group with a well established record for bravery, lawlessness and general disregard for all Bráhmanical standards of purity. As eaters of beef they are shunned by the Dhárálás who strongly resent the application of the name of Koli, which in Kaira always denotes Pátanwádia. The Dhárála Talábda of Kaira is a poor, mean-looking specimen entirely distinct from the Talábda Pateliás of Ahmedabad.

Panch Maháls.—Besides Khánt and Bária the local Koli aristocracy includes the Pateliás who refuses to answer to the title of Koli at all. They were probably the same as the Koli Pateliás of Ahmedabad.

Other Kolis of marked superiority are the Dhárálás or Talábdás who correspond to their Kaira brethren.

Broach and Surat.—Talábdás form the main group. In the south the highest Kolis are called Mandhata Sororária or Mánsororária. Bária Kolis are also met with and are accorded an equal status with that of the Talábdás. Dhárálás and Pátanwádiás are also found in Surat and Broach respectively, and new geographical names like Bhália (from Bhál, the black soil tract of Dholka and Dhandhuka in the Ahmedabad district) and Indoria from Indore are met with. Jahángadia and Kakapuri are also two special Broach tribes coming below the Talábdás.

The above is little more than a record of local names and their local significance and adds little to our ethnological knowledge of the various Koli groups.

As the Kolis now stand they are clearly a very mixed race, with too little pride in their descent to trace distant relationships or form large and distinct marriage groups. The infusion of Rajput and Bhil blood is most marked in some of the groups of Gujarát Kolis, and the distinction between Rajput and Koli and Bhil and Koli in extreme cases is almost non-existent.

History. The earliest records of Koli exploits are mainly the deeds of the coast dwellers of the Gulf of Cambay. In A.D. 1535 they pillaged the baggage and books of the Emperor Humayun.* In 1705 they captured Baroda†. Probably many of the pirates of the gulf were Kolis. These gave much trouble to the English, who in 1734 and 1771 sent expeditions against them, and on the second occasion captured their strongholds of Sultánpur and Tulája‡.

But historically the Kolis came into prominence more during the second to fourth decade of the nineteenth century than at any other period. At that time the regions of North Gujarát were particularly unsettled. There was no strong central power; the authority of the Gáekwár in Mahi Kántha was nominal only, and the petty Rajput and Koli chieftains were constantly fighting. The early writers of the 19th century described the Kolis as " bloody and untameable plunderers," uncivilized and filthy§.

In A. D. 1812 the Kaira Kolis were still addicted to gang robberies||, and were even sent for and employed as professional house-

* Bom. Gaz. Vol. IX, Part 1, quoting " Elphinstone's History, 443."
† Gaz. *ibid*, quoting " Watson, 88".
‡ Gaz. *ibid.* quoting " Bom. Qrly. Rev. IV 98 Aitchison's Treaties. VI, 263."
§ Gaz. *ibid*, p. 242, quoting " Hamilton's Hindustan, I, 609."
|| Gaz. *ibid*, p. 242, quoting " Hamilton's Hindustan, I, 692."

breakers by Surat persons, receiving as reward a share of the plunder*. Both in A. D. 1819 and A. D. 1825 the Chunvália Kolis of the Viramgám region were suppressed†. In the latter year Bishop Heber visited Gujarát on his Episcopal tour and has left an account of his impressions of the Kolis which is worth quoting *in extenso*: "These last" (Kolis) "form perhaps two-thirds of the population, and are considered by the public men in Gujarát as the original inhabitants of the country, a character which, I know not why, they refuse to the Bhils, who here, as in Malwah, seem to have the best title to it. I suspect, indeed, myself, that the Coolies are only civilised Bhils, who have laid aside some of the wild habits of their ancestors, and have learned, more particularly, to conform in certain respects, such as abstinence from beef, etc., to their Hindu neighbours. They themselves pretend to be descended from the Rajputs, but this is a claim continually made by wild and warlike tribes all over India, and that the Coolies themselves do not believe their claim, is apparent from the fact that they neither wear the silver badge, nor the red turban. Be that as it may, they are acknowledged by the Hindus as their kindred which the Bhils never are; and though their claim of being children of the sun is not allowed by the Rajputs who live among them, there have been instances in which intermarriages have taken place between Mahrattas of high rank and the families of some of their most powerful chieftains.

"Their ostensible, and, indeed, their chief employment is agriculture, and they are said to be often industrious farmers and labourers, and, while kindly treated, to pay their rent to Government as well, at least, as their Rajput neighbours. They live, however, under their own Thakoors, whose authority alone they willingly acknowledge, and pay little respect to the laws, unless it suits their interests, or they are constrained by the presence of an armed force. In other respects they are one of the most turbulent and predatory tribes in India, and, with the Bhils, make our tenure of Gujarát more disturbed, and the maintenance of our authority more expensive there, than in any other district of the Eastern empire. The cutcherries, and even the dwelling-houses of the civil servants of the Company, are uniformly placed within, instead of without, the cities and towns, a custom ruinous to health and comfort, but accounted a necessary precaution against the desperate attacks to which they might otherwise be liable. The magistrates and collectors have a larger force of armed men in their employ than any others of the same rank that I have met with;

* Gaz., *ibid*, p. 242, quoting "Hamilton's Hindustan, I-721,722".
† Gaz., *ibid*, S.V. Chunváliyas.

and the regular troops, and even the European cavalry are continually called out against them. Yet in no country are the roads so insecure,—and in none are forays and plundering excursions of every kind more frequent; or a greater proportion of, what would be called in Europe, the gentry and landed proprietors addicted to acts of violence and bloodshed. In these plundering parties they often display a very desperate courage; and it is to their honour that, rude and lawless as they are, they do not apparently delight in blood for its own sake, and neither mutilate, torture, nor burn the subjects of their cupidity or revenge like the far worse "decoits" of Bengal or Ireland.

"They are hardy, stout men, particularly those of the Catteywar and Cutch districts. Their usual dress is a pettycoat round the waist like that of the Bhils, and a cotton cloth wrapped round their heads and shoulders, which, when they wish to be smart, they gather up into a very large white turban. In cold weather, or when drest, they add a quilted cotton kirtle, or "lebada", over which they wear a shirt of mail, with vant-braces and gauntlets, and never consider themselves as fit to go abroad without a sword, buckler, bow and arrows, to which their horsemen add a long spear and battle-axe. The cotton lebada is generally stained and ironmoulded by the mail shirt, and, as might be expected, these marks, being tokens of their martial occupation, are reckoned honourable, inasmuch as their young warriors often counterfeit them with oil or soot, and do their best to get rid as soon as possible of the burgher-like whiteness of a new dress*. This is said to be the real origin of the story told by Hamilton, that the Coolies despise and revile all decent and clean clothing as base and effeminate. In other respects they are fond of finery; their shields are often very handsome, with silver bosses, and composed of rhinoceros hide; their battle-axes richly inlaid, and their spears surrounded with many successive rings of silver. Their bows are like those of the Bhils, but stronger, and in better order; and their arrows are carried in a quiver of red and embroidered leather. In their marauding expeditions they often use great secrecy, collecting in the night at the will of some popular chieftain, communicating generally by the circulation of a certain token, known only to those concerned, like the fiery cross of the Scottish Highlanders. They frequently leave their families in complete ignorance of as to where they are going; and the only way in which, should one of their number fall in battle, the survivors communicate his loss to his widow or parents, is by throwing before his door some sprigs of the peepul, plucked and disposed in a particular form.

* See text and foot-note above.

"On other occasions, however, their opposition to law has been sufficiently open and daring. The districts of Cutch and Catteywar have ever been, more or less, in a state of rebellion; and neither the Regency of the former state, nor the Guicwar, as feudal sovereign of the latter, nor the English Government in the districts adjoining to both which are under his control, have ever got through a year without one or more sieges of different forts or fastnesses *."

Though he refers to Cutch and Káthiáwár the authority just quoted wrote his impression mainly at Kaira; and some of the details do not agree with details given of the habits of the Chunvália Kolis of the Nal and Viramgám. Thus it is mentioned that here bows and arrows were not used. The arms were a matchlock, sword and spear, and to some extent the "*katár*" or crooked stick of very hard wood, with which they could stop and lame a man thirty or forty yards off. Selected champions only were dressed in chain armour in three pieces over a very thick quilted tunic. If on horseback these champions rode horses covered with an armour of hide or bamboo. The Chunvália Kolis used also to protect their villages with an almost impregnable fence of thorns†.

The distribution of the plunder taken in marauding expedition by the Central Gujarát Kolis was as follows:—Live-stock to the chief, coin mainly to the chief, all other articles to the individual captor ‡.

Bishop Heber's description quoted above may be supplemented by the following from the Rás Mála, though it is to be remembered that Forbes in this matter is not an original authority, but relates information given. "The Kolis or Bhils (for although the former would resent the classification, the distinction betweem them need not be here noticed), were, as has been observed, by far the most numerous of the inhabitants of Mahi Kántha. They were more diminutive in stature than the other inhabitants, and their eyes were an expression of liveliness and cunning. Their turbans, if they used any, were small; their common head-dress was a cloth carelessly wrapped round the temples; their clothes were usually few and coarse; they were seldom seen without a quiver of arrows and a long bamboo bow, which was instantly bent on any alarm, or even on the sudden approach of a stranger. The natives described them as wonderfully swift, active and handy; incredibly patient of hunger, thirst, fatigue

---

* Narrative of a Journey through the Upper Provinces of India, 2nd edn., London, 1828. III pp. 25 ff.

† Bombay Gazetteer, Vol. IX, Part I, and Bom. Gov. Sel. X, 78, there quoted.

‡ Bombay Gazetteer, Vol. IX, Part I, p. 243, foot-note, authority not cited.

and want of sleep ; vigilant, enterprising, secret, fertile in expedients, and admirably calculated for night attacks, surprises and ambuscades. Their arms and habits rendered them unfit to stand in the open field, and they were timid when attacked, but had, on several occasions, shown extraordinary boldness in assaults, even upon stations occupied by regular British troops. They were independent in spirit, and although all professed robbers, were said to be remarkably faithful when trusted, and were certainly never sanguinary. They were averse to regular industry, exceedingly addicted to drunkenness, and very quarrelsome when intoxicated. Their delight was plunder, and nothing was so welcome to them as a general disturbance in the country. The numbers of the Kolees would have rendered them formidable had they been capable of union, but though they had a strong fellow-feeling for each other, they never regarded themselves as a nation, nor ever made common cause against an external enemy * ".

In 1832 bands of Kolis from 50 to 200 strong, and bent on plunder, infested the Kaira highroads†. Three years later the Collector, almost in despair, wrote :—" Some special regulations must be made about the Kolis. No means of ordinary severity seem to have any effect. We never hear of a reformed Koli, or one whose mode of life places him above suspicion. All seem alike, rich or poor, those whose necessities afford them an excuse for crime, and those whose condition places them out of the reach of distress, are alike ready, on the first opportunity, to plunder ‡ ".

Matters came to a head in 1835. There had been for some years a standing feud between Gambhir Singh, Rájá of Idar, and one Fateh Singh, the Thákor of Rupál. Gambhir Singh had enlisted on his side against the Rupál Thákor one of his own feudatory Thákors, Suraj Mall ; and a desultory warfare had gone on between the two parties. Gambhir Singh died in 1833, and the power of the state was usurped by a bad character named Chajuram assisted by the Thákor of Mundeti. These two succeeded in securing the immolation as *satis* of some of Gambhir Singh's widows. A nominal regency was, therefore, set up by the Bombay Government. In 1835 the Rájá of Ahmednagar (modern Himmatnagar) died, and it became known to Mr. Erskine, Political Agent, that the heir to the *gádi*,

* Rás Mála edn., 1878, p. 441.

† Bom. Gazetteer, Vol. IX, Part I, p. 243, on authority of a letter of the then Collector to Govt.

‡ Bom. Gazetteer, Vol. IX, Part I, p. 243.

Prithvi Singh with the help of Hamir Singh (presumably the same Hamir Singh who was one of the Government's own Regency Council for Idar) intended to immolate the widows of the late chief. In spite of the presence of Mr. Erskine with a small force outside the town three of the widows were immolated, and a British officer was shot down. The state of the country was now very disturbed. As the Bombay Government said in their despatch of the 15th October 1835—"There were thus three parties of insurgents in arms in the Mahi Kántha: 1st, Pruthee Singh and his adherents; 2nd, the Thakor of Rupál and his associate, the Thákor of Ghorewara, and their followers; and 3rd, Soorujmul and his coadjutors."* Sir James (then Captain) Outram had by that date been sent to restore order. This he effectually accomplished with a British force collected from all the surrounding military posts and a detachment of the troops of His Highness the Gaikwar. Thereafter he was kept on for some years as Political Agent†. The Kolis were reported to have been peaceable and greatly subdued by 1844; but they are still liable to give occasional trouble, especially the Chunwália Kolis of Viramgám.

DHOR KOLIS, also called Tokre Kolis, are found chiefly in the north Konkan. The name Dhor comes from *dhor* cattle, because they eat beef. Tokre, from *thokar* a bamboo, refers to their calling as bamboo cutters. They are a very low tribe, ranking with Mahárs. They have no priests. Their marriage ceremonies are conducted by four or five of the tribal elders. They say that they do not worship Vághya, Hirva, Chita, Cheda or any of the deities or demons known to other wild tribes. They keep *Shimga* and *Diváli* as feast days. The dead are either burnt or buried. On the way to the burning ground the body is rested and a stone is laid to mark the place. If, as seldom happens, a copper coin is forthcoming, it is laid beside the stone, and again at the burning ground, if they have one, a copper coin and some rice are placed in the dead man's mouth. Water is sprinkled from an earthen jar on the burning pyre and the jar dashed on the ground. When the corpse is burnt the ashes and bones are raked together. On the fifth day after death the deceased's death day or *divas* is celebrated by feeding five children and setting rice bread and water at the burning place. Nothing is done with the stone that was laid at the resting place, but, if a copper coin was left there, it is taken away and spent on tobacco which is smoked by the mourners. In *Bhádrapad*, to feed the spirit of the deceased, cooked rice is thrown into the fire on the roof of the house. They live by day labour and

* Quoted in Rás Mála, Edn. 1878, p. 526.

† (1) Goldsmith's Life of Outram, 1880, I, 114 ff; (2) Rás Mála, Chap. XV.

are sometimes employed by Kunbis in mending banks between rice fields and in cutting brushwood for manure. They eat flesh including carcasses and drink liquor.

MAHADEV KOLIS are found in the valleys in the east slopes of the Sahyádris from Mulshi in the south-west of Poona to Trimbak in Násik, a distance of about 120 miles. They are also found westwards in Jawhár in the North Konkan, where one Pauperal, a Násik Koli, established a chiefship in the fourteenth century, and eastwards in the Báleghát or Mahádev hills in the Nizám's country, the traditional home of the Mahádev Kolis. They are, in most places, indistinguishable from Marátha Kunbis with whom they eat, and who in some places eat with them.

Exogamous divisions. According to Captain Mackintosh, Mahádev Kolis originally belonged to twenty-four clans or *kuls*, from each of which many off-shoots (*pot kuls*) numbering about two hundred and eighteen in all have sprung. They are as follows :—

Name of *Kul*.	Number of *Pot Kuls*
Aghási	3
Bhonsle	16
Budivant	17
Chaván	2
Dajai	12
Dalvi	14
Gáikwád	12
Gavli	2
Jagtáp	13
Kadam	16
Kedár	15
Kharad	11
Kshiraságar	15
Namdev	15
Pavár	13
Poleva	12
Sagár	12
Shaikhácha	12
Shiva	9
Soikhi	2
Suryavanshi	16
Uterecha	13
Vanakpál	17

Marriage. Marriage is prohibited within the limits of the *pot kul*, and in some places within the limits of the *kul* also. Sameness of *devak* also is considered a bar to intermarriage *. A Mahádev Koli may marry his mother's brother's daughter, but not his father's sister's or mother's sister's daughter. Marriage with two sisters is allowed and brothers are allowed to marry sisters. Polygamy is allowed and practised but polyandry is unknown. Girls are generally married between five and ten and boys between twelve and fifteen. Widow remarriage and divorce are allowed and practised. The marriage ceremonies of Mahádev Kolis resemble those of local Kunbis, their *devaks* also being the same as those of Marátha Kunbis.

Mahádev Kolis chiefly worship Khandoba, Bahiroba, Daryábái, Ghorpaddevi, Gunáivir, Hiroba, Kalsubái, Mhasoba, Navlái, Yellamma and Vyághrámbari, and make pilgrimages to the holy places in their neighbourhood. They observe all the leading Hindu fasts and feasts. They have great faith in witchcraft and sorcery. Their spiritual guides are Kánpháte Gosávis. Their original priests were Rával Gosávis, Lingáyats by religion, who were supplanted by Bráhmans during the reign of the third Peshwa Báláji Bájirao (1740-1761). Among the Mahádev Kolis of the Thána district, the death ceremonies are still conducted by Rával Gosávis. Following the example of the Maráthás, Sonárs and others, they have lately begun to exclude Bráhmans from their priestships and to employ members of their own tribe who have been taught the duties. Religion.

The dead are either burnt or buried. When buried, the head is turned to the south. The bodies of persons who die of a lingering disease are burnt, as such deaths are believed to have been caused by witchcraft. Either the same evening or the next morning they examine the ashes to see if they can find any unconsumed bits of cloth or some article of food. If they find a piece of cloth or some grain, they believe that what they have found was the cause of death and that it was worked into the dead man's intestines by a witch who had been employed to do this by some one from whom the dead man had stolen some cloth or some grain. Under Marátha rule, if the friends of the deceased found articles of this kind, the magician, unless he bribed some local officer, was sent for a time to some hill fort (1). The death ceremonies of Mahádev Kolis resemble those of local Kunbis. The deceased are propitiated in the latter half of *Bhádrapad* when rice mixed with milk is offered to the crow and a feast is given. Those who die in battle or in the Death.

* Thus the Koli family of Raste has for *devak* the mango, *jambhul* and *umbar* trees. Its members may not marry with the families of Lokhanda Balchimb and Wal Koli that have the same trees for *devak*. For a full explanation of these *devaks*, see MARATHAS.

(1) Mackintosh in Trans. Bom. Geog. Soc. I-225.

performance of an act of bravery are called *Virs* and are worshipped with the gods, a silver ball with two corners being offered to them and on the first day of *Phálgun* a fowl or goat is sacrificed to them. The *Shráddha* is performed only on the tenth to thirteenth day after death, and subsequently on the first anniversary.

The original occupation of Mahádev Kolis is supposed to have been that of an infantry soldier. They are now husbandmen, cattle-keepers and labourers. In some places they are boatmen, carrying passengers across rivers and streams during the rainy season. Some are hereditary ministrants at Mahádev temples and take to themselves the offerings laid before the god. In Kolhápur they also gather slake and sell lime nodules, and catch and sell fish. Many are land holders, and many till the lands of others though they are not so skilful as Kunbis. Many Kolis are employed as watchmen, a considerable number are *pátils* or village headmen, and a few are *deshmukhs* or hereditary district officers.

Food. Mahádev Kolis eat the usual kind of flesh except beef and pork and drink country liquor to excess. Their staple food is *nágli* or *sáva* bread and vegetables. In some outlying parts many, after finishing their stores of grain, live for a time on wild roots, herbs and fruits and on the flesh of game animals and birds. They eat with Maráthás and Kunbis, but no lower caste. Kunbis and Maráthás eat with them above ghâts, but below ghâts may only take water from them.

MALHAR KOLIS or the Kolis worshipping the god Malhár, also called Pánbhari or water-filling Kolis, are, according to Captain Mackintosh, one of the purest and most respectable of all Koli tribes (1). They are also called Chumlis from the cloth-fenders they wear on their heads as water-pot rests, and Kunum Kolis, because according to Mackintosh thy eat and associate with Kunbis. They are found in almost every village in the Deccan, in Bombay City and along the sea coast in the Thána district. Their common surnames are Bhoir, Jádhav, Kerav, Lánga, Povár, Sharanpad, Shelár, Sojval and Vekhande. In speech, dress, customs and ceremonies they do not differ from the Mahádev Kolis. As the name Pánbhari or water filler shows, their usual calling is to supply villagers and strangers with water and to clean out the village rest-house and office. Near Pandharpur many Malhár Kolis are *yeskars* or village door-keepers and in Khándesh and Ahmednagar a few are husbandmen. During the Marátha rule, to the south of Poona, Malhár Kolis were the hereditary guardians of the hill forts of Purandhar, Sinhgad,

(1) Trans. Bom. Geog. Soc. I, 191.

Torna and Rájgad [1]. According to Mr. A. M. T. Jackson Malhár Kolis in the Thána district frequently become Marátha Kunbis, and the process has been recognized in parts of the Poona district.

SON KOLIS [2] are found along the North Konkan coast from Bassein to Ratnágiri in the south. They are numerous in Kolába and form the most interesting of the castes found in the district. Distinguished physically from the other inhabitants by their light-brown complexion, the round curves of the face and their smiling expression, they are equally distinguished by their aristocratic constitution, their separate dialect and their occupation. History is not clear as to their arrival on the coast, but a probable inference from tradition is that a majority of the present Kolis is descended from immigrants from the hills who arrived some four hundred years ago. If this be correct it would certainly go far to explain the marked difference in type. But doubt is thrown upon the tradition by the difficulty of understanding the sudden conversion of hillmen into fishers.

The dress of the Son Kolis offers a few distinguishing peculiarities. The way in which the women's *sáries* leave the head bare and are tightly drawn round the thighs and between the buttocks with an effect like bathing drawers, is in itself distinctive of the caste. In respect of jewellery, anklets are never worn by man or woman. Apparently, however, this is a matter rather of fashion than of religion or superstition. On the right hand, women wear a silver bracelet of peculiar and heavy shape such as is worn by no other caste. No other bangle or bracelet, ornament or jewel is worn on that hand; and the absence of such adornments are for women as a sign of the covenant under which the deity protects fishers from the perils of the sea. On the other parts of the body on left hand and neck and head women wear ornaments as they please according to the wealth and enjoyment of their husbands. There is no custom of tattooing in the caste and men are never touched by the tattooer's point. Recently, however, a few women have begun to tattoo in imitation of other castes. Even these, however, do no more than tattoo a *tilak* on the brow.

The home tongue of Son Kolis is a patois of Maráthi gradually obsolescent under the grinding of the Local Board school and the newspaper. In the Koli home language the inflections of the verbs are syncopated or varied, certain variant substantives are used, and

(1) Trans Bom. Geog. Soc. I, 191-192.
(2) Contributed by Mr. O. Rothfeld, I.C.S.

formations of adverbs of place and other speech adjuncts from the standard language. Examples are " távåde " for " tikde ", "avåde " for " ikade", etc.

The administration of tribal affairs rests in the hand of the hereditary *Sar-pátil* whose residence is at Alibág. Under him, each village community has the subordinate administration of a hereditary *pátil* of the Kolis. These *pátils* are assisted in arriving at their decisions and in their promulgation by the deliberations of a *pancháyat* or caste meeting. The local *pátil* sends his invitation to the Kolis of his village. The *Sar-pátil*, when he fixes the date of hearing, invites the Kolis of four villages to attend, and at the request of the parties, may extend the invitation to eight, twelve or twenty villages. But the decision lies with the *pátil* or *Sar-pátil* and is not reached by any vote or referendum; and the position of the *pancháyat* is strictly that of asessors, not of a jury. Caste jurisdiction is exercised mainly in regard to the laws of navigation and fishing rights, or what are really professional questions. In respect to the sailing of ships and the crossing of one boat on the course of another, the rules framed and enforced by the *pátil* are as stringent as those of the Royal Yacht Squadron. The caste *pátils* with their assessors further deal with certain criminal offences, like assault, hurt and riot, and with certain torts like breaches of promise to marry. *The Sar-pátil* sitting by himself in " chambers " has further the right or duty of protecting women who become pregnant without being wives, of fining their paramours, and of finding them husbands.

The caste is divided into families, and marriage within the family is forbidden. But the forms of the family gods have become shadowy and their outlines are obscure in the mist of ages. Children of brothers and sisters do not intermarry. The son of a sister can marry the daughter of her brother, but the son of the brother cannot marry the daughter of his sister. Marriage with two sisters is permitted and two brothers are allowed to marry two sisters.

Marriage ceremonies.

Marriages are seldom entered upon till after puberty and the bridegroom is usually required to have attained at least twenty years, as a young man below that age is not considered to be fit for rowing if he have a wife to cherish. The bride is usually consulted by her parents and asked whether she be willing to accept her suitor. Recently, however, Bráhman influence and the desire to be fashionable have to some extent impaired this excellent rule and substituted the Bráhmanized marriage of compulsion. Widows are allowed to remarry. Full divorce is accorded only to a husband if his wife be taken in adultery. Otherwise only orders of what may be called judicial separation are allowed. Thus if a man becomes a leper or a Christian, he will be excommunicated and his wife will therefore obtain a "*sod-chitti*" or separation order from the *Sar-pátil* or head of the tribe. But until the separated husband die, the woman has no right to remarry. The same natural results follow this custom as in England arise from judicial separations. A noteworthy feature of marriage customs is that there is still a faint tradition that it is best if a younger brother marry his elder brother's widow. This is, however, no living, compelling tradition as among certain tribes of Gujarát Kolis. Such as it is, however, it may point to an earlier community of life with the other Kolis of Western India. This community of descent is so far recognised by the Son Kolis that they acknowledge their affinity to the Dongar Kolis, though intermarriages have for a long time been forbidden. The Son Kolis, however, claim a higher rank for themselves and will not eat food prepared by Dongar Kolis. Of a connection with the Gujarát Kolis they have no knowledge but they are freely prepared to admit the probability of such an affinity.

The tribe seems only recently to have entered the fold of Hinduism. Religion. The tradition of the Son Kolis themselves is that they were taught to know the gods properly by Kalu Bhagat, a Koli of Varsoli near Alibág, in the times of the Peshwás some two centuries ago. The teaching of Kalu Bhagat was especially directed to the adoration of the god that sits enthroned at Jejuri, the god, that is, Malhár and Mártand and is Khandoba. And so to this day Jejuri remains the chief shrine or centre of Koli worhsip. And the descendants of Kalu Bhagat are still the high priests of the tribe. Before they became the worshippers of Khandoba, the Kolis say they were in the state of ignorance (*adnyáni*). The parallel word *jahaliat* used by the Arabs to describe the loose animism that preceded Islám will at once occur to memory. That, therefore, the tradition relates to the first Hinduising of the Koli tribe, there can be little doubt.

The dead are either burnt or buried without distinction according to the wealth of the surviving relatives. But an invariable custom decrees that persons dying of contagious diseases like small-pox or cholera shall be buried.

The hereditary occupation of Son Kolis is fishing, in which practically all find sufficient and profitable employment. A few have now become wholesale fish suppliers and fish merchants and a very few are clerks or accountants in Government service. The sale of fish caught by fishing boats is done exclusively by the women of the caste. In consequence the women wield great power, manage household affairs entirely themselves, and look after the household funds. The Koli fish-wife is as fine and independent as her sister of Newhaven. Like her, she has her share of her husband's drink when there are guests in the house or the sorrow of the swirling driving rain is forgotton in a cheering glass.

Food. Son Kolis eat the flesh of goats, sheep and rabbits, but no wild animals nor any bird except the farmyard fowl. They drink liquor.

KOLI.—A sub-division of Uppars, Vaidus, Machhis, Khárvás, Bhois, Kabbaligars, Káchhiás ; a synonym for Bágdi.

KOLIGOR.—A sub-division of Audich Bráhmans.

Name and origin. **KOMARPAIKS** numbering 9,110 (1901), including 4,349 males and 4,751 females, are met with only in the Kanara district. About 900 are found in the above-Ghát *tálukas* and the rest reside below the Gháts. The former are followers of the Lingáyat religion ; the latter have certain Lingáyat practices which may be the result of their having formerly been Lingáyats and later reverted to Hinduism. Until twenty or thirty years ago the caste styled themselves Komárpaiks, but of late they have assumed the more grandiloquent title of '*Khetri Komárpanth*' and now claim to be Kshatriyas. The name *Komárpanth* or followers of Komár is probably taken from the Lingáyat teacher Komár Swámi, whose head-quarters are in Kaladgi ; * and the word *khetri* is a corruption of the Sanskrit Kshatriya. The name Komárpaik suggests their being connected with the warrior's profession, *paik* meaning a soldier.

The caste state that they came to Kanara from Kalburga in the Nizám's dominions. They appear to have formerly been soldiers in the service of the Sonda chiefs. After Hyder Ali's conquest of Kanara in 1763, they took to brigandage and became the terror of the country ; but since 1799, when the district came under British rule, they have become peaceful and orderly.

Komárpaiks speak a corrupt Kanarese with a mixture of Konkani words. The names in common use among men are, Kira, Chincha, Purso, Cháru, Chikka, Gutti, Sidrám, Kencha, Giryga, Rumo, Dánu, Siddappa, Munga, Lingappa, Chenna, Ira, Venku, and Mhádu ; and among women, Vorái, Vántái, Shivái, Chudái, Budái, Ganái, Sesái, Anande, Nágma, Neru, Reru, Govri, and Hemái. The men add the word *náik* or *metri*, meaning headman, to their names.

---

* Bombay Gazetter, vol. xv, p. 127.

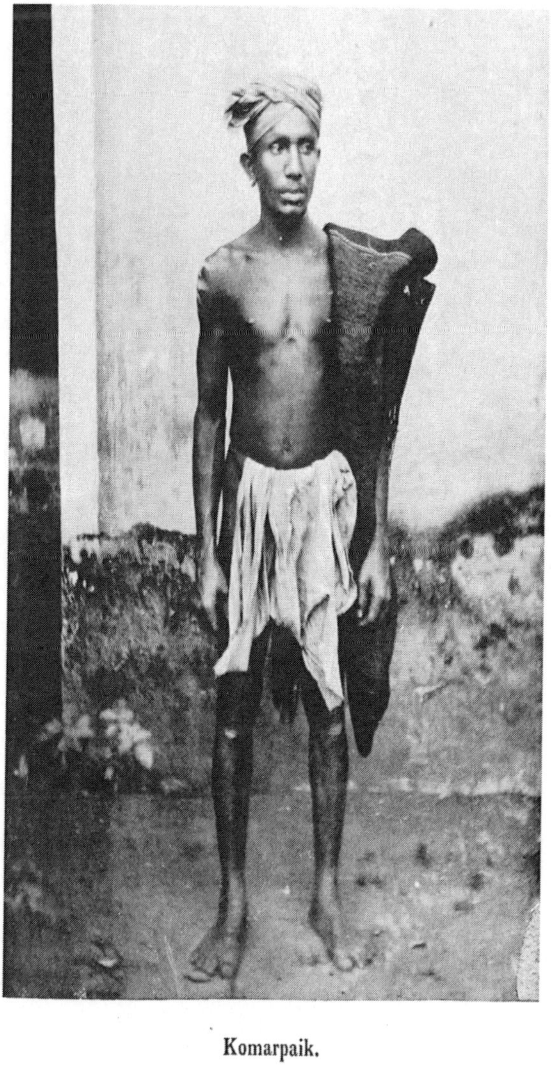

Komarpaik.

The caste is split up into eighteen exogamous sub-divisions, which are local in origin. They are as follows :— Divisions.

	Name.	Family God.
1.	Kárkonkar	Mallikárjuna.
2.	Phondekar	Mahádev.
3.	Talpankár	Nirankár.
4.	Mhálsaikar	Mhálsa.
5.	Mudgerikár or Shivnáthkar	Shivnáth.
6.	Majalkár	Rámnath and Dád-dev.
7.	Chitkulkar	Mahmayi.
8.	Kinmarkar	Mahádev and the village god.
9.	Bádkar	Mahádev and the village god.
10.	Nandangaddekar	Nágesh.
11.	Kadwadkar	Mahádev and the village god.
12.	Kadrekar	Mahmayi.
13.	Shiwekar	Sidram.
14.	Belurkar	Bindumadhav.
15.	Argekar	Mahádev and Satai Mhasti.
16.	Amdallikar	Mahádev and the village god.
17.	Ankolkar	Bhumidevata.
18.	Aursekar	Kátyáyani.

The caste head-quarters are at Bád near Kárwár. Every village has a *budivant* or local headman of the caste, above whom is the *Mahál budivant* of several villages, subordinate to the *Kalas* or supreme headman. The decisions of the latter on important caste questions such as re-admission to caste of offenders in social matters are subject to approval by the local Bráhman agent of the Shringeri *Math.*

Marriages are prohibited between members of the same section. Daughters of brothers can be given in marriage to sons of sisters. A sister's daughter may be married to her brother's son, if no other suitable match can be found; but in such cases the parents of the girl have to give her a silver chain during the marriage. The reason for this is said to be the girl's returning to the section from which her mother came. A man may marry a deceased wife's sister and brothers may marry sisters. Double marriages are sometimes arranged in order to curtail the marriage expenses. Girls are married from eight to twelve: boys from fourteen to twenty. Polygamy is allowed if the first wife is barren. Polyandry is unknown.

The offer of marriage comes from the boy's father. The day for the marriage is fixed by an astrologer and the ceremony is conducted by a Bráhman priest. The betrothal is celebrated on an auspicious day some time before the marriage when the boy's father goes to the girls' house with relations and friends and presents her with a robe and ornaments, which she puts on. Three or four days before the marriage the chief post of the marriage booth is planted at the houses of the boy and the girl. The post at the house of the body consists Marriage ceremonies.

of the wood of the *jámba* (Xylia dolabriformis) and that at the house of the girl of *kindal* (Terminalia paniculata). A lamp is kept burning near the post every evening for a month. A *devakárya*, or a feast in honour of the family gods, is given when the marriage booth is ready. On the morning of the marriage day the girl is rubbed with turmeric paste and oil. From this day to the end of the marriage the girl is attended by a Devli girl, who receives for her services a robe and the money waved round the girl. The boy is attended by his sister's husband. He is presented with a waist cloth and his wife with a robe. The marriages of Komárpaiks always take place at sunset. Festoons are hung at a distance of about forty yards from the girl's house, where the boy is received by the girl's father, and a hanging lamp is handed to him. When the party reach the girl's house, the boy's feet are washed by the girl's father and lighted lamps are waved round his face. Next the boy is led into the marriage booth over a cloth spread by a washerman, who is paid annas four. The lamp in the boy's hand is suspended from the booth and he is seated on a cot. The girl is brought and seated before him. A cloth is held between them; sacred verses are repeated; and at the end, the cloth is removed and the boy and the girl throw garlands of *bakul* flowers round each other's neck. The *dháre* ceremony and the marriage sacrifice are then performed, which are the binding portions. On the following day a ceremony known as *gavan* is performed, in which the bride and bridegroom with four other pairs are seated on a cot, and money presents are made to them by relations and friends, each waving a lighted lamp round their faces. The ceremony ends with a dinner to the caste people. On the third day the boy returns to his house with the girl. In the evening the girl's parents are invited, the ceremony of *gavan* again takes place, and the caste is feasted. On the fourth day the marriage coronet is removed from the boy's head, the pair are taken to the girl's house, the marriage garlands are taken off their necks, and a dinner consisting of flesh, fish, and *paisa*, is given to the boy's party. On the following evening a similar feast is given by the boy's father to the girl's party which brings the marriage festivities to an end.

The remarriage of widows is permitted. A widow cannot marry a member of her late husband's section. Widow remarriages can be celebrated during those months only when first marriages cannot take place. The widow has to return to the relations of her deceased husband the clothes and ornaments received by her from him. She has also to break the glass bangles on her wrists. This is done under the eaves of her deceased husband's house, when water is poured on her head by one of his relations. The widow then puts on a new robe presented to her by her new husband and goes to his house. The marriage takes place in the verandah. No priest is present. A remarried widow applies red powder to the widow's forehead and sticks thereto grains of boiled rice. The widow is then presented with clothes and ornaments by her new husband, which completes the ceremony. A remarried widow loses the privileges of taking part in marriages and other ceremonies, but her children's rights are in no way affected. A third marriage is also allowed. But it is believed that the partner of the man or woman who has been twice married is certain to die soon after the marriage. To prevent this, if the man has been twice married before, he is wedded to a plantain tree and fells it with a billhook immediately after the ceremony. If the woman has been twice married before, she is married to a cock whose throat she cuts with a knife as soon as the marriage is over. Divorce is not allowed. A woman taken in adultery is put out of caste. The caste follow the Hindu law of inheritance.

The few Komárpaiks residing above the Gháts are still staunch Lingáyats; those below the Gháts, though they profess to be Hindus, have certain Lingáyat practices. They honour Lingáyat priests, and at the time of the Holi festival, worship Basava and Shiva's bull; they also sing hymns in honour of Basava's defeat of Bráhmanism. These practices may have been acquired during their service under the Lingáyat Chiefs of Sonda. They are disowned by their own people above the Sahyádris and seem to have transferred much of their reverence from the Lingáyat priests to the Karnátak Bráhmans. The caste do not belong to any regular Hindu sect. The objects of their special devotion are Basava, Venkataráma, Kálbhairava, Mhálpuras or ancestral gods, and *mhástis* or ancestral *satis*, in honour of whom they hold yearly festivals. Fruit and flowers are offered to Bráhmanic gods, and blood-sacrifices to village and household gods, except to the spirits of *satis*. They observe all the Hindu holidays and make pilgrimages to Gokarn, Tirupati, Pandharpur, and Benares. On the first evening of the Holi holidays, at the full-moon nearest to the vernal equinox, all men and big boys, each with two wooden sticks, go to either of the temples of Basava, and falling before the idol, lay the sticks in front of it. Then the *ayya* or Lingáyat priest sanctifies the sticks by the touch of his feet. The man and boys then sing Kanarese songs in honour of Basava's triumph over Bráhmanism and dance, keeping time by clasping the sticks. The caste has great faith in soothsaying, and whenever there is illness in the family, soothsayers or *ghádis* **Religion.**

of the Ghádi, Komárpaik, and Kumbhár castes are consulted. The Komárpaiks on the coast acknowledge the supremacy of the head of the Shringeri monastery in religious matters and abide by the decisions of his agent at Gokarn. Their priests are Karnátak Bráhmans in and about Kárwár, and Ankola. In Gokarn and the outside villages of the Ankola *táluka* Haviks officiate as their priests while in the Yellápur *táluka* the Vaishnava Gaud Sárasvat Bráhmans are employed for religious and ceremonial purposes.

Death ceremonies. A century ago the Komárpaiks used to bury their dead in Lingáyat fashion. They now burn their dead, except children who have not cut their teeth, and those who have died of small-pox; these are buried in a lying position with head to the north. In the case of those who have died of small-pox a leaf of the *palas* tree (*Butea frondosa*) is burnt in the name of the deceased. The bones and ashes of the burnt are thrown in the sea or a river. The mourning ends on the eleventh day after death, when the mourners purify themselves by drinking water brought from the house of their priest, and a dinner is given to the caste people. On this day, as well as on every thirtieth day for a year, a person of the age and sex of the deceased is feasted. The ceremony of *mahál* is performed every year on a day in the latter half of *Bhádrapad* which corresponds to the death day of one of the deceased ancestors. In the case of violent death, in addition to the ordinary rites, the *nárayanbali* is said to be performed within forty-five days after death. The well-to-do perform the *shráddha.*

Occupation. The Komárpaiks state that they were originally soldiers by profession. They are now mostly husbandmen and cart-drivers, a few being palm-tappers and palm sugar-makers. Some are sawyers and petty contractors. The men are fond of acting and perform dramas written in Kanarese from passages in the Rámáyana and Mahábhárat. Some hold lands, a few paying a yearly assessment up to Rs. 500. Some are tenants of superior holders. Some are day-labourers and are paid in cash.

Food. They eat the flesh of goats, sheep, fowls, wild pigeons, wild boars and fish. Formerly they did not drink liquor; but of late some have taken to it, though moderately. They eat at the hands of Bráhmans Vánis and Maráthás. Low castes such as Bándis, Deolis, Chamárs Halleers and Mahárs eat at their hands.

KONGADI—A sub-division of Vanjáris.

KONKANASTH—A synonym for Chitpávan.

KONKAN DEVDIG—A snomym for Bándi.

KONKANI—A territorial name. A sub-division of Padtis, Guravs, Kalávants and Gáns, Khárvas, Nhávis, Shimpis, Gavlis, Kumbhárs, Kunbis, Sutárs, Lohárs, Sonárs, Chámbhárs, Kolis; a synonym for Sásashtikar Bráhman.

KONKNAS, numbering 72,678 (1911), are chiefly found in the southern parts of the Surat district and in the Dharampur and Bánsda States. They are a primitive tribe and resemble the Várlis of Thána in appearance. Their name indicates that they are a tribe from the Konkan, probably so named upon immigration, and the inference is that they are one of the hill tribes from Thána. That they originally belonged to the Konkan is clear from their dialect, which is a mixture of Gujaráti and Maráthi. It is said that they were driven northwards by the pressure of the Great Durga Devi famine (A. D. 1396—1408). Name and origin.

They marry their boys from sixteen to twenty, and their girls from fifteen to eighteen. Polygamy is allowed and practised and widows are allowed to remarry. On a man agreeing to pay her husband the amount he spent as dowry, a woman may leave her husband and go to live with the man. When he has found a girl likely to be a good match for his son, the boy's father with one or two friends, bearing a jar of liquor worth eight annas, goes to the house of the father of the girl. If the girl's father agrees, after five or six days the bride and her friends go to the boy's father's house. Liquor is drunk, and the boy's father gives two robes and a bodice to the bride, and to his son a turban, two cloths, and a loincloth, *lungoti*. The wedding-day is then fixed. For a few days before a wedding the bride and bridegroom are daily rubbed with yellow powder, and the bridegroom's father sends to the father of the bride eight or ten rupees as a dowry. On the appointed day, with music and singing, the bride's party goes in procession to the boy's house. Here they are met by the bridegroom's father and seated in a booth in front of his house. The bride and bridegroom are then made to sit on a blanket, and their skirts are tied by a woman, in front of a lamp. Each says the other's name and the knot is untied. After the men of the party have sung and danced, the bridegroom's father gives a dinner of rice, pulse and liquor. Her friends leave the bride and return home. After five days she goes to her father's house, and after five days more goes back to her husband. Among the Konknás the practice of serving for a wife *khandádio* prevails. Marriage.

Konknás worship Brahm and Vágh Dev. Brahm, a stone placed near a *shami* (Prosopis spicigera) tree, is supplied with a clay horse and Religion.

lamp-stand and a flag. Vágh, a wooden pillar with a tiger cut on it, is generally covered with red *sindur* powder. They do not respect Bráhmans or employ them as priests.

Death. Among the Konknás the dead body is bathed, rubbed with turmeric, and carried on a bier to the burning ground. The mourners bathe in the river. The pyre is kindled by a son or other near relation, and when it is half burnt the mourners return to the house of the deceased and drink toddy. On the third day eight or ten men go to the burning ground, gather the ashes, sprinkle water over them and return home. On the fourth day a dinner is given to relations and clansmen; at the end of the year a silver image of the dead is set up in the house, and in front of it a lamp is lighted every two or three days.

Konknás are labourers and cultivators. Most of them till fields, but have very little stock, and do the greater part of the work with their hands. Some, who, from want of bullocks, themselves drag the plough, are called *háthodiás* or hand-ploughmen.

KORAMA.—A synonym for Korava.

KORAR.—A synonym for Korava.

Name and origin. **KORAVAS,** also known as Korár, Korgár, Kormár (Korama) and Korchár, numbering, 19,364 (1901), including 9,672 males and 9,692 females, are found principally in the Belgaum, Bijapur and Dhárwár districts and in the Native States of the Southern Marátha Agency. They are a wandering tribe of hunters, fortune-tellers, cattle-breeders, carriers, musicians, basket-makers and thieves. They are immigrants from Mysore and the Tamil-speaking districts of Kurnool, Salem, South Arcot and Coimbatore in Madras, where they are generally known by the name of Kuravan and number 100,315 (1901). They appear to be an aboriginal tribe in the process of being Hinduised. Bráhmans do not take part in their ceremonies. Their women are not held unclean during the period of monthly illness. The dead are buried, and only a few of the leading Hindu holidays are observed. On the other hand, the tribe have many primitive practices, including the *couvade* (in Mysore) and trial by ordeal. Their home tongue is a mixture of Telegu, Tamil and Kanarese, indicating the country of their origin.

According to Buchanan* the Koravas once ruled South Kanara under a chief named Hubashika. The resemblance of his name to *Habshi* suggests an Abyssinian ruler (*see* HABSHI). He describes them in 1800 as wearing little but a bunch of grass, eating beef and offal,

* Buchanan's *Mysore*, Vol. III, p. 100.

and worshipping a stone called Buta. He also refers* to the Koramas of Mysore, an impure caste who made baskets and carried salt, and the Koravans, a wild tribe of Coimbatore.† Mr. Rice names the Koragas, Koramas and Korachas.‡ He describes them as thieves and robbers, moving with droves of cattle and asses, carrying salt and grain, and making bamboo mats and baskets. Abbé Dubois describes§ them as carriers and basket-makers, who were perpetually wandering about, and showed much affinity with the Gypsies of Europe, especially in telling fortunes. The women, according to him, were skilful as tattooers; but the tribe in his time had an evil reputation for thieving and house-breaking. A regiment of Koravas, known as *kalla-bants* or robber Bants was employed by Tippu Sultan to spy on and rob the enemy. To save themselves from the depradations committed by this tribe, the residents of the country paid regular blackmail, either in money or in kind. Koravas, besides speaking Telegu, Tamil and Kanarese, are said also to have a gypsy language of their own. The men wear the hair in a bunch on one side of the head in the style to be seen on figures on memorial stones; the women wear strings of red and white beads and shells covering the bosom, after the common practice of the lower castes in Kanara. In the remote forest they are said to wear little else, at most a leaf apron.

Endogamous divisions.

The Koravas in the Bombay Presidency have seven endogamous divisions. They are:—

1. Adivi or Kal Kaikádi.
2. Bid or Vir.
3. Dabbe or Uru.
4. Ghante Chor.
5. Kunchi.
6. Modi.
7. Pátrad.
8. Sanádi.
9. Suli.

The tribe contains four family stocks—Santipadia, Kavadia, Manpadia, and Menragutti. Persons belonging to the same stock do not intermarry. Bids and Dabbes eat together, and Bids will give their girls to Dabbes though they do not marry Dabbe girls. Of these the Sanádis, who are found in Dhárwár and are now of settled habits, are considered on that account to be the social superiors of the rest, with whom they neither eat nor intermarry. They are musicians by profession, and take the name from the *sanai* or horn which they blow at marriage and religious ceremonies. They also make baskets, cornbins, slings and grass ropes. The Kunch Koravas make weaver's

* Buchanan's *Mysore*, Vol. I, p. 249.

† *Id.*, Vol. II, p. 336.

‡ Rice's *Mysore*, Vol. I, pp. 312, 350, and Vol. III, p. 214.

§ *Hindu Manners and Customs*, Part I, Chapter 5.

brushes, and catch and sell game. The Adivis make baskets and brooms, and are notorious thieves. The Pátrads or shawl weavers (*patra* a scarf) are dancers, singers and prostitutes connected with Venkatgiri in North Arcot. The Sulis (Kan. *suli*) are prostitutes. The Ghante Chors seem to be refugees from the Bhámtás, who are known by this name. Most of the Koravas breed cattle and pigs and own large numbers of pack-bullocks.

Marriage ceremonies.

The Koravas marry their girls either before or after they come of age. Polygamy is allowed and practised, but polyandry is unknown. The betrothal is settled by the payment of Rs. 4 or 5 by the boy's father to the girl's father in the presence of relations and friends. He has also to pay a bride-price called *mahár* of not less than Rs. 30 to the girl's father. Exchanges of children in marriage are said to be arranged before their birth. The girl's father sometime makes the boy's father promise to give him two of his son's daughters or to pay a sum of money as their price. Half this sum is paid to the girl's maternal uncle. The marriages of Koravas generally take place on Mondays. On the Friday before the marriage Monday the relations of the bride take turmeric powder and oil to the bridegroom's, and the boy's relations take turmeric powder and oil to the girl's. Till Monday the fathers of the bride and bridegroom feast their friends and relations at their own houses, and on Monday the bridegroom's father leads the bridegroom to the bride's, where he is seated on the bride's right on a blanket covered with rice. *Kankans* or thread wristlets are tied round the right wrists of the bride and bridegroom and their garments are tied together. The guests throw grains of rice on their heads, the *mangalsutra* or lucky thread is tied round the bride's neck, and a feast is held. In the evening the *varát* or return procession starts from the bride's house to Maruti's temple. In front of the procession the bride and bridegroom walk, dressed in rich clothes, the bride's head being covered with a network of flowers; friends and relations follow, and the procession is closed by women waving lamps round the happy pair, to drive away evil spirits. When they enter the front door of the temple they stand near it, and the priest waves a piece of burning camphor before the deity breaks a cocoanut before him, and gives a piece of cocoa-kernel with some holy ashes to the bride and bridegroom, who put a little in their mouths as a god-gift. When they reach the bridegroom's, the lamp-carrying women wave the lamps about the heads of the bride and bridegroom. Afterwards, the bride and bridegroom are made to eat from one dish, and each puts five morsels into the other's mouth. In a marriage both the bride's father and the bridegroom's father give two different caste feasts.

In Kanara the day for the marriage is fixed in consultation with a Bráhman. On the evening before the wedding day, the bride is brought to the bridegroom's house. On the morning of the wedding day the bride and bridegroom are seated on a blanket in two circles, within which figures of the sun and moon have been marked in quartz powder, and a heap of rice with five *annas* in copper piled. Five married women come and rub the bride and bridegroom with turmeric paste, lead them outside the marriage booth, and bathe them thrice in water. Then a branch of the *khair* or catechu tree is felled and dropped into the nearest well. At midnight the five married women, singing songs, go to the well, and, after each has drawn a potful of water, take the branch out of the well. The branch is then planted opposite the front door. Close to it are piled two heaps of millet, two small water-pots, a large pot full of oil, and fourteen pounds of cotton seed. These are then set on fire, and when the flame is at its fiercest they take rice in their hands, rub some grains on the bride's and bridegroom's foreheads and sprinkle the rest on their heads. Early next morning the men take Rs. 4 from the bridegroom and spend it on liquor. The *khair* branch is thrown into running water. This ends the ceremony.

The re-marriage of widows is permitted. It is stated that a widow who has daughters may not marry until all the girls are married, and that a widow who has sons can never marry. Divorce is said not to be allowed. The Superintendent of Ethnography for Madras describes* the practice of the *couvade* as still prevailing among the Koravas. The husband awaits his wife's confinement, when he takes medicine consisting of chicken and mutton broth spiced. The clothes of both husband and wife are given to the washerman, and they themselves undergo purification. No evidence is forthcoming of this practice prevailing in the Bombay Presidency.

According to the same authority the Koravas also use the trial by ordeal, a favourite test being the extraction of a coin from a pot of boiling ghi†. A similar test is applied by the Bhámtás, Párdhis and other wandering tribes, who have much in common with the Koravas.

Religion.

The favourite gods of Koravas are Máruti, Yellamma, Mariamma, Maleva, Kallolyáppa, Huligeva and Sankalamma. They are specially devoted to Máruti. Of the Hindu holidays they observe only *Ugádi Nágpanchami*, *Dasara* and *Diváli*. They go on pilgrimage to

* Ethnographic Notes by Thurston, p. 549.

† Ethnographic Notes by Thurston, p. 424.

Huligeva in the Nizam's dominions and to the shrine of Yellamma in Saundatti. They have great faith in soothsaying, witchcraft and believe in evil spirits. They have no priests.

The dead are either burnt or buried, burying being more common.

Food. They eat the flesh of goats, sheep, fowls, hares, pigs and other game animals and birds and drink liquor. Although they hold a very low social position their touch is not considered defiling.

KORCHAR.—A synonym for Korava; a sub-division of Párdhis.

KORGAR.—A synonym for Korava.

KORMAR.—A synonym for Korava.

KOSARE.—A synonym for Kochare.

KOSHTI.—*See* Deváng, Hatkar, Jád, Koshti or Sáli.

KOT.—A sub-division of Havik Bráhmans.

Name and origin. **KOTEGARS** also called Metris, numbering 124 (1901), including 85 male and 39 females, are found entirely in the Kanara district, with the exception of a few emigrants in Belgaum. They are said to have once been a strong clan whose original seat was in the Karnátak uplands. They are also found in South Kanara, where they hold a good position among middle class Hindus and number nearly 4,000. There are no endogamous divisions of the caste. They are split up into exogamous sub-divisions known as *bedagus*. Marriages between members of the same *bedagu* are prohibited. Outsiders are not admitted into this caste.

Girls are generally married between ten and fourteen and boys between sixteen and twenty-five. The caste has no rule that girls must be married before attaining puberty. Sexual license before marriage appears to be tolerated to some extent, and girls who become pregnant before marriage are not turned out of the caste. Polygamy is allowed and practised. Polyandry is unknown. Their marriage ceremonies last six days. On the first day the boy and girl in their own houses are rubbed with cocoanut oil, bathed and dressed in new clothes. On the second and third day no ceremonies are performed, but daily feasts are held. On the fourth day the boy is decked in holiday clothes, adorned with the wedding garland, and led to the girl's house where an earthen pot called *airane moge* is brought from a potter's house, filled with water, and placed on a spot in the marriage booth. The bride and bridegroom are made to hold the pot with their hands, and four smaller pots are brought and placed on four sides of the couple;

a thread is then passed round them by an elderly member of the family, who takes the *airane moge* from the couple and pours its contents on their hands, thus ending the marriage ceremony. The boy is kept two days at the girl's house; on the sixth day he returns to his house with his bride. The remarriage of widows is allowed. The caste follow the Hindu law of inheritance.

Kotegars are Hindus and worship the village gods and goddesses, especially Maila, Gulyamma, Yellamma and Mariamma, and offer them sheep and fowls. They have strong faith in soothsaying, witchcraft and ghosts. They respect Bráhmans, but do not employ them as priests. All their ceremonies are conducted by members of the caste. The dead are generally buried in a sitting posture. Those who can afford it burn their dead. No death day is observed. Religion.

Kotegars are employed in burying paupers or strangers, sweeping the streets, carrying torches, acting as guides, removing and skinning dead animals, in basket-making, and in selling firewood and grass. They seem to have fallen socially beneath the main body of the caste in South Kanara who are petty shop-keepers and brick-layers. They allow prostitution in the case of both their married and unmarried women. Occupation.

They eat the flesh of sheep and fowls, beef, pork and fish of all kinds, and even carrion. They eat the leavings of other castes and drink liquor. Food.

KOTHARIA.—A sub-division of Khálpás.

KOTSANE.—A synonym for Kadu Gurav.

KOTTE VAKKAL—A synonym for Kot Vakkal.

KOT OR KOTTE VAKKALS, numbering about 2,000 (1901), are found above the Sahyádris in the Siddápur and Sirsi *tálukas* of the Kanara district. They take their name from the fact that they are employed in covering bunches of tender betel nuts with *kottes*, *i.e.*, bags made of the canvas like sheaths of the betel-palm, which shelter the fruit when tender from injury by heavy rain.

The caste has no endogamous divisions. It contains exogamous sections known as *balis* which closely resemble those of the Hálvakki Vakkal caste, and are totemistic.

In language, customs, ceremonies and other particulars the caste does not differ from the Hálvakki Vakkals. Polygamy is permitted with the consent of the first wife. If a man marries a second wife without the consent of the first, he is excommunicated. Widow remarriage is permitted, but is said to be looked upon with disfavour.

KOTWAL.—A sub-division of Kolis.

KRAMVANT.—A synonym for Kirvant.

KRISHNA.—A sub-division of Gaulis and Gollas.

KRISHNAVANSHI.—A synonym for Bhátia.

KRISHNORA.—A sub-division of Nágar Bráhmans.

KSHATRI.—A synonym for Khatri.

KSHATRIYA.—A synonym for Khatri.

KSHATRIYA YADUVANSHI.—A synonym for Bhátia.

KSHAURAK.—A synonym for Nhávi.

KSHIRASAGAR.—A sub-division of Mális.

KUDALDESHKAR..—A sub-division of Gaud Sárasvat Bráhmans.

KUDALE.—A sub-division of Vánis.

Name and origin.

KUDAVAKKALS. numbering 21,209 (1901), including 10,754 males and 10,455 females, are found mainly in Belgaum, Bijápur Dhárwár, Sholápur and the Southern Marátha Country. They take their name from the Kanarese *kudav* an iron field hoe and *vakkal* a cultivator, their occupation being husbandry. The caste tradition relates that the caste is named after their founder who was named Kudavakkal, and that their original home was in Coorg. But there is no historical foundation for this statement. The Raddis, another large cultivating caste, have a tradition that they were once connected with the Kudavakkals, which seems probable, *see* RADDI.

Endogamous divisions.

There are two endogamous divisions of the caste, Hindu and Lingáyat, the former numbering 1,486 and the latter 19,723. The Lingáyat Kudavakkals resemble Panchamsáli Lingáyats in religion and customs except that they keep the top-knot and are married byBráhmans. The former, though professing to be Hindus, are still greatly influenced by Lingáyatism inasmuch as they do not observe ceremonial impurity at birth, death or women's monthly illness. They bury their dead and abstain from flesh and liquor. They have four endogamous divisions, who eat together but do not intermarry. They are :—

1. Dandávatis or Fine-payers.
2. Minigadiks or Patched-shoe wearers.
3. Taddodis or Fools, with three sub-divisions. (1)
4. Yattiraks or Bull-wounded.

There are no exogamous sub-divisions of the caste.

(1) These are known as Huggiya, Bellyága and Navalyága. Among the last of these widow remarriage occurs.

Marriages are prohibited between descendants of a common ancestor. A member of the caste may marry his father's sister's or mother's brother's daughter. He cannot marry his mother's sister's daughter. A man may marry two sisters, and brothers may marry sisters. Polygamy is allowed and practised, widow remarriage and divorce are forbidden and polyandry is unknown. Girls are married before they attain puberty. Boys at any age. The offer of marriage comes from either side. The day for the marriage is fixed by a Jangam or Bráhman. The service is conducted by a Bráhman priest. The principal ceremonies are :— Marriage ceremonies.

Devakárga.—In which cooked food is offered to the god, and kinsfolk and a Jangam are feasted.

Simantpujan.—This ceremony takes place on the evening of the *Devakárya* day. The bridegroom is taken to a temple, where a priest applies red powder to his forehead, and the girl's father then presents him with articles of dress.

Lagna, or the marriage proper, is celebrated on the day following the *simantpujan*. First, cotton threads (*kankans*) are tied round the wrists of the bride and bridegroom. Next, five earthen jars containing betelnuts, dry coca-kernel and copper coins are placed on the floor, and the boy and the girl are made to stand near them. Sacred verses are repeated and grains of rice are thrown over the pair. The bride and bridegroom then worship the five jars, this being the binding portion of the ceremony.

Sáde.—This ceremony takes place on the day following the marriage, when the bride and bridegroom are taken on horseback to a temple, and thence to the boy 's house.

The caste follow the Hindu law of inheritance and belong to the Hindu and Lingáyat religions. Their family deities are Basavanna, Virabhadra and Yellavva. They also worship the village goddesses Dyamavva and Durgavva, and believe in sorcery, witchcraft and soothsaying. They observe the leading Hindu holidays, and make pilgrimages to Tuljápur in the Nizám's territory and to Golagiriling in the Bijápur district. On every Tuesday in the month of *Ashádha* their women worship the goddess Gulkava, and in the first half of the month of *Shrávan* the goddess Changalkavva is worshipped. The *Jeshtha* full-moon is called *karhunvi* and is held in great honour. The day before the full-moon, Indian millet is boiled, made into thick gruel and given to working bullocks; and on the full-moon day eggs are broken and mixed with oil and forced down the bullock's throats. Religion.

They are dressed in rich blankets or woollen cloths, decked with flowers, and their horns are painted red. In some cases rich husbandmen put their women's silver anklets on the bullock's legs. All the husbandmen meet together taking their white and red but not their black bullocks, and go in procession half a mile out of the village. A hemp rope is tied across the village gates about ten feet from the ground. The husbandmen form a return procession with the bullocks in front, and race their bullocks at top speed towards the village gates. If a white bullock is first to enter the gates, the white Indian millet crop will be plentiful, and if a red bullock wins, the red Indian millet crop will be plentiful. The owner of the winning bullocks is allowed to break the rope across the gate with his whip, a ceremony which is called *karihariyona* or the rope-breaking. Their marriages are conducted by Bráhmans and funerals by Jangams. The dead are buried in Lingáyat fashion. On the twelfth day after death Jangams are feasted. No ceremonies are performed for the propitiation of the deceased ancestors.

Occupation. The main occupation of the caste is husbandry. Some hold land under the *rayatvári* system. Some are tenants of superior holders. Some are field-labourers and are paid either in cash or in kind. Their women sell butter, milk and curds, the produce of their cows and shebuffaloes.

Food. They do not eat flesh or drink liquor.

KULACHARDAVRU.—A sub-division of Devángs.

KULAMAS numbering 37 (1901), including 13 males and 24 females, are found only in the Belgaum district. They take their name from the Kanarese *Kuluma* a forge. They have no sub-divisions. They worship the usual Hindu gods and goddesses, their family deity being Yellamma. They keep the regular Hindu holidays but do not fast or go on pilgrimages. They employ Bráhmans to conduct their birth and marriage ceremonies. They bury their dead. Their customs do not differ from those of Kunbis. They were originally iron-smelters. They have mostly abandoned this occupation owing to the competition of imported iron, and now work as husbandmen, some being tenants and others field-labourers. They eat fish and flesh and drink liquor. They rank below Kunbis, who do not eat from them,

KULIN MARATHA.—A synonym for Assal Marátha.

KULPARNA.—A sub-division of Kolis.

KULUM.—A sub-division of Vánis.

KULVADI.—A cultivator. A term applied to all cultivators in the Konkan whether Marathás, Bhandáris, etc.

KUMBHAR.—A sub-division of Gondhalis, Khándesh Kunbis, Saláts.

KUMBHARS or Potters, from the Sanskrit *kumbha* a water-pot and *kár* maker, numbering 239,265 (1901), including 120,288 males and 118,977 females, are found in all parts of the Presidency. **Name.**

They are divided into twenty-three endogamous groups as follows :— **Endogamous divisions.**

1. Ahir or Lahánchάke.
2. Balde.
3. Bhárdu.
4. Chag Bhaisa.
5. Garete.
6. Gujar.
7. Goremarátha.
8. Hátghade, Bhonde or Bhondkar.
9. Hátode.
10. Kadu or bastard.
11. Kanada
12. Karnátak, Pancham or Lingáyat.
13. Khambháti.
14. Konkani.
15. Lád or Thorcháke.
16. Ládbhuje.
17. Málvi.
18. Marátha or Gháti.
19. Pardeshi.
20. Rajput.
21. Sorathia
22. Varia.
23. Vátalia.

They are described below under Marátha, Konkani, Gujaráti and Pardeshi Kumbhárs.

None of the above 23 divisions eat together or intermarry. Maráthás, Konkanis, Kanadás, Sorathiás and Khambhátis are of the territorial type. Pardeshis, Rajputs and Málvis are immigrants from other provinces. Ahirs are part of the great Ahir tribe. They are called Lahánchάke because they work on *lahán* small *cháks* wheels. The Hátghades are so called because they have no wheels but work *ghad* with hands *hát*. Láds, like the Lád Vániás, are probably named from Lát, the old name for southern Gujarát. They are called Thorcháke because they work on *thor* large *cháks* wheels as opposed to the small wheels of the Ahirs. Lingáyats are those who have embraced Lingáyatism They are called Karnátaks because the bulk of the Karnátak Kumbhárs are Lingáyats. Gujar Kumbhárs, like Gujar Vániás, Gujar Sutárs, etc., are part of the tribe known as Gujar or Khazar, a late strain of invaders from Central Asia. Vátaliás, that is polluted, are said to be the offspring of a Bráhman by a Kumbhár wife.

Kadia Kumbhárs are those who have taken to the occupation of Kadiás or masons The origin of the other divisions is unknown.

Marátha Kumbhárs are found throughout the Deccan. Konkanis are found in the Konkan and Kanara. Lingáyats are met with in Sholápur, Dhárwár and Belgaum; Ahirs and Láds in Khándesh; Kanadás in Kanara; Pardeshis in Poona, Nasik, Sholápur and Belgaum; Gujars, Kadiás, Khambhátis, Sorathiás, Variás and Vátaliás in all parts of Gujarát and in the Konkan; and Bhándus at Panhála in the Kolhápur State.

The chief occupation of Kumbhárs is the making of tiles, bricks and earthern pots and figures of men and animals. In Kanara they have the privilege of making earthen figures of rural gods. In Poona they are famous for making children's toys. The pottery of Ahmedabad and Pátan is well burnt, glazed and ornamented with designs. In villages, Kumbhárs form part of the village establishment, and provide the villagers with earthern pots, for which they are paid in grain at harvest time or are allowed to hold village lands. The Konkani and Kanada Kumbhárs seem to have been local priests before the arrival of Bráhmans, and they still officiate in some of the temples of local deities. Besides acting as temple priests, the former perform the death ceremonies known as *Kumbhár-kriya* for all Shudras except the depressed classes. They serve as mediums between the gods and all classes of Hindus, and also act as sorcerers.

MARATHA KUMBHARS, look and dress like Marátha Kunbis. They speak Maráthi. They have in places an endogamous division known as Kadu for their illegitimate offspring. Their exogamous divisions are covered by surnames. The common surnames are:—

Adháv.	Divate	Kále	Sásvadkar
Bháleráo.	Gádhve.	Kápde.	Shirsát.
Buddhiván.	Gáikvád.	Lonkar.	Sinde.
Chaugule.	Jádhav.	Mánmode.	Sonavane.
Dalve.	Jagdale.	Mhetre.	Vágchaure.
Deshmukh.	Jondhale.	Pavár.	Vághmáre.
Devtráse.	Jorvekar.	Rokde.	Vágule.

Their *devaks* or marriage guardians are as follows:—

Poona .. { 1. A wristlet of the creeping plant called *mareta or maryádvel* (Ipomoa biloba) which grows by the sea side.
2. The potter's wooden platter or *phal*.
3. A hoe or *kudal*. }

Sátára	..	1. Mango. 2. *Jámbhul* (Eugenia jambolana). 3. Vad (Ficus bengalensis).
Sholápur	..	1 *Thápatne* or the potter's wooden platter. 2. *Pánchpálvi.*
Ahmednagar Khándesh Násik		*Pánchpálvi.*

In Násik, if leaves of the five kinds of trees, *i. e.*, the *pánchpálvi*, are not procurable, mango leaves are worshipped. This accords with the theory that originally each *devak* consisted of only one object, and that the composite *devak* was adopted later as the caste advanced in social progress and adopted the more advanced custom of prohibiting marriage between members bearing the same surname. That the *devak* was originally totemistic is suggested by the fact that the Ahir Kumbhárs, who, like the Pardeshis, have possibly borrowed many of their customs from the Maráthás, have to this day separate *devaks* for each family. Thus, the *devak* of Hivarkars is the *hivar* tree (Acacia leucophlea), of the Mores, peacock (*mor*) feathers, and of Vághs the *anjan* tree (Hardwickia binata).

Marriages are prohibited between members bearing the same surname. Sameness of *devak* is no longer a bar to intermarriage. Marriage with a mother's brother's daughter is allowed, but not with a mother's sister's or father's sister's daughter. Marriage with a wife's sister is allowed, and brothers are allowed to marry sisters. Boys are generally married from five to twenty, girls from five to twelve. Polygamy is permissible, but polyandry is unknowu. The remarriage of widows is permitted. A widow cannot marry her father's sister's, mother's sister's or mother's brother's son, or a member of her deceased husband's section. A bachelor is not allowed to marry a widow unless he first marries a *rui* bush (Calotropis gigantea).

In their religious beliefs Marátha Kumbhárs do not differ from Maratha Kunbis. Their family deities are Mahádev of Signápur, Jagadamba in the old fort of Sátára, Bahiroba of Sonári in Ahmednagar, Devi at Tuljápur in the Nizám's country, and Khandoba of Jejuri in Poona. Their priests are Deshasth Bráhmans.

Except that in Sátára they burn *vávading* or prickly-pear under the mother's cot and give her *kátbol* to increase her milk, and that in Sholápur they bury their dead in Lingáyat fashion, their birth, death and marriage ceremonies are the same as those of Marátha Kunbis.

Marátha Kumbhárs eat the flesh of goats, fowls and fish, and drink liquor. They eat food cooked by Koshtis, Dhangars, Nhávis, Kolis, Maráthás, Kunbis, etc., who all eat food cooked by Marátha Kumbhárs.

KONKANI KUMBHARS claim to be Maráthás in origin, and state that they formed a separate caste when they took to making earthen pots. This is extremely probable. They seem in many cases to have been local priests before the arrival of Bráhmans, and in Kanara they still officiate in some of the temples of the local deities. At Asnoti in Kárwár there is a temple dedicated to Rámnáth and another to Kattinbira, where none but a Konkani Kumbhár can act as ministrant. In Thána, among the lower classes, Kumbhárs are favourite mediums for consulting the spirits of the dead. When a Kunbi dies at a distance from his relations, a Kumbhár performs his funeral, the rite being known as the potter's obsequies, *Kumbhár-kriya.* The Kumbhárs also act as sorcerers. The Kumbhár, in fact, was a primitive medicine man. Kumbhárs have numerous *devaks.* In Thána, they require for their *devaks* the leaves of three kinds of trees, *umbar* (Ficus glomerata), mango, and *jámbhul* (Eugenia jambolana). The Ratnágari Kumbhárs appear to be more backward. Their *devaks* consist of the (1) *kalamb* (Anthocephalus cadumba), (2) *umbar* (Ficus glomerata), (3) *kocha,* (4) earth of an anthill, (5) peacock's feathers, etc. These *devaks* are held in great reverence, and, according to some, sameness of *devak* is a bar to intermarriage.

The exogamous divisions of Konkani Kumbhárs are local in origin, such as Ashtikar (those residing in Ashta), Kalyánkar, Nigvekar, and so on. In the Ratnágiri district families residing in one village form an exogamous unit, and intermarriages between them are prohibited. Marriage with a mother's brother's daughter is allowed, but not with a mother's sister's or father's sister's daughter. Marriage with two sisters is allowed. In Thána two brothers are allowed to marry two sisters. In Ratnágiri they are not allowed to do so. Divorce is not allowed among the Kumbhárs of the Thána district. In Ratnágiri it is allowed in the neighbourhood of Dápoli and Khed. A divorced woman is not allowed to remarry during the life-time of her husband. Adultery is punished by expulsion from the caste.

The remarriage of widows is permitted with the sanction of the caste headman. A widow cannot marry her mother's sister's or mother's brother's son or a member of her deceased husband's section. Among the Thána Kumbhárs a widow may marry her father's sister's son. In Thána a tax of rupees seven is levied on the marriage of a widow and is paid by her intended husband. The ceremony is conducted at night outside the village, under a mango tree. The widow is bathed and dressed in a white robe, Ganpati and Varuna are worshipped with the assistance of the caste priest, and the widow is married to a roll of white cloth. The widow hands the cloth to her intended husband, who wraps it round his turban. Red powder is then applied to his forehead and a lamp is waved round his face by the widow, and the ends of the pair's garments are tied into a knot by the priest. This completes the ceremony. In the Ratnágiri district the ceremony is different. The widow puts on new bangles and dresses in a robe and bodice presented by her intended husband. Next, a sum of Rs. 10 to Rs. 20 is sent to the house of the widow's deceased husband and a cock is waved round her face to free her from the hauntings of the spirit of her deceased husband. The pair are then seated side by side, and a widow marks the brow of the widow-bride and the knee of the bridegroom with red powder, thus completing the ceremony. In the Thána district a bachelor can marry a widow if first married to a *rui* bush (Calotropis gigantea). In Ratnágiri he is not allowed to do so on any account. Except that in Thána and Ratnágiri special ceremonies are performed to carry the spirit of the deceased to heaven, the birth, death and marriage ceremonies of Konkani Kumbhárs do not differ from those performed by Maráthás. These special ceremonies are as follows.

In Thána on the afternoon of the 11th day after death, a ceremony known as *dák kriya* is performed. A garland of flowers is hung from a peg, and a copper pot filled with water with its mouth closed by a cocoanut is placed under it. By the side of the pot is placed a bier made of twigs of cotton trees, and over it is laid an image of wheat flour representing the deceased. Next, a casteman plays on a drum called *dák*, singing songs in praise of Ganpati and holy men. The bier is then carried to a stream and immersed in water. In the Ratnágiri district, on the night of the twelfth day after death, six or seven Kumbhárs assemble at the chief mourner's house. A spot of ground is cowdunged in the central apartment of the house. A plantain leaf is laid on the spot, rice grains are strewn over it, and a metal pot filled with water is placed over the grains. Thirteen betel leaves with as many betelnuts are placed near the pot, its mouth is closed with mango leaves and a cocoanut and a flower garland is hung over it.

Close by is placed another leaf on which images of the following made of wheat flour, are seated :—

1. Pandu.
2. Ganpati.
3. Náráyan Swámi (two idols).
4. Deer.
5. Vaitarna (cow).
6. Peacock.
7. Eagle.
8. Flower.
9. The sun and the moon.
10. Nág or cobra.

Four lamps of wheat flour are kept burning on four sides of the above images. Then one of the Kumbhárs present worships the pot and the images, and recites verses known as *Pandu kriya.* When this is over, the chief mourner puts some water into the mouth of the image of the deceased and moves it to the tail of Vaitarna ; and a song known as Vaitarna is sung to the accompaniment of a drum called *dák.* The Vaitarná is then supposed to have carried the deceased to heaven, and the ceremony is over. All the images are then thrown in a stream or the sea.

In religion Konkani Kumbhárs follow Maráthás. Their priests are either Karháda or Chitpávan Bráhmans. In Kanara, Karnátak Bráhmans are also employed.

In food and drink they resemble Maráthás. They eat food cooked by Maráthás, Kunbis, etc. Kunbis, Nhávis, Agris, Thákurs, Kolis, etc., eat food cooked by them.

KANADA KUMBHARS are found only in the Kanara district. In origin they appear to be the same as Konkani Kumbhárs and performed the same functions in primitive society as the Konkanis. They marry their girls between six and twelve, and their boys between fifteen and eighteen. Polygamy and widow marriage are allowed but seldom practised. They worship the ordinary Bráhman gods, but the objects of their special devotion are the local deities known as *ammás* or mothers and *Jatga* or *Jattig* a wrestler. Their family goddesses are Márka Devate of Haldipur near Kumta and Durgádevi of Kumta. Their spiritual teacher is the Smárt head of the Shringeri Math in Mysore. Their priests are Havik Bráhmans. Their birth, death and marriage ceremonies do not differ from those of Nádors. They eat the flesh of goats, sheep, fowls and fish, but do not drink liquor.

GUJARAT KUMBHARS are also called Ghatghadás, Ojhás and Prajápatis. The term Ghatghada means maker of an earthen water jar (*ghat*). Prajápati is a name of Brahma or the creator of the Hindu trinity, and is applied to the Kumbhárs humorously on account of their profession of making earthern vessels which is likened to Brahma's creation of the world. The origin of the term Ojha is uncertain, but it seems to have some special connection with the Gujar trible, and may possibly be a form of Khazar or Gujar as Sir James Campbell suggests.

Gujarát Kumbhárs claim descent from the mythological king Daksha Prajápati. Some of their divisions claim to be Kshatriyas. They appear to be a functional caste evolved from Kanbis, whom they resemble in many respects. Tney have seven endogamous divisions, (1) Gujar, (2) Kadiya or Khedvaya, (3) Khambháti, (4) Lád, (5) Sorathia, (6) Varia and (7) Vátalia. Of these, Sorathiás, Khambhátis and Láds are territorial in origin. Gujars belong to the great tribe of Gujars who gave Gujarát its name, and to which the majority of the Gujarát Kanbis belong. Vátaliás or 'polluted' are said to be the offspring of a Bráhman by a Kumbhár wife. Kadia Kumbhárs are, properly speaking, a distinct caste formed by fission from Kumbhárs by those who gave up making earthern pots and took to masonry. They are known in many places simply as Kadiás. The origin of the other divisions is unknown.

Gujarát Kumbhárs have several exogamous divisions named after Rajput clans, such as Yádav, Chudásama, Chohán, Bhatti, Ráthod, etc. Marriages are prohibited within four or five degrees of relationship. Marriage with a father's sister's, mother's sister's or mother's brother's daughter is not allowed. A man may marry his deceased wife's sister. Marriage is infant as well as adult. Polygamy is allowed, but polyandry is unknown. The remarriage of widows is permitted. Except among some of the Sorathiás, a widow is not allowed to marry a younger brother of her deceased husband. Divorce is allowed. Divorced women are allowed to remarry. Except that among Gujars the bridegroom carries a sword in his hand and a Vátalia bridegroom a dagger, their marriage ceremonies do not differ from those of Kanbis. Among the Gujar Kumbhárs, in the case of a widow remarriage, the widow and her intended husband are seated on two low wooden stools side by side, the widow puts on the ivory bangles and dress presented by her intended husband, and the heads of the pair are brought into close contact, thus completing the ceremony. Among the Variás, in addition to the above ceremonies, the sister of the husband throws grains of rice over the heads of the pair.

Most of the Gujarát Kumbhárs are Hindus of the Vaishnav sect. Some are followers of Rámde Pir. Their religious beliefs are the same as those of Kanbis. Except that in some places among Gujar

Kumbhárs, an image of *pipal* wood called *surdhan* is placed in a niche in a wall of a house in memory of a person prematurely deceased and that among Sorathiás a stone called *khambhi* is erected instead of the *surdhan*, the death ceremonies of Gujarat Kumbhárs are the same as those of Kanbis.

In food and drink they resemble Kanbis.

PARDESHI KUMBHARS, also called Gavandis after the occupation of Gavandi (masonry) which is followed by some of their members, are chiefly found in Poona, Sátára and Ahmednagar. They are said to have come to these parts from Northern India about two hundred years ago, but have lost all connection with the parent caste, and now form a community by themselves. They still speak Hindustáni at home and employ Upper India Bráhmans to conduct their ceremonies. They have several endogamous divisions, the chief of which are :—

1. Balde.
2. Chag Bhaisa.
3. Garete.
4. Pardeshi proper.

Their exogamous divisions or *kuls* are covered by surnames, the chief of which are as follows :—

1. Basnivál.
2. Devalvál.
3. Jalindre.
4. Karole.
5. Kukadvál.
6. Kurnivál.
7. Maváne.
8. Morvál.
9. Pipude.
10. Tongare.
11. Udevál.

Each *kul* has a separate family deity which is known as *dhiradi*. The *dhiradis* also represent their *devaks*, which, according to their own admission, they have copied from the Maráthás. The *dhiradis* are worshipped with special ceremony on the occasion of a marriage. Some of the *dhiradis* are as follows :—

Kul.	Its *dhiradi.*
1. Devalvál	.. A clay figure of cobra besmeared with red lead.
2. Kurnivál	.. Fruit of the *bel* tree (Ægle marmelos).

Kul.		Its *dhiradi.*
3. Pipude	..	Two cocoanuts, two betel nuts and an idol of silver. (1)
4. Rájávali	..	Cocoanut.
5. Shekávali	..	Fruit of the *bel* tree.
6. Tongare	..	A cocoanut and a turmeric root.

The *dhiradis* form part of the household gods and are renewed on marriage occasions and on the *Dasara* day every year.

Marriages are prohibited between members of the same *kul* or *devak*. Marriage with a father's sister's, mother's sister's or mother's brother's daughter is not allowed. Marriage with two sisters is allowed, and brothers are allowed to marry sisters. Girls are generally married from seven to sixteen, thero being no rule that a girl must be married before attaining puberty. If a maiden commits sexual indiscretions with a caste-man either a fine or the giving of a caste dinner is imposed on both, and the man is compelled to marry the girl. Polygamy is permissible, but polyandry is unknown.

The offer of marriage comes from the boy'sfather. The day for the marriage is fixed by a Bráhman priest who conducts the service. A day or two before the marriage *five* unwidowed women go in procession outside the village to a dung-hill, worship it, and bring home some earth from its vicinity. The marriage *pandal* is next erected, in which is spread the earth brought by the women. A post known as *garu* is planted in the *pandal*, to which is tied, at the time of the installation of the *devak*, a yellow bundle of cloth containing turmeric roots, *juvári* and dry dates, and *five* wooden sparrows are hung from the roof of the *pandal*. On the day following, the *devak* is installed, and earthern jars are brought from a potter by *five* unwidowed women and placed near the *devak*. Next, the boy and girl are rubbed with turmeric paste at their respective houses, and a dough lamp is waved round the face of each by *five* unwidowed women and given over to a washerman with a few copper coins.

The marriages of Pardeshi Kumbhárs always take place at night. On the evening of the marriage day the boy is taken in procession to the girl's house and seated in the *pandal* near a post called *torankhámb*, cups containing sweetened water and a rupee each are exchanged and the contents drunk by the fathers of the bride and bridegroom. The girl's maternal aunt comes with a water jar on her head, and is presented with a rupee. The girl's mother waves a lamp round the

(1) The Pipudes do not wear silver ornaments, which shows silver to be their totem.

boy's face and receives a similar present. Next, the boy strikes the wooden sparrows with a stick. This is followed by the *hom* or marriage sacrifice. First, the boy alone walks four times round the sacrificial fire, and then the boy and girl together three times, marriage verses are repeated and the ceremony is brought to a close.

The remarriage of widows is permitted. A bachelor is not allowed to marry a widow. Divorce is not permitted. Except that they employ Kanoja Bráhmans to officiate at their ceremonies, they do not differ in any important detail from the Marátha Kunbis in religion, food, or birth and death ceremonies.

KUMRAVATA.—A synonym for Nemádi Bári.

KUNBI.—A sub-division of Gavlis and Vánis.

Name and origin.

KUNBIS corresponding to the Kanbis of Gujarát, numbering over two million (1901), so far as can be estimated from the census figures, are found all over the Presidency. Kunbi is commonly derived from Kulambi or Kutumbika and is a Maráthi term meaning a husbandman, Kanbi being its Gujaráti equivalent. The Bombay Kunbis are represented in the United Provinces by Kurmis, who are also known as Kunbis. There seems little doubt that, strictly speaking, the term Kunbi, like Rajput, denotes a status and not a caste, and may be compared in this respect with the latter term, which has no necessary ethnic significance. The fact that Marátha Kunbis are to a great extent homogeneous is clearly due primarily to their being Maráthás and not to their being Kunbis. It is of special interest in this connection to observe that in the Sávantvádi State, to the present day, the local cultivator, who would be known as a Kunbi in the Deccan, is known as a Marátha, the term Kunbi being little used. The meaning of the term Marátha Kunbi, in its ethnic significance, will be found more fully described under the head of MARATHAS.

The word Kunbi or Kanbi is derived by Pandit Bhagwánlal from the Sanskrit Kutumbin, that is, one possessing a family or a house. According to him, " From ancient times the title Kutumbin has been prefixed to the names of cultivators. This practice still obtains in parts of the North-West Provinces where the peasant proprietors are addressed as Grihasthas or householders. As cattle-breeding, not cultivation, was the original, as it still is the characteristic, calling of many North Indian Gujars, those of the tribe who settled down to cultivation came to be specially known as Kutumbin or householders. Similarly Deccan surnames show that many tribes of wandering cattle-owners settled as house-holders and are now known as Kunbis. During the last 20 years the settlement as Kunbis in

Khándesh of tribes of wandering Vanjára herdsmen and grain-carriers is an example of the change through which the Gujarát Kanbis and the Deccan Kunbis passed in early historic times. [1] "

Maráṭha Kunbis have much in common with Maráthás, who in some instances claim to be Kshatriyas; but there is much evidence to show that they are to a great extent the descendants of local tribes. (*See* MARATHAS.) The Talheri or Konkani Kunbis do not lay any pretensions to Kshatriya origin but are content to be called Shudras. In Gujarát the Leva and Kadva Kanbis appear to be Gujars by descent, the connection between whom and Rajputs is strikingly similar to the connection between Kunbis and the Maráthas proper in the Deccan. (*See* KANBI.)

Excluding the Gujarát Kanbis, Kunbis may broadly be divided into five territorial groups—Marátha, Konkani, Khándeshi, the Talheri Kunbis of Thána, and the Kále Kunbis of Kanara. All have Akarmáshe or Kadu divisions for their illegitimate offspring. Marátha Kunbis are said to be not infrequently recruited from the Malhari Kolis who take to cultivation and in time establish their claim to be classed as Kunbis.

Kunbis, as a class, are landholders and husbandmen. Some of the higher families are land proprietors, *deshmukhs* and *pátils* in the Deccan. Some of the Marátha Kunbis are employed in Native States, and a few in Government service. Many enter the army. The *deshmukhs* and those in service are well off, but the husbandmen as a class are poor. Marátha and Konkani Kunbis, like Gujarat Kanbis, are good husbandmen, and understand the growth of irrigated and of garden crops. They are assisted in their work by their women and children. Many are field labourers. They are paid in grain during the reaping season, and at other times in cash. When there is no work in the fields, they work as day labourers. They also grow fruit and vegetables in their back yards and sell them in the nearest markets. In towns they sell milk and curds and also work as domestic servants. In spite of their hard work, as a class Kunbis are in debt. Many earn enough to meet marriage and other expenses by seeking

(1) D. R. Bhandarkar remarks.—Both Dhanapálás *Paiyalachchhi* (A. D. 974) and Hemachandrás *Desinamamala* (Circa A. D. 1160) give *gahavai*, the Prakrit *grihapati*, in the sense of a husbandman or a rustic. A Karli Cave inscription speaks of a female donor's son as being a *gahata* (= *grihastha*), which is the same as *grihapati* These points, in my opinion, give strength to Pandit Bhagwanlal Indraji's view that the word *Kunbi* is derived from Kutumbin meaning a householder. It is true it may be argued that the Sanskrit word *Kutumbin* was chosen to denote a cultivator because it closely corresponds to the Dravidian word for 'labourer'. But the fact that not only *Kutumbin* but its synonyms such as *grihapati* and *grihastha* are also used in their Prakrit forms to denote the same class may be urged against the above argument. I have given all this in order that you might take it for what it is worth.

employment in Bombay, working as carriers, labourers, or garden or house servants, or in the spinning and weaving mills, where whole families find well-paid employment.

The divisions of Kunbis are described below separately under Marátha Kunbis, Konkani Kunbis, Kále Kunbis, Talheri Kunbis and Khándesh Kunbis.

MARATHA KUNBIS are generally regarded as originally the same caste as the Maráthás. The similarity of their social organization and *devaks* tends to support this view; and the apparently totemistic nature of the *devak* system suggests that they are very largely of non-Aryan origin. It is also noteworthy, in connection with their origin, that, as among Mahárs and other primitive tribes, the number *five* plays a prominent part in their birth and marriage ceremonies. An examination of the social organization and customs of the functional castes of the Deccan such as the Sutárs, Lohárs, Darjis, Kumbhárs, etc., seems to indicate that originally most of them belonged to one tribe or a group of tribes. The differentiation between Maráthás and Marátha Kunbis appears never to have become so complete as to result in two distinct castes. At present the terms Marátha and Kunbi, in many cases, are used synonymously. It is difficult to draw a line of distinction between the two communities. In some places there is no distinction, in others one caste blends into the other with no very distinct line of demarcation, while for the most part these castes hold themselves aloof so far as marriage is concerned. In Poona and its vicinity, the fusion is at its maximum; and if a Poona Bráhman were asked the distinction between a Marátha and Kunbi he would say "*Kunbi májla Marátha jhála*" *i.e.*, when a Kunbi attains to prosperity he becomes a Marátha, *i.e.*, by prohibiting widow marriage, putting on a sacred thread and enforcing the *purda*. Instances are not wanting, in which Kunbi families, owing to a fortunate turn in their circumstances, have formed connections with poor Marátha families and ultimately become absorbed into the general Marátha community.

Appearance. As a class, Marátha Kunbis are dark, middle-sized, with round faces, straight nose, thickish lips, and high, bare and protruding cheek bones. The poor among them differ very little from Mahárs, in appearance, which strengthens the view that they are of aboriginal descent. They are strong, hardy, enduring and muscular. The Kunbi women, like the Kunbi men, are strong and hardy. A Kunbi girl is slender, dark-skinned and generally graceful. She becomes a mother at fifteen or seventeen, and is past her prime at twenty. The men shave the head, except the mustache, and in a few cases, the whiskers.

Dress and ornaments. Marátha Kunbis are neat and clean in their dress. They are seldom rich enough to indulge their taste for finery; but the well-to-do are fond of gay clothes, the men wearing generally red or white turbans and the women red robes. Indoors the Kunbi wears a handkerchief passed between his legs, the ends fastened behind to a waistcord. Out of doors he rolls a loincloth round his waist, covers his body with a waistcloth or armless jacket, and wears a turban on his head and sandals on his feet. In cold and wet weather he throws a coarse blanket over his shoulders, or ties it in a hood and draws it over his head. Besides being worn as articles of dress, the blanket and waistcloth are used as sleeping mats and for carrying clothes and garden stuff. The women's dress is the full Marátha robe and the short sleeved bodice reaching to the waist and covering both the back and chest, the ends being tied in front.*

Language and names. The home tongue of the Marátha Kunbis is Maráthi. Each Kunbi has three personal names, a priestly name, a house name and a pet name. The priestly name which is known as the *rás náv* or star name, depends on the position of the stars at the time of the child's birth. The priestly names generally chosen for boys are Amritya, Ankorsa, Bábáji, Dungarji and Ráoji; and for girls, Saku, Bhágu and Chimi. The house name is chosen by the elders of the house; the commonest are, for men, Khandu, Pándu, Raghu and Vithu, and, for women, Kashi, Párvati, Rama and Sávitri. The pet or *ávadte* name is generally given by the child's parents or mother's relations. The commonest pet names, for boys, are Appa, Bábu, Bála and Nána; and for girls, Appi, Bái, Káki and Tái. The pet name sometimes clings to the bearer through life. When a boy grows up, *ji* or *ráo* is added to the name, and to the girl's name *ái* or *bái*. If a mother has lost several infants, she names the next child Dagad or Tipi, meaning a stone or a dung heap, apparently with the object of cheating the evil spirits into the idea that the child is not valued and is not worth carrying off.

Community. In each village, Marátha Kunbis have a head man, who settles caste disputes at meetings of the castemen. The office of the headman is neither hereditary nor fixed. Generally a man of wealth and position having the confidence of both parties is selected as headman for the time being. Breaches of social discipline are condoned by fines and caste feasts, and the decisions are enforced on pain of loss of caste.

* Bombay Gazetteer, Vol. XVIII, Part I, pages 287-88.

Social organization. Maráthа Kunbis have *kuls* or exogamous sections which are identical with those of Maráthás and their *devaks* similarly do not differ from those of Maráthás. (*See* MARATHA.)

Marriage rules. Marriages are prohibited between members of the same *kul* and *devak*. In some places however sameness of *kul* alone is considered a bar to intermarriage. A Marátha Kunbi cannot marry his mother's sister's daughter. He may marry his father's sister's or mother's brother's daughter. Marriage with a wife's sister is allowed after the death of the wife. Brothers are allowed to marry sisters. Polygamy is allowed and practised, but polyandry is unknown. Girls are generally married between three and twelve years, boys between sixteen and twenty-five. Girls can be married even after they attain puberty. Widows are generally allowed to marry, but some families consider widow-marriage disreputable and do not practise it. As a rule only widowers marry widows, and the children do not get so large a share of the property as those of first marriages. Divorce is allowed. Divorced wemen can marry again by the widow re-marriage form.

Pregnancy. When a woman is pregnant for the first time, her good longings are satisfied, and a special feast called *dohálejevan* or the longing dinner is held in the fifth or in the seventh month of her pregnancy. She is presented with a green robe and a green bodice, or a bodice only if her husband is poor, and some ten or fifteen unwidowed women are asked to dine with her. Lamps are placed by her side and the feast is made as grand as the giver can afford. To guard against the danger of miscarriage from violent movements or a sudden fright, a pregnant woman is made to sit in a sailing boat or a cart, is shown funeral processions, is made to cross the leather rope attached to the bag in a bullock draw-well, and to cross the boundaries of a village or a town.

Birth. For her first confinement a young wife generally goes to her parents' house. After delivery, the position of the woman is not changed for some time. If the child is a boy, the midwife beats a metal pot; if a girl, the father is told without any signs of rejoicing. The father notes the time of birth that the Bráhman astrologer may be able to choose a lucky name. The midwife cuts the child's navel cord with a knife, and, holding the cord in her left hand, passes it through the child's mouth. She puts the cord in an earthen jar along with the after-birth, a little turmeric and redpowder, and rice, and buries it in a hole in the mother's room. She touches with ashes the spot where the navel cord was cut and rubs the mother and the child with turmeric and oil, bathes them in hot water, and swathes the child in cloth bandages. The mother is given butter and myrrh pills, and the child is dosed with three or four drops of castor oil and honey. The mother is purified by burning Embelia Ribes, *Ova* Zigusticum ajwaen, and *Bálantshep* Anothus graveolus in the room, and then, with her child beside her, is laid on a cot, quite naked, under which a small fire of live coal is set. The mother is fed on fine rice, butter, pepper, and warm water. Near the door of the room an earthen pot of cow's urine is set with a *Nim* branch floating on it. That no evil spirit may come in with them, all visitors sprinkle a few drops of cow's urine on their feet before entering the room. At noon the mother is bathed in hot water, and elderly women begin to drop in and ask how she is. If the child is a boy, they congratulate her warmly; if it is a girl, they say "The first daughter is bread and butter" *Pahili beti tup-roti*. If the child's aunt is present at the time of delivery, she cowdungs the threshold of the room, places a packet of betelnuts and leaves near it, and says, looking towards the child, "This child is to be my son's wife." The mother smiles, and if she has a son says, "When you get a daughter she will become my daughter-in-law." In the evening the mother is again bathed, *Nim* juice is given to her to drink and she is fed, as in the morning, on rice, butter and pepper, and is given some hot water to drink. The child, as before, is dosed with three or four drops of castor oil, and laid by the mother's side on the cot. A lamp is kept burning during the night, and next morning, after rubbing them with turmeric and oil, both mother and child are bathed, the mother is purified with *vishesh* (frankincense), and the child is given a dose of castor oil. The mother takes some *Nim* juice, has a meal of rice, butter, and pepper, and is given some hot water to drink. At noon women neighbours and kinswomen begin to drop in. Each visitor touches the soles of her feet as if taking a pinch of dust therefrom, waves it round the child, and blows the dust partly into the air and partly into the ground. Then, cracking the finger joints of both her hands, she takes her seat, and is given turmeric and red powder. Should she be unlucky enough not to crack all her finger joints, she is thought to have no friendly feelings to the mother and child, and is not given the powder. In the evening, if the child takes to crying, frankincense is burnt in the names of Bahiroba and the goddess Satvái and they are prayed to, to save the child and prolong its life. On the third and fourth days, beyond bathing the mother in hot water, no ceremony takes place. On the morning of the fifth day the following articles are brought: a cocoanut, *five* pieces of cocoa-kernel, *five* dry dates, *five* grains of pepper, dry ginger, poppy, cardamoms, cloves, nutmeg, betelnut and leaves, catechu, scented and red powders, tooth powder a coloured cord with a small parcel of red and scented powder or *Nádá-pudi*, frankincense, turmeric, and a small copper or brass image of Satvái. Dishes of mutton and rice flour balls are cooked, and kinspeople and friends are asked to a feast. The women guests bring with them on a brass plate a few grains of rice, a cocoanut, and betel leaves, and set them before the goddess Satvái. Then the child's grandmother or some other elderly woman of the house sets a low wooden stool in the lying-in room, and places the image of Satvái on the stool. She sprinkles redpowder on the image, burns frankincense, offers fruit and cooked food, and, wrapping the child in a cloth, lays it before the goddess, and prays her to accept the offerings, to be kind to the child, and to overlook any shortcomings in the worship. The mother comes forward, bows before the image and eats of all the dishes. The other women bow before the goddess, and after eating, return to their homes. When the women have gone, the men begin to drop in. They are seated on blankets, and dinner is served outside as the woman is not allowed to see any man for twelve days. After dinner a pipe of tobacco is handed round, first to the *pátil* then to the senior guests, and then to the rest, but youths must go out if they desire to smoke. Singing, smoking and drinking go on till morning when all go home. The custom of the worship of Satvái varies according to family usage, which differs in different families. Next morning the mother and child are rubbed with cocoanut oil and bathed in warm water, and the former goes back to her special diet of rice, butter, pepper, and hot water. On the morning of the seventh day the cot and earthern waterpot are smeared with redpowder and turmeric, *five* lighted rice flour lamps are placed in the waterpot, and cooked food is offered. *Five* unmarried girls are rubbed with red powder and turmeric and their laps are filled with wet gram, a piece of cocoa-kernel, betel leaves and nuts, and small balls of powdered ginger mixed with molasses. After the mother has prostrated herself *five* times and bowed twice before the girls, a dinner is served to one or two women neighbours. On the morning of the eighth day the mother and child are bathed, and after eating her usual special food the former is given betel leaves and nut to chew, and a dish of live coals is placed under her cot. Cocoa-kernel and dry date (*khárik*) are pounded together and mixed with molasses, a little being given to the mother and the rest distributed among the neighbours. On the tenth day two or three women come and wash all the clothes and bedding, and in return are given breakfast. All the house walls and floors get a fresh plaster of cowdung, and when the singers come, cow's urine is sprinkled on their bodies and clothes. Then they, together with the house people, feast on bread, relishes, white *shepu* (Anethum foenic:tum), and green chillies. On the eleventh day preparations are made for the twelfth-day ceremony. Articles are laid in and the Bráhman priest and guests are invited

On the morning of the twelfth day the women of the house bathe the mother and again purify the walls and floor of the house with a plaster of cowdung. They take some cakes and begin to cook dishes of rice, vegetables, and pulse. A goat is killed, and its blood is gathered in a metal plate and mixed with spices and boiling water. This dish is called *rakti*. The bones and flesh are cooked into two separate pots and the liver or *kalij* in the third. A girl goes to tell the neighbours that the feast is ready, and when a few women have come the mother goes along with them to a spot outside the village and makes offerings to Satvái. On their return a bangle-seller puts green bangles round the mother's and black bangles round the midwife's wrists. Men guests have by this time begun to drop in, and, as they come, are seated on blankets, spread in the verandah. The Bráhman priest next arrives with his almanac, and he too takes his seat in the verandah. The women of the house tell the Bráhman the day and time at which the child was born, and he, spreading his almanac before him and counting his fingers, gives the child a name, and tells his fortune. The child is dressed in a new frock and cap. Soot is rubbed on his cheeks and eyelids, and he is set facing the east. The priest is given about two pounds of rice, and split pulse, a little molasses, and betelnut and leaves. A cradle is hung from the ceiling, and worshipped, turmeric and redpowder are thrown over it, cooked food is offered, and a blanket is spread in it with some wet gram a:d betelnut and leaves in the corners and a string tied in the middle. The mother sits near the cradle, and as they rock the cradle they sing songs. The mother lifts the child, and turning it thrice round the cradle they say: 'Take Harpál and give Gopál, take Govind and give Krishna, take Mahádev and give Rám, take Bharat and give Shatrughna.' The child is then laid in the cradle, and the paternal aunt of the child, the rest all the time slapping her on the back, puts her mouth close to the child's ear, and says,' Quietly quietly receive pulse and take Somji (the name given to the child) Patel to play.' Then the mother's lap is filled with a cocoanut, rice, glass beads, turmeric, pieces of cocoa-kernel and betelnut, and she is taken to bow to the family gods. A piece of thread is tied round the child's loins and the guests are feasted, the men and women in separate rooms. After they have done, they are given betelnut and leaves, wet pulse, and rice cakes. When the guests begin to leave, an old man and woman seat themselves in the doorway and refuse to let the women pass till each mentions her husband's name. After some coquetting the boldest of the women repeats some verses in which her husband's name occurs.

On the thirteenth day the mother begins to go about the house, washing, cooking and cleaning as usual. Except on the full and new moon the child is bathed every day. When two months old, as a safeguard against liver disease, the mother gives the child tooth-powder mixed with cow's milk and liquor, and rubs its stomach with black nut and ashes, while a sorcerer says a charm or a mystic verse. To increase her supply of milk, the mother is given rice, butter, and split peas. When the child is three months old, to help it to hold up its head the mother is given a cooked goat's head and round the child's neck is hung a black thread with two black nuts or *bajarbatus* and an image of the goddess Satvái. In this month a black thread is tied round the child's waist and copper rings are put on its feet, in order that teething may be accomplished safely, and to ward off the evil eye the eyelids of both the child and the mother are touched with soot. In the same month the mother and the child with other relations go to visit the shrine of the goddess Satvái, when a goat, tooth-powder, turmeric, redpowder, betelnut and leaves, soot, two cocoanuts, a robe and bodice, some grains of rice, dry cocoa-kernel, and frankincense are offered to the goddess and the goat is killed by a Mahár or Máng before her. The head and four legs are placed behind the goddess and the body is taken away presented to the goddess, cooked and eaten. The temple priest or ministrant tells the goddess the reason of the offering, and, taking a pinch of ashes, rubs them on the brow of the child and of its mother. After feasting on the flesh of the goat and on other dishes, the party buy back the goat's head, paying one to four annas, and go home. All the religious parts of this ceremony are performed by the temple servant, who is generally a Gurav by caste. On reaching the house the mother and child stand at the door, and a woman comes from the house and waves a piece of bread round them and pours water over the mother's feet.

When a child is four or five months old it is bathed outside of the house, and when it is about a year old and begins to walk, its head is shaved, except a tuft on the crown, and the hair is offered to the goddess Satvái. The barber gets a present of a pair of scissors, and the mother gives a feast to a party of married women. Six months later, when the child begins to eat, any flow of saliva is stopped by the mother passing a live fish three or four times round its face. When four years old the child begins to run about the streets and lanes and plays at marbles, bat and ball, tops, and hide and seek. After about seven the child begins to be of use to his parents, taking the cattle to graze and bringing them home in the evening. When ten or twelve years old he is branded as a cowherd either on the right or left hand or on both hands. A few pellets of hare's dung are brought from a hill, pounded and set in four or five places about the boy's wrist and burnt. The other boys hold the child so as to keep him quiet, and when he can no longer bear the pain the burning pellets are knocked off and the skin rubbed.*

Marriage ceremonies.

As a rule the proposals of marriage come from the boy's parents. Before accepting the offer the boy's father makes a full enquiry regarding the surname, family, and relations of the girl's father. When he is satisfied on these points, the boy's father goes with friends and kinsfolk to the girl's, marks her brow with redpowder, touches her brow with a rupee, and lays the rupee in her hands. The girl is given a small robe, a bodice, and some ornaments, and her grand mother and maternal uncle's wife are presented with two robes. The girl's father asks the boy's father and his kinsfolk, and his own friends and kinspeople, to a feast of cakes or *polis* either stuffed or unstuffed. When the feast is over, a Bráhman is called to fix the marriage day and is paid by both fathers. If the girl's father is poor, he takes Rs. 100 to Rs. 150 as her price; if he is rich, he gives Rs. 50 to Rs. 100 as her dowry. Before the marriage, in front of both the boy's and girl's houses, a marriage porch is built, and in the girl's marriage porch is set an earthen altar or *bahule*. The *muhurta-medha* or auspicious post of the marriage booth is planted on the marriage day. Supplies of clothes, grain, oil and other articles are also laid in. Not more than five days before the marriage, the bride and bridegroom are rubbed with turmeric powder. Three or four unwidowed women grind this turmeric in a handmill, and to the handle, in a yellow cloth, are tied a betelnut and three or four sprouted turmeric roots. In country parts, except the headman and other *mánkaris* or honourables, most of the men of the village take part in the turmeric grinding, sitting four or five at a handmill. They sing the women's corn-grinding songs. These handmills are not used till the marriage ceremony is over. On the morning of the marriage day a low wooden stool is set in

* Bombay Gazetteer, Vol. XVIII, Part I, pp 296-300.

the doorway and round the stool *five* metal water pots for bathing are arranged and a thread is passed *five* times round them. Some betelnuts and a few grains of rice are laid in the girl's hands, and a metal pot filled with cold water in the hand of the bridesmaid, or *karavli*, and the two go round the pots *five* times. Then the bridesmaid, walking behind the girl, pours a little water on the low wooden stool and the girl *five* times drops a few grains of rice on the water, and setting first her right foot and then her left foot on the stool, sits on it. Her head is rubbed with oil, and she is bathed. Meanwhile the girl bathes *five* little children who stand in front of her, and the musicians from time to time play their pipes. When all the children have been bathed, the girl's mother comes forward, and sitting close to her daughter on the low wooden stool, is bathed. When the bath is over, she is presented with a robe and bodice, and if she is not a widow, her arms are rubbed with turmeric, red powder is rubbed on her brow, and a cocoanut and rice are laid in her lap. The girl is dressed in a robe and green bodice and her clothes are stained with wet turmeric, her forehead is daubed with red powder and rice, her cheek and the space between the eyebrows are marked with soot, and in her lap are laid a cocoanut, *five* dry cocoa-kernels, *five* betelnuts, *five* turmeric roots, and some grains of wheat or rice. After this a chaplet, either of flowers or of tinsel, is tied round her brow, and her head is covered with her husband's blanket. Without letting the cotton thread that encircles them touch the girl, four women stand with water-pots in their hands, and a fifth loosens one end of the thread and ties it to the *muhurtamedha* and plants the post on one side of the doorway. By this time, at the boy's house, the Bráhman priest has come, and is given a cocoanut, pieces of cocoa-kernel, thread, turmeric, a piece of yellow cloth, a winnowing fan and rice. The priest sets two lighted lamps on a low wooden stool, and between the two lamps, a bathing tub or *ghangál*. He picks up a winnowing fan, lays grains of rice in it, and filling a metal water-pot with cold water, sets it on the rice. He spreads a few mango leaves on the water-pot or sets a cocoanut on it. He ties in a yellow cloth a few grains of rice, and some betelnut and turmeric. He daubs the bundle with red powder and lays it in the winnowing fan, beside the water-pot. The priest opens his almanac at a picture of Ganpati, tells the host to worship the picture, repeats verses, and the host sprinkles over the picture sandalwood, rice and red and scented powder, lays betelnut and leaves and a copper coin before it, offers it sugar and bows to it. When the worship of Ganpati is over, the priest rolls up his almanac and lays it beside him. Then, after worshipping the winnowing fan and its contents and seeing that it is put in a safe place, the priest goes home. A near relation of the girl, taking turmeric powder and accompanied by music, goes to the boy's house, makes over the turmeric to the people of the house and returns. The boy is seated on a low wooden stool in the midst of the *five* earthen pots, bathed, and dressed in a new waist-cloth, a turban and a shoulder-cloth. His forehead, like the girl's forehead, is marked with red powder, and over the powder a few grains of rice are stuck. A tinsel chaplet is tied to his brow, and, as at the girl's house, the thread that was wound round the earthen pots is tied to the *muhurtamedha*. The village barbers lay a cloth on the grinding stone or *páta*, and worship it by laying grains of rice before it. To the wooden pestle or *músal* are then tied a betel leaf, a millet stalk, and a needle, and it is set in the mortar. The women of the house seat the boy in front of the mortar on a low wooden stool, take cocoanut-oil in a metal cup, and dipping mango leaves in the oil let it drop on his head. The washerwoman, holding the pestle in her left hand, stands in front of the boy singing songs. A chaplet of flowers, a cocoanut, and a few grains of wet pulse are sent to the village god with the prayer that he may be kind, that the marriage ceremony may pass without mishap and that he may give the marriage guests a safe return to their homes. When this is over, the guests are treated to a dinner. During the two or three days, after the boy has been rubbed with turmeric, friends and kinspeople ask him to dine, and when he goes young girls sometimes go with him. If one of the friends is wealthy, he invites the boy and all the members of the boy's family to his house with musicians playing before them, feasts them on cakes and *polis*, and hangs flower garlands or *mundávals* round the boy's head. If the houses of the bride and bridegroom are in the same village or town, the installing of the *devak* is held on the marriage day. If the boy and girl live in different places, the worship is held two or three days before the marriage. In installing the *devak* the first step is to worship the house gods. After the house gods have been worshipped, a near kinsman of the boy's father and his wife have the skirts of their garments tied together, and, under a waist-cloth held over their heads by four persons, go, preceded by musicians, to the village Máruti. The husband carries on his shoulder an axe or some other iron field tool and a rope twelve to fifteen feet long, and his wife walks close behind him carrying a platter with the family *devak* and an offering of food. Behind the pair walk four or five unwidowed women, each carrying a brass water cup, filled with water. At Máruti's temple the Gurav or ministrant has a supply of *pānch pálvi* or sprigs of *five* trees, the mango, the *rui* (Calotropis gigantea), the *saundad* or *shami* (Prosopis spicigera), the Indian fig or *vad* and the *jámbhul* (Eugenia jambolana).*

The party bow before the god and lay sandal, flowers, frankincense, and food before him, and the ministrant presents them with the five sprigs or *pánch pálvis.* On their return to their house, they tie the five sprigs to a pole in the marriage porch and along with the sprigs tie a cake or *poli* and the spiced gram relish called *besan,* which is eaten with bread. On this day some ten to twenty friends and kinspeople are asked to a feast of unstuffed cakes. They sit on square blankets and after the serving of betel withdraw. When the guests are gone, the women of the house sit on the bare ground and eat. When a marriage party has to go to a distant village, they travel in bullock carts with music. On reaching the boundary of the girl's village or town, water is fetched and poured on the boundary by a Koli of the place, who is given a cocoanut and occasionally a turban. In some places, a lemon is cut, waved round the boy's head, and thrown away, and his eyes are touched with cold water or soot. On entering the village, if he has not ridden the whole way, the bridegroom mounts a horse and goes to the village Máruti with music, and halts there with his sisters or other young girls who are called *karavlis* or groom's maids. In the village the girl's father has provided a lodging or *jánvasghar* for the boy's party. In the evening, from Máruti's temple, the bridegroom's brother or other near relation, called the *vardhava* or groom-sent, mounts a horse and, with friends and music, goes to the bride's. On reaching the bride's, her father asks him to dine, and, if he is rich, gives him a turban. When the groom-sent has taken some food, the bride's father gives him, for the bridegroom, a tinsel chaplet, a turban, a red chintz overcoat, a pair of waist-cloths, a pair of shoes and a shoulder-cloth. The harbinger mounts his horse and starts for Máruti's temple with the bride's father and some of the bride's kinsmen, who carry *five* bodice-banners or *dhvajas* tied to poles and held over his head, and followed by a married unwidowed woman, with a cocoanut and betel-leaves in a platter. As he goes, the bride's brother pelts him with onions. At Máruti's temple the bride's father lays the platter with the dress before the bridegroom. A Bráhman priest, who is in attendance, tells the bridgroom to wash his eyes with water, loosens the brocaded end of the bridgroom's turban, and winds it twice or thrice round the bride-

* These five trees or shrubs vary, the mango, *rui* and banyan (*vad*) being frequently used but the *kadamba* (Anthocephalus cadumba) the *bel* (Ægle marmelos), the *sag* Indian teak and *pipal* (Ficus religiosa) being sometimes included in place of others mentioned in the text. For a discussion of the significance of the *panch palvi,* see Maráthás.

groom's neck. He sets up a betelnut Ganpati, and tells the bridegroom to wash it and lay sandal-powder and flowers before it. After this the priest touches the new clothes with turmeric powder, marks the bridegroom's brow with sandal-powder, and gives him the clothes. If the bridegroom's old turban is of little value, it is given to the barber who is to lead his horse; if the turban is rich the barber is given a cocoanut. Betel leaves are handed to all present, and money is given to the Bráhman. The bridegroom's left cheek is touched with lampblack. He lays before Máruti two betel leaves, a betelnut, and a copper coin and walks round him. He carries a dagger or poniard with a lemon stuck on its point. Before starting for the bride's a cocoanut is broken at the village gate to keep off evil influences and given to the Mahárs. The village Mahár stands before the bridegroom as if to stop him and is given a white turban or shoulder-cloth worth annas four to eight. When he reaches the bride's house, a Mahár woman comes with an iron lamp in a platter and waves it round his head, saying "May all your pains and troubles vanish and the riches of Bali be poured on you." For this she is given a cheap bodice cloth. Near the door of the bride's house the wife of her maternal uncle waves round the bridegroom's head a lighted lamp of wheaten flour with two wheat flour balls at its sides and is given a bodice and a robe. This lamp-waving is called *varoválni* or the bridegroom-waving. The boy's party are seated in the marriage porch, and the bridegroom is made to stand near the earth altar in the centre of which is placed a mango sprig stuck in a ball of mud and at each corner a coloured earthern pot called *vahi*. The bride is carried out of the house and set in front of the bridegroom facing him. The priest and some begging Brhámans come forward and divide into two parties. A cloth or *antarpát* is held between the bride and bridegroom, so that they cannot see each other's faces. They touch finger tips with the cloth between them. The two parties of Bráhmans hand the guests turmeric or red-coloured rice or millet to throw on the heads of the bride and bridegroom. The two parties of priests in turn recite *mangaláshtaks* or lucky verses, at the end of each verse throwing some coloured grains on the heads of the pair, and the guests, like the Bráhmans at the end of each verse, throw coloured grains. When the verses are over, the Bráhmans clap their hands and the guests clap their hands, and musicians raise a din of music. Shortly after the maternal uncles of the bride and bridegroom sit on stools with the bride and bridegroom on their knees and with their faces turned to each other. The priest tells the bride and bridegroom to fold their hands and touch finger tips, while he winds a yellow thread round their necks. This ceremony is called *sutavane* or thread-winding. When they are thus seated, the girl-giving or *kanyádán* is performed by the bride's maternal uncle, or, in his absence, by her father. When he gives her away, the uncle presents the girl with copper vessels according to his means. The priest, muttering some verses, cuts the yellow thread that was passed round the pair's necks and tells them to sit on the altar or *bahule.* The bride sits on the bridegroom's left. In front of the pair a burnt offering is made, called *lájáhom* of clarified butter, pieces of wood and fried rice. A winnowing-fan with rice, split pulse, wafer biscuits, fried rice cakes and vermicelli is laid before the bridegroom. The priest suddenly puts his hand over one of the articles on the fan and asks the bridegroom to say what he has hid. If the bridegroom guesses right, the priest says that his patron has got an intelligent son-in-law; if he answers wrong, he calls him a dull fellow. After this a low stool, covered with wheat flour and with lines drawn on it, is set before the bride and bridegroom, and they are told to say each other's name, money is given to the Bráhman, and he retires. On the same day, after the marriage is over, a party from the bride's go to the village Máruti, and, with the same rites as those described in the case of the bridegroom's party, bring and tie in the marriage porch the bride's father's *devak* or marriage guardian. After the bride's *devak* has been installed, a party of the bride's kinswomen go in procession to the bridegroom, with platters full of fried rice, cakes and rice vermicelli or *shevya.* They are received with honour and are given turmeric and red powder. They empty their platters, and in return, in one of them, the bridegroom's kinswomen put annas 8 to Rs. 10 in cash. This food-gift to the bridegroom is called *rukhvat.* Then some of the bride's near kinsmen with music go to ask kinsmen to dine, and bring them home with music, and in the same way the women of the bride's family bring kinswomen. The relations are feasted on unstuffed cakes or *polis,* rice, split pulse, *álan* or boiled rice flour, seasoned with spices, and fried rice cakes. Early next morning, with music and friends, the bride and bridegroom seated on a horse, the bride in front, are taken to a river or garden, and, after retiring, have their feet rubbed with wet turmeric powder and oiled red powder, and return with music. About ten, the boy and girl are bathed on low stools in the booth. Round the bathing place are set five *támbyás* or copper drinking pots with a white thread passed round their necks. At the time of bathing, the bridegroom is seated on a low stool and the bride on another low stool or a large platter. While bathing they fill their mouths with water and blow it over each other's faces.

The boy holds a betelnut in his hand and the girl using both her hands tries to force it out; then the girl holds the nut and the boy tries to force it out with his left hand. If the boy fails the guests jeer at him, calling him *bulga* or impotent. When the bathing is over, the bridegroom tries to lift the bride by his left hand and set her at his left side while the bride tries to prevent him lifting her from the ground. These struggles greatly amuse the guests and relations. The boy and girl are then dressed and their brows are rubbed with red powder and their bodies with turmeric. They are given a dish of *shevya,* that is milk, clarified butter, rice vermicelli, and raw sugar, and feed each other. After dinner they sit on the altar in the booth. In the evening the bride's father gives a caste feast, and on one of the days the boy's father treats the caste to rice, split pulse, vegetables, and unstuffed cakes or *polis*. On this day or, if this is not a lucky day, on the next, the bride's lap is filled. The priest folds a waist-cloth four times, covers it with rice or wheat grains, and tells the bride and bridegroom to sit on it. While the priest chants verses, the bridgroom fills the bride's lap with *five* half cocoa-kernels, *five* dates, *five* sprouted turmeric roots, *five* betelnuts, a quarter of a pound of rice, a comb, a small casket, and a variously coloured cord. The bridegroom's father presents the bride with the richest robe he can afford and the guests present the fathers of the bride and bridegroom with clothes or cash from eight annas upwards. These presents are called *aher*. After this the twelve *balutedárs* or village servants come in, and according to his means, the boy's father gives their wives bodice-cloths or cash. If he is rich, he gives the headman or *pátil* a turban. In the evening the bride's and bridegroom's skirts are tied together, and they walk to the bridegroom's house or lodging. After lamplight the bridegroom's mother, with a band of kinspeople, walks towards the bride's, on cloths spread by the village washerman, and at the same time the bride's mother starts with a band of friends to visit the boy's mother. When the parties meet, they stop ten or fifteen paces from each other. A waist-cloth is held in front of each party and they begin throwing red powder on one another. They jest with one another showing in front of the cloth a ladle, a rolling-pin, a dog or a cat. While this is going on, the bridegroom and his mother pretend to be offended and leave the party. The bride's father and mother follow them and appease them with presents. Then the two parties move on to the bride's where the bridegroom's mother is seated in the booth on a three-legged stool. Round her are arranged *five* metal drinking pots or *támbyás* with a thread passed round their necks, and the boy and girl are seated on her lap. *Five* women of the bride's family wash the feet of the bridegroom's mother. The bride's father gives a robe to the bridegroom's mother and the bridegroom's father gives a robe to the bride's mother. This interchange of robes is called *potjhákni* or stomacher. While the bridegroom's mother is seated on the stool, the *jhál* or handing ceremony is performed. A bamboo basket or round metal dish, with a comb, a looking-glass, a basket, a rolling-pin, *five* sweet things and *five* wheat flour lamps is set on the bridegroom's mother's head, and four or five women stand about her and sing the *jhál* song which runs : "The bridegroom has reached the village boundary, I will worship the boundary and win the bridegroom." Meanwhile a kinsman of the bridegroom's runs away with the basket or dish to the bridegroom's and is pursued and pelted with onions by the bride's people. The bride's father, mother and other near relations hold the bride and seated on their crossed hands set her on her husband's lap and then on the laps of his father, mother and other near relations. At the time of handing her over, the girl's relations with sobs and tears say, "Up to this time she was ours, now she is yours." This ceremony is seldom over till the morning cock-crow, and, after it is over sometimes as late as five, they sit to a feast. When the feast is over, the bride and bridegroom are led into the god-house and bow before the images. As he bows, the bridegroom steals one of the gods and refuses to give it until the bride's father makes him a present. All then go to the bridegroom's. In the evening the bridegroom's father gives betel leaves with nuts to the guests and bids them good-bye. If the bridegroom belongs to another village, the guests, who belong to his village, accompany him home. When they reach the village the bride and bridegroom are taken to the temple of the village Máruti. In the evening, about seven or eight, the bride and bridegroom are seated on a horse and led to his house with a procession, music, and, if they can afford them, fireworks. In the house a dish with cocoanuts, saffron, and betel leaves is waved round the image of Khandoba, a ceremony which is called the lifting of Khandoba's *tali* or plate. After the plate-waving, comes the *jhenda náchne* or flag-dance when one man sets the bride on his back and another sets the bridegroom on his back and they dance. Sometimes the bride sits on the bridegroom's back and a man dances with both on his back. After the dance the bridgroom, holding the full box of a seed drill in his hand, sprinkles grain on the ground as if sowing, and along with the bride, who carries resin in her hand, goes to the god room. At the door of the god room they find the boy's sister, who refuses to let them pass till they promise to give their first daughter in marriage to her son. They agree though the promise is practically never kept, and pass in, and laying a betelnut and copper coin before them, bow to the house gods. The girl is considered the goddess of wealth and her brow is marked with redpowder. Some wheat with a piece of gold in it is heaped between the bride and bridegroom, and they are told to divide the heap. If the bride gets the gold in her half she is applauded, and it is taken as an omen that the rule in the house will be hers. On the next or some other lucky day the bride and bridegroom are bathed and the turmeric is taken off. If she can afford it, the boy's mother for a fortnight longer feeds them on boiled rice and clarified butter.*

When a girl comes of age, her feet are rubbed with turmeric powder moistened with water and her brow with redpowder with or without oil; and she is fed on *varan* or split pulse cooked in water with turmeric powder, and salt, rice, vegetables, and unstuffed cakes or *polis*. If her father-in-law is rich, the girl is for four days seated in a gaily dressed frame called a *makhar*. On the fifth she and her husband are bathed, and while they bathe music is played. She is dressed in a green robe and green bodice, and her hands are adorned with fresh green glass bangles. Her father, if rich enough, gives her husband a waistcloth and turban and to his mother a robe and a bodice, and beds, a carpet, a set of betel dishes, and a *samai* or metal lamp for her and her husband's use. Some unwidowed women with relations are asked to feast on cakes or *polis*, and the girl and her husband are made to feed each other from the same dish. In the evening the girl is sent to sleep in a separate room and the wife's brother or other near relation leads the boy to the room and shuts him in.† Puberty.

The remarriage of widows is permitted, but some families think widow-marriage disreputable and do not practise it. As a rule only widowers marry widows, and the children do not get so large a share of the property as the children of the first marriage. A remarried widow is not allowed to perform religious rites with her husband, and her husband is not allowed to make offerings to the *manes*. If a widower marries a maid, he is not prevented from making offerings. A remarried widow is less honoured than other women. Widow remarriage.

A widow cannot marry a member of her late husband's section or her father's section. She must observe the same limitation as at her first marriage. The ceremony takes place on a dark night in a field

* Bombay Gazetteer, Vol. XVIII, Part I, pp. 300—307.
† Bombay Gazetteer, Vol. XVIII, Part I, p. 307.

outside the village where three roads meet. It is attended by a few of the relations of the widow and her intended husband and a Bráhman priest. The pair are seated on a low wooden stool facing east, and they are made to worship Ganpati represented by a betelnut. Next the Bráhman priest asks the widow whether she has received all her price or dower (which varies from Rs. 50 to Rs. 100) from the bridegroom. On her saying yes, the priest rubs the widow's forehead with a little cowdung and the bridegroom touches it with a rupee, which is given to the priest. Next, redpowder is applied to the widow's forehead, the couple are asked to turn their faces to the west and five *mangaláshtaks* or lucky verses are repeated by the priest and the relations of the couple who are present. The party then disperse except the newly married pair, who have to pass the night in a *mála* or field-hut outside the village. On the next morning their faces are not seen unless they have bathed and visited the temple of the local Máruti or some other village deity. The priest who performs the ceremony bathes as soon as it is over, washes the clothes worn by him at the time, and puts on fresh ones.

Religion.

Marátha Kunbis follow the Hindu law of inheritance and belong to the Hindu religion. They cannot tell whether they are Smárts or Bhágvats. Many of them are Várkaris who are also called Málkaris as they wear necklaces of basil beads. They worship all Bráhmanic gods and goddesses, but their chief objects of worship are Bhairav, Bhaváni, Biroba, Jákhái, Janái, Jokhái, Kálkái, Khandoba, Máruti, Metisai, Mhasoba, Mukái, Navlái, Phringái, Satvái, Tukái, Vághoba and Vetál, whom they greatly fear and whose images or *táks* they keep in their houses. Bhairav is the usual village guardian. He has two forms, Kál Bhairav and Bál Bhairav. Kál Bhairav is shown as a standing man with two hands, an hour-glass-shaped drum or *damaru* in his right hand, and a trident in his left. He is encircled by a serpent. Bál Bhairav lives in an unhewn stone covered with redlead or *shendur* mixed with oil. If kept pleased by a coating of oil and redlead and if he is given offerings of clarified butter, Bhairav is kindly. He cures snake-bites and tells whether an undertaking will do well or will fail. In the chest of the rough figure of Bhairav are two small holes. The person who wishes to consult the oracle places a betelnut in each of the holes and explains to Bhairav that if the right betelnut falls first it will mean that the undertaking will prosper, and that if the left betelnut falls first it will mean that the undertaking will fail. He asks the god, according as the event is to be, to let the lucky or unlucky nut fall first. He tells the god that if he will drop the lucky nut and if his undertaking prospers he will give the god a cock or a goat. Twice a year before they begin to sow and before they begin to reap, the villagers come in procession and worship Bhairav. Bhaváni, that is, Párvati the wife of Shiva, is known by many names such as Phringái, Tukái, etc. She shares with Bhairav the honour of being village guardian; she is generally shown as a rude image, either with two hands, a sword being in the right hand, or with eight hands holding a conch, a wheel and other articles the same as Vishnu holds. Like Bhairav she is asked the cause of sickness or ill-luck and to advise regarding the future, and like him, if she removes trouble or advises well, she is given a goat or a cock. Biroba is worshipped mainly by Dhangars or shepherds. He lives in an unhewn stone outside of the village. Like Mhasoba he is an unkindly spirit to whom people pray when they are anxious to plague or ruin their enemies. Jakhái, Janái, Jokhái, Kálkái, Motisái, Mukái and Navlái are all local mothers. According to the people's account they are unkindly forms of Bhaváni. With the help of two attendants, Náikji and Birji, they do much mischief. They blast crops of grain, plague men with sickness, and carry off travellers. People who owe their neighbours a grudge pray to Janái, Mukái, or one of the mothers to send them sickness, to kill their cattle, or to ruin their fields. Khandoba, literally swordfather, guards the country as Bhairav guards the village. Khandoba is the Ishvar Dev or guardian deity of the Deccan. As a guardian, he is shown sometimes at his chief shrine at Jejuri as a *linga*, the great protector, and more often as a horseman with a sword in his right hand, and his Mhálsábái sitting beside him. As a horseman, he is Malhári, the form he took when he came to destroy the demons Mani and Malla. As an animal, he is the dog who runs beside his horse, and in the Deccan is generally called Khandi. As a plant he is turmeric powder under the name Bhandár. His house image is always of metal, never of wood or of stone. He drives away the evil which causes sickness. No class honour Khandoba so highly as the Rámoshis. If a Rámoshi makes a promise while laying his hand on turmeric powder or *bhandár*, that is, on Khandoba, nothing will bring him to break his promise. Máruti, also called Hanumán, is the monkey god. No village in the Deccan is without a Máruti, a rudely embossed monkey figure, sometimes within the village and sometimes without, but generally near the gate. He is a kindly god, the great saver of those into whom evil spirits have entered. He is fond of cocoanuts, but does not care for blood offerings. Mhasoba or Mhaskoba is perhaps the commonest and most widely feared of the local evil spirits. He lives in an unhewn stone coated with redlead. These stones are all old dwellings of Mhasoba—some get forgotten. Then sickness falls on the village, and the people go to the village guardian and ask him a series of questions, which he answers by dropping a betelnut or by some other sign. In the end they find out from the guardian that there is an old neglected dwelling of Mhasoba. The villagers find the stone, cover it with oil and redlead, and kill a goat or a fowl in front of it. Besides, to prevent his working mischief, Mhasoba is worshipped by men who have a grudge to clear off or a wrong to avenge. They go to Mhasoba, name their enemy, and promise, if he ruins their enemy with sickness, that they will give him a goat or a fowl. So much is he feared that when a man knows that some one whom he has ill used has arranged to set Mhasoba on him, he makes such amends that the god is not forced to exert his powers. Satvái, or Mother Sixth, is the goddess of pregnant and lying-in women. She is worshipped by barren women, and by lying-in women on the fifth or sixth day after the child is born. Her image is an armless bust. Vághoba, or Father Tiger, lives in an unhewn stone. If he is cared for, he guards the village herds from the attacks of tigers. Vetál is the leader of demons and evil spirits. He seems to be the earliest form of Shiva, the leader of spirits, and Ganesh, the lord of spirit troops. Vetál lives in an unhewn stone, three or four feet high, surrounded at a distance of a few yards by a circle of smaller stones in which his leading attendants live. Unlike most shrines, the stones in which Vetál and his attendants live are covered both with white and red wash. Vetál and his guard are generally at some distance outside of the village. Vetal's great day is the *Maháshivarátri* or great night of Shiva on the full-moon of *Mágh* in February. On that night the villagers, each with a bundle of lighted straw in his hand, walk round the circle of stones howling and bawling. When a Kunbi or one of his family is possessed by an evil spirit, he goes to Vetál and promises, if he orders his spirit to give up troubling him, that he will give him a goat or a fowl. Vetál is the patron of wrestlers and athletes. On one of the holidays the villagers go and wrestle at Vetál's circle. Vetál's sign is a cane called *vet* or *bet*, from which he seems to get his name. From his apparent sameness with the early forms of Shiva, and from the resemblance of his circle of guards to a rude Buddhist rail, and to the circles of unhewn stones found in Western Europe and in other parts of the world, the worship of Vetál is specially interesting.

Kunbis observe all the Hindu holidays, the chief of which are the *Pádva* or Hindu New Year's Day, *Akshatritiya, Rámnavami, Nágpanchami, Navyachi punav, Gokuláshtami, Ganesh Chaturthi, Pola, Gavri, Dasara, Diváli, Champá-shashthi, Sankránt* and *Shimga* or *Holi.* Their fast days are the four Mondays and Saturdays of *Shrávan, Navrátra* the first nine days of *Ashvin*, the two *Ekádashis* or elevenths of *Ashádh* and *Kártik*, *Hartálika*, *Rishi Panchami* and *Shivarátra*. Besides on these days, some fast on all Mondays, Saturdays, Sundays or Tuesdays of the year. *Nágpanchami* or the Cobra's Fifth is the Kunbi woman's festival. In the afternoon all the women dressed in their best, go with music to a white ant-hill in which a cobra is believed to live, and lay milk and sugar near the ant-hill while the priest says prayers.* The women take hands, dance round the ant-hill in a ring alternately rising and kneeling and keeping time to a song which they sing in chorus. At intervals they take parched rice in a clenched hand, and putting it on each other's heads ask their husband's name. As they may not answer directly, they bring in his name in a rhyme. At the *Pola* festival the oxen have a rest. Their horns are covered with tinsel or red, and *palas* fibre tassels are tied to their tips. Garlands of flowers are put round their necks, they are fed with sugar, and their owners fall at their feet and worship them. In the evening after the headman's cattle, all the oxen are driven round Hanumán's temple. The day ends with a feast.

Besides the above holidays many field rites are practised by the Marátha Kunbis. About the end of April on the *Akshatritiya*, literally the undying third, offerings are made to three generations of dead warriors and a fresh year of field work begins. In some places, before beginning to plough waste land, cooked rice or *five* millet or Indian millet cakes, curds, a cocoanut and a he-goat or fowl are offered to the field spirit, Mhasoba, Navlái or Satvái. This is not done in other places. When the rice seedlings are ready to plant, the villagers meet on a Sunday, anoint their village god, who is generally Bahiroba or Hanumán, with oil and redlead, sacrifice a he-goat and ten fowls, and offer *five* cocoanuts, frankincense, fifteen lemons and camphor. They ask the god to give them good crops and walk round the village calling the name of their god. A feast is prepared, and the sacrifices are eaten near the temple. Each landholder on the Tuesday before he begins to plant his rice kills a fowl and sprinkles its blood over the field and offers the field spirit a cocoanut and a he-goat or fowl. Before setting up the *tivda* or central pole of the threshing floor, all ask an astrologer what wood they should use. Under the pole they bury their *devak*, frequently consisting of the twigs of the mango, *jámbhul* (Eugenia jambolana), *shami*

---

* Among many castes in the south of the Presidency the white ant heap is worshipped to this day. In Kanara near Dighi in Supa Mahál of Yellápur *táluka*, a temple built over a white ant heap has been found by the Editor. The local belief is that the ant heap is the home of a cobra.

(Prosopis spicigera), *arati* (Mimosa hamata) and *rui* (Calotropis gigantea) and an egg. They set up as a shrine or *devasthán* an earthern pot and seven pebbles, five for the Pándavs and one each for *Vandev* or the forest god and *Vansapatra* or the forest lord. The pot and the pebbles are smeared with redlead and frankincense is burnt before them. Kunbis sacrifice a sheep or a he-goat, a Bráhman or Gujarát Váni would offer five grains of wheat or five millet cakes and five each of betel, cloves, cardamoms, turmeric roots and pieces of cocoa-kernel. When the grain is threshed some husbandmen offer a sheep, a goat, a fowl or cakes. Before winnowing, an animal or cakes and fruit are offered at the Pándav shrine. Rice is also offered and scattered over the threshing floors, a rite known as *ráspuja*, that is the heap worship. When an animal is offered, the rice is steeped with blood before it is thrown. Before measuring the grain the astrologer is asked which of the husbandman's family should measure it. With a broom of early *juvári* stalks the grain is heaped round the central pole and incense is burnt before it, a two-*sher* or *adholi* measure is held in the incense smoke and handed to the measurer, who offers the first measureful to the village god. If a crop is attacked by rust, in some parts of the district a fowl is sacrificed or a cocoanut is offered to the village deity. At all these rites the village priest is present, recites texts and is given a cocoanut and a few coppers.

Marátha Kunbis make pilgrimages to Jotiba of Vádi, Ratnágiri, in the months of *Chaitra* and *Shrávan*, to Narsoba's Vádi on *Guru-dwádashi* in *Ashvin* and in the month of *Mágh*, to Pandharpur on the elevenths of the first halves of *Ashádh* and *Kártik*, to Alandi and Dehu in Poona and Tuljápur in the Nizam's country and to many other places where fairs are held, and even to Benares.

Marátha Kunbis believe in incantations, witchcraft, ghosts and evil spirits, oracles and the evil eye. Partly perhaps because they are much more sober, partly perhaps because fever is much less common, the Deccan Kunbis are much less afraid of spirits than the Konkan Kunbis. Still, the belief in spirits, witchcraft and the evil eye has a great effect on the lives of the Deccan Kunbis. If a Kunbi is seized with uncommon sickness, or suffers from any calamity, he first finds out whether his misfortunes are due to natural causes, to the displeasure of the gods, to witchcraft, to the evil eye, or to an evil spirit. To find out the cause the sufferer and his friends make several experiments. A flower is stuck on the breast of an idol and its fall on one side or the other determines the cause of the misfortune, or a sacrificial vessel is hung by a string, and, as is agreed beforehand, the direction to which it points when it comes to rest settles the cause of the evil. If these trials are not satisfactory, a *Jánta* or knowing man is asked. If the evil has come from the gods, the knowing man says how the gods are to be pleased; if the cause is witchcraft, either the knowing man breaks the spell by counter-charms, or the witch is caught and either forced to remove the spell or made to drink water from the hands of a cobbler, which destroys her power; if the cause is the evil eye, either the knowing man breaks the spell, or the mother of the sick child throws salt and red pepper into the fire saying, *Drisht-Misht áli gelichi, Bhut-khet pápi chándáláchi*, that is, 'The evil eye of passers-by, of evil spirits and filthy wights'. The evil eye is much feared. The owner of the eye is not thought to blame, but he is shunned and cattle are not driven past his door. To draw the evil eye from the crops a white-washed pot is stuck on a pole; the walls of houses are decked with figures and gaudy stripes; beautiful women and children wear neck-laces and cattle wear necklaces and anklets. A Kunbi never congratulates a friend on his prosperity, his fine oxen or his handsome wife. If he does, ill-luck will hear and carry away the excess of good fortune. Every place teems with ghosts and evil spirits, who are included under the general name *bhut*, literally a being. The male ghosts are called Keins or Jhotings, and the female ghosts Hadals. Among the worst female ghosts are the seven water-nymphs called Aija or Jaldevtás, who carry off handsome youths. There are distinct names for the ghosts of Bráhmans, Musalmáns and outcastes. A ghost wanders and ill-uses the living either because he was murdered or ill-treated, or because he hankers after a house, a wife or a treasure. Ghosts live in large trees, lonely places, empty houses and old wells. They are generally seen or heard at noon and at midnight. They take many shapes, a deer, a tall figure, or a strange ox or goat. If a person sleeps under a haunted tree, or cuts a branch of a haunted tree, or defiles the ghost's ruin or old wall, or jostles a ghost on a road, the person sickens or is unlucky. The ghosts of the murdered or of ill-used are chiefly dangerous to those who ill-treated them. The ghost enters into the culprit, maddens him, destroys his sleep, kills his family and turns his joy to sorrow. Many people make a living by appeasing or casting out angry spirits. One plan is for the excorciser to take the possessed person in front of an idol, to seize him by the top-knot, scourge him, and abuse him till the spirit says what offering or penance will satisfy him.

Marátha Kunbis have great faith in omens. They consider it unlucky if a crow flies to the right and *tás* or the blue jay Coracias indica to the left. On going out they think it lucky to meet an unwidowed woman with a full waterpot on her head, a milkmaid with milk pots, or anybody with a dish of cooked food. If a cat or a widow happen to pass before them while going out, they consider it unlucky and go back. They hold it very unlucky if a lighted lamp falls on the ground and goes out; or if a house lizard drops in front of them.*

The priests of Marátha Kunbis are the local or Deshasth Bráhmans. Their religious teachers are Gosávis, whose advice or *updesh* they take.

Death ceremonies.

Kunbis generally burn their dead. When a person is on the point of death, his son or his wife lays the dying man's head on his or her right knee and lets a few drops of water fall into his mouth. Money and grain are given to the poor and a cow or from annas 8 to Rs. 5 in cash is given to the family Bráhman to help the flight of the soul to heaven. When the dying man has breathed his last, the women of the house raise a loud cry and dishevel their hair. A small piece of gold is put into the dead mouth, and after an hour or two, friends and neighbours come and mourn. The dead body is bathed in water heated on a hearth set in front of the house. To carry the body a ladder-like bier is made of two poles, six or seven feet long, with three or four small cross pieces. Two new earthern pots, a large one for water and a small one for fire, redpowder, betel leaves and a cloth about seven and-a-half feet long are brought from the market or village cloth shop. Word is sent to the village Mahár, who carries cowdung cakes and firewood to the burning ground, which is generally on the river bank. Except the face the body is covered with a new waistcloth and a cord is passed several times round the body to secure the cloth firmly. Betel leaves and *gulál* or red powder are sprinkled over it and a basil leaf is put in the mouth and some rice, a copper coin and the quarter of a cake are laid beside the body. Four kinsmen of the deceased bear the body and the son bathes and walks in front carrying the firepot on a triangular frame fastened to a sling. Before setting out he is warned not to look back. About half way to the burning ground at a place called the *visávyáchi jága* or rest-place the party stops and the bearers set the bier on the ground and change places. They throw away the rice, the copper coin and the quarter of a cake which were laid on the bier beside the body and pick up a stone, which is usually called the life stone or *jiv-khada*. When they reach the burning ground, they raise a pile of four layers of cowdung cakes.

* Bombay Gazetteer, Vol. XVIII, Part I, pp. 289—296.

They then take off the waistcloth, cut the thread tied round the wrist, and loosen the loincloth. The body is laid on the pyre and is covered with other layers of cakes. When the mouth is being covered the son pours a little water into it. The son sets fire to the pyre, bathes, brings water in the large earthen pot, and stands at the head of the pyre. Another person comes and with a small stone makes a hole in the earthen pot. As the water spouts from the pot, the son goes five times round the pyre and at the end throws the pot on the ground at the head of the pyre, and calls aloud, beating his mouth with the back of his hand. He then goes and sits among the other men without touching them. After a short time the sound made by the bursting of the skull is heard and the chief-mourner and others, at least the four bearers, bathe. The stone with which the earthen pot was pierced is kept with great care somewhere in the burning place. On their return to the house of mourning the funeral party are given *nimb* leaves to eat; or they go to a temple and then to their houses. The mourners do not cook but are fed on that day by a relation or a friend with food prepared at his house.

In the evening after the funeral, a lighted lamp is set on the spot where the deceased breathed his last. Flour is strewn round the lamp, and the lamp is covered with a basket. Next morning the basket is moved and the flour is examined. If a human foot-print appears on the floor, the deceased is believed to be re-born as a human being; and if the foot-print is that of a bird or beast, the spirit of the person is believed to have entered that beast or bird.

Next morning the son with some friends and relatives goes to the burning ground with three small earthern pots with their mouths covered with three small wheaten cakes and three *pimpal* leaves. He places the small pots in a winnowing basket and fills them with milk, cow-urine, and honey or sugar, and lays some cowdung in the basket. On reaching the rest-place, the son lays on the ground a cake with a little raw sugar. He goes on to the burning ground and from the spot where the body was burnt, he takes the ashes except one bone which he puts aside and throws them into the nearest river. If he is rich, he gathers the bones and afterwards takes them to a holy river. After removing the ashes the son sprinkles the spot with cowdung and cow-urine and places the two pots with two cakes, one where the head lay and the other where the feet lay. When the ash-gathering or *rakshávádhne* is over, the son and the other mourners bathe and return home. On the third day the bearers' shoulders are rubbed with oil and they are given dry cocoakernel to eat. On the tenth all the household bathe and wash their clothes in the river; and the son shaves his moustache and bathes. While a Bráhman repeats verses the son washes with cow-urine, the life-stone or *jiv-khada* and the bone he kept, prepares ten balls and three little banners made of ochre-coloured cloths, each tied to a stick. The Bráhman is given some money, shoes, and sometimes even a cow, presents which are supposed to help the deceased on his way to heaven. After preparing the offering balls the son sits at a distance that crows may come and eat them. If a crow touches them soon after they have been laid out, the deceased is supposed to have died with no unfulfilled wish. If crows do not touch the balls, the son and his relations promise to fulfil the dead person's wish, and when the promise is given, the crows are believed to fall on the offe ing and eat it. After this is over, the son and the other mourners bathe and return home. On the thirteenth day the priest is given money and provisions, and a feast of unstuffed cakes or *polis*, rice, and split pulse is given to friends and relations in honour of the deceased. Some food is put in a platter and the platter is kept aside that crows may eat out of it. In the evening, one of his near relations ties a small white turban round the son's head and takes him with the other mourners and generally some of the villagers to Máruti's temple, where the son lays a copper coin and a betelnut before the god. Every month a man is asked to dine in the name of the deceased, and, after five months and a half, a feast of unstuffed cakes or *polis* is given to the near relations of the deceased. In the dark half of *Bhádrapad* the spirit of the deceased is worshipped on the day of the fortnight which corresponds with the death day.*

Food. The staple food of Marátha Kunbis is millet, rice and vegetables, and, in some places in the Konkan, *náchni*. They eat the flesh of goats, sheep, hare, deer, wild hogs, fowls and fish, and drink liquor.

KONKANI KUNBIS are mainly found in the northern *tálukas* of the Ratnágiri district and the southern part of Kolába. They are popularly called Tilori Kunbis but are quite distinct from the Talheri Kunbis of Thána. They neither claim to be Maráthás nor Kshatriyas, but are content to be called Shudras. As among Marátha Kunbis the number *five* plays a prominent part in their ceremonies, suggesting a primitive origin. They are smaller

* Bombay Gazetteer, Vol. XVIII, Part I, pp. 307-309.

and darker and more slightly made than Marátha Kunbis. The women are small, and as a class rather plain and hard featured. Their home tongue is Maráthi, spoken more roughly and less clearly than by Bráhmans, but differing little in words or grammar.

Konkani Kunbis have no *kuls* like the Marátha Kunbis. Marriages are prohibited between members bearing the same surname, the other restrictions on intermarriage being the same as among Marátha Kunbis. Girls are married either before or after puberty. Widow remarriage is allowed and practised and is not considered so disreputable as among Marátha Kunbis. Divorce is forbidden.

The marriage ceremonies of Konkani Kunbis are similar to those of Marátha Kunbis though not so elaborate. The widow remarriage ceremony is celebrated in the house of the intended husband. As among Marátha Kunbis it is attended by a few relations and a Bráhman priest. Five unwidowed women apply red powder to the widow's forehead and fill her lap with a cocoanut, betelnut and grains, which completes the ceremony.

The chief objects of worship of Konkani Kunbis are Bahiri, Zugái, Navlái, Pawnái and Bhagvati. They observe all the Hindu holidays and on the Nágpanchami day (cobra-fifth) worship a white ant hill. They visit some of the places of Hindu pilgrimage, and have great faith in incantations, witchcraft, ghosts, oracles and the evil eye, their beliefs in these respects being the same as those of Marátha Kunbis. Their priests are Chitpávan or Karháda Bráhmans, or rarely Devrukhás. Their death ceremonies, with a few differences, resemble those of Marátha Kunbis.

The staple food of Konkani Kunbis is *nágli* and *vari* cakes. They eat the flesh of goats, sheep, fowls, wild pigs and fish and drink liquor.

KALE KUNBIS* are chiefly found in the Khánápur *táluka* of the Belgaum district and in the villages of the western part of Supa *petha* in Kanara. They are also called Konkani Kunbis. They belong to the same class as the Kunbis of south-west Goa, whence, it is believed, their ancestors migrated in the sixteenth century on account of religious persecutions.

---

* The term Kale Kunbi is identical in meaning with Kare Vakkal, both meaning black or dark Kunbis. The castes bearing these names are distinct, the former speaking Konkani and the latter Kanarese. Their costume seems, however, to indicate a common origin.

Kále Kunbis, both men and women, are dark, middle-sized and spare, with regular features. In dress and ornaments they resemble Hálvakki Vakkals.

Their home tongue is Konkani.

Each village of Kále Kunbis has a *miráshi* and a *gávada.* The duties of the *miráshi* are religious while those of the *gávada* are social. It is the *miráshi's* office to offer prayers to the village god or goddess for the villagers. Other Kunbis are not at liberty to commence cultivation or harvesting before the *miráshi* does so in his own land, if he has any, and each Kunbi before commencing cultivation and harvesting offers a cocoanut to the spirits of his village through the *miráshi,* as it is a strong belief that failure to propitiate the spirits entails a serious damage to the crops. The *miráshi* has also to make a cut on the throat of an animal killed by the villagers in hunting before its flesh is portioned out among the villagers. This duty falls on the head of the family when an animal is killed by a single individual. By making the cut the animal is supposed to have been sacrificed to the village or family deity as it is killed by the villagers jointly or by a single person. The object of the sacrifice is to prevent illness to those who eat the flesh, as it is believed that flesh eaten without being sacrificed to the gods causes illness.

The village social head *gávada* is subordinate to another *gávada* who has control over a group of villages which goes by the name *kariyadi.* The *kariyadi gávada* is again subordinate to two *gávadás, sar* or *ráj gávada* and *pradhán gávada,* who exercise authority over a *mahál* which comprises of several *kariyadis.* It is the duty of the village *gávada* to watch the conduct of the villagers and communicate any infringement of an established custom to the *gávada* of the *kariyadi.* Matters of small importance are settled by him. Important social questions are decided in councils of the *kariyadi gávadás* presided over by the *ráj gávada* of the *mahál* concerned. The *ráj gávada* confers with the *kariyadi gávadás,* but is not bound by their opinion. The decision rests with him. The duty of the *pradhán gávada* is to communicate the decision passed by the *ráj gávada* to the parties concerned. The Kudlegi branch of the Shringeri *math* of Shankaráchárya occasionally levies contributions from the Kále Kunbis, but does not interfere with the social questions affecting the community. The unwritten law of the community is very strict and is never allowed to be broken with impunity.

They belong to a number of clans or *kuls,* each of which has special gods and goddesses whose shrines are in villages, which are the head stations of the clans. Persons of the same clan and family deity cannot intermarry. The chief clans with their family deities are as follows :—

Name of clan.			Family deity.
Dándalkár	..	..	..Bhutnáth.
Dingakár	..	..	.. Do.
Goirekár	..	..	..Náiki.
Irkolkár	..	..	..Bhutnáth.
Kajewkár	..	..	..Monái.
Kolálkár	..	..	..Bhutnáth.
Kumarkár	..	..	.. Do.
Kumgelkár	..	..	..Rámling.
Máinolkár	..	..	..Bhutnáth.
Mudekár	..	..	.. Do.
Nándkár	..	..	..Monái.
Nujekár	..	..	..Bhutnáth.
Pátankár	..	..	..Rámling.
Ráikár	..	..	.. Do.
Sanwarkár	..	..	..Bhutnáth.
Tirodkár	..	..	.. Do.
Turaikár	..	...	..Rámling.
Volkár	..	..	.. Do.

The only important ceremony observed by Kále Kunbis is marriage, at which a Bráhman or Lingáyat priest officiates. The boy's father has to pay to the girl's father Rs. 12 and twenty maunds of paddy, and articles of dress to the members of his family. The binding portion of the marriage ceremonies is the *dháre* ceremony, in which water is poured over the joined hands of the bride and bridegroom. Girls are married either before or after puberty according to the convenience of the parents, though as a rule they are seldom kept unmarried after the age of eighteen years. The remarriage of widows is permitted but is not much resorted to, as a remarried widow is lowered down in social estimation. Divorce is prohibited.

Kále Kunbis have no idea of a heaven or hell or of the different divinities of the Hindu pantheon. Their religion consists for the most part in spirit worship. They believe that every man, after death, becomes a good or bad spirit according to his good or evil deeds in his life-time. Soon after a death a Ghádi is employed to ascertain whether the deceased is likely to turn out a good or bad spirit and, if the former, to induce it to live in the family house for the good of the family. Good spirits are propitiated by offerings of cocoanuts and food, through the *miráshi*, bad spirits by the offerings of sheep and fowls through the Ghádi. All diseases and misfortunes are attributed to the workings of the evil spirits. Of the Hindu holidays they observe only the *Ganesh Chaturthi*, *Shimga*, *Dasara*, *Diváli* and the *Ashádh* and *Kártik Ekádashis*. Some appear to have been influenced by Lingáyatism and worship Basava or Nadin and employ Jangams as priests.

The dead are generally buried, those dying an unnatural death in a place different from the usual burying ground. Women dying during pregnancy or shortly after child-birth are buried beyond the hamlets to which they belonged, as it is believed that the spirits of such women become terrible ghosts. Parched grains of rice or some other corn are thrown round the place of burial of such a woman or along the road from this place to the house of the deceased. The object of this rite is to adjure the spirit not to leave the place until the seeds germinate, the idea being that the seeds being parched will never germinate and the spirit will consequently never leave its place. On the fourth day after death the mourners are purified by sipping three drops of *panchagavya* or five products of the cow brought by a Bráhman priest.

Kále Kunbis eat fish and the flesh of wild animals. They do not eat the flesh of domesticated animals or birds such as sheep, goats and fowls. The fowl is looked upon as so unholy that if a Kunbi is touched by it, he immediately purifies himself by bathing or at least by sprinkling on his head water mixed with cowdung. The touch of a dead sheep or goat is equally polluting, but not that of a living one. Drinking toddy or liquor is considered a great sin, so much so, that they would not drink even water or milk under a palm tree which has been tapped. They eat cooked food at the hands of Bráhmans only.

TALHER KUNBIS are found almost entirely in the centre of the Thána district along the basin of the Vaitarna between the Tal pass and the coast. The term Talheri seems to mean a lowlander, perhaps as opposed to Varáli uplander and Malhári a highlander. Talheris are composed of two main elements, a local one apparently little different from the Son Kolis, and a foreign. The early or local element is much stronger than in Gujárat and Marátha Kunbis. The foreign element is chiefly Marátha, traces of which are to be found in their surnames and *devaks* and in the similarity of customs between the two castes. The relations of Talheris with Maráthás are the same as those between Marátha Kunbis and Maráthás. They eat with Maráthás and Marátha Kunbis and to some extent intermarry, and do not differ from them in appearance, religion and customs.

KHANDESH KUNBIS have seven sub-divisions (1) Ghátole, (2) Kumbhár, (3) Madráj, (4) Loni, (5) Pánjna, (6) Tidole or Tirole, (7) Vanjári. Ghátoles are said to have come from above the Ghats, that is, from the south side of the Ajantha range. They eat but do not marry with the Tilole Kunbis. Lonis, regarded as an aboriginal tribe, dwell chiefly on the banks of the Girna and in small villages on the Tapti. They eat with Tiloles, Pánjnás, Gujars and Vánis, but marry only among themselves. The Kumbhárs are a small tribe and very poor. Vanjáris originally belonged to the great tribe of carriers of that name, but they have long formed themselves into a separate caste by taking to agriculture and by copying the manners and customs of the Kunbis. Pánjnás have four divisions, (1) Kandárkar, (2) Navghari, (3) Reva and (4) Thorgavhana. The Revás form the main stock, the other three originated in feuds and disputes. The Thorgavhánás take their name from Thorgavhan in Sávda, and the Kandárkars from Kandári on the Tapti in Bhusával. The Navgharis would seem to be the descendants of nine families or houses who left the main stock and settled in different villages throughout the district. All the divisions eat together, but on account of disputes as to which divisiom is the highest, they do not interma·ry. Tiloles are said to have come from Upper India and to have belonged to the class of Dádar Pawárs.

KUNCHI VAKKALS, also called Marenavas, numbering 967 (1901), including 475 males and 492 females, are a wandering tribe of buffalo breeders, found mostly in Dhárwár. They appear to be immigrants from Mysore and Madras, and are Dravidian in origin having *balis* or totemistic exogamous sections and the *dháre* ceremony (pouring water over the clasped hands of the bride and bridegroom) which is common among Dravidian castes. The *balis* commonly found are :— **Name and origin.**

Alunava.	Jánkalava.
Basláva.	Valkallava.
Jaldenava.	Yardukareyava.

Marriages are prohibited between members of the same *bali*. **Marriage.** A man may marry his wife's sister during the wife's lifetime if she does not beget children. Marriage is infant as welll as adult. Sexual license before marriage is tolerated to the extent that if a girl does not become pregnant she is not put out of caste. If a girl's marriage is delayed till after she attains puberty she is made to undergo a penance called *hasge,* which consists in giving her only one meal a day for two days among some and four days among others. Polygamy and polyandry are unknown. The remarriage of widows is not permitted. A husband can divorce a wife if she is proved to be unchaste. Divorced women are not allowed to marry. The caste follow the Hindu law of inheritance. Their chief deities are the god Bapráya and the goddess Tuppad. Besides these they also worship Bhutappa, Savdamma, Biru and other minor gods. Cocoanuts, plantains, etc., are offered to the former and goats and fowls to the latter generally on Tuesdays and Fridays, at harvest time and on the *Diváli* holiday. The priests of the caste are Bráhmans. The ministrant at the temple of Bhutappa is a Kare Vakkal called *Másházgonda.*

Death. The dead are buried, except those who have white or black spots on their bodies. The latter are burnt. The deceased is dressed in his every day dress and kept in the house in a sitting posture for a day. Next day he is carried to the burial ground accompanied by tomtoms and buried with head to the south. In the case of cremation, the bones and ashes are thrown into a river. The deceased are propitiated once every two or three years by feeding a few castemen. The main occupation of the caste is breeding and selling buffaloes. They wander long distances in the southern parts of the Bombay and Madras Presidencies and in the Mysore State carrying on their trade.

Food. They eat fish, fowls, wild boars, etc., but do not drink liquor.

KUNCHA BANDHANARE.—A sub-division of Kanjáris.

KUNCHEVALE.—A synomym for Mákadvále.

KUNCHI.—A sub-division of Koravas.

KUNJARA.—A synonym for Káchhia.

KUNUM.—A synonym for Malhár Koli.

KURAD.—A sub-division of Devángs.

KURNAVAL.—A sub-division of Devángs.

KURSALI.—A sub-division of Lingáyats.

KURUBA.—A sub-division of Gavlis and Jogis.

Name and origin. **KURUBAS**, or Shepherds, numbering 226,370 (1901), including 115,204 males and 111,166 females, are found all over the Karnátak and the Kanara district. Of this number 10,948 were recorded as Lingáyats, and are known by the name of Hande Kuruba or Hande

Vazir. In Mysore, 377,091 Kurubas were recorded at the Census of 1901, in Hyderabad 87,217, while in Madras 206,286 were returned under the name Kuruba, and 154,959 under the name of Kurumban which is the Tamil equivalent of the Kanarese Kuruba.

The term Kuruba is derived from the Kanarese *Kuri* a sheep. Origin. Sir W. Elliot[1] makes the Kurubas one of the most important elements in the early population of South India. They appear as Kurumbans in Tamil and Malayali, as Kurubas in Kanarese, and correspond to the Dhangars of the Maráthás and of Northern India. Some in Malabár are bondsmen; others in the Madras Karnátak bred horses and served as troopers in the Marátha armies. In early times, in the East Karnátak, they are said to have formed a federal community of twenty-four States, to have been converted to Buddhism, to have gained much skill in the arts and to have been overthrown by a Chola King of Tánjore in the fifth or sixth century. Sir W. Elliot notices that their truthfulness is proverbial. On this and other grounds he would trace a connection between the Kurubas and Santháls of Bengal, and through the Santháls with the Ahirs or Abhirs. He thinks they were the people who buried in rude stone tombs. Mr. Taylor[2] suggests that some of the South Indian dynasties who claim to be Yádavs may be Bráhmanical Kurubas. The Kurubas have a special interest in Kanara, if, as seems possible, Kadamba, the name of two of the leading dynasties of Banavási (A. D. 300—400 and A. D. 700—1,200) is a Brahmanical form of Kuruba. Mr. Rice[3] describes the Kurubas of Mysore as a numerous class scattered over the whole province. He notices[4] that Kurubas stretch as far south as the Nilgiris, where they are feared as sorcerers. Buchanan[5] describes the Kád Kurubas of South Mysore as dark and weak, and hair like mops and a few rags for clothes. They were famous for their honesty and for their courage in driving off wild elephants by rushing up to them and holding a blazing torch to their faces. The Kád Kurubas or wild Kurubas are known as a very primitive section of the tribe, in Mysore to this day.

The Kurubas tell the following story regarding the origin of their tribe :—

About the year 1690 of the current *Káliyuga* there was an incarnation of Shiva at Kalyán in the Nizám's territory whose name was Revana Siddheshvar. At this time there lived in Kolhápur a goddess named Máyi. She had incarcerated through her great prowess nine

(1) 1869 Jour. Eth. Soc. Lond. I. 104, 110.
(2) Madras Lit. and Scien., VIII, 261.
(3) Mysore, I. 333.
(4) Id. 311
(5) Mysore, II. 128.

crores of Siddhas or Lingáyat saints. Revana Siddheshvar, on coming to know this, invaded Kolhápur, defeated the goddess, and liberated the saints. Half of the saints he set at liberty, telling them to maintain themselves by begging alms in his name. The Lingáyat priests who beg in the streets at sunset ringing one or two bells in one or both hands and taking the name of Revana Siddheshvar as their *guru*, are said to be the descendants of these saints. As to the other half of the saints, Revana Siddheshvar did not know what to do with them, so he turned them into sheep, drove them all into a cave in a field and closed the mouth of the cave. This field belonged to a certain Padmanna and his brother. While ploughing his field, the end of Padmanna's plough struck against the stone fixed at the mouth of the cave, on removing which, the sheep came out and surrounded him. He drove them into a forest close by, and while feeding them saw a handsome girl who had been concealed in the forest by a giant. The girl, who was anxious to marry, came running to Padmanna and put a garland round his neck. At this moment Shiva came and performed the marriage ceremony. As cotton was not available in the forest, *unni* or wool was used for the *kankans* or marriage wristlets; and thus came into existence the division of Kurubas known as Unnikankan, who are supposed to be the descendants of Padmanna. The other main division of Kurubas named Hattikankan claim Padmanna's brother as their common ancestor. At his marriage *kankans* or wristlets of *hatti* or cotton were made.

In the Bijápur district, next to the Lingáyats, Kurubas are the most important and numerous class. In Muddebihál, they have a great majority of the village headships, and throughout the district they certainly hold more headships, than any other caste, perhaps more than all other castes put together.

Appearance, dress and ornaments.

The Kurubas are small, dark and strongly built, remarkably sturdy and independent. They are more like the Kabbaligars than any other class, and with them and the Musalmáns, as far as bodily vigour goes, they form the backbone of the people of Bijápur. In the Bijápur district the village wrestler is generally a shepherd; and they are fond of taking village service as *válekars* (watchmen). Among the men the rich wear the waistcloth and coat; but the poor of both divisions, village watchmen, small farmers and others are specially fond of knee-breeches and of a short loose shirt. These form a capital working dress. As his clothes are commonly dyed pink, and as his face and neck are daubed with yellow powder, his head swathed in a large white kerchief, and his ear decked with a flower, the Hattikankan wrestler or watchman is generally a rather picturesque figure. The hair is worn short, the top-knot being seldom more than an inch long, and the face is shaved all but the mustaches and eye-brows. There is nothing peculiar in the woman's dress. It is the ordinary short-sleeved and backed bodice and the full robe worn without catching the skirt back between the feet and the upper end drawn over the head. In Kanara, the men wear a narrow waistcloth which they fold lightly round the waist, a country blanket woven by themselves, and a head-scarf. The women wear the robe with the skirt hanging from the waist and with the upper end drawn over the head like a veil, and a bodice with a back and short sleeves in loose folds. Some women, when going out, wear a blanket on their shoulders, drawing the upper ends across the bosom and tucking them into the folds of the robe. The ornaments of the Bijápur Kurubas are like those of local Lingáyats. In Dhárwár, the men wear ear and finger-rings, and the women, ear, nose and toe-rings, glass bangles and necklaces. The male Kurubas of Kanara wear the girdle also, and the females wear flowers in their hair like all other castes of Kanara.

Language. The Kurubas speak an impure and indistinct Kanarese, and use some strange words such as *jámpra* for *kelasa* business, *bashatikáran* for *vágnischaya* a betrothal, *tabandi* for *tambana* a plate, *kodpána* for *koda* a pitcher, *haredage* for *munjháne* in the morning, and *chánji* for *sáni* in the evening. The names in common use among the males of the Karnátak Kurubas are Bharmappa, Karibasappa, Maritammappa, Mudkappa, and Sunkippa; and among females, Manava, Sunganbasava, Savakka, and Verava. In Kanara, the common names among men are Bora, Lingappa, Mallappa and Tirkappa; and among women, Gangavva, Gauravva, Irravva, Mallavva, Nagavva, and Puttavva.

Endogamous divisions. There are two main divisions of Kurubas, Hattikankans or cotton wristlet-wearers and Unnikankans or wool wristlet-wearers, who eat together but do not intermarry. In Dhárwár, two more divisions are found, *viz.*, Jande and Varsáliyava. The Hattikankans are divided into Khilári, Sangar, Hatkár and Hande Kurubas or Hande Vazirs. Of these, the first three eat together and intermarry. The Hande Kurubas are those who have embraced Lingáyatism, eschewed flesh and changed sheep-rearing for blanket-weaving. The Hande Kurubas are again divided into two classes, the initiated and the non-initiated. The initiated marry girls from the other Hattikankans or non-initiated divisions after initiation. The girls so married are never sent back to their parents' house.

Exogamous divisions. The exogamous subdivisions of the tribe are known as *bedagus*, the chief of which are as follows :—

Bangad.	Dosenava.	Halenava.	Poornayanava.
Banneva.	Gondinava.	Halmathenava.	Shásuldava.
Beinkinava.		Korenava.	

Marriage rules. Marriages are prohibited between members of the same *bedagu*. A man may marry his father's sister's, mother's sister's or mother's brother's daughter and even his sister's daughter. Marriage with a wife's younger sister is allowed during the wife's life-time as well as after her death. Infant as well as adult marriages are in vogue. Girls are sometimes married even when they are only three months old. Misconduct on the part of unmarried girls may be expiated by payment of a fine to the *guru* and touching his feet and pouring water over them; but such cases are rare. Among the Kurubas of Kanara girls can be divorced only for adultery with low-caste men. Adulteresses, widows, and girls who fail to find husbands are free to consort with men of all but the impure castes, with whom they live as concubines. These women are called Kattigaru or concubines. Though scorned by regular wives they are not put out of caste, and their children marry with the children of pure Kurubas. Adultery is often detected, but divorce is rare as the wives are useful workers, and because a man who puts away his wife is despised unless he gives a caste feast and persuades the teacher to speak to his caste fellows in his favour. Polygamy is allowed and practised, but polyandry is unknown.

Birth ceremonies. The birth ceremonies of the Bijápur Kurubas are like those of Lingáyats. In Dhárwár, on the birth of a child, its navel cord is cut and the mother and child are bathed. The midwife buries the after-birth in a corner of the back yard. On the fifth day the goddess Satvái is worshipped with an offering of food, and on the ninth day the child is named and cradled.

Marriage ceremonies. The offer of marriage comes from either side. The bridegroom's father has to pay to the bride a sum of Rs. 60 or upwards according to his means. The day for the marriage is fixed by the village astrologer. Among the Unnikankans, a *Váder*(1) or elder of the tribe conducts the service. Among the Hattikankans, the service is conducted by a *Váder* with the help of a Bráhman priest. The marriage ceremonies last four or five days. On the first day the *arashina* or turmeric-rubbing ceremony is performed. A *suragi* is formed by placing four jars on four corners of a square, and a *kalash*, *i.e.*, a tray containing a

(1) *Váder* is the Kanarese for an elder or old person, an ancestor.

lamp, incense, etc., is placed in the centre. Cotton thread is passed round the jars, the bride and bridegroom are seated near the *kalash* and bathed, and turmeric paste is applied to their persons by married unwidowed women. A dinner is held and the ceremony is over. On this day also, according to the division of the tribe to which the family belongs, the women tie wristlets of *hatti* or cotton or of *unni* or wool round the wrists of the bride and bridegroom. On the second day, *devarakárya* or *devarautta, i. e.*, the ceremony of god-propitiation, is performed, in which the family god is worshipped with offerings of food, and castemen are feasted. On the third day the marriage ceremony itself is generally performed. The *Váder* brings an idol of the god Berappa in a palanquin to the bridegroom 's house to which the bridal party go in procession with the bride. In front of the god a big umbrella called *jaggempa* is held and under it the bride and bridegroom are seated on a blanket spread on a raised seat. A *kalash* or water-pot with five betel leaves, some ears of corn, and a light in a platter is set before the pair. Round the water-vessel a string of cotton is five times wound, broken, and tied to the wrists of the couple. The lucky necklace or *mangalsutra* is then tied round the girl 's neck by a *Váder*, or in his absence, by a temple *pujári*. Texts or *mantras* are repeated and rice grains are thrown over the pair. Among the Unnikankans, a fire is made of sandal wood in front of the image of Birappa, and milk and *ghi* are poured into the fire. When the fire is ablaze the time is deemed auspicious to tie the *táli* or lucky necklace round the girl 's neck. The bride and bridegroom are seated in the middle of a square formed by setting on the ground four drinking vessels or *támbyás*. A string is passed five times round the vessels, broken, and tied to the wrists of the couple. The *Váder* fastens the lucky necklace round the girl 's neck, knots the hem of her dress to her husband 's and throws sacred rice over them. On the fourth day, the bride and bridegroom are carried on a bullock in procession through the village. On the fifth day, a feast is held and the marriage festivities end.

The remarriage of widows is permitted. A widow cannot marry a member of her deceased husband 's or father 's *bedagu*. The ceremony takes place in the presence of four leading members of the tribe and the priest. The widow is presented with a robe and bodice by her intended husband, and a dinner is given to the tribesmen, which ends the ceremony. In some places, a *táli* or lucky necklace is tied round the widow 's neck by the priest. A remarried widow is not allowed to take part in any auspicious or religious ceremony. She is not allowed even to enter a marriage *pandal*. A widow is only allowed to remarry thrice. A husband can divorce a wife for bad conduct or for eating with a member of a lower caste. According to some, divorced women cannot remarry in the tribe. According to others, they may remarry by the widow remarriage form. At the time of divorce the wife has to return to the husband the sum received by her at the time of her marriage with him. The tribe follow the Hindu law of inheritance.

Religion. Kurubas belong to the Hindu religion. Their chief god is Biráppa, who resides on a hill but they do not know where, whose ministrants are a class of Kurubas known as *Váders*, the Kurubas' hereditary teachers or *gurus*. They pay homage to Netteppa, whose shrines are at Nágnáth in Bijápur and at Ruji in Indi, and whose priest is a Kuruba. Their house gods are Biráppa, Nettappa, Yellamma, Margavva and Shaktavva. Offerings are made to these gods on Tuesdays and Fridays, which are eaten by married women of the tribe in a common dish. On great days, these gods are worshipped in house shrines under the form of little human metal figures. They keep the leading fasts and feasts both of Bráhmanical and Lingáyat Hindus, and rarely go on pilgrimages. They respect Bráhmans but their *gurus* or religious teachers are the *Váders*, who are also their priests. Unlike the laity of either division, the *Váders* eat no flesh and wear the *linga*. The *Váder* teachers of the Unrikankans live at Kandgal, Anagvádi and Budyal in the Bijápur district. They have a head priest who has power to fine, put out of caste and let back to caste. The high priest's office is elective and he is chosen from the *Váder* families by the respectable lay Unnikankans. All of them believe in soothsaying and witchcraft, and the god Birappa is the great saver of Kurubas who are possessed by evil spirits.

The chief gods of the Kanara Kurubas are Birappa and Batteddeva, and their chief goddess is Yellamma. The ministrants in the shrines of these deities are Kurubas of their own class and rank. On the days sacred to these deities, they propitiate them by offering fowls and sheep killed in some forests or on the bank of a stream or pond where the deity is supposed to dwell. The flesh of the victims is given to washermen or barbers. On ordinary days these deities are worshipped by offering fruit and flowers and by waving lighted lamps and burning incense before them. The spirits of men who die unmarried called *virkas* are held in great respect and much feared. Their friendship is sought by yearly offerings of red cloth, molasses and cocoa-kernel. If these offerings are forgotten, the spirits of the unmarried are believed to send pestilence among men and sheep, and to disturb people by dreams and nightmares. The hereditary teacher of the Kanara Kurubas is a Lingáyat priest called Revana Siddheshvar, whose headquarters are at Sárur near Kálgan Pattu in Mysore. He visits the Kuruba villages every year, and in return for cowdung ashes or *vibhuti* receives presents of money and fixed fees for marriage and other ceremonies, which are collected for him by agents. Neither the teacher nor his agent take any part in their ceremonies. Though they believe in the Lingayát religion and have a Lingáyat teacher, they are not allowed to wear the *linga*.

Death ceremonies.

The dead are buried in a sitting position with face to the north or east. The burial rites are like those practised by Lingáyats. Mourning is observed for five days. Special services are performed on the tenth day and a feast is given to the tribesmen on the twelfth. The *shráddha* is not performed. For the propitiation of the deceased ancestors, tribesmen are fed every year in the latter half of *Bhádrapad*.

Occupation.

The Kurubas are very honest, and have a great name for sturdiness and obstinacy. They are a cheerful, frank and decent people. Large numbers, both of the Hattikankans and Unnikankans, live as husbandmen. In the Karnátak, the Hattikankans have flocks of 500 to 600 sheep, weave blankets, till the land and lend money. The women of both divisions are hard working. They mind the house and help the men in the field and in carding and spinning wool. According to Buchanan(1) the Kanara Kurubas were formly shepherds, *khandakár* or hill militia, *allavana* or armed attendants and *ancheyáva* or post messengers.

Food.

The staple food of the Karnátak Kurubas is millet bread, a sauce of pulse boiled and spiced and pot-herbs, milk and curds; that of the Kanara Kurubas is cooked and strained rice, *rági*, vegetables and fish. They eat flesh except beef and pork and drink liquor. Among the Kanara Kurubas, animal food is forbidden for a month after weddings, during the first nine days of *Dasura*, and on the *Ganeshchaturthi* day. The Hande Kurubas or Hande Vazirs, who are Lingáyats, neither eat flesh nor drink liquor. They eat at the hands of none but members of their own community. In Bijápur, the Kurubas rank above Kabbaligars. In Kanara, they rank with Gaulis and Gollars.

KURVA.—A sub-divison of Karad Vániás.

KURVINARA.—A sub-division of Lingáyats.

KURVIN SHETTI.—A sub-division of Lingáyat Jáds.

---

(1) Mysore, I, 396.

KUSHASTHALI.— A synonym for Sárasvat.

KUSIA.— A sub-division of Dhedas.

KUSUBATANVALE.— A synonym for Kámáthi Kaikádi.

LABHANA.— A synonym for Vanjári.

LAD.— A sub-division of Vanjáris, Dhangars, Vániás, Kumbhárs, Telis, Sonárs, Udámbar Bráhmans.

Name and origin.

LADS, numbering, 3,175 (1901) including 1,541 males and 1,643 females, of whom 97 are Musalmans, are an interesting offshoot of some Gujarát caste, who appear to have wandered into the Southern Marátha Country and Mysore in the Great Durga-devi Famine in the fourteenth century. They are chiefly found in Belgaum, Bijápur, and Dhárwár. Lád or Lát is the original name for Southern Gujarát. Writing of the Láds in Mysore at the beginning of last century, Buchanan* remarks that they serve as cavalry, trade in horses, and own lands. They claim to be Kshatriyas and wear the sacred thread. He remarks that they have 14 *gotras*, and perform a sacrifice to the Shaktis, in the presence of a naked female. From their wearing the sacred thread and serving as cavalry they would seem originally to have been Rajputs, but in this Presidency they appear to have fallen from this position and are now engaged in trade. Some are employed as butchers to slay sheep and goats. But many still wear the sacred thread and claim to be Kshatriyas. They have a home tongue known as *Chaurasi* which, in the opinion of the Editor of the Bombay Gazetteer is a possible indication that they came from Chorási in Surat.

Endogamous divisions.

Láds have seven endogamous divisions, *viz.*—

1. Gujar
2. Halvekari
3. Kayit
4. Khátik
5. Márwári
6. Sav
7. Sherogar
8. Sugandi or Kshatriya
9. Suryavanshi.

These divisions neither eat together nor intermarry. The Suryavanshi division is the most numerous.

There are no endogamous divisions of the Suryavanshi Láds. Their exogamous sub-divisions are families bearing the same surname. The commonest surnames are Bilgikar, Bujurukar, Chendukál, Dharmkámfea, Govindkar, Parbhukar, and Rájápuri.

Marriage ceremonies.

Marriage is infant as well as adult. The offer of marriage comes from the boy's father. The betrothal or *báshtagi* is performed

* Mysore, Vol. I, page 422.

on a lucky day some time before the marriage either at the boy's or at the girl's house, when the girl is presented with a silver necklace, silver bangles, and a robe and bodice-cloth, and her lap is filled. A feast of sweet dishes to the guests ends the ceremony. Next, a Bráhman astrologer is consulted in order to fix a lucky day for the marriage. He writes the day and the names of the bride and bridegroom on two pieces of paper and gives to the boy's father the slip on which the boy's name is written and to the girl's father the slip on which the girl's name is written. At the time of marriage these slips of paper are wrapped in cloth and tied round the necks of the bride and bridegroom. On this occasion the boy's father gives the girl two white bodice-cloths and three and a half pounds of rice. Some days before the marriage day the bridegroom is rubbed with turmeric paste and bathed in a *surgi* or square with a drinking pot at each corner and a cotton thread wound round the necks of the pots. On the same day the ceremony of *devkárya* or god-pleasing is held, and the bridegroom and his party start for the girl's village. At the village he is met by the bride's father and relations, who lead him to a house which has been made ready for him and his party. On the marriage day the bride and bridegroom are bathed inside squares at their own houses and dressed in new clothes, the brides clothes being a white robe and a white bodice. The bridegroom is seated on a horse and led to the bride's in procession with music. At the bride's, he is led into the marriage booth, where he stands in a basket containing millet and a rope, facing the bride who stands on a grindstone. A cotton wristlet made of the thread that was tied round the four water-vessels is wound round the bride's left wrist and another round the bridegroom's right wrist; a curtain marked with a cross in the centre is held between them; and the priest recites the eight luck-giving verses, and, when the verses are ended, throws grains of rice over the couple; the guests join in throwing the rice. Then betel is served and the guests go. Next day the bride and bridegroom are bathed in the same square and dressed in new clothes. In the evening the *varát* or married couple's homeward procession starts from the bride's for the bridegroom's. On the way it halts at the temple of the village god, where the bride and bridegroom bow, and break a cocoanut before the god. In this procession the pair are seated on a bullock, the bride sitting in front of the bridegroom. At the bridegroom's her mother hands the bride to her mother-in-law, and the bridegroom's father gives Rs. 7 to the bride's party. On the third day the bride's father gives a caste-feast, presents suits of clothes to the bridegroom's father and mother, and gives Rs. 7 as a money present to his caste-people. On the fourth day the bridegroom's father gives a caste feast and makes similar presents to the father and mother of the bride, and a money gift to the caste-people double that given by the bride's father. The present of money is spent on liquor. On the fifth day the bridegroom with his party return to his house, which act terminates the marriage.

Religion. The Suryavanshi Láds belong to the Hindu religion. Their family deities are Durgavva, Dyámavva, Hulgavva, Máruti, Sidhráya, and Yellamma. The special object of their devotion is the Sun, whom as Suryavanshis or of the Sun-stock, they claim as their first ancestor. They make pilgrimages to Máruti's shrine at Tulshigiri, to Yellamma at Parasgad, to Shidráya in Bijápur, and to the tomb of a Musalmán saint named Daval Málik at Navalgund in Dhárwár. They observe most of the Hindu holidays. They employ Bráhmans to conduct their marriages.

Death ceremonies. Those who live among the Maráthás generally burn their dead; in Bijápur, under Lingáyat influence, most of them bury. The funeral party bathe after burying the dead body and return to the house of mourning with some blades of *durva* grass which they throw into a drinking pot full of water that is placed on the spot where the deceased breathed his last. On the third day the mourners place parched rice and grain, dry dates, dry cocoa-kernel, molasses, cooked rice, and small wheaten cakes on the stone slab that is laid over the grave. To these things the persons who accompanied the funeral add a few drops of milk, each dropping a little in turn. All go and stand at a distance till crows come and eat what has been offered. If crows do not come, they pray to the departed and promise to carry out all his wishes. If, even after this promise, the crows will not come, the food is given to a cow. The shoulders of the four corpse bearers are rubbed with curds and washed to remove the uncleanness caused by bearing the bier, and food enough for a meal is served to them all in a single platter. If they cannot eat the whole, what is left is given to a cow. In the evening a feast is given, of which mutton forms a part, and to which caste people are asked one from each family. On the eleventh day a silver image of the dead is made and worshipped along with other ancestral images kept in the house-shrine on a blanket stretched under a tree on the bank of a river. To the new image, according to the sex of the dead, a man's or woman's dress is offered. All who join the ceremony are asked to a feast. Some of them perform the *shráddha* on the bright third of *Vaishákh*. Among Dhárwár Láds if the death occurs on an unlucky day, the house in which the death took place is abandoned for three months, its doors being closed with bunches of thorns. It is believed that if the family lived in the house some fresh calamity would fall on them.

The main occupation of the caste is killing sheep and selling the flesh. A few are excise contractors and land owners who employ servants to till their fields.

They eat the flesh of goats, deer, hare, doves, domestic fowls and fish and drink liquor. They rank below Kurubas and take food cooked by them; Vaddás and Lamáns eat *kacchi* at the hands of the Suryavanshi Láds, but the latter do not eat food cooked by the former. Food.

Next in importance to the Suryavanshi Láds are the Sugandhi Láds, who call themselves Kshatriya Láds. They are dealers in perfumes, their name being derived from *sugandh* meaning fragrance. Their exogamous sub-divisions are Gadekar, Khatarmoli, Lalashe, Mogardaj, Unále, Shatibarangale, Ganjekar, Nawate, Basawekar and Surangmale. A member of the caste cannot marry his father's sister's daughter. He may marry his mother's brother's daughter. A man may marry two sisters and brothers may marry sisters. Marriage is infant as well as adult. Boys are girt with the sacred thread before they are ten years old, without performing any ceremony. Polygamy is allowed and practised, but polyandry is unknown. The offer of marriage comes from the boy's father, who has to pay a sum up to Rs. 50 to the girl's father. The essential portion of the marriage ceremony is the *lájáhom* or marriage sacrifice. The remarriage of widows is permitted. A widow cannot marry a member of her late husband's section. The ceremony takes place in a room at night. The caste members who are present sit at a distance and do not witness the ceremony. A Bráhman priest hands over to the widow a lucky necklace, which she ties round her own neck. Next, he ties into a knot the hems of the pair's garments, which completes the ceremony. A dinner is given to the caste people on the day following.

Divorce is allowed if the husband and wife do not agree or the wife's conduct is bad. A divorced woman may remarry. The Hindu law of inheritance is followed.

Sugandhi Láds are Hindus of the Shaiva sect. The minor gods worshipped by them are Ambábhaváni, Khandoba, Máruti, Khákisha Bowa, Vithoba, Bahiroba, Mhasoba, Dawal Malik, and Narsoba. Offerings are made to these gods on Tuesdays or Fridays, which are either received by the temple priests or eaten by the offerers themselves. Bráhmans are employed to conduct marriage and widow remarriage ceremonies. The dead are burnt, except children up to three years old, who are buried. The bones and ashes are consigned to water. The *shráddha* and *mahálaya* are performed for the propitiation of the deceased ancestors.

The hereditary occupation of the Sugandhi Láds is dealing in perfumes. Some are grain merchants and a few are husbandmen.

They eat the flesh of goats, sheep, fowls and fish, and drink liquor. The lowest well-known caste with whom they will eat *kacchi* are the Marátha Kunbis.

Khátiks, chiefly found in Bijápur, describe themselves as of two divisions, Sultáni Khátiks and Suryavanshi, apparently showing their original connection with the Suryavanshi division already described. It is uncertain how they came to be butchers ; but the name Sultáni seems to indicate that they took to slaying meat in the days of the Musalmán kings.

LADAKS are found only in Cutch and in the Jámnagar State in Káthiáwár. They are said to have been originally Rajputs. Their original home was Nagar Samoi in Sind. They came to Cutch and Káthiáwár with the Jádejás and with Jám Ráwal in the 13th and 16th century respectively. Their original occupation was military service, and they hold *girás* lands granted to them by former Jáms for such service. Many of them cultivate their lands themselves. They have two divisions, Cutchi and Káthiáwári, who neither eat together nor intermarry. They have several surnames borrowed from Rajput clans, which indicate exogamous groups. Boys and girls are generally betrothed in infancy, but actual marriage takes place at the age of fifteen to twenty. Widow remarriage and divorce are allowed. Ládaks worship all the Hindu gods and goddesses and employ Bráhmans to conduct their ceremonies. When a Ládak dies, a finger of his right hand is cut and burnt with Hindu funeral rites, and the rest of the body is buried, after the fashion of Musalmáns, and a tomb is erected on the place of burial if the deceased was well-to-do. It is said that this custom was introduced by Meraman Jassa out of respect for the Emperor of Delhi by whom he was induced to embrace Islám when he visited his court, but on his return reverted to Hinduism. Ládaks eat food cooked by Rajputs, Khavás, Kumbhárs, etc. Rajputs do not eat food cooked by Ládaks.

LADBHUJE.—A sub-division of Kumbhárs.

LADHAN.—A synonym for Ládvan.

LADJIN.—A synonym for Lád Vanjári.

LADSAKKA.—A sub-division of Vániás.

LADVAN.—A sub-division of Mahárs.

LAHANCHAKE.—A synonym for Ahir Kumbhár.

LAKARHARA.—*See* under Minor Musalmán Castes.

LAKHERA.—A synonym for Lákheri.

LAKHERIS or Lakheras are makers of lac bangles, and are an immigrant caste that seem to have come into the Presidency from Márwár. In 1901 they numbered 377 including 214 males and 163 females, and were found scattered over the Gujarát Native States on the border of Rájputána, a few families being recorded in the Ahmedábád, Kaira and Poona districts. Mr. Crooke* describes them as closely allied to the Manihars in the United Provinces, where they number several thousand. The Poona Lákheris (40) settled there in the time of the Peshwás. They are reported still to speak Márwári at home. According to the Bombay Gazetteer, Lákheris still go to Márwár to fetch their brides. This and their home tongue, as well as the fashion of wearing the hair and dress, support their claim to be Márwár Vánis. It is also alleged that they are Kshatris from Jeypore, Ajmere and Udaipur; but this seems improbable from their customs and manner of living. Name and origin.

There are two endogamous divisions of the caste, proper and bastards, who eat together but do not intermarry. They are said to belong to the Gautam, Káshyap, and Vashishtah *gotras*, but marriages are regulated only by surnames, which are exogamous. The commonest surnames are Bágade, Bháte, Chaván, Hatáde, Nágare, Padiyár, Ratvad, and Sálunke. Endogamous divisions.

Polygamy and widow marriage are allowed and practised but polyandry is unknown. Girls are married before they are sixteen, boys before they are twenty-five. The offer of marriage comes from the boy's father, who has to pay a sum of from Rs. 25 to Rs. 100 to the girl before the day of betrothal. The marriage guardians of Lákheris are an earthen image of Ganpati and a copper or brass image of Báláji, which are worshipped before the wedding day. The bridegroom is taken to the bride's on horseback, where a tinsel arch is raised before the house, the girl's head is decked with a net of false pearls, and a square is marked off by setting an earthen pot *Utarandi* at each corner. No coronet is tied to the bridegroom's Marrige ceremonides.

* Tribes and Castes of the N. W. P. and Oudh, Pt. III, p. 361.

brow. The boy and girl are seated in the square on a carpet, the hems of their garments are tied together, and they are made to hold each other's hands. The priest kindles the sacrificial fire in front of them, marriage verses are repeated, Márwári marriage songs are sung by women, and at the end grains of rice are thrown over the pair's heads, and they are husband and wife. Next day the bridegroom returns to his house with his bride, and the ceremony ends with a feast. Divorce is allowed.

Religion. Lákheris are Hindus of the Smárt sect. Their family god is Báláji, otherwise known as Venkatesh of Tirupati in North Arcot. They also worship Bhaváni, Ganpati and Rám and local Musalmán *Pirs*. They observe the leading Hindu holidays. They believe in soothsaying, witchcraft and evil spirits. They employ local Bráhmans to conduct their ceremonies.

Death ceremonies. The dead are burnt. Children up to one year old are buried. On the third day after death the chief mourner goes to the burning ground, removes the ashes, and places cooked rice and curds on the spot for the crows to eat. On the tenth day the *Dashpindi* or ten ball-offering is performed with the same details as among the Kunbis. On the twelfth day they place twelve earthen jars on the threshold of the front door of the house, worship them as they worship the house gods, and cast them away. The death ceremonies end with a feast on the thirteenth day when the chief mourner is presented with a new turban either by relations or caste-fellows. For the propitiation of the deceased ancestors the friends of the deceased are feasted at the end of six months and again at the end of a year, and a *Mahálaya* is performed annually on the corresponding death day during the latter half of *Bhádrapad*.

Occupation. The hereditary occupation of the caste is making and dealing in lac bangles. Since glass bangles have come into fashion the demand for lac bangles has greatly declined, and many of them have abandoned their occupation to work as day labourers.

Food. Some Lákheris do not take animal food, but others have no objection to eating flesh. They occasionally drink liquor.

LALAT.—A sub-division of Bráhmans.

LALBAJARVALE.—A synonym for Kámáthi Kaikádi.

LALBEGI.—A sub-division of Bhangis.

LALCHUDAWALA.—A sub-division of Kadva Kunbis.

Vanjari woman.

LALGOND.—A sub-division of Raddis.

LALGONDA.—A sub-division of Lingáyats.

LALLANGOTI.—A synonym for Solesi.

LAMAN.—A sub-division of Kaikádis; a synonym for Lamáni.

LAMANA.—A synonym for Lamáni.

LAMANIS or Vanjáris, also known as Banjárás, Banjáris, Brinjáris, Lamáns, Lambadis, Lambárs and Sukalirs, numbering 133,349 (1901), including 68,533 males and 64,816 females, are found in all parts of the Presidency. Of this number 143 were returned as Musalmáns at the last census. The tribe is found all over India under one or other of the above names. According to some authorities the term Vanjári is derived from the Sanskrit *van* forest and *char* to wander, the whole meaning wanderers in the forests. According to others, it is derived from the Persian *biranjár* or rice-carriers. Both these derivations seem untenable, as the Vanjáris are neither forest wanderers nor the carriers of rice only. The true derivation appears to be the Punjabi *banaj* or *vanaj* as suggested by Lieutenant (now Sir) R. C. Temple,(1) which means bargain or trade. *Vanaj* or *banaj* is derived from the Sanskrit *vánijya, i. e.* trade. The evidence of history establishes the fact that the tribal occupation has been for centuries the carrying of grain and supplies for armies in the field. Hence the designation Vanjári or trader is an obvious occupational description. Grain dealers are ordinarily known as Vánis or Bánjigs, which are etymologically identical with *vánijya, vanaj* or *banaj.* The term Lamáni is derived from *lavan* salt, the tribe being the chief carriers of salt before the opening of cart roads and railways. Mr. A. M. T. Jackson considered the name Lamán identical in origin with Lubána, the great trading caste in Sind. If this be correct, all the names for the tribe would appear to be mere variants of the two commonest descriptions for grain dealing castes in this Presidency, *viz.*, Váni or Banya, and Luhána. Inasmuch as the origin of the tribe appears to have been the demand for grain carriers to accompany the large moving camps of Indian armies, it is extremely probable that the tribe should have been named, from its occupation, grain dealers. There is no doubt that as such, the tribe has been recruited from varied elements of the population. Name and origin.

(1) Vide foot-note, p. 205, Ind. Ant. Vol. IX.

The identity of the Vanjáris with Lamánis is proved by the similarity of the social divisions. Thus, comparing the exogamous sub-divisions of Vanjáris and Lamánis we find the following:—

Vanjari.	Lamani.
Chaván—	*Chaván*—
Kelut.	Kelut.
Kurha.	Kurha
Lavadiya.	Lavadiya.
Muda.	Palathiya.
Palathiya.	
Pavár—	*Pavár*—
Amgot.	Amgot.
Jarabola.	Jarabola.
Lunasávat.	Lunasávat.
Vakdot.	Vakdot.
Ráthod—	*Ráthod*—
Banot.	Banot.
Bhukiya.	Bhukiya.
Jalot.	Jalot.
Manhavat.	Manhavat.
Muchial.	Muchial.

The tribe clearly has been recruited to some extent either from Rajput sources or from followers of Rajput clans who have adopted the clan names of their masters. According to Crooke, the Rajput origin is admitted in their traditions. The tribe is mentioned by Muhammadan historians in connection with Sikandar's attack on Dholpur in 1504 A. D.(1) It is a reasonable assumption that they increased and absorbed many foreign elements during the long wars between the Delhi Emperors and the smaller kingdoms of the Deccan from Muhammad Tughlak to Aurangzeb. Great numbers were attracted to the English Army during the third Mysore war (1789—1793),(2) and again during the fourth Mysore war in 1799 they did much harm by pillaging the country.(3) Crooke quotes a song referring to permission given to the tribe to commit not more than three murders a day, provided they kept the army supplied with the necessary provisions.(4) Sir Alfred Lyall(5) writing of the tribe in Central India considers that there can be no doubt that they are

(1) Dowson's Elliot, V., p. 100. Brigg's Ferishta, I, p. 579.
(2) Wilks' South of India, II, 209.
(3) Buchanan, I, 180, 182.
(4) Crooke's Tribes and Castes of the N. W. P., I, pp. 150-157.
(5) Asiatic Studies, I, p. 165.

of very mixed origin 'made up of contingents from various other castes and tribes which may have at different times joined the profession.'

In an editorial foot-note at p. 182 of the Indian Antiquary, Vol. IV, reference is made to a paper published in the transactions of the Medical and Physical Society of Bombay. In this paper an aboriginal descent is suggested for the tribe. In Ptolemy's list of Indian castes the name Lambatai is to be found. According to McCrindle these were the inhabitants of Lamghán, a tract lying along the northern banks of the Kabul river; but it seems equally probable that Lambatai is merely a form of the modern name Lambádi. An examination of the endogamous divisions of the tribe shown below tends to establish the conclusion that though in origin the tribe may have been an aboriginal section of the population with a distinct identity, named from its occupation of carrying supplies on bullocks, it has since been so overlain with additions from Rajputs, Maráthás, Mahárs, and a number of other well known tribes and castes, that it can only be described as a miscellaneous collection of the flotsam and jetsam of humanity that would be drawn into the wake of a large military expedition, of no distinctive type, though the tribe preserves for the most part a distinctive costume to this day.

In certain cases Vanjáris have abandoned the wandering life which the tribe for the most part leads, and have settled down as husbandmen or craftsmen. In such cases they tend to form an endogamous division of some caste such as Vanjári Kunbis, Vanjári Chámbhárs, Vanjári Nhávis, Vanjári Bháts, Vanjári Mángs and Vanjári Mahárs, in the same way as Ahirs, Gujars and Kolis. The process of sub-division is noticeable even before the separation, many *tándás* or bands of wandering Vanjáris containing bards or Bháts, barbers or Nhávis, shoe-makers or Chámbhárs as well as Vanjári Mahárs and Mángs. It is uncertain whether the latter are degraded Vanjáris or recruits from the Mahár and Máng castes. Musalmán Vanjáris, of whom few returned themselves as Vanjáris at the census of 1901, are known as Dhadis. The Vanjáris have a tradition that the great Durga Devi famine which lasted from 1396 to 1407 was named after Durga, a Lád Vanjári woman who had amassed great wealth and owned a million bullocks.(1) She is related to have brought grain from Nepal, Burma and China and to have saved many lives, thus gaining the title of 'mother of the world.' The story obviously indicates the extremely valuable nature of the

(1) Bom. Gazetteer, Vol. XVI, p. 62.

Vanjáris' services as grain carriers in a period of severe famine, before the days of roads or railways.

Vanjáris who have settled down as husbandmen, live in the ordinary Kunbi houses. Those who are still carriers either have brick-built houses or live outside villages in grass huts which they take with them from place to place. These grass huts are always moved after a death, in accordance with the widespread custom of primitive tribes. At first an opening is made in the back of the hut and no one enters it by the ordinary door, which is believed to have been polluted by the passage of the spirit of the deceased. Afterwards the hut is pulled down and set up at a distance from its former site.

Appearance, dress and ornaments.

Though as a class robust and well built, the several divisions of Vanjáris differ in complexion, the Máthurás being generally fair, the Láds Mehurunás and Lámghás somewhat duskier, and the Chárans and the Labhánás dark and martial-looking. Vanjáris dress in Rajputáni fashion though some have adopted the Kunbi costume. A peculiarity of dress among the Cháran women is that they draw their shoulder robe over the point of a narrow stick about eight inches long, cup-shaped where it rests on the head and narrow at the point, standing, like a huge comb, from the knot of hair at the back of the head. The rank of the women is said to be shown by the angle at which she wears this stick. They wear a coarse petticoat of blue and red, with a fancy pattern, and pendants of wool and pewter from the hair. Heavy brass and bone bangles and anklets are worn on their arms and legs. In the Kanarese districts, many of the Vanjári women may be noticed with pieces of copper strung round their necks. A fresh piece is worn during each confinement to propitiate the tribal goddess. They thus show the number of children born to the wearer.

Language.

The Vanjáris in the Deccan speak fairly correct Maráthi, but Chárans, Labhánás and Máthurás use a rough peculiar dialect full of Hindi, and, in some cases, Gujaráti forms. They know Hindustáni, and those in the Kanarese districts, also speak Kanarese.

Every settlement of Vanjáris has its hereditary headman known as *Náik*. He is bound to help the rest in time of need, and to be their representative and arbitrator in caste disputes; to accommodate all guests coming to his encampment or *tánda*; and to direct the movements of the caravan when travelling. The appointment of *Náik* is hereditary in one family. If the original family from which *Náiks* are drawn has no representative, a fresh selection is made. On election he is presented with a turban and clothes in token of allegiance.

At every council meeting, the *Náik* presides, with ten or twelve adult males as members.

The Vanjáris may be divided into two territorial groups, (1) Marátha and Kanarese Vanjáris and (2) Gujaráti Vanjáris. The former have the following endogamous divisions :— Endogamous divisions.

1. Agasa
2. Asátkar.
3. Bhusáre, Bhusháre or Bhusárjin.
4. Chámbhár or Rohidás.
5. Cháran or Gavár.
6. Dhádes (Musalmán followers of Vanjáris).
7. Dhálya, Mádig or Máng.
8. Hajám or Nhávi.
9. Jogi.
10. Kanherjin.
11. Khudáne.
12. Kongádi.
13. Lád, Ládjin or Vadi.
14. Mahár or Shingádya.
15. Marátha.
16. Máthura, Labhána, Lamána or Mathurájin.
17. Mehuruna.
18. Rávjin, Lámgha or Bombilvike.
19. Sonár.
20. Tamburi or Musalmáns, who are the bards of Vanjáris.

Of the above divisions, Agasás, Dhályás, Hajáms, Jogis, Mahárs, Sonárs, and Tamburis are found in the Kanarese districts, and the rest in the Deccan. None of the divisions in the Kanarese districts eat together or intermarry. In the Deccan, though some of the divisions eat together, as a rule, none intermarry. Máthurás eat food cooked by members of their own division only, and some are believed, like the Purbias, to refuse to eat food cooked by their women, who are privileged to eat with all Vanjári divisions.

The endogamous divisions mentioned above have the following clans, with sub-divisions shown below the name of each :— Exogamous divisions.

Chaván.

Alodh.
Banod.
Kolot or Kelut.
Korch.
Kurha, Kora or Kola.
Lávadiya.
Lovna.
Muda.
Palathiya or Pálalya.
Safánat.
Supánat.

Jádhav.

Ajmira.
Bábisivál.
Báhon.
Bhukiya.
Bolapaváravi.
Devijival.
Dhárávat.
Garigávat.
Ghogalut.
Jarabala.
Kora Kelut.
Lávadya.
Luniva.
Málávat.
Pada.
Pádatya.
Vadatya.
Vishálvat.

Pavár or Parmár.

A'mgot.	Gorháma.	Lombávat.	Vishalvat.
Bádávat.	Indrávat.	Mori.	Vinjarvat.
Bálnot.	Járábola.	Punávat.	Zarpala.
Bani.	Lokávat.	Orste.	
Charote.	Lonsavad or Lu-	Vadaleya.	
Dharabala.	nasávat.	Vákdot.	

Ráthod.

Alot.	Dharamsot.	Kilut.	Turi.
Bánot.	Gavál.	Mauhavat.	Vat.
Bhukiya.	Jálpot.	Muna.	Vartia.
Chatotri.	Jálot.	Muzal or	Vedi.
Dáhe.	Játhot.	Muchiál.	
Dálván,	Khátarot.	Peráj.	

Turi or Tuvar.

Has no sub-divisions.

Udatiya.(1)

Ajmira.	Boda.	Hála.	Lákha.
Báda.	Dhárávat.	Jethot.	Luna.
Bhárot.	Ghugalot.	Kunsey.	Málot.

The clans found amongst the Gujarát Vanjáris with their sub-divisions are :—

Bráhman.

Bángadia.	Halávat.	Kelávat.	Tagávat.

Dángar.

Mali.

Dhánki.

Has no sub-divisions.

Gojal.

Bohoria.	Keharod.

(1) These are called Burteeas by Briggs.

Goti.

Bal. Baredhia. Kharedia. Totaria.

Khasávat.

Bhopan. Gojal. Gora. Pachoria.

Musalia.

Maja. Mathávar.

Padvál.

Bhenávat.	Gorávat.	Nagávat.
Chormar.	Khandáyat.	Rangávat.

Pelya.

Baja.	Hadkarni.	Khatedia.
Ghanga.	Khaja.	Láli.

Saltána or *Sartána.*

Duri. Sartána.

Tagara.

Máli. Mathávana.

Zád.

Ajedia.	Hádi.	Marávat.
Atvái.	Katára.	Raghávat.
Bharkáda.	Lohia.	Satabhái.
Dátala.	Lonávat.	Vaddayál.

Sendhu.

The members of the Sendhu division are said to be converts from other castes. They have no connection in food or marriage with any of the above divisions.

Marriages are prohibited between members of the same clan or of allied clans. Thus, Devijivals are forbidden to marry not only with other Devijivals, but with Bahons, Babisivals and many other Marriage rules.

clans or *kuls* because they are branches of one stock. Marriage with a father's sister's, mother's sister's, or mother's brother's daughter is prohibited. Marriage with a wife's sister is allowed, and two brothers are allowed to marry two sisters. Polygamy is allowed and practised, but polyandry is unknown. In some divisions of the tribe such as Chárans, divorce is not allowed. In others it is allowed on the ground of the wife's misconduct. Sexual intercourse before marriage appears to be connived at in some places, while in others, the offending parties are compelled to marry. Among Chárans, Máthurás and Labhánás, who are of Upper India origin, girls remain unmarried to twenty and thirty; but among Deccan Vanjáris the marriageable limit for girls is from ten to twelve and for boys from twelve to twenty. In the Kanarese districts, marriage is mostly adult, and in some places, girls are kept unmarried permanently. Black glass beads are fastened to the left ankles of such girls, who frequently live immoral lives.

Birth ceremonies.

Among wandering Vanjáris, children are often born away from villages, and in the absence of midwives, women attend women and no ceremonies are performed. Afterwards, when the caravan, *tánda*, meets a Bráhman, a council is called. The time of the child's birth is explained to the Bráhman, who fixes the name, the father paying him for his assistance. Among settled families, when a child is born, the relations beat drums, fire guns, and distribute sugar among their friends, the Bháts and priests. On the fifth day women worship Sati and are given grain, pulse and flowers. Some sections of the Vanjáris in Gujarát and the Lád Vanjáris gird their boys with the sacred thread before marriage.

Marriage ceremonies.

The offer of marriage comes from the boy's father, who has to pay to the girl's father a sum varying from Rs. 15 to 150, and some bullocks. If he is unable to pay this amount, the bridegroom has instead to serve his father-in-law for two or three years. Marriage ceremonies differ among the different sections of the Vanjáris. In some places, when the bride-price has been fixed, the bridegroom's party distribute molasses and liquor. A part of the amount is paid in cash and a part in bullocks. On a convenient day fixed by a Bráhman astrologer, the boy goes in procession with his house-people and guests to the bride's house, where he is received by four or a larger number of men, and the bride's father feasts the bridegroom's party on boiled rice and curry. After the feast, the bride and bridegroom are led to a square marked out with quartz powder and stand opposite each other. A Bráhman gives coloured rice to the guests, the bride and bridegroom stand inside the square, the guests throw rice over them, and the priest repeats verses. If a Bráhman is not available, the ceremony is performed by an elderly Lamáni. When the rice-throwing is over, the bridegroom's father serves the bride's people with a meal of mutton and bread. Then the bridegroom returns with the bride to his house. At night he retires to some lonely part of the dwelling and lies on the ground with a cocoanut under his head, feigning to be asleep, while the bride sits in another part of the house near an elderly woman who rubs her feet. One of her husband's kinswomen walks to the bride and tells her that her husband wants her, and guides her to the place where he is waiting for her. The husband hands the woman the cocoanut and in return receives his wife. Among Lamáns the nuptials are often performed by married women, of whom the bride's mother or other nearest kinswoman is one. In the bride's house a square is traced with quartz powder. At each corner a large water pot or *ghágar* is placed, and the bride's mother winds a thread seven times round the necks of the water pots. The bride sits on a bag filled with rice in the centre of the square. The thread is taken from the necks of the pots and cut in two, one part being tied round the bride's neck and the other round her arm. One of the women splashes water on her and bathes her, another rubs her body with turmeric paste, a third takes off her wet clothes and dresses her in fresh clothes, and a fourth sprinkles her brow with rice. They join in lifting her off the bag of rice. The bridegroom then takes her place and undergoes the same ceremonies. At the end, the bride's mother marks both their backs with a Jain cross in turmeric paste. The boy and girl sit together, a tub is set before them and filled with water, and a couple of shells are dropped into it. The bridegroom takes the shells out seven times and again drops them into the water. The bride picks out the shells seven times and at the end of the seventh time keeps them. In some families, at each corner of the marriage parallelogram, branches of the *rui* plant (*Calotropis gigantea*) are stooped, bound together. Underneath each stoop are placed five water pots and a copper coin. In the heart of the parallelogram a cross with a circle round it is drawn. In the middle of the east and west sides of the parallelogram a rice pounder or *musal* is erected. The bride holds on her open palm a cowry shell and a rupee, and the bridegroom, placing his open palm over the bride's and over the cowry shell and rupee, leads her seven times round the two *musals*, from west to east. The bride and bridegroom then sit together in the square and eat molasses out of one dish. A new cotton thread is brought and divided in two. One-half is tied round the boy's wrist and the other round the girl's, and their clothes are marked on the back with turmeric paste. The next day passes in games and amusements. On the third day a kinswoman leads the bride to the b idegroom's chamber, thus ending the marriage.

In Khándesh, the boy's party go to the girl's village for the marrage, riding on ponies or walking, for carts are forbidden. On arrival they are given separate apartments facing a booth covered with mango and *nim* (Melia azadirachta) leaves. The marriage takes place at midnight. A post of *palasa* (Butea frondosa) or *umbar* (Ficus glomerata) is smeared with turmeric paste and fixed in the ground, and a lighted lamp is placed on the top of the post. Tne marriage ceremony, which is very simple, is performed near this post. Grains of *juvári* dipped in turmeric water are thrown over the bridal pair by the party, and the *homa* or marriage sacrifice is performed. The bride and bridegroom walk five times round the sacrificial fire, thus completing the marriage. In some places, two posts of *kher* (Acacia catechu) are fixed in the ground. On each corner of a square nine earthen pots are piled one on the other and are covered with leaves of the *rui* (Calotropis gigantea). The nine pots probably represent the nine planets, *navagraha*. Near the post sit the bride and bridegroom, who have been rubbed with turmeric and bathed. Then the Bráhman priest worships Ganpati, joins the hands of the pair, and ties the knot in the same way as at a Kunbi weddin? ; except that a rupee, given by the bride's father, is tied to the knot. Then, between the posts, the Bráhman lights the sacred fire, and muttering sacred verses, leads the pair seven times round the fire from right to left. This ends the nuptial ceremonies. The Lád Vanjáris have a *devak* consisting of the *pánchpálvi* or leaves of five kinds of trees, which they instal in Kunbi fashion. Among them the *devak* is installed also on the fifth day after the birth of a child. The *devaks* of the Rávjin Vanjáris consist of the *pánchpálvi*, the feathers of the *tas* or blue jay *Coracias indica* and of leaves of the *nágvel* betel-vine. In Násik, it is customary to carry the *devak*, consisting of the leaves of the mango, *jámbul*, *umbar*, *shami*, and *rui* and known as *pánchpálvi*, to Maruti's temple after which the *evak* is brought back and tied to the marriage booth. Without the *devak*, marriage cannot take place.

The marriages of Gujarát Vanjáris are celebrated in the months of *Jyeshtha* and *Ashádh*, the binding portion consisting in walking five times round the sacrificial fire. The bride goes to live with her husband three years after the marriage, when her father gives her a bullock laden with clothes and utensils and corn.

Except among Máthurás and Labhánás, the remarriage of widows is permitted. The levirate is allowed. Among the Chárans, if a widow marries an outsider in preference to her deceased husband's brother or relative, a fine is levied by the *panch*. The ceremony of widow marriage is extremely simple. It consists in locking up the widow and her intended husband for the night or in their eating from one plate. A bachelor is not allowed to marry a widow. In some sections of the Gujarát Vanjáris, the head of a widow is shaved ten days after the death of her husband, and she is forced to betake herself to a secluded place for one year, during which period she is only allowed one meal a day, which must be taken at night, without salt. **Widow remarriage.**

Vanjáris follow the Hindu law of inheritance and profess Hinduism. Their chief god is Báláji. Next to Báláji they revere Tulja Bhaváni, Ambábái, Mariamma, Mártal and Hingláj; their inferior deities being Shital, Lakdya, Vághya, Mhasoba, Bahiroba, etc. In Gujarát, their chief god is Shiva, whom they call Sallalla. They erect flags in the name of Báláji in front of their huts and worship them. In times of distress, or in consequence of a vow, these flags are replaced by new ones on the full-moon day of *Jyeshtha* and during the *Diváli* holidays. On these days bullocks and implements of husbandry are also worshipped. Cooked rice is then offered to rivers, and is received by the Dhálya Lamánis. Once a year the ground in front of the huts is cowdunged, and a needle or two or a four anna silver coin is worshipped in the name of the deceased ancestors. In some places, flesh is offered to male ancestors only, rice being offered to females. This ceremony is repeated when there is sickness in the family. Musalmán *Pirs* are venerated. Some of the tribesmen worship the so-called three and a half goddesses *sáde-tin-devis*, but never divulge the name of the half goddess. When an epidemic breaks out, Sivábái, Durgavva and Margavva are propitiated with offerings of water, rice and flesh. Vanjáris have great faith in soothsaying, ghosts and witchcraft. They observe all the ordinary Hindu holidays, but especially *Gokuláshtami* in honour of Krishna's birth-day. On this day the Vanjáris of Gujarát worship bulls and snakes. Formerly all the ceremonies of Vanjáris were conducted by themselves. Of late, some employ Bráhmans to conduct their marriages, who, in some places, are regarded as degraded on that account. **Religion.**

The married dead are burnt, the unmarried being buried without any ceremony. The deceased, if married, is covered with a new shroud, tied to a bier, and carried to the burning ground on the shoulders of four men. Before laying the body on the bier the carriers drop **Death ceremonies.**

a little clarified butter and molasses into the mouth and tie a copper coin in the folds of the shroud. Half-way to the burning ground the bearers halt, lower the body, and tearing off the knotted end of the shroud with the coin, drop the coin on the ground, change places, and go on. At the burning ground the body is laid on the funeral pile, the pyre being lighted by the chief mourner. When the body is burnt, the bones and ashes are gathered and thrown into water, and the funeral party return to the house of mourning. When they reach the house, water is poured on the ground before them. On the third day all the mourners go to the burning ground and eat clarified butter, wheat and molasses near water. In some places a feast is also held. In Gujarát, a cow is milked on the ashes and bones. Some feed friends with cooked rice and molasses at their own houses on the twelfth day; others hold that the *Shimga* holidays is the time for the yearly rites for the deceased, and, on those days, either feed crows or go in a body to the neighbouring waste land, where they make bread and eat it. They also feed a certain number of men, in order to propitiate the spirit of the deceased, and make many gifts to Bráhman priests. At these death-dinners animal food and liquor are not used. In some places, on the full-moon day of *Márgashirsha* a dinner of flesh is given. In others, on the thirteenth day after death, the tribesmen present the chief mourner with half a goat, to the flesh of which they are treated. If this is not done, the tribesmen are not allowed to eat flesh at the house of the deceased for twelve years. In Khándesh, in the first *Mágh* or *Vaishákh* after a death, a caste feast usually, but not always, is given to propitiate the *manes*, and the *Mahálaya* is performed every year in the month of *Bhádrapad*.

Though generally peaceful and well behaved, the wandering Vanjáris are under Police surveillance, and, in the Kanarese districts, are often accused of stealing cattle, kidnapping women and children, and using false coin. Some are professional robbers. Their carrying trade, noticed by almost all European travellers of the last three centuries, has greatly suffered since the opening of cart roads and railways. They once carried their wares on pack bullocks in bands or armies of 100,000 strong, to Surat, Navsári and Kalyán, on the west, and Nimbár, Nágpur and Jabalpur, to the north and east. From the inland districts they carried wheat, and from the Konkan, salt, dates, dry cocoa kernel and betelnuts. This traffic continues along the Ghat roads to the present day (1920). They also deal in cattle. Though many are now settled as husbandmen, a few find a living by driving carts, spinning coarse hemp *tág*, selling grass and fuel, and working as labourers.

The staple articles of food of the tribe are the two millets in the Deccan and Gujarát and rice in Kanara. Except the Máthurás and Labhánás, all eat the flesh of goats, sheep, hare, deer, fowls, fish and wild boar, and drink liquor. Amongst the Rávjins, and in some places among the Maráthás also, the women abstain from flesh and liquor. They rank below the cultivating classes and above the impure castes. Food.

LAMBADI.— A synonym for Lamáni.

LAMBAR.— A synonym for Lamáni.

LAMGHA.— A synonym for Rávjin Vanjári.

LANGHA.— A synonym for Mir.

LAVANA.— A synonym for Lohána.

LAVANIA.— A sub-division of Bháts.

LENKAVALE.— A sub-division of Maráthás.

LEVA.— A sub-division of Kanbis ; a synonym for Reva.

LEWANA.— A synonym for Lohána.

LIMBACHIA.— A sub-division of Hajáms.

LINGANGI.— A synonym for Lingáyat.

LINGAYATS.—Numbered in 1901,1,422,293 (males 716,411, females 705,882). At that census 71 subcastes were separately enumerated, and of these two were again sub-divided,—the Bánjigs into five, and the Devángs into two, groups. Out of the total number of 1,422,293 as many as 132,138 or 9·02 per cent. did not return a subcaste designation. In the 1911 census the subcastes were not separately enumerated, the main caste numbering 1,339,248 (males 683,472, females 655,776). The reduction during the decennium was attributed mainly to mortality from plague.

Lingáyats are found chiefly in the districts of Belgaum, Bijápur and Dhárwár as well as in Kolhápur and the Native States of the Southern Marátha Country. Beyond the limits of the Bombay Presidency they are numerous in the Mysore and Hyderábád States. They also form an important element in the population of the north-west corner of the Madras Presidency. Distribution.

Lingáyats, * who are also known as Lingawants, Lingángis, Sivabhaktas, and Virashivas, derive their name from the word *linga*, Name.

---

* The following account is in the main a reprint of matter which has already appeared in my article on *Lingáyats* in Dr. Hasting's Encyclopœdia of Religions and Ethics.

the phallic emblem with the affix *ayta*, and are 'the people who bear the *linga*' habitually. Their name literally describes them; for the true Lingáyat wears on his body a small silver box containing a stone phallus, which is the symbol of his faith, and the loss of which is equivalent to spiritual death.* The emblem is worn by both sexes. The men carry the box on a red silk scarf or a thread tied round the neck, while the women wear it inside their costume, on a neck-string. When working, the male wearer sometimes shifts it to his left arm.

Description. The Lingáyat group is not racial, but sectarian. It was the essence of the original faith that anyone might embrace it and become a Lingáyat. Hence the Lingáyats can only be said to be Dravidian on the ground that the sect was founded in and never spread beyond, the north-west portions of the Karnátak, where the majority of its adherents were necessarily racially of Dravidian origin. They are dark in complexion, in common with the races of Southern India, and speak Kanarese, a Dravidian language. They have been not inaptly described as a peaceable race of Hindu puritans, though it may be questioned how far their rejection of many of the chief dogmas of Bráhmanic Hinduism leaves them the right to be styled Hindus at all. As will be seen below, the faith has not remained pure but has gradually reapproximated to the Hindu faith. Of the Bráhmanic trinity—Brahma, Vishnu and Shiva—they acknowledge only the god Shiva, whose emblem, the *linga*, they bear on their persons. They reverence the *Vedas*, but disregard the later commentaries on which the Bráhmans rely. Originally they seem to have been the product of one of the numerous reformations that have been aimed in India against the supremacy and doctrines of the Bráhmans, whose selfish exploitation of the lower castes has frequently led to the rise of new sects essentially anti-Bráhmanic in origin. It seems clear that, in its inception, Lingáyatism not only rested largely on a denial of the Bráhman claim to supremacy over all other castes, but attempted to abolish all caste distinctions. All wearers of the *linga* were proclaimed equal in the eyes of God. The traditional Lingáyat teacher, Basava, proclaimed all men holy in proportion as they are temples of the great spirit, and thus, in his view, all men are born equal. The denial

*This *linga* is called *ishtalinga* or "*linga* of investiture" as opposed to the *Sthaviralingas* or "fixed *lingas*". The latter, which are stones of large size around which temples have been built, or which have been installed in temples, are numerous all over India. The twelve most famous at Benares, Rameshwaram and other holy places are called *Jyotirlingas*. It was a cardinal tenet of the early Lingáyat faith that the true believer should never visit or worship *Sthaviralingas*. But this precept, like many others, is now not strictly observed (Artal in J. Bomb. Anthr. Soc. vii 181,2.)

of the supremacy of the Bráhmans, coupled with the assertion of the essential equality of all men, constituted a vital departure from the doctrines of orthodox Hinduism. The belief in rebirth and consequently in the doctrine of *Karma* was also abandoned. Other im portant innovations were :—the prohibition of child marriages ; the removal of all restriction on widows remarrying ; the burial, instead of burning, of the dead ; and the abolition of the chief Hindu rites for the removal of ceremonial impurity. The founders of the religion could scarcely have forged more potent weapons for severing the bonds between their proselytes and the followers of the doctrines preached by contemporary Bráhmanic Hinduism.*

The reader must not assume that this brief description of the fundamental doctrines of a religious movement which dates from the 12th century A. D. conveys an accurate picture of the prevalent Lingáyatism of the present day. In connection with the attitude originally assumed towards caste distinctions, there has been a very noticeable departure from Basava's teaching. The origin of caste in India is as yet a subject requiring much elucidation. In its development no mean influence must be allotted to function, religlion and political boundaries. Nor can differences of race have failed materially to assist the formation of Indian society on its present basis. One of the most interesting phenomena connected with the evolution of modern caste is the working of a religious reformation in which caste finds no place on the previously existing social structure of caste units. If caste is largely a manifestation of deep-rooted prejudices tending to raise and preserve barriers between the social intercourse of different sections of the human race, it would seem not unnatural to expect that it would tend to reassert itself within the fold of an essentially casteless religion so soon as the enthusiasm of the founders had spent itself ; and it is not unlikely that the mere fact of converts having joined the movement at an early stage in its history would generate a claim to social precedence over the later converts, and thus in time reconstitute the old caste barrier that the reformers spent themselves in endeavouring to destroy. One of the most interesting pages in the history of caste evolution, therefore, must be that which deals with the evolution of caste inside

*Artalo (p. cit. p. 183) mentions that the Channabasava Purana refers to 64 "commandments", and gives a list of 63 obtained from a Lingáyat priest. Many of these are very curious; for instance, the prohibition against using medical drugs. But Artal remarks that only 14 out of the 63 are generally observed by all Lingáyats. These 64 Rules provide, among other things, that a Lingáyat must be shaved by a Lingáyat barber, he should wear cloth woven by a Deváng or Lingáyat weaver, his clothes should be washed by a Lingáyat Agasa, and his pots made by a Lingáyat potter.

the fold of a religious community originally formed on a non-caste basis. A remarkable instance of such evolution will be found in the history of Lingáyatism.

The Lingáyats of the present day are divided into three well defined groups, including numerous true castes, of which a description will be found in the section dealing with their social organization. With the rise of caste distinctions, numerous other changes occurred in the nature of the Lingáyat religion. The *ayyas* or *jangams,* the priests of the community, devised in time a ritual and ceremonies in which the influence of the rival Bráhman aristocracy can freely be traced. The more important of these ceremonies are described below. But it is essential to a thorough understanding of the nature of Lingáyatism that the most important ceremony of all, known as the *ashtavarna* or the eightfold sacrament, should be understood by the reader.

It is commonly asserted nowadays by prominent members of the Lingáyat community that the true test of a Lingáyat is the right to receive the full *ashtavarna,* and that the possession of a few of these eight rites only does not entitle the possessor to be styled a member of the community. The contention seems scarcely in harmony with the popular usage of the term 'Lingáyat'.

The *ashtavarna* consists of eight rites known as—

1. Guru.
2. Linga.
3. Vibhuti.
4. Rudráksha.
5. Mantra.
6. Jangam.
7. Tirth.
8. Prasád.

On the birth of a Lingáyat the parents send for the *guru,* or spiritual adviser, of the family, who is the representative of one of the five *ácháryas,* or holy men, from whom the father claims descent. The *guru* binds the *linga* on the child, besmears it with *vibhuti* (ashes), places a garland of *rudráksha* (seeds of *Elaeocarpus ganitrus*) round its neck, and teaches it the mystic *mantra* or prayer known as *Namah Shiváya*—*i.e.,* 'Obeisance to the god Shiva'. The child being incapable of acquiring a knowledge of the sacred text at this early stage of its existence, the prayer is merely recited in its ear by the *guru.* The child has then to be presented to the god Shiva, in the person of a *jangam,* or Lingáyat priest, who is summoned for this purpose. On his arrival the parents wash his feet, and the water in which the feet are washed is described as the *tirtha* or *charanatirtha* of Shiva. This water is next poured over the *linga* attached to the infant. The *jangam* is fed, and a portion of the food from the dish is placed in the child's mouth. This final ceremony is known as *prasád*. Occasionally the double characters of *guru* and *jangam* are combined in one person. When the child attains the age of eight or ten, the ceremony is repeated with slight modifications.

It will be seen that this eightfold ceremony forms a very concise test of a Lingáyat's religious status, and may be not unfitly compared to the rites of baptism and confirmation which are outward and visible signs of admission to the Catholic Church. But not all Christians are confirmed, and in the same way not all members of the Lingáyat community undergo the full ceremony of initiation. It would probably be safer to apply the term 'Lingáyat' to all wearers of the *linga*, whether they are entitled to the full *ashtavarna* on birth or conversion, or to a few only of the eight sacraments. In so doing, the lower orders, from a social standpoint, of the Lingáyat community, will not be excluded, as they would otherwise be, from the fold.

Lingáyats are not permitted to touch meat, or to drink any kind of liquor. The greater number of them are either occupied in agriculture or are traders. They are generally reputed to be peaceful and law-abiding; but at times they are capable of dividing into violent factions with such rancour and hostility that the dispute culminates in riots, and occasionally in murder. Among the educated members of the community there is a strong spirit of rivalry with the Bráhmans, whose intellect and capacity have secured them a preponderating share of Government appointments and often a preponderating influence in municipal affairs. This rivalry between the two sects may be said to dominate the whole social and political life of the Bombay Karnátak. Except for these defects the community may be described as steady and industrious, devoted to honest toil, whether in professional employment, or occupied in trading or the cultivation of the soil.

History.

Until the recent publication of two inscriptions, which have been deciphered and edited by the late Mr. J. F. Fleet, and throw an entirely new light on the probable origin of the Lingáyat religion, the movement in favour of this special form of Shiva worship was commonly supposed to have been set on foot by the great Lingáyat saint Basava, in the latter half of the 12th century. The acts and doctrines of Basava and of his nephew Channabasava are set forth in two *puránas* or sacred books, named, after them, the *Basavapurána* and the *Channabasavapurána*. But these works were not written until some centuries had elapsed since the death of the saints to whom they refer and it seems certain that the substratum of fact which they contain had by that time become so overlaid with tradition and miraculous occurrences as to render them of little historical value. The *Basavapurána* describes Basava as the son of Bráhman parents, Madirája and Madalámbika, residents of Bágewádi, usually held to be the town of that name in the Bijápur district of the Bombay Presidency. Basava is the Kanarese name for a bull, an animal sacred to Shiva, and thus a connection is traced between Basava and the god Shiva. At the age of eight, Basava refused to be invested with the sacred thread of the twice-born caste, to which he belonged by birth, declaring himself a worshipper of Shiva, and stating that he had come to destroy the distinctions of caste. By his knowledge of the Shaiva scriptures he attracted the attention of his uncle Baladeva, then prime minister to the king of Kalyán, Bijjala. Baladeva gave him his daughter Gangádevi in marriage. Subsequently Bijjala, a Kalachurya by race, who usurped the Chálukyan kingdom of Kalyán in the middle of the 12th century, installed Basava as his prime minister and gave him his younger sister Nilalochana as wife. The *puránas* further recount the birth of Channabasava from Basava's unmarried sister Nagalámbika, by the working of the spirit of the god Shiva. The myth in connection with this miraculous conception is interesting. Basava, while engaged in prayer, saw an ant emerge from the ground with a small seed in its mouth. He took the seed to his home, where his sister swallowed it and became pregnant. The issue of this unique conception was Channabasava. Uncle and nephew both preached the new doctrines, and in so doing encountered the hostility of the Jains, whom they ruthlessly persecuted. A revolution, the outcome of these religious factions, led to the assassination of king Bijjala and to the flight of Basava and his nephew. Basava is said to have been finally absorbed into the *linga* at Kudal Sangameshwar, the confluence of the Krishna (Kistna) and Malprabha rivers in the Bijápur district (Bombay Gazetteer, xxii, p. 104), and Channabasava to have lost his life at Ulvi in North Kanara. An annual pilgrimage of Lingáyats to the shrine of the latter at Ulvi takes place to this day.

Two important inscriptions bearing upon these traditions of the origin of the Lingáyats deserve consideration. The first was discovered at the village of Managoli, a few miles from Bágewádi, the traditional birthplace of Basava. This record (as also many others) shows that king Bijjala gained the kingdom of Kalyán in A. D. 1156. It also states that a certain Basava was the builder of the temple in which the inscription was first put, and that Madirája was *mahâprabhu*, or head of the village, when the grants-in-aid of the temple were made. Basava is further described as the grandson of Revadása and the son of Chandirája, and as a man of great sanctity and virtue. The second inscription was found at Ablur in the Dhárwár district and belongs to about A. D. 1200. It relates the fortunes of a certain Ekántada-Rámayya, an ardent worshipper of the god Shiva. Rámayya came into conflict with the Jains, and defeated them, both in dispute and, the inscription says, by performing a miracle—we may venture to say, by arranging matters so that he seemed to perform it—which consisted in cutting off his own head and having it restored to him, safe and sound, by the grace of Shiva, seven days later. All this came to the notice of the king Bijjala, who summoned Rámayya into his presence. And Rámayya, making his cause good before the king, won his support, and was presented with gifts of lands for the temple founded by him at Ablur in the new faith. The incidents related of Rámayya are placed shortly before A. D. 1162, so that he would have been a contemporary of Basava. No mention, however, of the latter or of his nephew is found in this record.

Accepting the contemporary inscriptions as more entitled to credit than the tradition overlaid with myth recorded at a later date, it seems clear that both Basava and Ekántada-Rámayya were reformers who had much to do with the rise of the Lingáyat doctrine, and that the event is to be placed in the 12th century. Lingáyat scholars of the present day, indeed, claim a far earlier date for the origin of their faith. But their contention that its origin is contemporaneous with that of Bráhmanic Hinduism has yet to be established by adequate evidence. The best opinion seems to be that of Fleet, who considers that there is no doubt that the present Lingáyat sect is more or less a development of the guild (mentioned in many inscriptions) of the 500 Swámis of Aihole, a village in the Bijápur district, the protectors of the Vira-Bananju religion, who were always more or less strictly Shaivas, but with a free-mindedness which is not now common, patronized also Buddhism. The movement, however, in which the 500 Swámis of Aihole joined seems certainly to have originated with Ekántada-Rámayya at Ablur. And probably the prevalent tradition of the present day, that Basava was the originator of it and the founder of the community, must only be attributed to his having quickly become acquainted with the new development of Shaivism started by Rámayya, and to his having taken a leading part in encouraging and propagating it in circumstances which rendered him more conspicuous than the real founder. Basava happened to be a member of the body of village elders at Managoli, and so to occupy a recognizable position in local matters, administrative as well as religious. Consequently, it seems likely that, when the first literary account of the rise of Lingáyatism came to be written, which was unquestionably an appreciable time after the event, his name had survived, to the exclusion of Rámayya's. Accordingly, the writer of that account was unable to tell us anything particular about Rámayya, beyond duly recording the miracle performed by him, and attributed the movement entirely to Basava, assigning to him an assistant, his nephew Channabasava, who is perhaps only a mythical person. But it must be also admitted that the early history of the movement may be capable of further elucidation, and that the present day claims of the leading Lingáyats for a very early origin for their religion, though lacking the support of historical evidence, have this much to rely on, that it is essentially probable that the Dravidian races of Southern India, whose primitive deities were absorbed by the Aryan invaders into the personality of their god Shiva, always leant towards the special worship of Shiva to the exclusion of the other members of the Bráhmanic trinity, and combined with this preference a dislike of Bráhmanic ritual and caste ascendency which is the real substratum of the movement ending in the recognition of Lingáyatism.

In dismissing the question of the origin of the Lingáyat religion it seems desirable to give an instance of the claims advanced by learned members of the community for a greater antiquity for their religion than historical evidence would afford it. Mr. Karibasavashástri, Professor of Sanskrit and Kanarese in the State College of Mysore, contends* that the Shaiva sect of Hindus has always been divided into two groups, the one comprising the wearers of the *linga* and the other those who do not wear it. The former he designates Virashaiva, and declares that the Virashaivas consist of Bráhman, Kshatriya, Vaishya and Shudra, the fourfold caste division of Manu. Quoting from the 17th chapter of the *Parameshwar ágama*, he declares that the Virashaiva Bráhmans are also known as Suddha Virashaivas, Virashaiva kings as Márga-Virashaivas, Virashaiva Vaishyas as Misra-Virashaivas, and the Shudras of the community are Anteve Virashaivas. In his opinion, the duties and penances imposed on the first of these classes are (1) the *ashtavarna*, (2) penances and bodily emaciation, (3) the worship of Shiva without sacrifice, (4) the recital of the Vedas. He further asserts that the Hindu *áshramas* or conditions of life of Brahmachári, Grihastha and Sanyási, *i.e.*, student, householder and ascetic, are binding on Virashaivas, and quotes from various

* R. C. Carr's Monograph on Lingáyats, Madras Government Press, 1906.

Sanskrit works, texts in support of this view. He furnishes a mythical account of the origin of Lingáyats at the time of the creation of the world. The importance of this summary of his view lies in the fact that it is completely typical of the claims that many members of the Lingáyat community have recently commenced to advance, to be included, in a sense, within the fold of orthodox Hinduism, with the mistaken notion of thereby increasing their social standing. They endeavour to divide themselves into Manu's fourfold caste scheme of Bráhman, Kshatriya, Vaishya and Shudra, regardless of the fact that theirs is in origin a non-caste religion, and that Manu's scheme, which can only with great inaccuracy be applied to the more orthodox Hindu castes, is totally unsuited to the Lingáyats. A sign of this movement towards Bráhmanic Hinduism among Lingáyats is to be found in the organized attempt made by certain Lingayáts at recent censuses to enter themselves as Virashaiva Bráhmans; and it seems probable that these claims to a great antiquity for their religion and for a caste scheme based on Manu's model are chiefly significant as signs of the social ambitions of the educated members, who are jealous of the precedence of the Bráhmans.

Appearance.

Lingáyats, being a very large community, vary to a considerable extent in appearance, height and colour. It has been seen above that they are for the most part dark in complexion, resembling the races of Southern India in this respect; but they are fairer than Bedars and occasionally differ little in appearance from the average Marátha Kunbi. Some high class Lingáyat women are remarkably fairskinned. The striking points in the appearance of a Lingáyat man are his *linga* which is worn either at his waist in a silver box hung round his neck, or tied in a red ribbon round the neck, or round the upper left arm; the absence of the sacred thread; and the shaven topknotless head.

Dress.

The men wear the waist-cloth, the shouldercloth, the jacket and the headscarf, and the women wear the robe and bodice. The robe is wound round the waist and allowed to fall to the ankles. The end of the skirt is not passed between the legs and tucked into the waist behind, but is gathered into a large bunch of folds in front to the left side. The upper end is passed across the bosom and over the head, and hangs loosely down the right side. The two ends of the bodice are tied in a knot in front, leaving the arms, neck and throat bare. Many of them have silk and brocade clothes for holiday use. They are fond of black either by itself or mixed with red. Some are as neat and clean as Bráhmans, but the dress of most is less neat and clean than the dress of Bráhmans. High class Lingáyat women wear glass bangles and the lucky necklace or *mangalsutra,* and the putting on of the lucky necklace plays a much more prominent part in a Lingáyat than in a Bráhmanical wedding. Some Lingáyat women whose first husbands are alive mark their brows with *kunku* or vermilion, and others with ashes. Even after her second marriage, no widow is allowed to put either vermilion or ashes on her brow. Lingáyat women do not wear false hair or deck their hair with flowers. Both men and women are fond of ornaments.

Ornaments. The men wear on the neck, the *kanthi, goph* and *chandrahár,* round both wrists *khadás* and *todás,* round the right wrist *usalbalis,* round the waist the *kaddora,* and rings on the fingers. A rich man's ornaments are of gold, a poor man's of silver. The women wear the ear-rings called *vali, bugdi, jamki, ghanti* and *bálighanti,* all of gold with or without pearls ; the noserings called *mug, nath* and *mugti,* all of gold with or without pearls ; round the neck *gejitikka, gundintikka, hanigitikka, karimanitikka, karipate, sarigi, kathane* and *putlisara ;* on the arm *váki, nágmurgi* and *bajuband* ; on the wrists *got, pátlya, todas, jave, havalpátlya, doris* and *kankans* ; round the waist the *kambarpatta,* either with clasps representing mouths of animals or simple clasps, on the ankles *sákhli, paijan, kalkadágas* and *kalungars,* all of silver ; and on the toes *pille, gejipille, minpille* and *gendus,* all of silver. Poor women generally wear silver bracelets and necklaces.

Language. The home tongue of most of the Lingáyats is Kanarese. Their personal names are generally either the names of the reputed founders of their religion, or of village gods and goddesses. The commonest names among men are Basappa, Chanbasappa, Isbasappa, Irappa, Sivappa, Kallappa and Virbhadrappa*, and among women Basavva Nágavva, Dyámavva and Sangavva. If a woman has lost several children she gives her next child a mean name, Tipáppa, from the Kanarese *tipi* a dungheap or Kálavva from *kalu* a stone, hoping to save the child from untimely death.

Social organization. The results of investigations undertaken in 1900 by committees of Lingáyat gentlemen entrusted with the duty of preparing a classification of the numerous social subdivisions of the Lingáyat community tend to show that the relation of these various groups to each other is one of some complexity. Broadly speaking, Lingáyats appear to consist of three

---

* The termination *appa* means father. It is frequently followed by the addition of *gauda,* meaning village headman, a hereditary office to which many families have claims. Thus Lingáyat names are very lengthy, as for instance Chanbasappagauda *bin* (*i. e.,* son of) Dwodbasappagauda. *Chan* means "the younger" and *Dwod,* 'the elder'" literally small and big.

groups of sub-divisions. The first, which for convenience may be named Panchamsális with full *ashtavarna* rites, contains the priests of the community known as *ayyas* or *jangams* and the leading trader castes or *banjigs*. It is probable that this group is the nearest approximation to the original converts, who, it will be remembered, could interdine and intermarry without restriction. The sub-divisions of this group may still dine together, but are hypergamous to one another. Members of the lower sub-divisions in this group may rise to the higher by performing certain rites and ceremonies. The Panchamsális, as they may be called for lack of a better name, are all entitled to the *ashtavarna* rites, and rank considerably above the remaining groups. One of the writers in the "Bombay Gazetteer" describes them as True Lingáyats.[1]

The next group is that of the non-Panchamsális with *ashtavarna* rites. This group contains numerous endogamous sub-divisions which are functional groups, such as weavers, oil-pressers, brick-layers, dyers, cultivators, shepherds and the like. It seems probable that they represent converts of a much later date than those we have styled Panchamsális, and were never admitted to interdine or intermarry with the latter. Members of one sub-division may not pass to another. The names of the sub-divisions are commonly indicative of the calling of the members, and it is of special interest to note here how the barriers erected by specialization of function have proved too strong for the original communal theories of equality which the Lingáyats of early days adopted. It is interesting to observe that considerable diversity of practice exists in connection with the relations of the sub-divisions of this group to the parent Hindu castes from which they separated to become Lingáyats. In most cases it is found that, when a portion of an original Hindu caste has been converted to Lingáyatism, both intermarriage and interdining with the unconverted members is finally abandoned, and the caste is broken into two divisions, of which one is to be recognized by the members wearing the *linga* and the other not. But in some instances, *e.g.*, the Jeers of the Belgaum district, the Lingáyat members continue to take brides from the non-Lingáyat section, though they will not marry their daughters to them; it is usual to invest the bride with the *linga* at the marriage ceremony, thus formally receiving her into the Lingáyat community.* In other cases the Lingáyat and non-Lingáyat sections live side by side and dine

(1) Bombay Gazetteer, Vol. xxiii, p. 220.

*It is a remarkable fact that these Jeers or Hugars contain a section wearing the *linga*, a section wearing the sacred thread, and a section wearing both the *linga* and the sacred thread—a curious instance of religious tolerance.

together at caste functions, intermarriage being forbidden. In this case, however, the former call in a *jangam* to perform their religious ceremonies, and the latter employ a Bráhman. The more typical case seems to be that of a caste sub-division given in the Indian Census Report.(1) In the last century a Lingáyat priest of Ujjini converted a number of weavers in the village of Tuminkatti in the Dhárwár district. These converts abandoned all social intercourse with their former caste brethren, and took their place as a new sub-division in the non-Panchamsáli group under the name of Kurvinaras. This second group or sub-division of the main caste, therefore, differs essentially from the Panchamsális, though the members also have the *ashtavarna* rites. It is described in the Bombay Gazetteer as "Affiliated Lingáyats".

The third group or sub-division is the non-Panchamsális without *ashtavarna* rites. It contains washermen, tanners, shoemakers, fishermen, etc., who would rank as unclean castes among the Bráhmanic Hindus. It is the practice among Lingáyats of the present day to deny that the members of this third group are entitled to be classed as Lingáyats at all. They maintain that, since the possession of the full *ashtavarna* rites is the mark of a Lingáyat, these lower divisions, who at most can claim three or four of the eight sacraments, are only the followers or servants of Lingáyats. The contention is not unreasonable. Yet it seems that these lower orders would be styled Lingáyats by the other Hindus of the neighbourhood and would describe themselves as such. A classification of the Lingáyat community would not, therefore, be complete unless they were included. On this point the evidence of the Abbé Dubois(2) is of interest. He wrote: "Even if a Pariah join the sect, he is considered in no way inferior to a Bráhman. Wherever the *linga* is found, there, they say, is the throne of the deity without distinction of class or rank". This testimony of an observer writing just a century ago seems to indicate that the disintegration of the Lingáyat sect is comparatively recent. Lingáyats of this third description only marry within their sub-division. They are described as Half Lingáyats in the Bombay Gazetteer.

The chief Lingáyat sub-divisions are as follows:—

1. Adibánjig or Divatigi.
2. Agasa.†
3. Ambig.†
4. Badig.†
5. Baligar.
6. Bánjig.

(1) Bombay Census Report, 1901, Chap. viii, p. 182.
(2) Hindu manners, customs and ceremonies (1906, p. 117).

Athnikar or Holiachibalki.
Chalgeribalki.
Dhulpávad.
Lokabalki or Lokavant.
Shilvant or Chilmi-agni.
7. Basuvi.*
8. Burud or Medar.†
9. Chalvádi or Holaya.†

10. Chatter.
11. Dás or Deodás.†
12. Dhor.†
13. Ganiger.†
14. Gauli.†
15. Gavandi or Uppár.†
16. Handevant.
Handevazir.
Handeyawa.
Handeraut.
Handeguruba.
17. Helav.
18. Hugar, Jeer, Gurav, Malgár or Totigar.†
19. Ilgar or Kalál.†

20. Jád, Neyakár, Koshti or Sáli.†
Bilijád. Devara-Dasmaya.
Deváng
Hatgar.
Kurvin Shetti.
Nilkant.
Padsáli.
Padmasáli.
Pattasáli.
Semasáli.
21. Jangam, Ayya or Maheshvar.
Ganakumár.
Ganáchári.
Guiushtala.
Kambeya.
Kayakada.
Mathapati.
Nandi Kola.
Pancha-Sinvásanádhish.
Pujári.
Sthavara.
Vastradavaru.
Vishuti.
Virakta or Dhasthala.
22. Kabbaligar.†
23. Káchári.†
24. Kalávant.†
25. Kammár.†
26. Kudavakkal.†
27. Kumbhár.†
28. Kurub or Dhangar.†
29. Kurusali.
30. Lálgonda.
31. Mallav.‡
32. Nadig or Nhávi.†
33. Náglik or Bangar.†
34. Nilgar.†
35. Nonabar.
36. Pancháchári.
37. Raddi.†
38. Sada.
39. Saib.
40. Samgár, Jingar or Chamár.†
41. Shiva-Shimpig.
42. Shivyogi.
43. Sungar or Chunár.
44. Támboli.†
45. Tilári or Tiráli.
46. Turkar.

* A class of prostitutes, which is disappearing, to judge by the census returns. In the Bombay Gazetteer, 1884, xxii, p. 191, they were said to number "probably 2,000" in the Dhárwár District alone. In the 1901 Census they were returned as only 7 (male 1, females 6) in the whole Presidency. But it is not unlikely that Basavis, as courtezans, return themselves under another name.

† Presumably the Malwaru and Muskin Mallava of the 1901 Census. For this sub-caste see below (p. 374)

Of the above, the divisions shown under Nos. 6 and 20 are Panchamsáli Lingáyats with full *ashtavarna* rites. The rest are for the most part non-Panchamsális with the full *ashtavarna* except for recent converts and divisions corresponding to Hindu unclean castes, *e.g.*, Dhors, Ilgars, etc., who are non-Panchamsális without *ashtavarna*.

Those marked with † are converts to Lingáyatism from Hindu castes of the same name. Of the rest, a few that require special notice are briefly described at the end of this article.

Within the endogamous sub-divisions just described, there are exogamous sections. Little accurate information is available regarding the nature and origin of these sections, but it appears that in the higher ranks they are named after five Lingáyat sages—Nandi, Bhringi, Vira, Vrisha and Skanda*—and in this respect closely resemble, and are probably imitations of, the ordinary Bráhmanic *gotras*, or exogamous groups, which are also named after mythical ancestors.

Marriage rules.

The Lingáyats do not allow the children of brothers to intermarry, nor may sisters' children marry together. Marriage with the children of a paternal uncle or maternal aunt is similarly forbidden. A man may marry his sister's daughter, but if the sister be a younger sister, such a marriage is looked on with disfavour. Marriage is both infant and adult. Sexual license is neither recognized nor tolerated, at least in theory, but is punished, if need be, by excommunication. Polygamy is permitted, but is only usual when the first wife fails to bear a son.

Birth ceremonies.

After a birth a Kabbaligar, Lingáyat, or Marátha midwife washes the mother and child in warm water, and lays them on a bedstead. The family priest ties a *linga* round the neck of the child and withdraws. The mother is given dry dates, dry ginger, anise-seed or *shep* (*Pimpinella anisum*), raw sugar, and clarified butter, and is fed on boiled rice which is eaten with garlic. She is kept warm by having a chafing dish set under her bedstead on which garlic rind is burnt. On the fifth evening the midwife places in the lying-in room an image of the goddess Jivati, sprinkles turmeric and redpowder on the goddess, lays cooked food before her, waves a lamp about her, and carries the lamp under cover, for if the lamp is seen by any one but the midwife the mother and child will sicken. On the twelfth day the child is cradled and named. Each of the women who comes for the naming brings with her a robe

* Artal (op. cit. p. 209) gives these as the names of the *gotras* but gives the names of the five sages as Revanávádhya, Maruáláradhya, Yeko Rámávádhya, Panditáádhya and Vishvavádhya.

or a bodice-cloth for the mother, a jacket or a cap for the child, and two halves of cocoakernel and a pound of Indian millet, wheat, or spiked millet.(1)

Aitan

The rite of *aitán* or initiation is performed on the unmarried sons of all Jangams. When *aitán* is performed on a youth he becomes fit to hold the highest religious posts; he may become a *mathadayya* or the head of a religious house. A Jangam who has no sons has the rite performed at his expense on one of the sons of a lay disciple who is not below the Panchamsáli group. The boy who is chosen from a lay Lingayát family should be of respectable parents, and his ancestors, both male and female, even to the eleventh generation should not be children of married widows. For this reason the sons of *mathpatis* or beadles and of *ganácháris* or managers seldom undergo initiation or *aitán*. A boy is initiated when he is between eight and sixteen years old. The ceremony takes place at night, so that no non-*linga*-wearing Hindu may see it. It should take place in one of the seven months from *Vaishákh* (April-May) to *Phálgun* (February-March) inclusive—on one out of eight days in either fortnight, *viz.*:—the second, third, fifth, seventh, tenth, eleventh, twelfth, or thirteenth—on either a Monday, Wednesday, Thursday, or Friday, and in one of the following lunar mansions or *nakshatras*, *viz.*—*Anurádha*, *Hast*, *Magha*, *Mrig*, *Mul*, *Revti*, *Rohini*, *Uttara*, *Uttaráshádha*, and *Uttarbhádrapada*. If the boy is to become a Virakt or celibate, his initiation is performed in the dark half of the month, and when he is intended to be a Grihasth or householder, the ceremony takes place in the bright half of the month. In an initiation the *bhushuddhi* or earth purifying is the first observance. Either in a religious house or a dwelling house a piece of ground eleven and a quarter, twelve, or twelve and three-quarters feet, by six and three-quarters, seven and a half, or eight and a quarter feet, is dug seven and half to eight and a quarter feet deep. Bits of stone and tiles and other larger objects which may be in the pit are removed, and it is filled with fine earth, which is afterwards beaten hard. At the same time the house is whitewashed and painted and its floor is cowdunged. On the day fixed a small bower with a canopy of silk cloth is raised on the sacred spot. At the entrance of the bower an arch is made of two plantain trees or sugarcane stalks. The floor of the bower is plastered with *gorochan* or bezoar, cowdung, clarified cow's butter, cow's milk, and cow's urine, and on it is drawn a large parallelogram with lines of quartz powder, and within it, three small parallelograms.

(1) Bombay Gazetteer, Vol. xxiii, p. 230.

Of these the first, which lies farthest from the entrance, measures three feet and a quarter by two feet and a quarter. It is covered with a folded silk or woollen cloth and is set apart for the *guru* or initiator. The second or middle one is six feet by two and a half feet. In the centre and at each corner is set a *kalash* or brass or copper vessel with a narrow mouth and a dome-shaped bottom. These five vessels represent the five mouths of Shiva and the five *gotras* or family stocks which are believed to have sprung from them. The names of the five mouths are Aghor, Ishánya, Sadyoját, Tatpurush, and Vámdev, and the names of the corresponding family stocks are Uddán, Panchvanigi, Padudi, Muthin-kanti, and Mali.* Of the five jars the Sadyoját is set at the corner next to the *guru's* right hand and the Vámdev at the corner next to his left hand. Opposite the Sadyoját is set the Tatpurush and opposite the Vámdev the Aghor. In the centre is placed the Ishánya. Each jar is covered with five pieces of cloth—white, black, red, green, and yellow, and before each of them are laid five halves of dry cocoa-kernels, five dry dates, five betelnuts, five turmeric roots, five betel leaves, and five copper coins. The third or last design, which is not a parallelogram but a square two-feet each way, is close to the entrance of the bower. This square is covered with a woollen cloth seat, and is occupied by the boy, whose head has been completely shaved in the morning, since when he has been naked and fasting. Near the *guru* are placed a small brass vessel called *gilalu*, a conch shell, and a cane. Behind the boy sits a man belonging to the boy's *gotra* with a cocoanut in his hands. This man bows to the *guru*, and says—"Excellent teacher, purify this body of flesh and blood." After him the boy bows also to the *guru*, and worships an earthen vessel filled with water, in whose mouth is a cocoanut covered with a piece of cloth. The boy first marks the vessel with sandal paste, burns frankincense before it, and offers it molasses, fruit, betelnut, betel leaves, and money. At the end of the jar worship, a string composed of five strands is wound five times round the jars, the *guru* and the boy in the following elaborate order, each object mentioned being encircled five times before passing on to the next:—

Ishánya, Sadyoját, Ishánya, guru Ishánya, Vámdev, Ishánya, Aghora, Ishánya, boy, Ishánya, Tatpurush.

When the *guru* and the boy are thus seated, the *mathpati*, or Lingáyat beadle, worships the *linga* which the boy wears and his

---

* In the elaborate scheme of five-fold classifications given by Artal (op. cit. p. 209 (*a*)) these names do not occur. For the *gotras* he gives Vira, Nandi, Vrishabha, Bhringi, and Skanda (see above). The names given in the text perhaps belong to his *pravaras* (family stocks) for all of which he curiously gives simply Virshaiva.

hand and head. He first washes the boy's *linga* with seven holy waters in this order, *Gandhodak* or sandal paste water, *dhulodak* or dust water, *bhasmodak* or ash water, *suvarnodak* or gold water, *ratnodak* or jewel water, and *pushpodak* or flower water. He then washes the *linga* seven times with the mixture called *panchámrit*, or five nectars, namely, milk, curds, clarified butter, honey and sugar. In the same way he washes the boy's hands and his head. The *guru* then gives the boy a *jholi* or beggar's four-mouthed wallet and a staff, and tells him to beg alms of those who have come to witness the ceremony. The boy is given *dhátubhiksha* or metal alms, that is, gold, silver or copper coins. After gathering the alms, the boy gives them with the bag to his *guru*, bows low before him, and asks him to return the bag, promising to obey all his commands to the letter. The *guru*, after commanding him to live on alms, to share them with the helpless, and to lead a virtuous life, returns his bag. The boy gives him gold, vessels, and clothes, and gives other Jangams money and clothes. Besides these gifts the *guru* takes a handful of copper coins from a heap worth Rs. 3-8-0, the rest of which is distributed to ordinary or Sámánya Jangams. The friends and kinspeople of the boy's parents present the boy with clothes and vessels; and he takes a light repast. Next morning the boy's father gives a caste feast to Jangams of all orders and to friends and kinspeople. *Aitán* can be performed on one or more boys at the same time and by the same initiator.(1)

Diksha, or cleansing rite, is performed on any Panchamáli Lingáyat entitled to the *ashtavarna* rites who wishes to enter into a grade higher than his own, or to readmit one who has been put out of caste. In the main points *diksha* does not differ from *aitán* or initiation; the only difference is that in the purifying it is not necessary that a celibate Jangam should be the performer. His place is often taken by a family priest. As the person on whom the rite is to be performed is old enough to pray for himself, no man of his family stock is required to sit behind him. The *diksha* rite can be performed on twenty or thirty persons at the same time. When a person has undergone this rite and has entered into a higher grade, he or she does not eat with his former kinspeople. But this contingency rarely arises except when a girl marries into a higher grade. The ceremony performed at the time of tying a *linga* on a child's neck or arm is also called *diksha*.(2) Diksha.

(1) Bombay Gazetteer, Vol. xxiii, pp. 230—3.
(2) Bombay Gazetteer, Vol. xxiii, p, 233.

Marriage ceremonies.

The choosing of the bride and bridegroom is managed entirely by the parents. Among Lingáyats marriage is much cheaper than among Bráhmanical Hindus, as no price is paid for the girl. The offer of marriage comes from the boy's parents. When a boy's father can afford to pay for his son's marriage, he goes to a family who have a daughter likely to make a suitable match. If the girl's parents agree, he returns home and tells his wife that he has secured a bride for their son. After some days the boy's father, with friends and relations goes to the girl's village, and, through a *Mathpati* or a Lingáyat Gurav, calls those of his castemen and Jangams who live in the village. When all have come and taken their seats at the girl's house, a blanket is spread, some grains of rice are strewn on the blanket, and the boy and girl are made to sit on the rice. A kinswoman of the boy's dresses the girl in a new robe bought by the boy's father, and gives her five pieces of bodicecloth, out of which one must be white, and the remaining four of any colour except black. The woman dresses the girl, puts on her a gold ring and other ornaments, and fills her lap with two cocoanuts, five lemons, five dry dates, five plantains, and a few betel leaves. The girl's father presents the boy with a complete suit of clothes, including a turban, a shouldercloth, a coat and a gold ring. The boy and girl then rise, bow to the Jangams and house gods, and resume their seats. The Jangams on both sides, naming the father of the boy and girl, declare to the people that the boy and girl are engaged; and the guests are dismissed with betel leaves and nuts. This ceremony is called the *sákshivike* or engagement. Next day it is followed by the *báshtagi* or betrothal. In the betrothal the girl's father gives a caste feast, presents clothes to the relations of the boy's father, and leads them out of the village in procession with music. When the boy's father reaches home he asks an astrologer to fix the days on which the wedding rite and other ceremonies relating to the wedding should take place, makes a list of the days, and sends a copy of it to the girl's father. Preparations then begin. On the first day the laps of five married women are filled with bits of dry cocoa-kernel, dry dates, soaked gram, and betel. A grind-stone and a wooden mortar are brought out, whitewashed with lime, and marked with stripes of *hurmanj* or red colour. Before them are laid bits of cocoa-kernel, dry dates, soaked gram and betel leaves and nuts, and incense is burnt. The women, whose laps have been filled at a lucky moment, begin to pound the turmeric roots in the mortar and grind them on the grind-stone. On another lucky day the marriage booth is raised, the number of posts in each row being always uneven. The ornamenting of the booth depends on the parent's means. When all preparations are finished, both parties invite their kinswomen to live with them during the ceremony. A marriage takes five days. It is held at the boy's house. On the first day the bride and bridegroom sit together on a blanket, and, about eight at night, a Jangam begins to rub their bodies with turmeric paste. The rubbing is completed by a party of married kinswomen, whose first husbands are alive, after which the bride and bridegroom rub turmeric on each other. The women wave a light before the pair and chant. This day is called the *arshan* or turmeric day; and when the *arshan* has been put on, the boy and girl are considered *madmaklu* that is husband and wife. The second day is called the *devkárya* or god-humouring day. The boy's father gives a great dinner to Jangams and friends; the marriage garments are laid beside the house god and worshipped; the *guru's* feet are washed, and the water is taken and drunk by the bride and bridegroom and all the family. In a house in which Virbhadra is one of the house gods, the third day is called the *guggul* or Bdellium gum day. A new earthern vessel is brought to the boy's house, the neck is broken off, and a piece of sandalwood set in it, tipped with oil, and lighted, and camphor and *guggul* are burnt. The earthen vessel is held by a Jangam, and the boy and girl stand in front of them with the image of Virbhadra in their hands. The Jangam takes up the vessel, and the boy and girl carry the god, and, with music playing in front of them and followed by a band of friends, they go to Basavanna's temple. In front of the musicians walks a *vadab* or bard, dressed in silk, with a dagger in his hand, and an image of Virbhadra tied at his waist, chanting the praises of Virbhadra. At the temple the pair worship Basavanna, break a cocoanut, lay down the earthen vessel, and then return to the boy's house. Next day the actual marriage ceremony, the chief feature of which is the tying on of the bride's lucky neck-thread or *mangalsutra*, is performed by a Jangam.

Other persons of special positions who ought to attend a Lingáyat wedding are the personal *guru*, the *mathadayya*, or head of the local religious house, and the *panchacharus* or "five pots" namely the *ganáchári* or manager, the *mathpati* or beadle, the *metigauda* or village head, the *desái* or hereditary district revenue superintendent, and the *deshpánde* or hereditary district revenue accountant. A dais or raised seat called *sheshikate* or rice-dais is made ready, a blanket is spread on the dais, and on the blanket women strew rice. On this rice-strewn blanket the bride and bridegroom are seated. In front of them lines of rice are arranged in the form of a square, and, at each corner of the square and in the centre, a *kalash* or drinking-pot is set with betel leaves and a betelnut on it, some molasses and twenty-five copper coins, five close to each pot. Round the necks of the four corner drinking-pots two strings are five times wound. One end of the strings is held by the bride and bridegroom and the other end by the *guru*, who sits opposite them beyond the rice square. Between the teacher and the rice square sits the *mathadayya* with the *metigauda* on his right and the *mathpati* on his left. In the row behind, on each side of the teacher who holds the threads, sit the *deshpánde* and the *ganáchári*, the *deshpánde* on the teacher's right and the *ganáchári* on the teacher's left. The bride and bridegroom do not sit opposite each other but side by side and no curtain is held between them. Near the drinking pot in the middle of the square is set an image of Ishvar or Basavanna, and the *mangalsutra* is kept in a cup of milk and clarified butter. The ceremony begins by the *mathpati* bowing to the *mangalsutra*, and proclaiming that it is about to be tied to the bride's neck. The bridegroom lays his right hand on the bride's right hand, the *mathpati* lays the lucky thread on the boy's hand, the *ganáchári* drops water, *vibhuti*, or cowdung ashes, and *kunku* or vermilion on the lucky thread, and marks the bride's forehead with red and the boys with sandal paste. The teacher gives the order to tie on the lucky thread and the *ganáchári* ties it on the girl's neck, and calls *Sumuhurta Sávdhán*, that is, the moment has come, beware. When the priest says Beware, the lucky time has come the guests throw rice over the boy and the girl. The *ganáchári* ties the hems of the bride's and bridegroom's robes together and, in the knot ties a little rice, salt and split pulse. The teacher lets go the end of the two strings, ties a piece of turmeric root into each of them, and binds one to the boy's right wrist and the other to the girl's left wrist. The married couple fall down before the teacher, who ends the rite by dropping sugar into their mouths. The rice is given to the beadle, and first he and then the other four *panchahcharus* are presented with five quarter-anna pieces which had been lying besides the *kalashas*. On the last evening the bride and bridegroom ride on one horse in state to a temple of Basava, break a cocoanut before the god, and return and take off the marriage wristlets. On their return, friends wave boiled rice and curds round the heads of the bride and bridegroom and throw the rice to the evil spirits. During the passage to and from the temple, when they reach a street crossing or when they pass a ruined house, they break a cocoanut to the evil spirits.(1)

---

(1) Bombay Gazetteer, Vol. xxiii, pp. 233—5.

According to their religion, the wearer of the *linga* cannot be made impure. As a matter of fact Bombay Lingáyats mostly observe ceremonial impurity during a woman's monthly sickness, and after a birth or a death. The feeling about ceremonial uncleanness, which has its basis in the fear of spirit possession, seems to be stronger in the north than in the south. Among the Lingáyats in the south, near Mysore a woman's monthly sickness is not considered to cause impurity, while to the north of Bijápur in some families women sit by themselves on the first day of their monthly sickness and in other families a woman has to bathe on the first day, and to mark her forehead with ashes. Hence the Maráthi proverb :—" The Lingáyat woman puts on ashes and is pure." Families in which this rule is kept do not let their women touch the house gods during their sickness. If a Lingáyat girl comes of age before she is married, the fact that she has come of age is kept secret. When a married girl comes of age she is seated gaily dressed upon a canopied chair for four to sixteen days. During this time her kinswomen feed her with sweetmeats and at the end she is sent to live with her husband. On the last day the boy's father feasts Jangams and kinspeople. The boy's father gives the girl a rich robe and the girl's father gives the boy a dress. In the fifth month of her first pregnancy her mother gives the girl, a green robe and a green bodice, and her kinswomen make similar presents.(1) Puberty.

The marriage of widows was one of the points on which Basava insisted, and was probably one of the biggest bones of contention with the Bráhmans. Widow remarriage is allowed at the present day, but the authorities at Ujjini see fit to disregard it. They say that amongst Jangams it is prohibited and that amongst the other classes of Lingáyats it is the growth of custom. Divorce is permissible. The ordinary law of Hindus is followed in regard to inheritance. A special feature of Lingáyat life is the frequency of adoptions. Widow remarriage, divorce, inheritance.

The origin and original tenets of the faith have been discussed above. What follows is mainly an account of current beliefs and practices. The three main objects of reverence are the *linga*, the Jangam and the *guru*. The *linga* is the stone home of the deity, the Jangam is the human abode of the deity, and the *guru* is the teacher who breathes the sacred spell into the disciple's ear. The *linga* worn by Lingáyats is generally made of light-gray slate stone, and consists of two discs, each about three-fourths of an inch in diameter, the lower one about Religion.

(1) Bombay Gazetteer, Vol. xxiii, p. 235—6.

one-eighth of an inch thick, the upper slightly thicker, and is separated from the lower by a deep groove about an eighth of an inch broad. From its centre, which is slightly rounded, rises a pea-like knob about a quarter of an inch long and broad, giving the stone *linga* a total height of nearly three-quarters of an inch. This knob is called the *bán* or arrow. The upper disc is called *jalhári*, that is, the water carrier, because this part of a full-sized *linga* is grooved to carry off the water which is poured over the central knob. It is also called *pith*, that is, the seat and *pithak* the little seat. Over the *linga*, to keep it from harm, is plastered a black mixture of clay, cowdung ashes, and marking-nut juice. This coating, which is called *kanthi*, or the covering, entirely hides the shape of the enclosed *linga*. It forms a smooth black slightly truncated cone, not unlike a dark betelnut, about three-quarters of an inch high and narrowing from three-quarters of an inch at the base to half an inch across the top. The stone of which the *linga* is made comes from Parvatgiri in North Arkot. It is brought by a class of people called Kambi Jangams, because, besides the *linga* stone, they bring slung from a shoulder-bamboo (*kambi*) the holy water of the Pátál-Ganga, a pool on Parvatgiri, whose water Lingáyats hold as sacred as Bráhmanical Hindus hold the water of the Ganges. A *linga* should be tied to the arm of a pregnant woman in the eighth month of pregnancy and to the arm of a child as soon as it is born. This rule is not strictly kept. The *linga* is sometimes tied on the fifth day but generally not till a day between a fortnight or three weeks after birth. A child's *linga* has generally no case or *kanthi*; the *kanthi* is sometimes not added for months, sometimes not for years. The *linga* is sometimes tied to the cradle in which the child sleeps, instead of to the child. It is rarely allowed to remain on the child till the child is five or six years old. Till then it is generally kept in the house shrine along with the house gods. The *linga* is worn either on the wrist, the arm, the neck, or the head. Some wear the *linga* slung from the left shoulder like a sacred thread and some carry it in the waistband of the lower garments. The last two ways are contrary to the rule that the *linga* should never be worn below the navel. It is worn either tied round by a ribbon or in a silver box fastened by a silver chain. Each family has generally a few spare *lingas* in stock. The *linga* is never shown to any one who does not wear a *linga* himself. It should be taken out three times a day, washed, rubbed with ashes and a string of *rudráksh* beads bound round it. A man or a woman keeps the same *linga* all through life, and, in the grave, it is taken out of its case and tied round the neck or arm of the corpse. If the *linga* is accidentally lost, the loser has to fast, give a caste dinner, go through the ceremony of *shuddhi* or cleansing, and receive a new *linga* from his *guru*. For the cleansing he bathes and washes a Virakt Jangam's feet, rubs cowdung ashes on his head, and bows before him. He sprinkles on his body the water in which the Jangam's feet were washed and sips a little of it along with the five cow-gifts. The Jangam places a new *linga* on his left palm, washes it with water, rubs cowdung ashes on it, lays a *bel* leaf on it, mutters some texts or *mantras* over it, and ties it round the neck of the worshipper. When a Jangam loses his *linga*, the case becomes serious, and many a Jangam is said to have lost his caste on account of losing his *linga*. The *guru* or religious teacher, the third watchword of the Lingáyat faith, is either a *Virakt* or celibate or a *Sámánya* (ordinary) Jangam. Their head teacher is the head of the monastery at Chitaldurg in North-West Mysore. Like other Hindu teachers, the head teacher during his life-time generally chooses a successor, who acts under his orders so long as he lives. The head teacher may belong to any of the higher classes of Lingáyats. He lives in celibacy in his monastery at Chitaldurg with great pomp, and receives divine honours from his followers. He goes on tour once every three or four years, receiving contributions, and in return giving his followers the water in which his feet are washed, which they rub on their eyes and drink. The ordinary *maths* or religious houses are under married or unmarried Jangams. When the head of a religious house is a celibate, or Virakt Jangam, he is succeeded by his pupil. These pupils remain unmarried and are the sons either of married clergy or of laymen, who, under a vow or for some other cause have, as children, been devoted to a religious house. Boys devoted to a religious house under a vow are called *maris* or youths. The *gurus* or teachers are of five kinds. The *guru* who ties on the *linga* is called the Dikshágugu (from *diksha* ceremonial purification). The *guru* who teaches religion is called the Shikshághuru (from *Shiksha* instruction), and the religious guide is called the Mokshguru (from *Moksha* absorbtion into the deity). The *guru* of the Mokshguru is called the Gurvinguru or the teacher of teachers and the highest priest is called the Paramguru or the chief teacher. According to tradition, Basava taught that there was only one God, namely Shiva. In practice, like their Bráhmanic neighbours, Lingáyats worship many gods. First among their gods comes Basava, Basvanna or Basvandev, the founder of their faith, whom they identify with Nandi or Mahádev's bull. They also worship Virbhadra and Ganpati, whom they consider the sons, and Ganga and Párvati, whom they consider the wives, of Shiva, and keep their images in their houses. Besides these members of Shiva's family they worship Yellamma* of Hampi in Bellari, and Saundatti in the Belgaum district, Malayya,† Mallikárjun, and Tulja Bhaváni‡ of Tuljápur in the Nizam's country.§ As a guardian against evil, that is against evil spirits, the great rival of the *linga* is the sun. Worship of the heavenly bodies was specially forbidden in the original faith. Shilvants and other strict Lingáyats veil their drinking water so that the sun may not see it; they say the sun is Brahma. But common Lingáyats worship the sun on new moon day, and the moon on full moon day. Again, according to the books, Basava removed fasts and feasts, penance and pilgrimage, rosaries and holy water, and reverence for cows. This change probably never passed beyond the sphere of books. At present Bombay Lingáyats all fast on *Shivrátra* or Shiva's Night on the dark thirteenth of *Mágh* (January-February), and on *Nágpanchmi* or the bright fifth of *Shrávan* (July-August) and follow their fasts by a feast. They keep partial fasts, that is, they take only one evening meal, on Mondays in *Shrávan* (July-August). They make pilgrimages to Gokarn and to Ulvi in Kanara where Basava died, to Sangameshvar, to Yellamma Hill in Belgaum, to Parvatgiri in North Arkot, to Hampi in Belláry, and to Tuljápur in the Nizam's country. Contrary to the rule forbidding the worship of the *Sthaviralingas* a few devout Lingáyats even visit the twelve Jyotirlingas at the famous shrines of Shiva in different parts of India. Many Jangams wear rosaries and tell their beads; the water in which a Jangam's feet have been washed is drunk as holy water or *tirth*, and Lingáyats show the cow as much reverence as Bráhmanic Hindus show her. As regards mediators, Basava's efforts to drive Bráhmans out of their place as mediators between men and god have been successful. No Lingáyats of the first two orders, except that they consult them as astrologers, ever employ or show respect to Bráhmans. But in practice the Jangam is as much a mediator to the Lingáyat as the Bráhman is a mediator to the Bráhmanic Hindu.

Lingáyats have two peculiar religious processions, the *Nandi-kodu* or Nandi's horn and the *Vyásantol* or Vyás' hand. The story

---

* The origin of Yellamma is obscure. She is now identified with Renuka, the mother of Parsurám. However, there is also a village godling, Yellavva or Yel-Makkaltai (mother of seven children, probably crop pests), represented by painted stones in fields (C. W. M. Hudson in Journ. Bomb. Anthro. Soc. vii, p. 110.)

† Presumably the same as Malikárjun who is a form of Shiva.

‡ A form of Párvati.

§ Lingáyats also worship the village goddess Durgavva and Dyamavva. The former is simply Párvati. The latter is said to have been a Bráhman girl who was seduced by and married a Holaya (one of the untouchable castes) and subsequently destroyed him on finding out the deception (Bombay Gaz., 1884, Vol. xxii, p. 807).

about Nandi's horn is that in a fight with a demon Nandi once lost a horn. His followers found his horn and carried it in procession. The horn is now a long bamboo pole wound round with strips of coloured cloth and the top is surmounted by a conical globe. About four and a half feet from each side of the pole a plank is fastened, and on each plank is set a brass bull. This is paraded chiefly in the month of *Shrávan* (July-August). *Vyásantol* or the hand of Vyás, the reputed author of the *Purâns*. is a hand made of rags which is tied to Nandi's horn, and is paraded in the streets. Though in theory the *linga* wearer is safe from evil spirits, Lingáyats are as much afraid of ghosts as other Hindus, and one of their five holy ashes is specially valued as a ghost scarer. When a person is possessed, his brow is marked with ashes from a censer placed before the house image of Virbhadra, or he is sometimes given charmed water to drink. They have also faith in soothsaying and astrology, and occasionally consult Bráhman astrologers to find the lucky time to hold marriage and other ceremonies.

Except in religious houses and when a priest is present, the different Lingáyat sub-divisions are socially as exclusive as the different Bráhmanical castes. Their feeling to the Mahárs, Mángs, and other castes deemed impure is in no way kinder or more generous than the Bráhman feeling. The theory that nothing can defile the wearer of the *linga* has toned down in practice. A coming of age and monthly sickness, a birth and a death are all believed to cause impurity, though, as among Jains, the impurity is much less thought of and is much more easily and quickly cleansed than among Bráhmanic Hindus. That the dead Lingáyat goes to Shiva's heaven seems to be a practical belief which has greatly reduced the rites to the dead, and probably the fear of spirits. Still in practice the *linga* has not been found to protect its wearers against all evil. Lingáyats consult astrologers, fear and get possessed by evil spirits, and employ knowing men to cast out spirits, lay ghosts, and counteract charms and spells. little if at all less freely than their neighbours among Bráhmanic Hindus. On the whole, Lingáyats are less fettered than Bráhmanic Hindus by ceremonial details and observances. They have fewer gods and have less fear of the dead, they perform no mind-rites—*Shráddha* and they allow the widows of laymen to marry. When you have said this, and said that they do not read Bráhmanic holy books, that they hate Bráhmans, that, when men meet instead of calling of Rám they say Sharnárthi that is Help Pray, and when you have added that they wear a *linga* and not a sacred-thread, that the men shave the topknot and do not shave the widow's head or the mourner's lip, you have about exhausted the difference between the two parties.(1)

It has been seen that the Lingáyats are believers in the god Shiva the third person of the Hindu trinity, signifying the creative and destructive forces in the universe. Thence they derive the phallus or *linga*, emblematic of reproduction, and the sacred bull, Nandi or Basava, found in all their temples, and in all probability the emblem of strength. The principal Lingáyat ceremony known as the *ashtavarna* or eightfold sacrament has been already referred to in some detail. The essentially Lingáyat beliefs and ceremonies, such as the wearing of the *linga*, the worship of the *jangam*, and the administration of *ashtavarna* rites are, however, as is usual in India, constantly mingled with many commonplace Hindu beliefs and customs. It is a common practice in India for Hindus to worship at the shrine of Musalmán *pirs* or saints, and in the same way Lingáyats will combine the worship of the special objects prescribed by Basava, with the worship of purely Hindu deities, such as Hanumán, Ganpati, Yellamma, Máruti and many others. The investigations hitherto conducted do not clearly show how far Lingáyat and Hindu rituals are liable to be combined; but it can be securely predicted that the lower orders of the community, who still keep in touch with the unconverted section of the caste to which, professionally speaking, they belong, will be found to adhere in many instances to the beliefs and customs of their unconverted fellow castemen, despite the teaching and influence of the Jangams.

Death ceremonies.

Lingáyats always bury their dead. They make no exception even in the case of a leper, or of a woman dying in child-birth. According to the Lingáyat theory, death is a cause of gladness, the dead has changed the cares of life for the joys of *kailás* the heaven of Shiva. When a Lingáyat dies and the few rites are performed he is believed by the people to go straight to heaven. It is well with the dead, and the Lingáyats are less nervous about the dead walking and coming to worry the living than most Bráhmanic Hindus. Still, the loss to the living remains. A Lingáyat death scene is a curious mixture. The Jangams feast with merry music, the widow and children mourn and bewail the dead. When fatal symptoms set in, a *mathadayya* or head of a monastery is called. When he comes, the dying person gives him ashes and a packet of betel leaves and nuts and says: I go to become one with your lotus-like feet. When the dying man has breathed his last wish, the Jangam whispers a text or *mantra* into his right ear, and

(1) Bombay Gazetteer, Vol. xxiii, pp. 225—9.

those who stand round say: His soul is cleansed. When all is over the body is bathed and set on the verandah (*katta* or *sopa*), and the brow is rubbed with cowdung ashes. In front of the body a Jangam sits reading passages out of the Lingáyat scriptures to help the soul in its flight to heaven. A feast is made ready in the inner room and the Jangams go in and eat. Before sitting, each Jangam sets his right foot on the dead head. When the feast is over the Jangams are given money and clothes. The body is dressed in fine clothes and ornaments and flowers are tucked in the head dress. The body is set in a *vimán* or gaily canopied chair and sprinkled with powder and betel leaves. The beadle takes a cloth, tears it in two, keeps one half and lays the other half on the dead face, and seats himself in front of the chair and and rings a bell. Properly on the day of the death, but sometimes not until two or three days have passed, the chair is carried to the grave. The chair is carried by any four castemen, and the procession is headed by a band of music. The poor, though contrary to rule, sometimes carry the dead on a bier. While the Jangam's feast goes on in the house of death, the length of the dead man's foot is taken and the grave is dug. The grave is of two kinds, a married person's grave and a celibate's grave. The grave is nine of the dead man's feet long and five of the dead man's feet broad. It is entered by three steps, the first step one foot wide and one foot deep, the second step two feet wide and two feet deep, the third step three feet wide and three feet deep. At the bottom of the grave is raised an altar one foot high and three feet broad. In the side of the grave, facing either east or north, a five-cornered niche is cut, each of the three sides measuring three feet and each of the two sides measuring one and a half feet. On either side of the large niche is a small niche one foot across, for keeping lamps. Such a grave is called *gomukh samádhi* or the cow-mouth grave, and is used for married men. A celibate's grave is called *shikhar samádhi* or the peak grave. The celibate's grave has three steps equal in breadth and depth to those of a married man's grave, but of unequal length. The first is one foot long, the second two feet, and the third three feet. When the funeral party come to the grave the body is stripped of its rich clothes and ornaments, which are either given to a Jangam or kept by the mourners. It is carried into the grave by two kinsmen and seated crosslegged on the central altar. The body is generally bare except for a loincloth and a face cloth. Sometimes it is shrouded in a sack. In either case the *linga* is taken out of its silver cover. The cover is given to a Jangam and the *linga* is tied either round the neck or round the upper right arm of the body. The large niche is partly filled with ashes and faded *bel* leaves and flowers that have been offered to Shiva, and the body is set in the niche, and the niche filled with cow-dung ashes and fresh *bel* leaves. The grave is then filled with earth. On the grave the beadle lays a stone, and on the stone the Jangam stands and the chief mourner washes his feet, lays *bel* leaves on them and gives him and the beadle each five copper coins. Sometimes the beadle washes the Sámánya Jangam's feet, lays *bel* leaves on them, and gives him five copper coins. Alms are distributed to all Jangams and poor people who are present. Those who have been at the funeral go home and bathe. After they have bathed, the mourners wash their teacher's feet and purify themselves by drinking the water in which his feet are washed. Strictly speaking, Lingáyat funeral rites end with the purifying of the mourners. In practice the rich, for five days after the funeral, daily send for a Jangam, wash his feet, and drink the water; and do not eat wheaten bread or sugar. On the eleventh day friends are feasted. Nothing is taken to the grave and there is no yearly mind feast (1).

Lingáyats are bound together by a strong religious * feeling. Social disputes are settled by the castemen in the presence of eight office bearers, namely, the *mathadayya* or monastery head, the *ganachári* or monastery manager, the *mathpati* or Lingáyat beadle, and representatives of each of the five *gotras*. In social disputes final appeals are made to the four lion-thrones or *simhásans*, the north throne at Ujjain in Málwa, the east throne at Shri Shail in North Arkot, the south throne at Balhali in Belláry, and the west throne at Kolhápur. The fifth throne which is filled by the childless Virakt, is known as the *shunya* or empty throne.* Appeals to the four thrones are rare.

Occupation.

The Jangams live by begging and on the offerings of the people; the Bánjigs and Shilvants are shopkeepers and money-lenders, and most of the Panchamsális are husbandmen. Lingáyats seldom entered the army or the police before the war, when a double company was founded and attached to the 105th Mahrattas at Belgaum Depot. Previously not many were in Government service as clerks, but that is probably because they find agriculture, shopkeeping and money-lending pay better than clerkship. Of late more high class Lingáyat youths have been entering Government service.

---

(1) Bombay Gazetteer, Vol. xxiii, pp. 236—8.

* Here again the constant harping on the number five. The *Sinhasans* are given by Artal (op. cit. p. 209) as "Rambhapuri (Balehalli), Ujainpuri, Shri Shaila Parvat Himavat Kedar and Kollipaki (Kashi)." The last is of course Benares.

Lingáyats are strict vegetarians, the staple food being Indian or spiked millet, pulse, vegetables, onions, garlic, condiments, milk curds, and clarified butter, rice replacing the millets in the Mallád. As regards eating, a member of any one of the main divisions will eat in the house of any member of his own or of any higher division. None of the divisions below the Jangam eat in the house of any member of an inferior division. But in a field, in a rest house, or in any place except the host's house, so long as the host has used a new set of earthern cooking vessels, they will eat food cooked by the host even though he is of an inferior division. In a *math* or religious house any Lingáyat without question will eat bread which a Jangam has gathered in his begging. If the Jangam has brought it, it is all right, if cooked by any *linga* wearer. Though the rule is that a member of a lower division is allowed to eat with members of higher divisions in a religious house when a Jangam is present, this privilege is not granted to all classes who profess Lingáyatism, but only to the higher of them. In the same way there is no objection to any *Linga*-wearing man coming into a Lingáyat's house and seeing the food; but if a Musalmán, or a Marátha or anyone without a *linga* sees the food it must be thrown away. This rule applies only to food in one's own house; it does not apply to food in the field or in the rest-house. Food.

It will be gathered from the foregoing sketch of the origin and present day social organization and customs of the Lingáyats that the community is virtually an original casteless sect in process of reversion to a congeries of castes holding a common religion. It has been held that, in the 11th century, a movement was set on foot by Lakulisa, and spread abroad later by two Bráhmans, Basava and Rámayya, devotees of Shiva, to abolish the ceremonies and restrictions that fettered the intercourse between the different ranks of orthodox Hindu society of the period, and to establish a community on a basis of the equality of its members irrespective of sex, by means of the purifying worship of the one god Shiva. It seems clear that the movement found special favour in the eyes of the Jain traders of the period, who would have ranked as Vaishyas, below both Bráhman priest and Kshatriya warrior under the Hindu scheme of social precedence. The community encountered the hostility of Jains who remained unconverted, but clung tenaciously to its simple faith on the worship of Shiva and in his emblem the *linga*. We must assume the probability that the Bráhman converts, of whose existence we possess historical evidence, tended by degrees to assert for themselves social precedence as Ayyás or Jangams, *i.e.*, the priests of the community, for which position their knowledge General remarks.

and descent would give them special fitness. In time, indeed, they came to be regarded as the very incarnations of the god Shiva, and thus they were holy, imparting holiness, in a special degree to the water in which they had bathed their feet, known as *tirth,* so that it plays a prominent part to this day in the Lingáyat ceremonies. Once the original notion of universal equality of rank had yielded to the priest a precedence incompatible with such equality, the way was prepared for the introduction of further social gradations, and the older members of the community commenced to claim over the later converts a precedence modelled on that which the priests had established against them. In such manner the essential doctrine of equality became completely undermined, and in the end gave place to certain rites and ceremonies as the test of Lingáyat orthodoxy. Thus, when the more recent cases of caste conversion occurred, a section of a Hindu caste became Lingáyat, not as the founders of the religion would have wished, by being admitted to a footing of equality on the common ground of the worship of Shiva and of his emblem the *linga,* but by investiture through certain rites and ceremonies with the *linga*, retaining their distinctive social status as a functional caste with which other Lingáyats would neither marry or dine. It must be admitted that in case of most of the Lingáyat sub-divisions the Jangam will take food in the house of the members. But here all trace of the original equality ceases ; and the Lingáyats of to-day present the curious and interesting spectacle of a religious sect broken into course of centuries into social fragments, of which the older sections remain essentially sectarian, and the more recent in origin possess the typical attributes of ordinary Hindu castes. As in the case of Christianity in some parts of India, the social barriers of caste have proved too strong for the communal basis of the orthodox religion.

ADIBANJIGS, also called Arebánjigs, or Adbanjigs derive their name from *ádi* first and Banjigs, (*see* below), meaning the first trading Lingáyats. They are Panchamsáli Lingáyats with the *ashtavarna* rites. Their main calling is to trade in grain, cotton and other articles and to retail opium, hemp-flowers or *gánja* and hemp-water or *bháng*. In the Bijápur district they hold a few village headships.

BANJIGS from one of the largest of the sub-divisions of Lingáyats. They derive their name from the Sanskrit *vanik* a trader, and are mostly traders, dealing in grain, spices, salt, oil, butter and molasses or sugar. They are also cloth-sellers, bankers, money-lenders brokers and husbandmen. They are Panchamsáli Lingáyats with the *ashtavarna* rites. They have five main divisions :—

(1) Shilvant or Chilmi-agni.

(2) Athnikar or Holiáchibalki.

(3) Dhulpávad.

(4) Chalgeribalki.

(5) Lokabalki.

Shilvants, meaning pure, are called Chilmi-agnis because they put a cloth over their water-pot when carrying it home. Holiáchibalkis derive their name from the Kanarese *holi* river and *achi* beyond and are commonly found in the towns south of the Krishna. Like the Shilvants, they put clothes over their water pots when carrying them home. Dhulpávads from the Sanskrit *dhuli* dust and *pád* foot, are so called, because they sprinkle their clothes with dust off a Jangam's feet. Chalgeribalkis derive their name from the Kanarese *chalgeri* village and *balki* people, their main occupation being husbandry. Lokabalki or Lokavant means of the people.

BASAVIS (1) or Lingáyat women devotees derive their name from Basava, whose devotees they chiefly are. They wear a silver *linga* box hanging from the neck and rub themselves with white cowdung ashes or *vibhuti*. Their main calling is to attend caste meetings and marriage and other ceremonies, to help women in performing religious rites, and to wave lighted lamps round the bride and bridegroom. But most of them act as courtezans.

CHATTERS are non-Panchamsáli Lingáyats entitled to the *ashtavarna* rites. They seem to be a branch of the Nágliks, though now they have no connection with the latter. They make and sell bodice clothes and also cultivate land.

JANGAMS, literally "moving," the Jangam being considered a human abode of the *linga*, are divided into *Virakts* or celibates, *Sámányas* or common Jangams, *Ganácháris* or managers and *Mathpatis* or beadles. *Virakts*, the highest class of Jangams, dedicate themselves to celibacy, and are not allowed to celebrate marriages. They are a comparatively small body and move about the country accompanied by their disciples. They stop at *maths* or religious houses, live on the offerings of the sect, let the hair and beard grow, and wear no

(1) As mentioned above only 7 persons returned as of this sub-caste in the 1901 Census. But this is almost certainly incorrect. Basavis probably return themselves by some other name.

cloth but the loincloth, a cap on their heads with a string of *rudráksh* beads in it, and a long salmon-coloured coat falling to the ankles. They never intentionally look on the face of a woman. The *Sámánya* Jangam is the ordinary Jangam, who has had the *aitán* or initiation performed on him. He is a married man, who conducts marriages, begs, serves in a temple or lives by agriculture. When a Jangam goes begging he wears a garter of bells called *jang* below his right knee, and carries a cobra cane or *nágbet* staff. Besides the regular *Sámányas* five classes of Jangam live by begging. The first of these is the *Kugimmaritandegalu,* who sits on a tree and rings a bell all day long; the second is the *Paháredkáyakdavru,* who begs from door to door, ringing a bell; the third is the *Mullaháyigekávyakdavru,* who, in the presence of Lingáyats, stands on a pair of wooden shoes, in whose soles are nails with their points up, and does not come out of the shoes till he is paid whatever sum he is pleased to ask; the fourth is the *Tekkikáyakdavru,* who throws his arms round men and does not leave hold until he is paid something; the fifth is the *Mukakáyak* that is the silent, who feigns dumbness. *Mathpatis* or beadles and *Ganácháris* or managers are Jangams who hold rent-free lands, and are considered rather inferior to the regular or *Sámánya* Jangams. They have not undergone the *aitán* or initiation. They sometimes marry with one another, but regular Jangams do not marry with them Their duties are humble. The *Mathpati* brings for the Lingáyats *bel* (*Aegle marmelos*) leaves on Mondays, Thursdays and holidays, and the *Ganáchári* celebrates widow marriages, an office which the *Sámánya* Jangam refuses. To these functions the *Mathpati* adds the office of corpse dresser, and the *Ganáchári* the duties of a messenger who makes known the wishes of the Virakt, the head of the religious house. If a *Ganáchári* or *Mathpati* boy has the initiation or *aitán* performed on him he becomes a *Sámánya* Jangam and abandons his former duties. Jangams eat not only in the house of any member of the Lingáyat sect, but in the house of any *linga*-wearing member of any other caste, except Lingáyat Chalvádis or Mahárs.

MALLAVAS are a Lingáyat caste found in Belgaum, Dhárwár and the Kanara districts. The name Mallava is by some derived from *malnád,* meaning hilly country, where the Mallavas are said to have formerly resided. Other Lingáyats allege that they were called Mallavas or dirty people, because they did not adhere strictly to the rules of the Lingáyat religion. The Mallavas, on the other hand, style themselves Virshaiva Kshatriyas, basing their claim to be twice-born warriors on the position that they formerly occupied at Sonda [(1)],

(1) Bombay Gazetteer, Vol. xv, part II, p. 120. In the genealogical tree of the Sonda chiefs are found the pure Lingáyat names Basawalinga Raja and Madholinga.

Bilgi and Ikkeri, whose chiefs were of the Mallava caste. Buchanan describes how the ruling family at Kilidi, which afterwards moved to Ikkeri and Bednur, were originally the heads of five or six villages near Kilidi, and were of the Mallava caste.(1) One of them, Bhadracondi, entered the service of Krishnaráya of Vijayanagar, and assumed the title of Sadáshiva Náik. Evidence seems to show that the Mallavas were originally Jains, and were converted to Lingáyatism in the 14th and 15th century. They will still admit Jains into their caste,or at least did so until quite recent times.

There are five endogamous divisions of the caste who eat together, but do not intermarry. They are :—

1. Muskin Mallava.
2. Nir Mallava.
3. Balsad Mallava.
4. Kodag or Coorg Mallava.
5. Bandi or Gaudi Santán.

Of these, the Balsad and Coorg Mallavas are not found in this Presidency. The Muskin Mallavas take their name from the Kanarese *Mushik*, a cover or veil, the name having apparently originated in the custom of their women covering their faces like Musalmáns. Another custom peculiar to this division is that women must carry water on the waist, and not on the head. The violation of this rule is punished with excommunication. The Nir Mallavas (Kanarese *niru*, water) are so named because they cover their water-pots with a cloth when bringing water from a well. The Bandi or Gaudi Santán Mallavas are the offspring of Mallava widows and women who have gone astray, the division thus corresponding to the Kadu or bastard divisions of other castes. Of the three divisions of the Mallavas found in the Presidency, the Muskins are the social superiors of the other two.

The Mallavas claim the five usual *gotras* of the Lingáyats, *viz.*, Nandi, Skanda, Vir, Bringi and Vrisha; but it is doubtful whether marriage is in any way affected by *gotras* so named. They have certain exogamous divisions named after the god worshipped by the section, such as—

Basava	Ishvar	Togarsi Mallappa
Gudda	Mailar	Virbhadra
Gutti	Nandi.	

(1) Buchanan's Mysore, III pp. 253-54.

of which the Gutti section is looked on as inferior, and marriage is not favoured with members of this section.

Mallavas are non-Panchamsáli Lingáyats entitled to the *ashtavarna* rites. Their priests are Jangams, but Bráhmans are also called in Dhárwár. They worship Shiva, Párvati, Ganpati, Basava and their *guru* or spiritual guide. Offerings of goats and fowls are made to Mariái through the medium of other persons. Bhutapa, Huliapa, Chawdi, Birupa, Jebapa are the powers, they think, that protect their farms. They are stones which are worshipped. Annually offerings of rice, plantains and even of food and of goats are made.

Most of the Mallavas are land-holders and *pátils* or village headmen. They own rice and sugarcane fields and betelnut gardens. None of them work as day labourers. Some are traders.

SAIBS are a class of Lingáyat courtezans, though nearly half described themelves as Hindus at the Census of 1901, and appear to have come from Gulburga in the Nizam's Dominions where some of their caste are still settled. The name is held by some to be a corruption of *Sáhib* and is the Hindustáni equivalent of *Náikin*, the local term for courtezans. But a more probable derivation is *Shaiva*, the letters V and B being interchangeable. They still eat and intermarry with the Saibs of Gulburga. Like Kalávants and other classes of courtezans, they recruit from all Hindu castes except the impure classes. Their surnames are Bhikshada and Parivarda. Families bearing the same surname do not intermarry. Good looking girls become prostitutes, the less favoured girls marry. Girls who are to become courtezans, when between 8 and 12 years old, are invested with anklets of small brass bells called *gage*. They are non-Panchamsáli Lingáyats entitled to the *ashtavarna* rites. Their religious teacher is the head of the Chitaldurg monastery.

The following occupations explain the nature of many of the subcastes shown on pp. 354-355 :—

Agasa	..Washermen.
Ambig	..Fishermen and ferrymen.
Badig	..Carpenters.
Baligar	..Copper and brass smiths.
Burud or Medar	..Mat and basket makers and bamboo splitters.
Chalvádi or Holaya	..Village watchmen and menials.
Dás or Deodás	..Religious beggars.
Dhor	..Tanners.

Ganiger	..Oil-pressers.
Gauli	..Milkmen.
Gavandi or Uppár	..Masons.
Handevant	..Husbandmen.
Helav	..Beggars.
Hugar, Jeer, Gurav, Malgár or Totigar.	Temple ministrants, musicians, flower sellers.
Ilgar or Kalál	..Distillers and liquor sellers.
Jád, Nayakár, Koshti or Sáli	..Weavers.
Kabbaligar	..Fishermen, boatmen, palanquin bearers.
Káchári	..Glass bangle-makers.
Kalávant	..Dancers and singers.
Kammár	..Blacksmiths.
Kudavakkal	..Husbandmen.
Kumbhár	..Potters.
Kuruba or Dhangar	..Shepherds and wool weavers.
Kursáli	..Weavers.
Lálgonda	..Cultivators.
Nadig or Nhávi	..Barbers.
Náglik or Bangar	..Cotton thread dyers.
Nilgar	..Dyers.
Raddi	..Husbandmen.
Sada	..Cultivators.
Samgár Jingar or Chamár	..Leather workers.
Shiva-Shimpig	..Tailors.
Sungar or Chunár	..Masons.
Támboli	..Betel-leaf sellers.
Tilári or Tiráli	..Husbandmen.

LINGAWANT.—A synonym for Lingáyat.

LODHAS or Lodhis, numbering 1,585 (1901), including 802 males and 783 females, are found principally in Ahmedabad, Káthiáwár and Pálanpur. A few families are found in other districts of Gujarát, and they have even penetrated in small numbers to the Deccan and Southern Marátha Country. The caste is well known in the Central and United Provinces. It has traditional connection with Ludhiana in the Punjab, and has been settled for a long time in Bundelkhand. From the extent to which the caste has assimilated local customs it seems probable that it came into Gujarát and Káthiawár

Name and origin.

in the time of the Mughal Emperors, or possibly earlier. Like their fellows in Lalitpur of the United Provinces, they claim the title of Thákur.l Hindustáni is still their home tongue. They are agricultura labourers.

Endogamous divisions. The caste contains numerous endogamous divisions, of which two, Jaria and Patariha, apparently are common to them and to the main body of the caste, while Junágadhi is named after the State of Junágadh in Káthiáwár.

Marriage ceremonies. Marriages are prohibited within five or six degrees of relationship. Marriage with the wife's sister after the death of the former is allowed, and two brothers are allowed to marry two sisters. Polygamy is allowed and practised, but polyandry is unknown. Girls are married before they come of age. There is no restriction of age in the case of boys. The offer of marriage comes from either side. Amongst the Gujarát Lodhás, the boy's father has to pay a sum of Rs. 50 to the girl's father as *stridhan* (woman's property). The day for the marriage is fixed by an astrologer. The ceremony is conducted by the caste priest. The *devak* or marriage guardian of the Gujarát Lodhás is a cobra, a picture of which is drawn on a low wooden stool and worshipped on the day before the marriage. The other ceremonies are as follows :—

1. *Viváha karvo* or the betrothal.—In which the marriage declaration is made in the presence of castemen and sugar is distributed.

2. *Sarbat pivun* (drinking syrup).—In which the girl is made to worship Ganpati, and marriage invitatoin cards are exchanged by the fathers of the boy and the girl, after which they drink water sweetened with molasses.

3. *Mandap muhurta.*—In which a *mandap* or marriage porch is erected and a bamboo post, to which are tied a bough of *shami* (Prosopis spicigera), a turmeric root, and an iron ring, is planted in the booth.

4. *Darechi.*—A white stick about one and a quarter yards in length and a wheat stalk are kept standing against a wall; and the priest, smearing the palm of his right hand with red powder, presses it on the wall over the top of the stick.

5. *Pithi cholvi.*—The rubbing the boy and girl with turmeric paste.

6. *Varát.*—The procession of the bridegroom.

7. *Lagna sádhana* or the marriage proper.—This does not differ from the standard marriage ceremony of the lower castes of Gujarát, the essential portion being *mangalphero* or walking round the sacrificial fire.

The marriage ceremonies of the Deccan Lodhás differ greatly from those of the Gujarat Lodhás. Their *devak* or marriage guardian consists of five pinches of earth picked from five places, which they bring home and place near the house gods. This ceremony seems to have been adopted by imitation from the neighbouring castes in the Deccan. On the marriage day the boy is rubbed with turmeric paste by his sister. Next, the boy's sister goes to the girl's house and rubs the girl with turmeric, and the boy's and girl's relations dine together. The girl's father presents the boy's sister and his own daughter with a robe and bodice, and they return to their houses. The boy's maternal uncle gives a dinner at the boy's house. The uncle comes leading a bullock with a bag of rice on its back, twenty-five earthen jars and two flower-pots. Red powder is rubbed on the bullock's brow and garlands are hung from its neck. One of the party walks into the house carrying the grain bag, followed by another who sprinkles water after him as he walks. The bag is laid in front of the house gods. The boy's father plants a *palas* (Butea frondosa) branch about three feet long in his own marriage porch and another in the girl's marriage porch. He cuts four holes in each branch, fixes a ladle or *pali* in each hole, and fills the ladles with oil and lights them. The twenty-five earthen jars are piled near the house gods. The boy is dressed in new clothes and a marriage coronet or *báshing*, he is seated on a horse, and taken in procession to the girl's. When the bridegroom reaches the bride's house, the girl's sister takes the girl in her arms and makes her throw five balls of rice and molasses at the boy's marriage coronet. The boy is taken off the horse, and the girl's father touches his brow with red powder and presents him with a new waistcloth and turban. Each of the boy's near male relations is presented with a waistcloth, and the boy is taken and seated in a neighbouring house on a cot, the other guests on a blanket round him. A dish of vermicelli or *shevaya* is brought for the boy, but it is all eaten by other children, the boy getting none of it. The girl's brother's wife comes with a wooden pestle, and asks the boy to help her in pounding rice. The boy touches the pestle, and the girl's brother's wife stands with the pestle, repeating a song. When the boys have done eating the vermicelli the bridegroom puts one anna into the dish, and, except the boy and girl, all eat and take a nap. At daybreak the five ladles in the *palas* branch are lighted and five earthen jars are placed near them, one of which is filled with cold water. In front of the jars the priest traces a square made with lines of wheat flour and red and yellow powder, and the boy and the girl sit on the square close to each other, the girl to the right of the boy. Then the boy's relations present the boy with clothes and money. This is called giving away of the bride, or *kanyádán*. The boy and girl go six times round the *palas* branch, and stopping, ask the guests if they should take the last or seventh turn. The guests say 'Take the turn,' and as soon as the turn is completed the priest utters the word *sávadhán*, or beware, and the boy and the girl are husband and wife. In the evening a feast is held. After the feast the boys goes to his house with the girl in a palanquin, himself walking on foot with the guests. When they reach the boy's house, curds and cooked rice are waved round their heads and the boy's father presents them with a couple of rupees, rice is piled in a heap, and the boy kicks the heap five times with his right foot. On the following day the marriage festivities end with a feast at the boy's house.

The remarriage of widows is permitted. The Gujárat Lodhás follow the custom of a widow marrying a brother of the deceased husband. Should a bachelor desire to marry a widow he is first married to a *shami* tree (Prosopis spicigera). Divorce is not permitted.

Amongst the Gujarát Lodhás the sons inherit the property of the father. If there is no son, the property is inherited by daughters. In the absence of both, it is inherited by nephews. And in the absence of all, it goes to the caste.

Religion. The Lodhás are Hindus of the Vaishnava sect. But their family deities are the *mátás* or goddesses. The family goddess of most of the Deccan Lodhás is the Bhaváni of Tuljápur. They observe all the Hindu holidays and make pilgrimages to all the sacred places of the Hindus. Musalmán saints are venerated. The Gujarát Lodhás offer a goat to *Devi* by cutting one of its ears and setting it at liberty near her temple, on the seventh day of the latter half of *Bhádrapad*. Goats and fowls are also offered to goddesses when an epidemic breaks out. Their priests are Upper India Bráhmans. The religious teachers of the Gujárat Lodhás are the *Achâryas* of the Rámánandi sect.

The dead are burnt. The ordinary funeral rites are observed. The *shráddha* and *mahálaya* are performed for the propitiation of the deceased ancestors.

The Lodhás earn their livelihood as cart drivers, thatchers, money-lenders, fuel-sellers, husbandmen and day labourers.

They eat fish and the flesh of goats and sheep and drink liquor. Food.

LODHI.—A synonym for Lodha.

LODHI ALKARI.—A sub-division of Alkaris.

LOHAGAR.—A sub-division of Kabbaligars.

LOHANAS, Lavánás or Luvánás, numbering 562,261 (1901), including 296,754 males and 265,507 females, are found principally in Sind, Gujarát and Cutch. "They are also found in the Punjáb, Baluchistán, Afghánistán, the eastern parts of Central Asia, and on the Arabian coast, amongst a barbarous and hostile people enduring all kinds of hardship and braving no little danger in pursuit of wealth".* They are also known as Vaishes, Vániyás or Baniás and Bháibunds in Sind. The more educated among them are generally called Amils in Sind. The term Lohána is said by some to come from Lava, son of Rám, the well-known hero of the Rámáyan, from whom Lohánás claim descent. There is another tradition regarding the origin of the term, which is as follows. Name and origin.

The sub-division of Kshatriyas known by the name of Ráthors were by reason of relentless persecution obliged to take up arms against Jaichand, Rája of Kanauj; being conscious of their weakness, they prayed to god Varuna and invoked his blessings. God Varuna, being pleased with their devotion, granted their prayer and spoke to them thus :—

> "Early tomorrow morning at a distance of a *kos* and quarter you will see a big iron fort. Go and take shelter inside it and after sixteen days you will subdue your enemy. After that time, leave the fort, which will disappear after twenty-one days. Then build another fort and tower and settle there and you will thenceforth be called Lohánás instead of Ráthors."

The prophecy was fulfilled in every detail. After the defeat of Jaichand the Ráthors built a tower on the site of the battlefield and called it Lohgarh (afterwards Láhor), and the Ráthors who lived there became known as Lohánás (belonging to the iron fort).

Lohánás probably belong to the Lohánis who formerly held the country between the Sulaimán hills and the Indus.† Mr. Beal identi-

* Burton's Sind, 314.

† Beal's Travels of Fa Hian (A. D. 400).

fies the Lohánás with the Lohas of the Hindus and the Loi of the Chinese. They are probably the same as Lamánis, the great tribe of carriers, as held by the late Mr. A. M. T. Jackson (*see* LAMANI). Their original home appears to be Lohokat in Multán in the Punjáb, whence they were driven by the Musalmáns into Sind, and afterwards, about the thirteenth century they migrated to Cutch.*

Exogamous divisions.

Lohánás have a number of exogamous divisions called *nukhs*, the chief of which are as follows :—

Ad Thakar.
Adora.
Aiya.
And Kath.
Anuda or Adhiya.
Asar Pota.
Atha.
Bat.
Bhagde.
Kotecha.
Mahidhar.
Mamotia.
Manak.
Mangeya.
Manikram.
Manda.
Nainsonaya.
Naram.
Bhajaj.
Bhala.
Bhinde.
Chanabhata.
Chanaran or Chug.
Chande Bhamar.
Chande or Chandam.
Chandeya or Chandebar.
Chandi Bhambhor.
Chhabriya.
Chhata or Chhabria.
Cholera.
Daiya.
Dauda.
Daudiya.
Dhabaum.
Dhadhu.
Dhaun.
Gandha.
Hidocha.
Hurmatia.
Joban Potra.
Kakada.
Kanabar.
Kariya.
Kesarya.
Kath.
Katra.
Kemtak.
Khakhar.
Pallan.
Pancham Ganetre.
Pandh.
Pandit.
Pandit Potra.
Pau.
Phulbandhwa.
Ponda.
Popat.
Ra (Kundhaliya).
Ravasiya or Ratandhaira.
Ruparel.
Sachdev.
Saja.
Saota.
Sejpar.
Sodha.
Som Pallan.
Somaiya.
Someshwar.
Sonagal.
Sonagela.
Sonaiya.
Soneta or Soneja.
Sonpar.
Sota.
Swar.
Talariya or Tola.
Thakra or Thakral.
Yaduwa.

Marriages are prohibited between members belonging to the same *nukh* and within five or six degrees of relationship on the mother's side. In Sind, the Amils take daughters from non-Amil Lohánás but do not give eirth daughters to them in marriage. A few instances are however known in which Amils have given their daughters to non-Amils on account of poverty. Among Gujarát Lohánás marriage is generally infant, in Sind it is adult. Polygamy is permissible, but polyandry is unknown. The remarriage of widows is permitted, though it is looked upon with disfavour by the higher sections of the

* Ind. Ant. V. 171.

community. A widow cannot marry a member of her deceased husband's or father's section nor can she marry either a bachelor or any resident of her deceased husband's village. In Sind, marriage with a deceased husband's brother is common, though it is not compulsory. Divorce is strictly prohibited.

Marriage ceremonies.

The marriage and other ceremonies of Lohánás are similar to those of Bhátiás. In Gujarát, the widow remarriage ceremony consists in the bridal pair looking at each other's face in an earthen pot containing water with a ghi-fed lamp kept burning in the pot. The widow also puts on new *chuda* bangles. In Cutch the ceremony consists in the widow filling a water pot from a well, tank or river in her new husband's village and going to his house with this water pot. In Sind, the ceremony is performed in a secluded spot outside the village. A virgin girl ties the ends of the couple's garments into a knot and sets fire to a *buto* or shrub. The couple walk three times round the shrub, thus completing the ceremony.

Religion.

Lohánás are Hindus of the Vallábhácharya, Swáminárayan, Devi and Daryápanthi sects. Most of the Sind Lohánás are followers of Guru Nának, the founder of the Sikh religion. Their family goddess is Randel Máta and they are devout worshippers of Darya Pir, the spirit of the Indus, who is said to have saved them when they fled from Multán. In Gujarát, every Lohána village has a place built in honour of this Pir, where a lamp fed with clarified butter is kept burning day and night, and where in the month of *Chaitra* a festival is celebrated. The Cutch Lohánás worship by preference Rám, being the father of Lava, from whom they claim descent. The priests of Gujarát Lohánás are the Gujarát Sárasvat Bráhmans, who are not received on terms of equality by other good Bráhmans as they eat with Lohánás. The priests of Sind Lohánás are the Sindi Sárasvat Bráhmans, who are not lowered in social estimation although they eat with their patrons, as the restrictions on eating with other castes are not so rigid in Sind as in Gujarát.

Occupation.

Lohánás believe that they were originally soldiers and statesmen and that when their power declined they took to trade and other callings. They are now bankers, merchants, grain dealers, shopkeepers, Government servants, agriculturists and labourers. Of the Sind Lohánás, Burton says, "Uncommonly acute in business, some have made large fortunes in foreign lands. In Afghánistán they are patient and persevering, little likely to start new ventures, cautious and perhaps a trifle apathetic."*

*Burton's Sind, 316-317.

Food. Those of the Gujarát Lohánás who are Vaishnavs do not eat flesh or drink liquor. Others eat the flesh of goats and sheep only and have no objection to taking wine, though in Cutch these practices have, recently been prohibited. The Sind Lohánás also eat the flesh of the deer, antelope, partridge, *talur* (Hoobara bustard) and *acli* (a water-fowl). They eat both *pakki* and *kachhi*, drink and smoke with Sonárs and Wánhans whom they consider as their social inferiors, and with Sárasvat Bráhmans, the highest well-known caste in Sind. According to one report the Sind, Lohánás admit outsiders into their caste provided they are not Bháts, Bhogris, Sonárs, Ods, Jájáks and other low caste men.

Name and origin. **LOHARS** (Luhars) or Blacksmiths, from the Sanskrit *lohakár* worker in iron, numbering 115,622 (1901), including 59,126 males and 56,496 females, are found in all parts of the Presidency. They have the following endogamous divisions :—

1. Gujaráti.
2. Kanada Lohárs or Kamárs.
3. Konkani.
4. Marátha.
5. Pánchál.

They are described below under Marátha, Konkáni, Kanada and Gujarát Lohárs.

The caste is known as Lohárs in the Maráthi-speaking districts, Lohárs or Luhárs in Gujarát, and Lohárs or Kamárs in the Kanarese districts. Though the Marátha, Gujarát and Kanada or Kanarese Lohárs follow the same occupation, they are three distinct castes, speaking a different language and neither eating nor marrying with one another. Besides these three, there are two more divisions closely allied to the Marátha Lohárs, (1) Konkanis, or those residing in the Konkan and (2) Pánchháls, a class of Marátha Lohárs claiming a superior status.

Occupation. The hereditary occupation of Lohárs is making and repairing agricultural implements, for which they are paid by the villagers in grain and sometimes hold land for service on a small quit-rent. They also make locks, key-latches and similar articles of iron. In the Belgaum district some are skilful workers in brass, silver and gold, and some make excellent images of Hindu gods. Owing to the decline in their trade, due to foreign competition, some of the Gujarát Lohárs have become silversmiths and carpenters. In Kanara also some have taken to carpentry.

MARATHA LOHARS claim decent from Manu, son of Vishwakarma, the architect of the gods. They are obviously an occupational caste evolved from the same tribe or tribes as the other occupational castes of the Deccan, and, like many of them, have still traces of *devaks* or gods of the exogamous sections. They appear to have no endogamous divisions except in Sholápur, where they are split up into seven groups (1) Akuj, (2) Kalsábad, (3) Kámle, (4) Pakalghat, (5) Parvále, (6) Shinde and (7) Tingáre, who neither eat together nor intermarry. Their exogamous sub-divisions are identical with surnames. The commonest surnames are as follows :—

Agár.	Chor.	Kále.	Popalghat.
Akus.	Gádekar.	Kámble.	Sálpe.
Ambekar.	Gáikvád.	Kángle.	Sonavane.
Ankush.	Gavli.	Kávare.	Suryavanshi.
Bhadke.	Javane.	Lokhande.	Thorát.
Bhoránt.	Jagtáp.	Máne.	Tingare.
Chámphakárande.	Jádhav.	Navugire.	Vasav.
Chaván.	Kalsáit.	Pavár.	

Marriages are prohibited between members having the same surnames. Marriage with a father's sister's or mother's sister's daughter is not allowed. A man may marry his maternal uncle's daughter. Marriage with a wife's sister is allowed, and brothers are allowed to marry sisters. Polygamy is allowed, but polyandry is unknown. Girls are generally married between seven and twelve, boys between twelve and twenty. Divorce is allowed if the husband and wife do not agree, if the husband suffers from an incurable disease or when the wife is unchaste. A woman divorced for adultery with a casteman can marry again by the widow remarriage form. If the offence is committed with a member of another caste, she is excommunicated.

The birth, death and marriage ceremonies of Marátha Lohárs are similar to those of the Marátha Kunbis. In some places, boys are girt with the sacred thread a couple of days before marriage. Their *devak* consists of *sándas* or a pair of tongs, the *hátoda* or hammer and the *pánchpálvi* or leaves of five kinds of trees. Some perform a ceremony called *Vir* on the day of the installation of the *devak*, in which a person becomes possessed of the spirit of a deceased ancestor of the family. A goat is sacrificed to the *Vir*, and his brow is marked with the blood of the victim.

The remarriage of widows is permitted with the sanction of the caste headman. A widow cannot marry her father's sister's, mother's sister's or mother's brother's son or a member of her deceased husband's section. The ceremony is attended by relations on both sides, the caste headman and the caste priest. The widow is dressed in a white robe and ornaments and is seated along with her intended husband on a *muth* or bullock's packsaddle or a low wooden stool used for preparing *shevaya*, vermicelli. Ganpati and Varuna are worshipped, the widow's lap is filled, and the ends of the pair's garments are tied into a knot by the priest, this being the binding portion of the ceremony. After this, in some places, the newly married pair are made to drink milk from the same cup. Next, they proceed to bow to the house gods and elders. On the following day a feast is given to the caste people. A bachelor is not allowed to marry a widow, except in Khándesh, where he can do so after marrying a *rui* (Calotropis gigantea) bush or a ring.

Marátha Lohárs follow the Hindu law of inheritance and belong to the Hindu religion. Their family deities are Bhaváni, Khandoba, Vithoba, Jotiba, Mahádeva, Janái, Bahiroba and Kálika. They observe all the Hindu holidays, worship all the plants and animals held sacred by the Hindus, and visit places of Hindu pilgrimage. Except in some places where they have priests of their own caste, they employ Deshasth Bráhmans for religious and ceremonial purposes. Except in Belgaum where they are vegetarians, they eat the flesh of goats, sheep, fowl, deer, hares and fish, and drink liquor. They eat *kachhi* and *pakki* and drink water with Maráthás, Mális, Vánis and Dhangars; and Mális, Kolis, Dhangars, Nhávis, etc., eat *pakki* and *kachhi* and drink with them.

In dress, language and other particulars they resemble Marátha Kunbis.

Konkani Lohárs.

KONKANI LOHARS are also known as Dhávads in the Sávantvádi State. Their exogamous divisions are mostly local in origin. The chief of them are—

Bháladye.		
Chámphekar.	Kolambekar.	Rávut.
Chándárkar.	Masurkar.	Savandekar.
Gulekar.	Pánálkar.	Shrivankar.

Marriage with a mother's sister's or mother's brother's daughter and their descendants is not allowed so long as kinship can be traced. A man may marry his deceased wife's sister. Instances of brothers marrying sisters are unknown. Girls are generally married from five to twelve, boys from five to twenty-five. The boy's father has to pay a bride price of from Rs. 5 to Rs. 50. The whole caste is said to have the same *devak*, viz., *kalamb* (Anthocephalus Cadumba) for which they show their reverence by not cutting it nor burning its wood, Their marriage ceremonies are similar to those of the Marátha Kunbis, but less detailed. Widows are allowed to remarry with the sanction of the caste *panch.* The intended husband of the widow feasts the members of the *panch* and presents the widow with a robe, the wearing of which makes them husband and wife. Then the widow starts for her new home, and on the village boundary a cock is sacrificed to appease the spirit of the deceased husband. A bachelor is not allowed to marry a widow. Divorce is allowed with the sanction of the caste *panch.* A divorced woman is not allowed to marry again. In religion Konkani Lohárs do not differ from Marátha Lohárs. Their priests are either Deshasth or Chitpávan Bráhmans. Those who can afford it, burn their dead. The rest bury them in a sitting position with face to the south. For the propitiation of childless ancestors and those who have died a violent death, one of the two ceremonies called *dánkevar kádhane* and *mál lávane* is performed on the thirteenth day after death or later. In the former ceremony the mourners go to the burning ground with the village Ghádi, who offers a cocoanut and sacrifices a cock on the spot where the corpse is burnt. The cocoanut and the trunk of the cock are given to the Ghádi, and the party return home. At night a Kumbhár fills a *mánd*, that is, spreads a square piece of cloth on the ground, over which are laid some rice grain, a cocoanut and some copper coins. Next, amid beatings of drums the Kumbhár makes certain invocations, in answer to which the spirit of the deceased is supposed to come and possess one of its relatives. The medium then tells the cause of death and the unfulfilled desires of the deceased. The ceremony of *mál lávane* is performed by a Náth Gosávi. After the cocoanut and cock have been offered by the Ghádi as described in the ceremony above, the Gosávi sprinkles the ground where the cremation took place with water and fills the *mánd* which, in this case, requires five betelnuts, plantains, dry dates, almonds and other fruits and nuts. These are laid on the four corners of the cloth, and a copper drinking water pot *támbya*, containing milk, with its mouth closed with a mango leaf and cocoanut is placed in the middle. A garland of flowers with a betel leaf tied to it is hung over the *támbya*, so that the betel leaf touches the cocoanut. The rest of the ceremony is similar to that already described.

In food and drink they resemble Marátha Lohárs.

Kanada Lohárs.

KANADA LOHARS or Kamárs are found principally in the Kanara district. They are called Achária or Badgis when they work in wood, and Lohárs when they work in iron. It appears from their sub-divisions, most of which are named after places in the Southern Konkan and Goa, and from the fact that their *Swámi* or high priest and family deities are in Goa, that they are a branch of the Konkani Lohars, supposed by some to have migrated there during the Portuguese inquisition in Goa. Some years ago, some of them became followers of the head of the Shringeri Monastery in Mysore, whereupon the other members stopped all intercourse with them, thus giving rise to a new division. The mother tongue of these two divisions is Konkani. There is a third division who speak Kanarese and claim to have the five *gotras* of the Pánchâls (*see* PANCHAL), but do not differ from the general mass of the community in any important detail, except that they employ Havik Bráhman priests in the coast *tálukás*. None of the above three divisions eat together or intermarry. Some members of the caste state that they have Bráhmanical *gotras*. These are stated to be Manu, Maya and Sánag, but few are able to state to which *gotra* they belong, which shows that they are as yet in the first stage on their march to Bráhmanhood, to which they aspire. Marriages are regulated by *kuls* or exogamous sections which are local in origin. They are as follows :—

First Division.

Name of *kul.*	Family deities.	Locality.
Ajgaonkár	..Mahákáli, Yetoba	..Savantvádi.
Andurlekár	..Mávli, Ravalnáth	.. Do.
A'snolkár	..Ravalnáth, Ganpati	..Kanara.
Bándekár	..Bándeshvar	..Sávantvádi.
Dábulkár	..Giroba, Sáteri	..Ratnágiri.
Elingkár	..Vetál, Devali	..Goa.
Ghátkár	..Ghoomkádevi	.. Do.
Gáonkdevikár	..Mallikárjuna	.. Do.
Hánkonkár	..Sáteri	..Kanara.
Kánkonkár	..Nirankár	..Goa.
Kinnarkár	..Mahámáyi, Náráyan, Paik.	Kanara.
Kuddekár	..Someshvar, Somnáth	..Goa.
Madkaikár	..Mhálsa	..Do.
Nárvekár	..Saptakoteshwar	..Do.
Páinjinkár	..Durgádevi, Vetál	..Do.
Pályekár	..Sáteri, Bhadrakáli	..Do.
Pársekár	..Morjáyi	..Do.
Parvatkár	..Chandreshwar, Bhutnáth,	Do.

First Division—continued.

Pednekár	..Ravalnáth	.. Goa.
Rathkár	..Vetál	.. Do.
Talpankár	..Ravalnáth, Mávli	..Ratnágiri.

Second Division.

Chandvankár	..Bhaváni	..Sávantvádi.
Dámápurkár	..Bhagvati	..Ratnágiri.
Devagadkár	..Mahálakshmi	.. Do.
Dhámnaskar	..Bhaváni, Bhairi-devata.	Do.
Nerulkár	..Sámb	..Sávantvádi.
Pávshikár	..Shambhu	..Ratnágiri.
Sátárdekár	..Ravalnáth	..Sávantvádi.
Tolsulkár	..Sant	..Ratnágiri.
Varávdekár	..Bharádi	..Sávantvádi.

As stated above, the third division claim to have five *gotras*, like the Pánchāls, which are exogamous.

The first claimant to a girl's hand is her father's sister's son. When a sister's daughter is married to a brother's son, a silver chain is put round the girl's neck by her mother, as she has to go back into the family from which her mother came. Marriage with two sisters is allowed. Girls are generally married between ten and twelve, boys between fifteen and twenty. Boys are girt with the sacred thread between ten and fourteen. The heads of widows are shaved and their marriage is forbidden. Divorce is not permitted. The offer of marriage comes from the boy's father. The *murkámedi* or auspicious post of the marriage booth must be of the *jámb* tree (Xylia dolabriformis). As in the case with many other castes in Kanara, the *dháre* ceremony is performed(1); but the essential and binding portion is considered to be the mutual garlanding of the bride and bridegroom, the garlands being made of the *avli* flowers (Mimusops elengi). The peculiarity in the marriage ceremonies of the Kanada Lohárs is that, unlike other castes, two lucky necklaces are tied round the bride's neck, one by her mother before marriage and the other by the bridegroom after the garlanding.

(1) *Dháre* is the pouring of milk over the joined hands of bride and bridegroom.

Kanada Lohárs belong to the Smárt sect, but worship both Shiva and Vishnu. They also worship the village gods and goddesses with offerings of cocks and goats, which they partake of themselves. They hold in special reverence the goddess Kálamma at Ankola. They observe all the Hindu holidays, and have great faith in soothsaying, witchcraft and omens. Their priests are generally Karnátak or Havik Bráhmans, but in Goa and the Ghát *tálukás* they have priests of their own caste. The dead are burnt, except children who have not cut their teeth, who are buried. The death ceremonies are of the standard type. They eat fish and the flesh of goats, fowls, wild pigs and venison. They drink liquor. They do not eat cooked food at the hands of any other caste. The highest castes who will eat at their hands are Ambis, Mukris and the like.

Gujarát Lohárs.

GUJARAT LOHARS are sometimes called Deva Tanakhi, meaning 'divine spark', which may have reference to fire (which is worshipped as a deity), which is indispensable for their work. They often address one another, especially those connected by marriage relations—as Luhár Sutár, which has its origin in the following story :—

Once a Gujar Sutár went to a Luhár, accompanied by his daughter, to sharpen his tools. It was meal time, and the Luhár, being alone, had to cook his own food. He therefore told the Sutár to wait till his meal was prepared. The Sutár was in a hurry, and asked his daughter to cook the Luhárs meal so that his work might not be delayed. The Luhár consenting, the Sutár's daughter prepared the meal. In the meantime, the tools were sharpened and the Sutár started to return home. He asked his daughter to come with him, but she declined to do so, remarking that as she had done a housewife's work for the Luhár, she could not marry another man. The Sutár saw his folly and married the girl to the Luhár. To commemorate the occurrence, the custom of addressing relations connected by marriage as Luhár Sutár came into vogue.

Gujarát Luhárs claim descent from Pithvo, who according to tradition was created by Párvati out of the dust adhering to Shiva's back for the purpose of forging weapons for use in Shiva's wars against the two demons Andhár and Dhandhkár. They have six endogamous divisions, (1) Bhávnagri, (2) Khambháti, (3) Parjia, (4) Pánchál, (5) Sirohia and (6) Surati, who neither eat together nor intermarry. Besides these, three more divisions are found in Káthiawár,

(1) Sorathia, (2) Machhukothia and (3) Jhilka. They have several exogamous divisions, some named after Rajput clans, others after places of residence. Of the former type the chief are—

Chávda.	Makvána.	Ráthod.	Vághela.
Chohán.	Parmár.	Solakni.	Vála.

Those of local origin are—

Afádia.	Deládia.	Kahalia.	Podhyár.
Asodia.	Devgha.	Karania.	Sándhav.
Bardia.	Dodia.	Kava.	Sirohia.
Bodána.	Harsura.	Maru.	Vanol.
Chiptada.	Háthodia.	Pati.	
Chitroda.	Jhilka.	Pithva.	

Except that in parts of South Gujarát, children of sisters or of brothers and sisters are allowed to marry, marriage between near relations is forbidden. Marriage with two sisters is allowed, and brothers are allowed to marry sisters. Marriage is generally infant. In some places, if a girl is not married before fifteen, a fine is imposed upon the parents of the girl or they are excommunicated. Divorce is allowed. Except among some Cutch Luhárs, the widow is allowed to remarry, but marriage with the younger brother of her deceased husband is rare.

Cutch Luhárs are girt with the sacred thread, but some wear it for a short time only. With one or two peculiarities, the mariage ceremonies of Luhárs are similar to those performed by Kanbis. The peculiarities are that, on the third day before a marriage, the mothers of the bride and the bridegroom go separately with music and female relations a little way from their house and drive an iron nail into the ground, and that on the day before the marriage at the house, both of the bride and of the bridegroom, seven women of the caste, take seven earthen pots filled with water from a river, pond or well.

Luhárs belong to many religious sects, Godiápanthis, Kabirpanthis, Márgipanthis, Meherájpanthis, Rámánandis, Shaivs, Swáminárayans and Vallabhácháryas. They worship all Bráhmanic and village gods and goddesses, but the special object of their worship is the goddess Bhavání. Some of them regard their bellows as a symbol or home of Devi, and on big days worship the bellows, placing near them a lamp fed with clarified butter. Most of them believe in witchcraft, exorcism and the ordinary omens. Their priests except in Cutch are a class of Audich Bráhmans, known as Luhárgors, and considered degraded as they do not scruple to eat food cooked by Luhárs. In Cutch the priests are Shrigauda Bráhmans who do not consider themselves degraded. They burn their dead with all Kanbi ceremonies.

In South Gujárat and Cutch they privately eat fish and flesh and drink liquor, but elsewhere they are strict vegetarians.

LOKA BALKI.—A sub-division of Bánjigs.

LOKAVANT.—A synonym for Lokabalki.

Name and origin.

LONARIS, numbering 19,222 (1901), including 9,672 males and 9,550 females, are found chiefly in Khándesh, Nasik, Poona, Sátára, Sholápur, the Sátára Agency, and the Southern Marátha Country. They are occasionally called Gádhav (donkey) and Reda (buffalo) Lonáris. They are now a caste of cement-makers and lime burners who seem once to have been Maráthás but to have formed themselves into a separate class by adopting the occupation of lime and charcoal burners. In Belgaum district they are divided into Mith (salt) and Chune (lime) Lonáris, who eat together but do not intermarry. In Ahmednagar, Poona, and Sholápur districts they are divided into Lonáris proper and *Kadu*, *Akaramáshe*, or bastard Lonáris, who eat together but do not intermarry. In the *Játivivek* they are described as the progeny of a man of the Mallat caste and of a woman of the Avart caste. Their Sanskrit name is Saumik, and their occupation appears at one time to have been that of preparing salt. In the *Mulstambha* they are described as Kshatriyas, possibly on account of their Marátha origin. The Lonáris of Poona district relate that they came into the district from Mandesh near Phaltan in Sátára district. They say that they were once Lingáyats, when their religious ceremonies were conducted by Jangams. There is little evidence of their former connection with Lingáyatism beyond the fact that when they bury they adopt the sitting position for the corpse. A mention of the caste-name occurs in the Mahábhárat when Dhritaráshtra is advised by Vidur to act like a Máli who grows trees and eats fruits, instead of like a Lonári who burns trees and prepares charcoal. This indicates charcoal burning as the original occupation of the caste. According to the Bombay Gazetteer the Lonáris are Maráthás and eat and marry with them. But evidence of such intermarriages is not now forthcoming. In Sholápur district, when a child is about a year old, a Dhangar cuts the hair, and is presented with five copper coins, five pieces of dry cocoa-kernel and a betel packet, for his trouble. Lonáris have a caste-council, and their social disputes are settled at meetings of the caste-men. The commonest surnames among them are Chorge, Dhone, Dangekar, Rakshe, Limite, Bondre, Karche, Tambe, Zadge, Kalarkar, etc.

Exogamous divisions

Except in Poona district, persons with the same surname cannot intermarry. The following are some of the exogamous groups in Poona district :—

- Dhone. Koparkar. Muthekar. Natkar. Midke. Mitke. Tambe.
- Dangekar. Vagdare. Navthare. Redekar. Landge. Alshi. Bomble.
- Vasimkar. Sopárkar. Sadphalkar. Kasavkar.
- Adáne. Deulkar. Thite. Botcháte. Khilare.
- Rakshe. Khavle. Karade.
- Limite. Divje. Khavane. Adalkar.
- Bondre. Bahàd. Kale. Toufe. Ajge.
- Karche Dangar. Buchade. Narke
- Murge. Nalge. Murkhe.
- Khade. Kokde. Kanade. Goyal. Piparkar.

Marriage with a mother's sister's daughter or father's sister's daughter is not allowed. It is allowed with a maternal uncle's daughter. Marriage with a wife's sister is allowed. Two brothers may marry two sisters. Girls are married before they are twelve. There is no limit of age for the marriage of boys. Sexual license before marriage is neither allowed nor tolerated. If a girl commits sexual indiscretions before marriage with a man of her caste, she is married to him. The man is compelled to undergo certain purifications and to pay a fine and give a dinner to his caste-men. They are then classed as *kadu, akaramáshe* or bastard, and treated as being of an inferior division. If a girl commits sexual indiscretions with an outsider she is excommunicated, and cannot be readmitted into her caste either by paying a fine or giving a dinner to her caste-men. Polygamy is permitted, but polyandry is unknown. A man marries another wife when his first wife is barren or is physically defective. There is no limit to the number of wives.

Marriage ceremonies.

The offer of marriage generally comes from the boy's father. It is arranged through the mediation of four or five men of their caste, who are termed *pudháit*. A Bráhman priest fixes an auspicious date for the marriage and also conducts the service. When an offer is received, two men of both the sides go to an astrologer with the bride and bridegroom's horoscopes and cause them to be compared. When the horoscopes are not available, the marriage is settled by the religious names of the bride and bridegroom. Twenty-seven heaps of rice corresponding to the twenty-seven stars are prepared. Over each heap a betelnut and a pice is placed. Red and turmeric powders are offered to these heaps, and a small girl is asked to pick up a betelnut. From the number of the betelnut the bridegroom's star is marked. Similarly, the bride's star is marked, and then the astrologer decides whether the proposed match will be happy and prosperous. The principal ceremonies are *kunku-lávne* or betrothal, *lagna-chithi* or fixing the date of marriage, turmeric rubbing, *devkarya* or the ceremony of enshrining the marriage guardian deity which consists of *pánchpálvi*, *i.e.*, leaves of the mango, *jámbul* (Eugenia jambolana), *shami* (Prosopis spicigera), *umbar* (Ficus glomerata), and *rui* (Calotropis gigantea), *vardhava* or taking the bridegroom to the bride's house, *simant-pujan* or the reception of the bridegroom by the bride's father, *kanyádán* or the bride-giving ceremony, *rukhvat* or offering food articles to the bridegroom's party, and *sáde*. Their marriage ceremonies do not differ materially from those of the Maráthás except that at the time of marriage the bride and bridegroom are made to stand on bamboo baskets, or the bride on a grindstone and the bridegroom on a coil of rope. The *saptapadi*, or taking of seven steps by the bride and bridegroom, or the throwing of rice over the bride and bridegroom's heads, is the binding portion of the ceremony.

Widow remarriage is allowed. A widow is not allowed to marry her maternal or paternal aunt's son, maternal uncle's son, or any member of her deceased husband's family. The ceremony takes place during the latter half of any month, or when the moon is not shining. The heads of the caste *pancháyat*, a Bráhman priest, and kinsmen on both the sides are present on this occasion. The widow and her new husband are seated on a square which the priest marks out with grains of wheat. The priest worships a betelnut, Ganpati, and a metal water-pot—Varuna—of which the mouth is covered with betel leaves and a cocoanut. The Varuna water-pot is applied to the brow of the widow thrice. Sandal-paste, flowers, turmeric and vermilion powders, and sweetmeats are laid before the betelnut and the water-pot, the hems of the pair's garments are knotted together, and the lap of the widow is filled with rice, cocoanut, betel, and fruit. She bows before the gods, and the priest marks her brow with vermilion, and leaves her. She is unlucky for three days after her remarriage, and must take care that no married woman sees her face during that time. The widower gives a feast to his caste-men the next day. A bachelor is not allowed to marry a widow.

Divorce is allowed. A husband can divorce his wife on the ground of incompatibility of temper or when the wife bears a bad character, and the wife can divorce her husband when he is impotent. A divorce deed is passed with the permission of the headman of the caste, by whom the deed is attested. A woman divorced for adultery with a man of her caste is allowed to marry a second time and the ceremony is conducted after the form of a widow remarriage.

Lonáris follow the Hindu law of inheritance, and belong to the Várkari, Shaiva, or Vaishnava sects. They worship all Bráhmanic and local gods, observe all Hindu fasts and feasts, and make pilgrimages to Alandi, Jejuri, Pandharpur, Tuljápur, Benares, etc. They also worship animals such as the cobra, bullock, horse, cow, and trees and plants like the banyan tree, *pipal*, *ápta*, *shami*, and sweet basil, and their working implements and religious and account books. Excluding *ekádashi*, on Saturdays and Mondays a sacrifice of a goat is made to Khandoba and is partaken of by the offerers. They worship Muhammadan saints and make offerings of *khichadi*, frankincense, and sweetmeats for their propitiation. When cholera and small-pox are prevalent they worship the deities Mari and Shitala respectively. They employ Bráhmans to conduct their religious ceremonies. Religion.

They bury or burn their dead. Persons dying of small-pox and red leprosy are buried. Children who have not cut their teeth are buried. At burial the deceased is put in the earth in a sitting position. The ashes and bones of the dead when burnt are sent to a holy place or are consigned to a river. As soon as a person has breathed his last, the body is washed with hot water and is laid on a bamboo bier covered with a new shroud. If the deceased be a woman whose husband is still living, the body is wrapped in a new robe and a bodice, and the brow is marked with turmeric and red powder. Wreaths of flowers are also offered, and the deceased is borne to the burial or burning ground by four men. The chief mourner walks ahead of the bier, taking fire in a porcelain pot. The bier is put down half-way to the burning or burial ground, and a Death ceremonies.

sweet ball and a pice are thrown on the spot. A pyre of cowdung is prepared and the body placed upon it. The chief mourner shaves his moustache and head and bathes. Then he wets his over-garment and squeezes a few drops of water into the dead person's mouth. The chief mourner then ignites the pyre. When it is half burnt, the chief mourner takes a porcelain pot filled with water upon his shoulder and walks thrice round the pyre. At the commencement of each round a hole is bored in the pot with a pebble. On completing the third round he throws the pot over his back, and striking his mouth with his hand, calls aloud. The relatives of the dead feed the mourners for three days. On the third day the ashes and bones are collected and cow's urine and dung are sprinkled over the place of burning. Three small porcelain pots are placed in a line from north to south, and on the mouth of each pot a cake is placed. The food most fancied by the deceased is offered, and camphor and frankincense are burnt. This is termed *smashánbali.* On the tenth day ten balls are offered to the dead. A crow must touch one of the balls, otherwise an artificial crow of *darbha* grass is prepared and the ball is touched thereby. The relatives of the dead then pour sesamum and water over the life-stone and it is then thrown into water. This is known as the *daspindi* ceremony. On the thirteenth day the caste-men are feasted and some charity for the propitiation of the dead is distributed. On the fourteenth day a female or male, according to the sex of the deceased, is feasted, and articles of raw food are given to Bráhmans. For one year the same female or male is feasted every month. For the propitiation of ancestors in general they observe the *shráddha* ceremony during the latter half of the month of *Bhádrapad.* When a person has died of violent death and the dead body is not found, an image of wheat flour representing the deceased is burnt with sticks of *palas* (Butea frondosa), and funeral rites as on an ordinary death occasion are performed.

Occupation. From the probable derivation of the word 'Lonari' (*lona* salt) it is likely that the hereditary occupation of the caste was once preparing salt, and Lonáris following that occupation are still found in Belgaum district. Most of them are now cement makers and charcoal burners. They buy lime nodules and burn lime with charcoal and cowdung cakes in a circular brick kiln. Some are husbandmen and labourers.

Food. They eat the flesh of goats, sheep, and fowls, as well as fish. They drink liquor. They eat pakki and kachhi and drink water and smoke with Maráthás, Dhangars, and Mális. Maráthás, Dhangars, and Mális also eat with them.

LONDHARI.—A sub-division of Gujar Kunbis.

LONI.—A sub-division of Khándesh Kunbis.

LOTLIKAR.—A sub-division of Gaud Sárasvat Bráhmans.

LUHAR.—Gujaráti name for Lohár.

LUHARGOR.—A sub-division of Audich Bráhmans.

LUNDA.—A synonym for Khavás.

MACHHI.—A sub-division of Gandhariás.

MACHHIS, also known as Tandels, numbering (1901) 37,987, including 18,164 males and 19,823 females, are found chiefly in Broach, Kaira, Panch Mahals, Surat, Thána, Surat Agency, and Rewa Kantha, in seaboard cities, towns, and villages. They appear to be Kolis, possibly crossed in places with Rajput fugitives, and derive their present name from their occupation of catching and living by the sale of *machhi* (Sanskrit *matsya*, fish). Name and origin.

Divisions.

Their endogamous divisions are—

(1) Dhebla.
(2) Dhimár.
(3) Khárva.
(4) Khoti.
(5) Koli.
(6) Machida.
(7) Mitna.
(8) Nadia.
(9) Proper.
(10) Solanki.

The Koli Machhis and Machhis Proper and the Dhimár Machhis and Khárva Machhis of Broach eat together. In Thána the Machhis Proper do not eat with the Mitna, Nadia, and Khoti divisions, as they are considered socially inferior to them. In south Surat there is also a colony of Deccan fishermen called Dhebras or Dhimárs (Sanskrit *dhivara*, a fishman) who dine with the Machhi sub-divisions. In the Panch Mahâls Machhis are divided into two groups, Khárva and Solanki, which do not generally intermarry. The latter claim to be Rajputs. The Bulsar Machhis say they were Rajputs, who, in seeking refuge with a sage named Bak Rishi from Parshurám, the Kshatriya slayer, were compelled to work as fishermen for their fish-eating preserver. Their Panch Mahâls tradition is that they are the progeny of the sage Gautama who converted a mermaid into a rational woman and lived with her. Another story is that Bhagwán, to punish the fish tribe for biting him when bathing in a river, produced a fish netter from his body, and assigned to him and to his descendants the occupation of fish catching to rid the world of the fish nuisance. Their Koli origin is suggested by the totemism that still prevails among them. Thus they consider it sinful to cut or burn the wood of the *apta* (Bauhinia racemosa), *bel* (Ægle marmelos,) *pipal* (Ficus religiosa), *shami* (Prosopis spicigera), *umbar* (Ficus glomerata), *vad* (Ficus bengalensis), and *beheda* (Terminalia belerica). These form their *devaks* and are strongly suggestive of the common Marátha *devak* the *pánch-pálvi* or leaves of five trees. The Thána Machhis appear to have come into the district from Bulsar in Surat district. They speak Gujaráti at home and Maráthi out of doors, but their pronunciation of neither language is correct. They have a headman, or *pátil*, who settles social disputes.

Marriage with a maternal uncle's daughter, father's sister's daughter, and mother's sister's daughter is not allowed. Marriage with a wife's sister is allowed. Two brothers may marry two sisters. Girls are married from ten and boys from twelve upwards. Girls are married even after they attain the age of puberty among the rich as well as the poor. Sexual license before marriage is not allowed. If before marriage a girl commits sexual indiscretions with a man of her caste, her father is fined, and she is married to a poor man of her caste. The man involved is fined or compelled to give a dinner to his caste-men. When a girl commits sexual indiscretions with an outsider she is excommunicated. Polygamy is permitted, but polyandry is unknown.

Marriage ceremonies.

The offer of marriage generally comes from the boy's father. The father of the boy pays from forty to one hundred rupees to the girl's father as the price of the bride. A Bráhman fixes the auspicious day for marriage and conducts the service of marriage. When a marriage is settled, the father of the boy treats the girl's party to liquor. A period of one or two years may intervene between the betrothal and marriage. The ceremonies of Ganpati worship, *telpithi*, *varghoda*, marriage and *kanyádán* are performed in order. A feast to the caste-men ends the marriage ceremony. The *telpithi* ceremony consists in anointing the bride and bridegroom with turmeric paste and bathing them. The bride and bridegroom fold their hands and place them over one another. This is known as *hasta-mela*, and is supposed to be the binding portion of the ceremony. They have the *pánch-pálvi* or leaves of five kinds for their *devak*. These are hung in the marriage pandal.

Widow remarriage is allowed. A widow cannot marry her maternal aunt's or uncle's son, or her father's sister's son. She may marry a younger brother of her deceased husband. Permission of the headman of the caste is usually essential for a widow remarriage. Widow remarriage is celebrated on Tuesday or Sunday at about ten at night. On that occasion the widow, her new husband, and a couple who have been remarried, are present. The widow gives liquor or food to her new husband and receives the same from him. The remarried couple then join their hands and the ceremony ends. The joining of hands is the binding portion of the ceremony. But in some districts this is substituted by the striking together of the bride and bridegroom's heads, or by both striking a cocoanut with their heads. A bachelor is allowed to marry a widow after first being married to a *shami* tree.

Divorce is allowed with the consent of the caste-men. The husband or wife may ask for a divorce, and permission is granted when it is proved that the husband is impotent or that the wife dislikes him for some adequate reason. A deed of divorce is passed on a stamped paper. A woman divorced for adultery with a man of her caste is allowed to remain in her caste and to marry a second time. But when she is divorced for adultery with an outsider, she is excommunicated.

Machhis follow the Hindu law of inheritance. They are strong believers in magic or *muth*, the evil eye, witchcraft, evil spirits, and omens.

They are Hindus by religion and favour the worship of Krishna, the eighth incarnation of Vishnu. They go on pilgrimage to Dwarka. They observe *Rámnavmi*, *Gokaláshtami*, *Diváli*, and *Shimga* holidays. They worship the minor deities such as Khandoba and Bahiroba. Their patron deity is Khatri. They worship animals such as tortoises and crocodiles. They make offerings of peas, milk and red-lead to crocodiles. They also make sacrifices of goats on Tuesdays and Sundays, which are partaken of by the offerers. They do not worship their dead ancestors and Muhammadan saints. For the subsidence of cholera and small-pox they worship the deity Shitala. They employ Bráhmans for religious and ceremonial purposes, who are received on terms of equality by the other Bráhmans. The Mitna Machhis of Thána do not worship Vishnu, Shiva, or other Hindu gods, but only Chaitya and Hirva. They have no images in their houses and employ no Bráhmans or other priests to officiate for them. Religion.

They burn their dead. In the Panch Maháls the half burnt limbs are thrown into the river, where they are consumed by muggers, turtles and fish. Persons dying of small-pox and leprosy are Death ceremonies.

buried. They believe that small-pox is a deity and that her victims should not be burnt. Children without teeth are buried. The ashes and bones of the dead are thrown into the sea. The dead body is borne to the burning ground with singing of hymns. It is washed on reaching the burning ground and placed on the pyre. The pyre is then kindled. When the body is completely burnt the relatives return to their houses. If the body of a person who has died a violent death is not found, an image of pea-flour and grass is burnt. Some Machhis observe the *shráddha* ceremony.

Occupation. They fish, let boats on hire, and work as sailors. Besides catching fish in pools, rivers, and the sea, Machhis Proper sell vegetables, turn tiles, cultivate, and work as labourers. Koli Machhis also cultivate, but are more enterprising. They serve as navigators or *malams* and captains or *nákhudás* on country craft and steamboats, earning Rs. 3 to 5 monthly with board for short voyages between Bombay and Karáchi, and Rs. 8 to 12 for long voyages to Malabár and other distant parts.

Food. They eat fish of all kinds, and the flesh of goat, sheep, fowls and ducks, and also drink liquor.

MACHHUA.—A sub-division of Ahirs.

MACHHUKOTHIA.—A sub-division of Luhárs.

MACHIDA.—A sub-division of Machhis.

MAD.—A sub-division of Vániás.

MADARI.—A synonym for Gárudi.

MADHAVIA.—A synonym for Pálimanga Bhát.

MADHAVPURA.—A sub-division of Girnára Bráhmans.

MADHMAITRA.—A sub-division of Bráhmans.

MADHYACHAL.—A sub-division of Bráhmans.

MADIG.—Kanarese term for Máng; a synonym for Dhálya Vanjári.

MADIWAL.—A synonym for Agasa.

MADKAR.—A synonym for Bhandári.

MADRAJ.—A sub-division of Khándesh Kunbis.

MAHADEV.—A sub-division of Kolis.

MAHANUBHAVA.—A synonym for Mánbháv.

MAHAR.—A sub-division of Murlis, Vághes and Vanjáris.

MAHAR or Mhár, a tribe or more properly speaking an assembly of tribal units, numbering 953,212 (1901), including 471,803 males and 481,409 females, found throughout the Maráthi speaking area of the Presidency, including the coast portion of the North Kanara district. The term includes over fifty tribal fragments that do not intermarry, and in reality connotes more a status than a tribe, being the broken residue of many former aboriginal tribes owning the country, of which they were dispossessed by successive waves of Aryan and *post*-Aryan invaders. Thus they became "hewers of wood" if not "drawers of water" for the new overlords, and perform menial services, such as crop guarding, scavenging and the carrying of messages for the village community to this day. Kolis, Bhois, Kátkaris, Rámoshis and Bedars have much in common with the Mahárs, who differ from them in having settled on the land at a period when these tribes were still in the nomad stage, as, in some instances, they are to this day. The Mahár lives on the village lands he once owned, but in a separate hamlet to the present owners of the soil. He differs only from the similar tribe of Mángs in that he will eat cow and not pig, while the Máng will eat pig and not cow. By all castes of standing he is considered untouchable. Name and origin.

The synonyms by which they are known are:— (1) Antyaja, (2) Atishudra, (3) Bhumiputra or Dharnicheput, (4) Bhuyál, (5) Chokhámela, (6) Dhed, (7) Domb, (8) Hulsáva, (9) Káthivále, (10) Mhetre, (11) Mirási, (12) Parvári, (13) Taral, (14) Thorlegharche and (15) Veskar. The origin of the term Mahár is lost in antiquity. It is popularly said to be derived from *maháhári* or great eater, in support of which a few traditions are quoted below. According to others, it is derived through Prákrit from the Sanskrit word *mrita-hári*, which is given as the name of the lowest caste, in the *Márkandeya purán* (chapter 35, verse 36). In verse 28 of the same *purán* they are also called Mritahárins. This name they are said to have earned by their occupation of removing carcasses of dead animals. The synonym Antyaja means last-born, that is, the lowest in the social scale. Atishudra means those below the Shudras, the last of the fourfold divisions of Manu, and is indicative of the primitive origin of the tribe. Thorlegharche is an ironical expression meaning noble born. These three names are applied to the Mahárs contemptuously by the members of the higher castes. Bhumiputra or Dharniche-put means sons of the soil, and indicates the original position of the Mahárs. Dheds and Dombs are respectively the Gujarát and Northern India representatives of the Mahárs. Káthivále or men with a stick is a word indicative of the profession of the caste in olden times and Synonyms.

to some extent even at the present time. To such an extent is the *Káthi* or stick recognized as indicative of a Mahár that, in many places it is used by him as his sign-manual, and is accepted in courts of law and in the registration department. The term Mirási means a landholder. Parvári, though often applied to all Mahárs by the Europeans, is said strictly to belong to the musical Mahár. The term Veskar means a gatekeeper and describes the Mahár's occupation of the night watchman. In Poona, the Mahárs, who are followers of the Várkari sect, are known as Chokhámela after the famous Mahár saint of that name. The term Hulsáva is peculiar to Kanara.

Status. Mahárs are held to be impure. Except at Pandharpur in the Sholápur district, their touch, even the touch of their shadow, is thought to defile. The *Bombay Gazetteer*(1) relates that in some outlying villages in the early morning, the Mahár, as he passes the village well, may be seen crouching that his shadow may not fall on the water-drawers. The village barber will not shave the Mahárs, nor are they allowed to draw water from the village well. Formerly an earthern pot was hung from their necks to hold their spittle, they were made to drag thorns to wipe out their footsteps, and, when a Bráhamn came near, were forced to lie far off on their faces lest their shadow might fall on him. Modern means of locomotion, however, by bringing all classes together, have led to the proximity of unclean classes being tolerated to an extent formerly unheard of. The Mahárs live outside villages in special *Mhárvádás* or Mahárs' quarters. Their houses are generally untidy and ill-cared for, made of mud and stone with thatched roofs, and the ground near by is dirty and strewn with bones and refuse.

Traditions of origin. According to a Hindu tradition, Mahárs were originally night rovers (*nisháchars*), whom the god Brahma turned to men lest they should eat his whole creation.(2) In Násik, it is related that the founder of the caste was Svarup Somáji Mahár, sprung from the sole of Brahma's foot.(3) The Ahmadnagar Mahárs claim to belong to one of the four cow-born castes. Their story is that the cow asked her sons how they would treat her after she died. The first three sons answered they would worship her as a goddess; the fourth said he would bear her inside of him as she had borne him. The horror-struck brothers called him *maháhár* or the great eater, which, according to the story, use has shortened to Mahár.(4) Another

(1) Bombay Gazetteer, Vol. XVIII, Part I, p. 441.
(2) Do. Vol. XVII, p. 172.
(3) Do. Vol. XVII, p. 172.
(4) Do. Vol. XVI, p. 67.

tradition regarding the origin of the Mahárs relates that, once, when Párvati was bathing, her touch turned some drops of blood on a *bel* leaf into a handsome babe. She took the child home and shewed him to Mahádev, who named him Mahámuni. One day, while still young, the child crawled out of the house and, seeing a dead cow, began to eat it. Mahádev was horrified and cursed the child, saying that he would live outside villages, that his food would be carcasses, that nobody would have anything to do with him, would look at him, or would allow his shadow to fall on anything pure. Párvati, who took great interest in her child, begged her lord to have pity on him, and Shiva agreed that the people would employ him to supply mourners with wood and dried cowdung cakes to burn the dead. As the child's appetite was so great, he, turned his name into Maháhári or the great eater.(1) These stories are mere puns on the word Mahár. Some state that the Mahárs were born of the left eye of the moon (Soma) and therefore one of their divisions has come to be called Somavanshi. The name of the original ancestor of the Somavanshis was Domba, whose son was Soma and grandson Satyasoma. The traditions regarding the origin of the Pán and Bel tribes of Mahárs are too indecent for publication.

Appearance, dress and ornaments. The Mahárs of the Deccan are generally tall, strong, muscular and dark, with regular features and low unintelligent foreheads; those in the Southern Marátha Country are darker than Kunbis, with gaunt cheeks, irregular features, a dreamy expression and flat noses: still, except in colour, they differ little from Kunbis. The Kanara Mahárs, both men and women, are tall, fair and regular-featured. The men dress in a loincloth or waistcloth, a blanket, coat or smock and a dirty Marátha turban. The women wear the full Marátha robe and bodice. The men carry in their hands a thick staff about four feet long with one end adorned with bells. The poor among them use Kunbi-shaped ornaments of brass, while the well-to-do use gold or silver ornaments.

Language. The Mahárs of the Deccan speak an incorrect and oddly pronounced Maráthi. Among themselves they have a few peculiarities. They say *nahi* for *náhi* (no), *toha* for *tujha* (thine), *maha* for *májha* (mine), *nagu* or *nai payaje* for *nako* (do not want), *samindar* for *samudra*(the sea), *samang* for *sangam* (the source), *mang* for *mag* (afterwards), etc. When he meets a man of his own caste

(1) The Bombay Gazetteer, Vol. XVIII, Part I, p. 439.

a. Mahár says *namastu* or a bow to you, and when he meets anyone other than a Mahár he says *johár*, said to be from the Sanskrit *yoddhár* or warrior, the usual Shrávak or Jain greeting. In Khándesh, like the local Kunbis, they speak a Khándeshi dialect, a kind of shortened Maráthi, *e. g. kathethum una* for *kothun álás* (whence have you come), *kathi jás* for *kothe játos* (whither are you going), etc. The home tongue of the Kanara Mahárs is Konkani. The names in common use among men are: Bálya, Bhágya, Gondappa, Khima, Kondu, Limba, Mahádji, Masa, Munjya, Nárya, Ráma, Sadya, Laka and Tukappa; and among women Aheli, Bhági, Bhimi, Chimi, Gági, Iji, Jaya, Kushi, Mani, Nagi, Rádha, Tuki and Yelli. The men add the word *nák*—probably *náik* or leader—to their names.

In the Khándesh district, in each group of villages there is a chief Mahár headman, who in Jamner is called *pándwár* and in the south *mehetar*. The office is, as a rule, hereditary. The most sensible and worthy of the sons is chosen in the room of his father. Failing sons, some other member of the family, and failing the family, an outsider is chosen. Caste disputes are settled by the men of the village with or without, the help of the headman. The offences punished by expulsion are :— the failure to give caste dinners, dining and smoking with one of lower castes such as a Máng, and adultery or concubinage. In other places, they have caste councils, the head of which is known in some places as *pátil* and in others as *mehetar*. The headman of the Kanara Mahárs is called *budvant*. In Sholápur and Thánea caste decisions are enforced by forbidding the caste people to smokc, or drink water with the offender, or by enacting a fine, whith is spent on drink. In Sátára, if a Mahár dines or commis adultery with a Máng or a Bhangi he is put out of caste and is not allowed back unless he shews that he was ignorant of the caste of the person with whom he associated. In Kolhápur, a *nimb* twig is thrown on the offender's house and all are enjoined to keep aloof from the offender's family on pain of losing caste. When an offender is re-admitted, he has to spend from Rs. 2 to 10 on a caste dinner. The high priest gives him *tirth* or holy water to sip, and he is allowed to eat in the same row with his castemen. The Mahárs in the Sávantvádi State have no recognized headman, but the Mahárs of certain villages have for generations been regarded as arbitrators in settling caste and other disputes. Taking food in the house of a Jingar or a Musalmán and adultery are said to be punished by expulsion from the caste.

The Mahárs have the following endogamous divisions:— Endogamous divisions.

1. Abne.
2. Andvan or Andhon.
3. Ananthkulya.
4. Autakámble.
5. Balhi.
6. Balkámble.
7. Bárke.
8. Bávan or Bávane.
9. Bávcha.
10. Bávise.
11. Bel, Bele or Belia.
12. Ben.
13. Bole.
14. Bunkar.
15. Chelkar.
16. Daule.
17. Dhed.
18. Dharmik.
19. Dom or Domb.
20. Gardi.
21. Gavasai or Gavase.
22. Ghadshi.
23. Ghatkámble.
24. Godvan or Gondvan.
25. Gopál.
26. Hedshi.
27. Holár or Huvale.
28. Jháde.
29. Jogti.
30. Junnare.
31. Kabule.
32. Kadvan, Kudvan or Kadu.
33. Kámble.
34. Kásare.
35. Kharse.
36. Kochare, Khosare or Kosare.
37. Ládvan or Ládhan.
38. Mathkámble.
39. Murli.
40. Niråle.
41. Pán or Pánya.
42. Pradhán.
43. Pular.
44. Rati.
45. Saladi or Saláde.
46. Silván.
47. Sirsálkar.
48. Soma or Somavanshi.
49. Somkámble.
50. Sonkámble.
51. Sonaibalkámble.
52. Sutad.
53. Tilvan.

Of these divisions the Somavanshis, who claim descent from Soma or the moon, are most numerous and are the social superiors of the rest. In the Sávantvádi State, Beles and Somavanshis are considered to be identical, and the Páns are said to include Mángs, Berads, Bhorpis and Rámoshis. The name Pán is said to be derived from the profession of working with leaves (*pán* leaf), of which umbrellas are made, and the name Bele from the profession of making mats and baskets from *bel* chips of bamboo.

The Gopáls, who are Mahár ascetics, and Ratis are considered in some places to be half castes. Gopáls, Ghadshis and Holárs have been described separately under those heads. The Murli Mahárs are the offspring of Mahár girls dedicated to the service of the god Khandoba; Gavasi Mahárs are said to be the children of Mahár parents born in adultery; and Jogti Mahárs are said to be descendants of bastard Mahárs who were devoted to the service of the Karnátak goddess Yellamma. The Kadvans or Kadus are bastards, and Andvans are those born of virgins.

In the Ahmednagar district, the sub-divisions Anantkulya, Andvan, Bávane and Bel eat together and intermarry. The Khándesh Mahárs consist of 12½ divisions, *viz*, Andhon, Bávane, Balhi, Bunkar, Gondvan, Holar, Kharse, Kochare, Ládhan, Pradhán, Soma, Tilvan and the half caste Gopál. Of these the first four eat together, but do not intermarry. The Násik Mahárs also have 12½ divisions, the names of which are:— Andvan, Bávacha, Chelkar, Dhed, Dom, Ghadshi, Gopál, Ládvan, Pán, Pular, Rati, Somavanshi and Sutad, Rati being considered half caste. The Mahárs of Poona are split up into Andvans, Daules, Junnares, Páns, Silváns and Somavanshis, who neither eat together nor intermarry. In the Sholápur district are found Abnes, Andvans, Bávanes, Bels, Bens, Bavises, Boles, Dheds, Godvans, Kadvans, Kámbles, Khochares, Ládvans, Niráles, Páns, Saládes, Soms and Tilvans. Most of these divisions except the Kadvans eat together and intermarry. The Sátára Mahárs have four divisions—Proper, Gavasi, Jogti and Murli—who eat together but do not intermarry. In Kolába the divisions are:— Belias, Doms, Gardis and Somavanshis. The divisions found in Thána are Daules, Páns and Somavanshis. The Ratnágiri Mahárs are mostly Kámbles. The Mahárs of the Southern Marátha Country have fourteen divisions, *viz.*, Andvan, Bele, Gavase, Ghadshi, Hedshi, Jháde, Jotgi, Kadvan, Ladvan, Murli, Pán and Saládi, who neither eat together nor intermarry. The Sávantvádi Mahárs have two divisions—Beles and Páns, who do not eat together or intermarry.

Exogamous divisions.

The Mahárs have numerous surnames which are exogamous. Some of the commonest surnames are as follows:—

Abhang.	Bagad.	Bhálerão.
Adhav.	Bagul.	Bhámbhal.
Adijádhav.	Báhelime.	Bhede.
Adsule.	Baikar.	Bhilang.
Aherrão.	Balkámble.	Bhingár.
Ahire.	Bansure.	Bhoi.
Auchat.	Básede.	Bhoir.
Autakámble.	Báyakar.	Bholke.
Bábre.	Bayat.	Bhosale.
Báchav.	Bhagat.	Chandanshive.

Chavân.
Chhettise.
Chikane.
Chitale.
Dáháne.
Dárule.
Detge.
Dhárpavár.
Dhede.
Dive.
Doble.
Dukare.
Gáde.
Gadre.
Gáikvád.
Gamre.
Garud.
Ghanvat.
Ghátkámble.
Ghode.
Godivale.
Gote.
Hátavate.
Jádhav.
Joshi.
Kadam.
Kákate.
Kákude.
Kále.
Kámble.
Kanoje.
Katre.
Khandágale.
Khandizad.
Kharat.
Kharode.
Khupate.
Kohale.
Kolge.
Ládav.
Lákde.
Lokare.
Lokhande.
Makásure.
Málve.
Matkámble.
Mehede.
Mhasge.
Mhaskate.
Mohite.
More.
Nikumbh.
Nirmal.
Pácharne.
Págar.
Pákhare.
Párdhe.
Patekar.
Pavár.
Pokade.
Puravne.
Sadávarte.
Sapkál or Sakpál.
Sálve.
Samidar.
Sarvagod.
Satpal.
Shelár.
Shelke.
Shevale.
Shinde.
Shirke.
Sisáte.
Sodjádhav.
Somaibalkámble.
Somkámble.
Sonávale.
Sonkámble.
Sonavane.
Sonkavale.
Surya.
Suryavanshi.
Suryakadam.
Tadke.
Talvatke.
Támbe.
Tápichere.
Tizad.
Thorvade.
Umbále.
Vádkar.
Vágh.
Vághchavre.
Vághmáre.
Vághpanje.
Vartak.
Yádav.
Yetum.
Zankar.

The evidence obtained in the course of enquiries tends to establish the fact that each of these exogamous sub-divisions originally owned and worshipped a *devak* or *totem*, closely corresponding to the *bali* of the Kanarese tribes (see MARATHA). The object represented by the *devak* is worshipped, protected from injury by the section owning the *devak*, and brought into prominence at the time of the marriage ceremony. Members of families with a common *devak* cannot intermarry.

A list of some of these *devaks* with the name of the *kul* or exogamous section owning the *devak* is given below :—

Kul.	*Devak.*
Bagad	.. *Umbar* (Ficus glomerata).
Bhagat	.. Cobra.
Gáikvád	.. Crab, sunflower, *kohala* (Cucurbita pivi).
Jádhav	.. Palm (Borassus flabelliferi, *pankánis* (Typha angustata), tortoise (*Kásav*).
Kadam	.. *Kadamba* (Anthocephalus cadumba).
Mhasge	.. Buffalo.
Mohite	.. *Umbar* (Ficus glomerata).
More	.. Peacock.
Satpal	.. Cobra.
Shevale	.. *Nágvel* (Piper betle).
Sonkámble	.. *Champa* (Mesua ferrea).
Suryavanshi	.. Sunflower.
Talvatke	.. Copper.
Támbe	.. *Umbar* (Ficus glomerata).
Zankar	.. Mango, *umbar*, *jámbul*.

Other common *devaks*, in addition to the above, are the *harina* (mousedeer), *nág* or cobra, *nándruk* (Ficus retusa), the doll *pithiche bávle* and the banyan tree.

In many cases the *devak* has become obsolete and has been replaced by a composite *totem* or *pánchpálvi* composed of the leaves of five trees, which are similarly worshipped and play a prominent part in the marriage ceremony. The number five has special value among the Mahárs, as will be seen in the full account of the birth and marriage ceremonies given below. It may be equivalent to the early numerical conception of many. The *vansh* or group of five ancestors is largely worshipped in outlying villages in the form of a stone carving of five caste or tribal elders, kept in the village temple, to this day.

The following *pánchpálvis* are worshipped by Mahárs in the districts shown :—

Poona—

1. Mango.
2. *Pipal.*
3. *Rui.*
4. *Shami.*
5. *Umbar.*

Násik—

1. Mango.
2. *Pipal.*
3. *Rui.*
4. *Shami.*
5. *Umbar.*

Khándesh.		Sátára ..	
1.	*Arkáthi.*	1,	*Bábul.*
2.	*Borkáthi.*	2.	Banyan or *vad.*
3.	*Jámbul.*	3.	*Jámbul.*
4.	Mango.	4.	Mango.
5.	*Ruchkin.*	5.	*Rui.*

Marriage rules.

The Mahárs of the different districts, though belonging to the same division, do not intermarry, unless some former connection can be traced between them. In the Sávantvádi State, each village group forms an exogamous unit, and consequently marriages between Mahárs of the same village are prohibited. Marriages are generally prohibited within three degrees of relationship. A Mahár cannot marry his father's sister's or mother's sister's daughter. He may marry his mother's brother's daughter. In some places, marriage with a sister's daughter is allowed. Marriage with a wife's sister is allowed, both during the wife's lifetime and after her death. Two brothers are allowed to marry two sisters. Polygamy is allowed and practised, but polyandry is unknown. Marriage is infant as well as adult, girls being sometimes married even when only a month old and sometimes after the age of sixteen. The cause of late marriages is in most cases want of money. Sexual intercourse before marriage is tolerated among the more helpless portions of the caste. But generally, if a virgin commits sexual indiscretions, she is allowed to remain in the caste on her parents paying a fine and giving a dinner to the castemen, if the seducer is a casteman or a member of a higher caste. If the seducer be a member of a lower caste the girl is excommunicated.

After the birth of a child the mother is held impure, generally for twelve days. In Poona, she is held impure for forty-one days, in Ahmednagar for eleven days, and in Kolhápur for eight days.

Birth ceremonies.

In Sholápur and Sátára, on the third day, a ceremony called *tirvi* or *tikondi* is performed, when *five* little unmarried girls are feasted on millet of *karri* made into lumps and eaten with a mixture of milk and molasses, or sugar, or with curds and buttermilk. On the *fifth* or *pánchvi* day *five* stone pebbles are laid in a line in the house and worshipped by the midwife and millet is offered. On this day, among the Kolhápur Mahárs, a few spots of sandal and turmeric paste are daubed on the wall near the mother's cot. The spots are marked with sandal paste and rice and a lamp is waved round them. On the sixth or *satvi* day the hole made for the bathing water in the mother's room is filled, levelled, cowdunged and sprinkled with turmeric and redpowder and flowers, and wheat cakes are laid before it.

The goddess Satvái is also worshipped on this day, or, in some places, on the evening of the *fifth* day. A silver image of the goddess is set on a stone slab or *páta*, and flowers, a coil of thread and food are laid before the goddess, and a wheat flour lamp is set at the bathing pit. *Five* married women are asked to dine at the house, and the child is not allowed to look at the wheat flour lamp at the bathing pit, as the sight at the lamp is said to make it squint. In Kanara, the child in named on the sixth day, in Kolhápur on the ninth. In the Deccan, it is named between the twelfth and any time within about two months in consultation with the village astrologer. When the child is a year old, if it is a boy, the hair-cutting or *Jával* is performed.

Marriage ceremonies.

The offer of marriage comes from the boy's father, who, in some cases, has to pay a sum of money to the girl's father. A few days before the marriage, the village Bráhman is asked whether there is anything in the names of the boy and girl to prevent their marrying. He consults his almanac and says there is no objection. He is then asked to fix a lucky moment for the marriage and for the turmeric rubbing. He again consults his almanac, tells them the days and gives them a few grains of rice to be thrown on the bridal pair. The marriage service is conducted either by a Bráhman priest standing at a distance, or by a Mahár *gosávi*. In Khándesh, it is sometimes conducted by a Dhangar. Marriage booths are erected at the houses of both the boy and girl, the *muhurta medha* or auspicious post of which is generally of *umbar* (Indian fig tree) wood. The booth is covered with leaves of mango, *umbar* and *pipri* (Ficus tsiela). The *devak* of the family stock is worshipped. Silver masks or *táks* are occasionally brought by a newly married couple from a goldsmith's shop and placed among the household gods and worshipped. The *devak* is tied to the *muhurta medha* along with wheat bread and an axe. In some places, the *Pándhari* (Randia uliginosa) is worshipped by the bridegroom before the installation of the *devak*. The few particulars in which the marriage ceremonies of Mahárs differ from those of Kunbis are that the boy and girl are made to sit in bamboo baskets at the time of marriage and that a yellow thread is passed seven times round their necks. In Khándesh, while the marriage verses are being recited, the baskets are twisted round five times, and, when the priest claps his hands to shew that the moment for marriage has come, the baskets are turned a sixth time, the cloth is snatched aside and the bride and bridegroom throw garlands round each other's necks. In most places, from the beginning of the marriage ceremony to the end, the bride has to hold a knife in her hand and the bridegroom a dagger. Among the Mahárs of the Thána district, the marriage ceremony is performed without the help of a Bráhman, unless the boy's father is a follower of Chokhámela, when the services of a Bráhman are necessary. Some Mahárs also call in a Bhát. On the day before the marriage, a medium, *bhagat*, is called to the bride and bridegroom's houses and consulted whether the next day will be lucky. If the medium says the day is favourable, the marriage is celebrated on that day. The binding portion of the marriage service seems to be, in all places, the throwing of sacred grains of rice over the bride and bridegroom.

Among the Mahárs of the Sávantvádi State, a composite *devak*, consisting of one or two *sers* of rice grains, one cocoanut, five pice, a betelnut and leaves, plantains, and leaves of the *kadamba* (Anthocephalus cadumba) is put into a basket and worshipped with flowers and sandal paste by the bridegroom and his parents. The *muhurta medha* or auspicious post of the marriage booth, with mango leaves tied to its end, is then planted at the entrance to the house along with a post of the *sávar* tree (Bombax malabaricum) and it is worshipped. Next the ceremony of *shesa bharne* is performed, in which rice grains are applied to the foreheads of the bridegroom and his parents by *five* married pairs, and the *devak* is brought and placed into the house with a lighted lamp by its side. The bridegroom is then taken back into the marriage pandal and rubbed with turmeric paste by *five* married pairs. Next a triangular frame of the branches of the *sávar* or *kivan* tree is raised, outside the pandal, cotton thread is passed round the frame and to its top is hung a cloth bag containing *five vadás* (cakes fried in oil). The bag is filled with water by *five* married unwidowed women and the bridegroom is seated under it so that the water trickles over his head. The bridegroom is then taken out of the frame and bathed, and carried by his maternal uncle or some other near relation to the door of the booth, whence he throws *bel* leaves over the booth. In many districts, water is poured over the joined hands of the bride and bridegroom (the *dháre* ceremony). The marriage is completed after the fashion of the Kunbi caste marriages.

Widow remarriage. The remarriage of widows is permitted. A widow cannot marry her father's sister's, mother's sister's or mother's brother's son, or a member of her late husband's *kul*. In some places, marriage with a mother's brother's son is allowed, in others, it is prohibited with a member of the widow's father's *kul*. In Khándesh, a widow is said to be allowed to marry a younger brother of her deceased husband. The intended husband has, in some places, to pay a sum of money called *dej* to the father of the widow and to the relatives of her deceased husband. A widow remarriage is always celebrated at night except on a new-moon day. It cannot take place on those days on which first marriages are celebrated. In some districts, it is not allowed to be celebrated in the months of *Ashádha, Paush* and *Bhádrapada*. The ceremony takes place in a lonely locality and is generally attended by remarried widows, a caste *gosávi* or *pandit*, and sometimes a Bráhman priest. The widow is dressed in the clothes and ornaments presented by her intended husband, the pair are then seated on a carpet or a bullock's packsaddle, the ends of their garments are tied into a knot, the widow's brow is marked with redpowder, her lap is filled, and the ceremony is over. In some places, molasses are put into the mouth of both. Sometimes the god Varuna or Ganpati is also worshipped. In the Sávantvádi State, a widow remarriage is celebrated only on a Wednesday, Thursday or Friday. It is attended by the relations of both parties, neighbours and friends. The ceremony consists only in applying rice grains to the foreheads of the pair by the party assembled, which is followed by a feast. Next, the married pair with the party start for the widow's new husband's house. Before they reach the place, a cock is killed and a piece of the widow's robe is cut off and Rs. 2, wlth a *ser* of rice grains and a cocoanut or five *Nágchampa* leaves tied into a piece of cloth are sent to the house of the widow's deceased husband and placed in the basin of the *tulasi* plant in the courtyard. This offering is made to appease the spirit of the widow's deceased husband, The cock offered cannot be eaten by the remarried pair. It is cooked and eaten by the members of the party attending the pair before they reach their destination. On arriving there, the couple bow to their family god, and rice grains are applied to their foreheads by *five* married unwidowed women, which ends the ceremony. A bachelor is not allowed to marry a widow unless he is first married to a *rui* plant or a ring. The marriage with the *rui* plant is performed with full marriage rites. The plant is then chopped up and buried in a burial ground, thus indicating that the first wife, *i.e.*, the tree, is dead, and putting the bachelor, as a widower, on a footing with the widow. Divorce is allowed on the grounds of the wife's unchastity, the husband's illtreatment of the wife, or the contraction of an incurable disease by either. Divorced women are allowed to remarry by the widow remarriage form, unless the cause of the divorce be adultery with a member of a lower caste, in which case, they are excommunicated. The caste follow the Hindu law of inheritance.

Religion. The Mahárs profess Hinduism. They are both Shaivs and Vaishnavs. Some of them, in the Ahmednagar district, belong to the Mátangapatta sect, and many are followers of Kabir, Giri and Náth. Those who are followers of Chokhámela (Várkaris) wear sweet basil or *tulsi* bead necklaces and make periodical pilgrimages to Alandi and Pandharpur, passing their nights in praying or singing sacred songs or *abhangs*. In the Deccan, the pious among them have singing clubs where they sing in praise of some Hindu god, especially of Rám or of Vithoba of Pandharpur. Both men and women are good singers and go in bands of two or more, singing and begging.

The favourite deities of the Deccan Mahárs are Bhaváni, Mahádeva, Chokhoba, Jnyánoba, Khandoba, Vithoba and Mhaskoba. The objects of their special worship are the cobra or *nágoba*, the small-pox goddess Satvái and the cholera-goddess Mariái, whose shrines are found in all Mahár quarters. The family deities of the Kanara Mahárs are Shántariamma, Maridevi, Bhumidevi and Mahádeva. The Mahárs of the Sávantvádi State worship gods in the form of cocoanuts or betelnuts called Bráhmans and Purvás. In every village, close to the chief temples, there is a Mahár shrine where they workship a stone idol of Talkhba. The family deities of the Mahárs of Thána are Mhaskoba, Janái, Gauri, Bahiroba, Khandoba, Chokhoba, Bhaváni, Yellamma, Giroba, Bábdev, Chedoba, Jakhái, Somnái, Kalkái, and Jokhái. Besides the above deities all the Mahárs worship the usual Hindu gods and goddesses and Musalmán saints, and some have *táks* (embossed images) of deceased ancestors. They observe all the Hindu holidays and make pilgrimages to the holy places of the Hindus, specially to Pandharpur, Alandi, Jejuri and Tuljápur.

When cholera rages in a village, the people raise a subscription and hand the money to the headman. The headman brings a robe and bodice, some rice and flour, a he-buffalo or a sheep, and flowers, camphor, frankincense, red powder and betelnut and leaves. He takes three carts, fills one with cooked rice, a second with cakes and in the third places the other articles of worship, and, leading the he-buffalo, takes the carts through the village accompanied by music and a band of the villagers. The carts then go to the Mahárs' quarters outside of the village, where is the shrine of Mariái, the cholera goddess. The headman and the other villagers stand at a distance, while a Mahár bathes the goddess, dresses her in the robe and bodice, fills her lap with rice, betelnuts, dry dates and a cocoanut, waves burning frankincense and camphor before her, and with joined hands begs her to be kind. All the villagers lift their joined hands to their heads and ask the goddess to be kind and retire, leaving the Mahárs and Mángs in peace. The buffalo is led in front of the goddess and a Mahár chops off its head with a sword or a hatchet, and touches the goddess' lap with a finger dipped in its blood. The cart-loads of food and meat are shewn to the goddess and are distributed among such of the villagers as do not object to eat them. This concludes the sacrifice. They say that the goddess truly partakes of the sacrifice, as the food and meat become insipid and tasteless.

The religious teachers and priests of Mahárs are members of their own caste, who are called *gurus*, *sádhus*, *váchaks*, *pandits*, *gosávis*, or *mendhe joshis*. In Khándesh, there is a class of beggars known as Mahár *thákurs*, who also act as their priests. The *gurus* are those who have been initiated by other *gosávis*, and who have devoted themselves to a religious life, chiefly to the worship of Vithoba. The Mahár *thákurs* are probably Bháts who have been degraded by mixing among Mahárs. Their form of greeting is different from the Mahár saying *rám rám* to each other and *brahma* to strangers. Besides officiating as their priest the *thákur* acts as the Mahár's banker. He eats from a Mahár but no Mahár will eat from him. Besides *gurus* and *thákurs*, Bráhmans are sometimes employed to conduct marriages in the Southern Marátha Country. The *Jangams* also officiate at times.

In the time of Námdev and Tukárám, the Mahárs were admitted to the Várkari cult of the *Bhakti Márg*. Their great saint Chokhámela has a shrine at Pandharpur close to Námdev's preaching place.

The *sádhus* read and explain their sacred books, the *Bhaktivijaya*, *Dásbodh*, *Jnyáneshvari*, *Harivijaya*, *Rámvijaya*, *Santlila*, and the poems of Jnyánoba, Tukoba and others. Some of them are very fluent preachers and expounders of the *puráns*. Every Mahár, both a male and female, has a *guru*. If one has no *guru* he is not allowed to dine in the same line with the *gurus*. A child is first brought to be taught by its *guru* when it is about a year old, the rite is called *kánshrávni* or ear-whispering and more commonly *káuphnkne* or ear-blowing. About seven or eight at night, the parents take the child in their arms and go to the teacher's house, carrying frankincense, camphor, red and scented powders, flowers, betelnut and leaves, a cocoanut, dry dates and sugar. In the teacher's house a room is cowdunged and a square is traced with white quartz powder. At each corner of the square a lighted lamp is set, and in the middle on a wooden plank or on a low wooden stool is a metal pot or *ghat* filled with cold water. Another board or stool is set facing the square and the teacher sits on it cross-legged. He sets flowers, sandal paste and rice on the waterpot and takes the child in his lap, resting its head on his right knee. He shrouds himself and the child in a blanket or a waistcloth, mutters the sacred verse into the child's right ear, pulls off the blanket and hands the child to its parents. The priest is presented with money gifts and, if they are well-to-do, the parents give him a waistcloth, one or two metal water vessels and a plate. A feast is given to the teacher and a few near relations, or, if the parents cannot afford a feast, sugar is handed round. After the dinner the parents retire with the child.

The Mahárs believe in sorcery, witchcraft and soothsaying and attribute all diseases to the working of evil spirits. They have many spirit scarers or exorcists among them, some of whom are *gosávis*, and the rest *potras* or devotees of Lakshmi, who cover their brows with red powder and carry a whip with which they lash their bodies while they beg, singing and dancing.

The dead are generally buried. A few, who have the means, burn. At burial the corpse is either seated or laid with head to the north or south. The body is carried to the burning ground either on a bamboo bier or in a sling. In Khándesh, the thumbs are tied with a piece of silver wire over the breast, the body is shrouded in a new cloth, and grains of rice are tied to one of the hems of the cloth. The chief mourner walks in front with fire in a new earthen jar and music if he has the means. The mourners follow. On the way to the grave the party halts and the rice from the hem of the deceased's robe is laid on the ground. A pit five feet deep is dug, and the body is stripped of all its clothing, even the loincloth, according to the saying "Naked hast thou come and naked shalt thou go." In some places, the clothing is not removed. The body is then lowered into the grave, the chief mourner scatters a handful of earth on the body, the rest also scatter earth, and the grave is filled. In Poona, a few *bel* leaves are scattered on the head before the grave is filled. The chief mourner fills the fire pot with water, sets it on his shoulder and goes thrice round the grave, crying aloud and striking his open mouth with the palm of his right hand. At the end of the third turn he pours water from the jar on the grave and dashes the jar to pieces on the ground. All bathe in running water, and go to the mourner's house each carrying a *nim* branch. At the house an earthen pot of cow's urine is set on the spot where the deceased breathed his last. The mourners dip the *nim* branches into the urine, sprinkle it over their heads and bodies, and go to their homes. On the third day a few of the deceased's kinsmen go to the burial ground, the chief mourner carrying in his hands a winnowing fan with two pieces of cocoa-kernel and some molasses in each piece. At the rest-place, where the bearers halted, they lay a piece of cocoa-kernel with molasses on it under five stones. The other piece is laid on the heaped grave. They beat

Death ceremonies.

the grave down to the level of the rest of the ground, bathe, and go to the chief mourner's house. The four bearers are seated in a line on the bare ground in the front room of the house. Each holds a *nim* branch under his arm, the chief mourner drops a little molasses into his mouth, and they go to their homes. On the third, seventh or eleventh day a bread and vegetable caste feast is given. In the Sávantvádi State, on the eleventh day after death, an earthen jar is worshipped with an offering of a cock, the people assembled put coins into the jar, sing praises of gods all the night, worship a flour image of a cow and at daybreak the chief mourner gets his face and moustaches clean shaved, and the flour image is taken and thrown into a pool.

For the propitiation of the deceased ancestors *mahálaya* is performed in the dark half of *Bhádrapada*, when crows are fed and castemen are feasted. The ceremony of *shráddha* is not performed.

Occupation.

The Mahárs are hereditary village servants and are considered authorities in all boundary matters. They escort Government treasure, act as guides and messengers to public officers, call landholders to pay the land assessment at the village office, watch boundaries and the village office, repair the village office and village gate or *gaonkusu* and sweep the village roads. Most of them enjoy a small Government payment, partly in cash and partly in land. The chief source of their income is the yearly grain allowance or *baluta*. They say that they used to have fifty-two dues, but now the number is greatly reduced. Some of these dues, which were allowed by the Muhammadan and Marátha Governments, are as follows :—

1. *Sita-devi* or a part of a standing sugarcane crop.
2. Village or town gate offerings.
3. *Holi* food offerings on the full-moon day of *Phálgun*.
4. *Bendur* grain gifts on the full-moon of *Ashádha*.
5. Hides of dead cattle.
6. *Hátshekne* or hand-warming, a money gift for watching the fire made for boiling sugarcane juice.
7. *Ghar-takka* or home money.
8. Money paid for digging graves.
9. Grain lying on and about the threshing floor when the floor is used for the first time.
10. Grain at the bottom of a *pev* or grain-pit.

11. The rice thrown on the two low stools which are set for the bride and bridegroom.
12. A yearly pair of sandals for watching the village or town gate.
13. *Rukka* or marriage gift including two coppers in cash, a piece of cocoa-kernel and a handful of rice.
14. *Oti-pati* or lap-tax, that is handfulls of grain put into the laps of Mahár women at the first treading of the grain.
15. Money thrown into her platter when a Mahár woman comes to wave a lamp round the head of the bride's or bridegroom's mother.
16. *Madhe-pade* or carcass tax.
17. *Manguli* or gifts for winding a string round the village on the new-moon of *Ashádha* and of *Kártik.*
18. *Ránsodvan* or forest-leaving, that is, grain ears given to Mahárs on the first cutting and stacking.
19. *Pendha* or straw.
20. *Lagin-takka* or marriage rupee, that is, four annas given to the village Mahár when the booth is raised.

The duties of the Mahárs to the villagers are to cut firewood, carry letters, sweep and clean the yards in front of their houses, carry cowdung cakes to the burning ground and to dig graves. For their private services they are paid in cash, or, what they like better, in cooked food. They have a monopoly of the dead village animals, of the shrouds used in carrying the village dead, and of the copper coins which in the name of the dead are thrown to one side at the resting place or *visáviáchi jága.* Mahárs are largely employed by Europeans as domestic servants, and as grooms, or syces, they perform service in all parts of India. Recently they have taken readily to attending motor-cars and earn high wages in that capacity. As unskilled labourers they are employed in very large numbers. Of recent years complaints have arisen in villages near large centres of industry that the Mahárs have been so depleted in numbers by emigration to the cities as to leave an inadequate staff for village requirements. Some are husbandmen. Many are contractors and money-lenders, and manage their business without the help of any high caste clerk. Mahárs make excellent railway gang labourers, and have gained almost a monopoly of the unskilled railway labour market in some districts. The Mahárs of Kanara and Sávantvádi plait bamboo mats, baskets and fans, and play kettle-drums at some of the religious festivals and at the marriages of some of the lower castes. The Parvári or musical Mahár plays on a double drum called *sambal*, a small flute or trumpet called *sanai*, a long trumpet or flute called *sur* or *surani* with a palm-leaf mouth-piece, a thin drum-stick called *buk*, and a horned or crooked stick called *cháp*. These, with a wooden flute (*alguzár*), are the chief instruments used by the musical Mahár. Occasionally he blows the horn (*singa*), but never beats the tambourine or blows the big trumpet (*karna*) these being exclusively Máng instruments.

Food.

The staple food of the Mahárs of the Deccan is millet bread, split pulse, pounded chillies, cheap vegetables and occasionally fish ; that of the Konkan Mahárs—*kodra* and coarse rice. They eat the leavings of the higher castes, and when cattle, sheep or fowls die they feast on their carcasses, eating strips of the flesh roasted over a fire, often with nothing else, but sometimes washed down by liquor. They do not eat pork, crocodiles, monkeys, jackals, horses, serpents, rats, squirrels and lizards. They hate the Mángs for eating the pig and the Mángs hate them for eating the cow. They are very fond of liquor and palm-juice. They do not eat cooked food at the hands of Buruds, Jingars, Kaikádis, Vaddas, Parits, Mochis, Bhangis, Mángs and Ghadshis, The Holárs and Mángs eat food cooked by them. Socially, Mahárs are slowly making progress owing to the increasing earnings which the industrial development of the country affords them an opportunity of securing.

MAHAR DOMBAR.—A sub-division of Kolhátis.

MAHATMA.—A synonym for Mánbháv.

MAHAWAT.—*See* under Minor Musalmán Castes.

MAHESHRI.—A sub-division of Meghváls.

MAHESHVAR.—A synonym for Jangam.

Name and origin.

MAHIAS* numbering 1,944 (1901), including 1,051 males and 893 females, are chiefly found in the Sorath Prant of Káthiáwár. The head of the caste is the owner of the village of Shergadh under the Halia Malia Mahál of Junagadh. In descent they appear to be Jádhav Rajputs and to have accompanied the Bábriás, with whom they have many things in common, into Káthiáwár ; they were probably hired soldiers and labourers. It is a common belief among the people of the caste that they came from Chitor to Gujarát in the reign of Mahmud Begada. Not finding enough territory for themselves, they

* In the census of 1891 the caste is shown as "Maiya", numbering 2,621.

went over to Thán, which they occupied under the leadership of two brothers, Dunto and Mahio. Dunto subsequently marched on to Dedan and ruled there under the name of Kotillo. Mahio marched through Pánchála and occupied Shergadh. The latter won the Chorwád *mahál* for the Junagadh State, in recognition whereof that state conferred 24 villages upon the Mahiás. Later a misunderstanding arose between the State and the Mahiás regarding the payment of tribute, which ended in a cruel and treacherous slaughter of many of the caste on Kaneda hill near Khodiyar. According to the Bombay Gazetteer, it seems that the Mahiás claim Káthi origin, and were in revolt in 1867, when they established themselves in the Gir hills. Afterwards, on being pardoned, certain lands were made over to them on service tenure. They were disarmed in 1873.

Endo-gamous divisions.

Originally the Mahiás contained 15 sub-divisions, eight of whom *viz.*, Dhuya, Makhana, Gonia, Titvela, Lungha, Lunára, Lunjhária and Ládak, have become extinct. The existing sub-divisions are :—

	Sub-division.		Clan-name.		Founder.
1.	Daiyátar.	..	Jádeja	..	Lákho Phulám.
2.	Makka	..	Chaván	..	Prithvi Ráj.
3.	Dángar	..	Chudásma	..	Javgád.
4.	Páderi	..	Jethva	..	(Unknown).
5.	Bábria	..	Bábria	..	Babruváhana.
6.	Dhána	..	Dhánk	..	(Unknown).
7.	Chalávda	..	Solanki	..	Sidharáj.

The corresponding names for the seven above-noted among the Bábriás are, *seriatim*, Varu, Murmul, Chudásáma, Kátyál, Kotilla, Dhankda and Solanki. Intermarriage between members of the same sub-division is strictly prohibited.

Exo-gamous divisions.

The exogamous sub-divisions are identical with the seven surnames enumerated above. Sameness of patron deity is a bar to intermarriage. Each sub-division has a separate patron deity, as follows :—

Daiyátar	..	Mahamaya and Asápara.
Makka	..	But and Bálvi.
Dángar	..	Khodiyar.
Páderi	..	Rájbai.
Bábria	..	Chámunda.
Dhána	..	Pithad.
Chalávdá	..	Váchro.

Marriage ceremonies.

Marriage with a maternal uncle's daughter is allowed. It is prohibited with a father's sister's daughter and mother's sister's daughter. A Mahia may marry two sisters. Two brothers may marry two sisters. Boys and girls are married between twelve and fourteen. Sexual intercourse before marriage is neither allowed nor tolerated. If a girl commits sexual indiscretions before marriage, she is fined, as well as the man involved, if he belongs to the caste. Polygamy is permitted, but polyandry is unknown. The offer of marriage is generally made by the girl's father, and the marriage negotiations are carried on through a priest or by two respectable men of the caste. When a marriage is settled the ceremony of *sagái* is performed. The boy's father makes a present of clothes and ornaments to the girl. This is known as *samurtum*. Then an auspicious day for the marriage is fixed by the girl's father, and the day is made known to the boy's father in a letter sent through the family priest. This is known as *lagna lakhavun*. The acceptance of the date is signified by the boy's father giving a cocoanut to the priest and marking the boy's forehead with red paste. This is termed *lagna vadhávavu*. In the morning, a day previous to the marriage day, a fruit known as *mindol* is tied to the wrists of the bride and bridegroom and they are anointed with turmeric and saffron-paste at their respective houses. These ceremonies are known as *mindol bándhavun* and *halad chadhávavi*. In the evening the bridegroom and his party proceed to the bride's house, where they are received by the bride's party. A woman taking two earthen pots, one over the other, on her head, and placing a cocoanut at the mouth of the upper pot, receives the bridegroom's party first. The family priest too remains present, having with him saffron and red powder. The bridegroom's brow is marked with red powder, rice grains are applied to it, and he is offered a cocoanut. He offers a cocoanut in return. The couple are then led to a lodging specially prepared for them. Molasses or date fruit are distributed among those present. The bride is offered clothes and ornaments. On the morning of the marriage day men on both sides assemble in the marriage booth. At each corner of the marriage booth seven earthen pots are arranged in a row and called *chori bándhavi*. In the marriage booth Ganpati and local gods are established on an altar as the presiding deities of the ceremony. At the appointed time the bride's father gives his daughter to the bridegroom; this is the *kanyádán*. The couple then walk round the altar four times, this being the binding portion of the ceremony. The bride and bridegroom return to their house after making a bow to the presiding deities. Turmeric-paste is then washed off and the wristlets (*bhindols*) are untied,

Widow remarriage is allowed. A widow can marry her maternal uncle's son or a member of her caste by paying a fine of 200 to 700 *koris* (a *kori* equals nearly a quarter rupee). A widow may cohabit with the younger brother of her deceased husband. This course is commonly adopted when she has no issue, or when her deceased husband possessed some landed property. The previous consent of the husband's relations is required if a widow wishes to marry out of the family, when her first husband's line is likely to become extinct. A widow remarriage can be effected on any day. On the remarriage day the widow's weeds are removed and new clothes are put on. The widow puts on such ornaments as her new husband chooses to give her. The brows of the widow and her new husband are then marked with red powder, and sugar or molasses are distributed. A bachelor is allowed to marry a widow with all the forms of a widow remarriage.

Divorce is allowed, but it is not very common. A woman divorced for adultery is fined from 200 to 500 *koris*, and a portion of the head-dress of the husband is torn as a mark of divorce.

Religion. Mahiás are Hindus by religion. Some of them adore Mahákáli while others believe in Rámdepir. The religious preceptor of Mahákáli is Atit, while that of Rámdepir is Margi Sádhu. They worship the *Shaktis* and Khijadia. The offerings made by them are received by the servants of the respective deities.

Death ceremonies. Mahiás generally burn their dead. *Sádhus* (ascetics), and small children who have not cut their teeth, are buried. The *Sádhus* are buried in a sitting posture facing the north. Children are buried on their backs, the head being turned towards the north. Persons dying of small-pox and leprosy are buried, as it is believed that small-pox already consumes the body and that additional burning is unnecessary.* It is also thought that leprosy is infectious, and that the smoke from a leprous corpse is dangerous. The ashes and bones of the dead are thrown into a river or are sent to a holy place. On the eleventh day an image of the dead is prepared of wheat flour and worshipped by a river. For the propitiation of ancestors in general they observe the *shráddha* ceremony. When an accident is the cause of death a stone image of the deceased is prepared, and it is either worshipped with the household gods or worn round the neck. For the propitiation of childless ancestors a he-calf and a she-calf are formally married. This marriage ceremony is known as *lil parnavi.*

---

* Another common theory is that small-pox being a god should not be consumed by fire.

The people believe themselves to have once been soldiers rather than labourers. Some of them own lands, while others are agricultural labourers ; some are servants.

Food. They eat flesh and drink liquor. They eat with Ahirs, Rabáris, Bharwáds, and Margi Sádhus and Kumbhárs ; the Hátis, Káthis, Rajputs, Bábriás, and Chárans eat with them.

MAIRALS, numbering 123 (1901), including 76 males and 47 females, are found mostly in Poona. They are ministrants at Khandoba's temple, and live by begging alms at the houses of the rich worshippers of the gód. Their religious and social customs are like those of local Kunbis.

MAKADVALE.—A sub-division of Kaikádis.

MAKHIYAR.—A sub-division of Bhangis.

MAKKALSANTAN.—A sub-division of Suppaligs, Mogers and Gánigs.

MAKVANA.—*See* under Minor Musalmán Castes. Also a subdivision of Thoris.

MAKVANIYA.—A sub-division of Rávals.

MALA.—A sub-division of Bhois.

MALABANJARI.— A sub-division of Alkaris.

MALAI.—A sub-division of Kattais.

MALAO.—A sub-division of Kachhis.

MALGAR.—A synonym for Hugar.

MALHAR.—A sub-division of Kolis.

MALI.—A sub-division of Vaidus and Kachhiás.

Name and origin. **MALIS** or Gardeners, from the Sanskrit *mála* a garland, numbering 290,972 (1901), including 145,605 males and 145,367 females, are found in large numbers all over the Deccan and North Gujarát, and in small numbers in the Konkan, Kanara and Karnátak. They seem to have been originally Kunbis who took to gardening, and by degrees formed a separate community. Máli being a functional term is sometimes applied to other castes following the occupation of gardening, *e.g.*, Pánchkalshi, Agri, Bhandári, Káchi, etc., and also to the Musalmán Bágbáns. Mális are husbandmen, gardeners and day labourers, and their women help them in tilling and by selling flowers, fruit and vegetables. They are divided into three territorial groups, Marátha, Gujaráti and Kanarese, who have nothing in common except their occupation. These are described below.

MARATHA MALIS have thirteen endogamous divisions as follows :—

Endogamous divisions.

Adhaprabhu.	Kshiraságar.
Adhasheti.	Lingáyat.
Bávane.	Páde.
Halde, Bankar or Kás.	Phul.
Jire.	Ránt.
Kácha.	Unde.
Kadu.	

Of the above, Phul Mális, Halde Mális, Jire Mális, and Kácha Mális form the bulk of the caste. Phul Mális are found chiefly in Ahmednagar, Sátára, Poona and Násik, Jires and Haldes in Ahmednagar, Poona and Násik, Káchás in Ahmednagar; Lingáyats in Poona, Sátára and Sholápur; Pádes, Bávanes, Adhaprabhus, Adhashetis and Undes in Ahmednagar, Khándesh, Sátára and Sholápur; Ránts and Kshiraságars in Sholápur; and the Kadus all over the Deccan.

The Phul Mális are, as their name indicates, florists. They will not wear a flower or bunch of flowers in their turbans and will not have a flower pattern (of silk) on their shoes. They are considered to be the social superiors of the other three main divisions mentioned above. Jire Mális take their name from *Jire* (cumin seed) which they grow. Haldes grow *halad* or turmeric, and Káchás are cotton braid weavers. Káchás and Phul Mális dine together, but they will not eat with Jires or Haldes, who eat food cooked by Phuls and Káchás. Haldes are looked down upon by the other divisions of Mális, and are said to be treated as Mahárs, because they boil bulbs of turmeric and prepare them for market. A fanciful resemblance between a part of the turmeric flower and a cow's head is given as the reason for considering this occupation to be degrading. In many cases they have actually given up this work and passed it on to Mahárs. None of the above divisions intermarry. Kadu Mális consist of the illegitimate offspring of Mális and of the progeny of the crosses between the divisions. It is stated by some that a Máli girl may be kept by a Marátha as his mistress, when she becomes a Kunbi.

Exogamous divisions.

The *kuls* or exogamous divisions of Marátha Mális are covered by surnames. Sometimes a group of surnames is supposed to represent one *kul* as having descended from a common ancestor, and marriages between members belonging to one or other of them are prohibited. They have numerous *kuls*, the chief of which are as follows :—

Abang.	Garde.	Korde.	Pánsare.
Aher.	Ghádge.	Kore.	Párkhe.
Anárse.	Gharat.	Kudale.	Phule.
Bankar.	Gholap.	Lag.	Rásal.
Bhágvat.	Gite.	Lokhande.	Ráut.
Bhujbal.	Hirve.	Londhe.	Sasáne.
Boráde.	Jádhav.	Malange.	Shinde.
Chaudhari.	Jagtáp.	Mandlik.	Suryavanshi.
Chipáde.	Jamdáde.	Mule.	Tájne.
Dáke.	Kájle.	Navase.	Thorát.
Dalve.	Káthe.	Nikam.	Vágh.
Doke.	Khaire.	Páchure.	
Gáikvád.	Koke.	Páṅdhre.	

Adháv. } Povár.

Borband. } Dhadge.

Bulkunde. } Parvat.

Chápheker. } Sángle.

Bhopale. } Raut.

Gore. } Shevkar.

Koke. } Mehre.

Pándhre. } Shinde.

The Halde Mális of Khándesh have also *gotras* such as Atri, Kátyáyami, Kaundinya, Kaushik, Márkandeya, Muni, Vashishtha, etc., but in settling marriages only *kuls* are considered, which suggests that the *gotras* have been adopted at a later date in imitation of Bráhmans, like many other castes anxious to raise themselves in the social scale. It is interesting to note that the Haldes are the lowest of the Máli divisions, treated almost like untouchables, and therefore it seems natural that the desire on their part to rise in the social scale should be greater than the other divisions who hold the same social position as the Marátha Kunbis. Originally every *kul* or a number of *kuls* had a separate *devak*, and marriages were prohibited between members having the same *devak*. There are still some *kuls* having such *devaks*, instances of which are the following :—

Kuls.	*Devaks.*
Aher	The *maryádvel* (Ipomœa biloba).
Pándhare	
Sinde	
Bhujbal	A feather* of the *Sálunki* (Coracias Indica).
Gáikvád	The *suryakiran* grass.
Jádhav	*Pánkanis* (Reed mace).
Kudale	
Jamdade	The *Pánchpálvi.*
Koke	
Korde	
Lag	
Phule	
Ráut	
Suryavanshi	The sunflower.

Even among the above, sameness of *devak* is no bar to intermarriage, the *pánchpálvi* having now become the common *devak* of the whole caste. Only among the Jire Mális of the Násik district has the totemistic significance of the *devak* still survived, sameness of *devak* among them being still a bar to intermarriage. The *devaks* commonly found amongst them are :—

1. *Devnál*—Phragmitis communis.
2. Feathers of the *Sálunki* or blue jay (Coracias Indica).
3. *Kunda*—Andropogon intermedius.
4. *Maryádvel*—Ipomœa biloba.
5. Peacock feathers.
6. *Vásanvel*—Cocculus villosus.

Marriage rules.

Marriage with a maternal uncle's daughter is allowed. Marriage with a father's sister's daughter is allowed in some places. Marriage with a mother's sister's daughter is nowhere allowed. In Sátára and Sholápur instances are found of Mális having married their sister's daughters. A man may marry two sisters and brothers may marry sisters. Polygamy is common, some of the Mális at Kothrud near Poona having three to six wives. Polyandry is unknown. Marriage is infant as well as adult. Widow remarriage and divorce are allowed and practised.

* At Sangamner in the Ahmednagar district a feather made of silver.

The family deities of Marátha Mális are Bahiroba of Sonári and Agadgaum in Ahmednagar, Devi of Tuljápur in the Nizám's territory and of Saptashring in Násik, and Khandoba of Jejuri in Poona. At Mungi Paithan the Phul Mális have their *guru* called *malgand* who has with him all the literature about the origin of their caste and a genealogy of their whole caste. He travels every third or fourth year, when he goes to every family in the caste and records in his books a complete census of the family and all the changes since his last visit—additions and omissions, births, deaths, etc. He is paid his expenses and a rupee or two as *dakshina* by each family. He does not visit the houses of illegitimates. In all other details, Marátha Mális follow Marátha Kunbis as regards religion, customs, ceremonies, food and drink. They eat with Maráthás, Kunbis, Shimpis, Dhangars, Vanjáris, etc., who will eat food cooked by Marátha Mális.

GUJARATI MALIS are found mostly in north Gujarát. A few among them are from Márwár, but most seem to have been Kanbis, whom they resemble in appearance and dress. As a rule marriages are prohibited between near relations though in Ahmedábád the children of brothers and sisters marry. The remarriage of widows is permitted. A widow may marry a younger brother of her deceased husband. Divorce is granted in some places and not in others. In religion Gujarát Mális are Kabirpanthis, Rámánujis, Shaivas, Swáminaráyans and Vallabhácháryas, and in north Gujarát a few are Jains. They worship the cobra and other snakes. They are gardeners and flower-sellers, a few in Ahmedábád being traders, ministrants in Shrávak temples and domestic servants. They eat the ordinary grains, and, in the Panch Mahâls, fish, fowls and the flesh of goats and sheep after offering them to a goddess. In south Gujarát they drink liquor. Except that in the Panch Mahâls no ceremony is performed on the sixth day after the birth of a child, their customs at birth, marriage pregnancy and death do not differ from those of Kanbis.

KANARESE MALIS are also called Kámtis or Kunchgi Vakkals. They take their name Kunchgi Vakkal from the cloak or *Kunchgi* which they wear during the rains. They seem to have come from Mysore, as the shrine of their patron goddess Chandragutti is in Sorab in Mysore. They have neither clans nor family names. Children are married generally after the age of five years. Polygamy is permissible, but polyandry is unknown. Widows are allowed to remarry. Their family deities are Venkataráma, Yellamma, Guttiamma and Hanumant. Their priests are Bráhmans. They burn their dead except children under five years who are buried. They eat fish, mutton, poultry and game and drink liquor.

MALIK.—*See* under Minor Musalmán Castes.

MALIKWAL.—A sub-division of Bráhmans.

MALLAVA.—A sub-division of Lingáyats.

MALU.—A sub-division of Hajáms.

MALVI.—A sub-divisions of Bajániás, Kumbhárs, Sonárs, Shrigaud Bráhmans.

MANBHAV.—A sub-division of Mángs.

MANBHAVS[1] are a religious order, the members of which are scattered over the Deccan and Berars, a few being found in the Punjab and Afghanistan. At the census of 1901, they numbered 22,716, including 11,630 males and 11,086 females. In the case of a loosely knit community of the nature of a religious order, the census figures cannot be relied on. Many Mánbhávs must have returned themselves under their original caste names. Name and origin.

It would appear that the term Mánbháv is a corruption of the Sanskrit Mahánubháva, meaning great-souled. The other names of the sect met with in books and current in the different provinces are, (1) Sanyási, (2) Yogi, (3) Hansa, (4) Paramahansa, (5) Yati, (6) Muni, (7) Mahátma, (8) Mahánubháva, (9) Bhikshuk, (10) Dnyáni, (11) Achyutpanthi or Jayakrishniya.

In Maháráshtra they are known chiefly as Mahánubháva, Bhikshuk, Mahátma and Sanyási. In Bundelkhand they are known by the names Achyutpanthi, Muni, Mahátma, Dnyáni, Sanyási and Paramahansa; and in the Punjab and Afghanistan the chief names are Jayakrishniya, Sanyási, Mahátma and Yogi.

Mr. D. R. Bhandarkar points out that there is in certain points a striking resemblance between this sect and the Manichœans. Thus Mani, the founder of the latter, invented an alphabet of his own in which the scriptures were written. He forbade the killing of plants, plucking of fruit or breaking twigs, to avoid taking life. Idolatry was forbidden. An empty chair was worshipped. The ceremonies were kept secret. These are all Mánbhav customs, and there seems probability in the theory that they are Manichœans.

According to the Mánbhávs, the tenets of their order were promulgated by God himself through eight incarnations, two of which were born in each of the four *yugs* or ages. Of these incarnations Shri Náráyan and Shri Hansa were born in the *Krit yug*, Shri Nar and Shri Datta in the *Treta yug*, Shri Rishabh and Shri Krishna in the *Dwápár yug*, and Shri Prashánt and Shri Chakra-

(1) The materials for this article were supplied by Mr. D. R. Bhandarkar.

dhar in the *Kali yug*. Shri Chakradhar is said to have imparted the secret doctrine (*Brahmavidyáshástra*) to Nágadeva Bhatta in the Prakrita (old Maráthi language), which originated in the *Krit yug*.

In the original edition of the Imperial Gazetteer the sect is represented to have been founded in the fourteenth century by Kishen Bhat (Krishnabhatta), who married the daughter of a Máng and had four sons by her, called Mángbhávs, which, in the corrupted form of Mánbháv, is said to have become the name of the sect. Sir W. Hunter was obviously misled into giving a highly inaccurate account of this order. Dr. R. G. Bhandarkar, who has studied their literature and especially had access to their *Liláсharitra*, the most sacred of their scriptures, has come to the conclusion that the sect was founded by Shri Chakradhar, a Karháda Bráhman, who is looked upon as an incarnation of Shri Dattátraya, their god, but was propagated by his disciple Nágdevbhatta, a Deshasth Bráhman, also called the First Preceptor. Various stories have been narrated in that work which make Shri Chakradhar a contemporary of the two Yádav princes Krishna and Mopádev, and Nágdevbhatta of Rámchandra. Chakradhar is represented to have finally retired to Badrikáshram in Saka 1194 or A.D. 1272. This date is quite in keeping with the period (A.D. 1247—1271) when his contemporary Yádav sovereigns are known from inscriptions to have flourished. The same remark applies to the case of Nágdev and his contemporary prince, Rámchandra. This shows that the account of Chakradhar and Nágdevbhatta given in the Mánbháv scriptures is not only traditional but is confirmed by history. The account, therefore, deserves credence. The statement that the sect was originated by Kishenbhat in the 14th century, nearly a hundred years later than their reputed founder, thus falls to the ground. Kishenbhat is himself referred to in their works as the founder of a diabolical creed called Mátangpatta, which is therein held up to ridicule and opprobrium. Kishenbhat cannot, therefore, have any connection with the Mánbháv sect. The followers of Kishenbhat's creed are still in existence in the Ahmednagar district, and are never confounded with Mánbhávs. Lastly, Mánbháv is, as shown above, a corruption not of Mángbháv, but of Mahánubháv, which, like the alternative title of *Mahátma* means "high-souled".

Within the last hundred years three new sects have sprung from the Mánbháv sect. One of them known as Jayánandi was founded by the descendants of Shri Kavishvar Amnáy Dikshit Gopál Pandit, and has a good deal of following in Berar. The second is

Bnown as Lálpanth, and was founded by a Kunbi Pátil Lálji of kábarváda in the Vardha district of Berar. It has also many followers in that province. The third was founded by a Sanyási named Bhikshumuni at Nyálkal, a village in the Bedar district of the Nizám's territory, and has many Bráhmans amongst itsf ollowers.

The principal tenets of the sect are as follows :— Tenets.

1. *Brahmacharya* or celibacy.
2. *Bhikshávritti* or maintenance by begging alms.
3. *Ahinsa* or abstaining from killing life.
4. *Abhakshyábhakshan* or abstaining from flesh and liquor.
5. *Ishvarbhakti, i.e.*, devotion to God.
6. *Nitya atan, i.e.*, constant wandering.

The chief religious book of the order is the *Brahmavidyáshástra* which is a collection of 11,700 precepts divided into two heads, *viz.*, *Shruti* and *Smriti*, and incorporated in their famous sacred book the *Lilácharitra*. They also revere the *Bhagavadgita* and the *Upanishads*, the first of which is studied by all members of the sect and discourses on it are given by the learned among them who are termed Pandits. They do not worship idols and have no faith in the *shrutis* and the *puránic* religion of the Hindus. Of the Hindu gods, they recognise only Dattátraya and Krishna, whose birthdays are celebrated with great pomp. The Mánbhávs have built temples at places where Dattátraya, Krishna and Chakradhar are said to have performed miracles. Such temples are at Phaltan, Paithan, Máhur, Verool, Pánchálеshvar, Mathura and other holy places, at most of which they have quadrangular or circular whitewashed terraces which they worship in the name of God. They neither worship other gods, nor stay, or even drink water, in other temples. The principle of abstaining from taking animal life is carried so far that they do not cut grass or pluck leaves or fruits from trees, thinking that there is life in these things. For the same reason, in the absence of a flowing stream, they avoid bathing, and only clean their bodies with a wet cloth, and drink water after it has been strained through linen. They have monasteries at Kabul, Peshawar, Amritsar, Jalandar, Lahore, Rawalpindi, Mathura, Broach, Sátára, Indore, Raher, Nandor and many other places.

Admission.

The Mánbhávs are recruited from all castes of Hindus except the impure classes. Children vowed to Mánbháv saints are brought up by the brotherhood, and at the age of fifteen or sixteen, if they are found fit for admission, are initiated into the doctrines of the sect.

If not, they are allowed to leave. Adult men and women are kept on trial for some time before admission, and if they stand the test, are initiated. If a man and his wife join the sect, the man is kept in one *mela* and the woman in another for fifteen years.

Initiation ceremony.

A novice is generally admitted into the order at the age of ten or twelve. The time of entering the order is at any season, but on an auspicious day, and the place is the temple of Krishna. On the day of entering the order, the Mánbhávs meet at the temple of Krishna, and the boy has his head and face clean shaved. He is then bathed and presented with a waistcloth and shouldercloth dyed black* with lampblack, a square piece of cloth for filtering drinking water, a bag for begging alms, a rosary, and articles of worship. His head is marked with white sandalpaste, and garlands of *tulsi* or sweet basil wood are tied round his neck and wrists. He bows before the image of Krishna and before the monk who acts as his religious teacher, and tells him the five chief rules of the order. Next day the ceremony ends with a dinner to all Mánbhávs at the expense of the novice or of his teacher. The novice has to wait on his teacher or *guru*, and follow him wherever he goes. Women are admitted by nuns in the same way as men. They call their teacher *ái guru* or mother teacher, and the other nuns sisters.

Divisions.

There are four main divisions of the Mánbhávs. They are :—

1. *Vairági.*—These include both men and women. They have to lead a strict celibate life. They do not observe caste distinctions. Both men and women have to shave their heads clean, and the former also their mustaches and beards.

2. *Angvanshil* or *Gharbhári* are those who put on the dress of the order and live in monasteries. They marry by the *gándharva* or love marriage form.

3. *Bhopi* or *Pujári.* These are temple servants and worshippers of gods.

4. *Bhawál, Shishya or Upadeshi* observe caste restrictions. They are initiated into the order by the mystic words or *mantras* being whispered into their ears by Bairági Mánbhávs. Of all the tenets of the order they observe only one, that of abstaining from flesh and liquor. The members of this division, though belonging to different castes, eat together but do not intermarry.

---

* In the Punjab ochre coloured clothes are presented.

The Mánbhávs have thirteen schools known as *Amnáys* founded by thirteen celebrated disciples of Nágdevbhatta, which are as follows :

1. Amrite.	5. Jayadev.	9. Maheshvar.
2. Dámodar.	6. Kavishvar.	10. Párámbndalya.
3. Divákar.	7. Kumár.	11. Shálkar.
4. Haridev.	8. Mádálas.	12. Upádhye.
	13. Yakshadev.	

Of these the disciples of Upádhye and Kavishvar alone are much in evidence.

The Vairági Mánbhávs have four divisions, which are as follows :—

1. *Patadhári* are those who wander from village to village in assemblies of 50 to 200 persons under the guidance of the Mahant or the pontiff of the order.

2. *Vandhári* are those who wander singly in forests. The number of these is very limited.

3. *Mathdhári.*—These are old and infirm persons who are unable to travel, and who, therefore, stay in *maths* or monasteries.

4. *Dharmabhrashtasanyási* are those Vairági Mánbhávs who violate the principles of the order. They are turned out of the order and live by begging alms.

As stated above, the Patadháris wander in assemblies of 50 to 200 persons under the guidance of their Mahant. These assemblies are called *melás.* All duties such as begging alms, cooking, bringing water, etc., are carried out by the members of the *melás* by turns, and it is remarkable that all are done regularly without complaint or quarrel. In their wanderings they are careful to avoid a place where a murder has been committed, and will not eat food for three days in any place where an accidental or violent death has happened. As they wander, they receive into their order grown up men and women, and children dedicated to a Mánbháv life by their parents. The Mahant has emblems of royalty such as a palanquin (*pálkhi*), an umbrella (*chhatra*), and a fan (*chámar*) ; and he is taken from village to village in procession in a palanquin or litter by his disciples. They encamp, as a rule, under the shade of trees, a mile or a mile and a half away from villages, to keep aloof from allurements, and some of the party go to the surrounding villages to procure food by begging. The monks and nuns live separately, and the nuns never serve the monks, however high their position may be. The nuns and monks usually travel separately. If a band of nuns meets a band of monks and travels with them, they put up at a great distance from each other, generally in a separate village. The women hold a separate service for themselves, visiting the temple at noon, or other fixed hours, when no men are allowed to attend. Women and men never hold a joint service.

The members both of a monastery and of a nunnery are divided into five grades. The five grades of the Mánbháv monks are the head or *mahant*, the teacher or *pandit*, the manager or *kárbhári* who provides the inmates with food, the food-server or *pálekar*, and the disciples or *chelás*. The five grades of *Mánbháv* nuns are, the head or *bidkar ái*, the young women's guardian or *lasrukar ái*, the teacher called either *pandit* or *videshkar ái*, and the tood divider or *bhojan ái*.

After the death of a Mahant, such of his disciples as have a reputation for holy conduct or learning offer themselves as candidates for the post. The most competent is elected after examination by Pandits. The newly-installed Mahant, before assuming his powers, visits the temple of Páncháleshvar in the Nizám's country, and, after worshipping Dattátraya, gives a feast to the Mánbhávs, dry food to such as do not eat from their hands, and alms to beggars.

The Mahant inquires into and punishes offences committed by the monks, and the *guru* mother inquires into and punishes offences committed by the nuns. When a dispute arises which she cannot settle, the *guru* mother takes the parties before the Mahant. The head nun or *guru* mother keeps a strict watch over the sisters, and any monk or nun who commits adultery is put out of the house.

Inheritance. All movable property left by a Mánbháv, except the insignia, clothes, ornaments, articles of worship, etc., is given in charity to deserving men. The Angvanshils are not entitled to any share.

If a Mahant builds a house for his own use in old age, the house is sold, and the proceeds are divided equally among his ascetic disciples. If the house is big, it is not sold, but portions of it are allotted to the disciples.

A Mahant has no claim to the property of the *math* over which he presides, even during his lifetime. If the income of the *math* exceeds the expenditure, he has the power to spend the surplus on charitable purposes. If a Mahant dies without any disciples, his property is used for charitable purposes. Among the Angvanshils the property is divided equally among male and female disciples.

The property of an Angvanshil woman does not go to her husband or daughters, but is divided among her male and female co-disciples.

All Mánbhávs bury their dead. Mánbháv nuns attend the funerals both of monks and of nuns. At a monk's funeral they walk far behind. At a nun's funeral, men dig the grave and then withdraw. The body is carried to the grave by nuns, the monks walking at a distance behind. When they reach the grave the nuns take the body out of the palanquin, strip it of its clothes except a waistcloth, lay it in the grave, cover it with earth and walk away. When the nuns retire, the monks who followed at a distance, come and fill the grave. When a Mahant dies, his body is washed, placed on a raised seat and worshipped by the monks. It is then tied to a palanquin in a sitting position. The palanquin is carried by the disciples on their shoulders to a place chosen for the occasion. As they walk, they ceaselessly repeat the names of Krishna and Dattátraya from the moment of the death till the body is buried. Mánbhávs do not use the ordinary burial grounds. They choose a clean spot, and a grave is dug lengthwise, north and south, and spread with salt. The body is taken out of the palanquin, stripped of its clothes, a loincloth of buff silk is tied round the loins, and it is laid in the grave with its head to the north and its feet to the south. It is laid on its left side so as to face the east. A sash or *shela* or other valuable cloth is spread over the body, and salt is spread on the sash and on this again, earth. After the earth has been spread on the salt, each of the mourners lays a cocoanut and a betel packet over it, and the grave is filled and the ground levelled so as to leave no trace of the burial. No tomb is ever raised over a Mánbháv. For ten days after the death the members of the religious house are fed. In the Punjáb the dead are immersed in water. **Death ceremonies.**

As stated above, the Mánbhávs maintain themselves chiefly by begging. Cash offerings are made to the Mahant by his devotees, which are spent in buying clothes and feeding members of the monasteries. Some of the monasteries have *inám* lands and *jhágirs* bestowed upon them. The Gharbhari and Bhawál Mánbhávs follow the occupations of the castes to which they belong. They also adhere to the religious and social customs of their castes except that they eschew flesh and liquor. **Occupation.**

MANDALIYA—A sub-division of Modh Vánis.

MANDHATA SARORIA—A sub-division of Kolis.

MANDVIA.—A sub-division of Dublás.

MANG.—A sub-division of Rámoshis and Dhálya Vanjáris.

Name and origin.

MANGS, known as Mádigs in the Kanarese districts and as Mángelás in Gujarát numbering 250,573 (1901), including 124,268 males and 124,305 females, are found in large numbers in the Deccan and Karnátak, a small number being recorded in Kanara and Gujarát. The tribe is described in Sanskrit literature by the name Mátang, of which Máng is a corrupted form. In the Kanarese districts, the Mádigs are often addressed as Mángs, and *vice versa.* In Gujarát the Mángelás, who follow the occupation of fishing, are now regarded as a separate caste. Regarding the origin of Mángs, it is held by them that they are descended from Jambrishi, who had seven sons, one of whom named Karkamuni was offered by him to the earth. Karkamuni had two sons, Madarchanaya and Niluchandaya. The former was sentenced to be a Mahár by Shankar for having eaten his cow, and the latter to be a Máng for having gone before Shankar with his body sprinkled with the blood of the cow. Their dark complexion, features, and the fact that they are held impure, point to their being one of the aboriginal tribes whom the later settlers reduced to slavery.

The Mángs have three main territorial divisions, (1) Marátha Mángs known as Mángs, (2) Kanarese Mángs or Mádigs, and (3) Gujarát Mángs or Mángelás, who neither eat together nor intermarry. The three divisions will be described below separately.

Status.

The Mángs rank lowest among Hindus. They live by themselves in a quarter known as *Mángváda,* separate from the Mahárs, the hereditary rivals and enemies of the tribe. The Máng Gárudis or snake-charmers being a wandering class of jugglers, have no fixed dwellings and live under a stretched awning tied to pegs fixed in the ground. They keep dogs and use donkeys and buffaloes as pack animals. Being an impure caste, the Mángs are not allowed to draw water from the village well or enter the village temple. They have their own wells and temples. The village barber will not shave them and the village washerman will not wash their clothes.

Appearance, dress and ornaments

As a class, Mángs are tall, coarse-featured, and strongly made and the whites of their eyes are generally bloodshot. They can be easily recognised from Kunbis by their darker complexion. The hair on their face and head is lank and thick. Most of the men wear the top-knot, moustache, whiskers and beard. Some men in the Ahmednagar district allow their hair to grow to its natural length.

Women tie the hair in Kunbi fashion. They do not use false hair or flowers. Their hands and arms are profusely tattooed, the figures of a cypress, scorpion and snake being preferred. A mark III will often be found tattooed on all fingers of the right hand, except the thumb, and a sun-flower on the back of the same hand. In dress and ornaments they resemble the Mahárs.

Endoga-mous divisions.

The Mángs have the follwing endogamous divisions :—

1. Assal Mángs, Gastis, Maráthás or Mángs proper.
2. Bále.
3. Burud.
4. Chapalsande.
5. Dabkar.
6. Desur.
7. Dhakalvár, Dakalvár, Dakkalgar or Vájantri Mángs.
8. Dhor.
9. Ghadshi.
10. Holge or Holár.
11. Jingar.
12. Jiráits.
13. Kákar.
14. Kokalvár.
15. Mánbháv.
16. Máng Gárudi or Mhaisbhádre.
17. Mochi.
18. Náde, Nudar or Khotra.
19. Parit.
20. Pend or Ped.
21. Shivate, Shevte, Valar or Páthantánas.
22. Telangi.
23. Tokarphode.
24. Zare.
25. Musalmán.

Of these some have an Akarmáshe or bastard division. The Assal Mángs are considered to be the highest in social rank. In Sholápur their leavings are eaten by the Holár Mángs and the Dakalvárs. In some places, the Tokarphodes and Kákars call themselves Marátha Mángs, but they do not eat together. The Dakalvárs are the Mángtes or bards and priests of the other Mángs. They state that they are the highest branch of Mángs, and that the others profess to despise them to punish the Dakalvárs, etc., because they refuse to touch the other Mángs. This seems unlikely, as Dakalvárs eat the leavings of Mángs proper and the Náde Mángs, and no Máng will touch them. They are not allowed to drink water from a well or stream used by the other Mángs, but must take water from the other Mángs. At the same time, some sanctity or power attaches to the Dakalvárs as no Máng will ever swear falsely by a Dakalvár. The Kokalvárs are the Mángtes of Dakalvárs than whom they are lower in status. A separate account of the Dakalvárs is given below.

The Máng Gárudis are so called, because they were originally snake-charmers (*Gárudis*). They are called Mhaisbhádres in Khándesh after their occupation of shaving buffaloes (*mháis*, a she-buffalo, and *bhádrya*, one who shaves roughly). The Tokarphodes take their name from *tokar*, bamboo, and *phod*, to split, their occupation being bamboo-splitting. The Nádes are so called after their occupation of making *nádás* or ropes. The Mochis are leather workers (*mochi*, a tanner). Kákars make ropes of untanned leather (*kákar*, a rope of untanned leather). The Shivates are cobblers. The Holges or Holárs, Dhors, Buruds, Parits, Ghadshis and Jingars are doubtless representatives of these castes admitted by the Mángs. The Mánbhávs are probably members of the Mátangapatta sect, popularly known as Mángbháv, which was founded by Krishnabhatta. The origin of the other divisions has not yet been traced.

In the Ahmednagar dstrict, Chapalsandhcs, Gárudis, Holárs, Jiráits, Maráthás and Tokarphodes are found, the bulk consisting of the Jiráits. In Khándesh there are said to be 13½ divisions of Mángs, *viz.*, Marátha, Gárudi, Dakalvár, Pend, Dhor, Burud, Jingar, Parit, Telangi, Mochi, Ghadshi, Desurs, Mánbhávs and Musalmáns, the last being considered half a division. In Násik the only three divisions of Mángs are Assal, Pend and Gárudis. The divisions met with in the Poona district are the Assal Mángs, Gárudis, Holges and Tokarphodes. The Mángs of the Sátàra district are said to have no divisions. The Sholápur Mángs consist of Assals, Gárudis, Pends, Holárs, Mochis, Dakalvárs, Tokarphodes, Kákars, Shevtes, Nádes and Kokalvárs. In Thána, the Gárudis, Záres and Báles are found. The Belgaum Mángs include Dabkárs, Gárudis and Nádes. In the States of the Southern Marátha Country Mángs are represented by the Dakalvárs, Gárudis, Nádes, Páthantanás, Maráthás and Shivtes.

Exogamous divisions.

The exogamous divisions of Mángs are identical with surnames. The common surnames are as follows :—

Admáne.	Jagtáp.	Nánde.
Alhát.	Jánavare.	Netke.
Apte.	Jogdand.	Pálute.
Avle.	Kable.	Párdhi
Avár.	Kálukhe	Pavár.
Bhise.	Kámble.	Pitáre.
Bhode.	Khade.	Rájguru.
Bhore.	Khavade.	Satáne.
Chaván.	Kote.	Sáthe.
Dhongade.	Kunchekar.	Shenge.
Divate.	Lákade.	Sinde.
Gáikvád.	Lokhande.	Thokar.
Gavli.	Londhe.	Vairásgar.
Hunde.	Mohite.	Vavrát.
Jádhav.	More.	

Marriage rules.

Marriages are prohibited between members of the same sub-division. A Máng cannot marry his father's sister's or mother's sister's daughter. He may marry his maternal uncle's daughter. In some places a wife's sister can be married during the wife's lifetime; in others, she can be married only after the wife's death. Two brothers are allowed to marry two sisters. Polygamy is allowed and practised, but polyandry is unknown. Marriage is infant as well as adult. Children are sometimes married as babes, when the marriage garlands (called *báshing*) are tied to the cradle instead of to the brow. In some places, in the Belgaum district, girls remaining unmarried till after the age of puberty are not allowed to marry afterwards. They become Jogtins and follow prostitution. Sexual license before marriage is not tolerated. If misconduct on the part of a maiden with a casteman is brought to light, the parties are married, if possible, and are relegated to the Akarmáshe or bastard division. If a girl is guilty of misconduct with a member of a lower or higher caste, she is expelled from the caste, and becomes either a Murli or a prostitute. Divorce is allowed on the ground of the wife's unchastity, incompatibility of temper, the husband's impotence and an incurable disease, such as leprosy, in the case of either. A divorced woman is allowed to marry again by the widow remarriage form. A woman taken in adultery is allowed to remain in the caste on her paying a fine or giving a dinner to the caste people. If the offence is committed with a member of a lower caste, she is excommunicated.

Language. The home tongue of Mángs is Maráthi. In Sholápur, they speak among themselves a language known as *pároshi* or out of use, which is unintelligible to a Marátha stranger. In Ahmednagar, their home tongue is a dialect of Maráthi. They cannot pronounce nasals properly or two consonants joined by a single vowel. Among their peculiar words and expressions are *rákas* for *rákshas*, demon; *puris* for *purush*, a male; *map* for *majapáshin*, with me; *tap* for *tujapáshin*, with you; *maha* for *májha*, mine; *tuha* for *tujha*, thine. In Khándesh, they speak a dialect of Máráthi like the local Kunbis and Mahárs. The names in common use among men are Abhimán, Arjuna, Bápu, Bhágu, Bhiva, Ithu, Kavtik, Krishna, Kushába, Laksha, Mahádu, Mayáji and Málu; and among women, Báji, Bhágu, Chanda, Ganga, Gaya, Harku, Jái, Kami, Málshi, Putadi, Rakhma, Saguna and Sayi. As among other Hindu castes, when the male children of a man are short-lived, they are given opprobrious names such as Dagdya, Kerya, Maharya, Kacharya, etc.

Community. Mángs have two kinds of leaders, Mehetrias and Sarnáiks. The former are religious and social heads, the latter, leaders in crimes. The Mehetrias settle caste disputes in consultation with the adult male members of the caste. The offenders are fined from Rs. 1-4-0 to Rs. 5, which are spent on a caste feast. Till the feast is given the offender is not allowed back into caste. The offences punished by expulsion from caste are failure to give caste dinners, dining and smoking with a Dakalvár, Máng Gárudi, Vaddar or Phánse Párdhi, and adultery.

Birth ceremonies.

A woman is held impure for five weeks after childbirth, but after the twelfth day she is touched, though nothing is eaten from her hands. On the fifth day, after a child is born, they worship a dough image of Satvái or simply five pebbles arranged in a line in the mother's room and offer them cooked rice and split pulse or *dálbhát.* Two dough lamps are kept burning the whole night and a feast is held. On the twelfth day the mother and child are bathed, her clothes are washed, and the lying-in room is cowdunged. Seven pebbles are then placed outside the house in a line and worshipped by the mother in the name of the goddess Satvái. The child is named on the same day, the name being given by the Bráhman astrologer. Female guests are called and boiled gram or wheat is distributed among them. A month later new bangles are put round the mother's wrists. The boy's hair is cut at any time when he is between one and three years old and relations and friends are feasted.

Marriage ceremonies.

The offer of marriage comes from the boy's father, who has to pay a bride-price of from Rs. 5 to Rs. 10 to the girl's father. A lucky day for the marriage is chosen by a holy man or *sádhu* of their own caste. Each *sádhu* has a group of from twelve to thirty villages in his charge. In Khándesh the marriage service is generally conducted by a *sádhu* though his presence is not essential. In his absence, the headman, *mehetar,* who must be present at all weddings, and if not he, some members of the marriage party perform the marriage. In other places, the marriage is conducted by a Bráhman priest standing at a distance. Máng marriages resemble in many details the marriages of Mahárs. On marriage occasions, new images of gods, such as Bahiroba, Khandoba, Kalubai, etc., are made of gold, silver, or copper, or the old ones in the house are cleaned. Daily for five days before the marriage, the girl is rubbed with turmeric at her house, and the rest is sent with music to the boy. On the afternoon of the third day at both houses a sheep is offered to the family god and slain in the marriage hall. In the evening the boy's paternal uncle, cousin or brother, with music and kinspeople, goes to the temple of Máruti carrying a hatchet in his raised hands, four men hold a cloth over his head, and cooked food or *naivedya* is carried with them. At the temple the *gurav* or ministrant has ready as *devaks* or marriage guardians, mango, *jámbhul* (Eugenia jambolana), *rui* (Calotropis gigantea), *shami* (Prosopis spicegera), and *umbar* (Ficus glomerata) branches. The cooked food and a copper are laid before the guardians and they return with the *devak* and tie it to one of the posts in the marriage hall. Goats are then offered to the *devak* at both houses and a feast is held. Next, the boy, with kinspeople and music, goes either on a horse or a bullock to Máruti's shrine when the girl's father meets him, and presents him with a waistcloth and turban, which he puts on and is led to the girl's and seated in the marriage hall. Then two baskets are taken, hides and ropes are placed in them and the boy and girl are seated face to face and a curtain is held between them. The officiating priest repeats verses, and the guests who stand with rice grains in their hands throw them over the heads of the couple, and, when the verses are ended, they are husband and wife. In some places instead of a hide a grindstone is placed in the girl's basket and a rope in the boy's, and instead of a cloth a quilt called *jamnika* is held, and instead of rice, *juári* is thrown. The newly-married pair are then made to stand side by side on the ground and are covered with the cloth which was held between them. Cotton thread is passed five times round them and divided into two pieces and one piece with a turmeric root is tied to the boy's right wrist and the other piece to the girl's left wrist. The couple are made to stand on an earthen altar or *bahule* and thrice change places. Their faces are rubbed with turmeric and the boy spends the night at the girl's house sleeping with the other male guests in the marriage hall. The boy and girl play with betelnuts and beat each other's backs with twisted waistcloths. On the second and third the girl's parents feast the boy's and their own relations and caste fellows, and on the fourth the boy's father presents the girl with a bodice and robe and ties marriage ornaments to their brows. They are taken in procession to the village Máruti and thence to the boy's house. Next day the couple are sent round the villagers' houses, and the marriage ceremony is at an end.

Widow remarriage.

The remarriage of widows is permited. Among the Poona Mángs, widow remarriage is not allowed among those families who bear Marátha surnames. A widow cannot marry her mother's sister's or maternal uncle's son or a member of her deceased husband's section. A widow remarriage is celebrated on a dark night. In some places, the service is conducted by the village priest, in others by the *mehetar* or headman of the caste. The widow bathes and wears a new robe and bodice and ornaments brought by her intended husband. The pair are then seated on a bullock's packsaddle and the widow's forehead is marked with red powder, her lap is filled and the hem of her garment is tied to that of her intended husband. A feast to the castemen on the following day ends the ceremony. A bachelor desiring to marry a widow is first married to a *rui* bush or a ring.

Religion.

The Mángs profess Hinduism. Most of them are Shaivas, their chief god being Mahádeva. Their favourite goddess is Mariái or the cholera goddess. Their family deities are Bahiroba, Khandoba, Mhasoba, Ambabái, Bahiri, Janái, Taki, Vithoba and Yamái. They are not allowed to enter the village shrine, but stand at a distance and bow to the god. Goats and fowls are offered to the goddesses on Tuesdays or Fridays and to the gods on Sundays. Musalmán saints are venerated. Embossed images of deceased ancestors are installed and worshipped with offerings of cooked food. They make pilgrimages to Alandi, Kondanpur, Dehu, Pandharpur, and Singnapur. They observe the leading Hindu holidays, such as *Shivrátri*, *Holi*, *Rámnavami*, *Ashádhiekádashi*, *Gokuláshtami*, *Dasara* and *Diváli*. When cholera rages in a village, an offering of a goat is made to the goddess Mariái by the villagers through the village Mángs. They have a strong faith in soothsaying, witchcraft and sorcery. Their priests are the village Bráhmans. In some places, Gosávis, Bháts or Sádhus of their own caste officiate at all their ceremonies. In the Southern Marátha Country, Jangams are also sometimes employed. Unlike Mahárs who use the word *johár* that is 'Oh Warrior' in saluting, the Mángs say *pharman* probably the Persian *Farmán* or command to their caste fellows; to others they say *Maháráj*, at the same time passing the right palm to their forehead.

Death ceremonies.

Mángs generally bury their dead. The corpse is bathed and dressed in a waistcloth, turban and coat and laid on a bier. Red powder and betel leaves are sprinkled over it and a copper coin and some grains are tied to the hem of its garment. The chief mourner walks in front with an earthen firepot and his own turban under his arm, and music and the mourners follow. The musicians belong to the Máng caste. On the way to the burying ground the bearers halt, but the firepot is not allowed to touch the ground lest it should become impure, and the copper coin in the shroud hem is thrown away. On reaching the burying ground a hole is dug and the body is lowered into the hole and laid on its back. The chief mourner dips the end of his turban in water, squeezes a little water into the dead mouth, and strikes his own mouth with his open hand that the gods may hear and open the gates of heaven, *Svargi ghát vájte*, that is, the bell of heaven rings. The grave is filled and the mourners bathe in a river or stream close by and return to the deceased's house each carrying some grass and *nimb* branches. At the house of mourning cow's urine is sprinkled on the spot where the deceased breathed his last and the grass and *nimb* leaves are thrown over the urine. The mourners return to their homes. On the third day the chief mourner with the four bearers and a kinsman or two goes to the burial ground taking three *juári* cakes, cooked rice and curds, or only milk if the deceased is a child. They leave one of the cakes at the rest-place and the other two on the grave. They bathe, return to the deceased's house, and are sprinkled with cow's urine. The four corpse bearers sit in a line and their shoulders are touched with *nimb* leaves dipped in sweet oil. They are then fed on *juári*, molasses, oil and *sánja*, a sweet preparation of wheat flour, red sugar and *ghi*. The chief mourner is held impure for twelve days. On the thirteenth day he goes to the burying ground with his friends, has his whole face and head shaven, and bathes. He sets thirteen leaf saucers or *drons* side by side, fills them with water, and returns home with his friends. On the same day friends and kinsfolk are asked to dine at the house of mourning. They present the chief mourner with a turban and the mourning is at an end.

Occupation.

The Mángs are hardworking, but dirty, unthrifty, passionate, revengeful, and greatly feared as sorcerers. They make and sell leather ropes called *nádás*, thin cords or *charáts* of *ambáda* (Hibiscus cannabinus) or hemp and of *kekti* sweet pandanus, ropes, date brooms, *shinkes* or slings for hanging pots in, *gophans* or slings for throwing stones with, bamboo baskets, tent screens and ropes. They are musicians, songsters, scavengers, husbandmen, messengers, beggars, labourers, sellers of cowdung cakes, grass and firewood, bricklayers, carpenters and hangmen. The proudest moment of a Máng's life is said to be when he hangs a Mahár, the hereditary rival and enemy of his tribe. Several of them are village watchmen and guides. In some places, they have one-fourth share in every head of cattle that dies, while the Mahárs have three-fourths and, besides, own the skins and horns. Dakalvárs, who are the bards of Mángs, move from place to place begging from Mángs. They also tell fortunes and breed peacocks. Nádás are tanners and make hide and hemp ropes, brooms and bamboo baskets. Shivtes are cobblers, Vájantris are Máng musicians who play on the tabor and clarion. The Holár Mángs make shoes, slippers, whips, water-bags, saddles, harness and horses' grain-bags. Gárudis or sorcerers catch and pretend to have power over serpents, profess to know something of witchcraft, and earn their living by moving about the streets and preforming to any audience they can find on the road. Under the pretence of cattle-dealing and begging they often lift cattle, sheep and goats, which they catch at night or kill while grazing during the day. All, except the Dakalvárs, are hereditary robbers.

Food. The staple food of Mángs is Indian millet, *juári*, split pulse and chillies. They eat fish and the flesh of sheep, goats, fowls, dead cattle and hogs, but not that of horses or donkeys. They are exceedingly fond of drinking liquor. They eat the leavings of Bráhmans, Maráthás and other higher castes.

KANARESE MANGS or Mádigs have the following endogamous divisions :—

1. Asádarus.
2. Channa Holiya.
3. Dakaleru.
4. Dabke Mádig.
5. Dalaya.
6. Dhor.
7. Mángs Gadderu.
8. Máng Gadiger.
9. Mini Mádig.
10. Mochigar or Mochi.
11. Ped or Phed.
12. Máng Ráut.
13. Sanádi or Vájántri.

Most of these have representatives among the Marátha Mángs, which suggests that originally the two communities formed one caste.

The Mochis, Pheds and Sanádis eat together, but do not intermarry. The rest neither eat together nor intermarry.

The exogamous divisions of the caste are known as *Bedagus.* They are as follows :—

Aivallanavaru.
Avale.
Bhandáryavaru.
Ganikenavaru.
Gantenavaru.
Heganenavaru.
Honichiryavaru.
Hule.
Hutre.
Iragad.
Káblyánavaru.
Kengár.
Kumbalenavaru.
Máshál.
Ojenavaru.
Pándur.

Marriages are prohibited between members of the same *bedagu.* Marriage with a father's sister's or mother's sister's daughter is prohibited. Polygamy and widow remarriage are allowed and practised, but polyandry is unknown. Marriage is infant as well as adult. In some places, girls remaining unmarried till after the age of puberty, are not allowed to marry. They become *jogtins* and follow prostitution. Divorce is allowed if there is disagreement between husband and wife. In some places, the husband has to pay a sum of Rs. 12

to the wife at the time of the divorce, and he performs funeral rites in her name considering her to be dead. Divorced wives may remarry by the widow remarriage form.

Marriage ceremonies.

The offer of marriage comes from the boy's father who has to pay a sum of Rs. 22 to Rs. 30 to the girl's father. The marriage day is fixed in consideration with a Bráhman astrologer. In some places Bráhmans are employed to conduct the marriage service; in others, an elderly woman chosen for the occasion from amongst the guests conducts the service. At the girl's house the boy and the girl are rubbed with turmeric paste in two separate *surgis* or squares, with a drinking pot at each corner of the square and a thread wound round their necks. Both are bathed and the girl is dressed in a white robe and yellow bodice and the boy in a new dress. The girl stands in a basket containing rice opposite the boy who stands on a low stool. A curtain is held between them, marriage verses are repeated, and grains of rice are thrown over them by the priest and the guests. An unwidowed married woman of the boy's family fastens the *mangalsutra* or lucky necklace round the girl's neck and the ceremony is over. In Dhárwár, the ends of their robes are tied together and they are seated on rice spread on a raised seat, at the time of performing the marriage. In Belgaum, they are seated on a blanket. In Dhárwár, after the marriage is over, the bride and bridgroom and five other married unwidowed women are made to eat together out of one dish filled with food and sweets. In the evening a feast is given to the guests, and the married couple are taken in procession to bow to the village god.

Religion.

The Mádigs of the Karnátak do not worship the regular gods worshipped by the higher castes. Their favourite deities are Yellamma, Durgavva, Taladava, Dyámavva, Margái, Thaloba, Bharmaya, Khandoba, Mailár and Máruti. Their patron saints are Channaya, Haraly and Kakkaya. Goats and fowls are offered to the deities on Fridays and Tuesdays and are partaken of by themselves. Brass images of the family dead are seated along with the house gods. Mádigs observe the leading Hindu holidays. Some fast on the *Maháshivrátri* day and on the *Shrávan* Mondays. They make pilgrimages to the shrine of Yellamma in Parasgad in Belgaum and to the tomb of the Musalmán saint of Yamnur in Navalgund in Dhárwár. In some places they employ Bráhmans to conduct their marriages, who perform the ceremony standing at a distance. In others Jangams are employed. The other ceremonies are conducted by the castemen themselves.

The chief god of the Kanara Mádigs is Venkatráma. They are staunch devotees of Mariamma or mother-death. Once every two or three years they raise subscriptions, make a small shed, buy a brass pot which represents the goddess Mariamma, stop it with a cocoanut, cover it with flowers, and keep it for three days, which they spend in feasting and drinking, sacrificing lambs and fowls. At the end of the third day the pot is thrown into a river or pond. They do not employ or respect Bráhmans, but have priests of their own called *gurus* whom the laity support and who eat but do not marry with them. They have also a religious teacher named Jambu, whose monastery is at Kadapa in Madras where they go on pilgrimage.

Death ceremonies.

The dead are generally buried, the married in a sitting position and the unmarried in a lying position. The dead body is washed, dressed in its every day dress, and set leaning against a wall in a sitting position. It is carried to the burial ground in an old blanket. The mouth of the grave is closed with three stones to which, on the second day, are offered rice, molasses and clarified butter on a castor-oil leaf. When a crow has pecked this offering, the chief mourner bathes and returns home. On the fourth day a sheep is killed, its flesh is offered to the spirit of the deceased and a feast is given to the caste people. In some places, the castemen are feasted on *polies* or sugar rolly-polies on the fifth day. For the propitiation of the deceased a feast is given every year in the latter half of *Bhádrapad*.

Like the Marátha Mángs, the Mádigs also are notorious highway robbers. Their main occupation is working in leather. The Dálya Mángs, when they travel with Lamán caravans, make and mend their shoes and sandals, and beat drums. Mochi Mádigs make sandals, leather whips, nose-bags, girths, and many other articles useful to husbandmen. Ped Mádigs are village watchmen and attend upon travellers. They sweep the village *chávdi* and the *dharmashála* or rest-house. Sanádi Mádigs act as musicians to all other Mádigs and attend their marriage and other ceremonies. The Ráuts are leech-sellers. Asádarus dance before and abuse the goddess Dyamavva during her fair. When they dance, both men and women wear long, curiously worked, and dirty gowns. The women dance and the men hang large drums round their necks, beat them, and make a horrible noise. One of them is supposed to represent the brother of the Holaya who married Dyámavva under false pretences and was killed by her. This man stands before the idol, beats his head and chest and shows all signs of grief, and curses and loads the goddess with the vilest abuse. Besides their distinctive callings, most of these classes are husbandmen and some are field labourers who are paid in grain. They are also considered specially skilful in spinning cotton thread.

The Mádigs eat fish and all kinds of flesh except pork. They eat carrion. They are extremely fond of drink. They rank lower than Holayas, from whom they eat. **Food.**

GUJARAT MANGS or Mángelás are found in Bánsda and other States to the south-east of Surat. They stand lowest in the social scale. No Hindu will touch them and even the Vitoliás, themselves impure, will not eat at their houses. Their occupation is making baskets and winnowing fans. They worship Hanumán and Mari Máta. They never make use of a Bráhman's services, nor pay him any respect. Among them is a class of men called Bhats who claim to be of Bráhman descent and act as their priests. More than other wild tribes, their ceremonies resemble those of high class Hindus. On a fixed day in the seventh month of a woman's first pregnancy five women fill her lap with cocoanut kernels and rice or wheat. Friends are fed on rice and pulse or thick cakes, mutton and liquor. On the sixth day after birth the goddess Chhathi is worshipped. On the inner wall of the house lines of red powder *kanku* and turmeric are drawn. Rice is thrown at the drawing, a lamp is lighted before it and a dinner is given. The same day the priest names the child and is paid annas eight. When a Mángela finds a girl suited to be his son's wife he asks her father. If the girl's father is willing, the boy's father feasts the village on liquor spending about Rs. 6, when the day for the marriage is fixed. Some days after, the girl and her friends go to the boy's father's house, she receives two robes, a bodice, and a silver ornament. For two days, before the marriage, the bride and bridegroom are rubbed with turmeric powder. On the marriage day, in the afternoon, with music and accompanied by a party of his friends, the bridegroom rides to the girl's house. Here he is met by the bride's party and led to the entrance of a booth, inside of which the girl is seated. A lighted lamp representing the fire-god is placed on a raised square or *chori* in the centre of the booth, and the bride and bridegroom kneel before the lamp, while the women of the party sing songs. The priest ties the hems of their garments and joins their hands. Then the knot is unfastened and the marriage is over. A dinner follows. The bridegroom and his party stay three days with the girl's father and then take leave, the bride going with them. After four days she comes back to her father's and after four days more goes to her husband. The father of the bride gives a silver or brass ring or a cow or heifer to the bridgroom. Polygamy and widow marriage are allowed and practised.

Death ceremonies. Mángelás bury their dead on the fourth day after death; early in the morning rice is cooked, rolled into small balls or *pinds* and covered with the heart of a cock. The rice-balls are placed in the deceased's house and after lying for a few hours are thrown into running water. In the afternoon a dinner is given. A silver image of the deceased is kept in the house and in front of the image every seven or eight days a lamp is lighted. Each family keeps small silver plates each with an embossed figure of the deceased.

Food. The staple food of Mángelás is bread or porridge made of *nágli* (Eleusine coracana), rice and pulse. Except the dog, the cat and the ass, whose dead bodies they will not touch, Mángelás eat all animals. They drink liquor to excess.

DAKKALGARS are found in very small numbers in some of the villages of the Bijápur district and in the Nizám's dominions. They generally carry with them dogs and bitches. They cut off the ends of the ears of one dog and one bitch, and disguise them in male and female dress respectively. They carry with them a musical instrument called *kinnari*, at one end of which is fixed an artificial peacock. They are called Dakkalgárs probably because they use a lute called in Sanskrit *dakkari*. They sing songs in honour of Mahárs and Mángs to the tune of the *dakkari* or *kinnari*. The latter give them alms, etc., in return, for which the Dakkalgárs bless them.

Dakkalgárs occupy the lowest position in the social scale of the Hindu society. They are also called Sopachas or Svapachayyas meaning men of very low or degraded caste—outcastes—dog-feeders. They are not allowed to enter a village nor even its Mángváda. They live in places far away from a village and also from the quarters occupied by Mahárs and Mángs, who consider the very touch of the Dakkalgárs polluting. It appears therefore that custom has rightly and justly imposed upon the village Mahárs, Mángs, and Ganácháris of the diocese called in Kanarese Katti-mani the duty of supplying the Dakkalgárs with food, clothes, money, etc., whenever the latter happen to encamp within the limits of their villages. Dakkalgárs are not even allowed to touch the sources of water-supply from which Mahárs and Mángs fetch drinking water. Should Mahárs and Mángs and their Ganácháris ever fail to look to their comforts and conveniences, the Dakkalgárs retaliate by adopting the following method of procedure :—

The chief of the gang of Dakkalgárs goes in anger to the quarters occupied by the Mahárs and Mángs, and calls the dog dressed in male attire by the name of the male chief of the Mahárs or Mángs and the bitch dressed in female attire by the name of the wife of the chief Mahár or Máng. They are then alternately called forward slowly, the Dakkalgár chief meanwhile walking slowly backward, facing the dog and bitch. This goes on for some time and the Mahárs and Mángs, who have failed in their duty towards the Dakkalgárs, are in effect excommunicated.

On hearing of this degradation, the Ganáchári or the head of the diocese of the Mahárs and Mángs visits the Mahárváda or the Mángváda at once and applies cowdung to the doors of the house of the family. This amounts to an absolute excommunication of that family. As a result of this, none of the castemen are allowed to take food and water from that family until the matter is settled by a big caste committee after a long and protracted enquiry involving much trouble and a large expenditure. It is on this account that Mahárs and Mángs are afraid of Dakkalgárs and take every possible care to propitiate them.

Dakkalgárs have *bedagus* which are exogamous. Marriage is generally infant. Every Dakkalgár has two wives, which is probably due to the difficulty of finding husbands for all the girls in the community. Married women wear lucky badges and toe-rings called *kalungares*. Widow remarriage is allowed. Their chief deities are Hanumanta and Yellamma. Their patron saint is Siva-Nágamayya. They have no priests. The dead are buried.